QUANTITATIVE METHODS FOR PUBLIC DECISION MAKING

McGraw-Hill Series in Quantitative Methods for Management

Consulting Editor

Martin K. Starr, *Columbia University*

Gohagan: *Quantitative Analysis for Public Policy*
McKenna: *Quantitative Methods for Public Decision Making*
Swanson: *Linear Programming: Basic Theory and Applications*

QUANTITATIVE METHODS FOR PUBLIC DECISION MAKING

Christopher K. McKenna, Ph.D.
Associate Professor of Management Science
Pennsylvania State University–Capitol Campus

McGraw-Hill Book Company
New York St. Louis San Francisco Auckland Bogotá Hamburg
Johannesburg London Madrid Mexico Montreal New Delhi
Panama Paris São Paulo Singapore Sydney Tokyo Toronto

This book was set in Times Roman by Progressive Typographers.
The editors were Charles E. Stewart, Donald G. Mason, and Edwin Hanson;
the production supervisor was Leroy A. Young.
The drawings were done by Danmark & Michaels, Inc.
Fairfield Graphics was printer and binder.

QUANTITATIVE METHODS FOR PUBLIC DECISION MAKING

234567890 FGFG 83210

Library of Congress Cataloging in Publication Data

McKenna, Christopher K
Quantitative methods for public decision making.

(McGraw-Hill series in quantitative methods for management)
Includes bibliographies and index.
1. Public administration—Decision making—Mathematical models. I. Title.
JF1525.D4M32 350′.0001′51 79-22049
ISBN 0-07-045351-9

To Kathleen,
who made it not only possible but worthwhile

CONTENTS

PREFACE

A few years ago the chairman of our public administration program asked me to develop an administrative models course. In gathering materials I came to two conclusions: (1) There was no text with applications from and the perspective of public administration, and (2) many descriptions of models that have been or could be applied to public decision making appear in the literature, although not always in the form and forum most accessible to public administrators and students of public administration.[1] In such circumstances, I did what many others have done. I used one of the many "quantitative methods for business decisions" texts and supplemented it with handouts and additional exercises to foster a perspective other than profit and loss. The present text will hopefully avoid having to "make do."

The need was further emphasized when The National Association of Schools of Public Affairs and Administration (NASPAA) published its curriculum guidelines. "Applications of quantitative tools" is specifically mentioned as a recommended topic for the last year of a baccalaureate program.[2] "Quantitative decision methodology: e.g., . . . linear programming, modeling" is specifically recommended for the masters degree program.

The general purpose for writing this book was to fill a void. There are many texts that generally fit into the category, "quantitative methods for business decision making." None is for students and practitioners of public administration. One might argue that any good quantitative methods text is appropriate for students in any application area. However, the motivation for any of the tech-

[1] One hundred and seventy references supported this claim and comprised the bibliography of Christopher McKenna, "A Survey of Operations Research/Management Science Applied to Public Administration," a paper presented at the National Meeting of ORSA/TIMS, Atlanta, Ga., November 1977. This survey helped to identify which techniques should be included in a text such as this.

[2] NASPAA, "Guidelines and Standards for Baccalaureate Degree Programs in Public Affairs/Public Administration." Washington, D.C., 1976, p. 7.

niques comes not from the technique itself but from the applications through which it is presented. Students interested in the service sector can learn something about decision theory, linear programming, simulation, and so on more easily when the problem environment is related to public policy or the use of public resources than when it is restricted to profit and loss. The problems and illustrations in this text come entirely from the realm of public and quasi-public activity. This, I trust, will provide students with applications to education, health, criminal justice, regional planning, municipal operations, emergency vehicle distribution, and general public administration.

Specific purposes evolve from the general purpose. They are:

1. To develop a basic understanding of the role of quantitative models in general. This goal is pursued through examining a few specific commonly used types of models and explicitly relating their use to decision making.
2. To go beyond the results of a model solution. This objective is sought through emphasizing "what if" questions, and through the exercises that extend chapter examples.
3. To develop a broad view of applications of the different techniques. I pursue this objective in the chapter examples themselves and in the "Other applications" exercises.
4. To show that quantitative methods are really applicable to public decision making. This is addressed through applications presented within the chapters and through "Project problems" at the end of the chapters.
5. To develop familiarity with the literature. I try to achieve this by presenting the essential features of published studies without all the details, through project problems based on published studies, and through the chapter bibliographies.

The topics include those of particular value to the multiple-objective setting of public decision making: relation of models to decision making in general and public decision making in particular, utility theory and multiple objectives, cost-benefit analysis, goal programming, and simulation. Other topics usually treated in the standard quantitative methods course are presented in a public-decision-making setting.

The topics are presented in a way that permits great flexibility of selection and sequencing. The book serves as a stand-alone text in a one-semester course on administrative models or management science or as a second text in public management. With greater use of readings, the text serves as the basis for a two-term course. A curriculum in a specific application area such as health, education, or regional planning would use the text in conjunction with selected readings, many of which appear in the bibliographies.

Chapter 1 introduces the role of models in public decision making. As such, it provides a starting point for whatever combination of chapters will be included. A policy analysis course might use Chapters 1, 4, 5, 6, 7, 8, 9, 12, and 14, and a course in public management might use Chapters 1, 4, 6, 7, 8, 9, 11, 12, 14 and 15, although not necessarily in that order.

Sequencing can be chosen with no constraints other than those for the programming section. Chapter 9, "Linear Programming II: Sensitivity Analysis," can be covered after Chapter 8, "Introduction to Linear Programming: Formulation and Graphic Solution," without requiring that the computational details of the simplex method, Chapter 10, be done. Chapter 11, "Goal Programming," can be presented at one of three levels: an introduction requires only Chapter 8; sensitivity analysis requires Chapters 8 and 9; and a full presentation, including the goal simplex method, requires Chapters 8 to 10.

Because of the relative independence of the various chapters, the text is suitable also for use in short courses, professional development, and continuing education. Some samples are: a policy analysis short course might include Chapters 1, 4, 6, and 7, and an applied programming workshop would include Chapters 1, 8, 9, and 11.

Among those to whom I am especially grateful are: my parents whose attitude toward education was both practical and lofty; two master teachers, Brother Charles A. Lynam, C.F.C., and Brother Edmond R. Kiely, C.F.C., Professors Emeriti of Iona College, who are models of the learned learning; Penn State's Capitol Campus, whose tradition of sharing faculty among academic programs provided me with the right mix; Professor Daniel Poore, Chairman, Graduate Public Administration at Penn State—Capitol Campus, whose work on the NASPAA Curriculum Committee led him to ask me to develop the course that led to this book; Professor Robert J. Brown, Chairman, Graduate Business Administration at Penn State—Capitol Campus, whose attitude toward personnel administration is more helpful and productive than he can know; my many colleagues who reviewed parts of the manuscript and made many excellent suggestions, especially Professors Terence Brown, Robert Munzenrider, James Skok of Penn State—Capitol Campus; Martin K. Starr and Kathy A. Lewis of Columbia University; Henry C. Lucas, Jr., of New York University; James A. Fitzsimmons of The University of Texas; Barnett R. Parker of the University of North Carolina; Marvin Rothstein of the University of Connecticut; and Gerald E. Sullivan of Kent State University; the many students who have used draft versions of this book and have made helpful suggestions; Mrs. Patricia Souders who typed (and retyped) much of the manuscript; Mrs. Ann Ediger who not only typed much of the manuscript but also proved to be a remarkable coordinator; and my wife and children for their patience and endurance.

Christopher K. McKenna

QUANTITATIVE METHODS FOR PUBLIC DECISION MAKING

CHAPTER
ONE

INTRODUCTION: PUBLIC DECISION MAKING AND MODELS

This book is concerned with public decision making. There are many aspects of public decision making; the key aspect with which this book will concern itself is the appropriate use of quantitative models in public decision making. In this chapter we attempt to provide the framework by describing the elements of quantitative analysis in the general context of public decision making. By doing so we hope to suggest the use of quantitative analysis not only as a tool to generate specific information concerning a decision, but also to develop a useful approach to decision analysis in general. The mode of presentation of material throughout the book will be within the context of specific public sector applications. Hence, in this chapter we will present some examples of the kinds of decision situations that may benefit from the appropriate use of quantitative analysis.

PUBLIC DECISION MAKING

Nigro and Nigro[1] present a brief summary of many relevant points in coming to a definition of public administration. By paraphrasing that summary we form a description of public decision making, realizing that any one of the points might be suitable debate material.

[1] Felix A. Nigro and Lloyd G. Nigro, *Modern Public Administration,* Harper & Row, Publishers, Inc., New York, 1973, p. 18.

Public decision making:

1. Is a process and a result of cooperative group efforts in a public setting.
2. Is the responsibility of all three branches of government at federal, state, and local level and is affected by their interrelationships.
3. Takes place within the political process.
4. Is different in significant ways from business decision making.
5. Affects and is affected by the actions of private groups which also provide services to the public.

While some do not see a difference of any real importance between public and business management (decision making), Keeling has summarized the main differences.[2] With some caution about giving them more weight than they deserve, they are:

1. The size, complexity, and the allocative functions of the public realm
Allocating resources among major program areas such as health, education, and defense seems to have no parallel in business. The size and complexity of the organizations conducting any one of those programs, however, certainly has a counterpart in the larger multinational corporations. The presence of multiple objectives holds true for the large business organization but is central to public service agencies. While profit maximization may not be the only objective of a corporation, it can be considered prime, in the sense that there is a profit level below which all of the other corporate objectives, including survival and growth, may be threatened.

2. The politics of public decisions
Public management must be sensitive to political considerations and to outside pressure from the public at large and from special interest groups. However, it is no longer true that corporations are relatively immune from these forces. Maintaining a good public image is considered by some to be of great importance for preserving the independence and safeguarding the future of a corporation.

3. The immeasurability of public service
The private sector has a bottom line by which the organization can be evaluated overall; the public sector has no such bottom line. However, finding operational assessments of efficiency and effectiveness is not always a simple task even in the production environment, and it is more difficult in a service environment. It may be that the immeasurability is a more applicable distinction between product and service organizations than between public and private ones.

4. Organization and personnel management
The bureaucratic form is commonly attributed to government; by no means is it restricted to government. As organizations become large, they tend to become bureaucratic; private corporations tend to have their own bureaucracy. Greater

[2] Desmond Keeling, *Management in Government*, George Allen and Unwin Ltd., London, 1972, p. 145.

movement in and out of public service tends to reduce the contrast in personnel management. The federal civil service reforms initiated in 1978 have the potential for further reducing the difference.

Alvin Drake[3] suggests some ways in which public systems are different:

1. The clientele of a public issue, the most relevant administrators, and a relatively complete overview of the issue itself are harder to find.
2. Measures of effectiveness for various public policy alternatives are hard to specify, much less measure and evaluate.
3. The problem itself, the available data, and the time available for analysis make only a most approximate and aggregate sort of analysis possible.
4. Only in exceptional cases is there a need for the development of analytic techniques not currently available.
5. Solutions to quantitative models of decision situations have to be modified for many good reasons. A careful political analysis of an issue may be no less structured than the quantitative analysis.
6. At the state and local level especially by the time a problem is analyzed, the many involved parties will already have taken sides, often based on their own definitions of the situation and their own objectives.

We include in the public sector nongovernmental organizations such as hospitals, charitable organizations, or nonprofit corporations that serve as funding streams for service providers, and other organizations often characterized as quasi-public. Situations that are categorized as public decision making include the assignment of emergency vehicles to particular areas, the determination of appropriate levels of participation in a national health insurance program, the use of busing in school desegregation, assignment of personnel to a medical clinic, choosing the media mix for an educational campaign or program, awarding of government contracts, and planning for a referendum. These applications and others will be the context within which we will present various quantitative techniques that have proved useful in providing information to decision makers.

THE DECISION PROCESS

As the decision process unfolds, recognizable phases emerge. John Dewey[4] described these as the stages of problem solving:

What is the problem?
What are the alternatives?
Which alternative is best?

[3] Alvin W. Drake, "Quantitative Models in Public Administration: Some Educational Needs." in Alvin Drake, Ralph Keeney, and Philip Morse (eds.), *Analysis of Public Systems,* The M.I.T. Press, Cambridge, Mass., 1972, pp. 78ff.

[4] John Dewey, *How We Think,* D. C. Heath and Company, New York, 1910, chap. 8.

These are the phases that Simon[5] calls *intelligence,* searching the environment for conditions calling for decisions; *design,* finding and assessing alternatives; and *choice,* selecting an alternative from those available.

The so-called rational model of decision making closely parallels Simon's phases of decision making and Dewey's description of problem solving. The steps proposed in the rational model are generally appropriate for decision situations and are as follows:

1. Define the problem; a need is recognized and that need is formulated as a problem. A problem exists when there is a discrepancy between what ought to be and what is.
2. Search for alternatives; possible courses of action are sought. The search is limited by time and resources available, by current level of information and technology, and by the value placed on resolving the problem.
3. Evaluate alternatives; the consequences of each alternative are assessed according to previously defined criteria.
4. Select an alternative; the alternative that yields consequences which are the most favorable according to the criteria is chosen to be implemented.

Figure 1-1 presents the rational model as it relates to Simon's phases of decision making. This model provides the framework for decision making that we

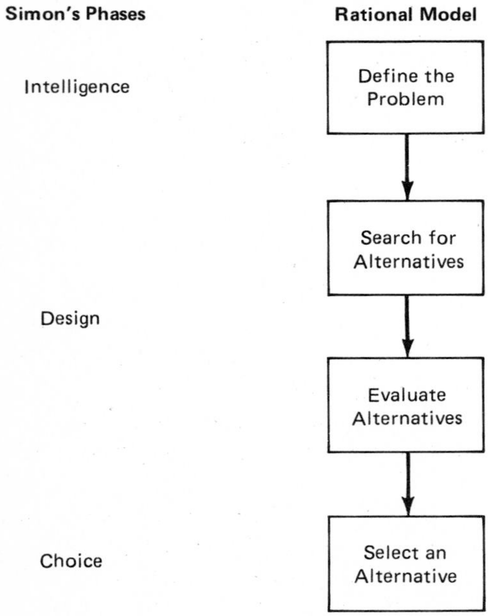

Figure 1-1 The decision-making process according to Herbert Simon and the rational model.

[5] Herbert A. Simon, *The Shape of Automation for Men and Management,* Harper & Row, Publishers, Inc. New York, 1965, p. 54.

will rely on in presenting the various analytical techniques and in indicating how each can be useful to the decision maker.

Implementation of the chosen alternative is considered by Simon to be the setting for a new round of decision making, with the need for intelligence, design, and choice at a greater level of detail. Implementation is considered by others to be a fifth phase in the rational model, although not one particularly aided by quantitative analysis. For this reason it is excluded from our basic decision-making model, but is included in Figure 1-2 which presents various paradigms of decision making.

The decision process is presented here as a sequence of fairly well-defined discrete steps. In reality decision making takes place rather in a continuum, although the emphasis may shift from one task to another along that continuum. The sequence of emphases is likely to be something like the following:

Define the problem.
Search for alternatives.
Reconsider the problem.

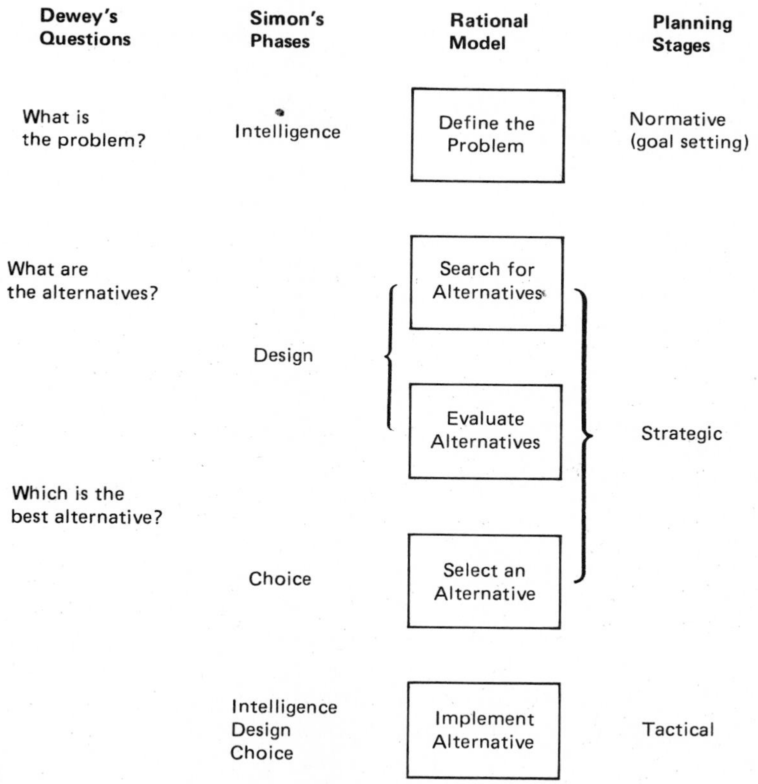

Figure 1-2 The decision-making process represented in various paradigms.

Continue the search for alternatives.
Evaluate alternatives.
Consider whether any alternative is worthwhile implementing.
Further refine the problem definition.
Implement an alternative or a combination of alternatives, or drop the issue.
Evaluate the implementation relative to the original problem.

Figure 1-2 shows the relationship between planning and decision making. Defining the problem requires learning how things are and how we would like them to be. Planners sometimes refer to this stage as "normative planning." Consideration of what is, what we can do, and what we shall do is referred to as "strategic planning." The implementation of decisions is necessary if anything is to be done. Simon sees implementation not as a separate phase but as an initiation of a new cycle of decision making on a more detailed level. Planning the execution of the chosen alternative is referred to as "tactical planning."

The *incremental approach* to public decision making is suggested as an alternative model. In this approach the decision maker includes in the list of possible alternatives only those which are incremental modifications of current government activities. Whether this is, in fact, a different decision model, or whether it is the application of conservatism to the search for alternatives, is less important than the recognition that agreement is easier to achieve when: (1) the elements of a dispute are only slight modifications to existing undertakings; (2) there is less uncertainty in the consequences; and (3) previous and present commitments make drastic change politically unwise.

The steps outlined above are for the ideal situation; real decision situations often do not follow the tidiness of the ideal. What is recognized as a need by some may not be such in the eyes of others; for example, some see national health insurance as a need, others see it as a superfluity. Different segments of the population have different value systems and therefore tend to have different goals. Equality of educational opportunity is a goal shared by most; however, school desegregation through forced busing elicits very different responses from the community depending upon whether values such as ethnic purity and neighborhood integrity are preferred over those of broader societal equality. Typically the sources of goals are the organization, the individual, and the environment. The goals of government, the organization, originate with those of the people but come to include strictly organizational goals such as survival of an agency regardless of the value of its services. Such organizational goals may be in conflict with the people's goals, which are themselves terribly difficult to identify. Organizational goals are affected by and affect individuals' goals. The individual decision maker's (law maker, administrator, appointed official, career professional, potential candidate, and so forth) goals of self-realization, recognition, acceptance, security and survival, and physical well-being will at times support and at other times detract from seeking the common good. The environment of any organization consists essentially of the other organizations and individuals with whom there is contact. In the public sector the environment consists of the people as taxpayers and service recipients, both as individuals and as specific interest groups.

Identifying alternatives requires time, but decisions must be made. The search for alternatives cannot go on forever. In fact, particularly in crisis situations, the search for alternatives is often only too brief. Consider the case of an expanding school-age population. It might seem that the only alternative is the construction of new buildings. In fact, however, it may be wiser to rent space if the school-age population has been growing, but is about to start a decline.

The examination of consequences, like identification of alternatives, takes time, foresight, and intuition. Examining the consequences of reducing the staff at a medical clinic may reveal that although staff idle time will be reduced, the patients' waiting time will be increased far more than reason permits. Choosing an alternative, according to the established criteria, is relatively simple if the criterion or criteria have been agreed upon, or if the criteria are not conflicting. Positioning ambulances in various depots throughout a hospital service area may provide very good response time and patient care in critical instances. However, such a choice precludes the hospital attendants from assisting with other hospital duties. The choice of an alternative requires a compromise among the conflicting objectives.

The process of coming to a decision requires the analyst to identify competing value systems, develop factual information, make tradeoffs of some values for others, and choose among a limited number of alternatives, ultimately advocating the implementation of one preferred course of action. Information, generally distorted in its natural state, must be gleaned from a number of different sources, namely, the citizenry as clients (often organized into interest groups), the citizenry as taxpayers (generally unorganized but becoming less so since California's Proposition 13 in 1978), and government officials at the policy and operations levels. Under normal circumstances, information is available to decision makers in limited amounts, usually distorted, often muddling fact, value, and opinion indiscriminately. As far as possible, it is the role of an analyst to separate the fact from the opinion, not to discard one in favor of the other, but to identify each for what it is. The analysis will be both *qualitative,* based upon managerial experience and judgment, and program experience and judgment, and *quantitative,* based upon mathematical techniques.

Without devaluing the former, the intent of this text is to focus on the latter. The *representation* of the decision situation that is the medium for analysis is called a *model.* Our attention now shifts to the advantages of using models and then to the steps generally employed in developing a model.

MODELS

Insofar as a *model is a representation of the relevant features of the real decision situation,* no model can be a precise replica. In the public realm, in particular, concern is often with approximate, highly aggregate models. Models may assume many forms, from a verbal description of how an individual passes through the criminal justice system to a technical mathematical investigation of the consequences of various flood-control alternatives.

Benefits of Formal Models

Regardless of its form a carefully developed model will usually be more useful than a vaguely defined one insofar as the more formal model:

1. Makes explicit its problem definition, identifying those aspects of the situation which are and are not included.
2. Supplies a focal point for discussion of the problem, generally leading to a better understanding of the problem itself.
3. Provides the framework for empirical assessment and improvement.
4. Fosters the use of more technical analysis, when appropriate.
5. Can help in keeping the discussion and search for alternatives problem oriented rather than personality oriented.

Model Development

The main stages in the construction and use of a model are:

1. Abstraction, the identification of the main features of a problem
2. Formulation, expressing the relationships among the main features
3. Execution, manipulation of the model, yielding a solution
4. Sensitivity analysis, the process of determining the effects of changes in one component on other components
5. Validation, the determination of whether the model behavior correctly corresponds to real behavior

The general stages of developing a model are now briefly considered. In later chapters, discussion of specific types of models will provide greater detail.

Abstraction

A real-world problem tends to be extremely complex. The enormous number of facts and interactions with all of the cause-effect relationships are literally unfathomable. The decision maker must abstract from the decision situation those factors which are deemed most relevant and express them relative to the recognized need in a well-defined problem. This is the process of *abstraction*. Providing well-rounded education is a recognized need, but it must be more clearly defined before actions are taken. A school district cannot choose the appropriate curriculum without limiting its focus to the most relevant needs and the services that are technologically available. After limiting the focus in this way and noting the very basic facts (number of pupils at each grade level, location of each school building, transportation costs, and available resources, personnel and financial), pupils can be assigned to classes in order to provide them with the greatest opportunities to satisfy their needs within the many constraints of the school district.

Model Formulation

After the most important factors have been identified, their relations are expressed verbally and then symbolically. This process of *model formulation* results in a representation or model of the real-problem situation. The level of complexity of the model can vary greatly. An extremely simple model having only a few variables is easily understood by the decision maker, is economically constructed and used, and can be readily altered. The very simple model represents only the most salient features of the problem. As more features are included, the model becomes more complex, and consequently more expensive to construct and to use; it becomes less easy to understand, and more difficult to modify.

Execution

Symbolic manipulations are performed in the *execution* phase. This includes solving equations and making statistical analyses. This stage results in a *solution* to the model. Conclusions are then made about the behavior of the model and thence inferred about the behavior of reality itself.

Sensitivity Analysis

Sensitivity analysis is a process of determining the effects of changes in one variable on others, and especially on resulting decisions. In abstracting the problem and in formulating the model, uncertainties are encountered and estimates have to be made. Wherever values and relationships are not known with certainty or where they are likely to change, the effects of such modifications should be investigated. In a university enrollment model one key item is the proportion of college-aged people actually attending college. Since this value varies from year to year, it is not known for certain in advance. Thus it makes sense in examining the solution to determine the effects of changes in the proportion of college-aged youths actually in college on projected university enrollment. The decision makers are trying to determine the *sensitivity* of the college's enrollment to the proportion of college-aged youths attending college. If slight changes in that proportion lead to a different decision, then we say that the decision is very sensitive to the estimated proportion. Conversely if large changes in the proportion do not result in any different decision, then the decision is not sensitive to the estimated proportion.

Validation

In drawing conclusions about the original problem, it should be carefully noted that the solution is the *solution to the model.* The *validation* of a model comes about when the model solution leads to correct inferences about the real situation. Since this validation is possible only by comparing model behavior with real behavior, it sometimes cannot be undertaken until well after the decision-making point. Such a situation strongly indicates the need for a thorough sensitivity analysis.

Role and Limitations of a Model

The basic role of a model is to help decision makers understand a problem situation. Figure 1-3 represents two underlying ways of gaining knowledge of real behavior; they are direct observation of the real situation and the use of a model or representation of the real situation. Where the situation of interest is relatively simple, direct observation is advised; where the elements and their relationships are more involved, use of a model may be more effective. Usually the more complex model more closely represents the original problem. This is the tradeoff between the simple model and the more complex but more representative model. A model to be used by an association of hospitals in planning their growth is worthy of greater complexity than a model designed to indicate the appropriate assignment of staff in the neighborhood clinic. Essentially the decision maker and the supporting analyst should look for the simplest model that *adequately* represents the problem situation.

As with any management or decision-making aid, there are limitations such as the following:

1. Development of models is time consuming; an elaborate model may produce results long after the decisions it was supposed to support have been made.

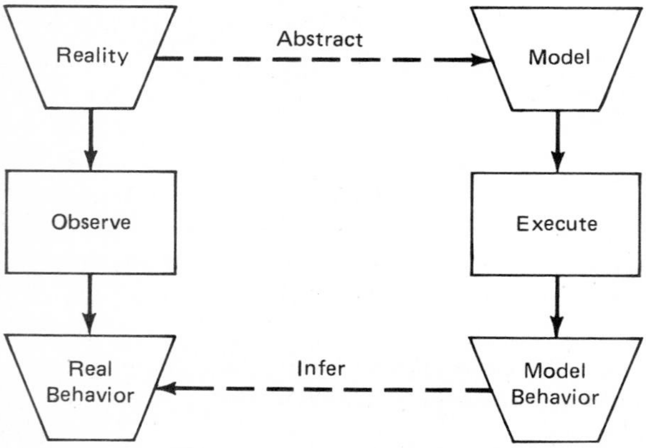

Figure 1-3 The role of a model: helping to understand reality.

2. Decision makers are often disinclined to accept model-based conclusions; some effort must be made by the decision maker to gain an understanding and appreciation of the role that models can play, and some effort must be made by the specialists to realize that models are not the be-all and end-all of decision making, and that ultimately it is the real problem, not the abstracted one, that is of importance.
3. Models can be very expensive; data collection, analysis, and model formulation and solution can require a considerable amount of human effort, and therefore financial resources.
4. Models can be so oversimplified that they distort the real decision situation.
5. Completed model studies may be totally ignored, either because the analysis was untimely, was simplistic, or assumed away the main features of the problem, or because the decision makers had already decided to ignore the analysis. The whole effort may turn out to be a futile intellectual exercise.

The decision maker, with the aid of the analyst, must weigh the expected benefits against the recognized limitations, to determine whether the expenses of developing a model are likely to be a productive investment in improved decision making.

MODEL DEVELOPMENT AND DECISION MAKING

Quantitative models are either *descriptive* or *prescriptive*.

Descriptive Models

A descriptive model describes the way a system operates. Commonly used descriptive models are queuing (Chapter 12), simulation (Chapter 13), and cost-benefit analysis (Chapter 6). Cost-benefit analysis is more properly an application for which many techniques may be useful, rather than a technique itself. Nevertheless, there are some features specific to cost-benefit analysis, and so we will treat it as a particular model.

Normative Models

Other mathematically based models aim at finding "the best" alternative—the best according to some previously identified criterion. This process is referred to as *optimizing,* and this type of model is referred to as *normative* or *prescriptive*. Examples of normative models are linear programming (Chapters 8 to 10), goal programming (Chapter 11), and network analysis (Chapter 12). Decision theory (Chapters 4 to 6) is sometimes included here, although it is more than a particular model since it provides a framework for analyzing decisions generally.

Models and Decisions

The role played by normative models in aiding decision making varies slightly from the role played by descriptive models, as Figure 1-4 indicates. Insofar as the latter type merely describes the situation of interest, alternatives are identified outside the model and incorporated at the formulation stage. Thus each alternative requires some modification in the model itself.

Example Queuing is the study of waiting lines. As such it has been used to analyze toll bridges. The model does not directly find the "best" number of lanes to have open. Rather the model's formulation is modified for each alternative that is identified. It then determines the waiting time of automobiles and the idle time of toll takers for each alternative number of lanes. Its

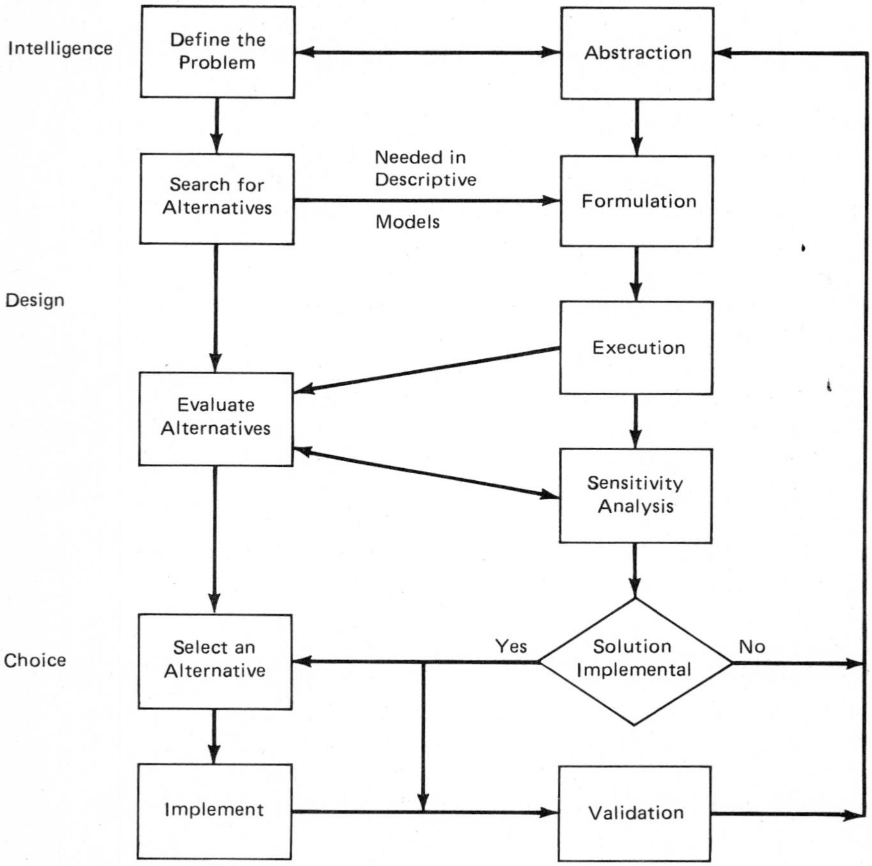

Figure 1-4 Use of models in the decision process.

purpose is to describe the consequences of any alternative; that is, queuing is a descriptive model.

In some normative models, alternatives do not have to be identified outside the model. In the execution phase of model development and use, alternatives are generated and tested in seeking the best alternative.

Example Linear programming is used when there is a single quantified objective (keep total travel distance to a minimum) but many restrictions that must be adhered to (school capacity, desegregation quotas, balanced busing, and so forth). Alternative busing schemes do not have to be separately identified, because the model seeks the scheme that has the least travel distance from among those that satisfy the restrictions. Linear programming is a normative or prescriptive model.

In other normative models, the alternatives are identified outside the model, and the "best" one is found within the model.

Example Alternative bid proposals are identified as part of the decision-making process. A decision theory formulation may assist in determining the "best" of the proposed bids. Decision theory models are normative ones.

As we have already noted, real-world problems tend to have many criteria, none of which may be tidy or measured without argument. Hence, while solving the model may generate an optimal solution, relating that solution to the real problem may generate a solution that is not optimal, but that is satisfactory and sufficient. In a real-world problem, it is often extremely difficult, perhaps impossible, to find *the* optimal solution. Hence, the goal becomes achieving a satisfactory and sufficient solution rather than an optimal one; *satisficing* replaces *optimizing* as the objective. In one sense, then, a limitation on the use of models is that the solution aims at optimizing in the model but only at satisficing in reality. On the other hand, using a model may generate a real-world solution that is more satisfactory and more sufficient than would have been possible without the use of the model. In the regional planning application of Chapter 4, the procedure used is an optimum-seeking one. There are conflicting criteria: providing needed hospital capacity and maintaining lowest costs. The decision theory model does not indicate the alternative that should be chosen, but it does identify the alternatives and their consequences in a rather clear and distinct fashion so that the decision makers are able to choose a solution that *satisfices,* perhaps more so than would have been possible without employing the model.

One of the most widely heard criticisms of quantitative models is the claim that numbers are used to represent essentially subjective judgments. Models do involve quantities and variables that represent truly measurable entities (number of people employed by a county government, number of dollars spent in the delivery of a particular service, amount of time that clients spend waiting for service, the rate at which judges are able to adjudicate the cases before them, and so forth), and quantities and variables that appear to represent essentially qualitative and subjective value judgments (importance of a regional recreational facility, feeling of security generated by an "effective" police force, degree of desocialization engendered by long-term incarceration, and so forth). If it is true that a particular model does not distinguish between these, then it is the fault of the model builder, and it behooves the decision maker to understand the assumptions on which the model is based, and the way in which qualitative or subjective value judgments are quantitatively assessed. The decision maker with some basic understanding of the role of quantitative models in public decision making will at least know the questions to pose. In a cost-benefit study of alternative uses of an urban plot, there would be considered, among other things, the total cost of each alternative, effects of each alternative on revenue to the city and to merchants in the surrounding area, on air quality and on visual appearance. If the model representing the situation has a quality-of-life variable that includes visual quality and water quality, one would certainly want to know how the esthetic aspect is measured and how that measurement is treated in the model. This is not a suggestion that such essentially value-judgment entities be measured and included in a model by a specific quantitative variable. Rather it is a caution that if such a value judgment is included, then the decision maker must know how it is represented if the model is to be meaningful. Our own thought on the subject is to exclude any such variables from the model and present them as separate entities along with the results of the model. This provides the decision makers with the opportunity to view the judgmental qualities as such and prevents deterioration of the model, by excluding those qualities with dubious quantitative measure.

APPLICATIONS OF QUANTITATIVE TECHNIQUES

The quantitative techniques that will be included in this text are part of what is frequently referred to as *operations research,* or *management science.* Although a scientific approach has been used for decision making for hundreds of years, the birth of operations research, as it is known today, is generally accepted to have taken place during World War II in Britain. Interdisciplinary teams of scientists representing various fields, including psychology, mathematics and physics, cooperated with British military personnel in research to make the use of radar operational. This description gave rise to the British term "operational research." Not long after, operations research was used in the United States in the development of new types of mine tactics for use in the war against Japan. After World War II, operations research was applied in the more peaceful activities of business, government, and the military. From these applications in a management environment, the term "management science" came to be used. Although there is some discussion on the similarities and differences between the two terms, we will be satisfied to use them interchangeably. In practice, operations research or management science is usually carried on by teams of individuals so that various relevant disciplines can be represented. On such teams, the role of the quantitative specialist is an important one, and the productivity of such teams is greatly enhanced if each of the members is at least able to understand the basic concepts of the other disciplines.

This multidiscipline approach allows for focusing not only on the specific problem that is raised but also on the larger environment in which the specific problem exists. This larger field of focus is the essence of what is referred to as *systems analysis. A system is described as a purposeful collection of entities which interact*. The systems approach to decision making views each decision as related to a larger frame of reference. Needless to say, in the interest of arriving at a decision before the need for the decision disappears, the whole state of the world cannot become the actual field of focus for every decision. However, the field of focus should be at least greater than the specific decision and should include at least those elements that can be productively and efficiently related to the decision at hand.

In discussing various public-decision-making applications of the quantitative techniques, we necessarily focus on a span of attention somewhat smaller than the entire decision-making environment, just as the decision maker must focus his attention on a field smaller than the entire decision environment. At the same time, however, we encourage looking beyond the decision itself.

Automation or computerization should not be confused with operations research, management science, or even systems analysis. The systems approach to a decision does not require computer assistance; however, one's approach to some decisions is different if there is available a tool that can rapidly process many pieces of data and perform many mathematical computations. The use of a computer has made possible some applications of operations research and systems analysis that would otherwise have been impractical or impossible. Hence we say that systems analysis is quite distinct from, but in specific instances is quite dependent on, the use of a computer.

The use of quantitative models in decision making in actual practice is viewed by some as not having lived up to its expectations. Reasons for the shortfall include the following:

1. Expectations have been unrealistically high; decisions do not and should not depend entirely on a quantitative analysis any more than on any other single source of information.
2. People in authority tend to resist change; relying on familiar procedures is much more comfortable than becoming familiar with new ones.
3. The quantitative analysts often seem to be communicating with each other rather than with the decision makers. In my survey of over 200 journal ar-

ticles investigating quantitative applications in the public sector, the vast majority appeared in journals written for quantitative analysts rather than in journals written for public administrators.

In spite of these shortcomings, however, quantitative analysis of public decision making is an expanding reality. Government departments and agencies have their own systems analysis staffs. Small jurisdictions use the services of consulting organizations. Colleges and universities engaged in educating future public decision makers, with the encouragement of The National Association of Schools of Public Affairs and Administration, have included applications of "quantitative tools" in the list of required or recommended courses. Some of the areas of the public sector that have been recently addressed by quantitative analysis include criminology, school districting, educational planning, election campaigns, emergency vehicle location, health planning, hospital administration, land use, law enforcement, pollution control, family planning and population growth, procurement, local government financing, and water resources management. These application areas will receive further attention as they are addressed by various quantitative methods in later chapters.

DO SNOWPLOWS FAVOR MANHATTAN? AN APPLICATION

New York City has been the scene of many crises, private and public, financial and social, meteorological and, above all, political. New Year's Day, 1969, was the occasion of a particularly heavy snowfall that took the administration, the snow-removal force, the meteorologists, and the public by surprise. The combination of the holiday, the unpredictability of the storm, and the speed of the downfall led to great delays in mobilizing the snow-removal force. Days after the snowfall, portions of the city were still snowed in. Manhattan, however, was relatively clear and passable well before many areas of the other boroughs were even touched. Queens and Staten Island residents clamored that the better snow-removal service in Manhattan merely typified the favoritism with which that borough was treated by His Honor, John V. Lindsay. Bias or not, the fact was that Manhattan was cleared considerably before sizable portions of Queens and Staten Island. Whether this was a coincidence or somehow built into the snow-removal system was left to be investigated by the First Deputy City Administrator, Mr. E. S. Savas.[6]

Under his direction, the analytical staff collected relevant data on previous snowfalls in New York City. On the basis of the relative frequencies of different sized storms, they were able to classify this storm as a rarity. Further, that a storm of this size would be unforeseen by the meteorologists was an even greater rarity. A nonmeteorological factor that was nonetheless significant was

[6] A more complete account of the incident and the analysis can be found in E. S. Savas, "The Political Properties of Crystalline H_2O: Planning for Snow Emergencies in New York," *Management Science,* vol. 20, October 1973, pp. 137–145.

that 1969 was a mayoralty election year, in which the then-current Mayor would seek reelection. Such a sizable and unpredicted storm, occurring on a holiday when needed work crews would be far from their place of employment, in a relevant election year, was indeed a rather unlikely combination of events. Nevertheless, it happened. That the occurrence was a freak was little consolation either to the snowed-in citizens of Queens and Staten Island, or to the politicians whose jobs were threatened by the perceived injustice of the snow-removal system.

Attempting to dissociate the facts of the situation from the claims and hurt feelings, analysts reviewed the actual plan that was used in removing snow from the city streets. The most significant finding of their study was that a bias in favor of the Island of Manhattan was built into the plan. Many of the snow-removal vehicles were garbage trucks that were equipped with snowplows in times of need. Garbage trucks were assigned to sections of the city according to population density. Snow does not fall according to population density. The less densely populated areas were appropriately assigned fewer garbage-removal vehicles, but thereby unjustly assigned fewer snow-removal vehicles. A relatively simple reassignment of snow-removal vehicles in a more reasonable and equitable fashion, according to a revised priority listing of the city streets, which came about as a second result of the study, was adequate to ameliorate the situation. A simple reassignment, however, does not get much public attention, especially when the reassignment comes 6 months or more after the crisis itself. There was considerable public attention given, however, to new, bigger and better snow-removal vehicles that were unveiled in Queens before a gathering of reporters and onlookers not long before election day.

The problem solving conducted in the snow-removal illustration serves as an example of applied quantitative analysis. Aside from or because of public outrage, a need was recognized. Separating fact from fury and identifying key elements were part of abstraction. Formulation of a model involved collecting data on those elements: snowfalls, street usage, and the method of assigning snow-removal vehicles. Execution of the model estimated rates of clearing arteries for such large snowfalls under various vehicle assignments. Sensitivity analysis revealed that results would not vary greatly with moderate changes in prevailing conditions. The solution of the model gave rise to a plan to clear the streets in their order of use and importance, and to reassign some snow-removal vehicles. Subsequent snowfalls revealed the validity of the model and the solution implemented. The setting of the problem in an election year merely typified the political environment in which public decision making takes place. What is done and what is decided are supplemented by what is perceived by the public as solutions to identified problems.

DIFFICULTIES IN PUTTING ANALYSIS TO WORK

Difficulties in applying quantitative analysis in the public sector have many sources. In the first place, viewing every negative aspect of society as a problem to solve may be considerably less productive than viewing them as conditions to cope with. Solving a problem that is oversimplified is not nearly as useful as muddling through the mess that is real.[7] The process of public sector decision making is less a sequence of separate decisions than it is a "continuous flow of decisions, large and small, that make up the seamless web of policy formulation and administrative action. The dynamic flux of the policy process makes the job of the advisor [or analyst] particularly difficult."[8]

The process of analysis itself may limit the implementation of recommendations that come from analysts; the mere fact that a particular issue has been identified as potentially benefiting from analytical study reflects that someone has judged that the chosen area has problems. This in turn may be viewed as a threat by the bureaucracy involved. The implementation of a rational solution may be politically unacceptable; a political analysis is as valuable and as needed as a rational analysis.

Resistance to change, certainly not unique to public organizations, often finds itself verbalized in one of four classic defenses. The resister claims that the recommendation (1) simply cannot be done, (2) has been tried before and did not work, (3) already is being done, more or less, or, finally, (4) even if it were done, it would not do any good.

The subject of an analysis cannot be the entire environment in which a problem situation exists. Reality is simply too complex to have every facet and detail examined in a model or an abstraction. The analyst, therefore, is confronted with conflicting demands: He is supposed to expand his perspective which brings about the growing risk of failure, but he must also narrow his scope which increases the chances that the analyst and the analysis will simply be ignored.

The environment in which a public sector application exists and is studied is *public,* not only in the sense that it is public servants who administer and decide, but also in the sense that it is by, for, and of the people. This gives rise to constituencies who, if loud enough, shrewd enough, or well enough organized, will have as much or more influence on an ultimate decision as the recommendation that comes from a rational analysis.

Concern of analysts for the theoretical and technical niceties of model development leads to two difficulties. The first is that the problem situation may be artificially categorized so that it can be handled with a particular technique. This is a contradiction of a basic principle of operations research or management science, that the perspective and analysis should be problem-oriented rather than technique-oriented. The second difficulty is that the solution to the model may not give any indication for "how" an alternative is to be acted upon. The process for implementing the solution as well as the solution itself is

[7] Further commentary on this and other difficulties can be found in E. S. Savas, "New Directions for Urban Analysis," *Interfaces,* vol. 6, no. 1, November 1975, pp. 1–9.

[8] D. E. Kash, "Research and Development of the University," *Science,* vol. 160, June 21, 1968, pp. 1313–1318.

needed. Given the involvement of the various levels of decision makers that are necessary for implementing anything, and given the public nature of the decision environment, how the recommendations are handled will have much to do with their acceptance and implementation. Just as it is recommended that analysts become involved early in the problem definition stage and remain involved through the implementation stage, so too the public decision makers should be involved, in some respects, in the analysis phase, as well as in the problem definition and implementation stages. Without this user involvement, models will retain their "black box" image, and not provide the assistance of which they are capable.

CONCLUSION

It is our contention that fruitful application of quantitative analysis in the public sector requires a twofold effort: first, of specialists to communicate the results of their efforts to decision makers who are not necessarily quantitative specialists, and second, of decision makers to gain some basic understanding of the approaches used by the analysts.

This book is written to sustain the latter effort, a need identified by many in public administration and public decision making, including Nicholas Henry:

> This is not to say that every public administrator should be as fully steeped in operations research, systems theory, statistical analysis, computer science, or whatever, as are full time professionals in those fields. But the public administrator should know at least some of the basics of these subjects, so that he will be able to cut through the verbiage of technical analysis and recognize the underlying value choices that the jargon often obscures. Politics pervades all endeavors, and to recognize the politics of expertise requires an understanding of the languages and the symbols of the experts. All too frequently public administrators have copped out in this regard with the phrase, "We can leave that to the engineers." They can no longer afford to be so flippant, or if they are, then public administrators must accept the consequences of their having taken such a position: the social deficiencies that result when "engineering mentalities" are placed in positions of political power; the dangers of technocracy; the political disregard for "people problems" by a new managerial elite trained in science but not in social science; and—last but not least—the undermining of their own usefulness in the governmental hierarchy.[9]

BIBLIOGRAPHY

Drake, Alvin W., Ralph L. Keeney, and Philip M. Morse: *Analysis of Public Systems,* The M.I.T. Press, Cambridge, Mass., 1972.

Henry, Nicholas: *Public Administration and Public Affairs,* Prentice-Hall, Inc., Englewood Cliffs, N.J., 1975.

Hoos, Ida: "Systems Techniques for Managing Society: A Critique," *Public Administration Review,* March–April 1973, pp. 157-164.

[9] Nicholas Henry, *Public Administration and Public Affairs,* Prentice-Hall, Inc., Englewood Cliffs, N.J., 1975, pp. 126–127.

Kash, D. E.: "Research and Development of the University," *Science,* vol. 160, June 21, 1968, pp. 1313–1318.

Keeling, Desmond: *Management in Government,* George Allen and Unwin Ltd., London, 1972.

Lucas, Henry C., Jr.: *Toward Creative Systems Design,* Columbia University Press, New York, 1974.

Nigro, Felix A., and Lloyd G. Nigro: *Modern Public Administration,* Harper & Row, Publishers, Inc., New York, 1973.

Rising, Edward J., Robert Baron, and Barry Averill: "A Systems Analysis of a University-Health-Service Outpatient Clinic," *Operations Research,* vol. 21, September–October 1973, pp. 1030–1047.

Savas, E. S.: "The Political Properties of Crystalline H_2O: Planning for Snow Emergencies in New York," *Management Science,* vol. 20, October 1973, pp. 137–145.

Savas, E. S.: "New Directions for Urban Analysis," *Interfaces,* vol. 6, no. 1, November 1975, pp. 1–9.

Simon, Herbert A.: *The Shape of Automation for Men and Management,* Harper & Row, Publishers, Inc., New York, 1965.

Starling, Grover: *Managing the Public Sector,* Dorsey Press, Homewood, Ill., 1977.

CHAPTER

TWO

BASIC PROBABILITY CONCEPTS

The material presented here and in Chapter 3, "Probability Distributions," is intended as a review. The reader familiar with these ideas should move ahead. The reader who needs only a brief reminder can go through these chapters quickly and easily. The reader who has been barely introduced to probability, or who has not dealt with such notions for some time, will benefit from a fuller reading of these chapters.

This chapter explores and illustrates the most elemental concepts of probability. Chapter 3 is a sequel, dealing with probability distributions, random variables, and two commonly used measures, the mean and standard deviation.

In this chapter we draw upon common experiences to introduce basic notions of probability. As we consider these experiences, we recognize underlying differences in two types of probability, subjective and objective. Expressing the basic ideas in fundamental statements and laws makes using them much easier.

The basic ideas are explained within the context of a political election, and further illustrated by a school board trying to assess the effects a particular high school course has on subsequent study.

BASIC CONCEPTS

Probability is the chance that something will occur. If a thing cannot occur, it is assigned a probability of zero and represented by $P = 0$. If a thing always occurs or will occur with certainty, it is assigned a probability of one and represented by $P = 1$. Events whose occurrence or nonoccurrence is less certain are assigned probabilities between zero and one; that is, $0 < P < 1$.

An *outcome* represents the most basic result of doing something; it is so elementary that it cannot be further divided. An *event* is a collection of one or more of the basic outcomes, usually grouped together because they have something in common. In these terms the toss of a six-sided die results in one of six outcomes, 1, 2, 3, 4, 5, or 6. The event "even number" occurs when one of the outcomes 2, 4, or 6 occurs.

Two or more events are *mutually exclusive* if only one of them can occur at a time. Referring to the toss of the die, "even number" and "odd number" are mutually exclusive, since they cannot both be the result of a single toss of the die. However, "even number" and "number larger than 3" are not mutually exclusive, since the outcomes 4 and 6 are both even and greater than 3.

A list of events is *exhaustive* if the list includes every possible outcome. In our previous example of a die, the list "even and odd" is exhaustive.

In a political campaign if each party has its own candidate, then "Republican candidate" and "Democratic candidate" are mutually exclusive because they cannot both be elected, but they are not exhaustive if there are Independents, Liberals, Conservatives, or other candidates.

OBJECTIVE AND SUBJECTIVE PROBABILITY

Perhaps without really knowing it, we are all fairly familiar with some basic laws of probability. A few minutes at a fund-raising bazaar provides some simple examples of various kinds of chance or probability. "Round and round she goes, where she stops nobody knows"; the game wheel is a simple example of *objective probability*. We note that the numbers 1 to 10 are on the wheel. Assume the wheel is well balanced, so that any number is as likely to win as any other number. Hence, when we put a quarter down on a number, we calculate that we have a 1 in 10 chance of winning. Other ways of expressing this "1 chance in 10" are: the odds against winning are 9 to 1, and the probability of winning is one-tenth. This is written as

$$P(\text{win}) = \frac{1}{10} = \frac{\text{number of outcomes that will win}}{\text{number of possible outcomes}}$$

This kind of probability is found by dividing the number of *favorable* outcomes by the *total* number of outcomes. It is not necessary to observe a number of trials in order to assess this *a priori objective probability*.

As we move on to the next booth at the charity bazaar, we find a new game. This one involves six goldfish, each in its own long tubular tank. The purpose of this game is to move the piece of mesh screening behind the goldfish to encourage it to be first to cross the finish line, without letting it slip back through the large holes in the mesh. If the goldfish are all of equal ability, the probability of winning would be one-sixth for each goldfish. Being somewhat sophisticated in games of chance, however, we pause for a few moments and watch a few plays of the game. We note that goldfish 3 seems to win half the time. We conclude that it is more likely to win in the next race than any one of the others. Casually and informally we have observed the relative frequency with which each goldfish wins. Based on the observed relative frequency we arrive at a probability of winning:

$$P(\text{goldfish 3 will win}) = .5$$

$$P(\text{any other fish will win}) = .5$$

These probability statements are based on empirical evidence and defined by the observed relative frequency. This type of probability is referred to as *empirical objective probability*.

Moving to the next booth we find another new game, a modified version of basketball. All we have to do to win one of those nice big stuffed pandas is put the ball through the basket. We note, however, that the ball is a bit larger than the ordinary basketball, and the hoop is considerably smaller than the ordinary basket. We now make an assessment of our chances of being able to put the ball through the basket. In arriving at our chances of success, we call upon our prior experience in related activities. The probability that we arrive at is a *subjective probability*. There is no theoretical framework for this situation, nor is there any historical evidence to provide us with an objective probability. Personal belief and whatever evidence is available are the only bases for the probability assessment.

Application: Dr. Spock and Women Jurors

When we think of Dr. Benjamin Spock, we probably think of him in either of two roles. His work and publications as a pediatrician-author were so popular that the phrase "Dr. Spock says" all but became a household word. In 1968, Dr. Spock and others were tried for conspiracy to violate the Selective Service Act by encouraging resistance to the war in Vietnam. Because of his work in his former capacity, it is understandable that he would want a number of women on the jury for his trial. However, even though more than half of all eligible jurors were women (the scene of the trial was Boston District Court), Dr. Spock's jury was totally devoid of women. For this reason the defense challenged the legality of the jury selection method.

The Spock trial judge's jury selections generally averaged about 15 percent women. The proportion of women on the juries of the other trial judges were all very close to the overall 29 percent average. It was concluded that the jury lists, each numbering 300 or more potential jurors from which juries are ultimately chosen, also included about 29 percent women. Either by chance or by design—even unintentional design—the Spock trial judge managed to have juries that were comprised of only 15 percent women, while the lists that were used to choose jurors contained approximately 29 percent women. It was hypothesized that having such a difference based purely on the luck of the draw was "extremely unlikely." To make the degree of unlikelihood more precise, some statistical computation was performed. The result showed that the trial judge's low proportion of women could occur strictly by chance only 1 in 1,000,000,000,000,000,000 cases. The conclusion drawn on the basis of this probability assessment was: The trial judge did indeed employ a system that was inherently biased against the inclusion of women jurors.[1]

In the Dr. Spock trial challenge, the three types of probability are illustrated. Historical data on the proportion of women jurors provided the empirical objective probability:

$$P(\text{juror is female}) = .29$$

That sheer chance would provide the Spock trial judge with only 15 percent women was based on the possible outcomes and found to be

$$P(15\%\ \text{women}) = .000\ 000\ 000\ 000\ 000\ 001$$

This is an a priori objective probability. (The size of the probability value has nothing to do with the type of probability. That the probability value is so close to zero means the event is next to impossible.)

The defense's belief that women would be more likely than men to be favorably disposed to Dr. Spock was based neither on counting the possible outcomes nor on observed relative frequency. As such its basis was in subjective probability.

There are relatively few instances in the realm of decision making in which one can base a probability statement on a priori objectivity. There are many such instances in which probability statements are based on historical evidence. Since there are many new situations in public decision making in which only past personal experience, not historical data, can be brought to bear on the situation, subjective probability statements are quite common. Although subjective, such probability statements serve a useful purpose. They provide the decision maker with the opportunity to examine various consequences of decisions in light of the relative likelihood of their occurrence. Subjective probability statements do not have the support or conviction of history; they do not pretend to have it, they should not be interpreted as having it, but the role they play should not be summarily dismissed.

[1] This brief illustration on the use of probability in law is taken from Hans Zeisel, "Dr. Spock and the Case of the Vanishing Women Jurors," *University of Chicago Law Review*, vol. 37, 1969, pp. 1–18. This illustration and other simple examples of the application of probability and statistics to law are discussed in Hans Zeisel and Harry Kalven, Jr., "Parking Tickets and Missing Women: Statistics and the Law," in Judith M. Tanur, et al. (eds.), *Statistics: A Guide to the Unknown*, Holden-Day, Inc., San Francisco, 1972, pp. 102–111.

Table 2-1 Probabilities for mayoralty election

Event	Probability
Election of:	
Democrat	.30
Republican	.40
Conservative	.10
Liberal	.20

BASIC PROBABILITY STATEMENTS

There are two fundamental probability statements:

1. A probability value is always greater than or equal to 0 and less than or equal to 1; symbolically, $0 \leq P \leq 1$.
2. The probabilities of mutually exclusive and exhaustive events total 1. Symbolically, $P(A) + P(B) + P(C) = 1$, where A, B, and C are mutually exclusive and exhaustive.

Example In a mayoralty race, there are four candidates. A political analyst has estimated the probability that each candidate will win. Table 2-1 presents the subjective probabilities ascribed by the political analyst to each candidate.

Each of these four events has a probability value between 0 and 1. Each candidate has a chance of winning; none is certain of winning or losing. The four events are mutually exclusive since no two of the candidates can both win; exactly one event will occur. The four events are exhaustive since they comprise all of the possible outcomes; the vote casting will result in the election of one of these and not some other candidate. Since these events are mutually exclusive and exhaustive, the sum of their probabilities equals 1.

BASIC PROBABILITY RULES

There is often interest in events other than the very simple ones. Basic probability rules provide a way to determine the probability of such events.

Addition Rule for Mutually Exclusive Events

The probability that one thing *or* another will happen is given by the addition rule. If the events are mutually exclusive, then

$$P(A \text{ or } B) = P(A) + P(B)$$

$P(A \text{ or } B)$	$P(A)$	$P(B)$
Probability of A or B happening	Probability of A happening	Probability of B happening

Example Using the mayoralty election probabilities, determine the probability that a major party candidate will be elected.

$$
\begin{aligned}
P(\text{Democrat or Republican}) &= P(\text{Democrat}) + P(\text{Republican}) \\
&= .30 + .40 \\
&= .70
\end{aligned}
$$

The probability that a major party candidate will be elected is .70.

Addition Rule for Events that Are Not Mutually Exclusive

If two events are not mutually exclusive, they can both occur. The addition rule must be modified to avoid double counting the probability that both will occur. This rule is

$$P(A \text{ or } B) = P(A) + P(B) - P(A \text{ and } B)$$

$P(A \text{ or } B)$	$P(A)$	$P(B)$	$P(A \text{ and } B)$
Probability of A or B happening—not mutually exclusive	Probability of A happening	Probability of B happening	Probability of A and B both happening together

Example In the mayoralty election, the Democratic and Conservative candidates are men; the Republican and Liberal candidates are women. Revising Table 2-1 to incorporate sex yields Table 2-2.

Find the probability that a major party candidate *or* a male will be elected. We first note that $P(\text{major}) = .70$ and $P(\text{male}) = .40$; the Democrat is *both* a major party candidate and a male. Using the addition rule,

Table 2-2 Probabilities for mayoralty election

Event	Sex	Party class	Probability
Election of:			
Democrat	M	Major	.30
Republican	F	Major	.40
Conservative	M	Minor	.10
Liberal	F	Minor	.20
			1.00

$$
\begin{aligned}
P(\text{major or male}) &= P(\text{major}) + P(\text{male}) - P(\text{major and male}) \\
&= .70 \qquad + .40 \qquad - .30 \\
&= .80
\end{aligned}
$$

INDEPENDENT AND DEPENDENT EVENTS

Events may be either *independent* or *dependent*. We should be careful to note at this point that we are speaking of probabilistic or statistical independence and dependence, rather than causal independence or dependence. If two events are statistically *independent*, then the occurrence of one event has no effect on the probability that the other will occur. If events are dependent, then the occurrence of one event alters the probability that the other event will occur.

When two or more events are under consideration, there are three types of probability that are of interest: marginal, joint, and conditional.

Marginal Probability

Marginal probability is the probability that one event occurs, without reference to the other event.

Example In the example, $P(\text{Democrat}) = .30$ is a marginal probability; it is the probability of just one simple event.

Joint Probability: Independent Events

The probability of two or more events occurring is called the *joint probability*. When two events are independent, the probability of both events happening is equal to the product of the two marginal probabilities. This *multiplication rule* is represented symbolically by:

$$P(A \text{ and } B) = P(A) \times P(B)$$

$P(A \text{ and } B)$ ↑	$P(A)$ ↑	$P(B)$ ↑
Joint probability of both A and B happening	Marginal probability of A happening	Marginal probability of B happening

Example On the same election day there is a referendum concerning limiting real estate taxes. Since each of the four candidates has spoken in favor of the proposition, it might be safe to say that the mayoralty election and the tax limitation proposition referendum are independent.

The same political analyst has assessed the feelings of the public with regard to the tax limitation proposition. Her subjective estimates of the

Table 2-3 Probabilities for tax limitation referendum

Event	Probability
Yes	.60
No	.40
	1.00

probabilities that the proposition will be supported or defeated are represented in Table 2-3.

The probability that the Democrat will be elected and the tax limitation referendum will be passed is the joint probability:

$$
\begin{aligned}
P(\text{Democrat and yes}) &= P(\text{Democrat}) \times P(\text{yes}) \\
&= .30 \qquad\qquad \times .60 \\
&= .18
\end{aligned}
$$

Conditional Probability: Independent Events

Another approach to independent events involves *conditional probability:* the probability of event A on condition that event B has occurred. Symbolically this is

$$P(A/B)$$

Probability of A happening — On condition that — B has occurred

If A and B are independent events, then the occurrence of one event has no effect on the probability of occurrence of the other. Symbolically this is

$$P(A/B) = P(A)$$

Example If the mayoralty election and the tax limitation referendum are independent, then regardless of who wins the mayoralty election, the probability that tax limitation will be supported is .60. Knowing there has been a Liberal victory in the mayoralty election, the probability that the tax limitation will be supported is still equal to .60. Symbolically for independent events,

$$
\begin{aligned}
P(\text{yes/Liberal}) &= P(\text{yes}) \\
&= .60
\end{aligned}
$$

Probability of "yes" on condition that the Liberal candidate has been elected — Probability of "yes"

Similarly, support of the tax referendum does not affect the probability that the Liberal candidate will be elected.

$$P(\text{Liberal/yes}) = P(\text{Liberal})$$
$$= .20$$

Probability of a Liberal victory knowing that a "yes" vote has occurred (for $P(\text{Liberal/yes})$)

Probability of a Liberal victory (for $P(\text{Liberal})$)

Conditional Probability: Dependent Events

Two events are *dependent* if they are not independent. A more positive description of dependence is that the occurrence of one event does affect the probability of the occurrence of the other. To find the conditional probability for dependent events, we use the general formula

$$P(A/B) = \frac{P(A \text{ and } B)}{P(B)}$$

$P(A/B)$: Conditional probability of A happening given that condition B has occurred

$P(A \text{ and } B)$: Joint probability of both A and B happening

$P(B)$: Marginal probability of B happening

Example Refer to Table 2-2, the probabilities for the mayoralty election. We want to know the probability of a major party victory on condition that a male is elected; that is, we want to know

$$P(\text{major party/male}) = ?$$

To use the general rule

$$P(\text{major party/male}) = \frac{P(\text{major party and male})}{P(\text{male})}$$

we first note the joint probability

$$P(\text{major and male}) = .30$$

The Democrat is the only candidate *both* major party and male. We note also that

$$P(\text{male}) = .40$$

Now

$$P(\text{major}/\text{male}) = \frac{P(\text{major and male})}{P(\text{male})}$$

$$= \frac{.30}{.40}$$

$$= .75$$

There is a .75 probability that a major party candidate will be elected *on condition that* a male is elected. This is different from $P(\text{major}) = .70$, the marginal probability.

As expected, the occurrence of one event, male, does affect the probability that the other event, major party, will occur.

Joint Probability: Dependent Events

For dependent events it is not true that the joint probability equals the product of the marginal probabilities. However, the general rule for conditional probability provides a *modified multiplication rule.* If we solve for $P(A \text{ and } B)$ by cross multiplication, then the relationship

$$P(A/B) = \frac{P(A \text{ and } B)}{P(B)}$$

is written as

$$P(A \text{ and } B) = P(A/B) \times P(B)$$

- $P(A \text{ and } B)$: Joint probability of both A and B happening
- $P(A/B)$: Conditional probability of A happening on condition that B has happened
- $P(B)$: Marginal probability of the condition B happening

Example On the same election day the candidates for Controller are a Democrat and a Republican; their probabilities of election are presented in Table 2-4. The election is dependent on the mayoralty election, and vice versa. We emphasize that this dependence is a statistical one that repre-

Table 2-4 Probabilities for Controller election

Event	Probability
Election of:	
Democrat	.60
Republican	.40
	1.00

sents an association between the two elections but not necessarily a cause-effect relationship.

It may be, for example, that if the Democratic mayoralty candidate is elected, the Democratic Controller candidate is almost a sure thing. This might be quantified by

$$P(\text{Democratic Controller}/\text{Democratic Mayor}) = .90$$

The joint probability of both Democrats being elected is

$$\begin{aligned} P(\text{Dem Cont \& Dem Mayor}) &= P(\text{Dem Cont/Dem Mayor}) \times P(\text{Dem Mayor}) \\ &= .90 \times .30 \\ &= .27 \end{aligned}$$

The multiplication formula

$$P(A \text{ and } B) = P(A/B) \times P(B)$$

and the conditional probability formula

$$P(A/B) = \frac{P(A \text{ and } B)}{P(B)}$$

relate the three types of probabilities: marginal, joint, and conditional. If any two of these are known, the basic formula can be used to find the third one. If only one of the probabilities is known, then more information must be gotten before the formulas can be used. The relationships among the three types of probabilities are illustrated in the next section.

ILLUSTRATION: JOINT, MARGINAL, AND CONDITIONAL PROBABILITIES

A school district is in the process of doing some long-range planning. There are forecasts of continued but small decline in enrollment, and of continuous tight-budget situations. It has decided to assess the effectiveness and the basic needs of many of its curriculum components, so that when cutbacks become necessary, they can be made according to some well-thought-out plan rather than in the heat of impending crisis. As part of the feedback system that it is attempting to develop, it has compiled questionnaire responses from its alumni. One block of questions on the questionnaire attempted to assess the relationship between taking high school chemistry and succeeding at college chemistry. Based on the relative frequency of responses, a joint probability table was developed. It is presented in Table 2-5. The table shows that 70 percent of the responding students received a grade of C or better in college chemistry. Thirty percent had previously taken high school chemistry *and* earned a grade of C or better in college chemistry. The relative frequency provides the basis for objective probabilities.

Table 2-5 Joint probabilities for taking high school chemistry and grade in college chemistry

	Grade in college chemistry		Marginal probability of taking high school chemistry
High school chemistry	C or better (B_1)	Less than C (B_2)	
Yes (A_1)	.30	.10	.40
No (A_2)	.40	.20	.60
Marginal probability of grade in college chemistry	.70	.30	1.00

To determine whether taking high school chemistry affects the probability of success in college chemistry, one compares *P*(C or better/high school chemistry) with *P*(C or better/no high school chemistry). Using the symbolism of the table,

$$P(B_1/A_1) = \frac{P(B_1 \text{ and } A_1)}{P(A_1)}$$

$$= \frac{.30}{.40}$$

$$= .75$$

This means that 75 percent of those who *took* high school chemistry earned C or better in college chemistry. To complete the comparison, one finds

$$P(B_1/A_2) = \frac{P(B_1 \text{ and } A_2)}{P(A_2)}$$

$$= \frac{.40}{.60}$$

$$= .667$$

and about 67 percent of those who did *not take* high school chemistry earned a C or better in college chemistry.

From this brief analysis it appears that a student who has had high school chemistry is just slightly more likely to get a C or better in college chemistry than a student who has not had high school chemistry. One interpretation offered for the school board's consideration follows. Since taking the high school chemistry course seems to have little effect on success in subsequent related courses, the course should be among the first to be dropped in times of need.

In response, it is pointed out that one of the purposes of high school science courses is to generate interest as well as to impart basic knowledge. Therefore, the more pertinent question is not whether a good or poor grade is received for college chemistry, but whether college chemistry is taken at all. Interest should

Table 2-6 Incomplete Joint probabilities of taking high school chemistry and college chemistry

	College chemistry		
High school chemistry	Yes (C_1)	No (C_2)	Marginal probability of high school chemistry
Yes (A_1)	.08	—	—
No (A_2)	—	—	—
marginal probability of college chemistry	.20	.80	1.00

be directed at the probability that a student took college chemistry on condition that (1), he had previously taken high school chemistry and (2), he had not previously taken high school chemistry.

Let C_1 represent the fact that college chemistry has been taken and C_2 that college chemistry has not been taken. The probabilities to be compared are

$$P(C_1/A_1) \qquad \text{and} \qquad P(C_1/A_2)$$

Reexamining the questionnaire responses reveals that

$$P(C_1) = .20 \qquad \text{and} \qquad P(C_2) = .80$$

The preceding analysis, Table 2-5, revealed that 40 percent of the students who took college chemistry had previously taken high school chemistry; that is,[2]

$$P(A_1/C_1) = .40$$

The probabilities of interest are $P(C_1/A_1)$ and $P(C_1/A_2)$. To find these, we first must get the joint probabilities. Using the multiplication rule to find the joint probability of taking high school chemistry *and* college chemistry yields:

$$\begin{aligned} P(A_1 \text{ and } C_1) &= P(A_1/C_1) \cdot P(C_1) \\ &= .40 \cdot .20 \\ &= .08 \end{aligned}$$

We can now partially complete a table of joint probabilities relating the taking of high school chemistry and the taking of college chemistry. This table is presented in Table 2-6 Incomplete.

It is noted from the responses that of those who did not take college chemistry, 75 percent had not taken high school chemistry either. In probability terms, this is $P(A_2/C_2) = .75$. With this we find the joint probability that a res-

[2] It might seem strange that the condition, college chemistry, occurs later in time than the primary event, high school chemistry. Recall that there is no cause-effect relationship expressed even if the events are found to be dependent. Some find it easier to understand if "knowing" is used in place of "on condition." That is, $P(A_1/C_1)$ is the probability that a student had had high school chemistry knowing that the student later took college chemistry.

pondent did not take college chemistry *and* had not previously taken high school chemistry as follows:

$$P(A_2 \text{ and } C_2) = P(A_2/C_2) \cdot P(C_2)$$
$$= .75 \cdot .80$$
$$= .60$$

We include the joint probability of A_2 and C_2 in Table 2-6. In order to complete the table, we note that the marginal probability is equal to the sum of all of the joint probabilities involving the relevant event. For example:

$$P(C_1) = P(C_1 \text{ and } A_1) + P(C_1 \text{ and } A_2)$$
$$.20 = .08 + P(C_1 \text{ and } A_2)$$

and so

$$P(C_1 \text{ and } A_2) = .12$$

We note also that

$$P(A_2) = P(C_1 \text{ and } A_2) + P(C_2 \text{ and } A_2)$$
$$= .12 + .60$$
$$= .72$$

This enables us to complete Table 2-6, giving all the joint and marginal probabilities.

Table 2-6 Joint probabilities of taking high school chemistry and college chemistry

	College chemistry		
High school chemistry	Yes (C_1)	No (C_2)	Marginal probability of high school chemistry
Yes (A_1)	.08	.20	.28
No (A_2)	.12	.60	.72
Marginal probability of college chemistry	.20	.80	1.00

Using this new table of probabilities, we are able to determine whether taking high school chemistry has any effect on the probability of taking college chemistry. In order to do this, we determine the following conditional probabilities:

$$P(C_1/A_1) = \frac{P(C_1 \text{ and } A_1)}{P(A_1)}$$
$$= \frac{.08}{.28}$$
$$= .286$$

and
$$P(C_1/A_2) = \frac{P(C_1 \text{ and } A_2)}{P(A_2)}$$
$$= \frac{.12}{.72}$$
$$= .167$$

Based on this sample, taking high school chemistry greatly increases the probability that the student will take college chemistry. We wish to emphasize here that the probabilities should not be inferred as indicating that taking high school chemistry somehow causes one to take college chemistry. It could very well be that taking both high school chemistry and college chemistry is dependent on some third factor that is not measured here, for instance, an underlying interest in science or an ambition to be a doctor. More properly we would say that taking high school chemistry is associated with taking college chemistry.

The preceding illustration, with the probabilities summarized in Tables 2-5 and 2-6, serves to point out to the decision maker and user of analysis that the questions at which analysis is directed are more important than the actual analysis and the computations. Table 2-5 implies that taking high school chemistry has no effect on ultimate success in college chemistry; however, Table 2-6 indicates that taking high school chemistry has some effect on whether a person will ultimately take college chemistry. The former suggests taking high school chemistry has no effect, while the latter suggests that taking high school chemistry does have an effect. We conclude that the overriding question rests not on the probabilities involved but on the choice of an appropriate measure. Once the measure and required information are decided and agreed upon, relative frequencies and probabilities can be used to shed light on the situation. The school district's planning process depends more on the supposed purpose of any particular course than on the probability values that are derived; the probability values, however, can assist in determining whether certain purposes are being satisfied.

Using one kind of conditional probability, $P(A_1/C_1)$, and marginal probabilities to find the opposite conditional probability, $P(C_1/A_1)$, is the foundation of *Bayes' theorem*. The use of conditional probabilities and Bayes' theorem are useful in revising probabilities on the basis of new information. This subject will be treated in Chapter 4 in some detail.

SUMMARY

Many events have some chance or probability of occurring. Probability can be either *subjective*, based on personal belief, or *objective*. Objective probabilities are either (1) *a priori*, arrived at by understanding the chance process, or (2) *empirical*, arrived at by finding the relative frequency of the event.

Fundamental notions of probability are expressed in a few statements and rules.

Two basic statements

$0 \leq P(A) \leq 1$	for any event A
$P(A) + P(B) + P(C) = 1$	for A, B, and C mutually exclusive and exhaustive

Addition rules

$P(A \text{ or } B) = P(A) + P(B)$	for A and B mutually exclusive
$P(A \text{ or } B) = P(A) + P(B) - P(A \text{ and } B)$	for A and B not mutually exclusive

Multiplication rules

Independent events: $P(A \text{ and } B) = P(A) \times P(B)$

$$P(A/B) = P(A)$$

Dependent events: $P(A \text{ and } B) = P(A/B) \times P(B)$

$$P(A/B) = \frac{P(A \text{ and } B)}{P(B)}$$

BIBLIOGRAPHY

Boot, John C. G., and Edwin B. Cox: *Statistical Analysis for Managerial Decisions,* McGraw-Hill Book Company, New York, 1974.

Sanders, Donald H., A. Franklin Murph, and Robert J. Eng: *Statistics: A Fresh Approach,* McGraw-Hill Book Company, New York, 1976.

Schlaifer, R.: *Probability and Statistics for Business Decisions,* McGraw-Hill Book Company, New York, 1959.

Tanur, Judith M., Frederick Mosteller, William H. Kruskal, Richard F. Link, Richard S. Pieters, and Gerald R. Rising (eds.): *Statistics: A Guide to the Unknown,* Holden-Day, Inc., San Francisco, 1972.

White, Orion, and Bruce Gates: "Statistical Theory and Equity in the Delivery of Social Services," *Public Administration Review,* vol. 34, January–February 1974, pp. 43–50.

Zeisel, Hans: "Dr. Spock and the Case of the Vanishing Women Jurors," *University of Chicago Law Review,* vol. 37, 1969, pp. 1–18.

Zeisel, Hans, and Harry Kalven, Jr.: "Parking Tickets and Missing Women: Statistics and the Law," in Judith M. Tanur et al. (eds.), *Statistics: A Guide to the Unknown,* Holden-Day, Inc., San Francisco, 1972, pp. 102–111.

EXERCISES

Extensions of chapter examples

2-1 In the 10-number game-wheel example (see p. 22), what is the probability that:

(*a*) An even number will win?
(*b*) A number over 7 will win?
(*c*) An even number over 7 will win?

2-2 In the goldfish example, *P*(goldfish 3 will win) = .5; assume the other five fish are equally likely to win. What is the probability that:

(*a*) Goldfish 1 will win?

(*b*) An odd-numbered goldfish will win?

(*c*) An even-numbered goldfish over 7 will win?

2-3 Assume that the population is half men and half women; hence, in picking a person at random, the probability that the person is a woman is .50. In picking 12 people for a jury, what is the probability that:

(*a*) The jury will have no women?

(*b*) The jury will have twelve women and no men?

(*Hint:* Assume that picking successive jurors are independent events.)

2-4 In the same population as in exercise 2-3, suppose two juries are being chosen, independently of each other. What is the probability that there will be no women on either jury, assuming that jurors are chosen at random from the entire population.

2-5 In the mayoralty election (Table 2-2) what is the probability that:

(*a*) A minor party candidate will be elected?

(*b*) A Conservative or a woman will be elected?

(*c*) A Liberal and a male will be elected?

2-6 Using Tables 2-1 and 2-3, find the probability that:

(*a*) A major party candidate will be elected and the tax limitation referendum will be passed.

(*b*) A Republican will win on condition that the tax referendum is passed.

2-7 Using Tables 2-1 and 2-4, can you find the probability that both Republicans will win? If not, what further information is needed?

2-8 Assume *P*(Republican Controller/Republican Mayor) = .80. Now answer exercise 2-7.

2-9 Recall that the joint probability of both Democrats being elected is .27. It is further believed that if the Liberal mayoralty candidate wins, there is no chance that the Republican will win the controllership. Using Tables 2-1 and 2-4, and exercise 2-8, construct a complete joint probability table for the mayoralty and Controller elections.

2-10 Refer to Table 2-6. The text specifically indicates how most of the probabilities were derived. Where did the .20 and .28 come from?

2-11 In the school district's analysis of the relation between high school and college chemistry courses, an antagonist of high school science courses (they are expensive, it is argued) uses Table 2-5 as the basis for his argument: "Of the students who have done well in college chemistry (C or better), the probability that they had not had high school chemistry is .40/.70 = .57, whereas the probability that they had had high school chemistry is only .30/.70 = .43. It seems pretty obvious that a prospective chemistry student is better off skipping the subject in high school." Discuss the claim, using the same table to point out the emptiness of the argument. (*Hint:* Consider "of the students who have not done well in college.")

Other applications

2-12 An attempt is being made to establish formal job links by the Civil Service Commission. The skill scores of those who have attempted typing-proficiency examinations and keypunch-proficiency examinations are being investigated. The following results have been found: 50 percent passed both exams, 40 percent failed the keypunch exam, and 20 percent failed the typing exam.

(*a*) What is the probability that if a person passes typing he will also pass keypunch?

(*b*) What is the probability that a person fails keypunch knowing that the person has failed typing?

(*c*) Are the two exams independent or dependent? Justify your answer using probabilities, and discuss whether this dependence or independence is as expected.

2-13 The Civil Rights Commission is investigating the hiring policy of a municipality. The municipality has a stated policy that where the number of adequately qualified candidates for a particular position(s) exceeds the number of openings, the position will be offered to the candidate chosen by lot. The record shows that in each of the past 4 years, there were five eligible candidates for a particular position in the municipality. Of the five eligible candidates, there were two minority candidates last year and the year before, while there were three minority candidates in the 2 preceding years. However, not one of the four positions was, in fact, offered to a minority candidate. The municipality maintains that that was "the luck of the draw." What is the probability that the luck of the draw would yield such apparent bias? As an investigator or other involved party, on the basis of that probability would you be willing to either draw a conclusion or recommend any action?

2-14 In recent years a particular state has become known for its failure to pass a state budget by the start of a fiscal year. Some banks within the state have become extremely sensitive to the budget decision, since they lend money to some state-related institutions if the budget is not passed on time. The current assessment is that there is a .6 probability that the House will pass a budget, a .4 probability that the Senate will pass a budget, and a .3 probability that they will both pass a budget on time.

(*a*) What is the probability that the Senate will pass the budget, on condition that the House passes it?

(*b*) What is the probability that the House will pass the budget, on condition that the Senate passes it?

(*c*) What is the probability that neither will pass a budget on time?

2-15 In Traho Village there is only one intersection of main streets that has a traffic light. In the past year, there have been 23 pedestrians hit by vehicles at that intersection. The State Safety Commissioner has decided to investigate those accidents. Through accounts of the injured, the motorists, and witnesses, she has been able to determine that 16 of those accidents occurred while pedestrians were crossing with the light, and only 7 occurred while the pedestrians were crossing against the light. She seems a bit perplexed since it seems that one should be safer when crossing with the light, rather than being twice as likely to be hit than when crossing against the light. Can you resolve her perplexity?

2-16 A neighborhood medical clinic offers examinations for the detection of stress. It has found that 70 percent of those requesting the test are, in fact, suffering from stress. The test it uses is not perfect (what test is?). If a person is suffering from stress, there is only an 80 percent chance that the test will detect it. If a person is not suffering from stress, there is a 10 percent chance that the test will erroneously indicate stress. Given a positive test result, what are the chances that the person being tested is suffering from stress?

Project problems

2-17 Refer to E. S. Savas, "The Political Properties of Crystalline H_2O: Planning for Snow Emergencies in New York," *Management Science,* vol. 20, October 1973, pp. 137–145. What events were assigned probabilities, and were these a priori, empirical, or subjective? For which conclusions was the assumption of independent events useful? Do you believe the assumption was justified?

2-18 Many states have lotteries and number games. Choose one such game from your state or some other state. What are the winning events? Determine the probability of each such event. Use either data or published odds in finding the probabilities.

CHAPTER
THREE
PROBABILITY DISTRIBUTIONS

This chapter, like Chapter 2, serves as a review of basic material on probability distributions, random variables, and the mean and standard deviation. One discrete distribution, the binomial, and one continuous distribution, the normal, will be treated in some detail because of their widespread applicability. The reader familiar with such matter is encouraged to move ahead. Readers less familiar can benefit from a fuller reading.

INTRODUCTION

To introduce the notion of a probability distribution, we go back to the simple wheel game of Chapter 2. Table 3-1 presents the possible outcomes of a spin of the wheel together with the probability of each.

Once we have decided to bet on a particular number, the events of interest are winning, when our number comes up, and losing, when any other number comes up. A *probability distribution* associates a probability value with each of the mutually exclusive exhaustive events. Table 3-2 presents the probability distribution of the possible results of spinning the wheel. These probability distributions are based on objective probabilities.

We can refer to the list of candidates and their probabilities in Table 2-1 as the probability distribution of the possible events in the mayoralty election.

Table 3-1 Outcomes of one spin of the wheel and their probabilities

Winning number	Probability
1	.1
2	.1
3	.1
4	.1
5	.1
6	.1
7	.1
8	.1
9	.1
10	.1
	1.00

Similarly, Table 2-3 presents the probability distribution of the tax limitation referendum results. These probability distributions are based on subjective probabilities.

It should be emphasized here that a probability distribution does not describe what actually happens in a relatively few occurrences. Rather it provides information on what we would expect in the long run, or provides an assessment of the likelihood of each event.

Example Table 3-2 gives the probability distribution on winning a prize. It *does not* mean that in ten attempts, we would lose exactly nine times and win exactly once. It does mean that in the long run, we would expect to win 10 percent of the time.

Example Table 2-1 gives the probability distribution for the mayoral candidates. In the election only one candidate will win. That the Republican candidate has a higher probability than the other candidates does not mean that she will win. It does mean that the analyst who assigned the subjective probabilities believes she is more likely to win than the others. The election will occur only once. Thus the probability values cannot be meaningfully interpreted ''in the long run'' in this case.

Table 3-2 Probability distribution of the results of one spin of the wheel

Event	Probability
Lose	.9
Win	.1
	1.0

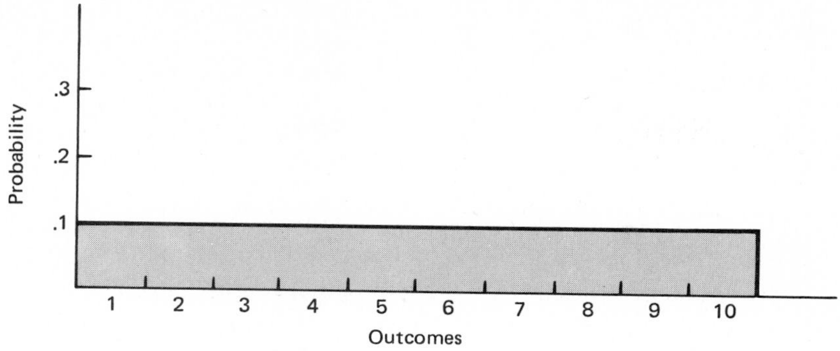

Figure 3-1 Uniform probability distribution: The game wheel.

A probability distribution can also be represented graphically. Figure 3-1 depicts the probability distributions corresponding to Table 3-1. This probability distribution is an example of a *uniform probability distribution,* one in which all outcomes have equal probability.

Figure 3-2 depicts the probability distribution corresponding to Table 3-2. This probability distribution is an example of a *Bernoulli probability distribution,* one in which there are only two possible outcomes. As we shall soon see, this distribution is the basis for many probability applications in public decision making.

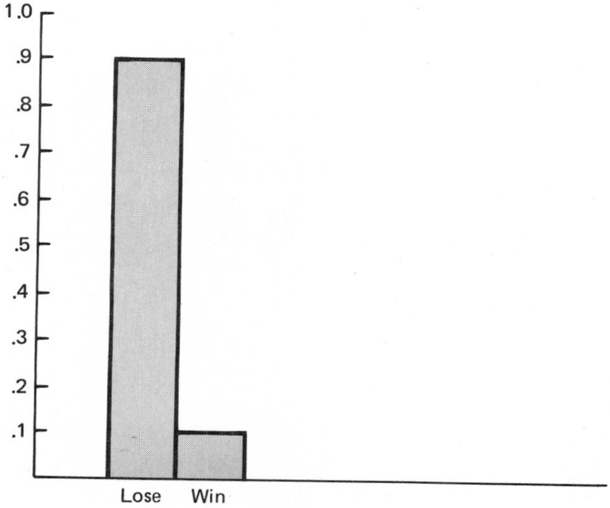

Figure 3-2 Bernoulli probability distribution: Win or Lose at the game wheel.

RANDOM VARIABLES

A *random variable* is a variable that takes on numerical values as a result of random events. The "winning number" on the spin of the wheel (Table 3-1) is an example of a random variable. "Lose" or "win" on the spin of the wheel (Table 3-2) is not an example of a random variable since there is no numerical value that results from the various possible events. However, "number of prizes won" is a random variable that takes on numerical values as a result of the events "win" and "lose." Table 3-3 illustrates how the random variable corresponds to the events, and how the probability distribution corresponds to the random variable.

Some events are meaningfully associated with the values of a random variable while some are not. It would not make very much sense to say in Table 2-1 that the election of a Democrat could be given a numerical value of 1, the election of a Republican a numerical value of 2, the election of a Liberal the numerical value of 3, and the election of a Conservative the numerical value of 4.

One of the questions asked in a census is the age of the head of the household. This is a characteristic to which is associated a meaningful numerical value. The number of residents per household is another example of an attribute that is meaningfully represented by a numerical quantity; thus the number of residents per household is a random variable. The various responses to the question are the values that the random variable can take on. As the census taker approaches a household, he or she does not know beforehand what value the random variable "number of people in household" will assume; however, the probability of any one value occurring is known, or at least is estimated on the basis of prior censuses. Some examples of random variables, their descriptions, and the values they can assume are presented in Table 3-4.

Discrete and Continuous Random Variables

Random variables are classified as either *discrete* or *continuous*. A discrete random variable can take on only a limited number of values, usually whole-number values. Examples of discrete random variables are number of residents in a household, profit on a $1 lottery ticket, number of township employees in each township of Tiger County, and others as in Table 3-4.

A continuous random variable can take on any value—not just whole

Table 3-3 Probability distribution of random variable "number of prizes won" on one spin of the wheel

Event	Random variable	Probability
Lose	0	.9
Win	1	.1
		1.0

Table 3-4 Examples of random variables

Random variable	Description	Type	Values
R	Number of residents in a household	Discrete	1, 2, 3, . . . , 20, . . .
X	Number of arrests in a precinct in each hour	Discrete	0, 1, 2, 3, . . .
Y	Ultimate profit on a $1 lottery ticket	Discrete	−$1, $49, $99, $999, and $999,999
N	Number of positive reactions by an individual to a drug screen on a single occasion	Discrete	0, 1
W	Number of positive reactions by a group of 20 people to a drug screen on a single occasion	Discrete	0, 1, 2, . . . , 20
S	Score on a standardized aptitude test	Discrete*	200, 201, . . . , 800
P	Proportion of the population in favor of a particular candidate	Continuous	Any number between 0 and 1; that is, $0 \leq P \leq 1$
C	Concentration of noxious gases in atmosphere (in parts per million)	Continuous	Any number within a range of values, say $0 \leq C \leq 1000$
A	Absenteeism rates in a training program	Continuous	Any value from 0 to 100

* Variable S, although discrete, is often treated as if it were continuous because it has many possible values.

numbers—within a given range. Examples of continuous variables are proportion of voters in favor of a resolution, crime rate, and others as in Table 3-4. Discrete random variables with many possible values are usually treated as continuous ones. Some examples are test scores, annual income per household, and number of voters in favor of an issue.

A characteristic of random variables that is very useful in decision making is the expected value or mean.

The Expected Value, or Mean, of a Random Variable

The concept of a mean or counting average of a bunch of numbers is probably a rather familiar one; to find it, add all the numbers involved and divide by however many numbers there are. The *expected value,* or the *mean,* of a random variable is similar. Instead of taking the simple average of all possible values, take the weighted average, where values that are more likely to occur are weighted more heavily. Specifically, the *expected value of a random variable is the sum of the products of all possible values times their probability.*

Example Based on available records, the number of township employees in each township of Tiger County has the probability distribution given in

Table 3-5 Probability distribution of number of township employees

Value of random variable T, number of employees	Probability
2	.10
4	.30
5	.20
8	.30
12	.10
	1.00

Table 3-5. We find the mean or expected value of the number of employees per township by finding the weighted average, with the probability values as the weights. The calculations for finding the mean or the expected value of the number of employees are presented in Table 3-6. We say, then that in Tiger County each township employs, on the average, six employees. Figure 3-3 is a graphic presentation of the probability distribution of Table 3-5.

In the example above, available records were used to find the mean. In cases where the probability distribution is based on subjective assessment, the expected value is one expression of the personal belief.

Probability distributions are discrete or continuous, depending on whether their random variables are discrete or continuous. There are many probability distributions of both types. We will briefly examine one frequently occurring example of each type.

THE BINOMIAL DISTRIBUTION

When an individual is asked whether he or she favors a particular issue, the response can be either "yes" or "no." When an individual is screened for a

Table 3-6 Calculation of expected value

Value of random variable T, number of employees T_i	Probability that T will take on the particular value, $P(T = T_i)$	Weighted number of employees $T_i \cdot P(T_i)$
$T_1 = 2$	.10	.20
$T_2 = 4$	.30	1.20
$T_3 = 5$	.20	1.00
$T_4 = 8$	.30	2.40
$T_5 = 12$	.10	1.20
	1.00	$E(T) = 6.0$

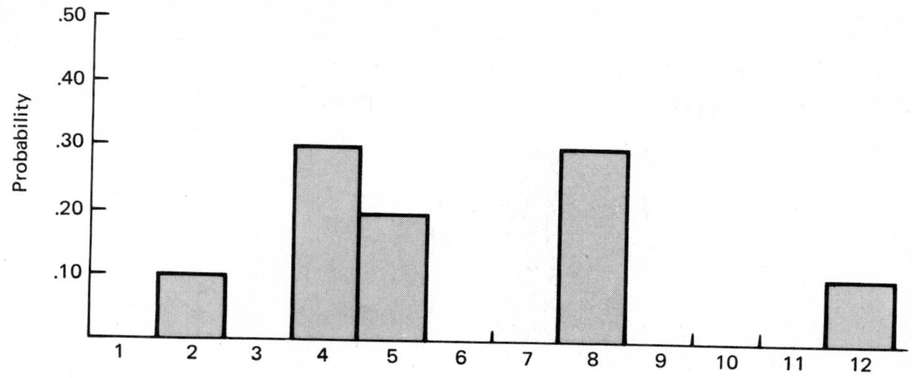

Figure 3-3 Probability distribution of number of township employees.

particular symptom, or reaction, either there is a reaction or there is no reaction. When a person holds a term insurance policy, either the person (or beneficiaries) collects on the policy or he or she does not collect on the policy. These are examples of no-yes, zero-one, failure-success occurrences. Each such occurrence or trial has exactly two possible outcomes.

In decision making it is often of interest to analyze the results of many such trials. As a consequence, such trials frequently take place or are executed in bunches. For example, a pollster may ask a number of people whether they are in favor of a particular issue. A regional health agency may screen a number of individuals for a particular condition. An insurance company or an insurance commission will examine a number of policies. The binomial distribution is useful in analyzing such situations provided that the repeated trials are an example of a Bernoulli process.

The Bernoulli Process

The process of repeated trials is called a Bernoulli process if the following characteristics apply:

1. Each trial has exactly two possible outcomes.
2. The probability of a success on any trial is the same as on any other trial.
3. The outcome of any trial is independent of the outcome of any other trial.

Example Winning a prize or not in the spin-the-wheel game follows a Bernoulli process:

1. On each trial, we either lose or win.
2. On each trial, $p(\text{winning}) = .10$, and this does not change as the wheel is respun.
3. The outcome on any prior spin has no effect on the current trial.

The Binomial Distribution Formula

When there is a specific number of Bernoulli trials involved, then the random variable "number of successes" follows a binomial probability distribution. The probability of r successes in n trials is given by the binomial formula:

$$P(r \text{ successes in } n \text{ trials}) = \frac{n!}{r!(n-r)!} \cdot p^r q^{n-r}$$

where n = number of trials
r = number of successes
p = probability of success on each trial
$q = 1 - p$ = probability of failure on each trial
$r!$ = r *factorial*, which means $r(r-1)(r-2) \cdots 3 \cdot 2 \cdot 1$

The calculations in using this formula for any but a small number of trials are extremely tedious, and so, as is the case with most commonly occurring probability distributions, probability tables are available when and where needed.[1]

Example What is the probability of winning 2 times in 5 spins of the wheel?

$$n = 5$$

$$r = 2$$

$$p = .1$$

$$q = 1 - p = .9$$

$$P(2 \text{ successes in 5 trials}) = \frac{5!}{2!(5-2)!}(.1)^2(.9)^3$$

$$= \frac{5 \cdot 4 \cdot 3 \cdot 2 \cdot 1}{2 \cdot 1 \cdot 3 \cdot 2 \cdot 1}(.1)^2(.9)^3$$

$$= 10(.01)(.729)$$

$$= .0729$$

The binomial distribution gives the probability value for the random variable "number of successes" in a specific number of trials. As with any distribution, it can be presented graphically as well as numerically. The distribution for the above spin-the-wheel example is presented graphically in Figure 3-4. The values have been calculated using the binomial formula.

[1] The binomial probability distribution formula is composed of two parts. The first factor $n!/r!(n-r)!$ is the number of combinations of n things combined r at a time. The second factor $p^r(1-p)^{n-r}$ represents the probability of having r successes, and $n - r$ failures in a particular order in n trials. Most basic probability textbooks provide a more detailed explanation of combinations and the mathematical basis for the binomial probability formula.

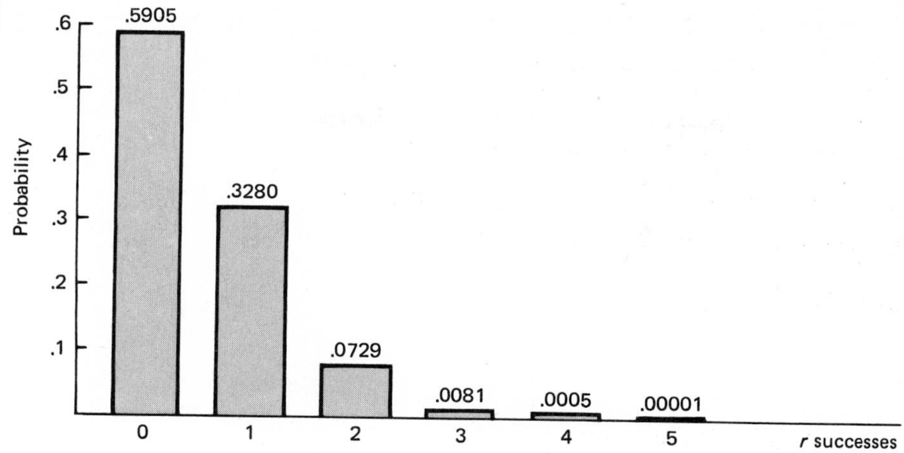

Figure 3-4 Binomial distribution for $n = 5$, $p = .1$, $q = .9$.

Example What is the probability distribution of the number of successes in 5 spins if a wager is placed on 4 of the 10 numbers for each spin? This problem differs from the previous one in the probability of success on each spin: $p = .4$. The distribution is represented in Figure 3-5.

Cumulative Binomial Distribution

In decision making, there may be more interest in knowing the probability of r *or more* successes than *exactly* r successes. A pollster may want to know whether half *or more* people favor an issue. A regional health agency may screen to see if there is one *or more* positive reactions.

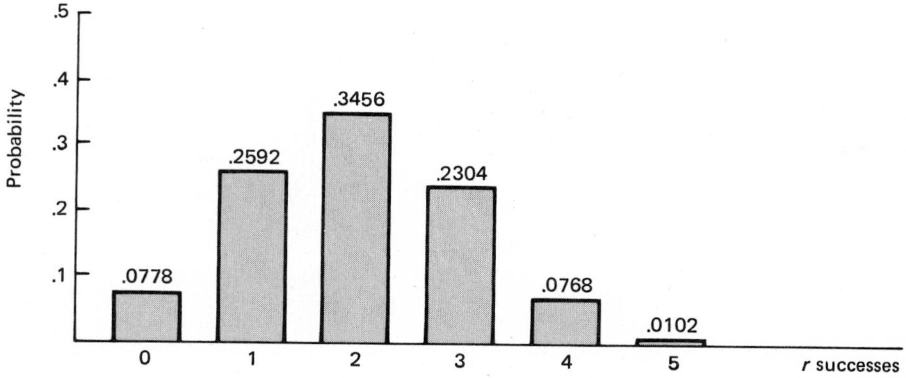

Figure 3-5 Binomial distribution for $n = 5$, $p = .4$, $q = .6$.

This *cumulative binomial probability distribution* is defined as:

$$P(r \text{ or more successes in } n \text{ trials}) = P(r \text{ successes}) + P(r + 1 \text{ successes}) + \cdots + P(n \text{ successes})$$

Example Find the probability of winning 2 or more prizes.

$$n = 5$$

$$r = 2$$

$$p = .1$$

$$q = 1 - p = .9$$

$$\begin{aligned} p(2 \text{ or more}) &= p(2) + p(3) + p(4) + p(5) \\ &= .0729 + .0081 + .0005 + .00001 \\ &= .0815 \end{aligned}$$

Cumulative binomial tables For convenience, tables of binomial and cumulative binomial probability values are generally available. Calculating a cumulative probability value from a binomial table requires adding all the separate values. Calculating a simple probability value from a cumulative binomial table requires only a single subtraction. For this reason, the cumulative table is presented in the Appendix. We now illustrate the use of the table.

Example Alcoholism is a recognized problem among national politicians and their spouses. One estimate is that 25 percent of them have a problem. In a group of 10, what is the probability that 2 or more have an alcohol problem?

$$n = 10$$

$$r = 2$$

$$p = .25$$

Use the table as follows:

1. Look in Appendix Table 1 for the $n = 10$ table.
2. Look through the $n = 10$ table for the column headed by $p = .25$ (printed as 25).
3. Move down that column to the $r = 2$ row, where we find the value 7560. This means $P(2 \text{ or more alcohol problems}) = .7560$.

The same cumulative binomial table can be used to find the probability of an exact number of occurrences, as is now illustrated.

Example In the previous example, find the probability of exactly 2 alcohol problems.

$$n = 10$$

$$r = 2$$

$$p = .25$$

$$\begin{aligned} P(\text{exactly } 2) &= P(2 \text{ or more}) - P(3 \text{ or more}) \\ &= .7560 - .4744 \\ &= .2816 \end{aligned}$$

The binomial probability table presents values only for $p \leq .50$. If a particular situation has $p > .50$, a slight rewording of the problem statement will put it into a form for which the table can be used. We here illustrate that process.

Example It has been noted that after attending a "by invitation only" federal agency security seminar, a person has a probability of .6 that he or she will ultimately be promoted to the assistant secretary level or better. Of the current class of 10 participants, what is the probability that exactly 7 of the 10 will ultimately be so promoted? We note that the salient features of the problem are:

$$n = 10 \qquad r = 7 \qquad p = .60$$

Since the table does not contain probability values for $p = .60$, we restate the problem. Instead of looking for the probability that 7 will be promoted where the basic individual probability is .60, we look for the probability that 3 will not be promoted, where the individual probability of not being promoted is .40. Now the salient features of the problem are:

$$n = 10 \qquad r = 3 \qquad p = .40$$

We can now use Appendix Table 1 to find the probability of this event.

$$\begin{aligned} &P(3 \text{ not promoted}) \\ &\quad = P(3 \text{ or more not promoted}) - P(4 \text{ or more not promoted}) \\ &\quad = .8327 - .6177 \\ &\quad = .2150 \end{aligned}$$

Thus the probability that 7 of the 10 will ultimately be promoted is .2150.

So far we have been concerned with the binomial distribution, one of the many discrete probability distributions. Since it does not suit our purpose to examine many distributions, we now turn our attention to a continuous distribution, the normal probability distribution. In the normal distribution, the mean and standard deviation play integral roles. We examine them before introducing the normal distribution.

THE MEAN AND STANDARD DEVIATION

Most of us have found and used the *mean* (or average) of a set of values. The *mean* is also a measure of central tendency of a probability distribution. It is a way of measuring the center of the data or the distribution. To find the mean, add the numbers and divide by how many there are. Symbolically this is:

$$\mu = \frac{\Sigma x_i}{n}$$

Σ — Symbol meaning "the sum of"
x_i — Values of the random variable in the distribution
n — Number of values used to find the mean
μ — Greek letter mu, the mean of a distribution

Example Tiger County has 10 townships. The number of employees of the various townships is as follows:

2, 4, 5, 8, 12, 4, 5, 8, 4, 8

The mean number of employees is:

$$\begin{aligned}\mu &= \frac{\Sigma x_i}{n} \\ &= \frac{2 + 4 + 5 + 8 + 12 + 4 + 5 + 8 + 4 + 8}{10} \\ &= \tfrac{60}{10} = 6\end{aligned}$$

The mean is a useful measure. In this example it gives the average number of township employees. Looking at the values, we see that the number of employees is centered around 6. The mean gives no information, however, about how the values are spread out. A measure of dispersion or variation is needed.

The most commonly used measure of dispersion is the *standard deviation.* The standard deviation is calculated by following these steps:

1. Subtract the mean from each value.
2. Square each difference of step 1.
3. Add all the squared differences of step 2.
4. Divide the sum of step 3 by the number of values.
5. Take the square root of the quotient of step 4.

$$\sigma = \sqrt{\frac{\Sigma(x_i - \mu)^2}{n}}$$

Greek letter sigma, the standard deviation of a distribution

Another and related measure of variation is the *variance*. The variance is the quotient of step 4; that is, the variance is the average of the squared differences. One of the interpretive difficulties in using the variance arises from the fact that the units are squared. For example, if the random variable and the mean are measured in dollars or in employees, then the variance is measured in squared dollars or in squared employees, neither of which is very meaningful. The standard deviation is measured in the same units as the random variable itself; consequently, it is more easily interpreted.

The greater the dispersion of the values, the greater will be the standard deviation. A more meaningful interpretation of the standard deviation will be given in the discussion of the normal distribution.

Example Find the standard deviation of the number of township employees in Tiger County.

Step 1	Step 2
$2 - 6 = -4$	16
$4 - 6 = -2$	4
$5 - 6 = -1$	1
$8 - 6 = 2$	4
$12 - 6 = 6$	36
$4 - 6 = -2$	4
$5 - 6 = -1$	1
$8 - 6 = 2$	4
$4 - 6 = -2$	4
$8 - 6 = 2$	4
Step 3	78
Step 4	$\frac{78}{10} = 7.8 =$ variance
Step 5	$\sqrt{7.8} = 2.79 =$ standard deviation

Example In a neighboring county, the number of employees in each of its eight townships is 5, 7, 5, 7, 5, 7, 5, 7. The mean number of employees is found to be 6. The standard deviation is calculated as before $\sigma = \sqrt{\frac{8}{8}} = 1$. There is less variation in the number of township employees here than in Tiger County; as a result, the standard deviation is smaller. The variance in either of these examples is not easily interpreted.

THE NORMAL PROBABILITY DISTRIBUTION

The normal distribution is represented by the familiar bell-shaped curve. Many variables tend naturally to be approximately normally distributed. Such things as score on standardized aptitude examinations and measure of success at a particular skill task are examples of random variables that are very well represented by a normal probability distribution. Other variables are not normally distributed unless the field of interest is restricted. Personal income and dollar value of loss due to a fire are not normally distributed random variables. However, the income of a particular classification of employees may be normally distributed; the income of government-employed computer programmers and of hospital-employed pharmacists are examples of variables approximately normally distributed. The loss due to fires, electrically ignited, in single-family houses, for which the alarm was received by telephone, is so restricted that the variable is fairly well represented by the normal distribution.

Properties of the Normal Distribution

The familiar bell-shaped curve, depicted in Figure 3-6, indicates several important properties of the normal distribution:

1. It has a single peak.
2. Its mean is at the middle of the distribution.
3. The distribution is symmetric about the mean.
4. The tails extend indefinitely.

The above are properties of the theoretical normal probability distribution. Empirical distributions seldom, if ever, perfectly match the theoretical one. However, the approximation is often good enough to be quite useful.

There are actually very many normal distributions; they are distinguished only by their means and standard deviations. Figure 3-7 shows three normal

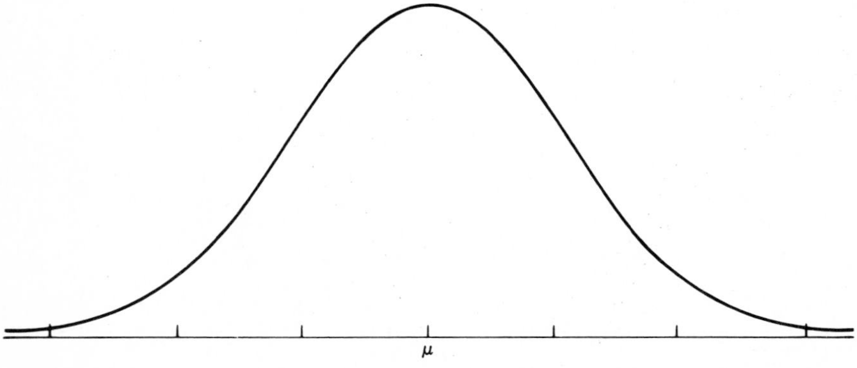

Figure 3-6 The familiar bell-shaped curve of the normal probability distribution.

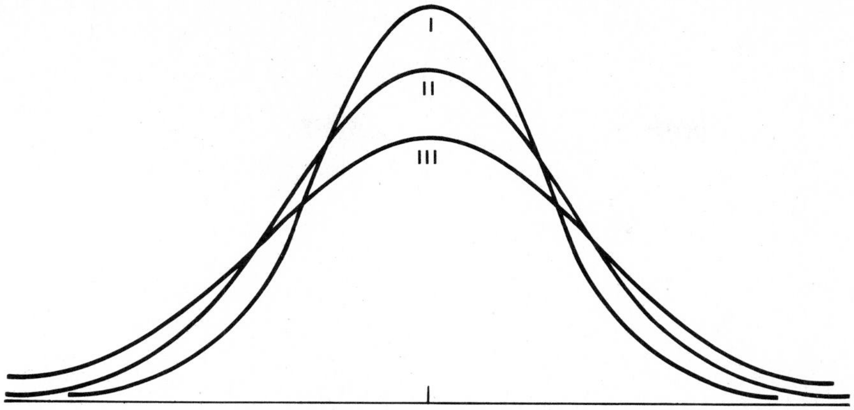

Figure 3-7 Normal probability distributions with the same mean but different standard deviations.

distributions, with the same mean but different standard deviations. The three normal distributions represented in Figure 3-8 have different means but the same standard deviation.

Regardless of what the mean or standard deviation is equal to, it can be shown mathematically that in any normal distribution:

1. About 68 percent of all values are within 1 standard deviation of the mean.
2. About 95 percent of all values are within 2 standard deviations of the mean.
3. About 99.7 percent of all values are within 3 standard deviations of the mean.

These three statements are illustrated in Figure 3-9. These and other probability statements apply to all normal distributions. Thus, one can use one standard normal probability table, Appendix Table 2, with any normal distribution.

Standard Normal Probability Table

Appendix Table 2 illustrates the probability—the area under the curve—between the mean and any point to the right of the mean. The table uses Z to represent the number of standard deviations from the mean. To use the table to

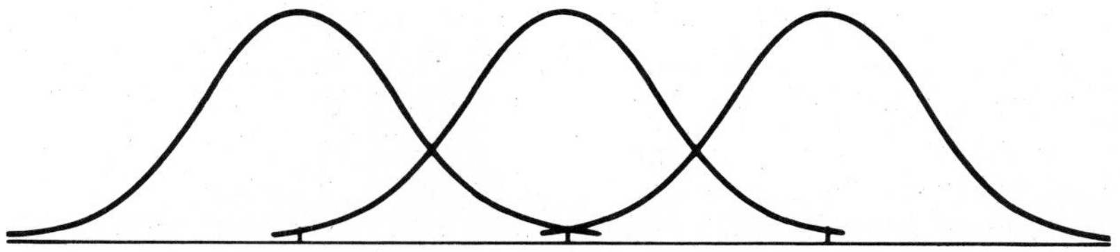

Figure 3-8 Normal probability distributions with different means but the same standard deviation.

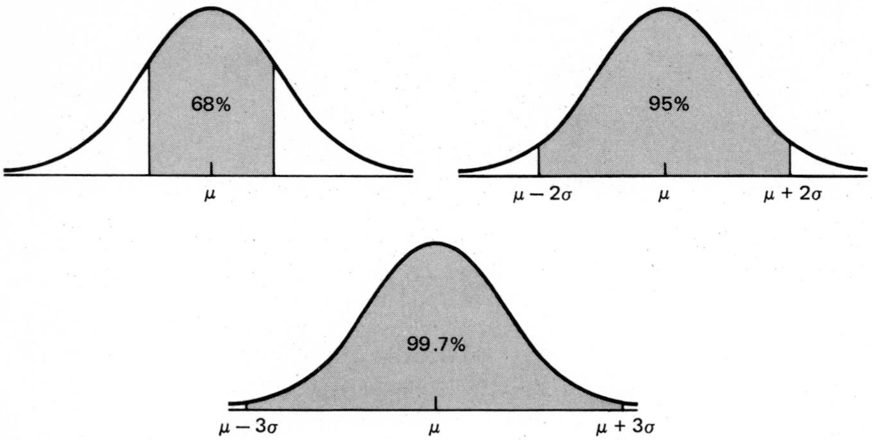

Figure 3-9 Approximate areas under selected portions of any normal curve.

find the probability that a normal random variable has any value between the mean and number x:

1. Find the Z corresponding to x according to the equation $Z = (x - \mu)/\sigma$
2. In Appendix Table 2 locate the row and column for that value of Z.
3. Find the probability value at the intersection of that row and column.

A few examples will develop familiarity with the normal probability distribution.

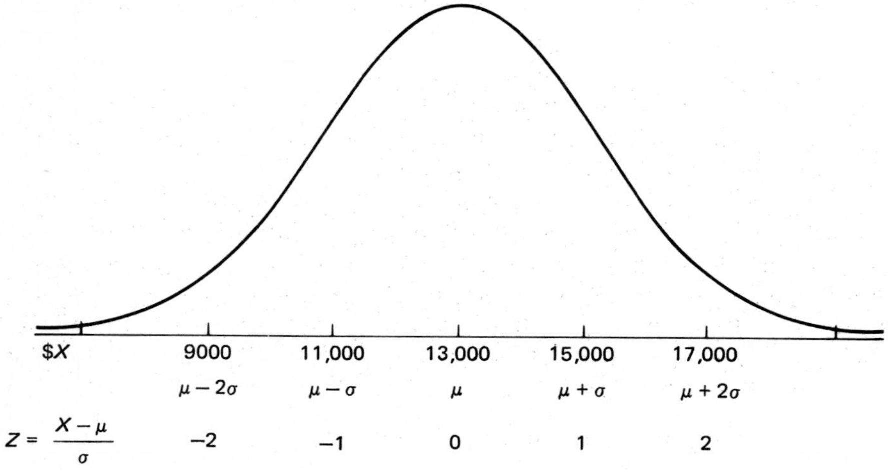

Figure 3-10 Transforming a normal variable into a standard normal variable.

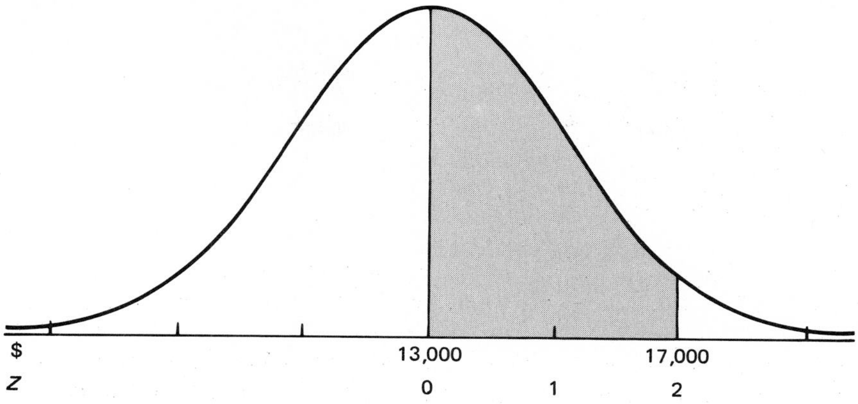

Figure 3-11 $P(\$13{,}000 \le \text{analyst's income} \le \$17{,}000) = P(0 \le Z \le 2) = .4772$.

Example Income is generally not a normally distributed random variable. When restricted it may be normally distributed. The income of individuals with the title "systems analyst," employed by a governmental (federal, state, or local) unit in the Southeast has been found to be normally distributed with a mean μ of \$13,000 and a standard deviation σ of \$2,000.

Figure 3-10 illustrates the relationship between the income variable and the Z variable and shows how to transform the income variable into the Z variable.

Example What is the probability that an individual selected at random will have an income between \$13,000 and \$17,000? The desired probability is represented by the shaded area of Figure 3-11. Following the three rules:

1. $Z = \dfrac{\$17{,}000 - \$13{,}000}{\$2{,}000} = 2$. That is, the end of the interval is 2 standard deviations above the mean.
2. In Appendix Table 2, the 2.0 row and the .00 column correspond to $Z = 2.00$.
3. The probability value at the intersection of the 2.0 row and the .00 column is .4772. Thus $P(\$13{,}000 \le \text{analyst's income} \le \$17{,}000) = .4772$.

Example What proportion of analysts earn between \$9,000 and \$17,000? This situation is represented in Figure 3-12. By the symmetry of the normal distribution we note that

$$P(\$9{,}000 \le \text{income} \le \$13{,}000) = P(\$13{,}000 \le \text{income} \le \$17{,}000)$$

$$\text{or that } P(-2 \le Z \le 0) = P(0 \le Z \le 2)$$

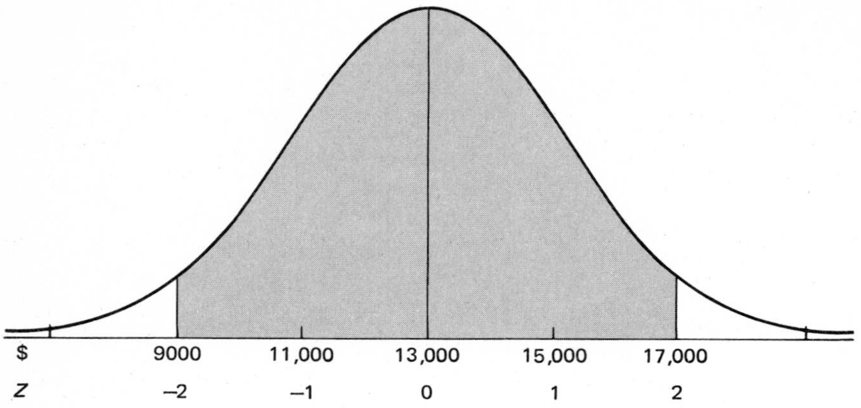

Figure 3-12 $P(\$9{,}000 \leq \text{analyst's income} \leq \$17{,}000) = P(-2 \leq Z \leq 2) = .9544$.

In the previous example we found that latter probability to be .4772. Then also

$$P(\$9{,}000 \leq \text{income} \leq \$13{,}000) = .4772$$

$$\text{Thus } P(\$9{,}000 \leq \text{income} \leq \$17{,}000) = .9544\ (= .4772 + .4772)$$

Example What is the probability that an analyst's income is above \$18,000? The appropriate probability is represented by the shaded region of Figure 3-13. In order to determine the probability, first transform the \$18,000 into the corresponding Z value, just as before.

$$Z = \frac{x - \mu}{\sigma} = \frac{\$18{,}000 - \$13{,}000}{\$2{,}000} = 2.5$$

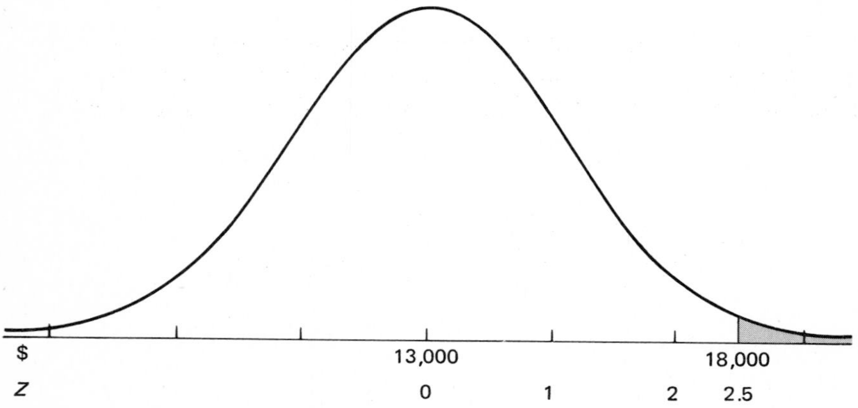

Figure 3-13 $P(\$18{,}000 \leq \text{analyst's income}) = P(2.5 \leq Z)$.

Use Table 2 of the Appendix to find the probability

$$P(\$13{,}000 \leq \text{income} \leq \$18{,}000)$$

which is

$$P(0 \leq Z \leq 2.5) = .4938$$

Since the entire curve to the right of the mean has a probability value of .5, by subtracting .4938 from .5, we find that

$$P(\$18{,}000 \leq \text{income}) = .0062$$

This means that only about 6 of every 1000 analysts earn more than $18,000.

Limitations in Using the Normal Distribution

There are three limitations that do not discourage the use of the normal distribution but do suggest some caution in interpreting probability values.

A real-world distribution usually only approximates a theoretical distribution. Probability values taken from a theoretical equation or table are therefore only approximately correct.

The theoretical normal distribution extends indefinitely to the left and right. Empirical distributions usually have bounds on the range of possible values. In the systems analysts' income example there may be no analysts with an income less than $5,000 but the normal table indicates that .00003 of the analysts earn such an income. The small tail-probabilities have to be thoughtfully disregarded in such applications.

Finally, the normal distribution is a continuous one. Many of the real-world distributions that approximate the normal distribution are actually discrete. In a continuous distribution probability values are assigned to intervals, and the probability that the random variable will be exactly equal to any one value is zero. The probability that the discrete random variable will exactly equal one particular value may be a positive number. In the analysts' income example, there may be analysts who earn exactly $13,000, although according to the theoretical distribution, *P*(an analyst earns $13,000) = 0. The way around this difficulty is to relate the particular value to an interval and then find the probability associated with that interval.

Example Find the proportion of analysts who earn $13,000, assuming that income information was recorded to the nearest $200. This means that when we say an analyst earns $13,000 we mean any value from $12,900 to $13,100 (this range is depicted in Figure 3-14). Thus about 4 percent of the analysts earn $13,000. If income had been recorded to the nearest $100, or $1, or even $.01, the interval would more closely represent the actual $13,000 amount.

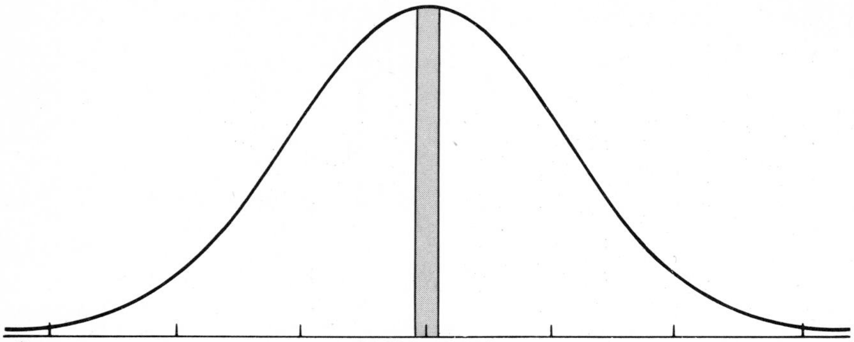

Figure 3-14 $P(\$12{,}900 \leq \text{analyst's income} \leq \$13{,}100) = P(-.05 \leq Z \leq .05) = .0398$.

SUMMARY

A probability distribution associates a probability value with each possible event. A random variable takes on a numerical value as a result of random events. A discrete random variable can take on a limited number of values; a continuous random variable can take on any value in a given range. A discrete probability distribution is associated with a discrete random variable; an example is the binomial distribution. An example of a continuous distribution is the normal probability distribution. These are only two of the many probability distributions that occur; their many applications prompted their inclusion here.

BIBLIOGRAPHY

See the Bibliography for Chapter 2.

EXERCISES

Extensions of chapter examples

3-1 Verify the values in the binomial distribution example of Figure 3-4 by using:
- (*a*) The binomial probability formula
- (*b*) The binomial probability table, Appendix Table 1

3-2 Verify the values in the example of Figure 3-5 using:
- (*a*) The binomial formula
- (*b*) The binomial table, Appendix Table 1

3-3 In the analysts' income example of Figures 3-10 to 3-14, find the probability that an analyst earns:

(*a*) Between \$13,000 and \$16,000
(*b*) Between \$13,000 and \$14,000
(*c*) Between \$14,000 and \$16,000
(*d*) Between \$10,000 and \$14,000

3-4 Refer to exercise 3-3. Regional economists would like to include the lowest 10 percent in a personal consumption study. What is the highest income earned by the lowest 10 percent of the systems analysts?

3-5 A jury is not actually chosen by just picking 12 people at random from the entire population of eligible jurors. The process actually involves a few stages. First, the clerk of the court is supposed to select 300 names at random from the entire population. The second stage begins prior to a trial when 30 or more are drawn from the 300 names. Of the 30, some can be eliminated by the prosecution or the defense for a specific stated reason, and some may be eliminated by either for no stated reason (this is referred to as a *peremptory* challenge). The group of 30 or more that is chosen at the second stage is referred to as a *venire*. Supposedly, the lists of 300 that were used by the U.S. District Court in Boston contained approximately 29 percent women. Assume that the proportion of women on these lists was in fact .29. Find the probability that a 30-person venire would contain:

(*a*) Zero women (is that really the probability?)
(*b*) 1 woman
(*c*) 4 or fewer women
(*d*) 5 or fewer women

3-6 Refer to problem 3-5.

(*a*) Find the probability that two 30-person venires, chosen independently from two different lists of 300, would each contain 5 or fewer women?

(*b*) What is the probability that four successive venires chosen from separate lists would contain 5 or fewer women?

This is essentially the process used to establish the remote possibility (that is, extremely small probability) that chance alone would consistently provide the Spock trial judge with venires on which there were relatively few women.

Other applications

3-7 On a particular aptitude test, the scores are normally distributed, the mean is 400, and the standard deviation is 50.

(*a*) If your score is 460, what *portion of the test scores would be lower than yours?* (This is your *percentile* score.)

(*b*) What score is higher than 50 percent of all the scores; that is, what score corresponds to the 50th percentile?

(*c*) What score corresponds to the 90th percentile?

3-8 The probability that a person picked at random has a positive reaction to a particular drug test is .01. Thirty people are tested. Find the probability that there are:

(*a*) No reactions
(*b*) 1 reaction
(*c*) 2 reactions
(*d*) 3 reactions
(*e*) 4 or more reactions

3-9 Suppose 30 individuals are screened, and there are 3 positive reactions. What conclusion would you draw about the underlying reaction rate of .01?

3-10 The probability of measurable rainfall on any day in August in the river valley is .30. A particular 20-day experiment being conducted at the Department of Agriculture requires between 4 and 8 days inclusive on which there is some rainfall. What is the probability that the experiment's conditions will be satisfied?

3-11 A question of interest to HUD is how far people usually travel to do their major food shopping. A study in one city revealed that urban dwellers' travel distance was normally distributed with a mean of 1.5 miles and a standard deviation of .75 mile. What proportion of the people traveled

(*a*) More than 2 miles?

(*b*) Less than 1 mile?

(*c*) The curve suggests that about 2.5 percent of the people traveled less than 0 mile. Obviously this is not true in reality. Can you account for the "error"?

3-12 Refer to exercise 3-11. A similar study of suburbanites revealed that their shopping travel distance was normally distributed with a mean of 2.5 miles and a standard deviation of 1.25 miles.

(*a*) What proportion of the urban dwellers traveled more than the mean suburban distance?

(*b*) What proportion of the suburban dwellers traveled more than the mean urban distance?

(*c*) In a recent press interview, a city official claimed: "Food markets are no longer readily available to city folk. In fact, a large number of them must travel farther than most suburbanites to get to the food stores." Comment on his statement, noting (1) whether a "large number" do so; and (2) if this means they *must* do so.

Project problems

3-13 In the 1980 American census, find two questions that generate random variables, and two questions whose answers cannot meaningfully be represented by random variables.

CHAPTER
FOUR
DECISION THEORY: A FRAMEWORK FOR DECISION MAKING

Decision theory provides a method for rational decision making when the consequences are not fully known. Decision makers apply various criteria to decision situations. For specific criteria, decision theory identifies the best alternative. When the criteria are vaguely defined, or not unanimously held in group situations, decision theory provides a framework for evaluating alternatives. In this chapter we explore various specific criteria. So that our attention will not be diverted, the context is one with easily compared dollar consequences. Many decisions, especially in the public sector, have consequences that are less easily measured or compared. The use of decision theory in such a setting is shown in a health-planning application. Other applications are considered in the exercises.

DECISION THEORY AND THE DECISION-MAKING PROCESS

A decision involves choosing one alternative from among a set of alternatives. The decision situation often involves uncontrollable factors and many consequences. Two brief examples will illustrate the essential features of a decision.

Examples

1. A state has to choose from among many bids to drill for natural gas on certain state-owned properties. The amount of natural gas present is an uncertainty. The consequence for the state, the full-bid payment, depends on the alternative chosen, the particular bid, and on the uncontrollable, the volume of recoverable gas.

2. The federal government through its Department of Health has to decide whether to support an influenza vaccination program for the entire nation, or for a selected portion of the population, or not at all. The outbreak of an epidemic is a possibility, but not a certainty. The consequences for the nation, illness, death, avoidance of illness, and reaction to the vaccination, will depend on the alternative program chosen by the government and on the uncontrollable possibility of an outbreak of influenza.

The role of decision theory in decision making is twofold: first it provides a framework for better understanding the decision situation, and second, it can furnish a way to evaluate alternatives in light of the uncertainty. The relationship between decision theory and decision making is depicted in Figure 4-1. If a decision is to be made on the basis of one of the decision criteria to be examined here, then the selection of an alternative is a direct effect of decision theory. If alternatives are to be compared relative to considerations other than the so-called pure criteria, then decision theory aids in the evaluation of alternatives. Decision theory can indirectly assist in defining the problem and in identifying alternatives, while directly helping to evaluate the alternatives.

Decision situations can involve one objective or a number of objectives. The latter is more realistic, especially in the pluralistic setting of public decision making. We first examine a decision-making framework for a single objective. While some of the particulars of the single-objective situation can be trans-

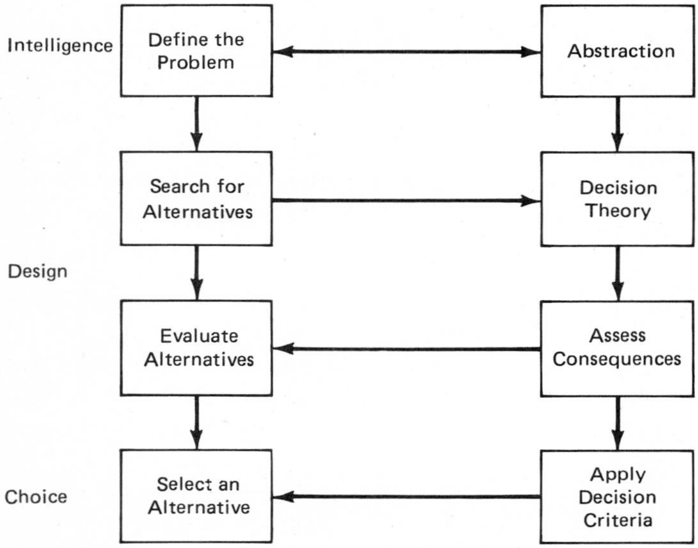

Figure 4-1 The role of decision theory in decision making.

ferred only with difficulty to multiple-objective situations, the framework can often be used with benefit. Later in this chapter we shall illustrate just such a decision situation. In Chapter 6 we will consider an extension of the decision framework to cover multiple-objective situations more appropriately.

THE ELEMENTS OF A DECISION

Assuming there is some underlying value system and a set of objectives, the set of decision alternatives is the prime ingredient of decision making. Some examples of decision alternatives are:

1*a*. To establish a graduated local income tax
1*b*. To establish a flat-rate local income tax
1*c*. To establish no local income tax at all
2*a*. To repair the potholes in a roadway
2*b*. To repave the entire roadway
2*c*. To construct an alternate parallel roadway
3*a*. To establish a system of completely government-supported medical care
3*b*. To establish a user-supported national health insurance program
3*c*. To avoid direct government support of medical care

If there were but a single possibility that could be chosen, there really would be no decision to make; the "decision maker" would simply go along with the inevitable.

In most decision situations there are many factors beyond the control of the decision maker. These uncontrollable factors are often referred to as "states of nature." This name comes from making a decision in the face of such uncontrollable natural factors as weather, the presence of oil, and the extent of viral growth. The name continues in use even though it is recognized that there are many uncontrollable factors that are not simple natural occurrences or "acts of God." Some examples of states of nature or uncontrollable factors are:

1. The future employment level
2. The future traffic patterns in a particular area
3. The level of demand for medical care

The uncontrollable factors can be studied for a better understanding of the decision situation, but they can neither be controlled nor chosen by the decision maker.

The alternative that is chosen by the decision maker is not usually chosen for its own sake, but rather for what will occur as a consequence. In fact the purpose for a decision choice can be found in the envisioned consequences, whether they be realistic or fantastic, beneficial to many or a select few, essential or cosmetic. Some examples of consequences of a decision act and a state of nature are:

1*a*. A continuous budget deficit
1*b*. A depression of new industry
2*a*. Accelerated deterioration of a roadway
2*b*. The public generally avoiding a roadway
3*a*. Deterioration of the health of a significant portion of the population
3*b*. Huge budget deficit

Consequences occur as the result of both the decision act that is chosen and the uncontrollable factors that occur. Hence, in analyzing a decision situation, the decision maker tries to identify the possible uncontrollable factors or *states of nature* and the consequences associated with each factor and each decision alternative. The extent of the knowledge one has about the uncontrollable factors is the basis for different approaches to decision making.

THE CONTINUUM OF UNCERTAINTY IN DECISION MAKING

The decision-making environment is characterized by the extent of knowledge one has about the states of nature. At one extreme we have:

Decision making under ignorance The decision maker knows absolutely nothing about the states of nature, including not even knowing the possibilities.

This extreme is seldom if ever presented so openly. A slightly more subtle presentation of it has been seen, however.

Example After discussing the future needs of a school district's youngsters, school planners decide on a particular architectural plan from the many considered. The plan chosen holds the most promise for providing the greatest opportunity for a sufficiently large portion of the future school population. Just as the cornerstone is laid, however, the declining birth rate of 6 years ago has its impact on the school population. The decision makers realize they were concerned with the wrong states of nature. Their concentration on the specific needs of future students allowed them to ignore the more basic uncontrollable, namely, the size of the school population. Perhaps the new building can serve as an adult education center, or be sold to the state university for use as a satellite campus to recoup some of the public money. Nonetheless, as far as the actual states of nature are concerned, the decision makers were operating in a relatively knowledge-free environment.

Although the "ignorance" in the heading "decision making under ignorance" refers to the lack of knowledge of the states of nature, in such an environment it is just as applicable to the consequences, and, more than likely, to the decision alternatives as well.

At the other extreme of the continuum we have:

> **Decision making under certainty** The decision maker knows exactly the state of nature that will occur.

This rather blissful situation allows the decision maker to examine the available choices and the single consequence of each. The most desirable consequence dictates the decision alternative to be chosen.

> **Example** If the nutrient content of various foods does not vary from day to day, then the nutritionist can prescribe a particular diet in order to maintain desired levels of nutrient intake. If there are many combinations that will yield the desired levels of nutrition, then the nutrition decision maker can choose the alternative that is the optimum according to some characteristic. For example, the dietician might choose the diet on the basis of providing the greatest variety of foods to patients, whereas the zoo keeper might choose the diet on the basis of lowest cost. In either case, the nutrition content is assumed to be completely known so that the decision can be made on the basis of the most desirable assured consequences.

Between the two extremes are decision-making environments in which there is incomplete knowledge of the states of nature:

> **Decision making under uncertainty** More than one state of nature is known to exist, but the probability of any state is unknown.

> **Decision making under risk** More than one state of nature is known to exist, and the probability of each state is known.

There is more information available in the latter category, but neither situation is completely known. These categories are the real subject matter for decision theory.

The four decision-making environments can be depicted on a continuum of knowledge about the states of nature, as in Figure 4-2. The first and the last environments are dismissed from further consideration here, albeit for different reasons. If the decision maker realizes his ignorance, attention can be given to moving to one of the other environments. If the decision maker possesses certain knowledge of the state of nature, attention can be directed to some other facet of the decision process. For example, if it is known that there will be an outbreak of influenza, then attention can be directed to estimating the cumula-

Decision Making Under –

Ignorance | Uncertainty | Risk | Certainty

None | Incomplete | Complete

Amount of information about states of nature

Figure 4-2 Knowledge of the states of nature on a continuum.

tive effects of any vaccination decision. The two environments of incomplete knowledge will be presented in a prolonged illustration.

DECISION MAKING UNDER UNCERTAINTY

Natural resources are ordinarily considered to be the property of the owner of the land in or on which the natural resources are present. Exceptions to this occur when the agreement, by which ownership of land is transferred from one party to another, contains a clause indicating that mineral rights are retained by the former owner. When the minerals are present on federal- or state-owned lands, they are considered to be publicly held resources. The public at large cannot undertake the actual resource recovery, and the government, whether federal, state, or other, is not in the business of mineral recovery. The publicly held resources are recovered through a cooperative venture between the public, represented by the responsible officers, and a private operator who has the technical capability to recover the minerals and transform them into usable products. Under the cooperative venture, the government transfers the right to recover the minerals to the private operator in exchange for a share in the ultimate profits of the venture. The profits are therefore the public's share in the mineral recovery operation and as such are considered like other public money, to be used for public purposes. The mineral profits due to the people through their government depend on the value of the minerals recovered. The government may use the money to replace funds that would otherwise come from taxation or may use the money for some specific purpose that would not otherwise be served from the general fund, for instance, housing subsidies to the elderly.

Natural gas is currently considered to be a rather valuable resource. As with many other natural resources that are valuable and of restricted occurrence, the region that finds and develops the natural gas thereby generates for itself a fair supply of the national currency. Suppose that a geologist has discovered, on state-owned land, certain types of rock formations that suggest the possibility of a natural gas field. There is believed to be a reasonably good chance that a gas recovery operation would be successful.

Since the state itself is not in the gas recovery business, it enters into a cooperative arrangement with private industry to recover the available gas and transform the gas in the ground into gas in the pipes and money in the till. One way to enter into such an arrangement is for the state government, through its appropriate contracting agency or administration (a general services agency, for example), to invite bids from individual private developers or groups of private developers. In so doing the state would stipulate its requirements and conditions, perhaps indicating that the land shall remain the possession of the state, that the operation shall take place during a specific number of years, and that afterward the use of the land will revert to the discretion of the state without further obligation to the private contracting party.

It is not entirely unrealistic to assume that the state invites bids in each of three categories:

1. A fixed price for the length of the lease, regardless of the outcome of the gas recovery process
2. A fixed percent of the profits, in which the eventual lease amount depends on the profitability of the recovery operation
3. A combination of fixed amount plus a variable amount dependent on the success of the venture

Upon receipt of the sealed bids in each of the three categories, the state can choose any bid that was best in its category. Thus, the state can reduce the set of alternatives to three.

Assume further that the results of the gas recovery venture can be expressed as complete success, moderate success, or failure. A team of geologists and natural resource economists has estimated the quantity and value of the gas that would be present for each of these three gas recovery possibilities. The gas would be recovered over a long period of time. During each year of the operation, a certain volume of gas, and therefore a certain value of gas, would be recovered. Monetarily speaking, the operation is represented by a stream of dollar amounts in successive years. From that stream one can determine what is called the *present value* of the operation. (The actual determination of the present value of future amounts of money is a topic to be considered in Chapter 7.)

Note that the values involved in this decision situation are very much dependent on a number of estimates. The quantity of gas actually present in the gas field is estimated. Whether the actual venture will be successful is estimated; the speed of recovery is estimated. The future value of natural gas is estimated. Since there are so many estimates, the decision maker should be very cautious in accepting recommendations based on a single analysis. "What if" questions should be posed so that the simple decision model will be the subject of sensitivity analysis, in order to determine the effect of modifications in the estimates on the ultimate decision. We explore such sensitivity analysis in extension exercises 4-1, 4-2, and 4-3.

Table 4-1 Consequences (payoffs) of lease alternatives (millions $)

	Decision alternatives		
State of nature	Percent of profit	Fixed lease	Combination
Complete success	2000	600	1200
Moderate success	600	600	540
Failure	60	600	300

The present values of the lease for each alternative and each state of nature are presented in the decision matrix or payoff table, Table 4-1. When consequences are money amounts, they are usually referred to as *payoffs*.

Although the value of the lease to the state for each of the decision alternatives for each of the possible states of nature is completely specified in the table, note that the decision must be made in the face of uncertainty. The consequence of the decision is not known at the time the decision must be made.

For the same set of alternatives and the same states of nature, different decision makers might very well make different decisions. In effect, the decision makers are making use of different decision-making philosophies or different decision-making criteria. We now explore some of these criteria.

Maximax Decision Criterion

The maximax decision criterion is the one used by the optimistic decision maker. Underlying the maximax philosophy is either of two implicit thoughts. The first is that no matter which decision he makes, the best possible consequence will follow, and so he might as well choose the alternative that has the highest possible value associated with it. The second is that no matter what decision he makes, a poor consequence will not be very disconcerting. In either case, the maximax decision maker will choose the alternative with the highest possible payoff. For the current problem the highest payoff is $2 billion, a possible consequence of the *percent-of-profit* alternative. Hence, the maximax decision maker will choose as his decision alternative the percent-of-profit contract. *Maximax is the criterion used by a decision maker who chooses the act which makes possible the maximum payoff.*

If the payoff table contains losses rather than profits, the maximax decision maker would choose the act which would *make possible the minimum loss*. Here again the decision maker would be choosing the act which could yield the best possible consequence.

Example Most people use the maximax decision criterion in specific situations. An example is the purchase of a lottery ticket. Table 4-2 presents the payoffs associated with the two decision alternatives concerned with purchasing a ticket and the two possible states of nature concerning whether

Table 4-2 Lottery-ticket decision matrix

	Decision alternatives	
State of nature	Purchase ticket	Do not purchase ticket
Number not drawn	($1.00)	$0
Number drawn	$1000	$0

the purchased ticket's number is drawn. If the decision is to purchase the ticket and if the number is not drawn, there is a loss of $1.00 (represented in the table in parentheses, the usual accounting symbolism for a negative quantity). For that same decision, the state of nature "number drawn" generates a positive payoff of $1000, the lottery prize.[1]

Minimax Decision Criterion

The decision maker who is more a pessimist than an optimist will choose his decision alternative on the basis of some form of Murphy's law. Murphy's law suggests that no matter which alternative is chosen, the worst that can possibly happen will happen. Hence, the minimax decision maker examines the possible payoffs for each alternative and takes particular note of the smallest payoff for each alternative. He then chooses the alternative that yields the greatest of those minimum payoffs. In the leasing example, the minimax decision maker notes that the percent-of-profit alternative might wind up yielding only $60 million, the *fixed lease* has a minimum of $600 million, and the *combination* might have a yield as low as $300 million. The greatest of those minimum payoffs is $600 million, and so the minimax decision maker chooses to accept the contract for the fixed lease worth $600 million. *The minimax decision maker tries to maximize the minimum gain.*

If the payoffs are losses rather than gains, the minimax decision maker identifies the greatest loss associated with each alternative, and chooses the alternative that has the smallest of those maximum losses. In other words, *the minimax decision maker would try to minimize the maximum loss.* His guiding principle is to choose the alternative that has the best of the worst possible payoffs.

Actually, it is not only Murphy's law that urges one to use the minimax decision criterion, but also a conservative decision approach that may generate the same decision-making philosophy.

Example Whenever we purchase optional (not legally required) liability insurance for our automobile or home, we are making use of the minimax

[1] Actually if the lottery prize is $1000, then the positive payoff would be $999 since we should deduct the cost of the lottery ticket from the gross prize to yield a net payoff. In order not to confuse the example, we disregard this small difference.

Table 4-3 Liability-insurance decision matrix

	Decision alternatives	
State of nature	Purchase	Do not purchase
Accident occurs	($100)	($10,000)
No accident	($100)	0

decision principle. Table 4-3 presents the payoffs of purchasing or not purchasing liability insurance with or without the subsequent need for insurance.

If the insurance is purchased (we assume there is no deductible amount in the insurance policy), then whether an accident occurs or not, the cost of the decision is the insurance premium, say $100. Table 4-3 presents this as a negative $100 payoff. If the decision is not to purchase the insurance, and if the insurance is not needed, the payoff is $0. However, if there is an accident and we are held liable, then we may suffer a substantial loss; assume that the loss is $10,000. Note that the greatest loss associated with the "purchase" decision is $100, and the greatest loss associated with the "do not purchase" decision is $10,000. Opting for the smaller of these, the minimax decision maker chooses to purchase the insurance. *The minimax decision maker tries to minimize the maximum loss.*

In the state's leasing example, the minimax decision maker tried to maximize the minimum gain. The insurance purchaser sought to minimize the maximum loss. These two objectives are different expressions of the same philosophy. Using that philosophy, one determines the worst payoff for each alternative, and then chooses the alternative that has the best of the worst payoffs. If the payoffs are gains, one seeks to maximize the minimum gain. If the payoffs are losses, one seeks to minimize the maximum loss. In either version, the criterion is referred to as the minimax criterion.

Minimax Regret Decision Criterion

The presence of a second guesser is usually made painfully obvious. Such a presence becomes all the more painful when the second guesser has the power, either political, supervisory, or psychological, to punish an errant decision maker. Such a decision maker may find himself or herself in the position of making a decision based not on the payoff associated with the decision but rather on the regret associated with making the wrong decision. For example, suppose the decision maker in the gas recovery problem decided to accept a fixed-lease contract, and suppose further that the result of the gas recovery operation was a complete success. The actual payoff to the state would be $600 million; had the decision been made to choose the percent-of-profit contract,

Table 4-4 Regret, or opportunity loss, of lease alternatives (millions $)

	Decision alternatives		
State of nature	Percent of profit	Fixed lease	Combination
Complete success	0	1400	800
Moderate success	0	0	60
Failure	540	0	300

then the payoff to the state would have been $2 billion. In this situation the decision maker would regret having made the wrong decision, regret in the sense that the actual payoff was less than the payoff for what turned out to be the right decision. The acceptance of the fixed-lease contract followed by a completely successful gas recovery operation would generate a regret of $1400 million. In economic terms, this is commonly referred to as the *opportunity loss,* which can be described as the *difference between the payoff following the right decision and the payoff following the actual decision.*

Table 4-4 presents the regret, or opportunity loss, associated with each alternative for each of the possible states of nature. Choosing the percent-of-profit alternative may generate a regret of $540 million if the gas recovery venture turns out to be a failure. That is, the payoff of $60 million for percent of profit is $540 million less than the payoff would be for fixed lease with the "failure" state of nature. The fixed-lease contract may generate a regret as big as $1400 million while the combination contract may generate a regret as big as $800 million. The smallest of the three maximum regret values is $540 million. Hence a minimax regret decision maker would choose the percent-of-profit decision alternative. Essentially *the minimax regret decision maker tries to minimize the maximum regret;* if he is to be wrong, he does not want to be "too wrong."

Average Payoff Decision Criterion

A kind of middle-ground approach considers all the payoffs for each alternative. One such approach takes the average of the payoffs for each alternative. In finding and using the average payoff, one tacitly assumes that all states of nature are equally likely. *The average payoff criterion says that the alternative with the best average payoff should be chosen.*[2]

For the leasing problem, the average payoffs as in Table 4-1 Revised, are: $886.67 million, $600 million, and $680 million; the average payoff criterion points to the percent-of-profit alternative. If there is reason to believe that not all states of nature are equally likely, then it is reasonable to make use of a

[2] The average payoff criterion is based on the principle of insufficient reason, which assigns equal likelihood to all possible states of nature.

Table 4-1 Revised Payoff (present value) of lease alternatives (in millions $)

	Decision alternatives		
State of nature	Percent of profit	Fixed lease	Combination
Complete success	2000	600	1200
Moderate success	600	600	540
Failure	60	600	300
Average payoff	886.67	600	680

weighted average, with the more likely states of nature more heavily weighted. Knowing the probability distribution of the states of nature distinguishes "risk" from "uncertainty." The criteria just described are appropriate for decision making under uncertainty. Very frequently probability values for the states of nature can be assigned, if not objectively then at least subjectively. Knowing or estimating probability values allows the use of other decision criteria.

DECISION MAKING UNDER RISK

After the states of nature have been identified, the decision maker tries to determine the likelihood of each. There is usually some basis for believing that one state of nature is more likely to occur than another. For this reason rarely must one rely entirely on the decision criteria for uncertainty; rather one incorporates the likelihood in selecting an alternative. As described in Chapter 2, the probabilities can be objective or subjective.

Objective probabilities are preferable but not always possible. Seldom is there a theoretical or a priori basis for assigning probabilities in a decision situation. Records of past performance are useful in finding empirical objective probabilities. Such records would be useful, for example, in estimating which of two bidding vendors is more likely to deliver contracted supplies by the contract's required date. If neither kind of objective probability is possible, subjective estimates are used. The following procedure can be used to develop a subjective probability distribution:

1. Rank the states of nature in order of their likelihood of occurrence.
2. Assign a probability to the most likely state of nature.
3. Assign a probability to every other state of nature by comparing its likelihood to that of the most likely state.
4. Make sure the probabilities total 1, adjusting them up or down as necessary.

Example The geologists in the gas recovery venture do the following:

1. Rank the states: failure, complete success, moderate success.
2. Believe that a failure is a bit more likely than a success of any kind, and so they assign a probability of .55 to failure.
3. Believe that a complete success is slightly more likely than a moderate success. Realizing that success of either kind has a probability of 1 − .55 = .45, they assign .25 to a complete success and .20 to a moderate success.
4. Because of the way they assigned probabilities in step 3, the probabilities total 1; no adjustments are needed.

There are a few basic decision criteria that use probabilities of the states of nature.

Expected Value Decision Criterion

If there is some basis for believing that one state of nature is more likely than the others, a weighted average of payoffs is preferable to a straight average. The weighted average, in which the probabilities are the weights, is called the expected value of the payoff or simply the *expected payoff*. The expected payoff is the sum of the products of probability times payoff for each of the decision alternatives. *The expected value decision maker chooses the alternative with the greatest expected payoff*. The underlying rationale is that for repetitive decision situations this criterion provides the best long-run average payoff. In nonrepetitive situations the criterion leads to the best overall decision making provided there are many similar decisions. With a strictly one-time occurrence, the expected payoff criterion is a mechanism for incorporating into the decision-making process all payoffs and probabilities for each alternative.

Example The calculation of the expected payoff for each of the oil recovery lease alternatives is presented in Table 4-5. The expected value decision maker would choose the percent-of-profit alternative since its ex-

Table 4-5 Expected payoffs of lease alternatives (millions $)

	Decision alternatives		
State of nature	Percent of profit	Fixed lease	Combination
Complete success	.25 × 2000 = 500	.25 × 600 = 150	.25 × 1200 = 300
Moderate success	.20 × 600 = 120	.20 × 600 = 120	.20 × 540 = 108
Failure	.55 × 60 = 33	.55 × 600 = 330	.55 × 300 = 165
Expected payoff	653.0	600	573

pected payoff, \$653 million, is greater than either \$600 million or \$573 million.

Maximum-Likelihood Decision Criterion

There is another decision philosophy which makes use of the probabilities. *Using the maximum-likelihood criterion, the decision maker chooses the alternative that is best for the most likely state of nature.* While this criterion has the advantage of simplicity, strict adherence to it requires ignoring substantive information related to the less likely states of nature.

Example In the lease illustration failure is more likely to occur than either complete success or moderate success. Consider the payoffs associated just with failure. For the state of nature failure, percent of profit yields \$60 million, fixed lease yields \$600 million, and combination yields \$300 million. The maximum-likelihood decision maker would thus choose the fixed-lease alternative. However, failure is not much more likely than some kind of success:

$$P(\text{failure}) = .55 \qquad \text{and} \qquad P(\text{success}) = .45$$

One would be ill advised to use this criterion under such circumstances.

Applying the maximum-likelihood criterion is of questionable wisdom whenever the most likely state of nature is just slightly more probable than the others. Its use has better support when one alternative has a rather high probability, say .90.

The last criterion we examine applies the notion of expected value to the concept of regret or opportunity loss.

Expected Opportunity Loss Decision Criterion

A decision maker using this decision criterion will determine the regret or opportunity loss associated with all states of nature for each alternative. The expected value of these opportunity losses is referred to as the *expected opportunity loss.* Since the expected opportunity loss represents the expected difference between the payoff of the right decision and the payoff of the actual decision, *the expected opportunity loss decision maker will choose the alternative that has the smallest expected opportunity loss.*

Example Table 4-4 Revised presents the opportunity losses, together with the expected opportunity loss, for each alternative in the oil recovery lease illustration. Using this criterion, one would choose the percent-of-profit alternative, since its expected opportunity loss is the smallest.

Table 4-4 Revised   Regret or opportunity loss of lease alternatives

		Decision alternatives (millions $)		
State of nature	Probability	Percent of profit	Fixed lease	Combination
Complete success	.25	0	1400	800
Moderate success	.20	0	0	60
Failure	.55	540	0	300
Expected opportunity loss		297	350	377

A comparison of the expected opportunity losses in Table 4-4 Revised with the expected payoffs in Table 4-5 points out that the same decision is made under those two criteria. This does not come as a great shock when one considers that the opportunity loss is the difference between the payoff associated with the best decision and the payoff associated with the actual decision. Hence, the alternative with the highest expected payoff will be the alternative with the lowest expected opportunity loss, and vice versa. In summary, the expected payoff and expected opportunity loss are not distinct decision criteria but are rather two different ways of looking at the same decision philosophy.

HEALTH AND FACILITIES PLANNING: AN APPLICATION[3]

The planning council for a large portion of southeast Texas was recently faced with the task of setting a limit on the number of hospital beds in the region. About 5500 new beds were planned, but it was not unanimously believed that all these beds were needed. The planning period was 7 years.

In an attempt to identify the appropriate bases for deciding on the bed limit, a decision model was developed. The decision would ultimately be stated in terms of a reduction or increase in the number of planned beds. The uncontrollables were many, but using specific population forecasts and accepted occupancy rates, the states of nature were able to be expressed as the level of ''use rate.''

Different levels of future use rate were forecast on the basis of the use rates for different numbers of previous years. The projections and the number of years on which they are based are as follows:

[3] This illustration is taken from an article, ''Use of Decision Theory in Regional Planning,'' by Richard Grimes et al., which appeared in *Health Services Research,* Spring 1974, pp. 73–78.

Projected use rate	Number of previous years
Medium-low	1
Low	2
High	4
Medium-high	7

The critical consequences were that constructing too few beds would leave a portion of the sick of the community without adequate care, while constructing too many beds would place an unnecessary financial burden on the community.

The simply stated and widely recognized objectives conflicted: Provide adequate health care for all in need in the community, and keep health care costs to, if not a minimum, at least a bearable level. Attempting to use a stand-in measure to represent both health care and costs would unnecessarily conceal the impact of any decision on the two relevant factors. Although our decision framework has assumed a single objective or at least a single measure, the decision table format for presenting alternatives, states of nature, and consequences can be used to provide a good synopsis of the various relationships even in a multiple-objective decision situation. Rather than use an artificial factor to convert too few beds into dollars, that consequence was left in terms of beds. Excess beds could be realistically converted into dollars with the following rationale. There was a projection for the cost of occupied beds, and an accepted estimate for the relationship between the costs of occupied and unoccupied beds. Hence, the total operating cost for each excess bed for the 7-year planning period was estimated to be about $202,000.

The decision table for the problem is presented in Table 4-6. If the council

Table 4-6 Decision table for southeast Texas hospital planning*

	Decision alternatives			
State of nature	Major reduction in beds (I)	Slight reduction in beds (II)	Slight increase in beds (III)	Major increase in beds (IV)
Low use rate	OK	373 eb $75.3M	1095 eb $221.2M	1356 eb $273.9M
Medium-low use rate	373 bbn	OK	722 eb $145.8M	983 eb $198.6M
Medium-high use rate	1095 bbn	722 bbn	OK	261 eb $52.7M
High use rate	1356 bbn	983 bbn	261 bbn	OK

* eb = excess beds; bbn = beds below need; M = million.

chose alternative II, then the potential cost of overage would not exceed $75.3 million, but there could be as many as 983 beds too few. If the council decided to minimize the bed shortage, then they would choose alternative IV which could cost the region as much as $273,900,000 in excess beds over the 7-year planning period.

The council wanted to have some way of incorporating all the possible consequences of each alternative. Since there was no past experience that suggested any one use rate was more likely than any other, the four states of nature were assumed equally likely for the sake of making an aggregate comparison. Beds and dollars cannot be added, of course, and so the expected payoff contains both beds and dollars. The decision table with the average payoffs is presented in Table 4-7.

Although the assumption of equal probabilities left some of the council members a little uneasy, they saw the new payoff table as useful in comparing various alternatives. One comparison showed that reducing the expected bed shortage from 706 beds to 426 beds would bring with it an expected cost of $18,800,000.

As the discussion about the likelihood of projected use rates continued, there emerged a sense—albeit intuitive—that projections based on longer periods were more likely to hold over the relatively long 7-year planning period. Hence the council agreed to consider new probabilities based on length of trend to see if the bed shortage–cost relationship would be substantially altered. Each projection was given a rating equal to the length of the trend

Table 4-7 Decision table with average payoffs for southeast Texas hospital planning*

		Decision alternatives			
State of nature (use rate)	Probability	Major reduction in beds (I)	Slight reduction in beds (II)	Slight increase in beds (III)	Major increase in beds (IV)
Low	.25	OK	373 eb $75.3M	1095 eb $221.2M	1356 eb $273.9M
Medium-low	.25	373 bbn	OK	722 eb $145.8M	983 eb $198.6M
Medium-high	.25	1095 bbn	722 bbn	OK	261 eb $52.7M
High	.25	1356 bbn	983 bbn	261 bbn	OK
Average payoffs		706 bbn	426 bbn and $18.8M	65 bbn and $91.8M	$131.3M

* eb = excess beds; bbn = beds below needs; M = million.

Table 4-8 Finding subjective probabilities for projected use rates

Projected use rate	Number of previous years	Rating	Probability
Medium-low	1	1	$\frac{1}{14}$
Low	2	2	$\frac{2}{14}$
High	4	4	$\frac{4}{14}$
Medium-high	7	7	$\frac{7}{14}$
		14	

period. The sum of the ratings was 14. Dividing each rating by 14 yielded a probability for each projection. This process is summarized in Table 4-8.

Using these probabilities, a new set of expected payoffs resulted. These expected payoffs are presented in Table 4-9. Once more the council found the table useful for comparisons. Even a relatively small reduction in expected bed shortage would be accompanied by a relatively high dollar cost.

After due deliberation the council chose decision alternative I, not only for the possibly high dollar cost of other alternatives but also because a decision to curtail construction could be altered later if the need arose, whereas a decision to allow further construction could be altered only with great difficulty.

In this instance, the decision table certainly did not dictate the decision nor was any one of the criteria unambiguously preferable. However, decision theory did provide a framework through which the decision makers could iden-

Table 4-9 Decision table with expected payoffs for southeast Texas hospital planning*

		Decision alternatives			
State of nature (use rate)	Probability	Major reduction in beds (I)	Slight reduction in beds (II)	Slight increase in beds (III)	Major increase in beds (IV)
Low	$\frac{2}{14}$	OK	373 eb \$75.3M	1095 eb \$221.2M	1356 eb \$273.9M
Medium-low	$\frac{1}{14}$	373 bbn	OK	722 eb \$145.8M	983 eb \$198.6M
Medium-high	$\frac{7}{14}$	1095 bbn	722 bbn	OK	261 eb \$52.7M
High	$\frac{4}{14}$	1356 bbn	983 bbn	261 bbn	OK
Expected payoffs		962 bbn	642 bbn and \$10.8M	75 bbn and \$42.0M	\$79.7M

* eb = excess beds; bbn = beds below need; M = million.

tify the relevant factors and grasp the relationships among them. As a result of the decision and the recognized components of the decision situation, bed use rates are being monitored to assure that a greater bed use rate will in fact be responded to in an appropriate manner.

DECISION ALTERNATIVES WITH DIFFERENT PROBABILITY DISTRIBUTIONS: AN ILLUSTRATION

The state's Bureau of Management Services is considering entering into a contract with one of two firms that will supply technical assistance in a number of specialized areas. The need for assistance is not continuous within any one specialty; so it is not worthwhile for the state to maintain employee positions to satisfy each of the specialized needs.

The firms' bids indicate that the direct cost to the bureau is the same for either firm. The efficiency and completeness vary between the two firms, however. Any technical assistance must ultimately be transmitted to less technical decision makers. The bureau must prepare its own reports and develop recommendations based on the work that the firm provides. Hence, less efficient and complete assistance means greater in-house costs to the bureau. Both of the bidding firms have had previous contracts with the state, and so there is some empirical basis for estimating how close their actual work will be to the contract indications.

After some searching, the bureau learns that Flash, Inc. has had some extremely capable specialists as well as some trial-and-error devotees on its staff. The bureau estimates that there is a 60 percent chance that Flash, Inc. will do rather complete work, and the bureau will incur in-house costs of only $20,000 to support the specialized activities. If Flash, Inc. does unsatisfactory work, which has a 40 percent chance, then the bureau will spend $60,000 in support. On the other hand, Penser, Ltd. is much more consistent; it is not capable of either extreme. The bureau estimates that there is a 70 percent chance that it will have to spend $35,000 and a 30 percent chance that it will have to spend $50,000 in support of Penser, Ltd.'s technical assistance. Which firm should be awarded the contract?

The information can be summarized in a decision table, which is presented in Table 4-10. This problem statement and the payoff table differ from earlier ones in that the states of nature, satisfactory and unsatisfactory, have one set of probability values for the decision alternative Flash, Inc., and another set for Penser, Ltd.

If the decision maker, the bureau, is an expected value decision maker, then Flash gets the contract. If the decision is made with the more conservative minimax criterion, then Penser gets the contract. The maximax criterion indicates choosing Flash. The state of nature "satisfactory" is more likely for either alternative, but using the maximum likelihood criterion is questionable since the probabilities are not the same.

Table 4-10 Decision table of in-house costs for choosing a technical assistance firm

	Decision alternatives			
State of nature	Flash	Probability	Penser	Probability
Satisfactory	$20K*	.60	$35K	.70
Unsatisfactory	$60K	.40	$50K	.30
Expected cost	$36K		$39.5K	

* K = thousand.

When the state of nature is dependent on the chosen alternative, as it is here, the minimax regret and expected opportunity loss criteria are not appropriate. If Penser is chosen and does a satisfactory job, there is no regret that Flash was not chosen because there is no guarantee that Flash would also have done a satisfactory job. Hence even the idea of an opportunity loss is not applicable when the state of nature depends on the alternative.

SUMMARY

Decision theory provides a decision-making rationale when the decision situation is not fully known. The basic elements in a decision theory approach are: identify decision alternatives; identify uncontrollable factors or states of nature; identify the consequences of each alternative for each state of nature.

The decision situation is termed uncertain when the relative likelihoods of the states of nature are not known. Applicable criteria include maximax, minimax, average payoff, and minimax regret. The situation is termed risky when the relative likelihoods are known. Applicable criteria include expected payoff, expected opportunity loss, and maximum likelihood.

We have examined these criteria through simple examples in which the payoffs are not only quantified but are also well represented in simple dollar terms. Not all decision consequences in the public sector are as well represented by dollars, nor are decision criteria always so specifically stated. Often payoffs are better represented, for example, by improved health services or greater recreational opportunity or better educational enrichment. The purpose in developing a decision matrix there is as much to be sure that one has identified the alternatives, states of nature, and consequences, as it is to quantify the consequences. A health planning application typified this purpose.

A final illustration showed which criteria are applicable when the states of nature have different probability distributions for each alternative, and are dependent on the alternative that is chosen.

BIBLIOGRAPHY

Buchele, Robert B.: *The Management of Business and Public Organizations,* McGraw-Hill Book Company, New York, 1977.

Chance, William A.: "Study Program Determination by Incremental Analysis: An Alternative Approach," *Decision Sciences,* vol. 3, January 1972, pp. 129–135.

Grimes, Richard M., Catherine L. Allen, Ted R. Sparling, and Gerald Weiss: "Use of Decision Theory in Regional Planning," *Health Services Research,* vol. 9, no. 1, Spring 1974, pp. 73–78.

Gustafson, David H., and Donald C. Holloway: "A Decision Theory Approach to Measuring Severity in Illness," *Health Services Research,* vol. 10, Spring 1975, pp. 97–106.

Kraus, Jonathan: "Decision Process in Children's Court and the Social Background Report," *Journal of Research in Crime and Delinquency,* vol. 12, January 1975, pp. 17–29.

Schweitzer, Stuart O.: "Cost Effectiveness of Early Detection of Disease," *Health Services Research,* vol. 9, Spring 1974, pp. 22–32.

Weinberg, Charles B.: "The University Library: Analysis and Proposals," *Management Science,* vol. 21, Oct 1974, pp. 130–140.

Wendt, Dirk, and Charles Vlek (eds.): *Utility, Probability and Human Decision Making,* D. Reidel Publishing Company, Dordrecht-Holland, 1973.

EXERCISES

Extensions of chapter examples

4-1 Reconsider the drilling decision situation presented in Table 4-5. A reassessment of a complete success indicates that the payoffs have changed and are as follows:

	Percent of profit	Fixed lease	Combination
Complete success	1700	600	1400

(*a*) Using the expected payoff criterion, what is the preferred alternative?

(*b*) What does this suggest about the sensitivity of the decision to estimates of future revenues?

4-2 Arriving at the probability of each outcome in the drilling problem was in part a subjective process. Although we have numeric estimates, we should be attuned to their subjective origin. The reasoning that generated the probability values .25, .20, and .55 might just as validly have generated the values .21, .20, and .59, which are not all that different. Using this new set of probability estimates and the payoffs of Table 4-1, determine the alternative preferred by the expected value criterion. What does this suggest about the sensitivity of the decision to the estimated probability values?

4-3 Assume you are an expected value decision maker. Noting the results of exercises 4-1 and 4-2, what decision alternative would you choose?

4-4 In the southeast Texas hospital planning problem, the basis for the dollar value of excess beds is the $202,000 operating cost for each excess bed. Suppose the true cost is only $20,200 for each excess bed, or just 10 percent of the original estimate. Reconstruct the decision table and the expected payoffs, using the probabilities of Table 4-9. How might these changes have affected the council's choice of decision alternative I?

4-5 In problem 4-4, suppose the true cost is \$181,800 for each excess bed, or just 10 percent less than the original estimate. How might these changes have affected the council's choice of decision alternative I?

4-6 Assume your answer to problem 4-4 suggests that the council would have chosen an alternative other than alternative I, and your answer to problem 4-5 suggests they would have stayed with alternative I. Determine the level of "operating cost for each excess bed" at which they would change their decision. Discuss.

4-7 Refer to the last section of Chapter 4 and the illustration on choosing a technical assistance firm. It is sometimes claimed that in-house costs to support contractual services are sunk costs. They are costs already incurred and will not change whether the result of the contract is satisfactory or unsatisfactory. What may change is the delay in delivering required studies and the level of complaint and harassment. Reconstruct Table 4-10 with the following changes: The consequences of satisfactory work are no delays for Flash, Inc. and a 1-week delay for Penser, Ltd. The consequences for unsatisfactory work are a 4-week delay for Flash, Inc. and a 2-week delay for Penser, Ltd.

(*a*) What is the numerical expected payoff or consequence?

(*b*) What would the decision be according to the expected value, maximax, and minimax principles?

(*c*) What would your decision be?

Other applications

4-8 The following letter to the Editor appeared in *The New York Times* of February 28, 1971. The writer directed the theoretical division of the Los Alamos Scientific Laboratory from April 1943 to January 1946. Hans Bethe was the 1967 Nobel laureate in physics.

> Yalta: Lack of Communication on Bomb
> To the Editor:
>
> Under the title "The Truth about Yalta," C. L. Sulzberger [column of February 14] discussed the assessment by Ambassador Charles Bohlen of the chief problems that faced President Roosevelt and the U.S. delegation at the time of the Yalta Conference, February 1945. The third point of this assessment reads in part as follows:
>
> "While Roosevelt and a handful of advisers knew about the Manhattan Project, no one could be certain the atomic bomb would in fact explode or how effective a weapon it would be."
>
> This problem looked different as seen from the Los Alamos Scientific Laboratory charged with the development of the bomb. By February 1945, it appeared to me and to other fully informed scientists that there was a better than 90 percent probability that the atomic bomb would in fact explode, that it would be an extremely effective weapon, and that there would be enough material to build several bombs in the course of a few months.
>
> Thus even if the first bomb should have failed, the project was bound to succeed in a relatively short time. Few things in war and even fewer in politics have as good a chance as 90 percent.
>
> That the full flavor of this conviction of the scientists was not transmitted to the decision-makers was a failure of communication—excessive secrecy and the absence of direct channels between scientists and high Government officials were responsible. Because of this failure of direct communication, the U.S. at Yalta urged Russia to participate in the assault on Japan, with grave consequences for the future of the political situation in the Far East. Suppose there had been good communication. Should the U.S. Government have acted on a 90 percent probability of technical success? In my opinion, definitely yes.
>
> Again, in 1958 we had a chance to arrange a ban on the testing of nuclear weapons at a time when the U.S. had a clear advantage over the Soviet Union in weapon design. However, we were afraid of the possibility of clandestine underground Russian tests of small nuclear

weapons and insisted therefore on ironclad safeguards. These were unacceptable to the U.S.S.R., and no agreement was reached by 1961.

In 1961, the Russians conducted a series of nuclear weapon tests in which they managed to equal, in most of the important aspects, the performance of U.S. thermonuclear weapons. Thus here again, by insisting on certainty, the U.S. lost a clear advantage.

This letter is not meant to imply that our foreign policy should center on advantage over the U.S.S.R. I merely wish to argue that if and when the seeking of such an advantage is part of our policy, we should act on high technical probability rather than requiring certainty and should have easy communication between the knowledgeable persons and the decision-makers.

Hans Bethe
Ithaca, New York, February 16, 1971

Comment on the letter,[4] placing emphasis on the decision philosophies

(*a*) Apparently used at top levels of government
(*b*) Suggested by Bethe
(*c*) Recommended by you.

Support your recommendation.

4-9 The highway police patrol the interstate highways in order to prevent accidents and to service them when they do occur. Stopping speeders may be seen as a means to the end. Two types of patrol are available: (1) standard patrol, in which cars combine roadside standing to identify speeders and highway driving to catch them, and (2) cruising patrol, in which cars drive almost constantly at the posted speed limit to set a traffic pace. The operating cost per shift is $600 for the standard patrol and $800 for the cruising patrol. It is estimated that the mean cost to the patrol of servicing an accident is $100. In response to the right leading questions, the troop commander estimates that with the standard patrol, the chances of averaging 0 or 2 accidents per shift are about the same, and either is twice as likely as averaging 6 accidents. With the cruising patrol, averaging 0 accidents is four times as likely as 2 accidents, and averaging 6 accidents just will not happen. Assume no other average is possible.

(*a*) Develop a dollar-cost table for the two decision alternatives and the three states of nature.

(*b*) Determine the probabilities of the states of nature based on the given descriptive likelihoods. (Note that they are different for each decision alternative. If a state of nature for the first alternative has 0 probability for the second alternative, it is not considered a state of nature for the second alternative.) For each of the following criteria determine the better alternative;

1. Minimax.
2. Maximax.
3. Expected value.
4. Minimax regret. Comment on the appropriateness of this criterion.

4-10 It is suggested that the revenue that patrols generate in issuing citations to speeders should be taken into consideration. Reassess problem 4-9 if standard patrols generate 8 citations per shift (averaging $25 each) and cruising patrols generate only 2 per shift, because their cruising keeps traffic at a proper speed.

4-11 No matter how many relevant facts are considered, there are usually some that have been neglected. It is further noted that the cost of issuing and adjudicating a citation is about $50. Now reconsider problem 4-10. What other information should be considered in choosing the type of patrol? Should the dollar costs be considered at all?

4-12 Cy Linder is responsible for the medical supply room of a large medical center. Overall he is responsible for having supplies on hand as they are needed; however, he is also accountable for controlling expenses. Medicines acquired by him and subsequently requested for a patient are charged to that patient, and hence do not affect his budget. Supplies lost, stolen, or discarded do

[4] © 1971 by The New York Times Company. Reprinted by permission.

affect it. Cy has observed that a widely used but perishable medication has been overstocked for the past few weeks. Records reveal that the demand for the medication over the past 4 years (200 weeks) is as follows:

Vials of medicine used per week	Number of weeks
130	20
140	80
150	70
160	20
170	10
Total number of weeks	200

The medication costs $5 a vial and is ordered and delivered weekly. The shelf life of the medicine is 1 week. (Supplies on hand at the end of the week must be discarded.)

(*a*) Set up a loss table for the possible states of nature and decision alternatives.

(*b*) Keeping in mind Cy's overall responsibilities, what alternative would you recommend?

(*c*) What is his expected dollar loss for that alternative?

4-13 In problem 4-12, if Cy were able to arrange two deliveries per week, would his expected dollar loss be approximately halved? Discuss the overall effects of such an arrangement.

4-14 The U.S. Army Corps of Engineers has proposed to the Congress that the cost of maintaining the inland waterway system should be in part financed by the users of the system. They have also presented four different alternatives for assessing this charge: a tax on the fuel used by the tugs, a lockage fee for each time a barge passes through a lock, a toll on the barges for each ton per mile, and a license fee for each barge. While none of these alternatives will return the complete cost of maintaining the system, they were set at a level that would not significantly reduce the traffic. The corps also predicts that there is a 30 percent chance of a major increase of traffic, a 30 percent chance of a moderate increase, a 30 percent chance of a slight decrease, and a 10 percent chance of a major decrease. The consequences are displayed in the following table.

Decision table for inland waterway revenue*

		Decision alternatives			
State of nature	p	Fuel tax	Lockage fee	License fee	Toll
Major increase	.3	$3.7 B	$3.0 B	$2.7 B	$4.1 B
Slight increase	.3	3.0	2.5	2.3	3.3
Slight decrease	.3	2.4	2.1	2.1	2.4
Major decrease	.1	1.9	1.9	2.0	1.7

* B = billion.

(*a*) Which alternative is preferred according to each of the applicable criteria?

(*b*) Which alternative do you recommend? Why?

(*c*) Inasmuch as the probability for increases and decreases are estimates, what kind of sensitivity analysis would you recommend?

Project problems

4-15 Recent years have seen some wide-scale public efforts to prevent the occurrence of some epidemic that was considered a real possibility. An epidemic, obviously, is a widespread disaster. A public program taken to forestall or prevent it is necessarily a widespread program. A vaccination program carries with it not only the purported benefit of preventing the illness but also the recognized risk of a severe reaction in certain types of individuals.

Suppose the National Center for Disease Control indicates that there is a possibility of a widespread influenza epidemic within the next few months. Specifically, suppose there is a .02 probability that the epidemic will reach 20 million persons, a .08 probability that it will reach 2 million persons, and a 90 percent chance that there will be only a trace, that is, that the disease will reach 1,000 or fewer persons. Subjective estimates indicate that the influenza will be fatal to 1 in 1,000 persons afflicted. Hence, the death toll due to the influenza could go as high as 20,000 people without any prevention program.

In the face of such a dismal forecast, the federal government is faced with a decision concerning whether to fund a public vaccination program. It has three alternatives: to have no program; to have a select program, under which 20 million high-risk persons could be vaccinated; and to have a widespread vaccination program making the vaccine available to all who desire it. Estimates in this case are that 100 million persons would avail themselves of the vaccination. The cost is estimated to be $5 per vaccination. It is expected that there will be rather widespread reaction to the vaccine. It is believed that this reaction to the vaccine will occur only in those who have not been exposed to the influenza, so that the more widespread the influenza is, the fewer reactions there will be. The reaction is considered to be fatal to one of every 100,000 vaccinated people who are not also exposed.

If a selective vaccination program is undertaken, those considered most likely to get the influenza illness will be among those vaccinated. Since the influenza is believed to affect heart muscles, persons with chronic heart disease will be given the opportunity to be vaccinated.

All of the various estimates, although in part subjective, can be summarized in the following table. The entries for "epidemic = 1,000" and "no program" are derived from the above information. The remaining entries are estimated but are not directly calculable from the given information alone.

Decision table for influenza vaccination program; Number of fatalities due to influenza and vaccination reaction

		Type of program, Number vaccinated, Cost		
Extent of epidemic	Probability	Full program, 100 million, $500 million	Select program, 20 million, $100 million	No program, 0, $0
20 million	.02	1,000 + 200	10,000 + 50	20,000 + 0
2 million	.08	100 + 600	1,000 + 150	2,000 + 0
1,000	.90	0 + 1,000	0 + 200	1 + 0

(*a*) For purposes of comparison, find the alternative that would be chosen according to each of the decision criteria applied to estimated fatalities: maximax, minimax, minimax regret, expected value decision rule, maximum likelihood.

(*b*) What would your decision be and why? Did you consider the dollar cost in your decision?

4-16 Refer to problem 4-15. There are many subjective estimates in this decision situation and, hence, sensitivity analysis of the estimates is called for.

(*a*) If the probability estimates were corrected to be .01, .09, and .90 respectively, how would the expected value change for each alternative?

(*b*) Which alternative do you recommend?

(*c*) Did you make use of the cost in choosing your alternative?

(*d*) Would a decrease in cost to $1 per vaccination or an increase to $100 per vaccination have any effect on your decision choice? Is there any unit cost per vaccination at which you would include costs as a consideration?

(*e*) If you were a decision maker, or someone charged with making recommendations to the decision makers, what other information would you like to have before making a decision or recommendation? Would it take a long time to get this information? What effect might waiting have on decision making?

4-17 Refer to problem 4-15. Suppose that a consequence of the influenza and the vaccination reaction is not death, but rather critical illness. Since it is not completely known how the influenza affects the heart muscles, the severity of the illness is uncertain. The uncertainty includes whether the effect is temporary or permanent, whether the effect is on the heart muscles in general or on a particular muscle, and how the influenza in combination with some other preexisting condition will affect the individual. Presumably, some persons with particular respiratory or circulatory difficulties would succumb. Under these new conditions, which type of program would you recommend? (Assume no numeric changes from problem 4-15.)

4-18 Think of a decision situation in which you have been involved.

(*a*) Was there an identifiable objective?

(*b*) Was there a workable criterion?

(*c*) Were alternatives explicitly sought and found? List them.

(*d*) Were uncontrollable but related events (states of nature) uncovered? What were they?

(*e*) Were the consequences of the alternatives investigated? Summarize them.

(*f*) Can you summarize the decision situation in a decision table?

(*g*) Is there an appropriate probability distribution for the states of nature (the uncontrollables)?

(*h*) Which alternative would you pick based on the summary?

(*i*) Which alternative was chosen?

(*j*) If there is a discrepancy between the answers to parts *h* and *i*, is it due to a problem feature that cannot be adequately represented in the decision table?

(*k*) Discuss the role of such a summary in decision making.

CHAPTER

FIVE

DECISIONS AND REVISED PROBABILITIES

The search for and evaluation of decision alternatives often reveals new information. When new information concerns the identification of alternatives, there are revisions to and expansions of the list of choices. When it concerns the effects, consequences are restated. When the uncontrollable factors are involved, either the states of nature themselves are reconsidered or their likelihoods are revised. Here we will explore the fundamentals of how to revise probabilities on the basis of new information. The value of the new information is seen in its impact on the expected payoff. The expected value and the cost of the new information are compared to determine whether it is worth acquiring.

The ideas and techniques of probability revision are presented through a previously encountered (problem 4-15) government vaccination decision situation. The decision to fund and implement a widespread vaccination program has severe and long-lasting consequences. The sheer magnitude of the consequences is sufficient to suggest that efforts be made to acquire new information on the situation and use that new information, not to replace prior information and probabilities but to update them. By incorporating new information, probability estimates can be revised. This chapter focuses on the role of new information in revising rather than replacing previously estimated probabilities.

NEW INFORMATION AND REVISED PROBABILITIES

Problem 4-15 is used for illustrative purposes. The essence of the problem follows. There is a possibility of an imminent influenza outbreak. As a preventative step federal officials can choose one of three alternatives:

1. A full vaccination program in which vaccine would be made available to the entire population
2. A select program in which vaccine would be made available to high-risk individuals
3. No vaccination program at all

Estimates have been made of the likelihood of the extent of the epidemic, and the number of fatalities that will result from the epidemic itself and from reactions to the vaccine. The various estimates are presented in Table 5-1. Although many of the salient features, especially the numeric estimates, can be neatly presented in the table, the decision is anything but a neat or obvious one. That the consequences are numbers of impending deaths is certainly ominous; that the estimates of fatalities and their likelihoods are subjective generates some insecurity. Regardless of one's decision-making philosophy, especially in such a critical situation, the examination of the alternatives, states of nature, and their consequences is encouraged for gaining a fuller understanding of the problem. A sensitivity analysis of the estimates was suggested in problem 4-16. Here we are concerned with incorporating new information to revise the probability values.

Suppose prevailing weather conditions during the summer are capable of providing some information that would allow public health professionals to revise their estimates of the likelihood of an outbreak of influenza during the fall. How they might use the information to revise the estimates becomes a question of some interest.

Revision of probabilities depends on the basic notion of conditional probability:

$$P(A/B) = \frac{P(A \text{ and } B)}{P(B)}$$

The purpose for revising probabilities is to determine what effect new information B has on the probability of any state of nature A. Since the original

Table 5-1 Decision table for influenza vaccination program
Number of deaths due to influenza and vaccination reaction

		Type of program, number vaccinated, cost		
Extent of epidemic (number of cases)	Prior probability	Full program, 100 million, $500 million	Select program, 20 million, $100 million	No program, 0, $0
Extreme (E) (20 million)	.02	1,000 + 200	10,000 + 50	20,000 + 0
Serious (S) (2 million)	.08	100 + 600	1,000 + 150	2,000 + 0
Trace (T) (1000)	.90	0 + 1,000	0 + 200	1 + 0

marginal probability assessment $P(A)$ is arrived at before the new information, it is referred to as a *prior probability*. The conditional probability $P(A/B)$ that uses the new information is called a *posterior probability*.

Revised or Posterior Probabilities

In the epidemic illustration the prior probabilities are

$$P(\text{E}) = .02$$

$$P(\text{S}) = .08$$

$$P(\text{T}) = .90$$

The new information is the prevailing weather conditions in the summer preceding an outbreak. Assume a summer overall can be labeled either hot and humid (HH) or dry and moderate (DM). The objective is to determine the revised or posterior probabilities:

$$P(\text{E/DM}) \qquad P(\text{E/HH})$$

$$P(\text{S/DM}) \qquad P(\text{S/HH})$$

$$P(\text{T/DM}) \qquad P(\text{T/HH})$$

With this kind of information, decision makers can review the decision situation, incorporating new information in estimating the likelihoods of each of the uncontrollables.

In order to see whether there is a relationship between the extent of an epidemic and the prevailing weather conditions during the summer preceding the outbreak, many instances of recorded influenza outbreaks are examined. Suppose such an examination leads to the conditional statements that for occasions in which there were extreme epidemics, the probability of a hot, humid summer was .80, whereas the probability of a dry, moderate summer was only .20. Symbolically,

$$P(\text{HH/E}) = .80 \qquad \text{and} \qquad P(\text{DM/E}) = .20$$

Suppose that on the occasions in which there have been outbreaks of a smaller scale, the preceding summers were just as likely to be moderate and dry as they were to be hot and humid. Hence,

$$P(\text{HH/S}) = .50 \qquad \text{and} \qquad P(\text{DM/S}) = .50$$

By the multiplication rule, joint probabilities can be found. Two such joint probabilities are:

$$\begin{aligned} P(\text{HH and E}) &= P(\text{HH/E}) \cdot P(\text{E}) \\ &= (.80)(.02) \\ &= .016 \end{aligned}$$

and
$$P(\text{HH and S}) = P(\text{HH/S}) \cdot P(\text{S})$$
$$= (.50)(.08)$$
$$= .04$$

Suppose further that the probability of having a hot, humid summer is .40 and the probability of having a dry, moderate summer is .60. A joint probability table can now be completed to establish the relationship between the extent of an epidemic and the prevailing weather for the preceding summer. If there is such a relationship, then it can be used to revise the original prior probabilities.

Using the joint probabilities of Table 5-2, we can now determine the probability of extreme epidemic on condition that the type of summer weather condition is known. If the summer has been a dry, moderate one, then the revised probabilities of the three possible extents of epidemic are found as follows:

$$P(\text{E/DM}) = \frac{P(\text{E and DM})}{P(\text{DM})}$$
$$= \frac{.004}{.60}$$
$$= .0067$$
$$P(\text{S/DM}) = \frac{P(\text{S and DM})}{P(\text{DM})}$$
$$= \frac{.04}{.60}$$
$$= .067$$
$$P(\text{T/DM}) = \frac{P(\text{T and DM})}{P(\text{DM})}$$
$$= \frac{.556}{.60}$$
$$= .927$$

Table 5-2 Joint probabilities of extent of epidemic and summer weather conditions

	Summer weather conditions		
State of nature	Dry, moderate (DM)	Hot, humid (HH)	Marginal probability of extent of epidemic
Epidemic:			
Extreme (E)	.004	.016	.02
Serious (S)	.04	.04	.08
Trace (T)	.556	.344	.90
Marginal probability of summer weather	.60	.40	1.00

Table 5-3 Revised probabilities of extent of epidemic given the summer weather conditions

State of nature	Prior probabilities	Revised probabilities: Given summer weather $P(\ /DM)$	$P(\ /HH)$
Epidemic:			
Extreme	.02	.0067	.04
Serious	.08	.067	.10
Trace	.90	.927	.86
	1.00	1.00	1.00

If the new information is that the summer has been a hot, humid one, conditional probabilities would be determined in a similar way. Both of these sets of conditional or posterior or revised probabilities are presented in Table 5-3.

We have found the revised probabilities by completing the joint probability table and then finding the conditional probabilities. The use of the table can mask the fact that we are actually using *Bayes' law:*

$$P(B/A) = \frac{P(B \text{ and } A)}{P(A)} = \frac{P(A/B) \cdot P(B)}{P(A)}$$

Note that the new information does not affect the consequences themselves, but rather the likelihood of each state of nature, and hence, the likelihood of each consequence.

For purposes of comparison, we determine the expected value of the number of fatalities for each decision alternative, first with the prior probabilities and then with each set of revised probabilities. Note that not both sets of revised probabilities would apply to the same decision situation; either the new

Table 5-4 Influenza and vaccination-reaction fatalities and expected fatalities with prior and revised probabilities

State of nature	Type of program: Full	Select	None	Prior probability	Revised, given DM	Revised, given HH
E	1,200	10,050	20,000	.02	.0067	.04
S	700	1,150	2,000	.08	.067	.10
T	1,000	200	1	.90	.927	.86
Expected number of fatalities (prior)	980	473	561			
Expected number of fatalities (given DM)	982	330	269			
Expected number of fatalities (given HH)	978	687	1001			

information is a dry, moderate summer or the new information is a hot, humid one. It could not be both at the same time. Table 5-4 presents the number of fatalities for each alternative and each state of nature, and the expected number of fatalities using the prior probabilities and both sets of revised probabilities.

Table 5-4 reveals that the new information has little effect on the expected number of fatalities associated with a full vaccination program. This is essentially because the three possible consequences associated with the full vaccination program are not markedly different from each other. By contrast the new information has a severe impact on the expected number of fatalities associated with having no vaccination program at all. This is consistent with the extreme differences among the three possible consequences associated with having no program. The impact of the new information on the select vaccination program is certainly considerable, but not quite as extreme as on the no-program alternative.

In presenting the expected number of fatalities for each alternative using the three sets of probabilities, we are not implying that the expected value decision rule is better than all others. If one chooses to ignore the likelihood of each epidemic possibility, then one considers only the separate consequences. This approach, however, ignores rather useful information. On the other hand, if one chooses to consider the probabilities of each type of epidemic, then one must have some way of comparing the impacts of changes in those probabilities. Using the expected value provides one such mechanism for comparison.

Acquiring new information usually costs something. The cost may be monetary or otherwise. Direct costs are the most obvious. These include the costs of record searching, sampling, and data processing. Less obvious but often higher are indirect costs. In the influenza vaccination program decision, waiting until the end of the summer when the new information becomes available may bring with it a significant delay in implementing the program, if in fact the program is to be implemented. This delay may result in failure to vaccinate some of the potential influenza victims on time and therefore may cost lives. In order to delay making the final decision until the end of summer, some of the one-half billion dollars of the full-program cost may have to be spent. The federal agency may have to fund the development of the vaccine from cultures, to plan a distribution program, and perhaps even to contract for medical services. If these expenditures are incurred before the final decision is made, and if the decision is to implement no program at all, they would be sunk costs. Such costs are considered a cost of delaying the decision, and therefore of the new information.

Since there is usually a cost associated with new information, then either there is also a value to the new information or the decision maker should not bother with it. If the changes in the likelihoods of the possible extents of an epidemic and the changes in the expected number of fatalities are viewed as having no effect on the decision, then there is no value in putting off the decision. Hence, the new information has no value. If the decision makers indicate that they would in fact make a different decision for each of the two possible kinds of summer, then the new information has value. Whether its value exceeds its cost remains to be seen.

The actual value of new information cannot be determined until the new information is provided and a decision is made. The decision made with the new information can then be directly compared with the decision that would have been made with the old information. However, it is not at all helpful to have to wait until the new information is provided in order to be able to decide whether the new information is worth seeking. Consequently, the expected value of the new information is used as the basis for determining whether the new information should be sought. We now explore the expected value of information.

EXPECTED VALUE OF INFORMATION

If the decision makers indicate that regardless of the type of summer, their decision will be unchanged, then the new information has no value insofar as it does not affect the decision. On the other hand, suppose the decision makers indicate that with the currently available information—that is, with the prior probabilities—they would choose to implement a selective vaccination program because it appears to have the lowest expected number of fatalities. The decision makers further indicate that for any particular kind of summer, they would choose the alternative with the lowest expected number of fatalities. Table 5-4 Revised presents the expected number of fatalities for each alternative for the prior probabilities and for both sets of revised probabilities. The lowest expected number of fatalities based on prior probabilities is 473 for the select program. The lowest expected number based on the revised probabilities for a dry, moderate summer is 269 for no program. The lowest expected number based on the revised probabilities for a hot, humid summer is 687 for the select program. These three values are circled in Table 5-4 Revised.

Table 5-4 Revised Influenza and vaccination-reaction fatalities and expected fatalities with prior and revised probabilities

State of nature	Type of program: Full	Select	None	Prior probability	Revised, given DM	Revised, given HH
E	1,200	10,050	20,000	.02	.0067	.04
S	700	1,150	2,000	.08	.067	.10
T	1,000	200	1	.90	.927	.86
Expected number of fatalities	980	473	561			
	982	330	269		$P(\text{DM}) = .60$	
	978	687	1001			$P(\text{HH}) = .40$

Expected Value of New Information

On the basis of the new information the expected number of fatalities is either 269 or 687. Recall that

$$P(\text{DM}) = .60 \qquad \text{and} \qquad P(\text{HH}) = .40$$

These probabilities apply also to the lowest expected number of fatalities. If the decision makers plan on using the new information, then

$$P(269 \text{ expected fatalities}) = .60 \qquad \text{and} \qquad P(687 \text{ expected fatalities}) = .40$$

With these probabilities one can determine the expected number of fatalities with new information as follows:

Expected number of fatalities with new information

$$\begin{aligned} &= (\text{expected number of fatalities/DM}) \cdot P(\text{DM}) \\ &\quad + (\text{expected number of fatalities/HH}) \cdot P(\text{HH}) \\ &= 269(.60) + 687(.40) \\ &= 436 \end{aligned}$$

At this point one has the expected payoff using old information and the expected payoff using new information. The difference between these is the *expected value of new information* (EVNI).

$$\begin{aligned} \text{EVNI} &= \text{expected payoff based on new information} \\ &\quad - \text{expected payoff based on old information} \end{aligned}$$

If the payoffs in the decision table are benefits, then EVNI will be positive. If the payoffs are detriments, then EVNI will be negative.[1] In the vaccination-program illustration the payoffs are fatalities so the value of EVNI will be *negative,* indicating that the new information will *lower* the expected number of fatalities.

Expected value of new information

$$\begin{aligned} &= \text{expected number of fatalities based on new information} \\ &\quad - \text{expected number of fatalities based on old information} \end{aligned}$$

$$\text{or} \quad \begin{aligned} \text{EVNI} &= 436 - 473 \\ &= -37 \end{aligned}$$

As anticipated, EVNI is *negative*. This means that the new information will *lower* the expected number of fatalities by 37.

[1] EVNI = 0 if either (*a*) the posterior probabilities equal the prior probabilities, which means the new information and the states of nature are statistically independent, or (*b*) one alternative has the optimum expected payoff based on the prior and on all the posterior probabilities.

Note that this decrease in the expected number of fatalities does not mean that the actual program will be altered but rather that with new information the choice is more likely to be the right one. If this were a decision situation that would be repeated many times, then using the new information in each situation would lower the number of fatalities on the average by 37. If this is not a repetitive decision situation (and hopefully for this particular illustration it is not), then the expected value of the new information is an indicator of the relative worth of the new information as it affects the likelihoods of each consequence. It is up to the decision makers to decide whether the new information should be sought, considering both its cost in terms of delays, possible postponing of vaccination shots, sunk costs for the development of the vaccine, and so forth, and its expected value in the reduced expected number of fatalities. If the cost includes delays that are so extensive that many people would not be given the vaccine on time, and the expected loss of life would be greater than the expected saving of life, then certainly the expected value of the new information would not be worth the cost of the new information. When the cost and the value of the new information are in similar terms, a comparative judgment is fairly direct. When the value and cost of the new information are in different units, then the comparison and hence the decision are more difficult.

Associating prevailing summer weather with the extent of an epidemic can provide some new information, which essentially revises the probabilities of each kind of epidemic. It certainly does not provide a precise forecast of the extent of epidemic. If there were such information available, it would be termed perfect information.

Expected Value of Perfect Information

If the public health officials wait until mid-fall or later, the information that they have concerning the extent of the epidemic becomes better and better. Eventually, of course, they would wait themselves out of alternatives, or more correctly, they would have backed into the alternative of having no program at all. "Not to decide is to decide."

Suppose that by waiting until late November, the extent of the epidemic will be known with certainty. When the state of nature is known with certainty, the decision makers are said to be operating with *perfect information*. The prior probabilities still apply in the sense that each state of nature will occur with a relative frequency equal to the prior probability. For example, a widespread epidemic will occur in 2 percent of such situations. Having perfect information will not forestall the epidemic, but will predict exactly the occurrences of the epidemic. This, in turn, allows the decision makers to choose the alternative that minimizes the adverse consequences. There are still fatalities, but they are kept to a minimum by choosing the alternative that is best for the certain state of nature. If there is to be an epidemic, either widespread or small scale, a full influenza vaccination program would be implemented. If there is to be just a

Table 5-5 Influenza and vaccination-reaction fatalities
Decision making using perfect information

State of nature	Type of program: Full	Select	None	Prior probability	Calculations of expected value
E	1,200			.02	1,200 × .02 = 24
S	700			.08	700 × .08 = 56
T			1	.90	1 × .90 = .9
Expected number of fatalities using perfect information					= 81 (rounded)

trace of an epidemic, no program would be implemented. These are the best decisions for those certain states of nature.

Table 5-5 indicates the number of fatalities that will occur as the result of choosing the best alternative for each state of nature when that state is known with certainty. Even when the extent of the epidemic is known with certainty, there will be some fatalities. The prior probability of each state of nature is the probability of the best payoff of each state. The expected number of fatalities using perfect information is calculated in Table 5-5.

The expected value of perfect information is the difference between the expected payoff using perfect information and the expected payoff using old information.

$$\text{EVPI} = \text{expected payoff based on perfect information} - \text{expected payoff based on old information}$$

EVPI will be positive or negative depending on whether the payoffs are beneficial or detrimental.[2]

In the illustration the expected number of fatalities using perfect information is 81, and the expected number of fatalities using old information is 473. The expected value of perfect information is found as follows:

Expected value of perfect information

$$= \text{expected number of fatalities using perfect information} - \text{expected number of fatalities using old information}$$

or

$$\text{EVPI} = 81 - 473 = -392$$

As anticipated, EVPI is *negative;* this means that perfect information would *lower* the expected death toll by 392. Since perfect information is seldom, if ever, available, the usefulness of knowing the expected value of per-

[2] As long as the original states of nature are uncertain or risky, perfect information will improve the expected payoff; EVPI will never equal 0.

fect information rests in the fact that it represents a ceiling on the improvement that any new information can provide. Regardless of how sophisticated and expensive efforts might be, no information can have an expected value greater than EVPI. Just as there is a value to new information, whether perfect or not, so too there is a cost. The decision makers must weigh the value against the cost and determine whether the new information is worth acquiring.

We now employ another illustration to reinforce some of the notions involved in revising probabilities and using new information.

THE VALUE OF KNOWING THE AUDIENCE: AN ILLUSTRATION

A speaker trying to gain the approval of an audience is well advised to understand the audience and know what it wants. Attempts have been made recently to characterize an audience, so that a political candidate would be better prepared to understand the audience, to know the issues to emphasize, and even to use the phrases that would be more likely to gain support.[3]

It is not suggested that the candidate be two-faced, saying "yea, yea" to one audience and "nay, nay" to a second, but rather that he know which issues to choose to discuss and to emphasize for each particular audience. The candidate makes a number of appearances and speaks to many audiences, so that the process of facing different kinds of audiences and choosing from among different possible presentations is a repetitive decision situation. The consequences are revealed in the number of votes garnered, the level of volunteer activity generated, and the amount of campaign contributions pledged. A simple example will illustrate the way a candidate might determine whether gaining such knowledge of the audience is worthwhile.

The Decision Table

Assume that an audience can be characterized as either mainly concerned with social issues or mainly concerned with the role of government in private enterprise, and that the former audience type is considerably more likely than the latter. The candidate has three different presentations which he uses. The first emphasizes social issues and gains considerable support from a socially concerned audience, but little support from a private enterprise audience. The second emphasizes corporate issues and gains much support from the private enterprise audience but relatively little from the socially concerned audience. The third presentation type gains medium support from either audience.

[3] The process that has been used involves interviewing a sample of the audience and analyzing the results using a statistical technique called "factor analysis." The purpose of the analysis is to identify some underlying characteristics of the audience so that the candidate will be more likely to discuss issues meaningful to that audience.

Table 5-6 Decision table for campaign presentations (proxy units)

		Decision alternatives		
		Presentation		
State of nature	Probability	*A*	*B*	*C*
Audience type:				
Socially concerned	.60	90	30	70
Corporately concerned	.40	20	80	60
Expected number of units		62	50	66

The level of support that is provided by the audience for the candidate's campaign is a difficult one to assess. The extent of the volunteer effort and the level of political contributions that grow out of the presentation provide some measure. The ultimate measure is the number of votes generated, but it is difficult to determine which votes would have been favorably cast even without the presentation. We will assume there is a proxy measure that combines these three factors. The number of units of support generated by each of the three presentations for either of the two types of audience is presented in Table 5-6.

No doubt for some of the presentations, the candidate or his staff will be able to make a good educated guess about the audience type; based on this educated guess he will choose the presentation to be made. In such situations, other probabilities may be applicable. For all of the audiences which are not guessed about, assume the probabilities of Table 5-6 apply. Since the candidate makes many such presentations, it is reasonable to use the expected value criterion. Using this criterion, presentation *C* would be chosen since in the long run it provides a greater level of support than either of the other two presentations.

Perfect Information

Suppose a polling organization proposes a scheme by which they will scout the audience ahead of time and determine almost perfectly, they claim, the particular audience type. They will do this, of course, for a fee. If they are, in fact, able to identify the type of audience perfectly, then the candidate will make his choice of presentation based on perfect information. This means that when the audience has been identified as predominately socially concerned presentation *A* will be chosen, whereas when the audience has been assessed as predominately corporately concerned presentation type *B* will be used.

Table 5-7 summarizes the calculations for EVPI. Using the perfect information, the candidate will get 90 units 60 percent of the time, and 80 units 40 percent of the time. He will get 86 units of support from each audience on the average. This improvement of 20 units over the expected value, 66, of alternative *C* is the expected value of perfect information.

Table 5-7 Consequences of campaign presentations using perfect information

		Decision alternatives			
		Presentation			
State of nature	Probability	*A*	*B*	*C*	Calculations
Audience type:					
Socially concerned	.60	90			54
Corporately concerned	.40		80		32
Expected value using perfect information					86
Expected value of perfect information = 86 − 66 = 20					

The candidate weighs the cost of the service against the value of the service. The value of the service is at most 20 additional units per presentation. If the forecasting of audience type is not perfect, then the value of the information will be something less than 20 units.

Revised Probabilities

Agreeing that improving the response to each presentation by an average of 20 units is certainly valuable, the candidate poses a poignant question to the polling group. "You say you can predict the audience type almost perfectly. Just what do you mean by 'almost perfectly'?" In response to the query, the pollsters produce records of their past work which indicate that they can characterize a socially concerned audience with 90 percent accuracy and a corporately concerned audience with 80 percent accuracy. One of the candidate's staff members suggests that this means that the 80 to 90 percent accuracy would bring about an improvement of 16 to 18 units, since perfect accuracy would bring about an improvement of 20 units. Another aide suggests that that seems too simple.

In fact, it is too simple. What must be done is to determine the expected number of units of support based on the new information. In order to do this, we must first determine the revised probabilities based on new information, which requires the development of the joint probability table between the audience type and the forecast.

The pollsters have indicated that they can forecast with 80 or 90 percent accuracy as follows:

$$P(\text{forecast socially concerned/audience is socially concerned}) = .90$$

and P(forecast corporately concerned/audience is corporately concerned) $= .80$

or $\quad P(\text{SF/Soc}) = .90 \quad$ and $\quad P(\text{CF/Cor}) = .80$

Table 5-8 Joint probabilities for audience type and forecasted audience type

	Forecasted audience type		
State of nature	Socially concerned (SF)	Corporately concerned (CF)	Marginal
Audience:			
Soc	.54	.06	.60
Cor	.08	.32	.40
Marginal probability	.62	.38	1.00

Recalling from Table 5-6 that *P*(Soc) = .60 and *P*(Cor) = .40, we construct the joint probability table, Table 5-8. Using the joint probabilities and marginal probabilities, we can now find the needed posterior probabilities. These are the revised probabilities given that there is a socially concerned forecast and the revised probabilities given that there is a corporately concerned forecast. One example of the calculations follows:

P(audience is socially concerned/forecast socially concerned)

$$= \frac{P(\text{Soc and SF})}{P(\text{SF})}$$

$$= \frac{.54}{.62}$$

$$= .87$$

All the revised probabilities and all the expected number of units of support, based on the prior probabilities and on the revised probabilities, are presented in Table 5-9. In that table the highest expected number of units for each set of

Table 5-9 Units of candidate support

State of nature	Presentation *A*	*B*	*C*	Prior probability	Revised, given SF	Revised, given CF
Audience:						
Soc	90	30	70	.60	.87	.16
Cor	20	80	60	.40	.13	.84
Expected number of units	62	50	(66)			
	(81)	37	69		*P*(SF) = .62	
	32	(72)	62		*P*(CF) = .38	

probabilities is circled. We can now determine the expected value of the new information, that is, of the forecast.

$$\begin{aligned}\text{Expected number of units of support using the forecast}\\ &= (\text{expected number of units given SF}) \times P(\text{SF})\\ &\quad + (\text{expected number of units given CF}) \times P(\text{CF})\\ &= 81(.62) + 72(.38)\\ &= 78\end{aligned}$$

Therefore

$$\begin{aligned}\text{EVNI} &= \text{expected number of units using the forecast}\\ &\quad - \text{expected number of units without the forecast}\\ &= 78 - 66\\ &= 12\end{aligned}$$

As it turns out, then, the 80 to 90 percent accuracy of the forecast yields only 12 additional units of support, much less than the 20 units based on perfect information. EVPI provides the maximum improvement that new information can provide. EVNI provides an indication of the improvement that the forecasts would provide. This difference suggests that while knowing EVPI is useful in providing the ceiling, it is also necessary to have some indication of the validity of the new information in order to be able to estimate its worth. Without having any indication of its worth, even in qualitative terms, the only basis for acquiring it (and paying the acquisition costs) is hope.

The value of information, whether new information or perfect information, and how to assess that value is further illustrated in the next section. In a decision-making situation concerning whether to seed potentially devastating hurricanes, the use of prior and posterior probabilities is explored and the anticipated reaction of an uninformed public is considered.

AN APPLICATION: WHETHER TO SEED HURRICANES[4]

Property damage due to hurricanes averages about one-half billion dollars annually. Damage due to a single hurricane such as Betsy (1965), Camille (1969), and Agnes (1972), can be around one and a half billion dollars. Reducing the destructive force of hurricanes would have significant consequences.

Whether to seed hurricanes is a decision addressed at two levels of decision making:

[4] This material is based on R. A. Howard, J. E. Matthison, and E. W. North, "The Decision to Seed Hurricanes," *Science,* vol. 176, no. 4040, June 16, 1972, pp. 1191–1202.

1. A policy decision to permit or prohibit the seeding of hurricanes
2. A tactical decision whether to seed a particular hurricane at a particular point in time

This application addresses the policy decision.

Since injury and death are often dependent upon the storm warnings, the consequences of a decision to seed or not to seed are measured by property damage. Other consequences are the legal and social ones. If a seeded hurricane caused an extraordinary amount of damage even though it was less than would have been caused without the seeding, the public may associate the damage with the seeding. There would likely be great public outcry and possible legal action. The extent of the government's liability in such instances is not yet completely resolved. It is interesting to note, however, that almost all the government meteorologists surveyed for this study favored hurricane seeding if their homes and families were threatened, if they could be freed from professional liability. The technical experts see the uncertainty and possible detrimental effects less as a technical problem and more as a political one.

The damage caused by a storm is related to the maximum sustained surface wind speed. If a hurricane is to be seeded, it would be seeded about 12 hours before the hurricane is predicted to strike the coast. Whether or not the hurricane is seeded, great natural changes in hurricane intensity over a 12-hour period comprise one source of uncertainty. If a hurricane is seeded, the effect of the seeding comprises a second source of uncertainty. In deciding the policy decision concerning whether seeding should be permitted or prohibited, average effects are of prime importance. In the practical decision, characteristics of the particular hurricane become greatly important. Based on meteorological data and seeding experiments during hurricane Debbie (1969), probabilities for the possible assessment of seeding have been estimated. A nominal hurricane has been used as the basis for property-damage estimates. Table 5-10

Table 5-10 Decision table for hurricane seeding (losses in millions \$)

State of nature	Probability	Alternatives: Seed	Do not seed
Seeding is:			
Beneficial	.49	69.42	116
Neutral	.49	116.25	116
Detrimental	.02	167.61	116
Expected loss		94.33	116
Expected loss with perfect information		93.17	
EVPI		−1.16	

summarizes the elements of the decision theory representation of the decision.

The cost of seeding a hurricane is estimated at a quarter of a million dollars, which value is included in the losses in Table 5-10. On the basis of available information there is little likelihood that seeding the hurricane would be detrimental. Moderate changes in that likelihood have a notable impact on the expected loss of the seeding alternative.

The expected value of perfect information is relatively small, due primarily to the rather small probability that seeding is detrimental. Consequently, if experts accept at .02 the probability that seeding is detrimental, then on the basis of expected value additional information is of little use. If the experts are less than secure with the .02 probability, further information would be valuable because of the sensitivity of the expected value of seeding to the probability that seeding is detrimental.

The imputed cost to the government for assuming responsibility for seeding has not been included in this summary. In the original article the imputed cost is included in an alternate analysis. On that basis, the expected loss of seeding is higher, but it is still lower than the expected cost of the alternative not to seed. In that case, EVPI is considerably greater, because with perfect information the responsibility costs of seeding can be avoided when seeding is either neutral or detrimental. This alternate analysis is explored in exercises 5-5.

SUMMARY

In this chapter we have considered how new information can be incorporated into the decision situation. This is done primarily through revising the state of nature probabilities. Revision of probabilities depends primarily on the basic notion of conditional probability:

$$P(A/B) = \frac{P(A \text{ and } B)}{P(B)}$$

The expected payoff using the revised probabilities is calculated in the same way as the expected payoff using the old probabilities. The difference between these is the expected value of the new information (EVNI).

$$\begin{aligned} \text{EVNI} = {} & \text{expected payoff based on new information} \\ & - \text{expected payoff based on old information} \end{aligned}$$

If the new information completely removes the uncertainty of which state of nature will occur in each particular instance, it is called perfect information. The expected value of perfect information, EVPI, is found in much the same way as EVNI:

$$\begin{aligned} \text{EVPI} = {} & \text{expected payoff based on perfect information} \\ & - \text{expected payoff based on old information} \end{aligned}$$

EVPI is useful primarily in establishing a ceiling on the value of new information, since in practice perfect information is seldom if ever available.

The chapter's main ideas are illustrated in a hypothetical situation predicting audience characteristics and a real application taken from the literature.

BIBLIOGRAPHY

See the Bibliography of Chapter 4.

EXERCISES

Extensions of chapter examples

5-1 Refer to the gas recovery operation of Chapter 4. Suppose that a new test becomes available for determining the type of underground formation. The substructure formation is related to the volume of gas. Examination of past gas recovery operations has led to the following joint probability table:

	Substructure formation		
State of nature	I	II	Marginal probability
Gas recovery operation:			
Complete success	.20	.05	.25
Moderate success	.15	.05	.20
Failure	.15	.40	.55
Marginal probability	.50	.50	1.00

The cost of the tests is estimated at $10 million.

(*a*) What is the expected value of the new information that would be provided by the test?

(*b*) Assuming you are an expected value decision maker, would you opt for the test?

(*c*) If you were asked for a recommendation, would you recommend that the test be made? If so, why? and if not, why not?

5-2 Refer to problem 4-17 and to the revised probabilities of Table 5-4 (see Table 5-4 Revised). Suppose the consequences are given in terms of critical illnesses rather than fatalities.

(*a*) Would you recommend postponing a decision until the new information is available?

(*b*) For each of the sets of revised probabilities, what is your recommendation concerning the type of program to be implemented?

(*c*) As a decision maker, what other factors would you consider besides costs, extent of epidemic and reactions, and the likelihood of some deaths.

5-3 Verify the joint probabilities of Table 5-8, using the conditional probabilities

$$P(\text{SF/Soc}) \quad \text{and} \quad P(\text{CF/Cor})$$

and the prior probabilities of Table 5-6.

5-4 Refer to Table 5-9.

(*a*) Determine the preferred alternative according to the

1. Minimax criterion
2. Minimax regret criterion
3. Maximax criterion
4. Maximum likelihood criterion

for each of the probability distributions

i. Prior
ii. Revised, given SF
iii. Revised, given CF

Based on the information available in Table 5-9:

(*b*) Which presentation would you choose prior to new information? Why?

(*c*) Which presentation would you choose for each of the revised probability distributions? Why?

(*d*) Would you choose to get the new information?

5-5 Refer to Table 5-10. Suppose the probabilities are reassessed and the new values for beneficial, neutral, and detrimental are .42, .48, and .10, respectively. Determine how the expected loss for each alternative and EVPI are affected.

New applications

5-6 An insurance commission is investigating an automobile insurance company's request for an adjustment in premiums for first-year drivers, 40 percent of whom are female. Company records support their contention that claims average $1000, including administrative and overhead costs and profit contribution. Premium rates are established to recover total claims. Past records of all first-year drivers provide a probability distribution for number of accidents:

Number of accidents	Probability	Loss	Loss × probability
0	.70	$ 0	$ 0
1	.18	1000	180
2	.12	2000	240
	Expected loss		$420

Annual premiums are set therefore at $420.

The company is requesting different rates for male and female first-year drivers because:

1. Of all first-year drivers who have 1 accident, two-thirds are male.
2. Of all such drivers who have 2 accidents, three-fourths are male.

What premiums is the company justified in requesting?

Project problems

5-7 Read the article, "The Decision to Seed Hurricanes," referenced in footnote 4. Take particular notice of how government responsibility costs are determined.

(*a*) Reconstruct Table 5-10 so that the payoffs include the government responsibility costs. [*Hint:* Equation (15) gives the government-responsibility costs for neutral and detrimental seeding. Figure 9 gives \$110.92 million as the overall expected loss of seeding, including government responsibility cost.]

(*b*) From your table calculate EVPI and compare it with Eq. (15).

(*c*) Discuss the conclusions of the analysis, from both the technical adviser's and elected official's points of view.

CHAPTER

SIX

UTILITY THEORY AND MULTIPLE OBJECTIVES

What do you want? A simple question, yet an extremely complex one. Each of us wants many things. Some things are wanted for themselves. Others are wanted for what they can provide. How badly we want any one thing depends on what it is, what we already have, and whether it is wanted for itself or as a means to something else. What we want today may not be what we want tomorrow.

Some things are clearly wanted more than others, and the others will be sought only if progress toward attainment of the more highly desired object is not thereby thwarted. The parent wants security for the children; other wants—vacation, a new car, or new carpeting—will be sought only to the extent that the insurance program providing the security will not be adversely affected. In other instances we want things but not so badly that others will be given up entirely; we are willing to accept trade-offs in order to achieve some or all to a less than complete degree. A well-rounded recreation program, well-equipped fire department, and adequate police protection compete for the same resources; the community may be willing to forgo complete satisfaction of any one of them, but it demands at least partial attainment of each.

The desires of a group are considerably more complicated than those of an individual. The group is made up of individuals, each of whom has his or her own set of desires that change over time. The desires of society are often expressed by spokespersons; the spokespersons change over time. Time and the individuals themselves are two sources of change in a group's preferences.

The group's desires are wanted intensely by some, moderately by others. The establishment of their relative importance is accomplished only with debate, persuasion, collusion, value sharing, or other attempts at collective assessment.

The reality of many desires and multiple objectives can be approached in a number of different ways. No one way is completely satisfying in itself, nor always better than the others.

One approach to multiple-objective decision making combines the objectives into some single aggregate objective. This assumes there exists either a meaningful way of combining them, or a single standard unit by which achievement toward all the objectives can be measured. A commonly used standard unit is the dollar. Another unit with much theoretical underpinning but some practical difficulty is an arbitrary measure of *utility* or usefulness.

A second approach to multiple-objective decision making makes no assumption about measurability by a single unit, but rather evaluates the alternatives for their impacts on all the objectives, incomparable and conflicting though they be.

More than any other characteristics, the need for nonmonetary measures and the presence of multiple objectives typify public decision making. This chapter is concerned with two main topics. The first is the concept of the *utility* or *usefulness* of various levels of attainment of a particular objective; the second is techniques for addressing multiple objectives. Two of many possible ways are explored:

1. Trade off among the preferences to evaluate alternatives.
2. Rate objectives for their relative utility, and evaluate alternatives according to their expected effectiveness in attaining the objectives.

More specialized techniques are applicable when particular conditions are satisfied. When the elements (people, dollars, acres, days, person-hours, miles, and so forth) of a decision problem are not only measurable but linearly related (a change in one brings about proportional changes in the others), two other techniques that are discussed later in this book may be appropriately employed. When one objective can be identified as the one to be optimized and the others can be identified as "musts" rather than "shoulds," then linear programming may be useful. Chapters 8 to 10 present linear programming. When there are many objectives, each with a target to be reached as closely as possible, then goal programming, an extension of linear programming, may be applicable. This topic is treated in Chapter 11.

Our present concern is with the general notions of utility and multiple objectives.

UTILITY THEORY

Utility theory provides a means of expressing subjective assessments of worth. In Chapter 4 different decision-making criteria or philosophies represented the subjective element of decision making. Here the consequences themselves are evaluated not for their intrinsic value but rather for their worth to the decision maker.

Role of Utility Theory in Decision Making

As an extension of the decision theory of Chapter 4, utility theory's role in decision making is primarily at the evaluation stage as indicated in Figure 6-1. While one alternative may be objectively preferable based on one way of measuring consequences, another may be preferable based on another way that includes subjective worth. Hence the units in which consequences are assessed is an important part of evaluating alternatives. It is anticipated that techniques used or implied here will not be readily usable because of practical difficulties in establishing a reliable measure of the utility or worth of various consequences. The concepts are presented here for the light they shed on how individuals approach evaluative tasks.

Example Tom has a reasonably good and secure position with the state auditing department, earning $20,000 a year. He has the opportunity to direct a project. It has been hinted to Tom that if the project is successful he will be promoted to agency chief with a $40,000 salary, and if it is a failure he will be asked to resign. We will assume being fired has a 0 monetary value, even though unemployment and prospects for another job would give it a

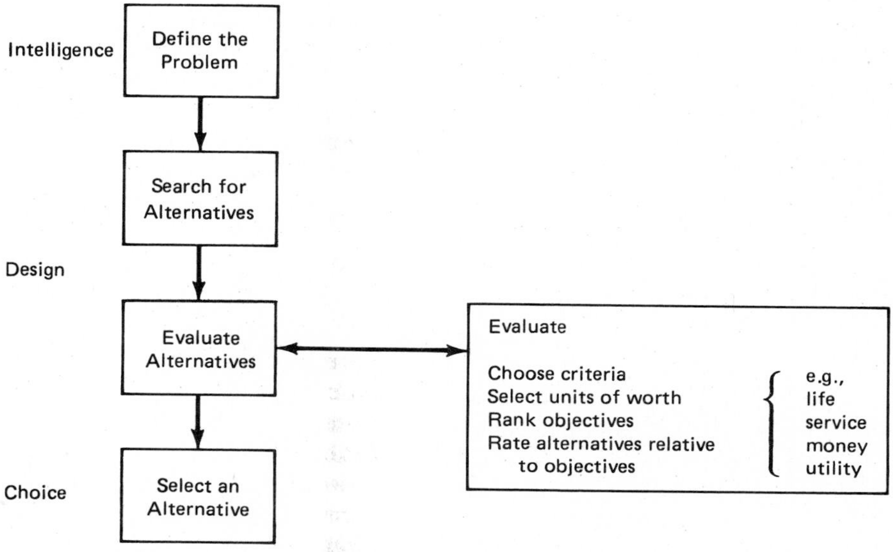

Figure 6-1 The role of utility theory and the treatment of multiple objectives in decision making.

positive value. The educated guess—with which Tom agrees—is that the project has a 50–50 chance of succeeding.

If Tom is an expected monetary value decision maker, he will be indifferent to taking on the project or not, since the expected value of the project is .50($40,000) + .50($0) = $20,000, which equals his current salary. If Tom prefers to avoid the risk, he will decline to direct the project. If Tom prefers to take the risk, he will accept the project.

These three attitudes toward risk are defined as follows. A situation with risk has a certain expected payoff. If a decision maker is faced with the choice of taking the expected payoff outright or facing the risky situation, then:

1. He is *risk-averse* if he prefers the expected payoff.
2. He is *risk-prone* if he prefers the risky situation.
3. He is *risk-neutral* if he is indifferent to the two alternatives.

Most people are generally risk-averse, although not in every situation. Two examples show this.

Example You are given a choice. You may choose to receive 50 cents outright or elect to follow the flip of a coin. On heads you will win $3 and on tails you will lose $1. Which do you prefer? Note that the expected value of the coin toss is twice the outright offer.

Example You are given another choice. This time the outright offer is $5000. With the toss, on heads you will win $30,000 and on tails you will lose $10,000. Which do you prefer? Note that the expected value of the coin toss is again twice the outright offer.

It is not unlikely that a person may choose the coin flip in the first example, and the outright offer in the second. Expected payoff alone does not explain the different choices.

The Utility Function

A utility function assigns utility values to payoffs. Developing utility functions helps to explain how people evaluate alternatives. One method of developing a utility function follows.

1. Give the best payoff a utility value of 1, and the worst a utility value of 0.
2. Ask the decision maker to identify a third payoff, so that he would be indifferent between getting the third payoff outright and a 50–50 gamble on the best and worst payoffs. The third payoff has a utility value equal to the expected utility of the gamble, .5.

3. Continue by making other 50–50 gambles between the best and second-best payoffs and between the worst and second-worst payoffs. When enough points have been obtained, determine the utility curve.

We now develop utility functions for the two preceding examples.

Example There is a 50–50 gamble of either winning \$3 or losing \$1.

1. Give winning \$3 a utility value of 1, and losing \$1 a utility value of 0.
2. Suppose the decision maker prefers the gamble to the 50 cents outright offer, but prefers an outright offer of \$2 to the gamble. By zeroing in, we find he is indifferent to the gamble or an outright gift of \$1.60. Give \$1.60 a utility value of .5.

3*a*. Consider the 50–50 gamble between winning \$1.60 or \$3; determine the outright offer so the decision maker would be indifferent to the gamble or the gift. Suppose he says he will take the gamble if the gift is under \$2.40, but he will take the gift if it is over that. \$2.40 is thus the point of indifference. The expected utility of the gamble is

$$.50(.5) + .50(1.0) = .75$$

Give \$2.40 a utility value of .75.

3*b*. Likewise consider the 50–50 gamble between losing \$1 and winning \$1.60. Suppose 60 cents is the point of indifference. The expected utility of the gamble is

$$.50(0) + .50(.5) = .25$$

Give 60 cents a utility value of .25.

3*c*. Continue until enough points have been found to sketch the utility function, as in Figure 6-2.

In Figure 6-2, the line joining (−\$1, 0) and (\$3, 1.0) is the utility function of a *risk-neutral* individual: The expected payoff of any gamble and the gamble itself have the same utility values.

The curve below the line is a *risk-prone* utility function: The expected payoff of a gamble has a lower utility value than the gamble itself.

A curve above the line is a *risk-averse* utility function: The expected payoff of a gamble has a higher utility value than the gamble itself.

Example There is a 50–50 gamble between losing \$10,000 and winning \$30,000. A risk-averse decision maker would have a utility function like Figure 6-3. Our decision maker prefers any outright gift to the original gamble, but takes the gamble rather than have to make any certain payment. He prefers a gift over \$6000 to the \$0 or \$30,000 gamble, but prefers the gamble to a smaller gift. He prefers to make any payment under \$6000

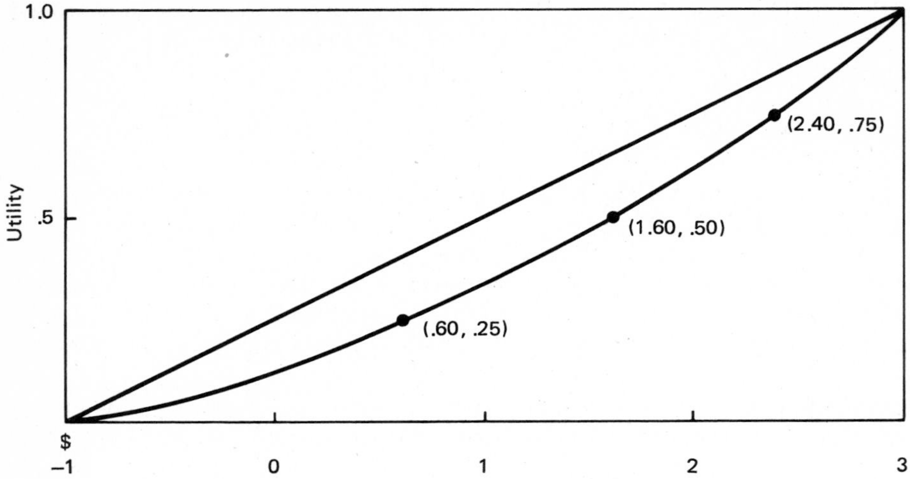

Figure 6-2 A risk prone utility function.

rather than take a chance on losing $10,000, but will take the gamble rather than make a larger payment.

The two utility functions just developed could be for the same individual, since the decision consequences are quite different. One of the limitations of utility theory is the need to develop a new utility function for each situation. However, similar functions would more than likely be exhibited in decision situations with payoffs in approximately the same range. A greater limitation is the difficulty in finding reliable points of indifference and thus establishing the

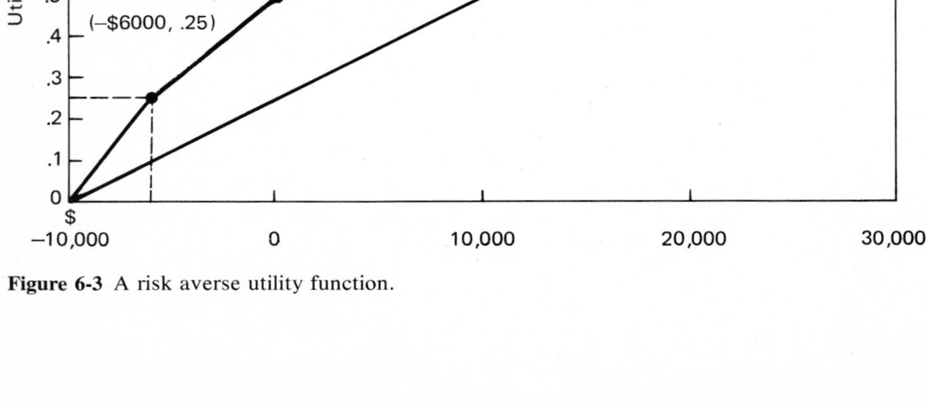

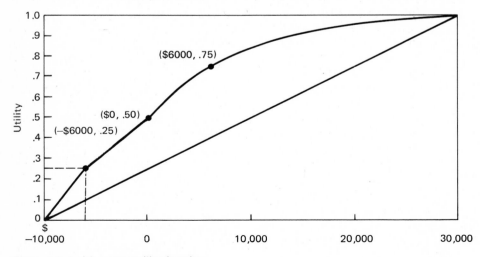

Figure 6-3 A risk averse utility function.

utility function. A utility function can provide some guidance in helping an individual or a group understand their own approach to decisions, especially nonmonetary ones.

Utility Theory and Curriculum Planning: An Application[1]

Students' performance in a subject area such as reading is measured by standardized tests. Such tests usually provide percentile scores. Using the scores, comparative assessments can be made for individuals, for classes, and for specific reading programs. The test scores thus provide a means of comparing reading programs.

A principal is deciding whether to initiate a new reading program. Articles, reviews, and published assessments of the new program lead him to the Table 6-1 probability estimates on the possible effects of the new program. He believes that performance will remain at the 50th percentile with the current program.

Whether he should adopt the new program depends on how he evaluates the consequences. The expected performance of the new program is the 53d percentile; on the basis of expected performance, the new program should be chosen.

However, a series of questions reveals his utility function, depicted in Figure 6-4. The abrupt change at the 50th percentile is readily explained. Dropping below the national average (50th percentile) will generate much criticism from the school board and parents, whereas performance above that level will not produce much noticeable reaction. Evaluating the new program by utility values rather than percentile scores is summarized in Table 6-2.

The expected utility of the new program, 77, is slightly lower than the expected utility, 78, of the old program. The old reading program would be retained on the basis of the principal's utility for test performance if only one could identify that utility. Aside from the theoretical foundation, there are operational requirements that must be satisfied before a utility function can be developed and applied.

Table 6-1 Possible effects of new reading program

Average performance will be	Probability
Increased to 65th percentile	.40
Unchanged (50th percentile)	.30
Decreased to 40th percentile	.30

[1] A fuller description of this application can be found in J. Dyer, W. Farrell, and P. Bradley, "Utility Functions for Test Performance," *Management Science*, vol. 20, December 1973, pp. 507–519.

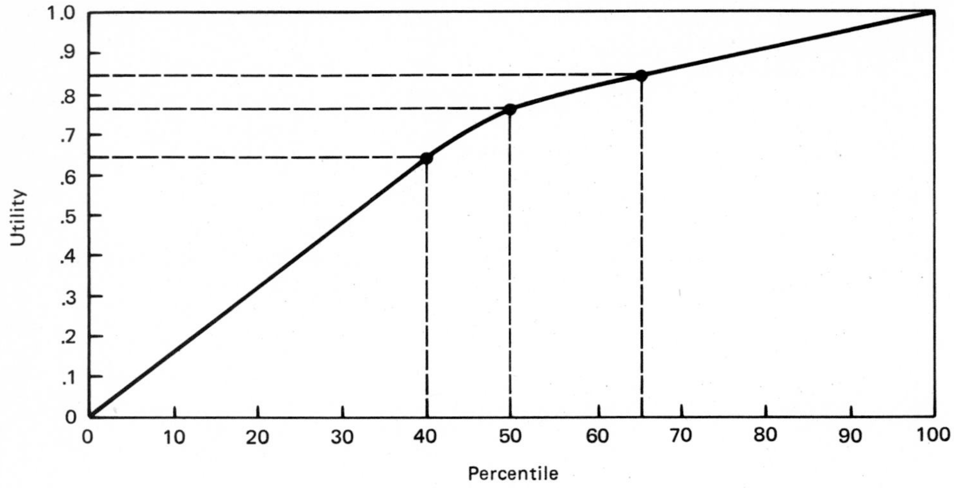

Figure 6-4 Utility function for performance on a reading test.

Operational Requirements

Using the maximum expected utility as a decision criterion leads to choosing the alternative with the greatest value to the decision maker. It includes the value intrinsic to the payoffs, and the value perceived by the decision maker, with his particular goals for this particular decision situation. The criterion is used less than frequently not because of problems with the underlying notions, but because of the difficulty in applying them.

The use of a utility function and employment of maximum expected utility as a decision-making criterion depend on four requirements:

1. A decision maker can *consistently* state preferences and indifferences.
2. His preferences are *transitive;* that is, if *A* is preferred to *B*, and *B* to *C*, then *A* will be preferred to *C*.
3. If he prefers *A* to *B* and *B* to *C*, then there is an *indifference probability p* so that he is indifferent between *B* and a gamble with a *p* chance of getting *A* and a $1-p$ chance of getting *C*.

Table 6-2 Utility values of effects of new reading program

Performance	Utility	Probability
65th percentile	.85	.40
50th percentile	.78	.30
40th percentile	.65	.30
Expected value = 53d percentile	.77	

4. If he is indifferent between A and B, then in any choice, A may be *substituted* for B (and vice versa) without altering the preference.

Decision makers may not satisfy all the requirements in every situation. The requirements do express what is intuitively acceptable as rational decision making—choosing alternatives in accordance with the decision makers' values and objectives.

The utility or usefulness of consequences can be taken into consideration without formally establishing an applicable utility function. This approach is part of our discussion of multiple objectives.

MULTIPLE OBJECTIVES

The complexity of many decision situations gives rise to multiple objectives. The framework for addressing situations with single objectives often falls short in such instances.

Movement toward one objective is ordinarily accompanied by effects on associated objectives. This is true even when only one objective has been explicitly identified. Singlemindedness can be dangerous when it blinds the decision maker to unintended effects. The speed limit was reduced to 55 miles per hour to save fuel and alert the public during the oil embargo. Other consequences included reductions in traffic accident fatalities, sharp and permanent increases in fuel prices, loss of revenue to those dependent on motor traffic, and a truckers' strike. That any of these was unintended does not diminish the effects. A system of interrelated multiple objectives most often has conflicting objectives; one is achieved only at the expense of the other. "Maximize services and minimize expenses" sounds nice, but it typifies conflicting objectives. The decision maker handles multiple-objective situations differently according to whether there is an individual or a group making decisions, and whether it is reasonable to consider partial satisfaction of objectives. The process of trading off satisfaction toward one objective for partial achievement of another assumes partial satisfaction is reasonable. This approach is more suited to individual than group decision making because of the many intermediate trade-offs necessary for a final comparison. The use of relative utilities, the second method we will examine, does not require that objectives be divisible. Its rating scheme is quite appropriate for group decision making.

Multiple Criteria and Trade-offs

Multiple objectives generate multiple criteria. Without formally judging the relative importance of the objectives and hence of the criteria, one can make trade-offs. Suppose there are two alternatives A and B, each with its own set of consequences relative to a list of criteria. A complete list of meaningful criteria is absolutely essential to the whole process of comparison based on trade-offs among preferences. Thoughtful attention to trade-offs is worthless—or close to it—if a most important criterion is omitted and the alternatives differ significantly on that criterion. Assuming complete criteria, the decision maker should take the time to consider each preference in the trade-off process. That process consists of:

1. Construct a "standard" alternative *C* with characteristics for all but one criteria.
2. Trade off *A* against *C* to determine what value for the missing criterion would make the decision maker indifferent between *A* and *C*.
3. Trade off *B* against *C* to determine what value for the missing criterion would make the decision maker indifferent between *B* and *C*.
4. The more favorable value inserted in *C* corresponds to the preferred alternative, either *A* or *B*.

Evaluating Employment: An Application

In evaluating employment options, a number of criteria are examined, including salary, climate, prospective commuting distance, and the nature of the work.[2] Suppose a recent graduate has two job offers, with characteristics as presented in Table 6-3.

A middle-ground standard alternate is constructed; it too appears in Table 6-3.

Step by step, job 1 is traded off against the standard. The decision maker says that he would be willing to give up $1000, but not more than $1000, to get warm, dry summers instead of hot, humid ones. Hence he is indifferent between

(*$15,000; hhs,* mw; 20; interesting and good)

and (*$14,000; wds,* mw; 20; interesting and good)

Table 6-3 Criteria and characteristics of job offers

Criteria	Job 1	Job 2	Standard
Starting salary	$15,000	$19,000	—
Climate	Hot, humid summers Mild winters	Warm, dry summers Very cold winters	Warm, dry summers Mild winters
Daily one-way commuting time	20 min	60 min	30 min
Nature of work	Interesting, good advancement opportunities	Routine, poor advancement opportunities	Routine, good advancement opportunities

[2] This application is further explained in J. R. Miller, III, *Professional Decision Making,* Praeger Publishers, Inc., New York, 1970.

Proceeding to the next characteristic, he says that an additional 10-minute commute each way would probably mean about 10 miles a day; estimating nonfixed costs (gas, oil, tires, and so forth) at 10 cents per mile, this is $1 a day. Figuring the wear and tear on himself at the same cost, he says 10 minutes per trip is worth about $500 a year. Hence he is indifferent between

(*$14,000,* wds, mw; *20*; interesting and good)

and (*$14,500,* wds, mw; *30*; interesting and good)

Finally he says a routine job would be worth about $1000; so he is indifferent between

(*$14,500;* wds, mw; 30; *interesting and good*)

and (*$15,500;* wds, mw; 30; *routine and good*)

The last is the description of the standard alternative with a salary of $15,500.

Similarly, job 2 is traded off. The summaries of both trade-offs are presented in Table 6-4. The subjective reasons for the job 2 trade-offs would very likely be similar to those for job 1; good advancement opportunities are valued at $2000 because a couple of good raises would return that much before very long.

As Table 6-4 shows, job 1 is indifferent to the standard with a $15,500 salary, and job 2 is indifferent to the standard with a $14,500 salary. Consequently job 1 is preferred to job 2.

The characteristics of the standard should be chosen so they are meaningful to the decision maker. A salary of $250,000 cannot be meaningfully considered by most people, so including it in the standard would be futile.

The underlying requirement of the trade-off approach to multiple criteria is that less than complete attainment toward one objective can be compared—qualitatively and subjectively—with less than perfect fulfillment in another dimension. Another approach does not have such a requirement but rather requires that one compare the utility for any one objective with the utility for any other. This approach is considered next.

Table 6-4 Summary of trade-offs

Job 1
($15,000; hhs, mw; 20; interesting and good)
($14,000; wds, mw; 20; interesting and good)
($14,500; wds, mw; 30; interesting and good)
($15,500; wds, mw; 30; routine and good)
Job 2
($19,000; wds, vcw; 60; routine and poor)
($17,500; wds, mw; 60; routine and poor)
($16,500; wds, mw; 30; routine and poor)
($14,500; wds, mw; 30; routine and good)

Multiple Objectives and Relative Utility

The single-objective decision theory framework of Chapter 4 presents the essentials of a decision situation in a table. A general decision table is presented in Table 6-5. The present framework for a multiple-objective situation[3] is represented by modifying the decision table; the modified table appears as Table 6-6.

As indicated in Table 6-6, the process requires two measures:

1. The relative utility of each objective
2. The probability that each alternative will achieve each objective

Assumptions necessary for the measures of utility to be meaningful are:

1. Every objective has a utility value.
2. More important objectives have higher utility values.
3. The utility value of achieving two objectives equals the sum of their individual utility values.

The last assumption does not admit of objectives expressed along a scale. For example, consider two objectives: O_1 to restrict morbidity to fewer than 1000 cases, O_2 to restrict morbidity to fewer than 2000 cases. O_1 implies O_2. If O_1 has a relative utility of 50 and O_2 a relative utility of 20, then achieving O_1 (and thereby also achieving O_2) has a utility of 50 rather than 50 + 20 = 70. Hence, this method is not applicable to such objectives.

Estimating the utility and probability measures is a critical part of the process. We will present the method within the context of a regional planning application.

Table 6-5 A single-objective decision table

		Alternatives			
State of nature	Probability	A_1	A_2	. . .	A_m
S_1	P_1				
S_2	P_2	Consequence, relative to the objective, for each alternative, on the occurrence of each state of nature			
.	.				
.	.				
.	.				
S_n	P_n				

[3] The effectiveness model, as the approach has been called, is the work of David H. Stimson and appeared as "Utility Measurement in Public Health Decision Making," in *Management Science,* vol. 16, October 1969, pp. B17–B30. The model uses the measure of value method of C. West Churchman and Russell L. Ackoff, "An Approximate Measure of Value," *Operations Research,* vol. 2, 1954, pp. 172–181.

Table 6-6 Multiple-objective decision table with relative utilities

		Alternatives			
Objectives	Relative utility	A_1	A_2	$\cdots$	A_m
O_1	U_1				
O_2	U_2	The estimated probability that each alternative will achieve each objective			
.	.				
.	.				
.	.				
O_n	U_n				

Land-use Planning: An Application

Determining the land-use plan for a large section of a rural county provides the setting for applying this multiple-objective decision methodology.[4] A large area of relatively undeveloped land was subjected to great devastation by a lashing hurricane in 1972. As a result the county had the opportunity to reconsider the use of the land, virtually from scratch. A planning commission was established. With some management guidance, the commission set out to establish meaningful objectives concerning the land. Four objectives were identified:

1. To provide for regional recreation, including overnight facilities (RR)
2. To provide for local recreation, without the need for overnight facilities (LR)
3. To encourage employment opportunities (E)
4. To conserve the region in a near natural state (C)

The actual list of objectives could indeed be much longer than this list. It often happens that a few objectives are seen by all to dominate the others; these become the objectives for further consideration.

The Nominal-Group Technique

The process of discussing the relative importance of the objectives can indeed be a thorny one. There may be much citizen participation or at least expression of citizens' views. An interacting group might be hard-pressed to arrive at acceptable relative utilities for the objectives. An interacting group responds to ideas as they are presented. There are two disadvantages to this: (1) the premature focusing of discussion before all reasonable alternatives have been identified and expressed and (2) the tendency for the discussion to become

[4] This application is based on Fredrick Davidson, "Dimensions of Utility in a Regional Planning Context," *Decision Sciences*, vol. 5, no. 1, January 1974, pp. 91–101.

person-oriented rather than idea-centered. An approach that is recommended for a planning session is the *nominal-group technique.*[5]

In the nominal-group technique, there is no interaction in the usual group-discussion sense, but rather there is interaction provided by identifying potential objectives without discussion, and then in a rather formal and orderly process, discussing the objectives in round-robin fashion. The process concludes with a secret vote on item importance. This mode of interaction facilitates concentration on the ideas, rather than on the persons participating, and allows for rating the objectives without undue pressure or interference from the other participants.

Assigning Relative Utility Values

The procedure followed by each individual in establishing the relative utilities for the objectives is as follows:

1. Rank the objectives in their order of importance. Suppose to one individual:

   C is most important

   RR next

   LR next

   E last

2. Assign the relative utility 100 to the most important objective. Assign to the others values that seem to reflect their relative utilities. Suppose the evaluator assigns:

   100 to C

   70 to RR

   50 to LR

   30 to E

3. To check the consistency of the relative utilities, compare the most important objective with the combination of the other three. Given the two choices C or the combination of RR, LR, and E, which would he prefer? Suppose he claims that C is preferable; he then should adjust downward the relative utilities for the other objectives. For example,

[5] The rationale for, some experiences in, and a step-by-step guide to using the nominal-group technique may be found in Andre L. Delbecq, Andrew H. Van de Ven, and David H. Gustafson, *Group Techniques for Program Planning,* Scott, Foresman & Company, Glenview, Ill., 1975.

100 to C

35 to RR

25 to LR

15 to E

Note that the utilities of RR, LR, and E relative to each other have been retained.

4. Further compare the second most important with the combination of the other two. Suppose he claims that RR is more important than LR and E combined. Another adjustment in their values is needed; for example,

100 to C

35 to RR

20 to LR

12 to E

Neither the process nor the final set of utility values is unique. The group utility values are arrived at by averaging the individual values. The exact value for each objective is less important than its relative size.

Alternatives and Their Efficiencies

Potential alternatives are proposed, not necessarily being related to only one objective. An alternative might be certain to achieve one objective (probability $p = 1$), have a chance of achieving another ($0 < p < 1$), and have no chance of achieving still another ($p = 0$).

In the land-use application, six alternatives were identified:

1. Full-range recreation, including the development of picnic areas, campsites, boating, and ball fields
2. Limited recreation, providing a preserve for hunting and fishing and thus retaining much of the natural character of the area
3. Conservation development, providing for the development of hiking trails, but very few facilities
4. Agricultural, providing for farming use of all tillable land and preserving the remainder in its natural state
5. Agricultural and natural resource industry, making use of the agricultural aspects of the preceding proposal, with timber and other natural resource removal where possible
6. Residential, developing a community of vacation homes requiring a traditional kind of land development

Table 6-7 Partial decision table for land use

Objectives	Relative utility	Decision alternatives: Full recreation	Limited recreation	Conservation	Farming	Farming and natural resource	Residential
Regional recreation	50						
Local recreation	25						
Employment	10						
Conservation	100						

Table 6-7 presents the incomplete model with the averages of the individuals[1] utility values. To complete the model, estimates must be made of the probability that each alternative will achieve each objective. These estimates are not easily arrived at, but their exact values are less important than their relative size; for instance, whether one of the probabilities is estimated at .20 or .25 will have little impact on the decision, but whether the estimated probability is .20 or .50 is much more likely to make a difference.

Consider the full-range recreation alternative. It is believed that this alternative will completely achieve the regional recreation and the local recreation objectives. It will generate some employment but has only a .50 chance of satisfying the employment objective. Little will be done in achieving the conservation objective. The first column of Table 6-8 presents the probabilities associated with choosing the full recreation alternative. On the other hand, if establishing a limited recreational area is decided upon, then the conservation

Table 6-8 Decision table for land use

Objectives	Relative utility	Decision alternatives: Full recreation	Limited recreation	Conservation	Farming	Farming and natural resource	Residential
Regional recreation	50	1.00	.70	.05	0	0	0
Local recreation	25	1.00	.80	.10	.10	0	.10
Employment	10	.50	.25	.05	.25	.70	.40
Conservation	100	.10	.80	1.00	.50	0	.10
Expected value		90	137.5	105.5	55.0	7.0	16.5

objective will be more greatly satisfied at the expense of the other three objectives. Each alternative is taken in turn, and estimates are made concerning how likely that alternative is to achieve each objective.

The residential alternative has little chance of satisfying any of the four stated objectives. Comparing the probabilities of that alternative with those of the full recreation alternative, we see that the latter is more, or just as, likely to achieve each of the four objectives. The residential alternative is said to be *dominated* by the full recreation alternative. It should be noted further that the residential alternative may be rather efficient in achieving an objective other than the four stated ones; the decision table can display probabilities only of the listed alternatives relative only to the stated objectives.

After the probabilities have been estimated, a weighted average is determined by weighting the individual probabilities by the relative utility of each objective. This yields the expected effectiveness of each decision alternative. A comparison of the expected values of the six decision alternatives indicates that limited recreation and conservation are the two most effective alternatives in achieving the stated objectives.

This model, which attempts to synthesize information and preferences for the decision makers, may suggest some contradictions between the decision makers' stated objectives and what they really want to accomplish. Suppose that in discussion the decision makers tend to speak against the limited recreation alternative because it has so small an impact on employment. Then they should reconsider the relative utilities assigned to the objectives. It may very well be that employment has been seriously undervalued.

One difficulty in using this kind of model is that much time, effort, and patience are needed to generate consistent relative utilities and meaningful probabilities, as well as to arrive at realistic objectives and feasible alternatives. Another is that objectives sometimes overlap, making the assignment of consistent utilities more difficult.

One advantage to this approach is that it clearly shows the interrelationships among the objectives and alternatives, underscoring the usefulness of, as well as the need for, compromise. Another advantage is that it readily admits of nonquantitative statements of objectives. Universal educational opportunity, adequate medical care, and rapid and fair adjudication of court cases are well represented by neither monetary equivalents nor other simple quantification. That the model has quantitative elements should not be allowed to mask their role in representing value judgments and subjective estimates of efficacy. The purpose of the model is to facilitate a comparison for making a rational choice.

SUMMARY

Utility theory provides a means of expressing subjective assessments of worth. In evaluating alternatives, the utility or usefulness of payoffs is a more important consideration than the payoffs themselves.

Decision makers exhibit different attitudes toward risk in different situations:

1. One is risk-averse if he prefers the expected payoff of a risk to the risk itself.
2. One is risk-prone if he prefers the risk.
3. One is risk-neutral if he is indifferent to the risk or its expected payoff.

A utility function assigns utility values from 0 to 1 to payoffs from the worst to the best. Developing a utility function for nonmonetary payoffs is of particular interest in public decision making. The use of a utility function assumes preferences are consistent, transitive, substitutable, and have indifference probabilities. A choice of educational programs provided an application.

Multiple objectives occur quite naturally in complex decision situations. One approach trades off achievement toward one objective for achievement toward another to determine the most preferred alternative. Employment options illustrated this method.

A second approach estimates the relative utility of the various objectives and the probability that each alternative will achieve each objective. A weighted average provides a measure of the efficacy of each alternative. The procedure was applied to planning land use.

BIBLIOGRAPHY

Churchman, C. West, and Russell L. Ackoff: "An Approximate Measure of Value," *Operations Research,* vol. 2, 1954, pp. 172–181.

Davidson, Fredrick: "Dimensions of Utility in a Regional Planning Context," *Decision Sciences,* vol. 5, no. 1, January 1974, pp. 91–101.

Delbecq, Andre L., Andrew H. Van de Ven, and David H. Gustafson: *Group Techniques for Program Planning,* Scott, Foresman & Company, Glenview, Ill., 1975.

Dyer, J., W. Farrell, and P. Bradley: "Utility Functions for Test Performance," *Management Science,* vol. 20, December 1973, pp. 507–519.

Fishburn, Peter Z.: *Utility Theory for Decision Making,* John Wiley & Sons, Inc., New York, 1970.

Huber, G. P.: "Methods for Quantifying Subjective Probabilities and Multi-attribute Utilities," *Decision Science,* vol. 5, July 1974, pp. 430–458.

Huber, G. P.: "Multi-attribute Utility Models: A Review of Field and Field-like Studies," *Management Science,* vol. 20, 1974, pp. 1393–1402.

Keeney, Ralph L., and Howard Raiffa: *Decisions with Multiple Objectives: Preferences and Value Tradeoffs,* John Wiley & Sons, Inc., New York, 1976.

Linstone, H. A., and M. Turoff (eds.): *The Delphi Method,* Addison-Wesley Publishing Co., Inc., Reading, Mass., 1975.

Miller, J. R., III: *Professional Decision Making,* Praeger Publishers, Inc., New York, 1970.

Stimson, David H.: "Utility Measurement in Public Health Decision Making," *Management Science,* vol. 16, October 1969, pp. B17–B30.

Torrance, George W., Warren H. Thomas, and David L. Sackett: "A Utility Maximization Model for Evaluation of Health Care Programs," *Health Services Research,* vol. 7, Summer 1972, pp. 118–133.

Turban, Efrain, and M. Metersky: "Utility Theory Applied to Multi-Variable System Effectiveness Evaluations," *Management Science,* vol. 19, February 1973, pp. 817–828.

Whitmore, G. A., and G. S. Cavadias: "Experimental Determination of Community Preferences for Water Quality–Cost Alternatives," *Decision Sciences,* vol. 5, no. 4, October 1974, pp. 614–631.

EXERCISES

Extensions of chapter examples

6-1 Reconsider the 50–50 gamble between losing \$10,000 and winning \$30,000 from the perspective of a very risk prone individual. Develop her utility function. (There is not a unique function.)

6-2 Paying a \$100 insurance premium against a \$10,000 loss that has a .001 chance of happening is not justified on the basis of expected payoff. Chapter 4 indicated that it is warranted by the minimax decision criterion. Justify it on the basis of a utility function.

6-3 Reconsider the curriculum planning application of this chapter. Suppose two reading teachers in the school have had considerable prior success in using the newly proposed program.

(*a*) How would the utility function be affected?

(*b*) How would the probability distribution be affected?

(*c*) Revise the estimates accordingly. (The estimates are still subjective; make reasonable revisions using the new information.)

(*d*) With your new estimates, which program would be chosen? Why?

6-4 Making preference trade-offs, as with establishing utility functions, requires individual value judgments. Refer to the employment evaluation application in the chapter.

(*a*) Without considering my trade-offs, do you prefer job 1 or job 2?

(*b*) By trading off salary against the other criteria, establish two salary levels for the standard alternative so you would be indifferent between:

1. Job 1 and the standard
2. Job 2 and the standard

(*c*) On the basis of these salary levels, do you prefer job 1 or job 2?

(*d*) Do your preferences in parts *a* and *c* agree? Why or why not?

6-5 Refer to problem 6-4.

(*a*) Do you prefer your present job to job 1 and job 2?

(*b*) Describe your present job according to the four criteria.

(*c*) Determine the salary of the standard alternative that would make you indifferent between your present job and the standard.

(*d*) In making your choice in part *a*, were you using criteria other than those listed?

(*e*) What are the implications of an incomplete list of criteria for the trade-off process?

Other applications

6-6 Victoria Johnson is one of two people running for county supervisor. Construct her utility function for proportion of votes received. Realistically, no matter what she does she will get not less than 25 percent nor more than 75 percent of the vote.

6-7 Lankhanna Township borders Capital City, the capital of the state. Capital City's population has decreased from 100,000 in 1950 to 80,000 in 1980, and the city is currently involved in redeveloping its downtown area. Lankhanna Township's population has doubled in the same period, reaching 20,000 in 1980. The support of the township's school system, with a rather stable enrollment of about 2700 since 1975, will shift from real estate taxes to income taxes over the next 5 years. About one-third of the land in the township has been zoned and used for farming. Much of that land is for sale, and the township is reconsidering its land-use plan.

(*a*) What are some possible objectives for the land-use plan?

(*b*) Does any one of these encompass any others?

(*c*) Rank the objectives for their importance.

(*d*) Establish relative utilities for the objectives.

Project problems

6-8 Suppose you were trying to get a group to determine the relative utilities of many (say, seven) objectives. How would you have them check their consistency by comparing their most important objective with the other objectives?

6-9 When David Stimson (see the Bibliography) applied the procedure, there were seven objectives. How did he have the public health agency members check their consistency in assigning relative utilities?

6-10 (*a*) Contact Affirmative Action officers, personnel officers, and Social Security officers to determine the objectives of having a retirement policy, and establish their relative utilities for their objectives. Summarize your findings and get a "pseudo-group" average.

(*b*) Consider alternative retirement regulations. Estimate how likely each alternative is to achieve the objectives of part *a*.

(*c*) Combine the relative utilities of part *a* and the probabilities of part *b* to get the expected effectiveness of each alternative.

CHAPTER

SEVEN

COST-BENEFIT ANALYSIS

Decision theory provides a conceptual framework for assisting decision makers in understanding the decision situation. Utility theory is an extension of that framework, insofar as it suggests, if not measures, the relative worth or usefulness of various alternatives. Cost-benefit analysis is another extension of the conceptual framework for systematically investigating certain problems of choice. Specifically, as the name implies, it investigates the costs and benefits of each of a set of alternatives so that the decision maker can better understand the consequences of a decision. Economic analysis—a more general term—studies the relationships between the resources consumed and outputs and impacts produced. Inasmuch as public agencies and public decision makers are at least as attentive to cost considerations as to impact assessments, economic analysis is an essential component of systematic public decision making. Cost-benefit analysis and cost-effectiveness analysis are prominent economic analysis approaches.

COST-BENEFIT AND COST-EFFECTIVENESS ANALYSIS COMPARED

As the use of these two economic analysis approaches has widened, the distinction between cost-benefit and cost-effectiveness analysis has become less clear. We will briefly compare the two approaches in their classic meanings, but then be less concerned with their differences than with more useful issues.

Does a drug-withdrawal program contribute to the welfare—in the sense of well-being, not in the sense of public assistance—of society? Does a rapid-rail project result in observable benefits to society, or a segment of society? Does vocational education produce desirable effects on society? Is society better off for having a defense program? Questions such as these that relate to the performance of public undertakings can be meaningfully evaluated at five different levels. To understand better the role of cost-benefit and cost-effectiveness analysis, the five levels are mentioned in brief:

1. Are the program's objectives *appropriate?* Are they desirable from a social welfare standpoint? (Addressed in policy analysis.)
2. Is the program *economically efficient?* Are the intended effects worth the costs? (Addressed in cost-benefit analysis.)
3. Is the program *effective?* Are the objectives being achieved? (Addressed in program evaluation.)
4. Is the operation *technologically efficient?* Are resources being used to get the maximum result? (Addressed in cost-effectiveness analysis.)
5. Is the scope of the undertaking *adequate?* Are objectives and results commensurate with the need? (Addressed by program analysis and program evaluation.)

These questions, moving from higher to lower levels of performance criteria, are addressed by various branches of program analysis.[1] Questions relating to efficiency are properly in the domain of economic analysis. Cost-benefit analysis is primarily concerned with *economic efficiency,* the consideration of whether total benefits outweigh the total costs of providing them. Cost-effectiveness analysis is concerned with *technological efficiency* and compares alternative approaches or projects in a program area.

As a consequence of that first formal distinction, cost-benefit analysis tends to have a global perspective resulting in a comprehensive investigation of related factors. Its primary question, whether involvement is economically justifiable, leads to long-term considerations, often of capital projects, rather than to programs already in operation.

On the other hand, the scope of cost-effectiveness analysis has tended to be narrower, resulting in a better focused and more detailed study. Focusing on how resources should be used within a program—given that the program is justifiable—leads to short-term considerations and includes strategies of ongoing programs.

Cost-benefit analysis has traditionally attempted to evaluate all costs and benefits in dollar terms, with a dollar having the same utility to one individual as any other. Benefits and costs are variable, so that relative productivity over a range of alternatives can be estimated. Benefits in many situations are less

[1] One must be careful not to impose too fine a delineation among the approaches of program analysis. See Theodore H. Poister, *Public Program Analysis: Applied Research Methods,* University Park Press, Baltimore, Md., 1978, chap. 1, for an overview of the five evaluative questions, and the relationship among policy analysis, program analysis, cost-benefit analysis, evaluation research, program evaluation, and cost-effectiveness analysis.

Table 7-1 A comparison of two economic analysis approaches

	Cost-benefit	Cost-effectiveness
Geared to	Economic efficiency	Technological efficiency
Measurement units	Dollars	Various measures
Variable components	Costs and benefits	Costs, with benefits fixed; benefits, with costs fixed
Main question	*Whether* the program is justified	*How* resources should be used in a program
Scope	Global, comprehensive	Narrow, focused
Usual application	Capital projects	Ongoing operating programs
Time frame	Long-term	Short-term

than easy to assess even qualitatively, difficult to quantify, and all but impossible to express in dollar terms. Cost-effectiveness provides an alternate method of analysis, wherein benefits may be assessed in their own units. In the absence of any method of assessing benefits, strategies can be compared by determining their cost differences for achieving a fixed level of effectiveness. Where budget amounts are fixed, strategies can be compared solely on the basis of their effectiveness. The comparison of cost-benefit and cost-effectiveness analysis is summarized in Table 7-1.

Cost-benefit and cost-effectiveness analysis lean on the same basic principles and employ the same processes. As cost-benefit analysis has considered activities whose effects are not readily or reliably equated to dollars, and as it has been applied to intraprogram choices, a level lower than its global context, the distinction between the two approaches has diminished. A cost-benefit analysis that presents descriptive benefits is, strictly speaking, a cost-effectiveness analysis. Since the precise name is only of secondary importance, our further discussion will consider applicable procedures and illustrations without distinguishing between the two approaches.

THE COST-BENEFIT PROCESS

The process of cost-benefit analysis consists of five elements: (1) objectives, (2) alternatives, (3) benefits and costs, (4) a model, and (5) a criterion. The relation between cost-benefit analysis and the decision-making process in general is depicted in Figure 7-1. *Objectives* are the desired effects intended to be brought about by the undertaking. *Alternatives* are the possible uses of resources, or possible approaches to employ. *Benefits* are results that improve society's welfare. *Costs* are resources consumed by the undertaking. A *model* represents the relationships between qualities of an alternative and the consequences. A *criterion* is the basis for selecting one alternative.

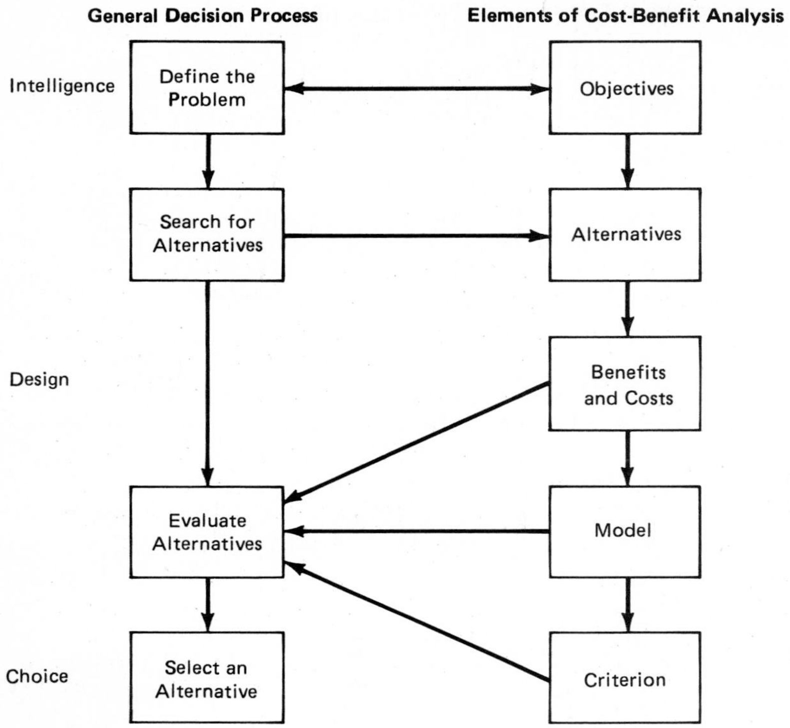

Figure 7-1 Cost-benefit analysis and the general decision making process.

Example With the objective of reducing recidivism, three prison-release alternatives are being considered: work placement, psychological counseling, and parole. Based on previous experience, estimated benefits and costs are as in Table 7-2. The model provides the estimates on the basis of data available from previous experience with the same or other prisoner populations. The choice of a criterion is not a simple matter. It is first decided that cost per nonrecidivous prisoner is more appropriate than cost per prisoner. Since it can be safely assumed that some prisoners would not repeat even without any program, the marginal cost[2] is believed to be more meaningful. Further, since parole is legally required even in the presence of either work placement or psychological counseling and is therefore incorporated in those alternatives, the decision is really whether to implement placement or counseling as well as the required parole. Consequently, the criterion finally decided on is the marginal cost for nonrecidivous prisoners beyond the effects of parole alone. By this criterion work placement by far surpasses counseling. Whether the additional benefit is worth the additional cost must be decided even for the more cost-effective alternative.

[2] Marginal cost is the cost of one additional unit; here, one additional prisoner.

Table 7-2 Costs and benefits of prison-release alternatives

	Alternatives		
	Work placement	Counseling	Parole
Number of prisoners	1000	1000	1000
Recidivism rate (for 5 years)	.15	.26	.37
Number not recidivous	850	740	630
Improvement over parole	220	110	—
Total cost	\$2,000,000	\$1,800,000	\$1,000,000
Additional cost over parole	\$1,000,000	\$ 800,000	—
Cost/prisoner	\$2000	\$1800	\$1000
Cost/nonrecidivous prisoner	\$2353	\$2,432	\$1587
Marginal cost per additional nonrecidivous prisoner	\$4545	\$7272	—

In the process of identifying alternatives and pursuing the analysis, assumptions will be made and constraints encountered that help to define the scope of the problem and the boundary of the analysis.

Assumptions

An assumption is a statement not necessarily of fact but of what will be held without demonstration. An assumption involves a certain amount of uncertainty. Sensitivity analysis does not remove the uncertainty, but it does provide an indication of the effects of changing the assumption. Assumptions underlying an analysis should be identified as such, for undocumented assumptions lead the decision maker astray. Assumptions, not having the strength of facts, should not be used in place of facts that are readily available. For example, a cost-benefit analysis of solid-waste disposal that assumes the presence of sufficient land for a land-fill operation, would be much stronger with a factual statement of whether there is sufficient land for such an operation.

With regard to cost-benefit analysis, there are basic technical assumptions that are part of every study; they are concerned with the economic life of a project and the period of comparison.

Economic life The *economic life* of a project is the period of time during which benefits can reasonably be expected to accrue. If the project represents a physical entity, then the greatest possible economic life would be the *physical life*.

> **Example** The construction of a building with a useful life of 40 years is part of a project. The economic life of that portion of the project cannot exceed that 40 years.

Often the economic life is considerably less than the physical life. Equipment will generally become obsolete before it deteriorates physically. The economic life of equipment, therefore, should not be assumed greater than the *technological life*.

Example A health care project requires the acquisition of certain specialized equipment. It is expected that in about 6 years new technology will render the present equipment obsolete, even though it will not have physically deteriorated. The economic life of that portion of the project should not exceed 6 years.

Other considerations may suggest that an economic life of shorter duration be assumed. Some portions of an undertaking may have an economic life that is theoretically without an end; for example, a new curriculum might be assumed to generate benefits for the duration of the lives of those who participate in that curriculum. A health care program might claim that the period of benefits goes beyond the generation participating in the program; that is, future generations will benefit not only from the health care but from the attitude development and education that accompany the health care program. Not only is it true that various components of a project will have different economic lives, but, even more so, different alternatives will have different economic lives. For the purpose of comparing alternatives, or assessing the costs and benefits of a single alternative, an assumption must be made concerning the period of comparison.

Period of comparison The period of comparison is the time during which a service will be rendered; comparisons shall include all costs and benefits occurring during the period. The alternative with the longest life may determine the comparison period; alternatives with shorter lives must be assumed to be reinitiated, with all the start-up and maintenance costs and benefits, in order to provide similar periods of comparison. On the other hand, the alternative with the shortest economic life may determine the comparison period; the residual values of longer-lived alternatives should be taken into account. However the period of comparison is arrived at, it should be explicitly stated.

As an alternative to identifying a particular period of comparison, the costs and benefits of each alternative can be adjusted to get uniform annual costs and benefits. The alternatives can then be compared through their annual costs and benefits.

Which benefits shall be included and which excluded is ultimately resolved in assumptions. Just as assumptions limit the scope of the analysis of a situation, constraints serve as forces acting upon the decision situation itself.

Constraints

As part of the boundary of the decision situation, restrictions must be considered. There are many kinds of constraints, and one way of categorizing them follows:

1. *Resource constraints.* Ordinarily the resources that are available are translated into an operating budget, so that resource scarcity shows up as a budget constraint. Frequently one is limited to optimizing benefits with a fixed budget, which may be translated into seeing which alternative will yield the greatest benefit for the same cost.

   Example Adding a relatively low-costing physician's assistant to the staff of a medical clinic may substantially increase benefits. However, if resources provide only for a physician and a nurse, the strategy of using the physician's assistant must be viewed as infeasible, at least temporarily.

2. *Political constraints.* Decision making generally and public decision making especially occur in a political environment. Good theoretical solutions may not be feasible in the practical political world. Political constraints are not as easily included as resource constraints in an analytical formulation, but they are just as real.

   Example Recognizing that closing certain armed forces bases is cost-effective is one thing; deciding to do so admidst the political reality of powerful legislators and their constituencies is quite another.

3. *Technological constraints.* At any given time there are limits to what technology and production can offer; theorizing beyond the bounds of technology leads nowhere fast in cost-benefit analysis.

   Example It is unreasonable to expect the medical care facility to be operable on the site of an abandoned used car lot within 36 hours.

4. *Legal constraints.* Existing laws, rights, and rulings must be considered in the search for alternatives.

   Example Building a highway through someone's kitchen requires time and due process.

5. *Administrative constraints.* Alternatives often require training and/or hiring those who will implement the alternatives.

   Example Implementing a utopian court management system is futile in a region without personnel trained to administer it.

6. *Distributional constraints.* Programs that involve payments or services to individuals may be limited by how they are distributed among regions, income classes, and so forth.

   Example College tuition loans are not available to many "middle-class" families, who may genuinely need such assistance.

7. *Social, religious, and traditional constraints.* What is generally acceptable to society on the basis of its values and traditions has a continual influence on the feasibility of alternatives.

   Example In some regions developing a school calendar requires observing both religious holidays and the first day of hunting season.

Understanding the constraints may require reconsidering the original objectives. Alternatives within the bounds of assumptions and constraints are means to an end, the objective. (There are instances in which the means is an end, for example, due process.) In viewing each alternative as a process, we can consider the costs as inputs into that process and the benefits as outputs of that process. These eventually become the focal points of the analysis.

COST-BENEFIT PROCEDURES

The heart of a cost-benefit analysis is the identification and assessment of the costs and the benefits of each alternative. To arrive at this point in the analysis, we have assumed that the things that matter, the *internalities,* can be identified; the *externalities*[3] are those that have no effect on the decision.

Costs

Identifying costs as inputs, and benefits as outputs, is arbitrary but not irrational. Such an identification makes cost determination relatively simple, at the expense of complicating the assessment of benefits. Another approach would be to consider negative consequences as social costs and include them in the total cost of the alternative. From the point of view of determining the excess benefit over cost it does not matter whether we subtract the negative benefits from the positive benefits, or add the negative benefits to the costs. The present convention has the advantage of identifying as costs only actual expenditures; administrators are usually required to identify the actual expenditures for budgetary reasons.

Agreeing to put the negative effects on the benefit side of the comparison provides a partial list of costs.

Initial costs

- Research and development
- Planning
- Testing and evaluation
- Training
- Land acquisition (may be offset by the eventual sale of redeveloped land, as in urban renewal)

[3] The term "externalities" is often applied to spillover effects, those that accrue to other than the producers or intended users; a purpose of cost-benefit analysis is to internalize the relevant externalities.

Buildings and facilities
Vehicles and equipment

Recurring costs

Personnel (salaries, wages, fringe benefits, and ongoing training)
Materials (e.g., medicines in a clinic, books in a training program, and meals in a residential program)
Rental of buildings and equipment
Maintenance of buildings and equipment
Direct contributions
Payments for supplied services
Administrative overhead
Public relations, education
Security and insurance

Different kinds of public programs will have varying proportions of their total costs in each of the previous categories; a publicly supported cancer control program will spend sizable amounts in research and development, whereas an urban renewal project will have huge expenses in the purchase of land and existing improvements. These and all costs, and benefits, occur or are incurred at different points in time. It is useful for purposes of comparison to be able to take into account the time value of money.

The Time Value of Money

A dollar today will be worth something more than a dollar 1 year from now. Based on simple savings account interest it will be worth about $1.05. Similarly, a dollar next year is worth only about 95 cents today. If we decide not to save the dollar but spend it now, it is because there is a greater preference for something now than for what $1.05 could purchase next year. Thus, even if money is not being saved, there is a time value associated with what it can purchase. This underlying time value of money is the basis for employing interest rates, or *discount rates,* in assessing the present value of future costs and benefits.

Whether today's dollar is worth $1.05 or $1.10 next year depends on whether the rate of interest is 5 or 10 percent. There is no universally accepted procedure for determining the appropriate discount rate at which public projects should be evaluated. However, there are two commonly proposed approaches: the opportunity-cost approach and the social-time-preference approach.[4]

[4] There exists a vast literature on the subject of the appropriate discount rate for public projects. See, for example, William J. Baumol, "On the Social Rate of Discount," *American Economic Review,* vol. 58, September 1968, pp. 788–802; and M. S. Feldstein, "The Social Time Preference Discount Rate in Cost Benefit Analysis," *Economic Journal,* vol. 74, June 1964, pp. 360–379. A number of readings on the subject appear in Harley H. Hinrichs and Graeme M. Taylor (eds.), *Program Budgeting and Benefit-Cost Analysis,* Goodyear Publishing Co., Inc., Santa Monica, Calif., 1969.

The opportunity-cost approach takes note that public funds are withdrawn from private sectors where they would otherwise earn some *return*. Hence, by devoting them to or investing them in some public project, there is an opportunity cost associated with the investment. The return that is foregone when public projects use otherwise private funds is the minimum interest rate or discount rate that should be used in evaluating public projects.

The social-time-preference approach emphasizes the *consumption* that is foregone by investing in a public project rather than the *return* on investment that is foregone. If a public project displaces investment in a private undertaking, then the foregone stream of consumption that would have followed the investment in the private undertaking serves as the basis for calculating the appropriate interest rate. Although the social-time-preference approach might be attractive from the social consumption point of view, it is not very operational, since it is impossible to determine the stream of consumption that would have followed an investment that was actually never made. The opportunity-cost approach is quite operational. In arriving at the discount rate by the opportunity-cost approach, one should take into account the social opportunities as well as financial returns that are foregone.

Since there is no optimal discount rate, the decision maker would be well advised to beware of strong arguments for either a very high or very low discount rate, and be cautious in using cost-benefit analyses in which the preferred alternative is very sensitive to slight variations in the discount rate.

Computing Present Value

The foundation of present value calculations is compound interest. A simple example will help to recall this simple concept.

Compound interest: An example If we deposit \$100.00 at 5 percent interest per year, then 1 year from now we will have \$105.00. That is, we will have the \$100.00 deposited, the *principal,* plus 5 percent of the principal. If we decide to keep the \$105.00 as principal in the account for the second year, then at the end of the second year we will have the \$105.00, plus 5 percent of that amount, which is \$5.25. If we decide to leave the account untouched at the end of the second year, we will have a principal of \$110.25 in the account. During the third year the interest will be 5 percent of that amount, which is \$5.51; hence, at the end of the third year, our account will total \$115.76. Table 7-3 summarizes these calculations.

In general the future amount S, depends on the present amount P, the interest rate i, and the number of years n, according to the formula:

$$S = P(1 + i)^n$$

Table 7-3 Future values of $100.00 at 5 percent interest

Year	Principal amount at beginning of year, P	Interest earned during year at 5%, Pi	Total amount at end of year, S
1	$100.00	$100.00(0.05) = $5.00	$105.00
2	105.00	105.00(0.05) = 5.25	110.25
3	110.25	110.25(0.05) = 5.51	115.76

Here this is

$$S = \$100(1 + .05)^3$$
$$= \$115.76$$

Single payment present worth The same underlying notion of compound interest can be used to determine the amount that we must have now in order to have $1000.00 six years from now, assuming a 5 percent rate of interest. In this case, P is the unknown quantity, and the future value S is $1000.00 which we will need 6 years from now. Solving for P in

$$S = P(1 + i)^n$$

we get

$$P = S\frac{1}{(1 + i)^n}$$

Here,

$$P = \$1000\frac{1}{(1 + .05)^6}$$
$$= \$1000(.7462)$$
$$= \$746.20$$

Alternately we say that the $746.20 is the present value of a single payment of $1000.00 six years from now, at a 5 percent rate of interest. The factor, .7462, is referred to as the "single payment present worth" factor for 5 percent and 6 years. To obviate the need for calculating such factors, they are presented in Table 3 of the Appendix.

Example To illustrate further the use of the table, find the present value of $50,000 eight years hence, assuming an interest rate of 6 percent.

$$P = \$50{,}000\frac{1}{(1 + .06)^8}$$

$$= \$50{,}000\begin{pmatrix}\text{SPPW}\\ i = .06\\ n = 8\end{pmatrix}$$

$$= \$50{,}000(.627)$$

$$= \$31{,}350$$

We say that \$31,350 is the present value of \$50,000 with $n = 8$ and $i = .06$.

To get some sense of the effect of different rates of interest, we calculate the present value of \$50,000 eight years hence at alternate interest rates of 8 and 10 percent.

For $S = \$50{,}000$ and $n = 8$, if

	$i = .06$	.08	.10
then	$P = \$31{,}350$	\$27,000	\$23,350

As the example shows, the present value of a fixed future amount decreases as the interest rate increases, or, in order to have a certain amount at some time in the future, a higher interest rate means less is required now.

Operating costs and recurring benefits sometimes occur in constant or uniform amounts year after year. Hence, it is useful to understand the present value of a uniform series of future amounts.

Uniform series present worth How much must we have on hand now if it is foreseen that we will need \$1000 each year for the next 4 years, assuming an interest rate of 6 percent? Here we determine the present value of a series of uniform amounts. We could find the present value as follows:

$$P = \$1000\,\frac{1}{(1 + .06)^1} + \$1000\,\frac{1}{(1 + .06)^2} + \$1000\,\frac{1}{(1 + .06)^3} + \$1000\,\frac{1}{(1 + .06)^4}$$

which is

$$P = \$1000\begin{pmatrix}\text{SPPW}\\ i = .06\\ n = 1\end{pmatrix} + \$1000\begin{pmatrix}\text{SPPW}\\ i = .06\\ n = 2\end{pmatrix} + \$1000\begin{pmatrix}\text{SPPW}\\ i = .06\\ n = 3\end{pmatrix} + \$1000\begin{pmatrix}\text{SPPW}\\ i = .06\\ n = 4\end{pmatrix}$$

or its equivalent

$$P = \$1000 \frac{(1 + .06)^4 - 1}{.06(1 + .06)^4}$$

$$= \$1000(3.465)$$

$$= \$3465$$

Hence \$3465 is said to be the present value of a 4-year stream of \$1000 amounts. The factor, 3.465, is called the "uniform series present worth" factor for $n = 4$, $i = .06$; these USPW factors are presented in Table 4 of the Appendix.

Example To further illustrate uniform series present worth calculations, we find the present value of future maintenance costs, estimated at \$5000 per year for the next 20 years, at an interest rate of 8 percent.

$$P = R \begin{pmatrix} \text{USPW} \\ i \\ n \end{pmatrix}$$

$$= \$5000 \begin{pmatrix} \text{USPW} \\ i = .08 \\ n = 20 \end{pmatrix}$$

$$= \$5000(9.818)$$

$$= \$49{,}090$$

\$49,090 is the present value of a 20-year series of \$5000 amounts, assuming an 8 percent interest rate.

When the uniform series is to continue indefinitely, as when a service is to be provided forever, its present value is called its *capitalized* value.

Capitalized cost The present value of annual costs is called the *capitalized cost*. To capitalize permanent annual costs, first recall that at 6 percent interest, \$10,000 will earn \$600 in interest each year. Conversely, \$10,000 is needed at present to meet an annual payment of \$600, when the interest rate is 6 percent. Generally P is needed at present to meet a payment of R every year forever with an interest rate of i.

$$P = \frac{R}{i}$$

In the above example,

$$P = \frac{\$600}{.06}$$

$$= \$10{,}000$$

Capitalizing can be applied not only to actual dollar costs but also to benefits. If an alternative will provide a continual service at a savings, the savings will be realized every year forever. The present value of the stream of annual savings is determined by capitalizing the benefit.

In comparing alternatives, it is imperative to make whatever adjustments are necessary so the alternatives will have similar periods of comparison. An extended illustration will help to reinforce some of the present value ideas.

Cost Comparison: An Illustration

A community is considering installing a supplementary pumping station to maintain adequate water pressure at time of peak demand. Two alternatives have been presented; the effectiveness of the two alternative stations are assumed equivalent, and so the decision is essentially a cost comparison. Alternative A has a purchase and installation cost of $120,000 and estimated annual maintenance costs of $10,000. Alternative B has an initial cost of $190,000 with annual estimated maintenance costs of $4000. Either station is expected to be operational for 20 years. Based on the opportunity cost of capital, the appropriate interest rate is accepted to be 8 percent. Which alternative should be chosen?

The salient pieces of information are first summarized.

Alternative A		*Alternative B*
$120,000	Initial cost	$190,000
10,000	Annual cost = R	4,000
	$i = .08$	
	$n = 20$	

$$P = \$120{,}000 + \$10{,}000\begin{pmatrix}\text{USPW}\\ i = .08\\ n = 20\end{pmatrix} \qquad P = \$190{,}000 + \$4{,}000\begin{pmatrix}\text{USPW}\\ i = .08\\ n = 20\end{pmatrix}$$

$$= \$120{,}000 + \$10{,}000(9.818) \qquad = \$190{,}000 + \$4{,}000(9.818)$$

$$= \$120{,}000 + \$98{,}180 \qquad = \$190{,}000 + \$39{,}272$$

$$= \$218{,}180 \qquad = \$229{,}272$$

Based on purely economic considerations, alternative A is preferable by a present value of about $11,000. We note that the economic life of each alternative is 20 years; so the period of comparison is easily arrived at. If the economic life of either alternative is other than 20 years, some adjustment would have to be made, as we see next.

While the community decision makers were embroiled in assessing the alternatives, a third alternative was identified. The third alternative requires an initial cost of $140,000 for purchase and installation of a sealed pumping station that is guaranteed maintenance-free for 10 years. At that time, however, the pumping station would have to be replaced. Is this alternative preferable to alternative A? Since the economic life of alternative A is 20 years and the economic life of alternative C is 10 years, a period of comparison can be arrived at by assuming that with alternative C the pumping station will be replaced at the end of 10 years. The present value of alternative C follows:

Alternative C

$$\text{Initial cost} = \$140{,}000$$

$$\text{Future cost} = S = \$140{,}000$$

$$i = .08$$

$$n = 10$$

$$P = \$140{,}000 + \$140{,}000 \begin{pmatrix} \text{SPPW} \\ i = .08 \\ n = 10 \end{pmatrix}$$

$$= \$140{,}000 + \$140{,}000(.463)$$

$$= \$140{,}000 + \$64{,}820$$

$$= \$204{,}820$$

Based on economic considerations with the assumption that the three alternatives are equally effective, alternative C is preferred. Here alternative C was found, while alternatives A and B were being compared. It is not uncommon that while some alternatives are being compared, others may be encountered.

The various phases of cost-benefit analysis are not locked into a time sequence. However, certain constraints may eliminate from consideration alternatives identified late in the process. In a legal request for bids, for instance, a deadline would preclude considering even preferable bids submitted after the prescribed time.

In our illustrations, thus far, the effect of inflation has been notably ignored. The issue deserves some attention.

The Effect of Inflation on Present Value Analysis

The effects of inflation are not usually taken into account in comparisons in cost-benefit analysis. Basic principles require that costs and benefits be considered on the same basis, which ordinarily involves initial price levels. However, if the rate of inflation is expected to be greater (or smaller) for some particular costs and/or benefits than for costs in general, then the discount rate for these items should be appropriately adjusted downward (upward).[5]

[5] It goes against intuition that higher rates of inflation should lower the applicable discount rate. Consider a simple example. \$100 is deposited at 5 percent interest for 1 year. The inflation rate is 3 percent. At the end of the year there is \$105, but its purchasing power is only about \$102. The real interest rate is only 2 percent.

Example Suppose equipment costs in the preceding illustration are expected to increase at a rate that is 3 percentage points higher than the general inflation rate, which governs maintenance costs. The discount rate applicable to alternative C should be lowered by 3 percentage points, while alternatives A and B need no adjustment. The adjusted present value of alternative C follows.

Alternative C

$$\text{Initial cost} = \$140{,}000$$

$$\text{Future cost} = \$140{,}000$$

$$i = .08 - .03 = .05$$

$$n = 10$$

$$\begin{aligned} P &= \$140{,}000 + \$140{,}000 \begin{pmatrix} \text{SPPW} \\ i = .05 \\ n = 10 \end{pmatrix} \\ &= \$140{,}000 + \$140{,}000(.614) \\ &= \$140{,}000 + \$85{,}960 \\ &= \$225{,}960 \end{aligned}$$

With the uneven effects of inflation, alternative C is no longer preferable to alternative A.

Where benefits can be given dollar values, the same present value calculations apply. There are some qualitative issues to be dealt with first.

BENEFITS

Benefits in the comprehensive sense include all outputs of the process, or consequences of an alternative. Benefits involve the tangible and the intangible negative unintended consequences; positive consequences, intended or unintended; direct services provided and their effects on human life. Here we address the essentials of benefit assessment and leave the finer points to a more detailed presentation.

Tangible and Intangible Benefits

Benefits include all the additions to and subtractions from social welfare. Tangible benefits are the additions to and subtractions from social welfare which can be valued in dollar terms. However, assigning a dollar amount to intangible benefits may substantially detract from the validity of the cost-benefit analysis by masking the fact that the assignment is essentially based on a subjective value judgment. Even when the basis for the assignment is made explicit, there is a tendency to look past the value judgment and focus on the numbers rather than on the original benefits.

Example The benefits associated with eliminating or controlling some disease may include preventing lost productivity and earnings, and avoiding pain and discomfort. There may be other benefits, but we consider only these for the purpose of illustration. There is considerable objectivity possible in assessing the worth of the lost productivity and earnings; not so for the pain and discomfort. An analysis that excludes the latter because of measurement difficulties would severely bias the conclusion. Assigning a dollar value to the avoidance of pain and discomfort facilitates its inclusion in the analysis, but it presents the risk that decision makers may look at only the dollar value. An alternative approach provides a qualitative analysis of the intangibles as a companion to the quantitative analysis appropriate for tangible benefits and costs.

Decision makers can judge how the net difference between quantifiable costs and quantifiable benefits compares with the sum total or accumulation of intangible benefits. As another example, a newly proposed method of police patrol, with its appropriate public relations effort, may generate the benefit of providing a sense of security to the community. This sense of security should be included as a benefit, although its dollar value may be a mystery.

Negative Effects

Some of the consequences of a particular alternative may be negative. This concept of a negative benefit may contradict the dictionary definition of benefit, but since benefit refers to the outputs of the process of implementing an alternative, there is really no contradiction. Intangible negative effects have the same assessment difficulties as intangible positive ones. A kind of critical value assessment can be made. This critical value is the estimate of the level of an intangible consequence that will just offset the excess tangible benefits of a project.[6]

Example Giving landing rights to a supersonic transport may cause already existing airplanes to operate at lower levels of passenger use, and it may generate an increase in air and noise pollution near the airport. Both negative effects should be included in the benefit assessment. The first lends itself to monetary assessment. We will make a critical value assessment for the second. Assume that permitting the supersonic transport to land will

[6] E. J. Mishan, *Welfare Economics: An Assessment,* North Holland Publishing Company, Amsterdam, 1969. This concept, referred to as a contingency calculation by Mishan, and others relevant to cost-benefit analysis are discussed in some detail in E. J. Mishan, *Cost-Benefit Analysis,* Praeger Publishers, Inc., New York, 1971.

generate a net benefit over cost of $10 million per year for the foreseeable future, ignoring air and noise pollution. Suppose it is calculated that about half a million families will suffer the annoyance of the air and noise pollution. Paying annual compensation of as little as $20 to each family would entirely offset the benefits. The question can then be raised whether the families would consider the $20 payment sufficient to offset the noise and air pollution which they must suffer. While this approach does not attempt to determine the dollar cost associated with the pollution, it does permit at least a critical level assessment.

Inside and outside effects Deciding which spillover effects should be included in, and which should be excluded from, the analysis is similar to defining the system in a systems analysis approach to decision making. On one hand, looking only at the direct and intended benefits is certainly myopic; on the other hand, attempting to identify every possible ripple effect would lead both the analyst and the decision maker to a state of permanently pending. The view that some things are more important than others must ultimately decide which items should be included and which should not. A task for the public decision maker is to determine whether excluded items upset the balance of the abstract analysis.

The perspective from which the analysis is performed will influence which costs and benefits are to be included. Inside ones are those that occur within the jurisdiction requiring the analysis; outside ones occur elsewhere.

Example A municipality examining an intensified police patrol may see as a benefit reduced crime within its borders. The municipality may choose to ignore the increase in crime in adjacent areas caused by perpetrators changing their *locus operandi*. On the state or federal level, however, those spillover effects would be considered quite relevant.

Benefits are being identified and assessed while objectives, constraints, assumptions, and costs are being considered. It may well be that benefits first included may eventually be discarded, while others not considered relevant at first will ultimately be included.

Example A motor vehicle bureau, in choosing a data processing system for driver license applications, includes among the benefits of one alternative its capacity to handle 10,000 applications per day. Later, projections of the driver population indicate there would never be a need for more than 4000 per day. The excess capacity of the system should be deleted from the alternative's benefits.

Example An emergency communication network incorporating the widespread use of citizen band radios may at first overlook the benefit of obviating the need for expensive roadside emergency telephones. In the final analysis, such a benefit should be included.

The value assessment of goods provided to the public has many thorny problems. Depending on the nature of the goods, different approaches may be useful.

Market Goods and Public Goods

Two broad classifications of goods and services are market goods and services and pure public goods and services. *Market goods* are those that have a market price that can be used in value assessment.

Example A free dental clinic for families of low-income workers can use the current rate of private services in evaluating the benefits that the clinic provides.

There are some difficulties with the use of market prices in evaluating publicly provided goods and services. Prices may not reflect the true worth of the items in the first place; for example, taxes, monopoly, or unemployment may distort the market price. Another difficulty is identified in questioning whether *consumers' surplus* should be included in evaluating the goods. Consumers' surplus is the difference between what consumers are willing to pay for an item and what they actually pay.

Example A public transportation system charges 50 cents for a ride. Experience and the relationship between price and demand show that at least some individuals would be willing to pay more than 50 cents for the ride. In assessing the value of the service for purposes of cost-benefit analysis, should the ride be assessed at 50 cents, or at the average level of what users would be willing to pay? The presence of a market price, however, does identify the minimum value of the service; those who value the ride at less than 50 cents would not make use of the service.

Public goods benefit many people jointly. Individuals are not easily excluded from enjoying their benefits. Evaluation is overwhelmingly more difficult here. For example, since the benefits of national defense are not selectively bestowed on some and refused to others, there is no way of getting people to reveal their true evaluation of such benefits. In cases in which the benefits cannot be valued, and hence cost-benefit analysis becomes impossible, only the costs of alternative ways of providing the same benefits can be compared. Cost-effectiveness analysis as originally defined is thus used in defense, public health, and other programs with wide-ranging impacts that are not readily assessible.

Benefits of many programs relate directly to the saving or loss of human life. We now turn our attention to the evaluation of such benefits.

Human Life

Many programs concern themselves with health and safety; one objective they may have is to save lives. Other programs may increase the chances of dying for some individuals, as in bridge construction and fire fighting. Teaching, a component of a different public program, is less dangerous and does not affect the chances of dying. (The late 1960s and 1970s might generate specific counterexamples!) The analysis of saving a life corresponds to that of losing a life, and so we will consider the loss of life and then transfer conclusions as appropriate.

There is yet no one correct way to make proper allowance for changes in the incidence of death, whether it be the intended benefit or a side effect. However, in a world where different programs compete for the same dollars, some assessment of the value of lives is considered by many to be useful. A caution and operational guideline suggests that the prose portion of the analysis describe effects on human life in substantive terms.

One frequently used method of evaluating the economic value of life is to determine the present value of the individual's expected future earnings. An alternative method approaches the value of life from a social point of view. Inasmuch as there are programs and projects that involve some increase or reduction in the incidence of death, it is claimed that society has implicitly placed a value on human life. This approach requires looking at various programs and projects that have been implemented, and other alternatives that have been rejected, in the hopes of determining the critical value of human life for which decisions are actually made. Other approaches include calculating not the expected future earnings but the expected future consumption; calculating the expected future excess of earnings over consumption; determining the insurance premium a man is willing to pay and the probability of his being killed as a result of engaging in some specific activity. None of these methods is without severe and reasonable criticism.[7]

In most undertakings in which an effect on the incidence of death is foreseen, a specific person cannot be designated in advance as the one who will certainly die or will certainly be saved as a result of the undertaking. Therefore, in advance of implementing an alternative—at the point of choosing an alternative, for instance—the effect on the incidence of death may be more reasonably interpreted as an effect on the likelihood of death for all members of the community. Evaluating the change in the probability of death may then be a better way of assessing the value of the effect on human life. That most people volun-

[7] The reader interested in a detailed presentation of the various techniques, their rationales, and criticisms of them is referred to E. J. Mishan, *Cost-Benefit Analysis,* Praeger Publishers, Inc., New York, 1971, with particular reference to "Loss of Life and Limb," chaps. 22 and 23, and the many references given there.

tarily place themselves in situations with increased risk of death indicates that doing so is valued more highly than a less risky but more inconvenient or more expensive alternative.

Example Workers in a factory who are regularly exposed to some toxic substance may be well aware that such exposure is expected to cause 3 deaths from among the 3000 employees. In spite of this, the workers choose to continue at the factory. The increased risk of death is more than compensated for by the tangible and intangible benefits of working at the factory. However, if an individual knew for certain that he or she would die from the toxic exposure during the next year, almost certainly that individual would choose to relocate.

There is a notable distinction between the practical assessment of risk to life and the formal valuation of loss of life. The practical assessment is made implicitly and unhesitatingly by each of us every day. No matter how the formal evaluation is done, it is met with urgent pleas to stop putting a value on human life. Approaching the latter through understanding the former may help to resolve philosophical issues if not economic ones.

Treatment of Uncertainty

Consequences of any action are seldom known with certainty. Uncertainty in cost-benefit analysis arises from three sources.

1. *Uncertainty about cause-effect relationships.* Projection of benefits often depends on knowledge gained from similar but not identical experiences. The more dissimilar the experiences the less complete will be the understanding of relevant cause-effect relationships.

   Example The link between a public nutrition–education program and general health is less than fully understood.

2. *Uncertainty about the future situation.* The environment, formally represented in assumptions and constraints, may change. Benefits anticipated in the current situation may not be possible, or may not be as valuable in the future situation.

   Example Price and availability of fuel may significantly alter driving patterns. Benefits of a new roadway will then be different from anticipation.

3. *Uncertainty related to chance effect.* The random component is a constant source of uncertainty as regards the prevailing state of nature.

   Example The benefits of an influenza vaccination program depend on the extent of the outbreak, which is a random uncontrollable component.

Uncertainty can be treated in a number of ways. If probabilities can be estimated, then expected values can be used to make comparisons. Whether or not they can be estimated, another approach considers the consequences of uncertainties being at their worst. If one alternative stands out even if the listing of consequences is biased against it, a strong case has been made for that alternative.

Sensitivity analysis will help to determine the effect of changes in estimated values on the relative merit of the alternatives. A related approach, called *contingency analysis,* investigates how the alternatives will be affected by having to execute contingency plans. Such plans are needed in the event of somewhat severe, discrete changes in the situation.

In whatever way benefits and costs are identified and evaluated, eventually they must be compared. Comparison is the focal point of the process.

BENEFIT-COST COMPARISON

A necessity for any decision is the presence of various alternatives. When there is only one identifiable course of action, the alternatives are to accept or reject it. The benefits and costs of each alternative are first identified and then compared. The way in which the alternatives are compared depends in part on the selection criteria.

Selection Criteria

There are a few different means for identifying the preferred alternative. There are two basic positions which indicate whether a program should be undertaken in the first place.

Pareto improvement This rather conservative position requires that in any public investment no one is worse off and at least someone is better off. Under this essentially hypothetical requirement, few public projects would be implemented.

Net welfare improvement This position merely requires that total benefits exceed costs. Alternately expressed, the position states that the total improvement by the gainers outweighs the combined setback of the losers, or that the benefit-cost ratio is greater than 1.

Comparison Measures

In comparing alternatives that have the same intangible effects, different comparison measures are available. Care should be exercised in selecting the measure most appropriate.

Table 7-4 A comparison of net present value and benefit-cost ratio

	Alternatives	
Present value	A	B
Costs	$200,000	$300,000
Benefits	300,000	420,000
Net present value	100,000	120,000
Benefit-cost ratio	1.5	1.4

Net present value This is simply the present value of total benefits minus total costs. This measure is indifferent between putting negative social effects on the benefit side with positive effects, and putting them on the cost side with direct costs. This measure is not particularly appropriate when comparing undertakings of vastly different size.

Example There are two potential projects, summarized in Table 7-4. That B has a greater present value is strictly a consequence of its greater scale.

Benefit-cost ratio This is the present value of benefits divided by the present value of costs. This measure is not influenced by the size of the investment, and so it better compares different-sized alternatives, as shown in the preceding example. Since the benefit-cost ratio is dependent on the placement of social costs, there must be a consistent procedure for the various alternatives. If the ratio exceeds 1, including social costs with benefits yields a higher ratio than including them with direct costs. If the ratio is less than 1, the opposite is true.

Example A proposed project is summarized in Table 7-5. Depending on how social costs are counted, the benefit-cost ratio varies by about 10 percent.

Table 7-5 Benefit-cost ratio depends on how negative effects are counted

		Count negative effects with:	
Components	Value	Costs	Benefits
Costs	$300,000	$500,000	$300,000
Negative effects	200,000		
Benefits	600,000	600,000	400,000
Benefit-cost ratio		1.2	1.33

The benefit-cost ratio is a relative value; if it is to be the measure for a meaningful comparison, it must be similarly derived for all alternatives.

Internal rate of return Rather than select a particular discount rate for the present value analysis, various rates are tried until the stream of benefits exactly offsets the stream of costs. A project is economically worthwhile if its internal rate of return exceeds the cost of borrowing funds. The preferred from among a set of alternatives is the one with the greatest internal rate of return. This method is indifferent to the size of the alternatives or the placement of negative effects, but it tends to be more abstract than either net present value or benefit-cost ratio. The method also avoids the sticky and sensitive issue of choosing an appropriate discount rate.

We have attempted to deal with issues common to many cost-benefit situations. We now illustrate some of the ideas of cost-benefit analysis in a number of different settings.

WHICH BRIDGE SHOULD BE BUILT? AN ILLUSTRATION

A municipality is faced with replacing a bridge which passes over a stream through town. It can construct a wooden trestle bridge which is expected to last for 25 years. It will cost \$80,000 and will require annual maintenance costing \$4000. Another alternative is a steel bridge, which would last for 50 years, cost \$160,000, and require annual maintenance costing \$2000. Assume a discount rate of 6 percent. The wooden bridge will have to be closed to traffic for 1 month while it is being rebuilt 25 years hence. The steel bridge is expected to withstand any flooding conditions, whereas the wooden bridge would give way in a "100-year flood". For illustrative purposes we proceed with the analysis in stages.

Assuming both bridges are equally effective and ignoring having to close the bridge for reconstruction, the comparison becomes strictly cost-oriented.

The present value of steel-bridge costs is:

$$P_{\text{SB}} = \$160{,}000 + \$2000 \begin{pmatrix} \text{USPW} \\ i = .06 \\ n = 50 \end{pmatrix}$$

$$= \$160{,}000 + \$2000(15.762)$$

$$= \$191{,}524$$

The present value of wooden-bridge costs is:

$$P_{\text{WB}} = \$80{,}000 + \$80{,}000 \begin{pmatrix} \text{SPPW} \\ i = .06 \\ n = 25 \end{pmatrix} + \$4000 \begin{pmatrix} \text{USPW} \\ i = .06 \\ n = 50 \end{pmatrix}$$

$$= \$80{,}000 + \$80{,}000(.233) + \$4000(15.762)$$

$$= \$80{,}000 + \$18{,}640 + \$63{,}048$$

$$= \$161{,}688$$

The initial and somewhat superficial analysis indicates that the wooden bridge is more economical by a present value of about $30,000.

To assess the value of the negative effect of closing the wooden bridge to traffic while it is being rebuilt, two approaches are possible. The first assumes that in the absence of the wooden-bridge alternative the steel bridge would be preferable to none at all. This is used as the basis for determining the worth, not the cost, of having a bridge. The cost of the steel bridge, present value = $191,524, is the minimum that having the bridge for 50 years is worth. The present value of $191,524 is equal to what amount annually for the next 50 years, or what uniform series for the next 50 years is the same as the $191,524? This annual equivalent can be determined as follows:

$$P = R(\text{USPW})$$

$$P_{\text{SB}} = \$191{,}524 = R\begin{pmatrix}\text{USPW}\\ i = .06\\ n = 50\end{pmatrix}$$

$$\$191{,}524 = R(15.762)$$

$$\frac{\$191{,}524}{15.762} = \$12{,}150$$

Based on this annual value of having a bridge, the community's monthly value of having the bridge is estimated to be $1013. The present value of a month's use 25 years from now is:

$$P = \$1013\begin{pmatrix}\text{SPPW}\\ i = .06\\ n = 25\end{pmatrix}$$

$$= \$1013(.233)$$

$$= \$236$$

Hence the negative effect of being without a bridge for 1 month while it is being rebuilt 25 years from now has a present value of at least $236. This negative benefit would hardly be enough to offset the $30,000 difference in costs.

However, the worth of the bridge can be assessed alternatively. It is currently estimated that there are about 1000 necessary crossings per day, and about 500 unnecessary or at least postponable crossings per day. Without the bridge through the town, the closest alternate route from one side of the stream to the other requires using a bridge about 15 miles upstream. Assessing the cost of operating a vehicle at 15 cents per mile, the negative impact on the community of not having the bridge is:

$$\text{Daily cost} = 1000 \text{ trips} \times 30 \text{ mi/trip} \times \$.15/\text{mi} = \$4500$$

If the necessary crossings are assumed to be undertaken 20 days per month, the cost to the community of not having the bridge for 1 month is $90,000. The present value of the $90,000 negative benefit 25 years from now is calculated as follows:

$$P = \$90{,}000 \begin{pmatrix} \text{SPPW} \\ i = .06 \\ n = 25 \end{pmatrix}$$

$$= \$90{,}000(.233)$$

$$= \$20{,}970$$

Note that this $20,970 is considered a negative benefit since it is a cost to the members of the community that comes about as a consequence of the choice, rather than an expense of the implementation of the choice. The tangible negative social impact of not having the bridge is still not sufficient to offset the cost difference, but it indicates that the wooden bridge is not so overwhelmingly preferable as costs alone might indicate.

The inconvenience, an intangible negative impact, of not having the bridge might be more than enough to shift the preference to the steel bridge. Specifically, neither the time required for the longer alternate trip nor the inconvenience of postponing or eliminating the so-called unnecessary trips has been included.

As more salient features are included in the analysis, the model better represents the actual costs and benefits. The risk of a flood is the next item to be included in the model.

If the wooden bridge is damaged in a flood, the real cost of rebuilding will be paid by the town. (For simplicity we assume the bridge must be replaced if it is damaged; that is, if it is damaged beyond what ordinary maintenance can take care of, the bridge must be replaced.) Since a "100-year flood" would damage the bridge, we can say that there is a probability of .01 that in any year the bridge will be destroyed. Using binomial probability tables for $n = 50$ and $p = .01$, we find the probability of having any number of floods during the next 50 years.

Probability	*Number of "100-yr floods" in 50 yr*
.60	0
.31	1
.08	2
.01	3

If a flood does occur during the next 50 years, the additional cost incurred would be an extra $80,000 for constructing a new bridge (unless the flood happens to occur in the year in which the bridge is scheduled for reconstruction anyway) and an additional negative benefit of $90,000 for each month the town is without the bridge. The present value of the additional costs and negative benefits depends on when the flood occurs. Since the year in which the flood will occur cannot be forecast, we estimate the present value by averaging its time of occurrence; that is, we determine the present value of the additional costs and negative benefits for an extra bridge being built 25 years from now. Note that it is not being claimed that two bridges will be built the same year, but rather that their average time of construction is 25 years hence. The costs and negative effects for one flood, using this averaging-over-time assumption, follows:

One flood:

$$\text{Cost} = \$80{,}000 + \$80{,}000 \begin{pmatrix}\text{SPPW}\\ i = .06\\ n = 25\end{pmatrix} + \$80{,}000 \begin{pmatrix}\text{SPPW}\\ i = .06\\ n = 25\end{pmatrix} + \$4000 \begin{pmatrix}\text{USPW}\\ i = .06\\ n = 50\end{pmatrix}$$

$$= \$80{,}000 + \$18{,}640 + \$18{,}640 + \$63{,}048$$

$$= \$180{,}328$$

$$\text{Negative effects} = \$90{,}000 \begin{pmatrix}\text{SPPW}\\ i = .06\\ n = 25\end{pmatrix} + \$90{,}000 \begin{pmatrix}\text{SPPW}\\ i = .06\\ n = 25\end{pmatrix}$$

$$= \$20{,}970 + \$20{,}970$$

$$= \$41{,}940$$

In the event of one flood the sum of costs and negative effects for the wooden bridge is

$$P_{\text{WB, 1 flood}} = \$180{,}328 + \$41{,}940$$

$$= \$222{,}268$$

In the event that two floods occur, then whether four bridges or three bridges will have to be built depends on when the floods occur.[8]

A conservative estimate of the total cost for two floods is the same as that associated with one flood.

Although it is slight, there is a possibility that there would be three floods during the 50-year period. We will ignore the remote possibility that the three floods occur with such timing that four bridges would be necessary.

[8] If the second flood occurs after the construction of the third bridge (the initial bridge, the planned replacement bridge, and the flood-caused replacement bridge), then the analysis would have to account for the construction of a fourth bridge. For the moment we will ignore this possibility; we will come back to it only if the choice of an alternative depends on it.

Again making a simplifying assumption that the occurrence of the floods can be averaged over the 50-year period, the present value of the costs and negative effects for three floods follows:

Three floods:

$$\text{Cost} = \$80{,}000 + \$80{,}000 \begin{pmatrix} \text{SPPW} \\ i = .06 \\ n = 13 \end{pmatrix} + \$80{,}000 \begin{pmatrix} \text{SPPW} \\ i = .06 \\ n = 25 \end{pmatrix}$$

$$+ \$80{,}000 \begin{pmatrix} \text{SPPW} \\ i = .06 \\ n = 37 \end{pmatrix} + \$4000 \begin{pmatrix} \text{USPW} \\ i = .06 \\ n = 50 \end{pmatrix}$$

$$= \$208{,}488$$

$$\text{Negative effects} = \$90{,}000 \begin{pmatrix} \text{SPPW} \\ i = .06 \\ n = 13 \end{pmatrix} + \$90{,}000 \begin{pmatrix} \text{SPPW} \\ i = .06 \\ n = 25 \end{pmatrix}$$

$$+ \$90{,}000 \begin{pmatrix} \text{SPPW} \\ i = .06 \\ n = 37 \end{pmatrix}$$

The total for three floods is

$$P_{\text{WB, 3 floods}} = \$282{,}108$$

The present value of the sum of the expenses and negative effects for the two alternatives for each potential number of floods is presented in Table 7-6 along with the expected net dollar amount.

Other factors worth considering include the inconvenience to the community of being without a bridge while it is being rebuilt; if the bridge is destroyed, the community will probably be without a bridge for longer than 1 month since in such a situation construction does not begin immediately; the costs and negative benefits of the wooden bridge have been conservatively estimated.

Table 7-6 Present value of estimated costs and negative effects

		Alternatives	
State of nature	Probability	Steel bridge	Wooden bridge
0 flood	.60	$191,524	$182,658
1 flood	.31	191,524	222,268
2 floods	.08	191,524	222,268
3 floods	.01	191,524	282,788
Expected value (costs + negative effects)		$191,524	$199,107

Nothing short of a severe current budget constraint could prevent the steel bridge from appearing preferable to the wooden one.

The presentation of the situation in the form of a decision table serves to emphasize that cost-benefit analysis is a decision theory approach to a particular class of problems. The next application follows the same type of presentation, but it makes use of slightly different analysis.

EARLY DETECTION OF DISEASE: AN ILLUSTRATION

Cost-benefit analysis has been applied to medical screening projects administered to large segments of the population in order to detect disease while still in the early, more treatable stages. One applicable disease is lung cancer, a leading killer of men and women. Treatment in the early, potentially curable stages is critical, since the survival rate of those with the more advanced stages is extremely low.

On the basis of lives saved and suffering relieved, an early screening method such as sputum cytology is readily justified. In the face of competing projects, however, an economic analysis of tangible costs and benefits is necessary.[9] When given the opportunity, an individual can choose to take the test or not. The disease is either present or not. The initial decision table is presented in Table 7-7.

The approach taken here does not directly assess the value of a life. Rather we derive a critical value. Assessing a life at that value exactly offsets all direct costs and indirect negative effects.

The errors associated with the test are:

$$P(\text{false positive}) = .0025$$

$$P(\text{false negative}) = .30$$

The multiplication rule for dependent events (see Chapter 3) provides all the needed joint probabilities for test results and presence of disease. They appear in Table 7-8.

The direct cost of the sputum cytology is \$15; the indirect cost of a patient's 2 hours' waiting, travel, and procedure time, at an estimated \$5 per hour, is

[9] Some simplifications will be made in our presentation. Ordinarily a positive finding on the sputum cytology is followed by a bronchoscopy, or visual exploration of the lungs, to determine if both lungs are infected, and a bronchial washing to locate the source of the irregular cells. Next a mediastinoscopy, or visual exploration of the tissues around the bronchi and trachea, is performed to determine if the disease has spread into the lymph nodes. Actual treatment depends on the combination of test results. Here we are considering only the first stage of detection with its test and treatment costs, incidence, and test effectiveness. The lung-cancer application is taken from an unpublished Master's Professional Paper by Leona Abt, Pennsylvania State University, Capitol Campus, Graduate Program in Public Administration. The methodology is from Stuart Schweitzer, "Cost Effectiveness of Early Detection of Disease," *Health Services Research,* vol. 9, Spring 1974, pp. 22–32.

Table 7-7 Decision table for lung cancer screening test

		Alternatives	
States of nature	Probability*	Test	No test
Lung cancer	.0005	Pay for test Treated Lives	No payment Not treated Dies
No cancer	.9995	Pay for test Not treated Lives	No payment Not treated Lives

* The morbidity rate of 50/100,000 is taken from *Cancer Facts and Figures 1978,* American Cancer Society Inc., New York, 1977, for the entire United States population. Actually the rate varies with segments of the population according to smoking, sex, and age.

$10. The primary treatment of lung cancer is a pneumonectomy, the surgical removal of a lung. Fees for surgery, hospital, and laboratory tests are estimated at $3000. The salient features of the problem are presented in Table 7-8; the payoffs include the $25 test cost, $3000 treatment cost, and the unidentified value V of continuing to live.

The critical value of life, which exactly offsets other costs, is given by

$$.99985V - 33.55 = .9995V$$

and so

$$V = \$95{,}857$$

If the economic value of prolonging a life exceeds $95,857, the screening test is economically worthwhile.[10] If it is less than that, it is not so. This ap-

Table 7-8 Decision table for lung cancer screening test

				Alternatives	
Condition	Probability	Test results	Joint probability	Test	No test
Disease	.0005	Positive	.00035	V-25-3000	
		Negative	.00015	−25	0
No disease	.9995	Positive	.0024987	V-25-3000	
		Negative	.9970013	V-25	V
Expected value				$.99985V - 33.55$	$.9995V$

[10] For reference purposes, the present value of 20 years of future earnings for the $16,000 wage earner is $199,392 at a 5 percent discount rate and $136,224 at a 10 percent discount rate.

proach avoids making a direct assessment of prolonging a life and permits coming to a conclusion based on a simpler comparison.

This survey of cost-benefit analysis concludes with an application of cost-benefit analysis to urban renewal.

COST-BENEFIT ANALYSIS APPLIED TO URBAN RENEWAL: AN APPLICATION[11]

The objective and social benefits of urban renewal are (1) superior pattern of resource allocation, (2) social benefits of the removal of *blight,* and (3) improved local financial position. Although there may be a number of alternative uses for land being redeveloped, we are here considering the more aggregate alternatives, either urban renewal or no urban renewal in a particular section of the city. This is the level of evaluation appropriate for cost-benefit analysis. The alternatives would then be the particular urban renewal projects that should or should not be undertaken.

Among the constraints active on urban renewal is the legal requirement that a redevelopment agency must provide former residents of an urban renewal area with decent, safe, and sanitary housing that is conveniently located and within the means of the residents. Note that it is not implicitly assumed that relocation results in housing facility improvement for the residents.

The costs include those for relocation, survey and planning, administration, public improvements, demolition, and the value of improvements demolished. Benefits include those specifically associated with the stated objectives as well as noneconomic negative effects of relocation and possible land value write-down. The benefits and costs of urban renewal are summarized in Table 7-9. In urban renewal there are, of course, tangible and intangible benefits; since there is no definitive way of evaluating the intangibles, the present approach assesses the tangibles and arrives at a net for benefits minus cost. Decision makers can then judge whether that figure is commensurate with the identifiable intangible benefits, both positive and negative.

The East Stockton, California, Urban Renewal Project was officially approved by the federal government in July 1959. Table 7-10 displays the various costs associated with the renewal project and the time at which they occurred. Many of the costs were actually incurred over an interval of time; in such cases the center of the interval is used as the date of the cost. The cost of the land is not included in the list of costs since land purchased was later resold. In the East Stockton renewal project, the land was purchased for $669,129 over a period roughly centered at June 30, 1960. After clearing and renewal, the land was subsequently sold for $1,200,000 over a period roughly centered at June 30,

[11] This application is based on James C. T. Mao, "Efficiency in Public Urban Renewal Expenditures through Benefit-Cost Analysis," *American Institute of Planners Journal,* vol. 32, March 1966, pp. 95–107. This application is a post facto evaluation; however, it shows how cost-benefit analysis can be applied in urban renewal.

Table 7-9 The benefits and costs of urban renewal

Benefits	Costs
1. Better allocation of resources	1. Survey and planning
a. Change in property value	2. Administrative
b. Value of public improvements installed	3. Demolition
c. Aesthetic and cultural value of planned community	4. Value of improvements demolished
2. Social implications of slum clearance	5. Cost of public improvements
a. Reduction in crime, disease, fires, and juvenile delinquency	6. Relocation
b. Improvement in housing welfare	
c. Disruptive influence of relocation	
d. Savings in the cost of municipal services	
3. Changes in local finances	

1965. Employing a discount rate of 6 percent, the selling price was discounted to June 30, 1960, yielding a present value of $896,760; hence the redevelopment agency had a "profit" of $227,631 on the project area land. This amount is included in the list of tangible benefits in Table 7-11.

Other tangible benefits were not quite so easily estimated. The increase in the property value in the project area was the result of three factors: inflation, growth in real income and population, and urban renewal. To isolate the increase due to urban renewal, a comparison was made between increases in the project area and increases near the project area. The comparison led to an estimate of $415,500 as the increase in the value of neighborhood properties.

Table 7-10 Costs of the East Stockton renewal project

Cost	Amount	Date	Present value @ 6%, 12/31/58
1. Survey and planning	$ 113,190	12/31/58	$ 113,190
2. Project execution expenditures			
a. Administrative, travel, and office furniture	201,535	6/30/61	174,328
b. Legal services	113,800	12/31/60	101,282
c. Acquisition expenses, salaries of relocation staff, and other related items	387,466	12/31/60	344,845
d. Site clearance	93,135	6/30/61	80,562
e. Disposal, lease, retention costs	59,228	6/30/64	43,000
f. Project inspection	32,731	12/31/62	25,923
g. Cost of improvements demolished	2,342,418	6/30/61	2,026,192
3. Site improvements	701,315	6/30/64	509,155
4. Public and supporting facilities	551,980	12/31/67	326,772
5. Relocation payments	84,715	6/30/61	73,278
			$3,818,527

Table 7-11 Benefits of the East Stockton renewal project

Benefit	Amount	Date	Present value @ 6%, 12/31/58
1. Increase in the value of project area land	$ 227,631	6/30/60	$ 208,509
2. Increase in the value of neighborhood properties	415,500	6/30/64	301,653
3. Value of public improvements, schools and parks	822,980	6/30/66	531,645
4. Reductions in costs of municipal services			
a. Savings in fire protection cost	700,000	1/01/64	522,900
b. Savings in health protection cost	425,000	1/01/64	317,475
c. Savings in police protection cost	1,167,000	1/01/64	871,749
			$2,753,931

Public improvements such as schools and parks were estimated at a value equal to their cost.

Urban renewal is generally expected to reduce the cost of municipal services. The savings in the cost of fire protection was estimated by noting that prior to urban renewal the per person expenditure for East Stockton was about $2\frac{1}{2}$ times what it was for the rest of the city. Assuming that after renewal the residents of East Stockton would require only average protection, the reduced cost of fire protection was estimated to be $42,000 annually. Capitalizing the annual amount of $42,000 at 6 percent yields $700,000 as the present value of all future fire protection cost savings. The savings in health protection and police protection costs were estimated similarly.

The difference between the present value of the tangible costs and the tangible benefits is $1,064,596. In order to make the project worthwhile from a cost-benefit perspective, the intangible benefits must be judged worth the $1,064,596 tangible deficit. Among the intangible benefits are the hoped-for reduction in rates of crime, fire, disease, and juvenile delinquency; the tangible aspect of these has been included in the savings in costs of municipal services. An improvement in the housing welfare of those who were relocated was a hoped-for benefit, but it could not be assumed. In the particular case of East Stockton, a survey indicated a significant reduction in overcrowding and a significant improvement in the quality of housing. Realizing that the former residents would be paying more for housing after relocation, a survey asked the relocatees whether they believed that they actually benefited from the relocation. Eighty-five percent of the former East Stockton residents replied affirmatively.

In concluding this brief application of cost-benefit analysis to urban renewal, it is noted that no judgment is made concerning whether urban renewal should be undertaken; rather, the thrust has been to identify and subject to analysis those elements that are comparable, so that the planners and decision makers can better concentrate on those which seem immeasurable or incomparable. The effect of using a different discount rate is left for the reader to determine in exercise 7-1.

SUMMARY

The thrust of cost-benefit analysis, an extension of decision theory, is to assess the costs and benefits of the alternatives so that the decision situation can be better understood.

Although there are some differences between cost-benefit and cost-effectiveness analysis, their basic principles and actual applications make any distinction a fuzzy one. The cost-benefit process, involving objectives, alternatives, benefits and costs, a model and a criterion, closely parallels the classically formulated decision-making process.

Initial and recurring costs are ultimately compared with the positive and negative, tangible and intangible benefits for each feasible alternative. Present value analysis accounts for the time value of both costs and benefits.

Market goods are valued according to their market price. Public goods cannot be provided to some and be withheld from others; consequently, since a market price for them is not available, their value remains intangible, though not any less real.

The main ideas have been further presented through three major illustrations. One illustration focused on the details of present value analysis and probabilistic uncertainty, a second on one approach to the economic value of life in a disease-detection setting, and a third focused on identifying costs and benefits in the context of an urban renewal application.

BIBLIOGRAPHY

Barish, Norman N.: *Economic Analysis for Engineering and Managerial Decision Making,* McGraw-Hill Book Company, New York, 1962.

Barsly, S. L.: *Cost-Benefit Analysis and Manpower Programs,* D. C. Heath & Company, Lexington, Mass., 1972.

Baumol, William J.: "On the Social Rate of Discount," *American Economic Review,* vol. 58, September 1968, pp. 788–802.

Besen, S. M., A. E. Fechter, and A. C. Fisher: "Cost-Effectiveness for the 'War on Poverty,'" in T. A. Goldman (ed.), *Cost Effectiveness Analysis,* Frederick A. Praeger, Inc., New York, 1967, pp. 140–154.

Cretin, Shan: "Cost-Benefit Analysis of Treatment and Prevention of Myocardial Infarction," *Health Services Research,* vol. 12, 1977, pp. 174–190.

Feldstein, M. S.: "The Social Time Preference Discount Rate in Cost Benefit Analysis," *Economic Journal,* vol. 74, June 1964, pp. 360–379.

Goldman, T. A. (ed.): *Cost-Effectiveness Analysis,* Frederick A. Praeger, Inc., New York, 1967.

Gorry, G. Anthony, and David W. Scott: "Cost-effectiveness of Cardiopulmonary Resuscitation Training Programs," *Health Services Research,* vol. 12, Spring 1977, pp. 30–41.

Hannon, Timothy H.: "The Benefits and Costs of Methadone Maintenance," *Public Policy,* vol. 24, Spring 1976, pp. 197–226.

Hinrichs, Harley H., and Graeme M. Taylor (eds.): *Program Budgeting and Benefit-Cost Analysis,* Goodyear Publishing Co., Inc., Santa Monica, Calif., 1969.

Layard, Richard (ed.): *Cost-Benefit Analysis,* Penguin Books, New York, 1972.

Lichfield, N.: "Cost-Benefit Analysis in City Planning," *American Institute of Planners Journal,* vol. 26, November 1960, pp. 273–279.

Mao, James C. T.: "Efficiency in Public Urban Renewal Expenditures through Benefit-Cost Analysis," *American Institute of Planners Journal,* vol. 32, March 1966, pp. 95–107.

McClain, John O., and Vithala R. Rao: "Trade-offs and Conflicts in Evaluation of Health System Alternatives: Methodology for Analysis," *Health Services Research,* vol. 9, Spring 1974, pp. 35–52.

Mishan, E. J.: *Cost-Benefit Analysis,* Praeger Publishers, Inc., New York, 1971.

Mishan, E. J.: *Welfare Economics: An Assessment,* North Holland Publishing Company, Amsterdam, 1969.

Poister, Theodore H.: *Public Program Analysis: Applied Research Methods,* University Park Press, Baltimore, Md., 1978.

Prest, A. R., and R. Turvey: "Cost-Benefit Analysis: A Survey," *Economic Journal,* December 1975, pp. 683–735.

Schweitzer, Stuart: "Cost Effectiveness of Early Detection of Disease," *Health Services Research,* vol. 9, Spring 1974, pp. 22–32.

Smith, Warren F., "Cost Effectiveness and Cost-Benefit Analysis for Public Health Programs," *Public Health Reports,* vol. 83, November 1968, pp. 899–906.

EXERCISES

Extension of chapter examples

7-1 Reevaluate the present value, as of December 31, 1958, of the tangible benefits and costs of the East Stockton renewal project using discount rates of 4 and 8 percent. For each of these rates, what must the net worth of intangible benefits be? Discuss whether the East Stockton renewal project should or should not be implemented, with particular reference to the appropriate rate of discounting and the worth of intangible benefits. Note that the new rate applies to capitalizing the savings in municipal services and to calculating the increase in the value of project area land, as well as to the values of Tables 7-10 and 7-11.

7-2 Refer to Tables 7-7 and 7-8 for the cancer screening test.

(*a*) How is the critical value of life affected if the morbidity rate is 100/100,000?

(*b*) If the morbidity rate is 10/100,000?

7-3 Refer to Table 7-8. Suppose it is known that segments of the population actually have different morbidity rates as follows:

Population segment	Population proportions	Morbidity rate
A	.20	.0010
B	.55	.0005
C	.25	.0001

A publicly financed state agency has the capability of providing free screenings for half the population.

(*a*) Suppose the state establishes priority classes for the tests on the basis of cost-effectiveness? What should they be?

(*b*) What are some likely citizen reactions?

(*c*) Can the priorities be defended?

Other applications

7-4 A municipality wishes to build a city hall and a police station on the same site. City council asks you to evaluate two plans for construction. The first plan calls for the building of the city hall now and the builidng of the police station at the end of 8 years. Each structure will cost $500,000. The second plan involves construction of one building now, at a cost of $700,000, to serve both purposes. Both plans are considered to be equally effective after the eighth year. The buildings are assumed to have a usable life of 50 years from the present day. Maintenance costs are estimated to be $6000 per year for the first 8 years and $40,000 per year after that for the first plan; for the second plan they are estimated at $60,000 per year for the period. Determine which is the preferred alternative, first based on a 4 percent discount rate and then based on an 8 percent discount rate. What assumptions must be made in order for either plan to be feasible?

7-5 Argo Township is considering repaving a stretch of roadway with a new material. The new pavement has no maintenance costs for 5 years, $200 per year for the next 10 years, and $800 per year for the next 10 years. The current roadway has annual maintenance costs of $800.

(*a*) What expenditure for the new pavement is justified? Assume a 6 percent discount rate.

(*b*) How sensitive is the decision to the assumed discount rate?

(*c*) Which alternative would you recommend? Why?

7-6 Refer to problem 7-5. Suppose the new pavement will cost $5300 initially; its benefits are the cost savings over the present roadway. Calculate its internal rate of return.

7-7 Cost-benefit analysis has used the past 6 years' experience of a methadone maintenance treatment program (MMTP) to see if it is worth continuing for the next 6 years. Here decision makers are considering the basic two alternatives, to continue the program or not. Although the effects of the program are expected to last longer than the 6-year length of the program, only the benefits during these years are considered. All projections are based on the assumption that future experience will follow the patterns of the past.

The actual expenditures of the program include salaries for physicians, counselors, nurses, and administrators, and rent, supplies, and the cost of the methadone. The analysis includes a dropout rate; if a patient drops out there are no further costs or benefits for that patient. The total costs for the 6 years are summarized in the following table:

Costs of the MMTP

Year	Number of patients	Cost	Present value @ 10%, 1978
1978	1200	$2,220,000	$2,220,000
1979	1093	1,639,500	1,490,305
1980	983	1,474,500	1,217,937
1981	866	1,299,000	975,549
1982	814	1,221,000	833,943
1983	782	1,173,000	728,433
		Total	$7,466,167

In methadone treatment as in most social programs there are both tangible and intangible benefits. Here the intangibles are not included in the calculations; however, the decision maker must be aware of them when interpreting the results of the analysis. The benefits of MMTP include decreases in private protection expenditures, the costs of injury to crime victims, the negative value placed on fear of attack by an addict, criminal justice expenditures, expenditures on heroin by the addict, and expenditures for narcotic-related illnesses; and increases in legal earnings. The last three are tangible benefits and are summarized in the following table.

Benefits of the MMTP

	Increased earnings		Criminal justice savings		Reduced heroin consumption	
Year	Estimated	Present value*	Estimated	Present value*	Estimated	Present value*
1978	$ 414,000	$ 414,000	$1,367,000	$1,367,000	$6,716,000	$ 6,716,000
1979	1,445,000	1,313,505	1,381,000	1,255,329	6,000,000	5,454,000
1980	1,692,000	1,397,592	1,293,000	1,068,018	5,346,000	4,415,796
1981	1,923,000	1,444,173	1,201,000	901,951	4,870,000	3,657,370
1982	2,005,000	1,369,415	1,138,000	777,254	4,618,000	3,154,094
1983	1,934,000	1,201,014	1,094,000	679,374	4,433,000	2,752,893
Subtotals		$7,139,699		$6,048,926		$26,150,153
Grand total						$39,338,778

* Discount rate = 10%.

In this particular MMTP the maximum number of patients that can be served is 1200. The analysis is based on the original 1200, and not those joining at a later date as some of the original patients drop out.

(*a*) Determine the net present value of the MMTP.
(*b*) Determine its cost-benefit ratio.
(*c*) Is its internal rate of return less than, equal to, or greater than 10 percent?
(*d*) Comment briefly on the credibility of the estimated benefit values.

Project problems

7-8 Problem 7-7 is based on Timothy H. Hannon, "The Benefits and Costs of Methadone Maintenance," *Public Policy*, vol. 24, Spring 1976, pp. 197–226. Refer to the article.
(*a*) What are the stated objectives of MMTP?
(*b*) What are some of its legal constraints?
(*c*) How do the tangible benefit measures reflect the program's objectives?
(*d*) How are negative effects handled in the analysis?

7-9 Read a published cost-benefit analysis in your own particular field of interest.
(*a*) Identify the stated and implied objectives, assumptions, and constraints.
(*b*) Are intangible benefits (positive and negative) adequately treated?
(*c*) Does the quantitative summary (if there is one) fairly represent the decision problem?

7-10 Identify a state or local program or project.
(*a*) Identify its objectives, assumptions, and constraints, stated and implied.
(*b*) Has a cost-benefit analysis been developed for the undertaking?
(*c*) If the answer to part *b* was "yes," review it critically. If "no," develop one based on available information.

CHAPTER

EIGHT

INTRODUCTION TO LINEAR PROGRAMMING: FORMULATION AND GRAPHIC SOLUTION

The difficulties that people encounter often provide them with the opportunity to reestablish a wholesome relationship with their environment. A fuel crisis or an extremely cold winter, or both together, encourage us to reconsider our use of energy sources. In such a situation, it would not seem unrealistic or unreasonable for a municipality, an energy commission, or a power company to determine the level of wasted energy. The municipality, commission, or company will use its resources, in this case mostly manpower, to gather information about energy wasted in homes and commercial plants. The manpower available is most assuredly not unbounded, any more than the fuel itself. Within the bounds of available manpower, the municipality, commission, or company would want to gather as much information as possible. This problem typifies the setting for which linear programming may be appropriate.

THE LINEAR PROGRAMMING MODEL

Before examining the characteristics of the model, and its underlying assumptions, we will consider how it relates to the multiple-objective situation. After noting the assumptions of a linear programming model, we will relate it to our decision-making paradigm. Next we will focus on the formulation of a model, present the graphic solution to a few models, and then consider applications to a policy analysis of a national health insurance program and a school busing problem.

Multiple Objectives and Linear Programming

We have seen two approaches to multiple-objective decision making (Chapter 6). In one, preferences were traded off so that alternatives could be compared; in the other, objectives were assigned relative utilities, and alternatives were rated for their efficacy in achieving the objectives. Two other approaches are appropriate for certain kinds of problems.

The first of these approaches considers all but one of the objectives as "musts" rather than "shoulds," or as requirements rather than aims. The single remaining objective is treated as the only entity to be optimized. If certain quantitative conditions are also satisfied, this problem is suitably addressed by linear programming. This chapter introduces the linear programming model, the formulation procedure, and a graphic method of solving simple problems; Chapter 9 presents sensitivity analysis in linear programming; and Chapter 10 presents a computational procedure for solving the model.

The second approach considers none, one, or some of the objectives as constraints. The remaining objectives (more than one) are prioritized and sought after according to their priority level. If the same certain quantitative conditions are satisfied, then goal programming would be a suitable approach. Chapter 11 discusses the goal programming model and some applications.

Underlying Assumptions

Linear programming is a technique that provides the decision maker with a way of optimizing his objective within resource requirements and other constraints provided that the following basic assumptions apply:

1. The objective can be represented by a linear function.
2. Each constraint can be represented by a linear inequality.
3. Each variable is nonnegative (either positive or zero).

As the term implies, the graph of a linear inequality or equation is related to a straight line. The following are examples of linear functions:

$$Z = 2X + 3Y - 2Z$$

$$N = 4A - B + .5C - 6D$$

$$W = 2X_1 + 8X_2 - \tfrac{1}{2}X_3 + 1.7X_4$$

The following are not linear functions:

$$Z = X^2 + 2Y$$

$$M = 4A - 3B + \sqrt{D}$$

$$C = 3X - XY + Z$$

$$D = 2X_1 - \frac{6X_2}{X_3}$$

A linear inequality has a linear expression that is related to a constant by either "≤" (less than or equal to), "≥" (greater than or equal to), or "=." The following are linear inequalities:

$$3X + 2Y - Z \leq 8$$

$$4A - 3B + .5C - D = 14$$

$$X_1 - 2X_2 + 6X_3 \geq 0$$

$$X_1 \geq 0$$

The last inequality above is a nonnegativity constraint, requiring X_1 to be zero or positive. Most variables of decision-making interest are nonnegative; so this assumption poses no problem.

These basic assumptions have implications that we will consider a bit later.

An example of the basic form of a linear program is as follows:

Maximize (or minimize) the objective function

$$Z = 2w + 3x + 4y$$

subject to the constraints

$$\begin{aligned} 3w + 2x - y &\leq 20 \\ w + 3x + 5y &\geq 40 \\ w + x + y &= 18 \\ w &\geq 0 \\ x &\geq 0 \\ y &\geq 0 \end{aligned}$$

Linear Programming and Decision Making

The basic concept of linear programming is characterized by the decision maker who is attempting to accomplish something; he has limited resources with which to accomplish it. His immediate concern becomes using wisely the resources that are available, so that he can attain as much as possible of his objective. Aside from limited resources, there may be legal regulations, organizational restrictions, and accepted standards that in some way constrain the decision maker.

Regardless of the complexity of the model or the number of constraints, the essential steps in using linear programming stay the same: Formulate the problem as a linear program if appropriate, seek a solution, and interpret the solution in terms of the original problem statement. Insofar as linear programming yields a solution to the problem as formulated, it is classified as a prescriptive model. Alternatives do not have to be found outside the model itself; the

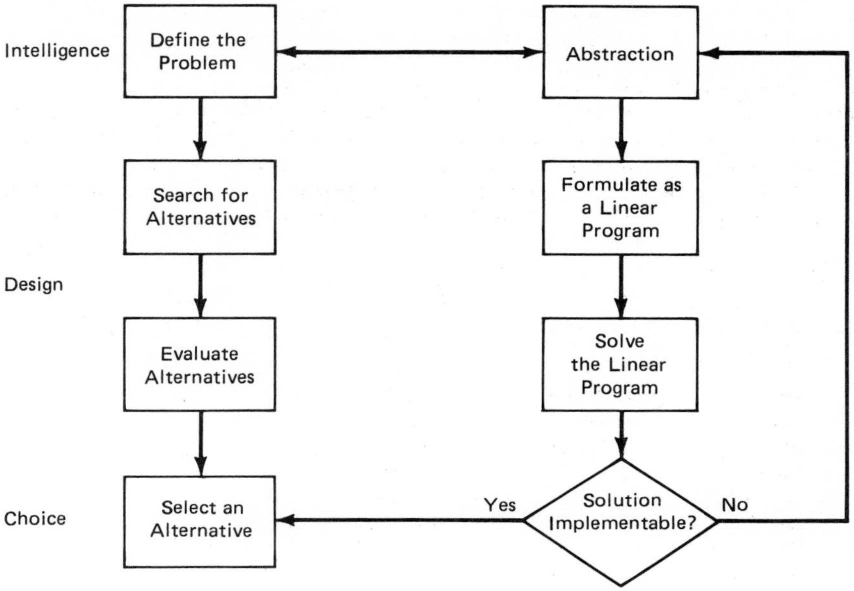

Figure 8-1 Linear programming and the decision-making process.

model generates allowable alternatives and identifies the best one relative to the formulated objective. Figure 8-1 depicts the role of a linear programming model in the decision-making process. We will explain these steps in using linear programming, first in simple examples and later in more complex and more realistic ones. Simple linear programs can be solved graphically; others require more sophisticated methods.

FORMULATION OF A LINEAR PROGRAM

Before becoming concerned with the solution to a linear program, it is useful to identify the salient ingredients of a linear program and to learn how to translate a problem situation into a linear program. Thus identifying and translating, we will also be better prepared to identify which problems are appropriately analyzed by this technique. A detailed illustration will serve as the vehicle for formulation and solution.

Assume that the Public Power Commission is undertaking a sample survey to estimate the extent of power loss in homes and industrial plants within its jurisdiction. Rather than being able to choose freely the number of homes and plants to inspect, the project has been assigned one person from each of the three relevant inspection categories for the duration of the project. These three people will inspect the insulation, the electrical wiring and circuitry, and the heating apparatus of the sampled homes and plants. In order for the information to be useful, a complete inspection must include all three types. The commission will try to have as many complete inspections as possible, either of homes or of plants.

The insulation inspector estimates that it will take 4 hours to fully inspect a home and only 2 hours to inspect a plant. She claims that insulation is usually more accessible in a plant than in a home. The electrical inspector estimates that it will take 2 hours to inspect a home and 6 hours to inspect a plant. The heating inspector estimates it will take 4 hours to inspect a home and 6 hours to inspect a plant. As might be expected, the more complex electrical and heating systems characteristic of industrial plants require more time to inspect them than the home systems. Not including the reports that must be completed and filed, it is estimated that the insulation inspector has 28 hours per week available for actual inspections; the electrical inspector has 30 hours per week available; and the heating inspector has 36 hours per week available. How should the commission assign the inspectors in order to complete as many inspections as possible?

The Objective Function

The commission realizes that although it wants to complete as many inspections as possible, it is restricted by the amount of time available to each inspector each week. It therefore attempts to assign the inspectors in such a way as to make the number of inspections per week as high as possible. In other words, it hopes to maximize the quantity

$$\text{homes} + \text{plants}$$

inspected each week. To simplify any further quantities or expressions, let

$$x_1 = \text{number of homes inspected each week}$$

$$x_2 = \text{number of plants inspected each week}$$

Then the objective is to maximize

$$N = x_1 + x_2$$

This expression is referred to as the *objective function* of the linear program. Here the aim is to maximize the objective function. If the objective function represented an expression of cost, then the objective would be to minimize it. The general term *optimize* applies to either maximize or minimize.

The Constraints

The constraints of the problem are represented by expressions not unlike the one that represents the objective function. The insulation inspection of a home requires 4 hours, and the number of homes inspected is x_1; so the number of hours spent inspecting homes is $4x_1$. Similarly, the insulation inspection of a plant requires 2 hours, and the number of plants inspected is x_2; so the number of hours spent inspecting plants is $2x_2$. The total number of hours the insulation specialist spends inspecting homes and plants is, therefore,

$$4x_1 + 2x_2$$

Since the insulation inspector has only 28 hours available, the number of hours she spends must be less than or equal to 28, that is,

$$4x_1 + 2x_2 \leq 28$$

Likewise, the electrical inspection of a home requires 2 hours, a plant requires 6 hours, and the electrical inspector has only 30 hours available; so

$$2x_1 + 6x_2 \leq 30$$

Finally, the heating inspection of a home requires 4 hours, a plant requires 6 hours, and the heating inspector has only 36 hours available; so

$$4x_1 + 6x_2 \leq 36$$

All of the constraints and the objective function satisfy the linearity assumptions.

Since it makes sense to consider assigning an inspector to inspect 2 homes or 5 homes or no homes, or 2 plants or 6 plants or no plants, but not to inspect -2 homes or -3 plants, the nonnegativity assumptions are applicable. Thus

$$x_1 \geq 0 \qquad \text{and} \qquad x_2 \geq 0$$

The full problem statement has now been translated into algebraic expressions; that is, we have formulated the linear program. In its complete form the linear program appears as:

Maximize the objective function

$$N = x_1 + x_2$$

subject to the constraints

$$4x_1 + 2x_2 \leq 28$$

$$2x_1 + 6x_2 \leq 30$$

$$4x_1 + 6x_2 \leq 36$$

$$x_1, x_2 \geq 0$$

A problem statement that is much more involved will yield a linear program that is considerably longer, with perhaps different kinds of constraints. The process of formulating the linear program would be essentially the same, however. After developing a solution to the present example, we shall examine other more involved problem statements and their associated linear programs.

GRAPHIC SOLUTION

A simple example such as ours can be solved graphically. The more complex problems could not even be represented graphically, much less solved graphically. Fortunately, there are techniques that can be applied quite directly to the larger problems. The graphic solution will hopefully provide an intuitive grasp that will be helpful in understanding if not solving the larger linear programs.

The basic approach of the graphic method of solution includes identifying solutions that are allowable or that are within the bounds of the constraints, and then choosing from among them the particular solution that provides the best value for the objective function. The specific steps of the method are:

1. Graph each constraint.
2. Identify the feasible region.
3. Graph the objective function for at least one value of N.
4. Consider lines parallel to the graphed objective function to find the one with the optimum feasible solution.

Graphs of the Constraints

The graph of each constraint is considered separately; then the graph of all the constraints taken together will be determined.

Recall that meaningful solutions require that

$$x_1 \geq 0 \qquad \text{and} \qquad x_2 \geq 0$$

These constraints are depicted in Figure 8-2. Each point in the graphed region

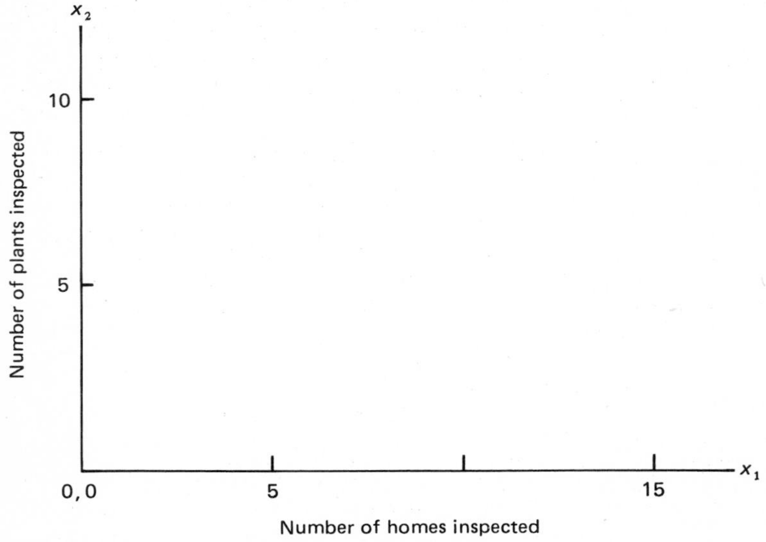

Figure 8-2 Region satisfying $x_1 \geq 0$ and $x_2 \geq 0$.

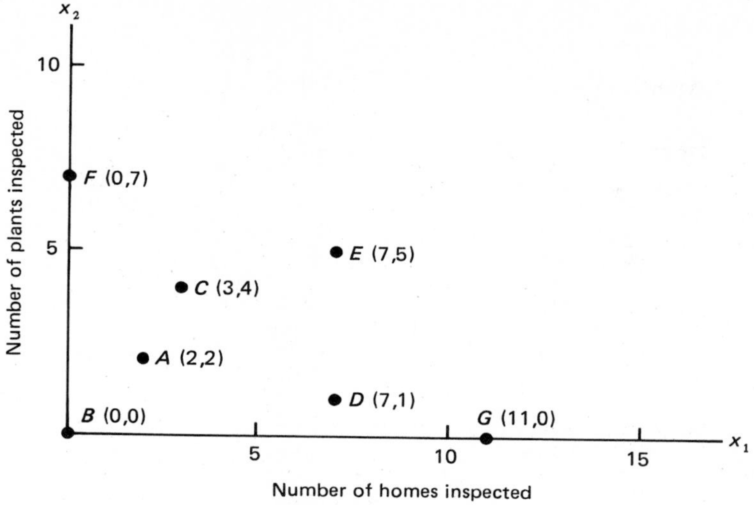

Figure 8-3 Points representing numbers of homes and plants inspected.

represents a particular number of homes inspected and a particular number of plants inspected.

Some examples of points and the numbers they represent are provided in Figure 8-3. The numbers represented by the points are usually referred to as *coordinates,* the horizontal and vertical distances of the point from the origin, the (0, 0) point.

By inserting the coordinates of the points in the three constraints, one can see that points *A*, *B*, and *C* satisfy all three constraints. This means that assigning each inspector to inspect (*A*) 2 homes and 2 plants, or (*B*) 0 homes and 0 plants, or (*C*) 3 homes and 4 plants would be within the time restrictions of each inspector. Such alternatives are said to be *feasible;* they satisfy all the constraints. On the other hand, point *D* is not feasible because 7 homes and 1 plant require 30 hours for the insulation inspection, more than the 28 hours available. Likewise point *E* is not feasible, since 7 homes and 5 plants require more time than any inspector has available; point *F* is not feasible since 0 homes and 7 plants require more time than is available for electrical and heating inspections; and point *G* is not feasible since 11 homes and 0 plants require more time than is available to the insulation and heating inspectors. Thus some of the points in the graphed region represent allowable alternatives and some do not.

The restriction on time available to the insulation inspector is given by the constraint

$$4x_1 + 2x_2 \leq 28$$

In order to represent this constraint on the graph, we will first find the graph of the related equation

$$4x_1 + 2x_2 = 28$$

An easy way to graph an equation in this form is to find the points at which the line will cross the x_1 axis and the x_2 axis. Such points are referred to as the x_1 *intercept* and the x_2 *intercept*. We know that the value of x_2 on the x_1 axis is always 0 (for example, point G in Figure 8-3). To find the x_1 intercept for an equation, simply determine the value of x_1 when $x_2 = 0$.

In $4x_1 + 2x_2 = 28$ if $x_2 = 0$, then $x_1 = 7$, and the x_1 intercept is 7. Similarly, if $x_1 = 0$, then $x_2 = 14$, and the x_2 intercept is 14. The two intercepts (or any two points, for that matter) completely determine the line. Figure 8-4 presents the line. Note that it is not being suggested that either intercept represents a feasible solution; the intercepts were found only to find the graph of the linear equation.

The constraint in the linear program is not the linear equation but rather the linear inequality

$$4x_1 + 2x_2 \leq 28$$

The graph of the linear equation was found as an aid to finding the graph of the inequality. In fact the graph of the inequality includes the line and the region below it. As you might have already inferred, if the constraint had a "$\geq$" instead of the "$\leq$," then the region above rather than below the line would be included in the graph. Figure 8-5 presents the graph of the constraint as it appears in the linear program.

The other constraints are handled in the same manner. In order to graph the constraint

$$2x_1 + 6x_2 \leq 30$$

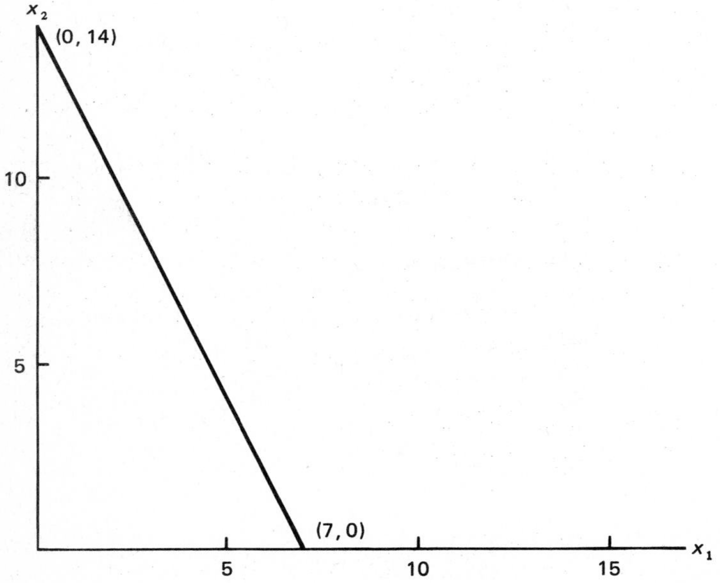

Figure 8-4 The graph of the linear equation $4x_1 + 2x_2 = 28$.

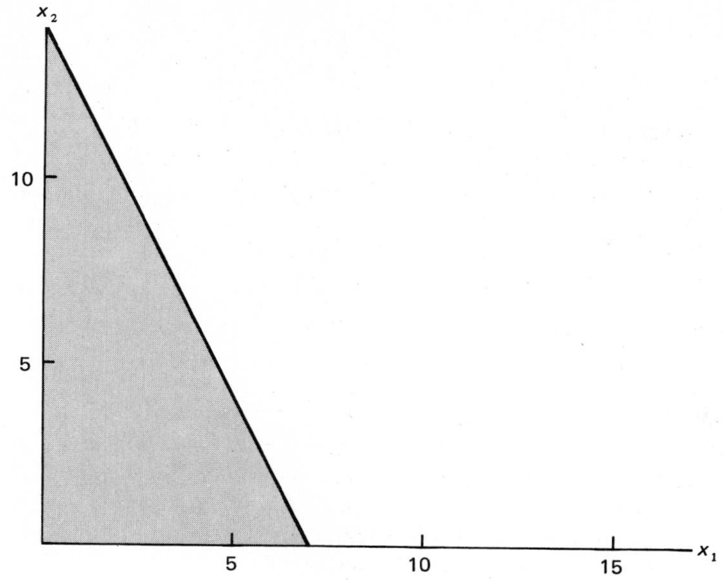

Figure 8-5 The graph of the constraint $4x_1 + 2x_2 \leq 28$.

first graph the equation

$$2x_1 + 6x_2 = 30$$

In this equation the x_1 intercept is 15 and the x_2 intercept is 5. The line and the region below it form the graph of the inequality constraint as in Figure 8-6.

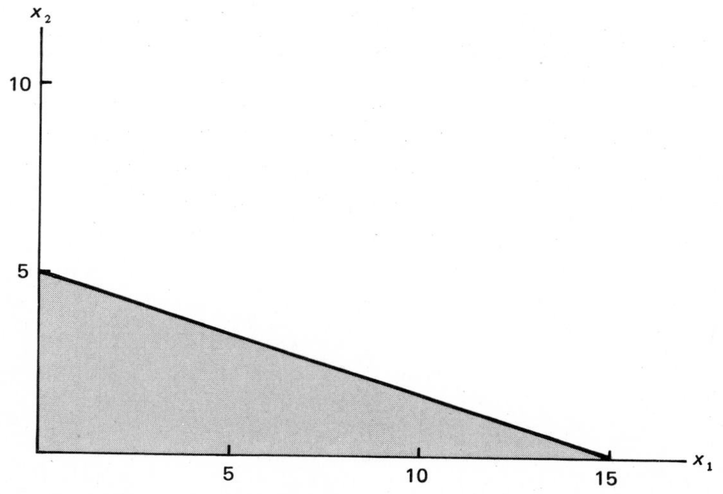

Figure 8-6 The graph of the constraint $2x_1 + 6x_2 \leq 30$.

Finally to graph the constraint

$$4x_1 + 6x_2 \leq 36$$

first graph the equation

$$4x_1 + 6x_2 = 36$$

In this equation the x_1 intercept is 9 and the x_2 intercept is 6. The line and the region below it form the graph of the inequality constraint as presented in Figure 8-7.

The Feasible Region

The graphs of the three constraints have been presented separately. Recall, however, that the number of homes and plants to be inspected must satisfy all three constraints. The region that satisfies all three constraints is that portion of the graph that is on or below all three lines. That region is presented in Figure 8-8. The region that satisfies all the constraints is called the *feasible region.*

Any point in the feasible region will satisfy all the constraints; each point represents a feasible alternative for the number of homes and plants to inspect. For example, 1 home and 4 plants, 5 homes and 2 plants, 4 homes and 3 plants, and 0 home and 5 plants all satisfy the three constraints. The Public Power Commission must choose the combination of homes and plants within the feasible region that yields the maximum number of complete inspections. That is, the objective function must now be considered in light of the constraints.

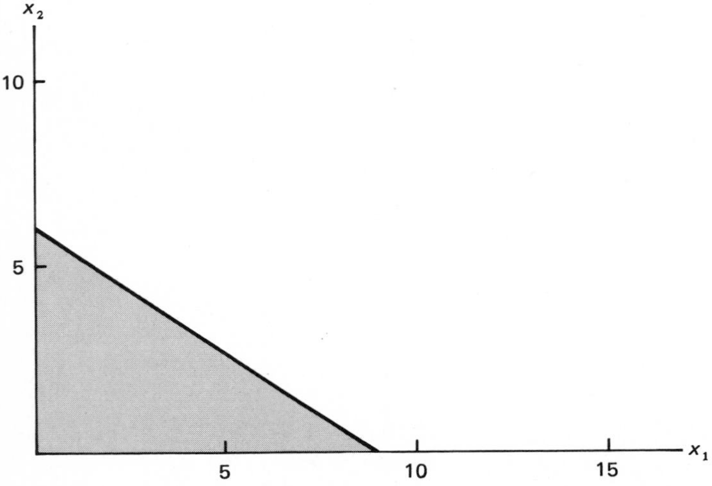

Figure 8-7 The graph of the constraint $4x_1 + 6x_2 \leq 36$.

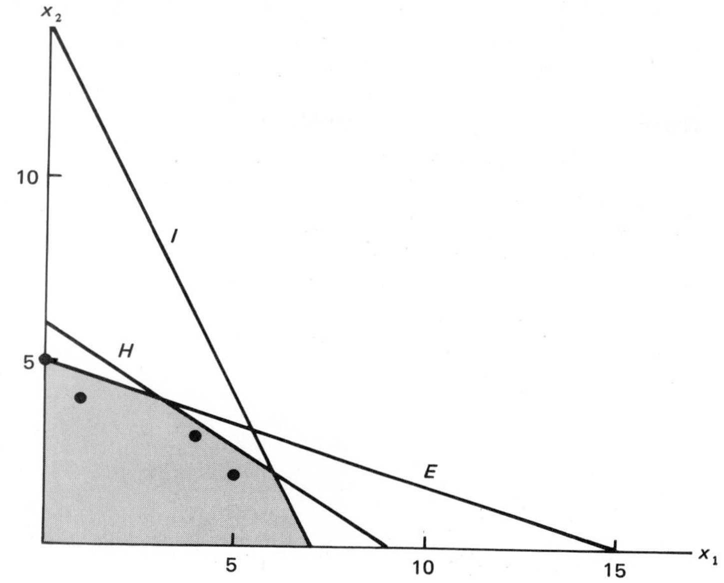

Figure 8-8 The graph of the feasible region satisfying $4x_1 + 2x_2 \leq 28$; $2x_1 + 6x_2 \leq 30$; $4x_1 + 6x_2 \leq 36$.

Graph of the Objective Function

The objective function

$$N = x_1 + x_2$$

has a different graph for each possible value of N. If $N = 8$, the objective function becomes

$$8 = x_1 + x_2$$

The graph of that equation can be found by finding the x_1 and x_2 intercepts; for this equation the x_1 intercept $= 8$ and the x_2 intercept $= 8$. Figure 8-9 presents the graphs of the objective function for various values of N, namely, $N = 2$, 3, 5, 8, and 12. Such a set of parallel lines is called a *family*.

Note that any point on the graph of

$$8 = x_1 + x_2$$

represents a number of homes and plants that together equal 8. For example, the point (5, 3) is on the line, and $5 + 3 = 8$. Similarly, any point on the graph of $5 = x_1 + x_2$ represents a number of homes and plants that together equal 5. By noting these points in Figure 8-8, one can see that the point (5, 3) is outside the feasible region; it corresponds to a number of homes and plants that is not allowable. The point (3, 2) is within the feasible region; it corresponds to a number of homes and plants that is allowable. The alternative (3, 2) is not the

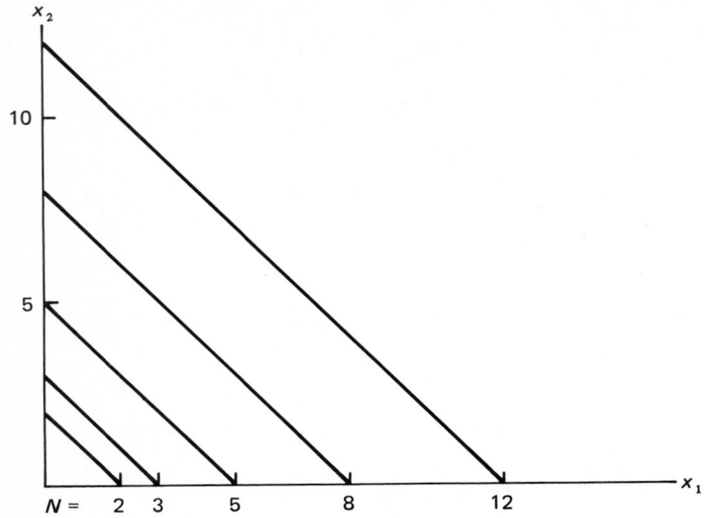

Figure 8-9 The objective function $N = x_1 + x_2$, for $N = 2, 3, 5, 8$, and 12.

solution that gives the maximum number of inspections, however, as there are feasible points beyond the line $5 = x_1 + x_2$.

The Optimum Feasible Solution

To find the *maximum* solution, we consider lines parallel to $5 = x_1 + x_2$ until we reach the *highest* line with a point in the feasible region. Figure 8-10 presents such a line. This line has only one point in the feasible region, namely, (6, 2). Any point beyond $8 = x_1 + x_2$ is outside the feasible region and therefore does not represent a feasible solution. Any point below $8 = x_1 + x_2$ yields fewer inspections. Hence the optimum solution is (6, 2), corresponding to 6 homes and 2 plants, or a total of 8 inspections per week.

It can be shown mathematically that the optimum solution to a linear programming problem always occurs at an extreme point, that is, a corner point. If it should happen that the optimum solution occurs at two extreme points, then every point on the line segment between those two points is also a solution. This means that an alternate method of finding the optimum solution is to graph the feasible region (by graphing all the constraints), identify the feasible points of intersection of the constraints (the extreme points of the feasible region), and evaluate the objective function for each extreme point. The point that yields the highest value in the objective function is the optimum solution. It should be emphasized that the graphic method of solution is appropriate only when there are only two variables in the linear program. Most real problems have more than two variables; so the graphic method is not used in practice. Our main purpose in using it here is to develop an intuitive understanding of a linear program,

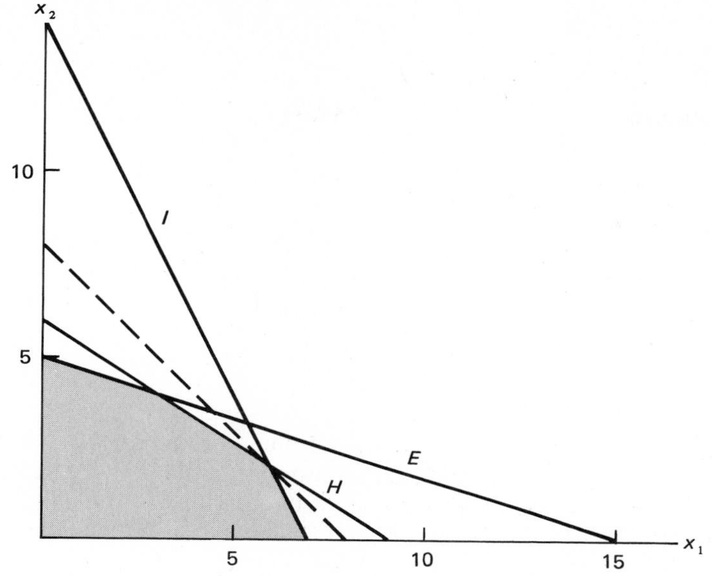

Figure 8-10 Finding the optimum solution to the energy inspection problem.

specifically of the relationships between the constraints of a problem, the ensuing feasible region, and the objective function. The basic relationships remain valid for linear programs of any size.

INTERPRETATION

In general, the solution provided by the linear programming model must be interpreted in terms of the original problem, not just with reference to the abstracted version. Conditions that were not quantifiable in the first place are necessarily omitted from the analysis. A qualitative analysis may indicate that the apparent optimum solution is not feasible for political or organizational reasons. Reconsideration of the solution in light of the whole situation may prompt a restatement of the problem that will alter the objective function and/or some constraints.

The reaction to the optimum solution in the wasted-power problem might be something like this: "Since industrial plants use more energy than homes, information about plants is more valuable. Surely plants should comprise more than 25 percent of the inspections." Consequently, the objective function should be altered to reflect this belief, which had not crystallized when the problem was originally stated. Such alterations are analyzed through a reformulation and new solution, or through sensitivity analysis of the old solution.

All linear programming models have certain common characteristics that are implications of the underlying assumptions, and that indicate limitations on the use of the model.

IMPLICATIONS AND LIMITATIONS

The basic assumptions of linear programming are:

1. The objective function is linear.
2. The constraints are linear.
3. The variables are nonnegative.

There are implications of these assumptions, which limit its use.

1. The model is *deterministic:* Each coefficient is assumed to be known with certainty. In practice, the coefficients are often estimated. Sensitivity analysis can be used to assess the consequences of fluctuations in the coefficients. If the coefficients are really random variables, however, then stochastic programming, a more advanced technique, should be used.
2. The model is *proportional:* The objective function and constraints change in proportion to each variable. For example, doubling the number of homes inspected x_1 doubles the time it takes each inspector to inspect them. In some situations, more or less of a resource may be used for higher levels of activity. For instance, each hour of a worker's time beyond a certain level may consume more dollars (time-and-a-half) than the basic amount. When proportionality holds over specific ranges of values, piecewise linear programming can be used; in other cases of nonproportionality, nonlinear programming may be needed.
3. The model is *additive:* The contribution of the various components are added to get the contribution of all of them together. A public health education program tries to reach as many people as possible through public relations–type television spot announcements (x_1 = how many) and through the distribution of informational brochures (x_2 = how many). It has found that each brochure is more effective if the recipient has seen the television message. The average effectiveness of a brochure depends on how many television spots there have been. Hence, in the objective function, the coefficient of x_2 would contain x_1, and the resulting term would not be linear. Linear programming could not be used for such a problem; nonlinear programming would be applicable.
4. The model is *divisible:* Fractional values for the variables are permissible. Some problems may require integer solutions. In such cases integer programming is the recommended approach, unless the linear program solution just happens to be in integers. An alternative is to round off the linear program solution to the nearest integer solution. Extreme caution must be exercised in rounding off because the result has three possibilities:

a. The rounded solution is the best integer solution.
b. The rounded solution is feasible but not the best.
c. The rounded solution is not even a feasible alternative.

Stochastic, nonlinear, and integer programming are more advanced techniques and are beyond the scope of this book. We will reinforce the basic ideas of linear programming with the graphic solution of another problem and in so doing introduce a minimization problem.

A MINIMIZATION PROBLEM

The County of Hillandale operates a small game park for the benefit of its residents, and to attract tourists during the summer. Among its many inhabitants is a pride of rare minilions. The County Recreation Board, and especially the curator of the game park, want to be sure that the animals' basic nutritional requirements are satisfied, but at the same time they do not want to spend more for their food than is necessary. Their necessary vitamins are provided in a supplement. Their daily diet must provide at least 500 units of protein and 960 units of mineral fiber. To keep the minilions from feeling hungry—and hence unhappy—they must be given at least 6 kilograms of food daily. There are also certain ceilings on the amounts of protein, mineral fiber, and total food provided, but we will assume that the objective of minimizing the total cost of feeding the minilions will keep the diet within the maximum allowable levels. The foods that they will be given are prime meat and ground bone meal. A kilogram of the bone meal provides 50 units of protein and 240 units of mineral fiber, and costs \$1 per kilogram. A kilogram of prime meat provides 250 units of protein and 80 units of mineral fiber, and costs \$2 per kilogram. The combined weight of the bone meal and the meat must be at least 6 kilograms. How many kilograms of each food type should be included in the diet of the minilions?

It is sometimes helpful to summarize the salient features of the problem statement prior to formulating the linear program. The content and cost of a kilogram of each food type is presented in Table 8-1.

Each of the minimum requirements generates a constraint. Each kilogram of bone meal provides 50 units of protein; so x_1 kilograms provides $50x_1$ units of protein. Similarly, each kilogram of meat provides 250 units of protein; so x_2 kilograms of meat provides $250x_2$ units of protein. Therefore the total amount of protein provided is $50x_1 + 250x_2$. Since this total must be at least 500, the protein constraint is

$$50x_1 + 250x_2 \geq 500$$

In a similar way the mineral fiber constraint is found to be

$$240x_1 + 80x_2 \geq 960$$

Table 8-1 Contents and cost of food types in minilion diet problem

	Food type		
	Bone meal	Meat	Minimum requirement
Protein units per kg	50	250	500 units
Mineral fiber units per kg	240	80	960 units
Weight, kg	1	1	6 kg
Cost per kg	1	2	dollars

and the weight constraint is

$$x_1 + x_2 \geq 6$$

The cost of providing the x_1 kilograms of bone meal is $1x_1$, and the cost of providing the x_2 kilograms of meat is $2x_2$; so the total cost in dollars of providing the daily diet is

$$x_1 + 2x_2$$

The cost is the quantity that the County Recreation Board wishes to minimize. The complete linear program is as follows:

Minimize $$C = x_1 + 2x_2$$

subject to
$$50x_1 + 250x_2 \geq 500$$
$$240x_1 + 80x_2 \geq 960$$
$$x_1 + x_2 \geq 6$$
$$x_1, x_2 \geq 0$$

The last constraints are the nonnegative constraints; it is senseless to consider providing a negative quantity of bone meal or meat!

To find the solution graphically, we first find the graphs of the constraints. The line associated with each constraint is found by finding the intercepts and the line that joins them. The graph of the constraint is the line and the region above the line. Figure 8-11 contains the graphs of the constraints. The feasible region satisfies all the constraints and is the shaded region.

The objective function for two values of cost is presented in Figure 8-12. Lines parallel to these are considered until we find the lowest line containing at least one point in the feasible region. Such a line is identified in Figure 8-13. The minimum solution is therefore (5, 1), which represents 5 kilograms of bone meal and 1 kilogram of meat for the daily diet of the minilions. The cost of such a diet is $5 \times 1 + 1 \times 2 = \$7$ per day per minilion. This is the least expensive diet that will satisfy the nutrition requirements.

The minimization linear program differs from the maximization program es-

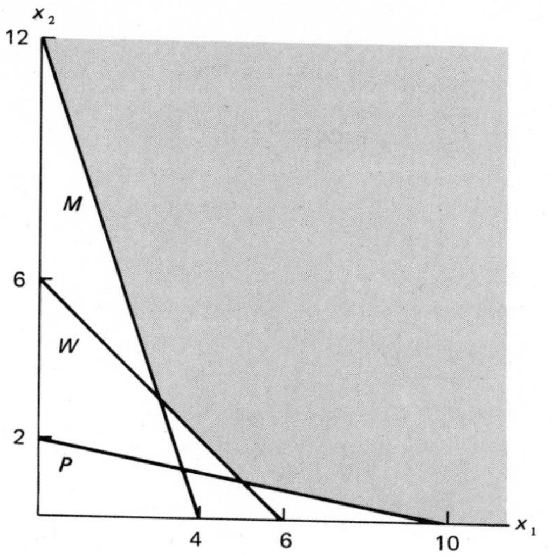

Figure 8-11 Graphs of the constraints: protein, $50x_1 + 250x_2 \geq 500$; mineral fiber, $240x_1 + 80x_2 \geq 960$; weight, $x_1 + x_2 \geq 6$.

sentially in its orientation. The specific steps in solving the two programs are similar, except for that difference in orientation.

The energy inspection linear program had constraints that are all of the "$\leq$" variety; the minilion diet linear program had all "$\geq$" constraints. In general, a linear program, whether it be a minimization or maximization problem, can have some constraints of each of the three types: "$\leq$," "$\geq$," and "$=$."

The next illustration is of such complexity that it does not permit a graphic solution. It contains constraints of all three types. Such a problem would undoubtedly be solved by the simplex method of solution using a computer.

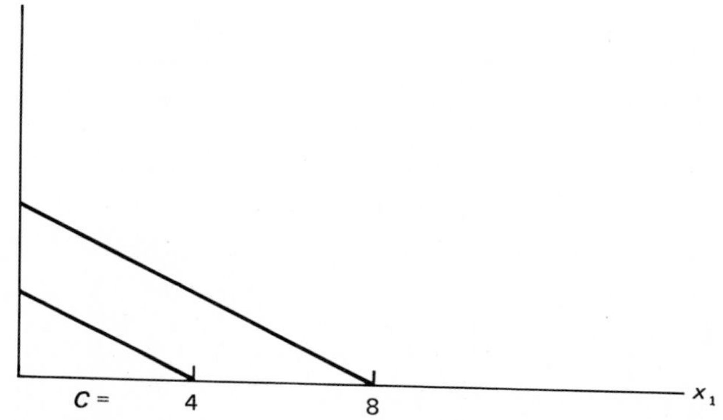

Figure 8-12 The objective function $C = x_1 + 2x_2$, for $C = 4, 8$.

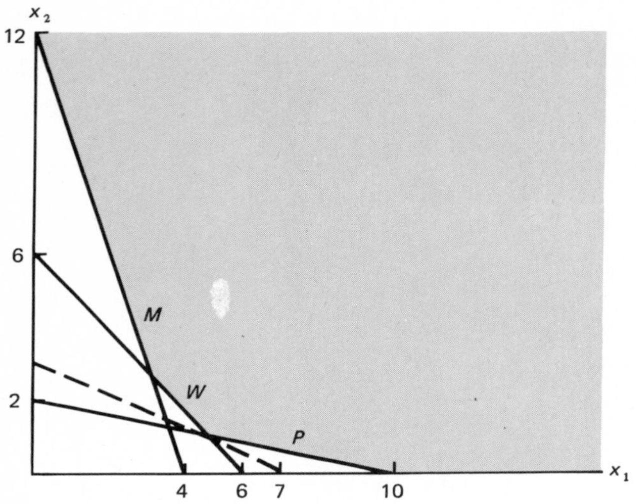

Figure 8-13 The optimum solution to the minilion diet problem.

The details of the simplex method, not essential for interpreting a solution, are presented in Chapter 10 for the reader interested in developing a deeper understanding of linear programming.

A POLICY ANALYSIS APPLICATION

Policy analysis is concerned primarily with examining the consequences of various alternatives. These alternatives may be different programs delivering different services to the public, for example, a reading readiness program for preschoolers and a dental clinic for preschoolers. They may be different strategies for delivering the same service, for example, to increase public safety by improving street lighting or by increasing the number of police officers assigned to foot patrol. Finally, they may be a single strategy's alternative levels of implementation. For example, a national health insurance program has many possible levels of funding by the federal government, contributions by individuals in the program, and benefits to the insured. The latter instance of policy analysis may well be profitably addressed by linear programming. At this point it should be emphasized that linear programming or any quantitative technique should neither be the sole basis for choosing public policy nor the prime reason for determining the specific levels of involvement of the various participants in the public program. The quantitative analysis can provide some information about the consequences of choosing particular levels of participation. This can help to provide an increased opportunity for rational decision making.

National health insurance, grants for education, and housing subsidies are some examples of attempts to redistribute income among income classes. Each such program consists of prescribed levels of participation and consequent impacts.[1] For the national health insurance program the prescribed levels of participation include (1) the deductible amount, or the initial expenditure that is paid by the individual; (2) the coinsurance rate, or the portion of each dollar of expenditure above the deductible that the individual must pay; and (3) the premium, the amount paid by each individual regardless of whether he or she ever needs the insurance. These prescribed levels are directly controlled by the government and as such may be referred to as the *program design variables.*

The impacts or effects of different levels of participation can be described in various terms, for example, the impact on the family expenditure within each income class or the value of the benefits received by each income class. These impacts are not directly controlled by the government; rather they are the effects of the specific prescribed levels of participation. These impacts may be referred to as the *distributional impact variables;* they are the measures of the redistribution of income that takes place as the result of the enactment of the program at the specified levels.

For the sake of simplicity we will assume that only lower- and middle-income classes are to be included in the program. However, in practice one would include in the same model many income classes defined as finely as is relevant and useful. Let all families with incomes under \$10,000 be class I, and all those with incomes from \$10,000 to \$20,000 be class II. The objective of redistributing income through the subsidized health insurance plan will generate various constraints, which we now consider.

Suppose the direct benefits are required to decrease at the rate of at least \$5 per \$1000 in additional income. Assuming a \$10,000 difference between the two income classes, the direct benefits to the average family in class I must be at least \$50 more than to the average family in class II. This generates the constraint

$$B_1 - B_2 \geq 50$$

To assure that the greater benefits are not accompanied by greater premiums, the premium paid by a family in class I should not be more than the premium paid by a family in class II:

$$P_1 - P_2 \leq 0$$

It is believed by some that maintaining reasonably high deductible amounts and coinsurance rates will prevent the generating of overwhelming levels of health care; not permitting them to be too large will prevent any family from bearing too great a burden. Finally, the deductible amounts and the coin-

[1] This illustration is based on the article, "Distributional Constraints in Public Expenditure Planning," by Martin Feldstein and Harold Luft, appearing in *Management Science,* vol. 19, August 1973, pp. 1414–1422.

surance rates should not be larger for the lower-income group than for the middle-income group. These considerations lead to three constraints for both the deductible amounts and the coinsurance rates.

$$D_1 \geq \$100 \qquad C_1 \geq .15$$

$$D_2 \leq \$300 \qquad C_2 \leq .40$$

$$D_1 - D_2 \leq \$0 \qquad C_1 - C_2 \leq 0$$

The constraint values \$100, \$300, .15, .40 and any other such values are called parameters. A *parameter* is a quantity that can vary from problem to problem but is constant for a specific problem. For example, the deductible amounts can vary according to the desires of the program designers, but once the choice is made they remain constant for all individuals in the same income class. Hence the choice of values is necessarily arbitrary, but hopefully not capricious. As we shall see shortly, the linear program will allow the decision makers to view the consequences of choosing any specific parameter values before the insurance program is implemented.

Since the program is voluntary, in order to enroll all the households, the program designers adopt the constraint that the premiums must not exceed 90 percent of the direct benefits at any income level. Hence

$$.90B_1 - P_1 \geq 0$$

$$.90B_2 - P_2 \geq 0$$

The final constraint relating to distribution of benefits comes from the amount of the subsidy. We assume the program is limited to the 4.8 million four-member (that is, two children) lower-income families, and the 2.4 million four-member middle-income families. In reality, of course, a program of this type would not be limited to such families. Including families of any size in the model would involve identifying the number of such families and perhaps adjusting the various program variables. Such is not difficult, but it would make our illustration more cumbersome than our purpose allows. If the limit on government subsidy is \$1 billion, then total benefits cannot exceed total premiums by more than that amount. Hence we have the constraint

$$4{,}800{,}000(B_1 - P_1) + 2{,}400{,}000(B_2 - P_2) \leq \$1{,}000{,}000{,}000$$

The relationship between the direct benefits and the deductible amounts and coinsurance rates is not one that is determined by setting program variable levels. Rather, it is a complicated one involving the stochastic nature of health expenditure. Hence an analytic form of the relationship can only be estimated through multiple regression based on available data. The equations that follow have been found to approximate the relationship rather well.

$$B_1 = 524 - .33D_1 - 300C_1$$

$$B_2 = 524 - .33D_2 - 300C_2$$

These equations complete the set of constraints for the problem statement. All that remains for the linear program is the objective function.

A dollar of direct net benefit to a lower-income family is considered to be worth more than a dollar of direct net benefit to a middle-income family. A way of expressing this consideration is to apply a greater weight to the class I benefits than to the class II benefits. For example, assuming the average income in the two classes to be \$5000 and \$15,000, the net benefits might be assigned the weights $\frac{1}{5}$ and $\frac{1}{15}$, respectively. If the objective is to maximize the total worth (not dollar value) of the program, then a suitable objective function would be

Maximize

$$W = \tfrac{1}{5} \cdot 4{,}800{,}000(B_1 - P_1) + \tfrac{1}{15} \cdot 2{,}400{,}000(B_2 - P_2)$$

Letting the weight be the reciprocal of the average income in each class quantifies the claim that the worth of a dollar decreases with increased income, an example of the so-called law of diminishing marginal utility. It also permits the easy extension of the model to any number of income classes, with each class covering any range of income.

Summarizing our translation from problem statement to linear program, we have the following:

Maximize

$$W = 960{,}000B_1 + 160{,}000B_2 - 960{,}000P_1 - 160{,}000P_2$$

subject to

$$\begin{array}{llllllllll}
B_1 & & & & -B_2 & & & & \geq & \$50 \\
 & P_1 & & & & -P_2 & & & \leq & \$0 \\
 & & D_1 & & & & & & \geq & \$100 \\
 & & & & & & D_2 & & \leq & \$300 \\
 & & D_1 & & & & -D_2 & & \leq & \$0 \\
 & & & C_1 & & & & & \geq & .15 \\
 & & & & & & & C_2 & \leq & .40 \\
 & & & C_1 & & & & -C_2 & \leq & 0 \\
.90B_1 & -P_1 & & & & & & & \geq & \$0 \\
 & & & & .90B_2 & -P_2 & & & \geq & \$0 \\
4.8B_1 & -4.8P_1 & & & +2.4B_2 & -2.4P_2 & & & \leq & 1{,}000 \\
B_1 & & +.33D_1 & +300C_1 & & & & & = & 524 \\
 & & & & B_2 & & +.33D_2 & +300C_2 & = & 524 \\
 & & & & \multicolumn{4}{r}{B_1,\ P_1,\ D_1,\ C_1,\ B_2,\ P_2,\ D_2,\ C_2} & \geq & 0
\end{array}$$

Table 8-2 Solutions to the national health insurance linear program

Income class	Variables	Solution A with $D_2 \leq \$300$	Solution B with $D_2 \leq \$200$
Lower:	Direct benefits	\$447	\$447
	Premiums	254	256
	Deductible	100	100
	Net benefits	193	191
	Coinsurance rate	.15	.15
Middle:	Direct benefits	\$306	\$339
	Premiums	275	305
	Deductible	300	200
	Net benefits	31	34
	Coinsurance rate	.40	.40
Objective function		190,880,000	189,810,000

We note that this linear program contains constraints that are not all of the same type; that is, some are "$\leq$," some are "$\geq$," and some are "$=$" constraints.

Needless to say, this linear program, much less the full-scale one from which this illustration was developed, could hardly be solved using graphic methods. Fortunately, there are methods that do not depend on the graphic representation, and such methods are available on most computers. The solution to our linear program was found by using a computer program; that solution is presented in solution A of Table 8-2. One of the main advantages of analyzing proposed program levels in this manner is to see the effects of altering some of the program variables. Solution B of Table 8-2 presents the solution to the linear program with one alteration. The limit on the deductible amount for the middle-income class has been decreased from \$300 to \$200; that is, the fourth constraint has been replaced by $D_2 \leq \$200$.

Interpretation

The interpretation of the objective function is best described in terms of aggregate worth to the families or, more technically, in terms of "uniformly distributed dollars." Changing the constraint on the middle-income-class deductible amount has little effect on the objective function and on the lower-income-class variables, but it does have an appreciable effect on the premiums and the direct benefits for the middle-income class. The small increase in their net benefits balances the decrease in net benefits to the lower-income class.

This model could be manipulated in many ways to determine the overall effect of altering one or more of the program variables. This type of "what if" analysis, referred to as "sensitivity analysis," is more fully treated in the next chapter. Aside from considering the effect of altering values, the model could be expanded to determine the effect of including other variables. The decision makers may wish to know the effect of including higher-income classes in the program, of accounting for regional differences in health care costs, of segmenting the population into narrower income classes or by other characteristics.

Linear programming has been used here in a simulation mode, in which the parameters can be modified to simulate program activity generated by various values for the program variables. Solving the program for each such modification shows the various impacts of such program variable values. The value of the specific program can then be assessed with reference to the nonquantitative factors that were not represented in the model.

Another application will conclude our discussion of linear programming.

AN APPLICATION TO SCHOOL BUSING

Busing students from one school to another to achieve racial balance has become a volatile social and political issue. In establishing policy there would undoubtedly be a number of higher-level goals (for example, to create the proper environment for the educational process) that would generate lower-level operational objectives. Among these might be to integrate schools according to some legally specified proportion, to transport children in order to satisfy the integration objective, and to avoid having the pupils spend an inordinate amount of time on the buses. Educational planners must be able to address the travel-time issue, while striving to satisfy other requirements. One approach to the problem is to consider racial balance, school capacity, and population of the school district as constraints, while striving to transport the children with as little inconvenience to them as possible. Suppose the Capital City School District has two elementary schools, with individual capacities as follows:

School	Capacity
I	600
II	300

For simplicity's sake, we assume there are three neighborhoods with the elementary school populations as summarized in Table 8-3. The distances in miles from the neighborhoods to the schools are:

	Neighborhood		
School	*A*	*B*	*C*
I	2.4	1.8	1.5
II	1.6	4.0	2.0

Table 8-3 Elementary school population by neighborhood and race

	Population		Percent	
Neighborhood	White	Nonwhite	White	Nonwhite
A	240	80	75	25
B	60	120	33.33	66.67
C	180	120	60	40
Total	480	320	60	40

The district has decided to integrate by school rather than by grade level. A school will be considered to be in racial balance when it deviates by no more than 10 percent from the district ratio of 60 percent white and 40 percent nonwhite. The district wishes to devise a busing plan that will transport pupils to any school in the same racial ratio as their neighborhood and will minimize the distance the youngsters must travel.

In order to formulate the linear program that would represent the problem, we let A_{I} stand for the number of pupils to be bused from neighborhood *A* to school I, A_{II} the number of pupils to be bused from neighborhood *A* to school II, and so forth.

The capacities of the schools are represented in two constraints:

$$A_{\mathrm{I}} + B_{\mathrm{I}} + C_{\mathrm{I}} \leq 600$$

$$A_{\mathrm{II}} + B_{\mathrm{II}} + C_{\mathrm{II}} \leq 300$$

The populations of the neighborhoods generate three constraints:

$$A_{\mathrm{I}} + A_{\mathrm{II}} = 320$$

$$B_{\mathrm{I}} + B_{\mathrm{II}} = 180$$

$$C_{\mathrm{I}} + C_{\mathrm{II}} = 300$$

Transporting pupils according to their neighborhood's racial ratio and the criterion for a school to be in racial balance generate two constraints for each school according to the following reasoning:

1. Racial balance requires that in school I white students comprise between 50 and 70 percent of the school population, that is,

   White students in school I $\leq$ .70(all students in school I)

   White students in school I $\geq$ .50(all students in school I)

2. Since 75 percent of the students in neighborhood *A* are white, racial ratio transportation requires that 75 percent of the students bused from neighborhood *A* to school I be white. Similarly, 33.3 percent of those bused from neighborhood *B* to school I must be white, and 60 percent of those bused from neighborhood *C* to school I must be white. Thus the number of white students being bused to school I is

$$.75A_{\mathrm{I}} + .333B_{\mathrm{I}} + .60C_{\mathrm{I}}$$

3. The total number of students being bused to school I is

$$A_{\mathrm{I}} + B_{\mathrm{I}} + C_{\mathrm{I}}$$

Putting the three relationships together yields the next two constraints. The same reasoning for school II yields the succeeding constraints.

$$.75A_{\mathrm{I}} + .333B_{\mathrm{I}} + .60C_{\mathrm{I}} \leq .70(A_{\mathrm{I}} + B_{\mathrm{I}} + C_{\mathrm{I}})$$

$$.75A_{\mathrm{I}} + .333B_{\mathrm{I}} + .60C_{\mathrm{I}} \geq .50(A_{\mathrm{I}} + B_{\mathrm{I}} + C_{\mathrm{I}})$$

$$.75A_{\mathrm{II}} + .333B_{\mathrm{II}} + .60C_{\mathrm{II}} \leq .70(A_{\mathrm{II}} + B_{\mathrm{II}} + C_{\mathrm{II}})$$

$$.75A_{\mathrm{II}} + .333B_{\mathrm{II}} + .60C_{\mathrm{II}} \geq .50(A_{\mathrm{II}} + B_{\mathrm{II}} + C_{\mathrm{II}})$$

Within these constraints, the objective is to minimize the total distance traveled; that is,

Minimize

$$D = 2.4A_{\mathrm{I}} + 1.8B_{\mathrm{I}} + 1.5C_{\mathrm{I}} + 1.6A_{\mathrm{II}} + 4.0B_{\mathrm{II}} + 2.0C_{\mathrm{II}}$$

The solution to the linear program, which merely indicates *the number of children* from each neighborhood to be assigned to each school, is as follows:

	Neighborhood		
School	*A*	*B*	*C*
I	56	144	300
II	264	36	0

In reality, not all youngsters from a given neighborhood are the same distance from a particular school. By defining neighborhoods small enough, a reasonable approximation to actual distances traveled is possible. However, if the pupils are widely dispersed over a large area, so that there are few pupils in any one "neighborhood" and very many neighborhoods, then linear programming would not be an appropriate tool for analysis. Other factors that would be present but which we have not considered are whether each grade within an integrated school should be integrated, different specific pupil needs that may be satisfied at one school but not at another, and costs of and resources available for transportation. These add to the complexity of the decision situation, the linear program (if, in fact, linear programming is considered appropriate), and the extent of the sensitivity analysis that would be conducted.

SUMMARY

Linear programming is particularly well suited as a decision-making aid in situations in which the decision makers have a specific linear objective function to be maximized or minimized, within fixed linear constraints. Linear programming is employed through problem formulation, solution, and interpretation. Simple programs may be solved by the graphic method; more complex programs require more involved methods, but the underlying concepts remain applicable. The linear constraints determine the feasible region, or set of allowable alternatives. The solution is a feasible alternative that optimizes the objective function. Applications vary from the operational level, as in aiding school bus assignments, to the policy level where the impacts of various program alternatives can be assessed through reformulation and re-solution.

BIBLIOGRAPHY

Austin, Larry M., and William W. Hogan: "Optimizing the Procurement of Aviation Fuels," *Management Science,* vol. 22, January 1976, pp. 515–527.

Barkan, Joel D.: "Operations Research in Planning Political Campaign Strategies," *Operations Research,* vol. 20, September–October 1972, pp. 925–941.

Barkan, Joel, and James Bruno: "Locating the Voter: Mathematical Models and the Analysis of Aggregate Data for Political Campaigns," *The Western Political Quarterly,* vol. 27, December 1974, pp. 710–730.

Belford, Peter C., and H. Donald Ratliff: "A Network-Flow Model for Racially Balancing Schools," *Operations Research,* vol. 20, May–June 1972, pp. 619–628.

Bruno, James E.: "A Methodology for the Evaluation of Instruction or Performance Contracts which Incorporates School District Utilities and Goals," *American Education Research Journal,* vol. 9, Spring 1972, pp. 175–195.

Feldstein, Martin, and Harold Luft: "Distributional Constraints in Public Expenditure Planning," *Management Science,* vol. 19, August 1973, pp. 1414–1432.

Franklin, Allen D., and Ernest Koenigsberg: "Computed School Assignments in a Large District," *Operations Research,* vol. 21, March–April 1973, pp. 413–426.

Gaballa, A. A.: "Minimum Cost Allocation of Tenders," *Operational Research Quarterly,* vol. 25, September 1974, pp. 389–398.

Hadley, G.: *Linear Programming,* Addison-Wesley Publishing Co., Inc., Reading, Mass., 1962.

Halloway, Charles A., Donald A. Wehrung, Michael P. Zeitlin, and Rosser T. Nelson: "An Interactive Procedure for the School Boundary Problem with Declining Enrollment," *Operations Research,* vol. 23, March–April 1975, pp. 191–206.

Harwood, Gorden B., and Robert W. Lawless: "Optimizing Organizational Goals in Assigning Faculty Teaching Schedules," *Decision Sciences,* vol. 6, July 1975, pp. 513–524.

Heroux, Richard L., and William A. Wallace: "Linear Programming and Financial Analysis of the New Community Development Process," *Management Science,* vol. 19, April 1973, pp. 857–872.

Hughes, A., and D. E. Grawoig: *Linear Programming: An Emphasis on Decision Making,* Addison-Wesley Publishing Co., Inc., Reading, Mass., 1973.

Koch, James V.: "A Linear Programming Model of Resource Allocation in a University," *Decision Sciences,* vol. 4, October 1973, pp. 494–504.

Kraft, D. H., and T. W. Hill: "The Journal Selection Problem in a University," *Management Science,* vol. 19, February 1973, pp. 613–626.

Ladany, Shaul P.: "Optimization of Pentathlon Training Plans," *Management Science,* vol. 21, June 1975, pp. 1144–1155.

Lehne, Richard, and Donald M. Fisk: "The Impact of Urban Policy Analysis," *Urban Affairs Quarterly,* vol. 10, December 1974, pp. 115–138.

Penz, Alton J.: "Outdoor Recreation Areas: Capacity and Formulation of Use Policy," *Management Science,* vol. 22, October 1975, pp. 139–147.

Ritzman, Larry P., and Leroy J. Krajewski: "Multiple Objectives in Linear Programming: An Example in Scheduling Postal Resources," *Decision Sciences,* vol. 4, July 1973, pp. 364–378.

Rothstein, Marvin: "Hospital Manpower Shift Scheduling by Mathematical Programming," *Health Services Research,* vol. 8, Spring 1973, pp. 60–66.

Stark, Robert M.: "Unbalanced Highway Contract Tendering," *Operational Research Quarterly,* vol. 25, September 1974, pp. 373–388.

EXERCISES

Extensions of chapter examples

8-1 Refer to the energy inspection example. (See p. 169.) If an additional 6 hours of the electrical inspector's time could be applied to the inspection project, the second constraint would become

$$2x_1 + 6x_2 \leq 36$$

The other constraints and the objective function would not be affected. Hence the new linear program would be:

Maximize the objective function

$$N = x_1 + x_2$$

subject to the constraints

$$4x_1 + 2x_2 \leq 28 \qquad \text{I}$$

$$2x_1 + 6x_2 \leq 36 \qquad \text{E}$$

$$4x_1 + 6x_2 \leq 36 \qquad \text{H}$$

$$x_1, x_2 \geq 0$$

(*a*) Solve the new linear program graphically.

(*b*) How does this solution compare with the solution to the original program?

(*c*) If another 6 hours of the electrical inspector's time (or a total of 42 hours) could be applied to the project, what would then be the number of homes and plants inspected? Base your answer not on a new graphic solution but on your response to parts *a* and *b*.

8-2 Refer to the minimization example in the chapter. (See p. 180.)

(*a*) How will the minilions' diet be altered if the cost of meat goes up to \$3 per kilogram?

(*b*) How will their diet change if the cost of bone meal goes up to \$3 per kilogram (with the cost of meat at \$2 per kilogram)?

(*c*) How will their diet change if the cost of bone meal goes to \$2 per kilogram and meat goes to \$4 per kilogram?

(*d*) What are the effects of the changes in part *c* on the objective function?

(*e*) Generalize the results of parts *c* and *d*.

8-3 Refer to the national health insurance policy analysis application. (See p. 184.) The equations for direct benefits are:

$$B_1 = 524 - .33D_1 - 300C_1$$

$$B_2 = 524 - .33D_2 - 300C_2$$

These are estimated through the multiple regression statistical technique. Comment on using such equations in linear programming, with particular reference to the implications of the underlying assumptions. How should such equations be treated in the linear programming model?

Other applications

8-4 Which of the following relationships might be found in a linear programming model?

(*a*) $2X_1 - 4X_2 + \frac{3}{2}X_3 \geq 100$

(*b*) $3X_1 + \dfrac{1}{X_2} \leq 50$

(*c*) $3X_2 - 6X_3^2 = 80$

(*d*) $X_1 - X_2 + X_3 \leq 40$

(*e*) $X_1X_2 - X_3 \geq 17$

8-5 (*a*) Solve graphically:

Maximize $Z = 4Y_1 + 10Y_2$

subject to

$$Y_1 + 4Y_2 \leq 20$$
$$8Y_1 + 2Y_2 \leq 40$$
$$Y_1 + Y_2 \leq 10$$
$$Y_1, Y_2 \geq 0$$

(*b*) Can any one of the constraints be eliminated without altering the feasible region?

8-6 Solve the following minimization problem graphically:

Minimize $C = 2X + Y$

subject to

$$Y \geq 6$$
$$X + Y \geq 10$$
$$X, Y \geq 0$$

8-7 Solve graphically:

Maximize $Z = 4X_1 + 6X_2$

subject to

$$X_1 + 2X_2 \leq 200$$
$$4X_1 + 3X_2 \leq 480$$
$$X_1 \geq 100$$
$$X_1, X_2 \geq 0$$

8-8 Refer to problem 8-7. Change the last constraint to

$$X_1 \geq 140$$

(*a*) What is the effect on the feasible region?
(*b*) What is the new solution?

8-9 Formulate and solve graphically: Food *A* costs \$2 per kilogram and food *B* costs \$3 per kilogram. A kilogram of *A* yields 2 units of vitamins, 10 units of starch, and 6 units of protein. A kilogram of *B* yields 6 units of vitamins, 2 units of starch, and 4 units of protein. The minimum requirements of each ingredient are 178, 200, and 240, respectively. What combination of *A* and *B* will give an adequate diet with least cost?

8-10 The American Safety Council has allocated \$220,000 to efforts to prevent automobile accidents. An assumed measure of the effectiveness of such efforts is the reduction in fatalities and property damage. The projects that have been suggested for funding and some relevant values are presented in Table 1. It is readily admitted that saving lives is the more important objective, but yet the decision makers are not willing to ignore the objective of averting property damage. Realizing

Table 1 Suggested safety projects and values

	Maximum allowable expenditure	Expected fatalities prevented per $1000	Property damage averted per $1000
Teen-age safety education	$160,000	.22	$20,000
Seat-belt advertising	130,000	.30	0
Lobbying for stiff DWI* laws	110,000	.28	15,000
Research in improved vehicle design	70,000	.16	40,000

* Driving while intoxicated.

that a human life cannot be equated to dollars, reference is made to other government agencies that use $300,000 for the value of a human life for internal analysis purposes.

(*a*) Formulate a linear programming model for the optimal allocation of the $220,000 based on the information given and the fatalities-prevention objective alone.

(*b*) Formulate another linear programming model that considers both lives and property and uses the assumed value of a life.

(*c*) Without solving either linear program, by comparing the two objective functions, how do you think the solutions will differ?

8-11 The demand for hospital services has been found to be quite seasonal. As a result, staffing the various services without frequent layoffs and rehirings requires some planning. The personnel director of Metropolitan Hospital is trying to decide how many orderlies to hire and train for the next 4 months. According to admissions forecasts, the demand for orderly-hours for the next 4 months is:

Month	Hours needed
Dec.	800
Jan.	1000
Feb.	900
Mar.	1200

The IOU (International Orderlies Union) has recently signed a contract calling for a guaranteed $37\frac{1}{2}$-hour work week, with overtime prohibited to maintain a high employment level. We will take that to mean each employed orderly is paid for 150 hours a month. Hospital records indicate that 10 percent of the orderlies quit their jobs each month.

Orderlies are given a 1-month training period to become familiar with hospital layout, patient handling, and emergency codes; hence they must be hired a month before being assigned regular duty. They are paid $400 a month while in training and $800 a month afterward. It takes approximately 10 hours of regular orderly time for each trainee during the training period; that is, the number of hours available for regular service by orderlies is reduced by 10 for each trainee.

Since there are currently six orderlies available, the hospital has 100 hours in excess of its needs for December. No one will be laid off; each orderly will work a few hours less, but be paid for full employment.

Formulate a linear program to solve the personnel director's staffing problem, identifying each symbol used. Do not solve the formulated problem.

8-12 The State Employees Credit Union makes various kinds of loans to members and invests up to one-third of its funds in market securities. Not more than 20 percent of money lent can be in unsecured (signature) loans. Furniture and expansion loans cannot be more than half of all secured loans. Signature and expansion loans may not exceed the market securities investment. The investments have the following yields:

Investment	Yield, %
Securities	10
Signature loans	13
Secured loans:	
Automobile	9
Furniture	11
Expansion	12

The credit union wants to determine the proportion of its funds to allocate to each category in order to maximize interest earned. Formulate (but do not solve) the problem as a linear program.

8-13 The state's Department of Administrative Services maintains a few light planes for official use. $10,000 has been allocated for fuels, which are purchased on a competitive bid basis. By adjusting the planes' engines, varying proportions of regular, super, and fuel additive can be used. The department wants to determine how many gallons of each type to purchase from each of the only two bidders, Poly Oil Co. and Petros Corp. The bids' summary follows:

	Price per gallon		Maximum to be supplied (gallons)	
	Poly	Petros	Poly	Petros
Regular	$1.00	$ .50	12,000	6,000
Super	1.50	2.00	1,000	8,000
Additive	5.00	6.00	200	200

A summary of the department's experience follows:

	Miles per gallon	Minimum number of gallons needed
Regular	5	8000
Super	10	2000
Additive	20	240

The department's objective is to maximize the number of air miles provided for by the total purchase. Formulate (but do not solve) the problem as a linear program.

8-14 The Department of Agriculture of a developing nation is encouraging better crop planning. The central region consists of three provinces, each with its own land availability and water capacity. The province specifics are presented in Table 1:

Table 1 Province data for the central region

Province	Available land (acres)	Water capacity (gallons)
A	800	600,000
B	1200	800,000
C	600	375,000

The Department of Agriculture has established a maximum planting for each crop in each region. Each crop has fairly well-established levels of water consumption and an expected return per acre. The crop information is presented in Table 2.

Table 2 Crop data for the central region

Crop	Maximum (acres)	Water consumption (gallons per acre)	Revenue (dollars per acre)
Millet	650	1000	$200
Cane	1200	3000	800
Cotton	1000	2000	600

The three provinces of the central region have agreed to plant the same proportion of available land. They want to determine how many acres of each crop should be planted in each province in order to maximize the total revenue to the region.

Formulate (but do not solve) this problem as a linear program.

Project problems

8-15 Observe any governmental or service agency process that consumes limited resources and/or has other restrictions.

(*a*) Describe the process. If specific data are not readily available, make up reasonable data.

(*b*) Formulate the process as a linear program, noting any assumptions.

(*c*) What (if any) aspects of the problem cannot be included in the linear program formulation?

8-16 Refer to any linear programming application from a journal in your own field of interest.

(*a*) Describe the problem verbally, including the objective and restrictions.

(*b*) What are the objective function and constraints of the linear program formulation?

(*c*) Is the problem directly presented as a linear programming model, or are modifications or assumptions made to convert it into a linear programming model?

(*d*) Does the original problem suffer for the conversion?

(*e*) What is the interpretation of the solution with reference to the original problem?

CHAPTER

NINE

LINEAR PROGRAMMING II: SENSITIVITY ANALYSIS

The situation that the decision maker encounters and resolves is often subject to changes in its basic characteristics. In some cases the decision maker has some control over the changes. Consider some examples: With appropriate persuasion the director of the power loss project (Chapter 8) may be able to acquire from the Public Power Commission some additional resources, namely, inspectors' time; the legislators may change the deductible amount in the national insurance program. In other cases the decision maker has no control over the basic characteristics, but must try to estimate what they are and how they might change. Some examples of this situation are: The zoo keeper does not control the amount of protein the animals need but uses accepted estimates in planning the animals' diets; the demand for health services is beyond the control of any program decision makers, and yet some estimates of demand are necessary in planning the insurance program.

When the decision maker can control some of the characteristics of the situation, knowing the effects of modifications may provide for more thoughtful decisions; when the decision maker cannot control certain characteristics, knowing the effects of variations may lead to more careful choices. The process of determining the effects of alterations in the original problem parameters is called *sensitivity analysis*. Just as we use a graphic method to solve a simple linear program and to gain some understanding of linear programming in general, so also we can apply the graphic method to sensitivity analysis. Sensitivity analysis of more realistic larger scale programs is beyond graphic methods, but the simplex procedure of Chapter 10 will provide a procedure for the sensitivity analysis of such problems. Sensitivity analysis in linear programming aims at determining:

1. The marginal effects of changes in the problem parameters
2. The range of parameter values over which the marginal effects appear

SENSITIVITY ANALYSIS: RIGHT-SIDE CONSTANTS

In Chapter 8 we formulated and solved a problem concerning allocation of human resources in the power loss project. The problem and graphic solution are repeated below, where x_1 and x_2 represent, respectively, the number of homes and the number of industrial plants inspected. We did not restrict the solution to integers; coincidence provided the integer solution.

Maximize the objective function

$$N = x_1 + x_2$$

subject to the constraints

$$4x_1 + 2x_2 \leq 28 \quad \text{Insulation}$$

$$2x_1 + 6x_2 \leq 30 \quad \text{Electrical}$$

$$4x_1 + 6x_2 \leq 36 \quad \text{Heating}$$

$$x_1, x_2 \geq 0$$

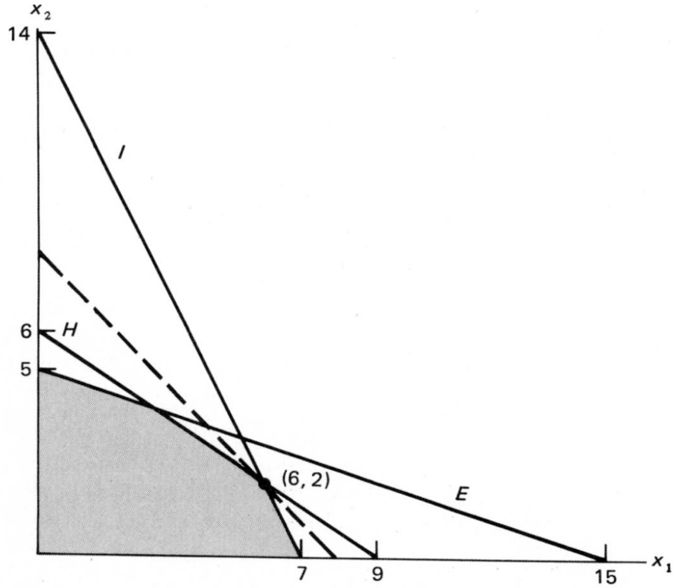

Figure 9-1 The optimum solution to the energy inspection problem.

The optimum solution is the combination of homes and plants that yields the maximum number of inspections within the constraints of the inspectors' time. How would that total number of inspections be affected by an increase in one inspector's available time?

In the graphic solution, presented in Figure 9-1, note that the optimum solution is at the corner point formed by the constraints

$$4x_1 + 2x_2 \leq 28 \qquad \text{I}$$

and

$$4x_1 + 6x_2 \leq 36 \qquad \text{H}$$

This suggests that a change in either of these constraints will alter the corner point and hence alter the optimum solution. That is, these constraints are actively restricting the solution or, more simply, are active. The remaining constraint

$$2x_1 + 6x_2 \leq 30 \qquad \text{E}$$

can be changed, provided it is not changed too much, without any effect on the corner point or on the optimum solution. There is another way of saying this: The constraint

$$2x_1 + 6x_2 \leq 30$$

is not actively restricting the solution or, more simply, is *inactive*. Sensitivity analysis of right-side constants differs according to whether the constraints are active or inactive.

Inactive Constraints

We have noted that the electrical inspection constraint,

$$2x_1 + 6x_2 \leq 30$$

is not actively restricting the solution; it is inactive. Hence, if there is additional electrical inspection time there will be no change in the optimum solution. The inspection of 6 homes and 2 plants requires 24 hours of electrical inspection time. Since there are 30 hours available, not all the available time is being used. There would be no improvement in the solution if additional time were provided. Figure 9-2 shows the electrical inspection constraint with the constant being changed from 30 to 36 hours. Note that there is no change in the optimum solution since it is the other constraints that are actively restricting the solution; that is, the solution is at the corner point formed by the other two constraints. Similarly, if the available time is decreased, there is no change in the optimum solution, at least not unless it is decreased "too much." In fact, the electrical inspection time available can be decreased to 24 hours without any ef-

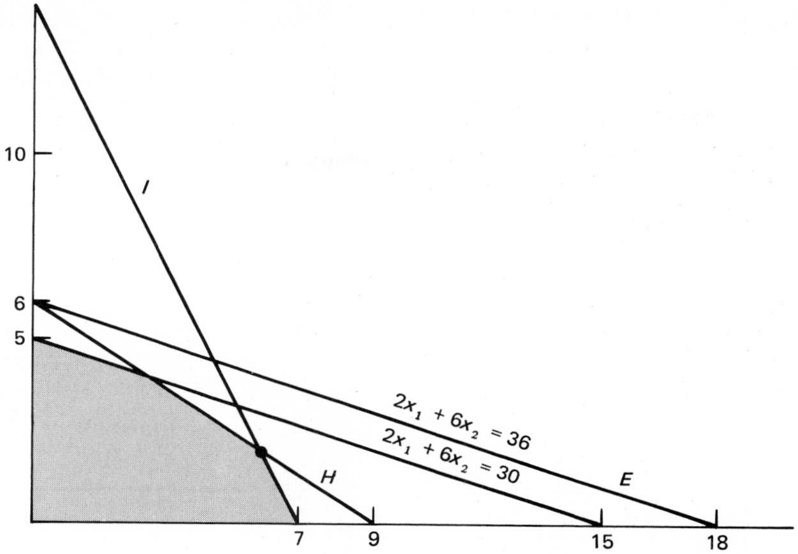

Figure 9-2 Increasing the right-side constant of the electrical constraint from 30 to 36.

fect on the solution. A decrease below that will affect the solution. Figure 9-3 shows the electrical inspection constraint with the constant being changed from 30 to 24 hours. Note that there is no change in the solution since it is the other constraints that are actively restricting the solution. Once the constant has been decreased to 24 hours, or once the constraint has been changed to

$$2x_1 + 6x_2 \leq 24$$

then it, too, is actively restricting the solution. Any further decrease in the available time for electrical inspection will bring about a reduction in the total number of inspections that can be completed. Determining the effect of such further reduction is sensitivity analysis of an active constraint.

The effect of altering the right-side constant of an inactive constraint can be summarized:

> The constant of an inactive constraint can be increased or decreased until the constraint becomes active with no effect on the optimum solution.

Active Constraints

Note again that in the graph of the linear program the optimum solution is at the corner point formed by the insulation constraint

$$4x_1 + 2x_2 \leq 28 \qquad \text{I}$$

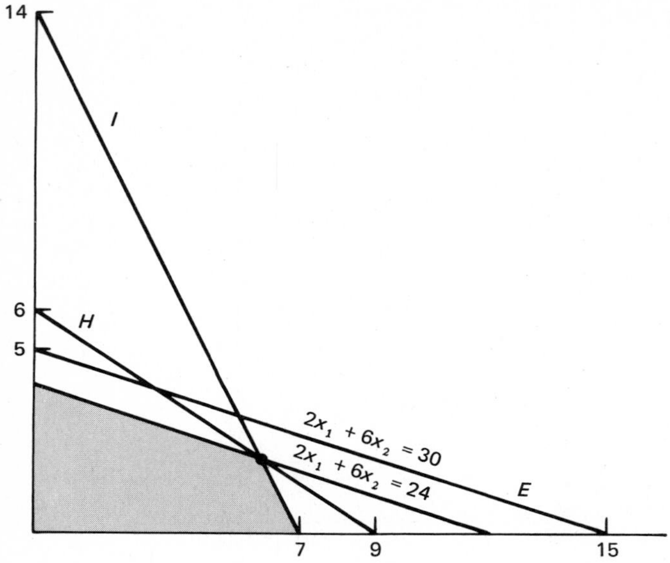

Figure 9-3 Decreasing the right-side constant of an inactive constraint.

and the heating constraint

$$4x_1 + 6x_2 \leq 36 \qquad \text{H}$$

A change in either of these constraints effects a change in the optimum solution. Thus it is appropriate to ask how the number of complete inspections would change if additional hours of insulation inspection time were made available.

As the constant of the constraint increases, the constraint moves further from the origin, and the feasible region expands accordingly. When the number of hours available for insulation inspection is increased from 28 to 32 to 36 to 40 hours, the graph of the constraint assumes the positions indicated in Figure 9-4. Each new position of the constraint becomes the boundary of an expanding feasible region. Once the available insulation inspection time exceeds 36 hours, the insulation constraint becomes inactive. Until it reaches 36 hours, the optimum solution is at the corner point formed by the insulation constraint and the heating constraint. Figure 9-4 shows the optimum solutions associated with the changing constraint.

For the constraint

$$4x_1 + 2x_2 \leq 32$$

the optimum solution is $7\frac{1}{2}$ homes and 1 plant, or $8\frac{1}{2}$ complete inspections. For the constraint

$$4x_1 + 2x_2 \leq 36$$

the optimum solution is 9 homes and 0 plants, or 9 complete inspections. As the right-side constant is increased beyond 36, the optimum solution remains 9 homes and 0 plants, or 9 complete inspections; that is, the optimum solution remains at the corner point formed by the heating constraint

$$4x_1 + 6x_2 \leq 36 \qquad \text{H}$$

and the nonnegativity constraint

$$x_2 \geq 0$$

When the insulation constraint becomes inactive, the x_2 nonnegativity constraint becomes active.

There is another way of describing the change: As the right-side constant of the insulation constraint is increased, the corner point—which is the optimum solution—slides along the heating constraint equation

$$4x_1 + 6x_2 = 36$$

until it coincides with the next corner point. The next corner point, (9, 0), is

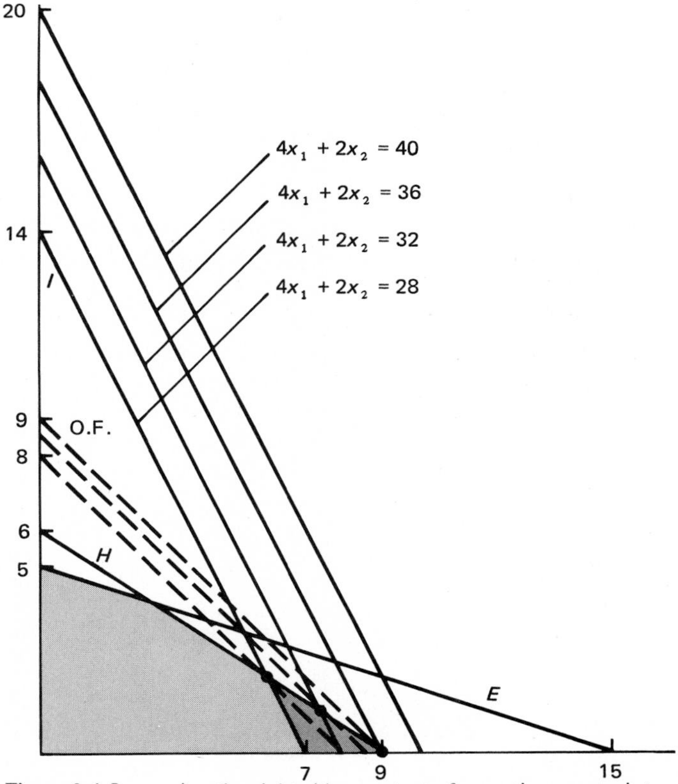

Figure 9-4 Increasing the right-side constant of an active constraint.

formed by the heating constraint and the nonnegativity constraint $x_2 \geq 0$. That corner point then becomes the optimum solution, so that further changes in the insulation constraint have no effect on the new optimum solution.

As the available time for insulation inspection is increased from 28 to 36 hours, the number of complete inspections changes. Table 9-1 presents:

1. The original solution
2. The new solution arrived at by increasing the right-side constant as much as possible without letting the constraint become inactive
3. The net change in each variable
4. The relative change in each variable with respect to insulation time

The change in the objective function per unit change in insulation time is referred to as the "shadow price" of insulation time. The particular value for the shadow price holds as long as insulation time does not change more than 8 hours. The maximum change to 36 hours establishes the upper limit on the range of insulation time for which the shadow price is applicable.

The *shadow price* is an economic term for *the value of an additional unit of any resource*. The value is not to be confused with the price that must be paid for that additional unit. The value of the additional unit is the effect that it has on the objective function. In the power loss project neither the resources nor the inspections have been given dollar values, and so the shadow price will not have a dollar value. Using the terms relevant to the problem, we say that the shadow price of insulation inspection time is $\frac{1}{8}$ of a complete inspection. In the same terms we say that the shadow price of electrical inspection time is zero, since we found earlier that changes in electrical inspection time have no effect on the optimum solution. Regardless of its cost, additional electrical inspection time should not be acquired since it has zero value. Whether additional insula-

Table 9-1 Effects of increases in the right-side constant of the insulation constraint $4x_1 + 2x_2 \leq 28$

Variable	Variable symbol	Original optimal solution	New optimal change	Total change	Change per hour
Right-side constant (insulation hours available)	b_1	28	36	8	
Number of homes inspected	x_1	6	9	3	$\frac{3}{8}$
Number of plants inspected	x_2	2	0	−2	$-\frac{2}{8}$
Objective function	$N =$				
Number of complete inspections	$x_1 + x_2$	8	9	1	$\frac{1}{8}$

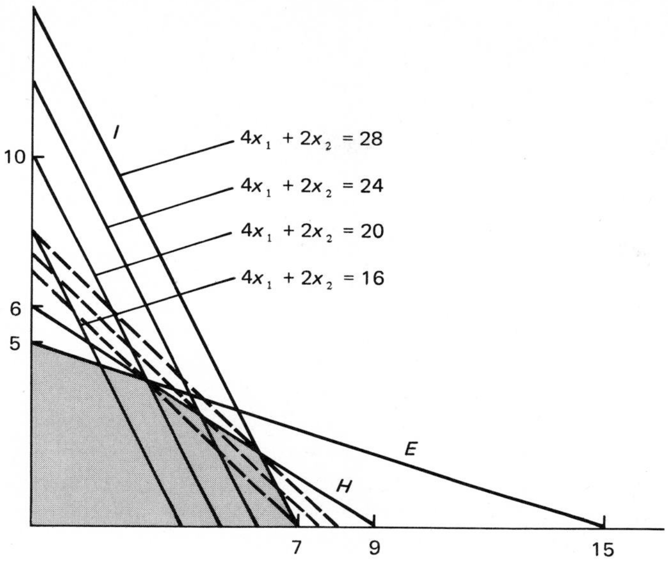

Figure 9-5 Decreasing the right-side constant of an active constraint.

tion inspection time should be acquired would depend on its cost—direct labor, fringe benefits, expenses, supporting services, and so forth—and whether an additional $\frac{1}{8}$ of an inspection is worth that cost. If the power inspection project is to last just 1 week, then an additional $\frac{1}{8}$ on an inspection is worthless; if 8 hours of insulation time can be purchased, then an additional inspection can be completed. Its value can be compared to the cost of the 8 hours.

The changes effected by a decrease in the right-side constant are the reverse of those effected by an increase. Figure 9-5 shows the insulation constraint as the right-side constant is decreased from 28 to 24 to 20 to 16. Each new position of the constraint becomes the boundary of a contracting feasible region. As the constraint moves closer to the origin, the optimum solution—the corner point formed by the insulation constraint and the heating constraint—slides along the heating constraint until it coincides with the next corner point. The next corner point (3, 4) is formed by the heating constraint and the electrical constraint. Decreasing the insulation right-side constant to 20 alters the solution; decreasing it below 20 keeps the insulation constraint active but the heating constraint becomes inactive and the electrical constraint becomes active. The optimum solution is then at the intersection of the insulation constraint and the electrical constraint. Table 9-2 presents the changes effected by the decreases as well as increases in the right-side constant. The first new solution is the solution presented in Table 9-1, with the number of hours available for insulation inspection increased to 36. The second new solution in Table 9-2 is the solution with the number of hours available for insulation inspection decreased to 20.

Table 9-2 Effects of changes in the right-side constant of the insulation constraint $4x_1 + 2x_2 \leq 28$

Variable	Original optimum solution value	First new solution: New value	Change	Change per hour	Second new solution: New value	Change	Change per hour
b_1	28	36	8	—	20	−8	—
x_1	6	9	3	$\frac{3}{8}$	3	−3	$\frac{3}{8}$
x_2	2	0	−2	$-\frac{2}{8}$	4	2	$-\frac{2}{8}$
N	8	9	1	$\frac{1}{8}$	7	−1	$\frac{1}{8}$

As long as the number of hours available for insulation inspection is between 20 and 36, sometimes called the "range of proportionality," the insulation constraint and the heating constraint are active, the optimum solution is at the corner point formed by them, and all other constraints are inactive. Within the range of proportionality, for every 1-hour change in the number of insulation hours available, the net effect on each variable is as in Table 9-2 ("change per hour" columns). These are termed the *marginal effects; they are the effects of a one-unit change in the right-side constant.* The shadow price and other marginal effects are valid only while insulation time is in the range 20 to 36. Beyond that range, either the insulation or heating constraint is inactive, and so new marginal effects would have to be determined.

In summarizing,

> changes in the constant of an active constraint generate proportional changes in the optimum solution within a range of values, until one of the currently active constraints becomes inactive. Changes in the constraint's constant beyond the range of proportionality either have no further effect or generate new proportional changes dependent on the new active constraints.

SENSITIVITY ANALYSIS: OBJECTIVE FUNCTION COEFFICIENTS

It is not entirely unlikely that the value of a complete plant inspection may be greater than a complete home inspection, or vice versa, depending on the amount of energy consumed by the two types of units, on the total number of plants and homes within the jurisdiction of the commission, and on other factors. The objective function should reflect the difference in value by using different coefficients for x_1 and x_2. Suppose the complete inspection of a plant is considered to be twice as valuable as the complete inspection of a home; then an appropriate objective function would be

$$Z = x_1 + 2x_2$$

If the opposite were true, then an appropriate objective function would be

$$Z = 2x_1 + x_2$$

In these objective functions, the difference in the perceived values is reflected in the different coefficients. The values are not assumed to be dollar values, but rather are expressions of the relative worth of the information to the decision makers.

Since the coefficients may be subject to change, it is reasonable to consider the effects of such changes on the optimum solution. Such is the role of sensitivity analysis of the objective function coefficients.

The solution to a linear program depends on the objective function and on the constraints. In the last section we were concerned with marginal effects of changes in the right-side constant of a constraint and with the range over which the marginal effects are valid. In this section we examine how changes in the coefficients of the objective function affect the optimum solution, and the range over which the optimum solution does *not* change.

In solving the Public Power Commission's linear program graphically in Chapter 8, we first developed the feasible region. Then we considered the family of parallel lines for the objective function $N = x_1 + x_2$ to determine the highest line with a point in the feasible region. Note that the objective function is represented by a *family of parallel lines*. This suggests that the direction of

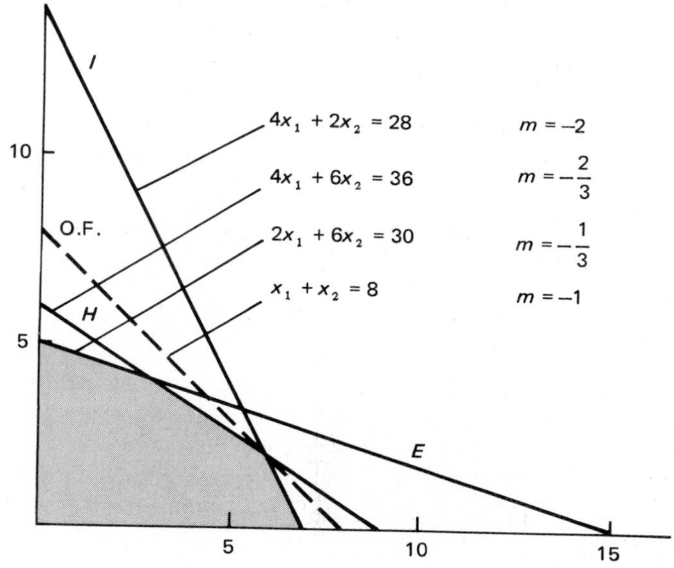

Figure 9-6 Slopes (m) of the constraints and the objective function of the energy inspection problem.

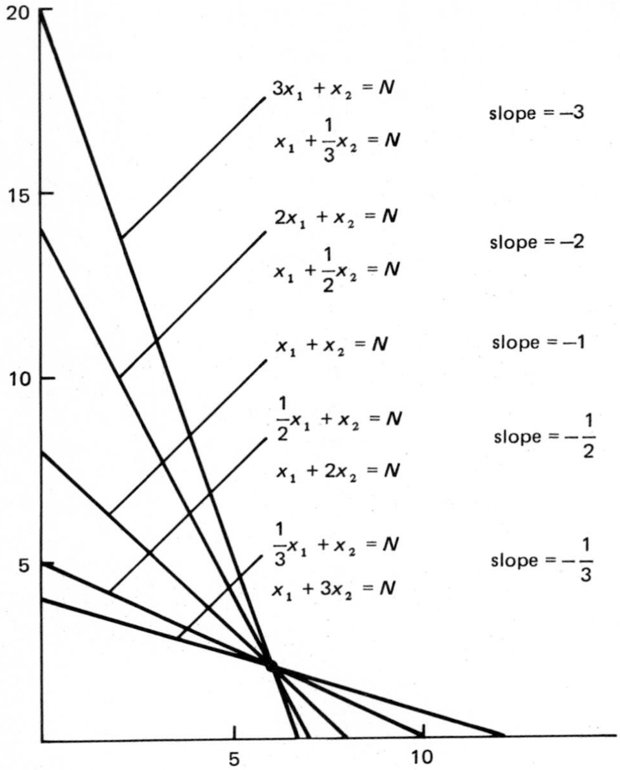

Figure 9-7 Effect of varying either coefficient in the objective function of the energy inspection problem.

the lines is crucial in the solution of the linear program. Figure 9-1 is repeated in Figure 9-6, showing the optimum solution and the slopes of the constraints and objective function. Sensitivity analysis of the objective function coefficients involves determining how much the direction of the objective function can be changed without changing the optimum solution.[1]

We now determine how much the coefficients of x_1 and x_2 (which we call c_1 and c_2, respectively) can change without affecting the optimum solution. Note in Figure 9-7 that as c_1 is increased or c_2 is decreased, the line becomes steeper and the size of the slope becomes greater; conversely, as c_1 is decreased or c_2 is increased, the line becomes flatter and the size of the slope becomes smaller. We find the effect of changes in the coefficients by determining the effect of corresponding changes in the slope, which is given by the quantity $-c_1/c_2$.

[1] The reader not familiar with the slope of a straight line might benefit from reading the brief appendix to this chapter before continuing.

Figure 9-8 depicts the feasible region and the objective functions with slope equal to -1, $-\frac{3}{2}$, -2, and -3. Since we are trying to determine whether the optimum solution is changed as the slope is changed, we draw the new objective functions $N = c_1x_1 + c_2x_2$ through the optimum solution (6, 2).[2]

As the slope is changed from -1 to $-\frac{3}{2}$ to -2, the objective function remains less steep than the insulation constraint (depicted by "I" in Figure 9-8), and the optimum solution remains (6, 2). Since one or both of the coefficients have changed, the *value* of the objective function is likely to change, but (6, 2) remains the solution. When we say there is no effect on the optimum solution, we are not implying that the value of the objective function is unchanged, but rather that the values of the variables are unchanged.

Once the slope becomes less than -2, the objective function becomes steeper than the insulation constraint and (6, 2) is no longer the optimum solution. We can see that (6, 2) is no longer the optimum solution when, for example, $c_1 = 3$ and $c_2 = 1$, since there is a portion of the feasible region beyond the line $3x_1 + x_2 = 20$. By considering lines parallel to $3x_1 + x_2 = 20$, we find the new optimum solution to be (7, 0).

When $c_1 = 2$, the objective function is parallel to the insulation constraint

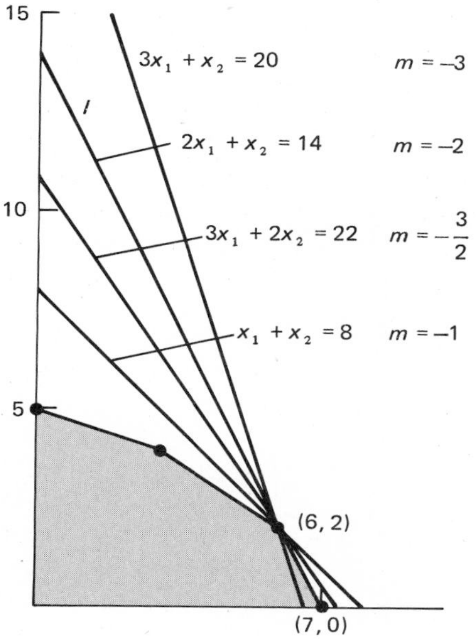

Figure 9-8 Decreasing the objective function slope in the energy inspection problem.

[2] The constant term of a line is found as follows: For the line passing through the point (6, 2) with $c_1 = 3$ and $c_2 = 2$, we have $3(6) + 2(2) = N = 22$. Therefore the equation of the line is $3x_1 + 2x_2 = 22$. Similarly the equation of the line passing through (6, 2) with $c_1 = 2$ and $c_2 = 1$ is $2x_1 + x_2 = 14$; and the equation of the line with $c_1 = 3$ and $c_2 = 1$ is $3x_1 + x_2 = 20$.

$4x_1 + 2x_2 \leq 28$, and so the optimum solution is both (6, 2) and (7, 0), and any other point between them; for example, $(6\frac{1}{4}, 1\frac{1}{2})$, $(6\frac{1}{2}, 1)$, and $(6\frac{3}{4}, \frac{1}{2})$ are other solutions. For any of these solutions, the value of the objective function $N = 2x_1 + x_2$ is 14.

Briefly, the optimum solution is insensitive to decreases in the slope above -2; any further decrease in the slope causes the optimum solution to switch to (7, 0).

Similarly we determine the effect of increases in the slope. Figure 9-9 shows the feasible region and the objective function with slope $= -1$, $-\frac{2}{3}$, and $-\frac{1}{2}$. As the slope is increased from -1 to $-\frac{2}{3}$, the objective function remains steeper than the heating constraint (H) and the optimum solution remains (6, 2).

Once the slope becomes greater than $-\frac{2}{3}$, the objective function becomes flatter than the heating constraint and the optimum solution is no longer (6, 2). For example, when $c_1 = -\frac{1}{2}$, there is a portion of the feasible region beyond the line $x_1 + 2x_2 = 10$. By considering lines parallel to $x_1 + 2x_2 = 10$, we find the new optimum solution to be (3, 4).

When the slope is equal to $-\frac{2}{3}$, the optimum solutions are (6, 2), (3, 4), and any point between them; for example $(3\frac{3}{4}, 3\frac{1}{2})$, and $(5\frac{1}{4}, 2\frac{1}{2})$ are other solutions. The value of the objective function $N = 2x_1 + 3x_2$ for any of these solutions is 18.

Summarizing the sensitivity analysis of the objective function coefficients, we note:

1. The optimum solution is at a corner point formed by two constraints.
2. The optimum solution, but not necessarily the value of the objective function, is insensitive to changes in objective function coefficients as long as the slope remains between the slopes of the two constraints.

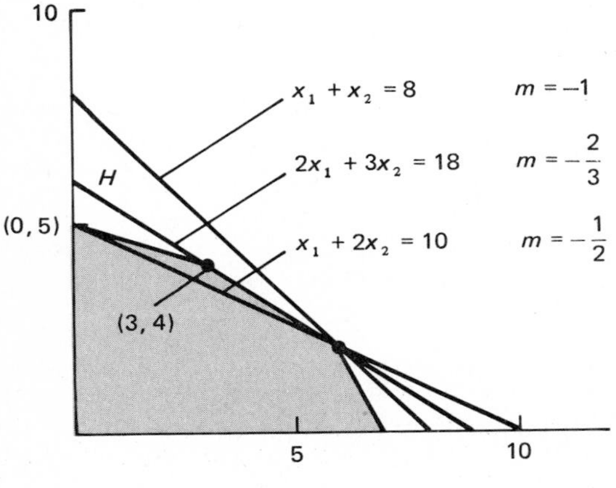

Figure 9-9 Increasing the objective function slope in the energy inspection problem.

3. The optimum solution shifts to an adjacent corner when the slope of the objective function is no longer between the slopes of the two constraints.

In our brief discussion of sensitivity analysis we have considered only two parameters: the right-side constant of a single constraint and the coefficients of the objective function. Changes in the objective function coefficients produce either no change in the optimum solution or a discrete "jump" to a new optimum; a change in the right-side constant of an active constraint produces a gradual change in the optimum solution; and a change in the right-side constant of an inactive constraint produces no change in the optimum solution.

Changes in other parameters or in more than a single parameter are indeed possible and may affect the solution. The methods appropriate for such sensitivity analysis are beyond the intent of our treatment, but a decision maker is well advised to raise questions concerning the effects of such changes.

The graphic solution of the minilion diet problem indicated that solving a minimization linear program is quite similar to solving a maximization one. We now illustrate sensitivity analysis applied to a minimization problem.

SENSITIVITY ANALYSIS: A MINIMIZATION PROBLEM

Nutrition or diet selection problems are essentially concerned with finding the blend of components that satisfies a number of ingredient constraints. The required level of each ingredient may change with the condition of the individual; for example, as the minilions (of the illustration in Chapter 8) grow, their nutritional needs may change. The costs of the components may change; in the same minilion problem, the price of meat is subject to considerable variation. It is worthwhile reconsidering the minilion diet problem as an illustration of sensitivity analysis applied to a minimization problem.

The illustration from Chapter 8 is:

$$
\begin{array}{lrl}
\text{Minimize} & C = x_1 + 2x_2 & \\
\text{subject to} & 50x_1 + 250x_2 \geq 500 & \text{Protein} \\
& 240x_1 + 80x_2 \geq 960 & \text{Mineral} \\
& x_1 + x_2 \geq 6 & \text{Weight} \\
& x_1, x_2 \geq 0 &
\end{array}
$$

where the diet consists of x_1 kilograms of bone meal and x_2 kilograms of meat, and the cost is C dollars. Its graphic solution is represented in Figure 9-10. The optimum solution (5 kilograms of bone meal, 1 kilogram of meat) is at the corner point of the protein and weight constraints. The mineral constraint is inactive; so the mineral requirement can change, but not too much, without affecting the optimum solution. The protein constraint is active; so the solution is sensitive to changes in the protein requirement. As the protein requirement is increased, the solution slides up the weight constraint until it reaches the mineral constraint at the point (3, 3). The point (3, 3) is the solution for the program with the protein requirement greater than or equal to 900 units.

$$50x_1 + 250x_2 \geq 900 \qquad \text{units}$$

The corresponding cost is $9.00 per minilion per day. These new solutions and the marginal effects of changes in the protein requirement are summarized in Table 9-3. The marginal effects, valid throughout the range 300 to 900 units of protein, are found as follows:

$$\frac{\text{Change in bone meal}}{\text{Change in protein}} = \frac{-2}{400} = \frac{-1}{200} = \frac{\text{change in } x_1 \text{ per unit}}{\text{change in protein}}$$

$$\frac{\text{Change in meat}}{\text{Change in protein}} = \frac{2}{400} = \frac{1}{200} = \frac{\text{change in } x_2 \text{ per unit}}{\text{change in protein}}$$

$$\frac{\text{Change in cost}}{\text{Change in protein}} = \frac{2}{400} = \frac{1}{200} = \frac{\text{change in cost per unit}}{\text{change in protein}}$$

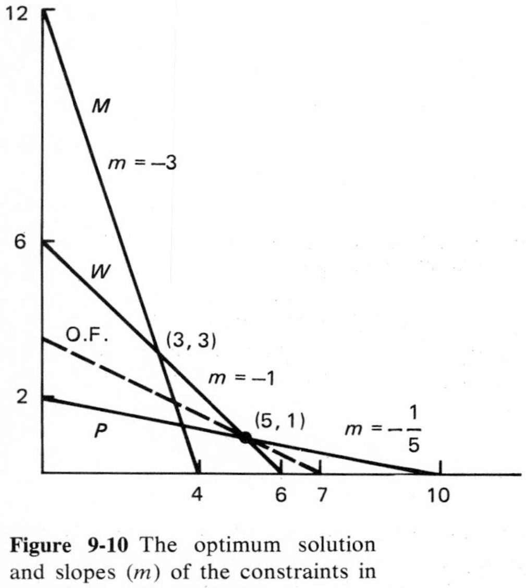

Figure 9-10 The optimum solution and slopes (m) of the constraints in the minilion diet problem.

Table 9-3 Sensitivity analysis of the right-side constant of the protein constraint $50x_1 + 250x_2 \geq 500$

Variable	Original optimum solution value	First new solution			Second new solution		
		New value	Change	Change per protein unit	New value	Change	Change per protein unit
b_1	500	900	400	—	300	−200	—
x_1	5	3	−2	$-\frac{1}{200}$	6	+1	$-\frac{1}{200}$
x_2	1	3	2	$\frac{1}{200}$	0	−1	$\frac{1}{200}$
Cost	7	9	2	$\frac{1}{200}$	6	−1	$\frac{1}{200}$

Throughout the range of proportionality the marginal effects remain constant; determining them relative to the second new solution of Table 9-3 will yield the same results. The shadow price, the value of an additional unit of a resource, does apply to "$\leq$" constraints that limit the availability of the resource but does not apply to the marginal effect on the objective function of a change in a "$\geq$" requirement constraint.

To determine the sensitivity of the solution to changes in the objective function coefficients, we again note that the solution is at the corner point of the protein constraint $50x_1 + 250x_2 \geq 500$ and the weight constraint $x_1 + x_2 \geq 6$. The slopes of these constraints are $-\frac{1}{5}$ and -1, respectively. The optimum solution is insensitive to changes in the coefficients of the objective function as long as the slope stays between -1 and $-\frac{1}{5}$. In this range the objective function is steeper than the protein constraint but flatter than the weight constraint. If the slope becomes greater than $-\frac{1}{5}$, the graph becomes flatter than the protein constraint and the solution jumps to (10, 0). Similarly, if the slope becomes less than -1, the graph becomes steeper than the weight constraint and the solution jumps to (3, 3). Hence the solution is insensitive to changes in the slope within the range -1 to $-\frac{1}{5}$. Changes beyond that range cause the optimum solution to jump to either (3, 3) or (10, 0).

As with maximization problems, changes in constraint constants have either no effect or a gradual effect on the solution depending on whether the constraint is inactive or active; changes in the objective function coefficients have either no effect or a discrete jump effect on the solution depending on whether the slope stays within the range or changes beyond the range.

SUMMARY

Generally, sensitivity analysis is concerned with the marginal effects of changes in problem parameters. Sensitivity analysis in linear programming considers the effects of changes in the coefficients and constants of the constraints, and coefficients of the objective function. We have considered only two relatively simple but illustrative cases involving changes in the constant term of a single constraint and changes in the coefficients of an objective function consisting of two variables.

1. If a constraint is inactive, changes in the constant term have no effect until the constraint becomes active. If it is active, then changes within a range of values produce proportional changes in the variables and in the value of the objective function.
2. The optimum solution is formed by the intersection of two constraints. Suppose their slopes are m_1 and m_2 with $m_1 < m_2$; the slope of the objective function is m_0. As long as $m_1 < m_0 < m_2$, the optimum solution is unchanged. For either $m_0 < m_1$ or $m_2 < m_0$, there is a discrete jump to a new solution. For either $m_1 = m_0$ or $m_2 = m_0$, any point between the old and new solutions is also a solution.

The last section of Chapter 10 will discuss other examples of sensitivity analysis. The reader wanting results and interpretation without going through the analysis can skip the simplex procedure; the reader wanting a more detailed understanding of both solutions and sensitivity will find it in the simplex procedure of Chapter 10.

BIBLIOGRAPHY

See the Bibliography for Chapter 8.

APPENDIX: THE SLOPE OF A STRAIGHT LINE

For different constants in the objective function, $N = x_1 + x_2$, different lines are generated. However, they are all parallel; that is, the constant term has no effect on the direction of the line. The coefficients of the variables determine the direction of the line. In this regard, the commonly used indicator of line direction is called the *slope*. The slope of a line can be found from its equation by rewriting the equation so the x_2 variable is isolated; that is, the equation is *solved* for x_2. Consider the equation

$$4x_1 + 2x_2 = 16$$

To put it in the desired form, rewrite it as

$$2x_2 = -4x_1 + 16$$

and then

$$x_2 = -2x_1 + 8$$

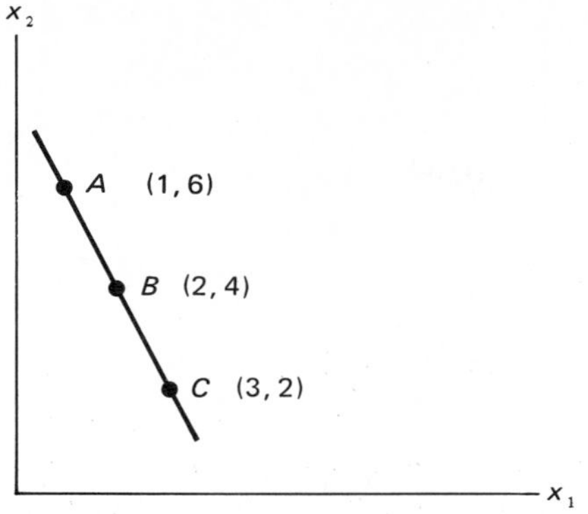

Figure 9-11 Slope $= \dfrac{\text{change in } x_2}{\text{change in } x_1}$

$= \dfrac{-4}{2} = -2$ and $\dfrac{2}{-1} = -2.$

With the linear equation in this form, the coefficient of x_1 is the slope. Graphically the slope represents the change in the x_2 variable per unit change in the x_1 variable. The slope of -2 indicates that when x_1 changes 1 unit, x_2 changes -2 units. The graph of this equation is represented in Figure 9-11. Note that in moving from one point on the line to another point on the line, a 1-unit change in x_1 is accompanied by a -2-unit change in x_2. For example, in moving from point B to point C, x_1 changes 1, from 2 to 3, and x_2 changes -2, from 4 to 2.

An alternative description is

$$\text{Slope} = \frac{\text{change in } x_2}{\text{change in } x_1}$$

for any two points on the line. For example, from point A to point C,

$$\frac{\text{Change in } x_2}{\text{Change in } x_1} = \frac{-4}{2} = -2$$

or from point C to point B,

$$\frac{\text{Change in } x_2}{\text{Change in } x_1} = \frac{2}{-1} = -2$$

The slope of this line is negative because an increase in x_1 is accompanied by a decrease in x_2; the graph of such a line decreases from left to right. A line with a positive slope will rise from left to right; on such a line, an increase in x_1 is accompanied by an increase in x_2.

Since it is the coefficients that determine the slope, changing the coefficient of either or both variables will therefore change the slope and hence the direction of the line. Changing the coefficients in the Public Power Commission ob-

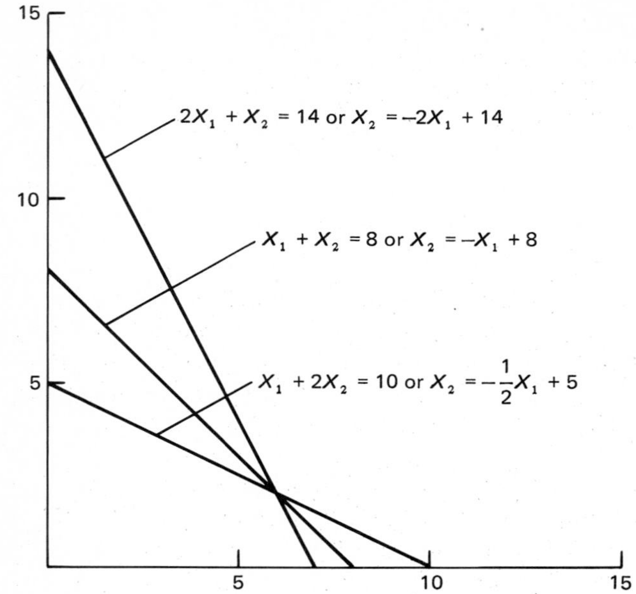

Figure 9-12 A change in the coefficient of X_1 or X_2 changes the slope and the direction of the line.

jective function generates graphs like those in Figure 9-12. The constant terms have no effect on the slope or the direction. For reference to that application, the lines have been drawn to intersect at the optimum solution. Note too that the constant term represents the x_2 intercept when the equation is written in the form just specified. Since the slope and the intercept are readily determined when the equation is in this form, it is often referred to as the "slope-intercept form" of a straight line. Common usage prescribes that the letter m represent the slope, and b the x_2 intercept. Hence the slope-intercept form is written as

$$x_2 = mx_1 + b$$

EXERCISES

Extensions of chapter examples

9-1 How are the optimum solution and the objective function affected when the heating inspection time available is changed in the power inspection problem of this chapter? (See p. 197.)

9-2 What is the effect of altering the mineral requirements in the minilion diet problem of this chapter? (See p. 209.)

9-3 What is the effect of altering the weight requirement in the same minilion diet problem?

Other applications

9-4 Refer to problem 8-5.

(*a*) Determine the effects of changes in the objective function coefficients of Y_1.

(*b*) Determine the effects of changes in the objective function coefficient of Y_2.

(*c*) Summarize your answers to parts *a* and *b* in a single specific statement.

9-5 Determine the effects of altering (both increasing and decreasing) the right-side constants of each of the constraints, one at a time, in problem 8-5.

9-6 Refer to problem 8-9. How will the optimum diet be affected if the minimum requirement of starch is decreased? Increased?

Project problems

9-7 Refer to your linear program for exercise 8-5.

(*a*) What are some likely and reasonable sensitivity analysis questions?

(*b*) What effect would such sensitivity analysis have on relevant decision making?

9-8 Refer to any linear programming application from a journal in your own field of interest (see exercise 8-16).

(*a*) What sensitivity analysis issues were raised in the article?

(*b*) How were they resolved (if they were) and what effects did they have on decision making?

(*c*) What might be some other sensitivity issues?

CHAPTER

TEN

LINEAR PROGRAMMING III: THE SIMPLEX METHOD

In the two preceding chapters, we discussed linear programming problems of varying degrees of complexity. The personnel assignment problem for the power commission and the diet problem for the minilions' zookeeper were solvable by simple graphic methods. The income redistribution problem in the national health insurance illustration and the school busing problem were not solvable through simple graphic methods. Problems of even this slight complexity require a less simple solution method. The commonly employed method is called the simplex method. The simplex method requires quite a bit of basic computation (addition, subtraction, multiplication, and division) so that most programs are solved with the aid of a computer. As we have seen in Chapter 9, the usefulness of linear programming does not stop when an optimum solution is found, but rather continues through sensitivity analysis. In order to better comprehend a solution in its fullest sense, we will discuss generally the basic simplex method before providing the computational details.

THE SIMPLEX METHOD

First we explain the general process of the simplex method through the graphic solution. Then we will focus on the computational details.

Overview

For purposes of illustration, we will use a slight modification of the Public Power Commission's problem from Chapter 8; the modification was actually solved in our discussion of sensitivity analysis in Chapter 9.

Maximize the objective function

$$N = X_1 + 2X_2$$

subject to the constraints

$$4X_1 + 2X_2 \leq 28 \qquad \text{I}$$

$$2X_1 + 6X_2 \leq 30 \qquad \text{E}$$

$$4X_1 + 6X_2 \leq 36 \qquad \text{H}$$

$$X_1, X_2 \geq 0$$

The solution to the linear program is found by first getting the feasible region. The feasible region for that linear program is presented in Figure 10-1. As we have noticed, a solution to a linear program is always a corner point of the feasible region. Therefore, one way of solving a linear program would be to identify all the corner points and then determine which corner point yields the highest value for the objective function. Such a point would be the optimum solution. For the simple two-variable problem, identifying the corner points and substituting them into the objective function are quite simple. If we did not

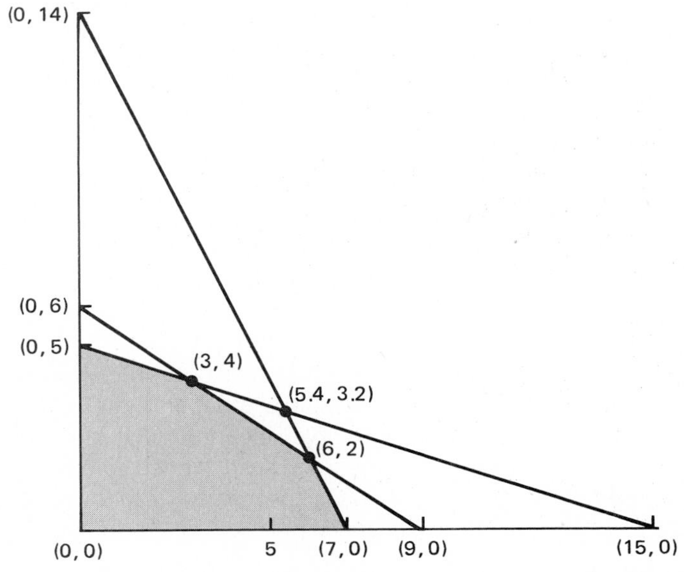

Figure 10-1 The feasible region and all constraint intersections for the energy inspection problem.

have a picture of the feasible region, we would first find all corner points; that is, we would find all the points of intersection of any two of the five constraints. We note in Figure 10-1 that there are 10 such points of intersection. Then we determine which corner points, or which points of intersection, solve or satisfy the other constraints. These are the feasible corner points. We see from Figure 10-1 that there are five such feasible corner points. Then we determine which of the five feasible corner points maximizes the objective function. With only two variables the complete enumeration approach is tedious.

With 15 variables and 20 constraints, still relatively small scale, there are more than 9 billion corner points. If a computer is able to generate 10 complete solutions every second, it would still take more than 9 years to determine the optimum. Something more efficient is fortunately available. The simplex method examines only some of the corner points, or points of intersection of constraint equations, that are feasible. If we are able to identify one feasible corner point that the simplex method can start with, it will then "move" from corner to corner around the feasible region until it identifies the optimum solution.

A simply found feasible solution in our illustration is the point (0, 0), the origin. With that as the starting point, the simplex method then considers the two adjacent corners, namely, (7, 0) and (0, 5), to see which one gives the objective function the greater marginal increase; that corner becomes the next solution. With any corner as the starting point, the simplex method compares all adjacent corners to see which gives the objective function the greatest marginal improvement. If none will improve the objective function, then the simplex method concludes that the current corner is the optimum.

Somewhat oversimplified, the simplex method can be considered a "search": Given a starting point the search continues through corners that will improve the objective function; when no further improvement can be made, the search concludes at the optimum solution. In Figure 10-1 we start the search at the origin; since X_1 improves the objective function one unit at a time (the coefficient of X_1 in the objective function is 1) and X_2 improves the objective function two units at a time (the coefficient of X_2 in the objective function is 2), the search continues to the point (0, 5). From that point, realizing that going back to the origin decreases the objective function but going to (3, 4) increases the objective function, the search moves on to (3, 4). From there, noting that moving to (0, 5) or to (6, 2) decreases the objective function, the search concludes at (3, 4), the optimum solution.

The simplex method is a step-by-step algorithm that seeks out the optimum solution and guarantees finding it (if one exists) in a finite number of steps. The process of moving from one corner to another involves algebraic manipulation that is not quite so simple as the visual image might suggest. Nevertheless, the preceding paragraph describes the essence of successive steps in the simplex method, and hopefully provides an intuitive grasp that will assist in understanding the details.

The Process

The simplex method consists of five basic steps:

1. Standardize the linear program by rewriting the inequalities as equations.
2. Get an initial solution.
3. Apply the optimality criterion and either (*a*) stop the process because an optimum solution has been found, or (*b*) select a new variable to enter the solution and go to step 4.
4. Select the variable to leave the solution.
5. Generate a new solution; go back to step 3.

We now describe and illustrate the basic steps.

Standardize the Linear Program

The first step in the simplex method is to convert all the inequality constraints to equalities, which is accomplished by creating variables as necessary. To convert the inequality

$$4X_1 + 2X_2 \leq 28$$

to an equality, or an equation, add a new variable which represents the amount of unused insulation inspection time. The equation can now be written as

$$4X_1 + 2X_2 + S_1 = 28$$

Variable S_1 is referred to as a *slack variable,* and it represents the unused capacity, or the amount by which the availability exceeds the need. In a similar way, the other two constraints are converted to equations; the three transformed constraints are

$$4X_1 + 2X_2 + S_1 + 0S_2 + 0S_3 = 28$$

$$2X_1 + 6X_2 + 0S_1 + S_2 + 0S_3 = 30$$

$$4X_1 + 6X_2 + 0S_1 + 0S_2 + S_3 = 36$$

The constraints $X_1 \geq 0$ and $X_2 \geq 0$ are not converted to equations, but the simplex method makes use of these nonnegative constraints by requiring that all variables be nonnegative. Since slack variables contribute nothing to complete inspections, their coefficients in the objective function are 0 and the objective function becomes

$$N = 1X_1 + 2X_2 + 0S_1 + 0S_2 + 0S_3$$

The constraints now are three equations with five unknowns. Where there are three equations, only three variables are needed to find a solution. If we let two of the variables be zero, then we can find values for the other variables.

Table 10-1 All points of intersection of the constraints of the revised power loss example

Variables set equal to zero	Solution variables and values	Objective function	Point in Figure 10-1
X_1, X_2	$S_1 = 28, S_2 = 30, S_3 = 36$	0	(0, 0)
X_1, S_1	$X_2 = 14, S_2 = -54, S_3 = -48$	Infeasible	(0, 14)
X_1, S_2	$X_2 = 5, S_1 = 18, S_3 = 60$	10	(0, 5)
X_1, S_3	$X_2 = 6, S_1 = 16, S_2 = -6$	Infeasible	(0, 6)
X_2, S_1	$X_1 = 7, S_2 = 16, S_3 = 8$	7	(7, 0)
X_2, S_2	$X_1 = 15, S_1 = -32\ S_3 = -24$	Infeasible	(15, 0)
X_2, S_3	$X_1 = 9, S_1 = -8, S_2 = 12$	Infeasible	
S_1, S_2	$X_1 = 5.4, X_2 = 3.2, S_3 = -4.8$	Infeasible	(5.4, 3.2)
S_1, S_3	$X_1 = 6, X_2 = 2, S_2 = 6$	10	(6, 2)
S_2, S_3	$X_1 = 3, X_2 = 4, S_1 = 8$	11	(3, 4)

For example, if we let $X_1 = 0$ and $X_2 = 0$, then $S_1 = 28$, $S_2 = 30$, and $S_3 = 36$. All the solutions, that is, all points of intersection of the constraints, are given in Table 10-1.

The infeasible solutions are identified by some of the solution variables having negative values, which do not satisfy the nonnegativity constraints. Listing all the points of intersection in order to determine which ones are feasible, and which of the feasible ones is optimum, is barely practical even in this small problem; in a more realistic problem it would be all but impossible. The simplex method evaluates just some of the solutions in its process of seeking the optimum.

An Initial Solution

The simplex method requires some corner point as the starting point and then proceeds step by step until an optimum solution is arrived at. A starting point is found with little effort by letting the real variables equal zero.

The slack variables then necessarily are equal to the right-side constants of their respective constraints. This yields what is referred to as an *initial solution*. The initial solution is on the first line of Table 10-1.

The Simplex Tableau

It is both conventional and convenient to represent the successive solutions of the simplex method in a table format, called the *simplex tableau*. Our initial solution is represented in Table 10-2. The top row of the table contains the objective function coefficients, and the body of the table contains the coefficients from the constraint equations. The solution variables are those variables which are not equal to zero; this initial solution was found by letting X_1 and $X_2 = 0$,

Table 10-2 Initial solution

C			1	2	0	0	0
	Solution variables	Solution values	X_1	X_2	S_1	S_2	S_3
0	S_1	28	4	2	1	0	0
0	S_2	30	2	6	0	1	0
0	S_3	36	4	6	0	0	1

which corresponds to the origin and to the first solution in Table 10-1. The first column consists of the objective function coefficients of the solution variables.

The constraint coefficients, the values in the body of the table, can also be termed *substitution coefficients*. If X_1 is increased by one unit from its current value of zero, then the values in the X_1 column correspond to the amounts of the solution variables that would be replaced; that is, 1 unit of X_1 requires or replaces 4 units of S_1, 2 units of S_2, and 4 units of S_3.

Since the units of S_1, S_2, and S_3, the excess time available to each inspector, contribute nothing to the objective function, reducing their values will have no effect on the objective function. This *indirect reduction in the objective function* or *opportunity cost* of increasing X_1 is found by finding the product of the X_1 column values times the C column values and adding the products. The result is entered in the Z row of the complete tableau. For the initial solution

$$Z_1 = 4(0) + 2(0) + 4(0) = 0$$

and

$$Z_2 = 2(0) + 6(0) + 6(0) = 0$$

Subsequent tableaus will have fewer zero entries; there the meaning of the Z values and the way they are found will be more easily seen.

The coefficients in the objective function represent the direct effect of one unit of X_1, or one house inspection, and of one unit of X_2, or one plant inspection. The difference between this *direct effect* on the objective function C and the *opportunity cost* Z gives the *net marginal effect* on the objective function, $C - Z$. Table 10-3 contains the complete initial simplex tableau. The last row, $C - Z$, is extremely important in the process of moving from one solution to another.

Apply the Optimality Criterion

Deciding whether the optimum solution has been found or a new solution should be sought depends on the net marginal effect row, $C - Z$. In a maximization linear program, the process tries to increase the objective function. The *optimality criterion* for a maximization linear program is:

1. If there are no positive values in the $C - Z$ row, an optimum solution has been found, or there is no feasible solution.

Table 10-3 Initial solution

C	Solution variables	Solution values	1 X_1	2 X_2	0 S_1	0 S_2	0 S_3	Direct marginal effect
0	S_1	28	4	2	1	0	0	Substitution coefficients
0	S_2	30	2	6	0	1	0	
0	S_3	36	4	6	0	0	1	
	Z	$N = 0$	0	0	0	0	0	Marginal opportunity cost
	$C - Z$		1	2	0	0	0	Net marginal effect

2. If there are positive values in the C − Z row, the *greatest* positive value identifies the *variable to enter the solution.*

From Table 10-3 we note that X_2 has the greatest positive value and hence the greatest positive effect on the objective function; therefore, X_2 is the variable to be increased from its current value of 0. That is, it will enter the solution. Graphically this corresponds to moving from the origin to the feasible corner point on the X_2 axis. As X_2 enters the solution, one of the present solution variables will leave the solution, or will become equal to zero. We now determine which variable will leave the solution.

Select the Variable to Leave the Solution

In Table 10-3, the substitution coefficients in the X_2 column (X_2 is the entering variable) indicate how much of each of the solution variables will be replaced by one unit of X_2. One unit of X_2 will replace 2 units of variable S_1; since the present value of S_1 is 28, 14 units of X_2 can be brought into the solution, forcing S_1 to become equal to 0 or to leave the solution. Continuing, 1 unit of X_2 replaces 6 units of S_2; since the present solution value of S_2 is 30, 5 units of X_2 can be brought into the solution. Finally, 1 unit of X_2 replaces 6 units of S_3; since the present solution value of S_3 is 36, 6 units of X_2 can be brought into the new solution. The smallest of these values, 5, is the most that X_2 can equal without forcing one of the solution variables to be negative, contrary to the requirements of linear programming. For example, if $X_2 = 14$, then 14 units of X_2 would replace 84 units of S_2 ($14 \times 6 = 84$). This would force S_2 to be reduced from its present value of 30 to -54. This would not be permitted by the nonnegativity constraint on all variables. Thus, X_2 will enter the solution and will equal 5, forcing $S_2 = 0$; that is, S_2 will leave the solution.

The key to determining the leaving variable is to divide each of the solution values by the corresponding value in the entering column; then the smallest of the positive ratios indicates the variable to leave the solution.

The smallest of 28/2, 30/6, and 36/6 is 30/6; thus S_2 will leave the solution.

In Table 10-3, the entering variable column and the leaving variable row are circled. The value that is in both of them, called the *pivot element,* plays a key role in generating the next solution.

Generate the New Solution

Replacing the leaving variable with the entering variable yields the new solution. Revising the tableau to reflect the change is done in two steps. Recall that the upper half of the tableau corresponds to the constraint equations of the linear program. The process will merely rewrite the constraints so that the current solution variables (the nonzero variables) are readily identified.

The process uses the two following basic rules of algebra:

1. An equation is essentially unchanged if it is multiplied or divided by a constant.
2. A set of equations is essentially unchanged if a multiple of one equation is added to or subtracted from another.

The steps of the process are:

1. Divide the leaving row by the pivot element. (This makes the pivot element become 1.)
2. For each of the other rows, call its value in the entering column the "key element." Multiply the leaving row by the quotient

$$\frac{\text{Key element}}{\text{Pivot element}}$$

and subtract it from each old row to get each new row. That is,

$$\text{New row} = \text{old row} - \frac{\text{key}}{\text{pivot}} \cdot \text{leaving row}$$

This makes all the key elements become 0 in the new solution. The Z row and $C - Z$ row are found in the same way as they were in the initial solution.

From Table 10-3, X_2 will enter and S_2 will leave to get the second solution. Replacing S_2 by X_2 and appropriately revising the tableau follow.

1. Divide each element of the leaving row by the pivot element, 6. This step appears in Table 10-4.

Table 10-4 Second solution—incomplete

C	Solution variables	Solution values	1 X_1	2 X_2	0 S_1	0 S_2	0 S_3
0	S_1						
2	X_2	5	$\frac{1}{3}$	1	0	$\frac{1}{6}$	0
0	S_3						

2. Revise the other rows. We shall revise the S_1 row first. 2 is the key element.

Old S_1 row		28	4	2	1	0	0
$-\dfrac{\text{key } (=2)}{\text{pivot } (=6)} \cdot$ leaving row	$-$	10	$\frac{2}{3}$	2	0	$\frac{1}{3}$	0
$=$ new S_1 row		18	$3\frac{1}{3}$	0	1	$-\frac{1}{3}$	0

Now we revise the S_3 row; 6 is the key element.

Old S_3 row		36	4	6	0	0	1
$-\dfrac{\text{key } (=6)}{\text{pivot } (=6)} \cdot$ leaving row	$-$	30	2	6	0	1	0
$=$ new S_3 row		6	2	0	0	-1	1

Table 10-5 presents the upper half of the second solution tableau.[1] From the revised constraints in Table 10-5 we determine the Z row. Its

Table 10-5 Second solution—incomplete

C	Solution variables	Solution values	1 X_1	2 X_2	0 S_1	0 S_2	0 S_3
0	S_1	18	$3\frac{1}{3}$	0	1	$-\frac{1}{3}$	0
2	X_2	5	$\frac{1}{3}$	1	0	$\frac{1}{6}$	0
0	S_3	6	2	0	0	-1	1

[1] There is an alternate and equivalent method for step 2 of revising the tableau. After the leaving row has been divided by the pivot element, it becomes the *entry* row of the new tableau. The other rows are revised by

$$\text{New row} = \text{old row} - \text{key element} \cdot (\text{entry row})$$

Consider an example, using the entry row from Table 10-4.

Old S_1 row		28	4	2	1	0	0
$-$ key $(=2)$ $\cdot$ entry row	$-$	10	$\frac{2}{3}$	2	0	$\frac{1}{3}$	0
$=$ new S_1 row		18	$3\frac{1}{3}$	0	1	$-\frac{1}{3}$	0

first entry is the value of the objective function for the second solution; it is the sum of the products of the objective function coefficients (the C column) and the solution values.

$$\text{Objective function} = 18(0) + 5(2) + 6(0) = 10$$

The values for the other columns are found by finding the sum of the products of the objective function coefficients and the corresponding values in the column; for example,

$$Z_1 = 3\tfrac{1}{3}(0) + \tfrac{1}{3}(2) + 2(0) = \tfrac{2}{3}$$

Subtracting the Z row from the objective function coefficients (the C row) leaves the $C - Z$ row, which is the net marginal effect on the objective function of changes in the variables. These rows yield the complete second solution, which is presented in Table 10-6.

Applying the optimality criterion reveals at least one positive value in the last row; the optimum solution has not been reached. Thus we go through the process of moving to the next corner, of finding a new solution once again. Having the only positive last-row value in the X_1 column indicates that X_1 is the variable to enter the solution.

To find the variable to leave the solution, divide each solution value by the corresponding value in the column of the entering variable. The resulting ratios are

$$\frac{18}{3\frac{1}{3}} \qquad \frac{5}{\frac{1}{3}} \qquad \frac{6}{2}$$

The smallest of these, $\frac{6}{2}$, shows that S_3 is the variable to leave the solution.

The pivot element 2 is circled in Table 10-6. The third solution is arrived at by following the exact same row operation process as before; the third solution is presented in Table 10-7. Since the last row of the third solution contains no

Table 10-6 Second solution

C	Solution variables	Solution values	1 X_1	2 X_2	0 S_1	0 S_2	0 S_3	Direct marginal effect
0	S_1	18	$3\frac{1}{3}$	0	1	$-\frac{1}{3}$	0	Substitution coefficients
2	X_2	5	$\frac{1}{3}$	1	0	$\frac{1}{6}$	0	
0	S_3	6	(2)	0	0	-1	1	
	Z	$N = 10$	$\frac{2}{3}$	2	0	$\frac{1}{3}$	0	Marginal opportunity cost
	$C - Z$		$\frac{1}{3}$	0	0	$-\frac{1}{3}$	0	Net marginal effect

Table 10-7 Third solution

C	Solution variables	Solution values	1 X_1	2 X_2	0 S_1	0 S_2	0 S_3	Direct marginal effect
0	S_1	8	0	0	1	$\frac{4}{3}$	$-\frac{5}{3}$	Substitution coefficients
2	X_2	4	0	1	0	$\frac{1}{3}$	$-\frac{1}{6}$	
1	X_1	3	1	0	0	$-\frac{1}{2}$	$\frac{1}{2}$	
	Z	$N = 11$	1	2	0	$\frac{1}{6}$	$\frac{1}{6}$	Marginal opportunity cost
	$C - Z$		0	0	0	$-\frac{1}{6}$	$-\frac{1}{6}$	Net marginal effect

positive values, we know that we have reached an optimum solution. From the "solution values" column we know that the optimum solution is:

$X_1 = 3$ Homes inspected

$X_2 = 4$ Plants inspected

$S_1 = 8$ Excess insulation inspection hours

$N = 11$ Value of objective function; the units have not been specified

This optimum solution agrees, as we would expect, with the optimum solution found by the graphic method of Figure 10-1 and the enumeration process in Table 10-1.

In this section we have illustrated the simplex method for a maximization linear program with "$\leq$" constraints. The simplex method for a minimization problem, and for linear programs with "$\geq$" and "$=$" constraints, has a few minor changes which we will illustrate in the next section.

THE SIMPLEX METHOD: A MINIMIZATION PROBLEM

The minilion diet problem from Chapter 8 serves as a suitable example of a minimization linear program. The linear program is

Minimize $C = X_1 + 2X_2$ Cost

subject to $50X_1 + 250X_2 \geq 500$ Protein

$240X_1 + 80X_2 \geq 960$ Mineral fiber

$1X_1 + 1X_2 \geq 6$ Weight

$X_1, X_2 \geq 0$ Nonnegativity

Following the basic five-step approach, we first introduce new variables to convert the inequalities into equations. The new variable added to a "≥" constraint is referred to as a *surplus variable*. This new variable represents the amount by which what is generated (the left side of the inequality) exceeds what is required (the right side). After this has been done, the constraints appear as

$$\begin{aligned} 50X_1 + 250X_2 - S_1 \qquad\qquad &= 500 \\ 240X_1 + 80X_2 \qquad - S_2 \qquad &= 960 \\ X_1 + X_2 \qquad\qquad - S_3 &= 6 \end{aligned}$$

As before, the simplex method needs an initial solution to get the process started. In the previous example, letting the slack variables equal the right-side constants provided the origin as an initial solution. However, in the present example if we let $X_1 = 0$ and $X_2 = 0$, then the surplus variables would be negative. This is in contradiction to the requirement that all variables be positive or zero. To get a simple initial solution, we introduce another new variable into each constraint. These variables are referred to as *artificial variables;* the artificial variables do not represent any quantity relevant to the problem, whereas the slack and surplus variables represent real excesses. With the artificial variables added, the constraints now appear as:

$$\begin{aligned} 50X_1 + 250X_2 - S_1 \qquad\qquad + A_1 \qquad\qquad &= 500 \\ 240X_1 + 80X_2 \qquad - S_2 \qquad\qquad + A_2 \qquad &= 960 \\ X_1 + X_2 \qquad\qquad - S_3 \qquad\qquad + A_3 &= 6 \end{aligned}$$

Since the artificial variables do not represent any relevant quantities, we want to be sure that they do not appear in the final solution. In order to guarantee their removal, they are given enormous coefficients in the objective function so that as the simplex method seeks to minimize the objective function, the artificial variables will necessarily be removed. The objective function then becomes:

$$C = X_1 + 2X_2 + 0S_1 + 0S_2 + 0S_3 + MA_1 + MA_2 + MA_3$$

where M represents a positive number larger than any number that might appear throughout the solution process.

From these revised constraints and the objective function, the initial simplex tableau appears as in Table 10-8.

The first departure from the simplex method of the last section is the need for artificial variables in the ≥ constraints. The other departure is that for a minimization linear program, the criterion for a variable to enter the solution is the one with the largest-sized negative value in the last row, rather than the largest-sized positive one. Remembering that M is a very large positive number, the column with the largest-sized negative value in the last row is X_2; therefore X_2 enters the solution.

The criterion to determine which variable leaves the solution is the same as in the case of the maximization program; whether the constraints originally

Table 10-8 Initial solution
Minimization problem

C	Solution variables	Solution values	1 X_1	2 X_2	0 S_1	0 S_2	0 S_3	M A_1	M A_2	M A_3
M	A_1	500	50	(250)	−1	0	0	1	0	0
M	A_2	960	240	80	0	−1	0	0	1	0
M	A_3	6	1	1	0	0	−1	0	0	1
	Z_j	$C = 1466M$	$291M$	$331M$	$-M$	$-M$	$-M$	M	M	M
	$C - Z$		$1 - 291M$	$2 - 331M$	M	M	M	0	0	0

were "≤" or "≥" or "=" does not matter at this point, since all the constraints have been made equations. Since $\frac{500}{050} < \frac{960}{80}$ and $(\frac{500}{250}) < \frac{6}{1}$, variable A_1 leaves the solution, and so 250 is the pivot element.

In moving to the next corner point, or the next solution, the same process that was used in the maximization program is used here. The two steps are:

1. Divide the leaving row by the pivot element.
2. For each of the other rows, use

New row = old row $- \dfrac{\text{key}}{\text{pivot}} \cdot$ leaving row. Apply this to the A_2 row as follows:

Old A_2 row	960	240	80	0	−1	0	0	1	0
$-\dfrac{\text{key }(=80)}{\text{pivot }(=250)} \cdot$ leaving row −	160	16	80	−.32	0	0	.32	0	0
= new A_2 row	800	224	0	.32	−1	0	−.32	1	0

The Z and $C - Z$ rows are computed from the top half of the tableau in the same way as before. The second solution is presented in Table 10-9.

Table 10-9 Second solution
Minimization problem

C	Solution variables	Solution values	1 X_1	2 X_2	0 S_1	0 S_2	0 S_3	M A_1	M A_2	M A_3
2	X_2	2	.2	1	−.004	0	0	.004	0	0
M	A_2	800	(224)	0	.32	−1	0	−.32	1	0
M	A_3	4	.8	0	.004	0	−1	−.004	0	1
	Z	$C = 804M + 4$	$224.8M$ $+.4$	2	$.324M$ $-.008$	$-M$	$-M$	$-.324M$ $+.008$	M	M
	$C - Z$		.6 $-224.8M$	0	.008 $-.324M$	M	M	$1.324M$ $-.008$	0	0

Table 10-10 Third solution
Minimization problem

C	Solution variables	Solution values	1 X_1	2 X_2	0 S_1	0 S_2	0 S_3	M A_1	M A_2	M A_3
2	X_2	1.29	0	1	−.0043	.0009	0	.0043	−.0009	0
1	X_1	3.57	1	0	.0014	−.0045	0	−.0014	.0045	0
M	A_3	1.14	0	0	.0029	.0036	−1	−.0029	−.0036	1
	Z	$1.14M + 6.15$	1	2	$.0029M$	$.0036M$	$-M$	$-.0028M$	$-.0035M$	M
	$C - Z$		0	0	$-.0029M$	$-.0036M$	M	$1.0029M$	$1.0036M$	0

Having at least one negative value in the last row shows we have not reached an optimum solution. Since the largest-sized negative value in the $C - Z$ row corresponds to variable X_1, it will enter the solution. Since

$$\frac{800}{224} < \frac{2}{.2} \quad \text{and} \quad \frac{800}{224} < \frac{4}{.8}$$

A_2 leaves the solution, and 224 is the pivot element.

The third solution appears in Table 10-10. The Z and $C - Z$ rows have been slightly modified by including only the very large M portion of terms containing M. Since M was defined as such a large number, any ordinary constant is negligible compared to any multiple of M (even $.0001M$). Note in Table 10-10 that A_3 is still in the solution. This means that we have not yet reached a solution that is feasible according to the original inequality constraints. Any solution containing an artificial variable is infeasible. The graph of the feasible region for the current problem is reproduced in Figure 10-2 (page 330); note there that the third solution, $X_1 = 3.57$ and $X_2 = 1.29$, is not within the feasible region.

As long as there are negative values in the $C - Z$ row, we have not obtained a minimum, and so the process goes on to the next solution. The fourth solution is presented in Table 10-11 (page 330). This is the first solution that is feasible according to the original constraints; note that the artificial variables are no longer in solution. The solution variables are X_1, X_2, and S_2. Since there is no negative value in the $C - Z$ row, the solution is optimum; it is circled in Figure 10-2.

Note in Table 10-11 that the last row for the artificial variables contains only the value M, disregarding the values of the Z row since they are small compared with M. Actually, since the artificial variables will not reenter a solution once they have left the solution, the column corresponding to any artificial variable may be eliminated from the simplex tableau once that artificial variable has been eliminated from the solution.

We noted that as long as there is an artificial variable among the solution variables, the solution is not a feasible one. This becomes the operational criterion for determining that a linear program has no feasible solution. There are also other special cases that warrant some brief discussion.

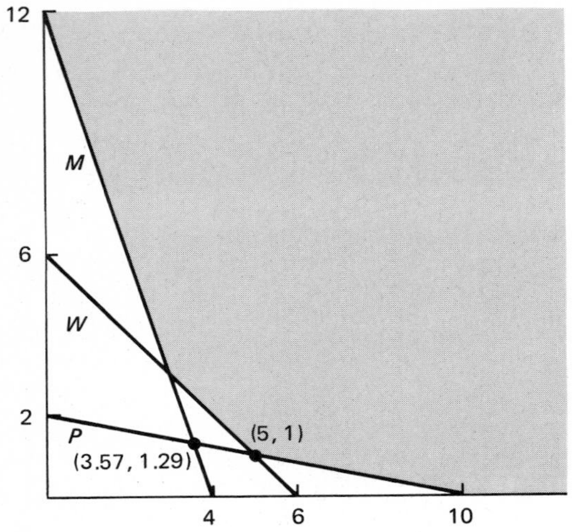

Figure 10-2 Graphs of the constraints: protein, $50X_1 + 250X_2 \geq 500$; mineral fiber, $240X_1 + 80X_2 \geq 960$; weight $X_1 + X_2 \geq 6$; the point (3.57, 1.29) from the third solution is infeasible. The point (5, 1) from the fourth solution is optimum.

LINEAR PROGRAMMING: SPECIAL CASES

The two problems that we have examined in this chapter and most of the problems that we have examined in the two preceding chapters led to a single optimum solution. There are certain special cases in linear programming that should prompt a reexamination of the problem situation. We now discuss these with brief illustrations.

No Feasible Solution

The presence of constraints having no common solutions results in the linear program having no possible solution. Detecting this situation is not always quite so simple as our illustration will suggest.

Example Consider the linear program:

Table 10-11 Optimum solution
Minimization problem

C	Solution variables	Solution values	1 X_1	2 X_2	0 S_1	0 S_2	0 S_3	M A_1	M A_2	M A_3
2	X_2	1	0	1	−.005	0	.25	.005	0	−.25
1	X_1	5	1	0	.005	0	−1.25	−.005	0	1.25
0	S_2	320	0	0	.8	1.0	−280	−.8	−1	280
	Z	7	1	2	−.005	0	−.75	.005	0	.75
	$C - Z$		0	0	.005	0	.75	M	M	M

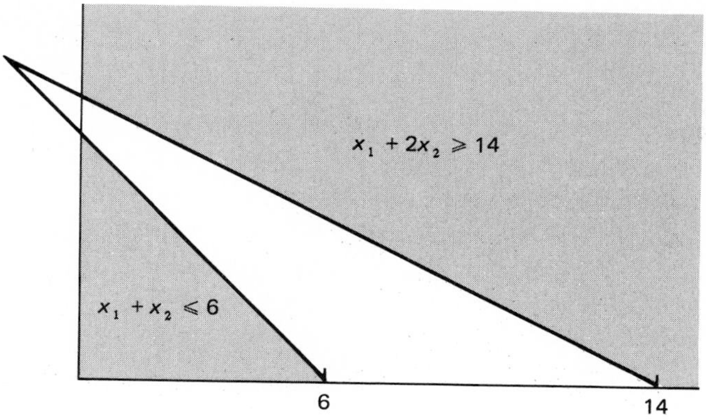

Figure 10-3 No feasible solution.

Maximize $\qquad Z = 3X_1 + X_2$

subject to

$$X_1 + X_2 \leq 6$$
$$X_1 + 2X_2 \geq 14$$
$$X_1, X_2 \geq 0$$

The graph of these constraints is attempted in Figure 10-3.

As we can see from the graph, it is not possible to find a point that is below the lower line and above the upper line; that is, there is *no feasible solution*. It is *not true* that every linear program with a "≤" constraint and a "≥" constraint has no feasible solution. The national health insurance application and exercise 8-7 from Chapter 8 are some examples.

If we had not graphed the problem, we might proceed with trying to solve it. In standardized form, the linear program, with equality constraints, is as follows:

Maximize $\qquad Z = 3X_1 + X_2 + 0S_1 + 0S_2 - MA_2$

subject to

$$X_1 + X_2 + S_1 = 6$$
$$X_1 + 2X_2 - S_2 + A_2 = 14$$

The second constraint requires an artificial variable to get a simple initial solution. Since we are maximizing the objective function, and we do not want the artificial variable to remain in the solution, we give the artificial variable a negative coefficient that is very large in size ($-M$). We proceed with the simplex tableau in the usual manner, continuing to go from solution to solution until the final row has no positive elements. The final tableau is presented in Table 10-12. The fact that the artificial variable remains in the

Table 10-12 No feasible solution

C	Solution variables	Solution values	3 X_1	1 X_2	0 S_1	0 S_2	$-M$ A_2
1	X_2	6	1	1	1	0	0
$-M$	A_2	2	-1	0	-2	-1	1
	Z	$6 - 2M$	$1 + M$	1	$1 + 2M$	M	$-M$
	$C - Z$		$+2 - M$	0	$-1 - 2M$	$-M$	0

final solution indicates that there is no solution satisfying the original constraints.

The source of such a conclusion is either that the problem was not properly formulated in the first place, or the set of requirements is self-contradictory. The first possibility is uncovered in checking the formulation. If the problem statement is properly formulated, then we cannot satisfy all the constraints simultaneously, much less find a solution that maximizes an objective function. One or more of the constraints must be relaxed to get any solution at all. One approach to the no feasible solution is to establish priorities among the constraints and treat them as goals rather than rigid requirements. The appropriate technique to employ then is goal programming, the subject of Chapter 11. Relative to decision making, this satisficing rather than optimizing approach at least yields a workable solution.

Unbounded Solution

Not identifying all the constraints in a decision situation may lead decision makers to expect more than can actually be realized, by leaving the feasible region unbounded in the direction of the objective function. The extreme of this kind of situation appears in linear programming as an unbounded solution.

Example The problem

Maximize $\quad Z = 3X_1 + 2X_2$

subject to $\quad 2X_1 + X_2 \geq 6$

$$X_1 \leq 4$$

$$X_1, X_2 \geq 0$$

has a feasible region represented by the graph of Figure 10-4. Considering the objective function leads to lines parallel to the three lines already drawn in Figure 10-4. We move upward without bound in looking for the farthest such line passing through the feasible region. This is referred to as an *unbounded solution;* that is, there is no finite solution.

the objective function leads to lines parallel to the three lines already drawn

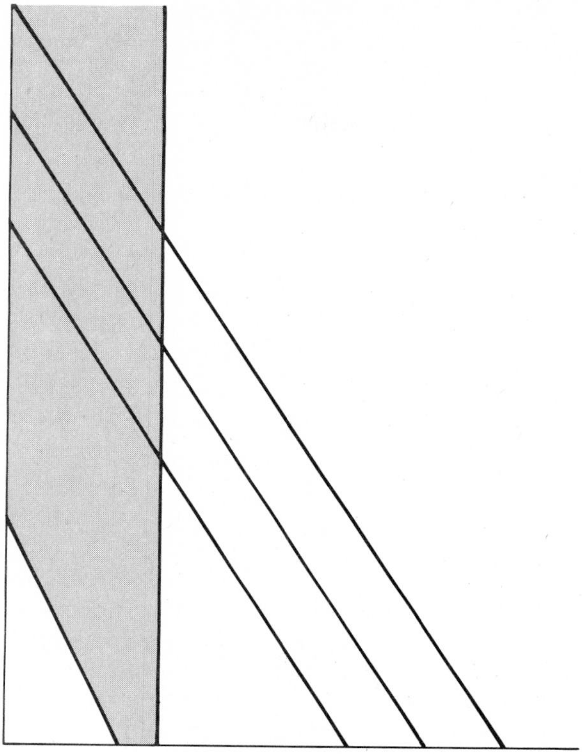

Figure 10-4 A feasible region, unbounded in the direction of the objective function, yields an unbounded solution.

This kind of problem usually results from an improper abstraction or formulation of the original problem. In fact, trying to find a real-life problem with an unbounded solution leads only to frustration. If we were to attempt to solve the example by the simplex method, we would eventually arrive at the tableau presented in Table 10-13. According to the last row, variable X_2 should be the next variable to enter the solution. In trying to determine which variable should leave the solution, we wind up trying to find the smallest positive ratio between $2/-1$ and $\frac{4}{0}$, which indicates that there is no variable to leave the solution. This means that as we increase the value of X_2, we would not have to change X_1 and we would actually increase the value of S_2, leading to a continually higher solution. The key in the simplex method to an unbounded solution is having no positive substitution coefficients in the column of the entering variable. Such is the case with X_2 in Table 10-13.

Multiple Solutions

In discussing sensitivity analysis of the objective function coefficients (Chapter 9), we noted that if the objective function is parallel to one of the constraints, then the two corner points on that constraint are optimum and any point between them is optimum.

Table 10-13 An unbounded solution

C	Solution variables	Solution values	3 X_1	2 X_2	0 S_1	0 S_2	$-M$ A_1
0	S_2	2	0	−1	2	1	−1
3	X_1	4	1	0	1	0	0
	Z	12	3	0	3	0	0
	$C - Z$		0	2	−3	0	$-M$

Example Modifying the objective function of the power loss project, but keeping the constraints, yields the following problem:

Maximize $N = X_1 + 1.5X_2$

subject to

$$4X_1 + 2X_2 \leq 28 \quad \text{I}$$

$$2X_1 + 6X_2 \leq 30 \quad \text{E}$$

$$4X_1 + 6X_2 \leq 36 \quad \text{H}$$

Note that the objective function has the same slope as, and therefore is parallel to, the heating constraint (H). Refer to the feasible region as depicted in Figure 10-1; the optimum solutions are (3, 4) and (6, 2). Since the objective function coincides with the line segment joining those two points, any point between them is also an optimum solution. For example, the point of ($4\frac{1}{2}$, 3) is another optimum solution.

Solving this problem by the simplex method eventually leads to the simplex tableau presented in Table 10-14. No last row value is positive; therefore we have reached an optimum solution at $X_1 = 3$, $X_2 = 4$. However, the $C - Z$ value for variable S_2 is 0. This means that variable S_2 can enter the solution without changing the value of the objective function; this in turn means that including S_2 in the solution will lead to an alternate optimum. Letting S_2 enter the solution will force S_1 out of the solution and will yield the other corner point $X_1 = 6$, $X_2 = 2$ as the alternate optimum.

In general, then, the presence of alternate optima in, or multiple solutions

Table 10-14 Multiple solutions

C	Solution variables	Solution values	1 X_1	1.5 X_2	0 S_1	0 S_2	0 S_3
0	S_1	8	0	0	1	1.33	−1.67
1.5	X_2	4	0	1	0	.33	−.167
1	X_1	3	1	0	0	−.5	.5
	Z	9	1	1.5	0	0	.25
	$C - Z$		0	0	0	0	−.25

to, a maximization linear program is indicated by a simplex tableau in which the last row has no positive values, but has a zero for a variable not currently in the solution. In a minimization problem, multiple solutions are indicated by the last row having no negative values, but a zero for a nonsolution variable.

Whenever there are multiple solutions, they should be identified for the decision maker. Ordinarily not all the elements of a decision situation can be included in the quantitative formulation of the problem. There is usually some reason why one alternate optimum would be preferable to the others; thus all the solutions should be found and reported.

Redundant Constraints and Degenerate Solutions

A constraint is considered redundant when the other constraints completely define the feasible region.

Example Suppose the heating constraint of the power loss problem is revised as follows:

Maximize $N = X_1 + X_2$

subject to

$$4X_1 + 2X_2 \le 28 \quad \text{I}$$

$$2X_1 + 6X_2 \le 30 \quad \text{E}$$

$$4X_1 + 6X_2 \le 48 \quad \text{H}$$

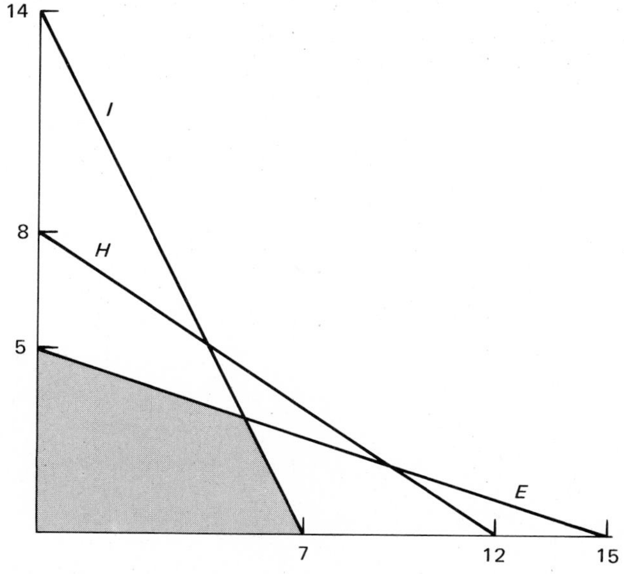

Figure 10-5 The feasible region with the heating inspection constraint changed to $4X_1 + 6X_2 \le 48$.

Table 10-15 Redundant constraint not revealed in final solution

C			1	1	0	0	0
	Solution variables	Solution values	X_1	X_2	S_1	S_2	S_3
1	X_1	5.4	1	0	.3	−.1	0
1	X_2	3.2	0	1	−.1	.2	0
0	S_3	7.2	0	0	−.6	−.8	1
	Z	8.6	1	1	.2	.1	0
	$C - Z$		0	0	−.2	−.1	0

That not all of the constraints are needed to identify the feasible region is not usually obvious from simply observing them. However, since this problem contains only two variables, the feasible region can be graphed. In Figure 10-5 the feasible region is completely defined by the first two constraints; the third constraint is redundant.

Solving the problem by the simplex method leads to Table 10-15, and the solution is quite an ordinary one.

Now consider the same problem with the third constraint changed slightly so that it becomes

$$4X_1 + 6X_2 \leq 40.8$$

With this modification, the feasible region now appears as in Figure 10-6.

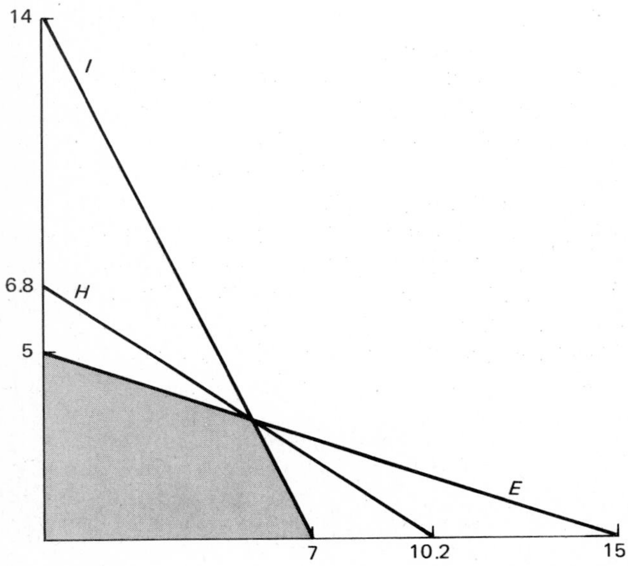

Figure 10-6 The feasible region with the heating inspection constraint changed to $4X_1 + 6X_2 \leq 40.8$.

Table 10-16 Redundant constraint and a degenerate final solution

C	Solution variables	Solution values	1 X_1	1 X_2	0 S_1	0 S_2	0 S_3
1	X_1	5.4	1	0	.375	0	−.125
0	S_2	0	0	0	.75	1	−1.25
1	X_2	3.2	0	1	−.25	0	.25
	Z	8.6	1	1	.125	0	.125
	$C - Z$		0	0	−.125	0	−.125

The three constraints all intersect at the point (5.4, 3.2). Since the constraint lines intersect at the optimum point, all the constraints are satisfied as equalities; all the slack variables should be zero. Solving the linear program by the simplex method yields a final tableau as in Table 10-16. Note that the solution variables include $S_2 = 0$. Such a situation is termed a *degenerate solution, one that contains a smaller number of nonzero variables than the number of constraints*. In the nondegenerate case, all the solution variables are nonzero.

Enroute to a final solution, the simplex method yields the second solution as in Table 10-17. According to the last row, variable X_2 should enter the solution. In determining which variable should leave the solution, we find that both $\frac{16}{5} = 3.2$ and $12.8/4 = 3.2$ are minimum, and hence either S_2 or S_3 can be chosen to leave the solution. To choose the leaving variable, any tie-breaking scheme can be employed; for example, simply select the variable with the higher position in the table, or use a random number scheme. Regardless of which variable is chosen to leave the solution, the simplex method will ultimately yield a final solution with a solution variable equal to 0.

There is a danger to having degeneracy. Usually the process leads to an optimum solution, but there are instances in which the new solution is a previously generated nonoptimal one. If this happens, the process stalls by repeat-

Table 10-17 Second solution with degeneracy

C	Solution variables	Solution values	1 X_1	1 X_2	0 S_1	0 S_2	0 S_3
1	X_1	7	1	.5	.25	0	0
0	S_2	16	0	5	−.5	1	0
0	S_3	12.8	0	4	−1	0	1
	Z	7	1	.5	.25	0	0
	$C - Z$		0	.5	−.25	0	0

edly cycling through the same sequence of solutions. There are advanced procedures, not discussed here, for handling this infrequent occurrence.

SENSITIVITY ANALYSIS

Finding the optimum solution is just one aim in linear programming. Identifying the effects of changes in the parameters through sensitivity analysis is another. We now revisit sensitivity analysis making use of the simplex method. Solving the energy inspection problem, with the original objective function and constraints, by means of the simplex method yields the final solution in Table 10-18. The optimum solution is $X_1 = 6$, $X_2 = 2$, and $S_2 = 6$, representing the 6 excess hours of available electrical inspection time.

Right-side Constants

For sensitivity analysis of the right-side constants of the constraints, we pay particular attention to the final row of the tableau. Note that the last row value for variable S_1 is $-.125$. Based on the meanings of these values, if S_1 were forced upward from 0 to 1 (that is, if the insulation inspector were required to leave one of her 28 available hours unused, or equivalently, if the insulation inspection time were cut back from 28 to 27 hours) the net effect on the objective function would be to decrease it by $\frac{1}{8}$. Correspondingly, if an additional hour of insulation inspection time were made available, there would be just the opposite effect on the objective function; that is, the objective function would be increased by $\frac{1}{8}$. In other words, an additional hour of insulation inspection time produces $\frac{1}{8}$ of an additional complete inspection. This is referred to as the *shadow price* of the resource, insulation inspection time. Similarly, the shadow price of heating inspection time is $\frac{1}{8}$. The last row value is zero for variable S_2, meaning that if the availability of electrical inspection time is decreased or increased, there is a zero net effect on the objective function. Thus the shadow price of electrical inspection time is zero. Each slack variable value in the last row is the negative of the shadow price of the corresponding resource.

Table 10-18 Final solution to the original energy inspection problem

C			1	1	0	0	0
	Solution variables	Solution values	X_1	X_2	S_1	S_2	S_3
1	X_1	6	1	0	.375	0	−.125
0	S_2	6	0	0	.75	1	−1.25
1	X_2	2	0	1	−.25	0	.25
	Z	8	1	1	.125	0	.125
	$C - Z$		0	0	−.125	0	−.125

Range

Since the body of the table contains substitution coefficients, the values there are used to determine the range for which the shadow price is valid. Forcing S_1 to go from 0 to 1 (or reducing the available insulation inspection time by 1 hour) replaces .375 unit of X_1, $-.25$ unit of X_2, and .75 unit of S_2. The number of units of X_1 that are replaced is positive; so the value of X_1 will be decreased. Since the number of units of S_2 that are replaced is also positive, the value of S_2 will also be decreased. We cannot let either of these variables become negative (negative values for any variables are infeasible), and so we determine the value of S_1 that would force either X_1 or S_2 to become 0. This is the same criterion that is used to determine which variable leaves the solution in moving from one solution to the next by the simplex method. Thus, to determine the maximum that S_1 can be increased (or the amount by which the number of insulation inspection hours can be reduced), we determine the minimum of $6/.375 = 16$ and $6/.75 = 8$. Increasing S_1 by 8 forces S_2 to become 0. As long as S_1 is less than 8 (or the insulation inspection time is reduced by less than 8 units), the solution variables will still be X_1, X_2, and S_2 (their values will change, of course, according to the substitution coefficients) and the shadow prices will remain valid. If S_1 is increased by more than 8 units (or the insulation inspection time is reduced by more than 8 units), S_2 will be replaced by another variable and a new set of shadow prices have to be determined.

To determine the amount by which insulation time can be increased and still maintain the shadow price, we proceed similarly. Since increasing the insulation time is the opposite of decreasing the insulation time, increasing insulation time is algebraically equivalent to decreasing S_1. Further, since increasing S_1 by one unit replaces $-.25$ of X_2, then decreasing S_1 by one unit will replace .25 unit of X_2, or X_2 will be decreased. Thus, to determine the amount by which the resource can be increased, we note the maximum amount that X_2 can be reduced. This is done by dividing its solution value, 2, by the size of the substitution coefficient, .25; and $2/.25 = 8$. Thus the insulation inspection time can be increased by 8 units while keeping the same solution variables and the shadow prices.

In summary, to find the range over which the shadow price of a resource is valid, we determine the ratio of solution value to substitution coefficient for all variables in the solution. The smallest of the positive ratios indicates the amount by which the resource can be reduced, and the smallest in size of the negative ratios indicates the amount by which the resource can be increased.

Applying this procedure to S_3 yields

Solution variable	Solution value	S_3 Substitution coefficients	$\frac{\text{Solution value}}{\text{substitution coefficient}}$
X_1	6	$-.125$	-48
S_2	6	-1.25	-4.8
X_2	2	.25	8

so that the heating inspection time can be reduced by 8 units or increased by 4.8 units, and the shadow price .125 will still apply to heating inspection time, and the solution variables will still be X_1, S_2, and X_2. Changing the right-side constants beyond the indicated range yields a different set of solution variables, and a different final row in the tableau, generating a new set of shadow prices.

Referring to the graphic description of sensitivity analysis and Table 9-2 may help to reinforce the relations between allowable range, substitution coefficients, and solution values.

Objective Function Coefficients

Just as it is worthwhile for decision makers to know the impact of changes in constraint constants, so too it is useful to know the effect of changes in the objective function coefficients.

Determining the sensitivity to changes in the coefficients is relatively simple for variables not currently in solution. If the objective function of the energy inspection project is altered to be

$$N = X_1 + 4X_2$$

then the final simplex tableau is as in Table 10-19. Variable X_1 is not in the final solution because its contribution (C_1) is not as great as its opportunity cost (Z_1), or $C_1 - Z_1$ is negative. In order for X_1 to come into the final solution, its contribution to the objective function must be greater than its opportunity cost; that is, $C_1 - Z_1$ must be positive. As long as the objective function coefficient C_1 is less than Z_1, the variable will not come into the solution. Changes in C_1 within this range therefore have no effect on the solution. In the present problem, as long as the coefficient of X_1 is less than $\frac{4}{3}$, the optimum solution will remain $X_1 = 0$, $X_2 = 5$.

For variables currently in the solution, the sensitivity analysis is not so simple. For the two-variable case we have seen in Chapter 9 that as long as the slope of the objective function is between the slopes of the active constraints, the solution remains unchanged. The detail of determining the ranges of the

Table 10-19

C			1	4	0	0	0
	Solution variables	Solution values	X_1	X_2	S_1	S_2	S_3
0	S_1	18	3.33	0	1	−.33	0
4	X_2	5	.33	1	0	.167	0
0	S_3	6	2	0	0	−1	1
	Z	20	1.33	4	0	.67	0
	$C - Z$		−.33	0	0	−.67	0

coefficients of an objective function with more than two variables is not within our scope. It is appropriate, however, that decision makers question the ranges over which the current solution is maintained.

SIMPLEX SOLUTION TO THE BUSING PROBLEM

The busing problem of Chapter 8 aims at minimizing the total distance students have to travel to school while satisfying a judicial order to integrate. The capacity of the two schools, the school-age population of the three neighborhoods, and the integration definitions generate the constraints; the total distance traveled constitutes the objective function. The linear program is:

Minimize

$$D = 2.4A_{\mathrm{I}} + 1.8B_{\mathrm{I}} + 1.5C_{\mathrm{I}} + 1.6A_{\mathrm{II}} + 4.0B_{\mathrm{II}} + 2.0C_{\mathrm{II}}$$

subject to

$$\begin{aligned}
A_{\mathrm{I}} + B_{\mathrm{I}} + C_{\mathrm{I}} &\leq 600 \\
A_{\mathrm{II}} + B_{\mathrm{II}} + C_{\mathrm{II}} &\leq 300 \\
A_{\mathrm{I}} + A_{\mathrm{II}} &= 320 \\
B_{\mathrm{I}} + B_{\mathrm{II}} &= 180 \\
C_{\mathrm{I}} + C_{\mathrm{II}} &= 300 \\
.05A_{\mathrm{I}} - .366B_{\mathrm{I}} - .10C_{\mathrm{I}} &\leq 0 \\
.25A_{\mathrm{I}} - .166B_{\mathrm{I}} + .10C_{\mathrm{I}} &\geq 0 \\
.05A_{\mathrm{II}} - .366B_{\mathrm{II}} - .10C_{\mathrm{II}} &\leq 0 \\
.25A_{\mathrm{II}} - .166B_{\mathrm{II}} + .10C_{\mathrm{II}} &\geq 0
\end{aligned}$$

Table 10-20 Final tableau for the school busing problem (abbreviated)

C			2	0	0
	Solution variables	Solution values	C_{II}	S_2	S_8
	S_1	100		1	
	S_9	60		.2	1
	S_6	80			1
1.5	C_{I}	300	1		
	S_7	20		−.2	−1
2.4	A_{I}	56	−.64	−.88	−2.4
1.8	B_{I}	144	−.36	−.12	2.4
1.6	A_{II}	264	.64	.88	2.4
4.0	B_{II}	36	.36	.12	−2.4
	Z	1410	1.78	−.44	−7.2
	$C - Z$		.22	.44	7.2

The final solution appears in Table 10-20 in a rather abbreviated form. The artificial variables introduced into the "=" and "≥" constraints have been deleted from the table since they have no effect once they have been replaced in the solution. The columns corresponding to the solution variables have been deleted since their substitution coefficients are all zero, except for a 1 in the row corresponding to the variable itself, and the last row value is always 0. The only useful columns are included in the final tableau.

The final assignment of pupils to the schools minimizes the total distance traveled at 1410 miles for the 800 students. Note that no pupils from neighborhood C are assigned to school II; assigning some there increases the total distance traveled by .22 mile per pupil assigned. Every three assigned there decreases C_{I} by 3, A_{II} by 2, and B_{II} by 1, and increases A_{I} by 2 and B_{I} by 1. These substitution quantities are based on approximations of the substitution coefficients because it is sensible to consider assigning only integral numbers of students, and the linear program is not restricted to integers.

The effects of altering the right-side constant of constraint 2 can be seen in the S_2 column. Increasing the capacity of school II by 10 (by mobile units, overlapping schedules, or any other means) will generate a marginal decrease of 4.4 miles in the distance traveled, and will alter A_{I}, B_{I}, A_{II}, and B_{II} by -9, -1, 9, and 1 pupils, respectively. Since the solution must remain in integers, rounding off the changes is necessary; the rounded solution values should be checked in the constraints to assure feasibility.

The range of values for the capacity of school II during which the marginal effects apply are determined as follows. The smallest of the positive ratios (solution value divided by substitution coefficient) is 100; the smallest-sized negative ratio is $56/-.88 = -64$. The capacity of school II can be reduced by as much as 100 or increased by as much as 64 without altering either the solution variables or the marginal effects. Whether it is worthwhile to increase the capacity is *not* revealed in the linear program, since the cost of doing so is not included in the problem. In this case, with individual distances already rather small, it is unlikely that increasing the capacity would be worthwhile.

It is not at all enlightening to consider altering variable S_8 for sensitivity purposes because the eighth constraint was originally expressed as a ratio; the right-side constant became 0 when the constraint was rewritten in the standard linear program form. A right-side constant other than 0 is not very meaningful in this kind of constraint. The effects of changing the required integration ratio can be assessed by altering the coefficients in the constraint. This kind of sensitivity analysis is suggested in exercise **10-4** for those readers who have a linear program computer program available.

Sensitivity analysis is employed to determine the effects of modifications in the formulation of the linear program. However, if a number of changes are being considered, or if the changes yield values outside the range of proportionality, then it is usually more efficient to re-solve the revised program than to investigate the consequences of modifications through sensitivity analysis.

SUMMARY

The simplex method is an algebraic-based algorithm for moving from corner to corner or solution to solution in a linear programming problem until the optimum solution (if it exists) is determined. The simplex method involves five basic steps:

1. Rewrite all constraints as equations, using slack, surplus, and artificial variables as needed.
2. Get an initial solution and put the problem in a simplex tableau.
3. Apply the optimality criterion and either end the process with an optimum or no feasible solution, or select a new variable to enter the solution.
4. Select the variable to leave the solution.
5. Generate a new solution; apply the optimality criterion of step 3.

Besides concluding the process with an optimum (maximum or minimum), other cases can arise. No feasible solution is the result of the constraints being self-contradictory. Assuming the problem has been correctly formulated, some of the constraints must be relaxed to get a solution. Goal programming may be appropriately used here.

An unbounded solution results from a feasible region unbounded in the direction of the objective function. This is the result of improperly abstracting or formulating the original problem.

Multiple solutions occur when the objective function is parallel to one of the constraints. All alternate optima should be found and reported.

Degenerate solutions occur when one or more of the constraints are unnecessary for defining the feasible region. Ordinarily this does not create any difficulty in arriving at a solution.

The simplex method provides not only an optimum solution, if it exists, but also the basis for sensitivity analysis. If many parameters are being changed it is usually more efficient to re-solve the problem than to perform a sensitivity analysis.

BIBLIOGRAPHY

See the Bibliography of Chapter 8.

EXERCISES

Extension of chapter examples

10-1 (*a*) How would the formulation of the busing problem be altered if pupils were allowed to travel no more than 3 miles?

(*b*) If you have the use of a computer with a linear program computer program available, solve the revised problem.

10-2 Use the simplex method to verify the final tableau of Table 10-14. Find the alternate optima.

10-3 Verify the final tableau of Table 10-12.

10-4 Suppose the judicial order in the busing problem were changed, requiring schools to deviate by no more than 5 percent from the district's racial ratio.

(*a*) How would the formulation change?

(*b*) How would the solution be affected? (Access to a computerized linear program is needed here.)

Other applications

Use the simplex method to solve exercises 10-5 to 10-9.

10-5 Exercise 8-5

10-6 Exercise 8-6

10-7 Exercise 8-7

10-8 Exercise 8-8

10-9 Exercise 8-9

Use a linear program computer program to solve the following problems, discussing sensitivity analysis implications. Indicate the marginal changes due to changes in right-side constants.

10-10 Exercise 8-10

10-11 Exercise 8-11

10-12 Exercise 8-12

10-13 Exercise 8-13

10-14 Exercise 8-14

Project problems

10-15 Read Martin Feldstein and Harold Luft, "Distributional Constraints in Public Expenditure Planning," *Management Science,* vol. 19, August 1973, pp. 1414–1422.

Review the simple formulation of the basic national health insurance application in Chapter 8.

(*a*) Expand the illustration to include three income groups, assuming reasonable parameters for the constraints. Use the same weighting scheme as in Chapter 8 in developing the objective function.

(*b*) Solve the newly formulated problem, if a linear program computer program is available.

Table 1 Welfare Agency personnel data

Position	MoE	Number currently employed	Expected minimum requirements next year	Expected salary
Case worker	.91	300	310	$12,000
Family counselor	1.00	40	44	14,000
Service coordinator	1.06	20	28	15,000
Juvenile specialist	1.08	20	30	16,000

(*c*) Through sensitivity analysis describe the effects of altering the deductible amounts.

(*d*) Reformulate the problem to account for two other levels of demand (expressed in the regression equations).

(*e*) Solve the revised problem.

(*f*) Comment on the implications of your various problem formulations, solutions, and sensitivity analyses.

10-16 Refer to exercise 8-15. Solve the formulated problem using the simplex method, either with or without computer assistance. Then reconsider the original problem now that you have seen the "solution."

10-17 A county welfare agency is planning its recruiting, training, and promotion activities for the next year, and therefore is studying its personpower requirements. An advisory council has established measures of average effectiveness (MoE) for each position.

These measures together with other salient data are presented in Table 1.

The salary budget for next year is $6 million. The only promotions being considered are from case worker to any of the other positions. The number desiring and eligible for promotion to each category are: family counselors (20), service coordinators (14), and juvenile specialists (14). Ten percent of staff in each category will retire or resign before next year. Not more than 50 case workers can be given training for promotion. There are 100 individuals who have passed the necessary civil service exams and can be hired as case workers.

(*a*) Determine the number of case workers promoted to each of the other three categories, and the number of new case workers to be hired.

(*b*) There is a movement to get more money for the personnel budget in order to provide better services for the clients. Based on your analysis, comment on the value of such a budget adjustment.

CHAPTER

ELEVEN

GOAL PROGRAMMING

"Shall coal continue to be a source of energy?" has generally been responded to positively. The positive response was merely casual in an era roughly centered in the 1950s, when the ready availability of oil and the convenience of using it prompted many industries and residences to switch from coal to oil. The "abundance" of natural gas not only prompted industry and residences to seek it as their source of energy but also prompted power companies to encourage its use. Somewhat later the promise of nuclear energy suggested that the coal question be answered less than enthusiastically, although it was still conceded that coal would continue to be a source of energy. The middle and late 1970s brought new vigor to the positive response. The oil embargo by the oil-producing nations underscored the oil-using nations' dependence. Natural gas was viewed as less abundant. With hints at the catastrophic consequences of nuclear accidents—Three Mile Island made "China Syndrome" a household word—widespread development of nuclear fission energy plants was discouraged. Although nuclear fusion as a source of energy was brought closer to reality in the late 1970s, it was still conceded to be decades away from implementation. Meanwhile technological advancements in controlling coal-caused pollution had made the use of coal more appealing. These characteristics of the energy picture prompted a more emphatic positive response to the continued use of coal. Thus, although conditions have prompted different degrees of enthusiasm, coal has continued to be seen as a source of energy.

With the increasing demand for energy and the rapidly diminishing reserves of, or the remoteness of, other sources, increased coal production is generally acceptable. The more difficult question concerning the use of coal as an energy source relates to how the coal is to be mined. Both conventional underground mining and strip mining have advantages and disadvantages. Strip mining is generally more economical, and less hazardous, but poses more of an ecological threat. On the other hand, underground mining may be inherently less of an environmental problem, but is a greater source of injury, illness, and death to miners. Barring some technological breakthrough, the demand for coal will be satisfied amid conflicting objectives and consequent different preferences.

In planning for the development or redevelopment of an area, the bona fide interests of environmentalists, residents, the Chamber of Commerce, sportspersons, and patrons of the arts will have conflicting objectives concerning how the area should be planned.

In developing an admissions policy, a state university must consider its mission to serve first the residents of the state, the academic standards required for its continuing accreditation and reputation, maintaining a student body large enough to support its many activities and small enough to be satisfied by existing and planned facilities and personnel. Again there is a decision to be made in the midst of many goals.

While it is true that in the private sector activities often have more than a single objective, it is perhaps the nature of the public sector that activities necessarily have more than a single objective. Realizing that the political environment of public decision making may supersede the conclusions generated by any analysis, it is nevertheless useful to identify appropriate methods for investigating decision situations with multiple objectives. If the objectives can be expressed in similar and comparable terms, then an aggregate objective might make the comparison of alternatives (Chapter 4) appropriate. Lacking that, the decision approach can be extended to include assessment of utility of the various objectives and hence of the various alternatives (Chapter 6). If the relationships among the requirements and objectives, and inputs and outputs, are linear, then the linear programming approach is appropriate if one objective can be identified as the one to be maximized or minimized, and the others can be considered necessities or constraints (Chapters 8 to 10). If it is not possible to identify a single objective amidst constraints or if the constraints yield no feasible solution, the value of linear programming diminishes. An extension of linear programming provides for maintaining multiple objectives as such and seeks to achieve the goals as closely as possible. This method of treating appropriate decision situations is referred to as "goal programming."

GOAL PROGRAMMING AND DECISION MAKING

As might be expected, the role of goal programming in decision making is similar to the role of linear programming. The similarities and differences between the two models distinguish the situations in which either can be better applied. A comparison of the two techniques helps to know when to use either.

Goal Programming and Linear Programming

The outstanding similarity is that all the objective functions, constraints, and goals are linear expressions and consequently are deterministic, additive, divisible, and proportional. The main difference is that in linear programming there is a single objective to be *optimized* and many constraints that *must* be satisfied, whereas in goal programming there are many goals to be reached, with the objective function formed from the under- and overachievement of the goals. Table 11-1 summarizes the main points of comparison. Goal programming is particularly well suited to public decisions because conflicting objectives, trade-offs, and its purpose of satisficing rather than optimizing are integral parts of the model use.

Goal Programming and the Decision Process

As one identifies a problem, defined as a discrepancy between what is and what is wanted, one also becomes aware of multiple, perhaps conflicting, objectives. Abstracting the salient features from the problem and formulating the problem as a goal program help to understand the problem even better. When one finds a solution and sees which goals are and which are not satisfied, one naturally reconsiders priorities and therefore redefines the problem. The specific steps of goal programming are more closely related to some phases of the decision process than to others, but all steps in model development and execution contribute to better understanding the basic problem. In following Figure 11-1 recall that even though we represent the decision process in discrete steps, we recognize that each phase feeds back to the prior phases.

In this chapter we will explore goal programming as an extension of linear programming, using as an example the admissions policy of a state university. After explaining goal programming through that particular example, we will consider other applications.

Table 11-1 Comparison of two programming models

Item	Linear programming	Goal programming
Purpose	Optimize	Satisfice
Quantitative expressions	Linear	Linear
Structure	One objective, many constraints	Multiple objectives, many constraints
Objective function	Decision variables	Deviational variables
Constraints/goals	All of equal importance	Prioritized by importance
Theory	Mature, many extensions	Relatively young
Applications	Many and varied	Few but varied
Computerized solutions	Generally available	Often not available

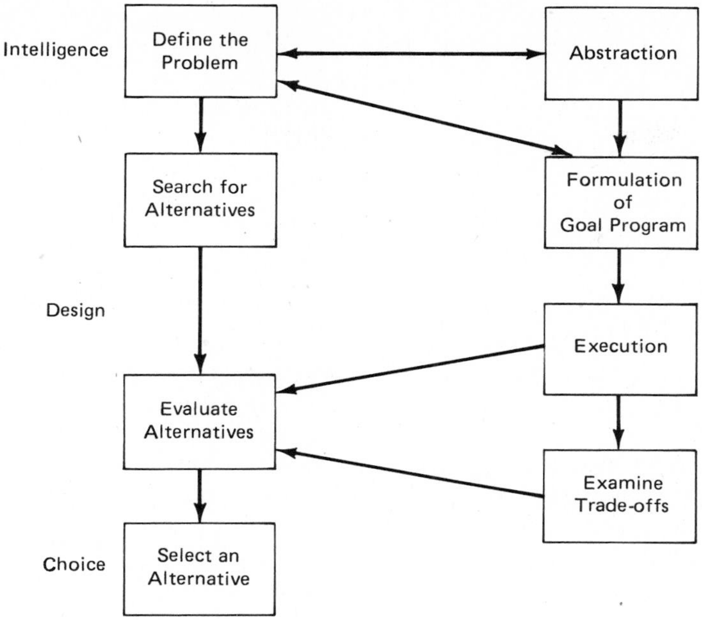

Figure 11-1 Goal programming and the decision process.

UNIVERSITY ADMISSIONS: A LINEAR PROGRAMMING FORMULATION

A medium-sized branch of a state university has recently had to reassess its admissions policy and plan. The reassessment has become necessary as enrollments declined, state funds leveled off, federal grants diminished, and costs greatly increased. By investigating the records of past applicants and noting the current high school graduation class population, and other related factors, the admissions officer has been able to assess quite firmly that the number of in-state eligible applicants is very close to 2400. This becomes the first constraint. The State Department of Education and the legislature have indicated that the mission of the state university demands that in-state students should represent at least 80 percent of the student body. Although the number of eligible out-of-state candidates applying for admission is not unbounded, it generally far exceeds the number who could be admitted on the basis of the 80 to 20 percent requirement. The campus' resident halls must be self-sufficient; that is, state funds may not be used to subsidize living costs of students simply because they happen to live on campus. The campus, then, has to have enough students to take care of operating expenses and amortization of debt. A full complement of resident students is 1600. Without considering whether any of these "requirements'' is flexible, a first crack at the admission policy might be based on trying to get as many students as possible while satisfying all of the constraints.

Let X_1 represent the number of in-state students to be admitted, and X_2 the number of out-of-state students to be admitted. The 80 to 20 percent requirement can be written as

$$X_1 \geq .80(X_1 + X_2)$$

$$\text{or } .20X_1 - .80X_2 \geq 0$$

This constraint appears as the second in the problem formulation.

Past admissions indicate that approximately 50 percent of the in-state students and all of the out-of-state students request on-campus housing. In order to satisfy the resident complement, the mix of in-state and out-of-state students should be such that 50 percent of the in-state students plus all the out-of-state students is at least 1600. This is the third constraint of the program.

With total enrollment as the objective function, the admissions problem, formulated as a linear program, appears as:

Maximize	$Z = X_1 + X_2$	Total enrollment
subject to	$X_1 \leq 2400$	Standards
	$.20X_1 - .80X_2 \geq 0$	In-state ratio
	$.50X_1 + X_2 \geq 1600$	Residence halls

A solution to the linear program is 2400 in-state students and 600 out-of-state students, as given in Figure 11-2. With the total number of students at 3000, the university administration realizes that so many students could not be handled with the present faculty complement and facilities. Although campus enrollment has generally been under 2500, it is believed that with minor modifications a student body of 2600 could be accommodated quite well, but certainly not more than that. Instead of being the objective function, therefore, the total number of students becomes another constraint. Without identifying an objective function, but including

$$X_1 + X_2 \leq 2600$$

as a constraint, the constraints are graphed in Figure 11-3. The arrows indicate the direction of the constraints; there is no feasible region. When the linear program encounters an infeasible set of constraints, the problem must be reformulated, letting some of the constraints be relaxed until a feasible region is identified. Goal programming, however, provides another and more appropriate way of handling the multiple-objective decision problem.

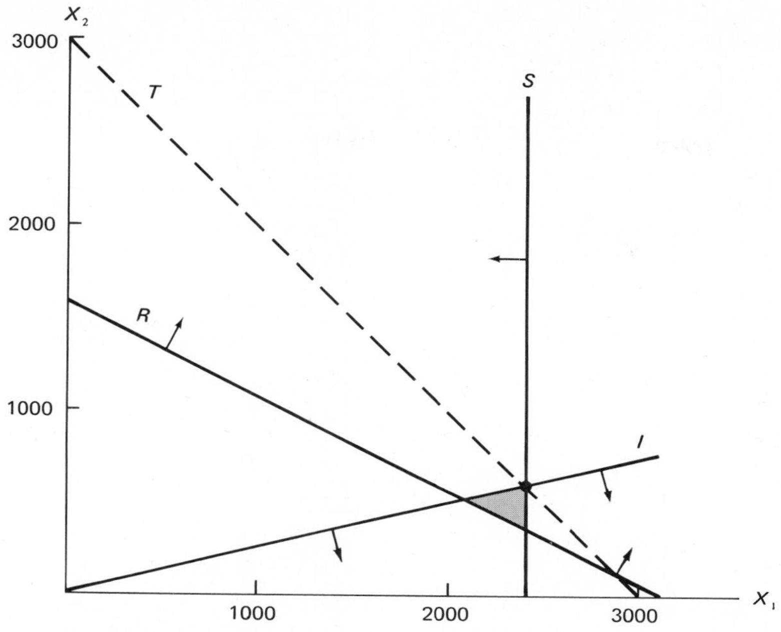

Figure 11-2 Optimum solution to university admissions linear program.

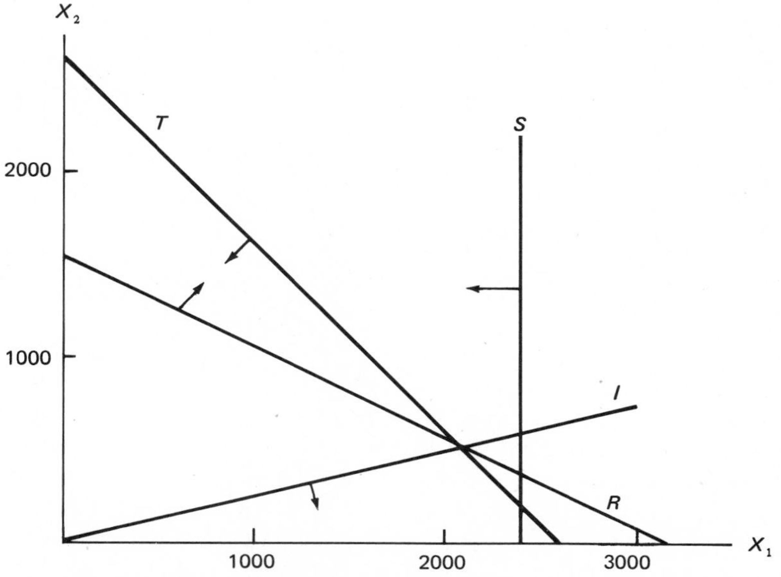

Figure 11-3 Constraints of the revised linear program; no feasible region.

UNIVERSITY ADMISSIONS: A GOAL PROGRAMMING FORMULATION

The formulation of a goal program involves three steps:

1. Identify goals with their deviational variables.
2. Prioritize the goals.
3. Construct the objective function using the deviational variables and priority levels.

These steps will be treated within the university admissions illustration.

Goals and Deviations

Upon reexamining the admissions situation, the university realizes that no one of the requirements is absolutely inflexible, but rather they are all goals to be striven for. Although it would be nice to achieve all the goals, getting close to them is satisfactory, especially if the more important ones are achieved. For example, instead of looking at the 1600 resident students as an absolute restraint, the 1600 can be considered a goal for achievement. Getting close to that is satisfactory. This approach provides a better representation of many constrained decision situations.

Based on academic standards it is indicated that not more than 2400 in-state students are eligible for admission. As a constraint this is represented as

$$X_1 \leq 2400$$

In preparing for a simplex solution to the linear program, a slack variable is added and the constraint becomes

$$X_1 + S_1 = 2400$$

where S_1 represents the amount by which the number of in-state students is under 2400. The goal programming approach considers the 2400 as a goal, and therefore the number of in-state students may be either less than 2400, equal to 2400, or greater than 2400. This goal statement is represented as

$$X_1 + d_1^- - d_1^+ = 2400$$

where d_1^-, the negative deviation, represents the amount by which the number of in-state students is less than 2400 and d_1^+, the positive deviation, represents the amount by which the number of in-state students is over 2400. d_1^- and d_1^+, therefore, are the amounts by which the number of in-state students deviates from the goal of 2400. In the final solution at least one of them will be zero.

Since the central notion of goal programming is to come as close as possible to the goal, goal programming attempts to minimize these deviations. With deviations below and above the goals, the constraints of the linear program become goal equations in the goal program and are written as

$$
\begin{array}{llr}
X_1 \qquad\qquad + d_1^- - d_1^+ = 2400 & \text{Standards (S)} & P_2 \\
.20X_1 - .80X_2 + d_2^- - d_2^+ = 0 & \text{In-state ratio (I)} & P_4 \\
.50X_1 \quad + X_2 + d_3^- - d_3^+ = 1600 & \text{Residence halls (R)} & P_3 \\
X_1 \quad + X_2 + d_4^- - d_4^+ = 2600 & \text{Total enrollment (T)} & P_1
\end{array}
$$

Goal Priorities

Although it may not be quantifiable, the relative importance of the goals varies. Goal programming permits assigning a priority level to each constraint without attempting to rate it on a scale. Accordingly, and after some debate and persuasion, the university assigns priorities to the goals as follows:

1. Minimize the overachievement of the admissions goal of 2600 students.
2. Maintain academic standards; that is, not more than 2400 in-state students are eligible.
3. Minimize the underachievement of the residence hall goal of 1600 students.
4. Minimize underachieving the goal of 80 percent in-state students.

These priorities are preemptive; no higher-level priority is sacrificed in the attempt to achieve a lower-level goal. The priorities associated with the four goals are represented by P_1, P_2, P_3, and P_4. The usual way of writing priorities is

$$P_1 \gg P_2 \gg P_3 \gg P_4$$

which means P_1 is very much greater than P_2, P_2 is very much greater than P_3, and so forth. This means that the first goal is so much more important than the second goal that no multiple of the second goal is sufficient to equal the first goal. If goals are considered to be of equal importance, they may be given the same priority level. If there is uncertainty or no agreement on the priority levels, trade-offs can be considered in postoptimality analysis. Thus, the great difference in priority levels should not be seen as a deterrent to applying goal programming, even if the priority levels are not certain.

The Objective Function

Goal programming seeks to minimize the weighted deviations from the goals; in the objective function the deviations are multiplied by or weighted with the priority levels associated with each goal. Based on the university's prioritized goals, the objective function for the goal program is

Minimize $$Z = P_1d_4^+ + P_2d_1^+ + P_3d_3^- + P_4d_2^-$$

Since the university does not want many more than 2600 students, the deviation above 2600 is included in the objective function. If the university also did not want many fewer than 2600 students, the deviation below, namely, d_4^-, would also be included in the objective function. Maintaining academic standards means that admitting more than 2400 in-state students is undesirable but admitting fewer than 2400 is perfectly all right; accordingly, then, only the positive deviation for the academic standards goal is included in the objective function. By similar thinking, only the negative deviations for the residence goal and the 80 percent in-state students goal are included in the objective function. It might very well be argued that the university would also want to guard against having too many students requesting on-campus residences since not being able to supply them might discourage those students from attending the university. In such a case the objective function should also include the positive deviation. For illustrative purposes here we prefer not to let the objective function become too cumbersome.

Thus far we have considered goal programming as an extension of linear programming in which the constraints are replaced by goals that are prioritized, and the objective function seeks to minimize the weighted deviations from the goals. Having formulated the goal program, we now examine a graphic solution followed by a more widely applicable simplex solution.

A GRAPHIC SOLUTION

Even a simple two-variable goal program can have many more than two variables in the objective function, none of which is an original variable. The special nature of the deviational variables permits a graphic solution without having to find a graph for the objective function. The process includes the following steps:

1. Graph all goals with the two decision variables and all deviational variables.
2. Define the feasible region by considering the deviational variables, one at a time, in their order of priority; lower-level goals entirely outside the already restricted feasible region cannot be satisfied.
3. Find the point in the feasible region closest to the highest-level unsatisfied goal; it is the most satisfactory solution.
4. The original problem should be reassessed in terms of the solution in order to evaluate trade-offs among the goals.

The Goals

The first step in developing a graphic solution is to plot all the constraints or goals, with the deviations indicated by arrows as in Figure 11-4.

The Objective Function

The next step is to assess the objective function on a term-by-term basis relative to the deviational variables. The objective function is:

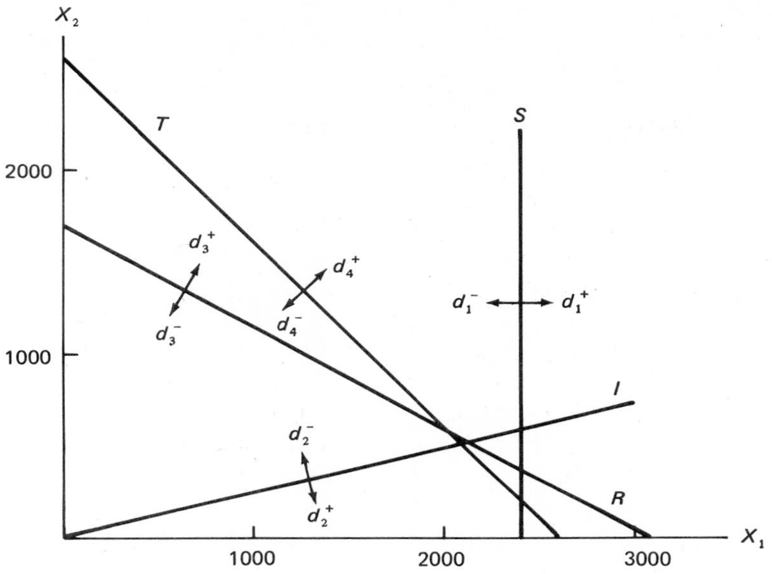

Figure 11-4 The goals in the university admissions illustration. S, academic standards; I, in-state ratio; R, residence halls; T, total enrollment.

Minimize $$Z = P_1d_4^+ + P_2d_1^+ + P_3d_3^- + P_4d_2^-$$

In goal programming the objective function is always to be *minimized*. P_1, being very large, makes the first term very much larger than any one of, or all of, the other terms. Thus, in minimizing the objective function, we must first let $d_4^+ = 0$; this is represented graphically in Figure 11-5.

Since the first goal is to avoid having more than 2600 students, the feasible region is now entirely below the constraint. The second goal is to maintain academic standards; having no more than 2400 in-state students eligible for admission means d_1^+ must be 0 and the feasible region is to the left of the constraint. The third goal is to minimize the underachievement of the residence goal; that is, d_3^- must be 0 and the feasible region is above that constraint. The region satisfying the first three goals is depicted in Figure 11-6.

A Satisfactory Solution

The feasible region indicates that satisfying the first three goals precludes the satisfaction of the fourth goal. Any point in the feasible region would satisfy the first three goals; point A is the feasible point most nearly satisfying goal 4. The solution at point A, 2000 in-state students and 600 out-of-state students, has about 77 percent of the student body comprised of in-state students. Point A represents the most satisfactory solution based on the given priority levels.

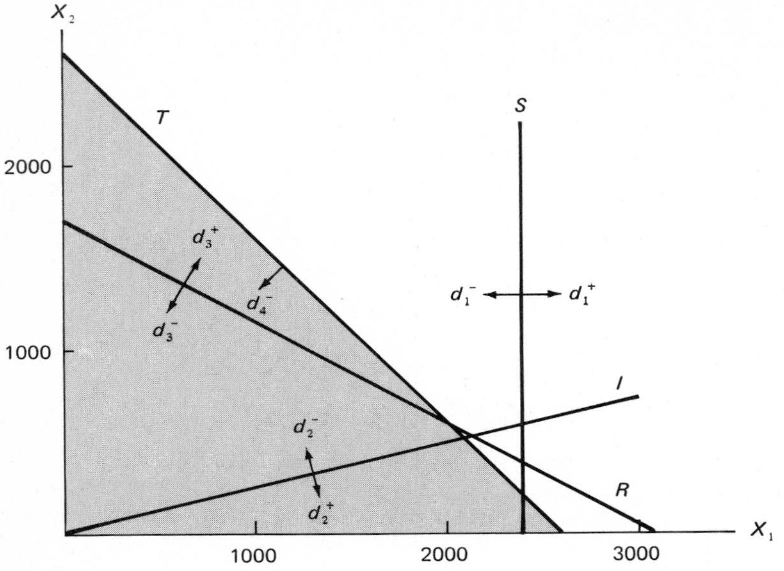

Figure 11-5 The top-priority total enrollment goal is satisfied in the shaded region $d_4^+ = 0$.

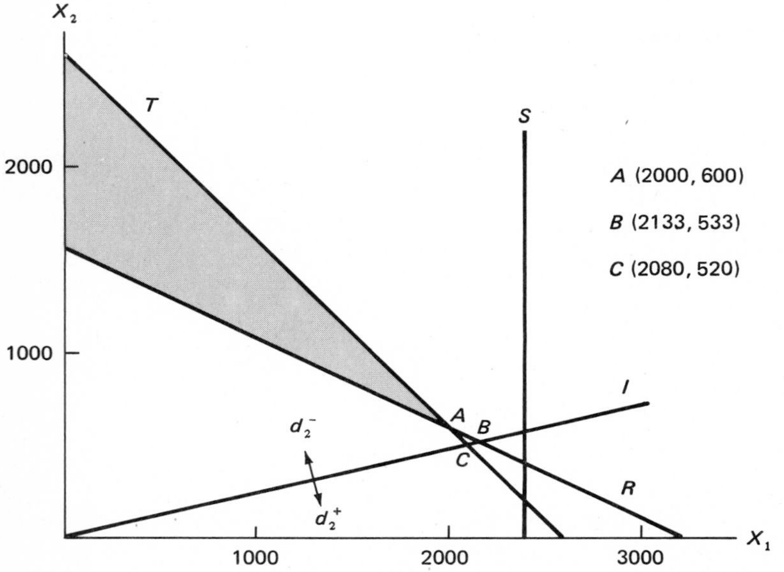

Figure 11-6 The three top-priority goals are satisfied in the shaded region. T: $d_4^+ = 0$; S: $d_1^+ = 0$; R: $d_3^- = 0$.

Trade-offs

If, in reconsidering, we require that the fourth goal be satisfied (that is, we reassess its priority to be higher than some other priority) then we consider points B and C.

Point B satisfies the academic standards goal, the 80 to 20 percent goal and the goal of 1600 resident students, but generates a student body of 2666, somewhat higher than the first goal prescribed.

Solution C satisfies the 2600 total enrollment goal, the academic standards goal, and the 80 to 20 percent goal but provides only 1560 resident students.

If the goals have their original priority levels, then the solution is point A, with the first three goals satisfied and the fourth goal almost satisfied. If the goals' priorities are reassessed, goal programming provides alternate solutions and indicates the trade-offs among the goals.

The graphic approach is appropriate for relatively small problems restricted to two decision variables (not including the deviation variables). As with linear programming, we rely on the graphic solution more to provide an understanding of the process of goal programming than to provide a method of solving a goal program. The linear program simplex method can be applied rather directly to a goal program in order to yield a method of solution that is of greater use than the simple graphic solution.

THE SIMPLEX SOLUTION TO A GOAL PROGRAM

The simplex method for goal programming closely follows the simplex method for linear programming. The process includes five steps:

1. Formulate the program in standardized form.
2. Select an initial solution.
3. Apply the optimality criterion, and either end the process or select a variable to enter the solution.
4. Select a variable to leave the solution.
5. Generate a new solution, and go back to step 3.

In formulating the program, one gives each goal a negative deviational variable; it then serves as a slack variable. A positive one is used if overachievement is permitted.

Once the goal program has been thus formulated, one finds an initial solution by letting the real or decision variables be 0 and letting negative deviations be equal to the right-side constants in the constraints. This process is identical to the one followed in arriving at an initial solution for a linear program. In determining admissions policy, the university has the following goal program:

Minimize $$Z = P_1 d_4^+ + P_2 d_1^+ + P_3 d_3^- + P_4 d_2^-$$

subject to

$$
\begin{aligned}
X_1 \qquad\qquad + d_1^- - d_1^+ &= 2400 && \text{Standards (S)} \\
.20X_1 - .80X_2 + d_2^- - d_2^+ &= 0 && \text{In-state ratio (I)} \\
.50X_1 \qquad + X_2 + d_3^- - d_3^+ &= 1600 && \text{Residence halls (R)} \\
X_1 \qquad + X_2 + d_4^- - d_4^+ &= 2600 && \text{Total enrollment (T)}
\end{aligned}
$$

Note that the number of variables in the goal program grows rather quickly. As a result the tableau contains quite a few columns. However, a great number of the entries in the tableau are 0 and many of the others are +1 or −1. This makes transformation from one solution to the next relatively easy. The simplex tableau corresponding to the initial solution of the university admission problem is presented in Table 11-2. The entries above the line correspond to the constraint coefficients. The top row and the left-most column contain the objective function coefficients. The many zeros in the tableau are not printed. The entries below the line are calculated in the same way as in the linear program simplex method. The Z row is the sum of the products of the numbers in each column times the corresponding numbers in the C column. As before, the last row, the $C - Z$ row, is found by getting the difference between the objective function coefficients and the entries in the Z row. The values in the last row correspond to the net effect on the objective function of increasing each column variable by one unit.

To identify the variable that should enter the solution, we proceed as in a minimize linear program. We determine the minimum value from among the negative values in the last row. In the present example the smallest (largest in size) of the negative values in the last row occurs in the X_2 column. Hence X_2 will enter the solution.

To determine the variable that will leave the solution, we compare the ratios of solution values over entering column values. The variable to leave the solution is d_3^- since

Table 11-2 Goal programming initial solution

C						P_2	P_4		P_3			P_1
	Solution variables	Solution values	X_1	X_2	d_1^-	d_1^+	d_2^-	d_2^+	d_3^-	d_3^+	d_4^-	d_4^+
	d_1^-	2400	1		1	−1						
P_4	d_2^-	0	.20	−.80			1	−1				
P_3	d_3^-	1600	.50	(1)					1	−1		
	d_4^-	2600	1	1							1	−1
	Z	$1600P_3$	$.2P_4$ $+.5P_3$	$-.8P_4$ $+P_3$			P_4	$-P_4$	P_3	$-P_3$		
	$C - Z$		$-.2P_4$ $-.5P_3$	$.8P_4$ $-P_3$	0	P_2	0	P_4	0	P_3	0	P_1

$$\frac{1600}{1} \quad \text{is the minimum of} \quad \frac{1600}{1}, \frac{2600}{1}$$

Because their values in column X_2 are either 0 or negative, d_1^- and d_2^- are not candidates to leave the solution. Only variables with positive values in the entering column are candidates to leave the solution, as was true also in the linear program simplex method.

The value that is in both the entering column, the X_2 column, and the leaving row, the d_3^- row, is the pivot element, which is circled in Table 11-2. The transformations necessary to move from one solution to the next are identical to those in the linear program simplex method.

1. Divide every element of the leaving row by the pivot element. Since our pivot element is 1, the values in that row remain unchanged, except that the solution variable is now X_2.
2. The other rows are revised by:

$$\text{New row} = \text{old row} - \frac{\text{key}}{\text{pivot}} \cdot \text{leaving row}$$

The new d_2^- row is:

Old d_2^- row	0	.2	−.8	0	0	1	−1	0	0	0	0
$-\frac{\text{key } (= -.8)}{\text{pivot } (=1)} \cdot$ leaving row	+1280	.4	.8	0	0	0	0	.8	−.8	0	0
= new d_2^- row	1280	.6	0	0	0	1	−1	.8	−.8	0	0

All of the remaining rows of the upper portion of the tableau are revised in a similar way. The second solution is contained in Table 11-3. The last two rows of the simplex tableau are based on the substitution coefficients and objective function coefficients and are calculated just as in the linear program simplex method. The Z values are the sum of the products of the substitution coefficients times the corresponding values in the C column. For example, the Z value in the X_1 column is

$$1(0) + .6(P_4) + .5(0) + .5(0) = .6P_4$$

The last row of the tableau is found by getting the difference between the objective function coefficient and the Z value. For example, the last row value for the X_1 column is

$$0 - .6P_4 = -.6P_4$$

An optimum solution has not been reached because the last row of Table 11-3 has at least one negative value. Actually, since $-.6P_4$ is the only negative

Table 11-3 Second solution

C	Solution variables	Solution values	X_1	X_2	d_1^-	d_1^+	d_2^-	d_2^+	d_3^-	d_3^+	d_4^-	d_4^+
						P_2	P_4		P_3			P_1
	d_1^-	2400	1		1	-1						
P_4	d_2^-	1280	.6	0			1	-1	.8	$-.8$		
	X_2	1600	.5	1					1	-1		
	d_4^-	1000	(.5)						-1	1	1	-1
	Z	$1280P_4$	$.6P_4$				P_4	$-P_4$	$.8P_4$	$-.8P_4$		
	$C - Z$		$-.6P_4$	0	0	P_2	0	P_4	P_3 $-.8P_4$	$.8P_4$	0	P_1

value in the last row, variable X_1 will enter the solution at the next step. Variable d_4^- will leave the solution since

$$\frac{1000}{.5} \quad \text{is the minimum of} \quad \frac{2400}{1}, \frac{1280}{.6}, \frac{1600}{.5}, \frac{1000}{.5}$$

The next solution is found by the usual transformations and is presented in Table 11-4.

Since the last row of Table 11-4 contains no negative value, an optimum solution is assured. Lest we think that the last row value of the d_3^- column is negative, recall that P_3 is very much larger than P_4 so that $P_3 - 2P_4$ is positive.

In the final solution 2000 in-state students and 600 out-of-state students will be admitted. Furthermore, that $d_2^- = 80$ indicates that the second constraint is underachieved by 80 students. Recall that the second constraint is

$$.20X_1 - .80X_2 + d_2^- - d_2^+ = 0$$

$$\text{or } X_1 + d_2^- - d_2^+ = .80(X_1 + X_2)$$

The number of in-state students is 80 fewer than 80 percent of the total student

Table 11-4 Final solution

C	Solution variables	Solution values	X_1	X_2	d_1^-	d_1^+	d_2^-	d_2^+	d_3^-	d_3^+	d_4^-	d_4^+
						P_2	P_4		P_3			P_1
	d_1^-	400	0		1	-1			2	-2	-2	2
P_4	d_2^-	80	0				1	-1	2	-2	-1.2	1.2
	X_2	600	0	1					2	-2	-1	1
	X_1	2000	1						-2	2	2	-2
	Z	$80P_4$					P_4	$-P_4$	$2P_4$	$-2P_4$	$-1.2P_4$	$1.2P_4$
	$C - Z$		0	0	0	P_2	0	P_4	P_3 $-2P_4$	$2P_4$	$1.2P_4$	P_1 $-1.2P_4$

body (80 percent of 2600 equals 2080; the optimum solution has only 2000 in-state students).

Since d_2^- is the only solution variable with a priority-level objective function coefficient, we conclude that the second constraint or goal is the only goal not met. Determining what has to be traded off in order to attain the second goal is addressed in the postoptimality analysis of the goal program.

In formulating the goal program above, we have inserted a negative deviational variable and a positive deviational variable into each constraint or each goal. This is not always necessary. For example, if the academic standard were viewed not just as a high priority goal but as a strict requirement, then a positive deviational variable should not be inserted into the equation. It would simply take the form

$$X_1 + d_1^- = 2400$$

and overachievement of the 2400 would not be feasible. Alternatively, a strict requirement may be handled by setting the deviational variable at P_1 priority. Here d_1^+ would have the coefficient P_1 in the objective function. Including the additional variable in the formulation provides information concerning trade-offs, at the expense of additional computation. Since the negative deviational variable is not included in the objective function, and admitting fewer than the 2400 who satisfy the academic standards is permitted without penalty, the role of d_1^- is really that of a slack variable.

Goal Program Format

The tableau format of a goal program is usually presented slightly differently from the linear program format that we have used. The upper half of the table is the same. The lower half of the table usually does not contain a separate Z row, and the last row is presented in a matrix, with a row for each priority level. With this convention our final solution is represented in Table 11-5. The

Table 11-5 Final solution
Goal Program Format

C						P_2	P_4		P_3			P_1
	Solution variables	Solution values	X_1	X_2	d_1^-	d_1^+	d_2^-	d_2^+	d_3^-	d_3^+	d_4^-	d_4^+
	d_1^-	400	0		1	−1			2	−2	−2	2
P_4	d_2^-	80	0				1	−1	2	−2	−1.2	1.2
	X_2	600	0	1					2	−2	−1	1
	X_1	2000	1						−2	2	2	−2
	P_4							1	−2	2	1.2	−1.2
$C - Z$	P_3								1			
	P_2					1						
	P_1											1

highest-priority goals appear at the bottom of the tableau. The optimality criterion is simply that the last value in each column be either zero or positive. This format also facilitates sensitivity analysis of priority levels.

SENSITIVITY ANALYSIS

As with most techniques for assisting a decision maker, finding the "optimum" is really only part of the solution. The decision maker or adviser is as interested in knowing "what happens if" as he is in knowing the "correct" answer to the formulated problem.

Understanding goal programming and, in particular, the subsequent sensitivity analysis, is not at as advanced a stage as linear programming. Although the questions may be similar, the techniques to find the answers are not as readily available; however, the effect of changes in the problem formulation can be determined by resolving the newly formulated problem. Our brief discussion of sensitivity analysis considers three commonly asked and relatively easily answered postoptimality questions. They concern trade-offs among goals, switches in priority levels, and changes in the right-side constants.

Trade-offs

The final solution to the admissions planning problem indicates that the second goal, the in-state ratio goal, is not completely achieved. The first question seeks to determine what would be required in order to completely attain the second goal. Figure 11-6 indicates the present solution at point A, and two alternate solutions that would achieve the in-state ratio goal at points B and C. Since point B is on the residence hall line, the residence hall goal would be satisfied but the total enrollment goal would not. This trade-off can also be seen in Table 11-5. The d_4^+ column has $-1.2P_4 + 1P_1$ in the $C - Z$ rows. This means that having d_4^+ enter the solution will improve the achievement of the in-state ratio (which has a priority level P_4) but at the expense of no longer satisfying the total enrollment goal (which has a priority level of P_1). We see, then, from the tableau that the in-state ratio goal can be satisfied at the expense of the total enrollment goal.

Point C in Figure 11-6 presents another way of satisfying the in-state ratio goal. Since point C is on the total enrollment line, the total enrollment goal would be achieved but the residence hall goal would not be achieved. In the last row of Table 11-5, the d_3^- column has $-2P_4 + P_3$; having d_3^- enter the solution will improve the achievement of the in-state ratio goal (with priority P_4) but at the expense of the residence hall goal (with priority P_3). Nearby points of intersection in the graphic solution and the last row of the tableau reveal the trade-offs necessary to satisfy an unachieved goal.

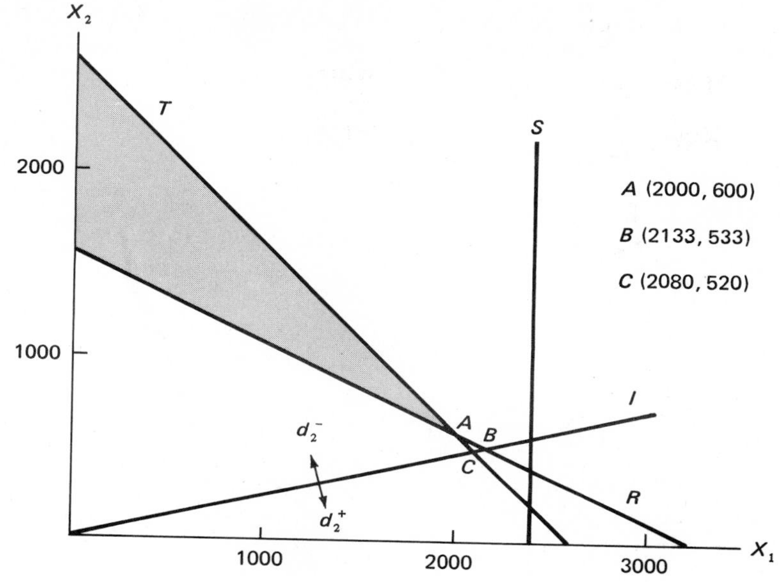

Figure 11-6 Repeated

Switching Priorities

The second question seeks to determine the effect of switching some priority levels. Among the solution variables d_2^- is the only one with a priority level. In the first place, this indicates that the second goal is the only goal not achieved. In the second place, it indicates that the priority levels of the other goals can be switched without affecting the final solution. For example, if the priority levels of the total enrollment goal and the academic standards goal are interchanged, then in the final tableau P_1 and P_2 will be interchanged. As a result the last value in each column will still be positive or zero, and so the current solution will still be optimum.

If the priority level of a deviation variable in the solution is exchanged with one not in the solution, then the optimum solution will change. Here, if the priority level of the in-state ratio goal and the residence hall goal are interchanged, then in the final tableau P_3 and P_4 will be interchanged. The last row value in the d_3^- column will become $P_4 - 2P_3$, which is negative; the variable d_3^- should enter the solution yielding a new optimum.

In summary, if the change in priorities affects a nonzero solution variable, there will be a new optimum; if it does not affect such a solution variable, the optimum solution will be unchanged.

Right-Side Constants

The third sensitivity analysis question considers how the solution is affected by changes in the right-side constants of the goals. Recall that the upper half of the

Table 11-6 Effects of a one-unit decrease in the residence hall goal

C	Solution variables	Old solution values	d_3^- substitution coefficients	New solution values
	d_1^-	400	2	398
P_4	d_2^-	80	2	78
	X_2	600	2	598
	X_1	2000	−2	2002

table contains substitution coefficients and that solution values must be positive or zero if the solution is to be feasible. Determining the effect of such changes is best explained through an illustration.

Suppose the residence hall constraint goal is decreased from 1600 to 1599. This is equivalent to increasing d_3^- from 0 to 1; the substitution coefficients in the d_3^- column show the number of units of each solution variable that will be replaced. The new values of the solution variables appear in Table 11-6. If the residence hall goal were decreased by more than 40, d_2^- would be reduced to a negative value, which of course is infeasible. Thus if the residence hall goal is decreased below 1560 (that is, decreased by more than 40), then the solution will contain a different set of variables.

Increasing the goal has the opposite effect. Thus if the residence hall goal is increased to 1601 (equivalent to increasing d_3^+ from 0 to 1), then the new solution will be as in Table 11-7. If the residence hall goal were increased by more than 1000, then X_1 would become negative, causing infeasibility. This means that such an increase in the residence hall goal would require a different set of solution variables. Therefore, the range of proportionality is (1560, 2600).

In this particular illustration, such a large increase in the residence hall goal would certainly not be permitted, since at that point the student enrollment would be comprised completely of out-of-state students. Such analysis is valuable in determining the effect of increases in the goal within a reasonable range. As long as the residence hall goal is 1560 or higher, then the optimum solution contains the same set of solution variables, and the same set of substitution coefficients applies.

If any goal value is changed so much that the solution will contain a different set of variables, then resolving the program is generally easier than

Table 11-7 Effects of a one-unit increase in residence hall goal

C	Solution variables	Old solution values	d_3^+ substitution coefficients	New solution values
	d_1^-	400	−2	402
P_4	d_2^-	80	−2	82
	X_2	600	−2	602
	X_1	2000	2	1998

making the necessary adjustments to transform the current solution to a new one.

Modifications in the goal program formulation other than the three we have examined are quite likely; the decision maker is well advised to raise any "what if" questions that are relevant. For our purposes these common and simple cases are sufficient to illustrate the basic concepts of sensitivity analysis in goal programming.

A kind of postoptimality analysis, other than sensitivity analysis, that is well addressed in goal programming involves purposely altering goal priorities. Although most public programs—and private undertakings—have a budget constraint, treating the cost as the lowest priority-level goal will determine the necessary budget amount to achieve all other goals to the maximum extent. A subsequent goal program solution might have the real budget amount included either as an absolute constraint or as the highest level goal. A personpower planning application will illustrate this use of goal programming.

MANPOWER PLANNING: AN APPLICATION[1]

Somewhat roughly described, manpower planning refers to the effort to fill positions that have varying requirements with persons who have varying characteristics. If all positions had the same requirement and all individuals had the same characteristics, then manpower planning would consist almost exclusively of maintaining the appropriate level of work force. Since such is not the case, due consideration must be given to the positions' needs and the individuals' strengths and shortcomings. Various factors affect individual hiring decisions and program hiring policy. Some of these factors are general economic climate, manpower availability, current level of social unrest, manpower needs, wage level, employer size and location, union management relations, and recruitment policies. These factors will enter into the manpower planning illustration in various ways.

Suppose that an agency's personnel office will place 100 people in department A and 50 people in department B. The potential work force is composed of skilled workers, unskilled workers, and hard-core unemployed. Represent the numbers of each group hired for each of the two departments as follows:

	Department	
	A	B
Skilled workers	X_1	X_2
Unskilled workers	X_3	X_4
Hard-core unemployed	X_5	X_6

[1] This illustration is based on Harvey Kahalas and Russell Key, "A Decisionally Oriented Manpower Model for Minority Group Hiring," *The Quarterly Review of Economics and Business,* vol. 14, no. 3, Autumn 1974, pp. 71–84. The author intends no sexist bias with the use of the word "manpower."

The total personnel requirements for the two departments generate the first two goals. We number the goals for easy reference later.

$$X_1 + X_3 + X_5 + d_1^- - d_1^+ = 100 \tag{1}$$

$$X_2 + X_4 + X_6 + d_2^- - d_2^+ = 50 \tag{2}$$

Because of the nature of the work, 80 percent of the department A employees must be skilled, while only 40 percent of the department B employees need to be skilled.

For department A:

$$X_1 + d_3^- - d_3^+ = .80(X_1 + X_3 + X_5)$$

or

$$.2X_1 - .8X_3 - .8X_5 + d_3^- - d_3^+ = 0 \tag{3}$$

For department B:

$$X_2 + d_4^- - d_4^+ = .40(X_2 + X_4 + X_6)$$

or

$$.6X_2 - .4X_4 - .4X_6 + d_4^- - d_4^+ = 0 \tag{4}$$

Manpower availability provides an upper limit on the number of employees from each group that can be hired. The agency in question uses applications, Civil Service lists, and a State Employment Service listing to generate its own list of candidates. These lists combine to form the available pool of 80 skilled workers, 120 unskilled workers, and 30 hard-core unemployed. These constraints, without positive deviational variables, are

$$X_1 + X_2 + d_5^- = 80 \tag{5}$$

$$X_3 + X_4 + d_6^- = 120 \tag{6}$$

$$X_5 + X_6 + d_7^- = 30 \tag{7}$$

Skilled workers in department A earn \$6.00 an hour, and skilled workers in department B earn \$5.00 an hour; all other employees earn \$3.00 an hour, but the hard-core unemployed require extra training and additional supervision, costing an additional \$1.00 per hour. Agency standards prescribe that department A's labor costs should not be more than \$400 per hour, and those for department B should not be more than \$350 per hour. These wage requirements and standards generate two additional constraints:

$$6X_1 + 3X_3 + 4X_5 + d_8^- - d_8^+ = 400 \tag{8}$$

$$5X_2 + 3X_4 + 4X_6 + d_9^- - d_9^+ = 350 \tag{9}$$

The personnel office has been allotted \$15,000 for a special training program for the hard-core unemployed; estimates indicate that \$700 will be spent on each such employee. Hence

$$700X_5 + 700X_6 + d_{10}^- - d_{10}^+ = \$15{,}000 \tag{10}$$

It is quite likely that education requirements for any position will have to be lowered to allow the hiring of the hard-core unemployed. If a labor contract forbids such a practice, then certain restrictions on hard-core hirings will be invoked. Here we assume that the union requires that no more than 30 percent of the employees can fail to meet the high school education requirement, and we further assume that such a requirement is lacking only in the case of the hard-core unemployed. These conditions yield the following constraint:

$$X_5 + X_6 + d_{11}^- = .3(X_1 + X_2 + X_3 + X_4 + X_5 + X_6)$$

or

$$-.3X_1 - .3X_2 - .3X_3 - .3X_4 + .7X_5 + .7X_6 + d_{11}^- = 0 \tag{11}$$

Note that the last constraint does not contain a positive deviational variable; we assume that the 30 percent limit is an inflexible upper bound. If it were flexible and something just above 30 percent were allowed, then a positive deviational variable would be included.

Not permitting the turnover rate to get out of hand is generally an objective of hiring practices. Assume the turnover rates based on historical data, for the skilled, unskilled, and hard-cores, are .1, .3, and .4, respectively. Limiting the expected turnover to 20 individuals yields the goal

$$.1X_1 + .1X_2 + .3X_3 + .3X_4 + .4X_5 + .4X_6 + d_{12}^- - d_{12}^+ = 20 \tag{12}$$

The final goal is to place a lower limit on the proportion of workers taken from the ranks of the hard-core. The desired rate is at least 20 percent, generating the goal

$$X_5 + X_6 + d_{13}^- - d_{13}^+ = .2(X_1 + X_2 + X_3 + X_4 + X_5 + X_6)$$

or

$$-.2X_1 - .2X_2 - .2X_3 - .2X_4 + .8X_5 + .8X_6 + d_{13}^- - d_{13}^+ = 0 \tag{13}$$

Although this set of constraints and goals is not complete, it is sufficient to indicate the conflicting pressures and consequent objectives brought to bear on the agency or organization trying to maintain a productive work force and satisfy social demands.

The objective function depends on the levels of priority associated with the various goals. We will discuss two different sets of priority levels. In the first situation the hiring agency is in an area of relative social calm but economic uncertainty. In the second situation the agency operates in an area of generally good economic conditions but near a region of recent social unrest. Applying these factors, two different sets of priorities follow; they appear in Table 11-8.

The priority levels for the two objective functions come from the two sets of priorities. The deviational variables to be included in the objective function depend on the sense of each goal. Specific total employment levels are to be met; therefore positive and negative deviational variables are included. Hourly labor costs should be within agency standards; being below the standards is acceptable; therefore, the objective function includes only positive deviational

Table 11-8 Manpower planning
Two sets of priorities

Goals	Equation number	Situation: Priority levels (I)	Situation: Priority levels (II)
Meet total personnel requirements	1, 2	P_1	P_2
Do not exceed training funds	10	P_2	P_6
Hourly labor costs within standards	8, 9	P_3	P_4
Acceptable turnover rate	12	P_4	P_3
20% or more from hard-cores	13	P_5	P_1
Meet or better skilled to unskilled ratio	3, 4	P_6	P_5

variables from equations (8) and (9). The two objective functions for the two different situations are:

$$\text{Minimize} \quad Z_{\text{I}} = P_1 d_1^- + P_1 d_1^+ + P_1 d_2^- + P_1 d_2^+ + P_2 d_{10}^+ + P_3 d_8^+ + P_3 d_9^+ + P_4 d_{12}^+ + P_5 d_{13}^- + P_6 d_3^- + P_6 d_4^-$$

$$\text{Minimize} \quad Z_{\text{II}} = P_1 d_{13}^- + P_2 d_1^- + P_2 d_1^+ + P_2 d_2^- + P_2 d_2^+ + P_3 d_{12}^+ + P_4 d_8^+ + P_4 d_9^+ + P_5 d_3^- + P_5 d_4^- + P_6 d_{10}^+$$

Constraints (5), (6), (7) and (11) are requirements that must be met and hence they were not given any positive deviational variables. An alternate approach is to insert positive deviational variables in the goal statements and then give them the highest priority level in the objective function. In either case those equations will be satisfied at the expense of all other goals.

The goal program solutions to the two sets of constraints and goals for the two different sets of priority levels are presented in Table 11-9. The upper portion of the table contains the decision variables; these are the components that the personnel office would directly control. The lower half of the table presents the goals as achieved or not, as a consequence of the decision variable values.

Placing a high priority on employing the hard-core unemployed provided the achievement of that goal in situation II at the expense of the two cost goals. By contrast, having a lower priority on the hard-core goal achieved nothing toward that goal in situation I; there the cost goals were satisfied. At this point some reassessing is in order, particularly as far as the costs are concerned. The allowable labor cost for department B is \$350 per hour; as we see from the situation II solution this is more than adequate to staff the department completely with skilled workers. The solution indicates that situation II does not satisfy the hourly labor costs in department A, but that is more than compensated for by the labor costs in department B. Some shifting of funds from department B to department A, if permitted, might not only keep labor costs within standards but may also provide a better distribution of skilled workers in the two departments. Making the same shift of funds in situation I may move the solution closer toward achieving the hard-core unemployment goal while staying within

Table 11-9 Solutions to manpower planning problems

	Situation			
	I		II	
Decision variables:	A	B	A	B
Skilled workers	33	47	30	50
Unskilled workers	67	3	40	0
Hard-core unemployed	0	0	30	0
	100	50	100	50

Goals	Achievement and Priority Level			
	I		II	
Meet total personnel requirements	Achieved	1	Achieved	2
Do not exceed training funds	Achieved	2	$d^+ = 6000$	6
Hourly labor costs within standards	Achieved ($d_A^- = 0$) ($d_B^- = 106.00$)	3	$d_A^+ = 20.00$ $d_B^- = 100.00$	4
Acceptable turnover rate	$d^+ = 9$	4	$d^+ = 12$	3
At least 30 employees from hard-cores	$d^- = 30$	5	Achieved	1
Meet or better skilled to unskilled ratio	$d_A^- = 47$ $d_B^+ = 27$	6	$d_A^- = 50$ $d_B^+ = 30$	5

the financial boundaries. Actually determining the effects of such monetary shifts is left as an exercise for the reader who has a computer program available.[2]

SUMMARY

Linear programming is an appropriate decision analysis technique provided that the basic relationships are at least approximately linear. If it is not possible to identify a set of "must be" constraints or goals, goal programming provides a suitable extension that can be applied, with the object of satisfying the goals as nearly as possible in some order of priority. Rather than identify a single optimum solution from among all the feasible solutions, the general approach is to shrink the feasible region so that the higher priority-level goals are satisfied. The goal programming simplex method closely follows the linear programming simplex method. Priority levels are assumed to be larger than any of the constants, and each level is very much larger than the next. Consequently, no higher-level goal will be sacrificed to achieve a lower-level goal. Appropriate applications of goal programming can be seen in academic planning, manpower planning, medical planning, and municipal planning, among

[2] The listing for such a goal programming computer program is provided in Sang Lee, *Goal Programming for Decision Analysis*, Auerbach Publishers Inc., Philadelphia, 1972, pp. 126–127. Some minor modifications to that program are needed to make it operational.

others. Some of these applications have been considered in the chapter while others are left for the reader in the exercises.

BIBLIOGRAPHY

Charnes, A., W. W. Cooper, D. B. Learner, and E. F. Snow: "Note on an Application of a Goal Programming Model for Media Planning," *Management Science,* vol. 14, no. 8, April 1968, pp. 431–436.

Courtney, James F., Theodore D. Klastorin, and Timothy W. Ruefli: "A Goal Programming Approach to Urban-Suburban Location Preferences," *Management Science,* vol. 18, no. 6, February 1972, pp. 258–268.

Field, D. B., "Goal Programming for Forest Management," *Forest Services,* vol. 19, no. 2, 1973, pp. 125–135.

Jackman, H. W.: "Financing Public Hospitals in Ontario: A Case Study in Rationing of Capital Budgets," *Management Science,* vol. 20, no. 4, December 1973, pp. 645–655.

Kahalas, Harvey, and Russell Key: "A Decisionally Oriented Manpower Model for Minority Group Hiring," *The Quarterly Review of Economics and Business,* vol. 14, no. 3, Autumn 1974, pp. 71–84.

Lee, Sang: *Goal Programming for Decision Analysis,* Auerbach Publishers Inc., Philadelphia, 1972.

——— and Edward Clayton: "A Goal Programming Model for Academic Resource Allocation," *Management Science,* vol. 18, no. 8, April 1972, pp. 395–408.

——— and Laurence Moore: "Optimizing University Admissions Planning," *Decision Sciences,* vol. 5, no. 3, July 1974, pp. 405–414.

——— and Laurence Moore: *Introduction to Decision Sciences,* Petrocelli-Charter, New York, 1975.

——— and William Sevebeck: "An Aggregative Model for Municipal Economic Planning," *Policy Sciences,* vol. 2, no. 2, June 1971, pp. 99–115. Also published in Sang Lee, *Goal Programming for Decision Analysis.*

Pitkanen, Eero: "Goal Programming and Operational Objectives in Public Administration," *Swedish Journal of Economics,* vol. 72, no. 3, pp. 207–214.

Schroeder, Roger G.: "Resource Planning in University Management by Goal Programming," *Operations Research,* vol. 22, July–August 1974, pp. 700–710.

Walters, A. J. Mangold, and E. G. P. Haran: "A Comprehensive Planning Model for Long-range Academic Strategies," *Management Science,* vol. 22, no. 7, 1976, pp. 727–738.

EXERCISES

Extension of chapter examples

11-1 Refer to the admissions planning problem. (See p. 252.) Suppose the university's first goal is changed to "achieve the admissions goal of 2600 students"; that is, minimize the underachievement and the overachievement of the 2600 goal.

(*a*) What changes would be made in the formulation of the goal program?

(*b*) How would the solution be affected?

11-2 Refer to the admissions planning problem of this chapter. As a result of a recent State Department of Education projection of sharply decreasing in-state applications, the state legislature has seriously relaxed its recommendations that 80 percent of the student body be in-state students. Instead, the legislature now *requires* that not less than one-half of the students be from the state. Heretofore, the number of eligible out-of-state students applying for admission did not seriously enter the problem since that number, which the Records Office estimates at 1200, far exceeded the number who could be admitted under the 80 to 20 percent recommendation. Now, however, the

1200 eligible candidates under the current academic standards becomes a relevant constraint. Based on the same set of priorities as before, formulate and solve graphically this new goal program.

11-3 Refer to problem 11-2. Since it is expected that the number of out-of-state students will rise under the new conditions, the claim that all of the out-of-state students will request on-campus housing is no longer tenable. Based on a brief survey of the applications of previously nonadmitted out-of-state applicants, the revised estimate is that 80 percent of the out-of-state students will request on-campus residence hall housing. How does this new estimate affect the formulation and solution?

11-4 Refer to problem 11-2. After some high-level, person-to-person research, the university learns that the legislature's decision to modify the in-state–out-of-state ratio will not affect the university's appropriation, which provides only a part of the university's financial requirements. Because of the rising costs and a relatively stable appropriation, the university has identified \$2250 per student per year as the cost not covered by appropriations and other sources. The university aims at recovering that amount through student tuition; in-state students pay \$1500 per year and out-of-state students pay \$3000 per year. The university views this goal on the same priority level as the goal to maintain full residence halls. How does this new goal affect the formulation and graphic solution?

11-5 Refer to the manpower planning illustration on pp. 265–269. Constraints 8 and 9 prescribe the standard hourly total labor rate for departments A and B. Suppose it is possible to pool these two so that the total hourly labor costs would be \$750?

(*a*) How would the new problem formulation appear?

(*b*) If you have an appropriate computer program available, determine how this new goal affects the solution for both decision situations described in the illustration.

11-6 Refer again to the manpower planning application. Suppose that based on expected long-term requirements to be placed on the agency, it is argued that maintaining an acceptable turnover rate and meeting or bettering the skilled to unskilled labor ratio should be given high priority. Assume that the other goals retain their relative priorities in both situations I and II.

(*a*) Determine how giving these goals the top two priority levels will affect the formulation.

(*b*) Find the solution to both new decision situations. (The solution requires access to a computer program; the formulation obviously does not.)

Other applications

11-7 Minimize

$$Z = P_1d_1^- + P_2d_2^- + P_3d_3^- + P_4d_4^- + P_5d_5^- + P_6d_5^+$$

subject to

$$\begin{aligned}
2X_1 + X_2 + d_1^- &= 32\\
2X_1 + 3X_2 + d_2^- &= 48\\
5X_1 + 6X_2 + d_3^- - d_3^+ &= 60\\
X_1 + d_4^- - d_4^+ &= 8\\
X_2 + d_5^- - d_5^+ &= 6
\end{aligned}$$

(*a*) Solve graphically.

(*b*) Solve graphically with the fourth constraint changed to

$$X_1 + d_4^- - d_4^+ = 16$$

(*c*) Solve graphically if both d_3^- and d_3^+ are included in the objective function at the same priority level, P_3.

11-8 A new Save the City (STC) federal organization is being formed, and there are 2000 technical and 800 nontechnical positions available. It costs \$1000 to successfully recruit a white male for each technical position and \$800 for each nontechnical position. Furthermore it costs 20 percent more to recruit a woman than a man, and 30 percent more to recruit a minority than a white. Based on urban population, employment records, and employment levels, it has been mandated that at least 40 percent of the positions should be filled by women and at least 50 percent by minorities. Formulate this as a goal programming problem, if the STC has established the following goal priorities:

1. Minimize the overexpenditure for recruiting, with a budget of \$3,000,000.
2. Minimize the underachievement of the goal that women fill at least 40 percent of the positions.
3. Minimize the underachievement of the goal that minorities fill at least half the positions.
4. Restrict the overachievement of the minority goal to 100 individuals.

(The last goal involves only deviational variables. If d_3^- and d_3^+ represent the underachievement and overachievement of the 50 percent minority goal, then the last constraint can be represented as $d_3^+ + d_4^- - d_4^+ = 100$; the objective function then includes d_4^+ with the priority level P_4.)

(*a*) Formulate the problem.

(*b*) If you have a computer program available, solve this goal program.

11-9 10,000 acres of state forest land are to be put to use in a manner which comes close to meeting specified goals. The state's goals relate to the four possible uses for the forest land: camping, hunting, raccoon sanctuary, and lumbering. Each acre of forest can provide 400 camper days, 100 hunter days, a sanctuary for 4 raccoons, or 12,000 cubic feet of timber. Operating costs for the entire 10,000 acres must be paid for out of the revenue received from leasing timber land to lumber companies at the rate of \$480 per acre per year. The operating expenses vary with the kind of activity; they are estimated at \$30 per acre for camping, \$40 for hunting, \$10 for a sanctuary, and \$8 for timber cutting. The following goals and priority order have been established by the State Bureau of Recreation:

1. Minimize the overachievement of cutting 3,000,000 cubic feet of timber.
2. Minimize the underachievement of 350,000 hunter days.
3. Achieve as closely as possible the goal of maintaining 20,000 raccoons.
4. Minimize the underachievement of 1 million camping days.

Formulate the goal program for this problem.

11-10 (*a*) Solve problem 11-9 if you have a computer program available.

(*b*) Determine the effect of interchanging the priority levels of the hunting and camping goals.

Project problems

11-11 Refer to the linear program you formulated in exercise 8-15 and solved in exercise 10-16.

(*a*) Reformulate the problem as a goal program, assuming a reasonable target level for the linear program objective function, and priority levels for the constraints.

(*b*) Is the linear program or goal program formulation more likely to better represent the decision situation? Why?

(*c*) Solve the goal program by the simplex procedure.

11-12 Choose a goal programming article in your own area of interest.

(*a*) Identify the salient features of the goal program formulation.

(*b*) Were the priorities readily identified and unquestionably accepted?

(*c*) What problems were faced in formulating the program, and what assumptions were made?

CHAPTER
TWELVE

PROJECT MANAGEMENT: A NETWORK MODEL

Projects that are undertaken and completed many times over are those that best lend themselves to tight control. The time, personnel, and other resources needed for completion are fairly well understood from past experience. Projects that are one-time-only undertakings are more difficult to plan and control. Many activities in the public sector are of this variety. The *overall project* may be a first, but the *components* or *tasks* of the project have been done many times before in similar projects. Some examples are: construction of a highway or a hospital; preparing for a municipal bond issue; development and implementation of a management information system; transferring operations from one site to another, as from one hospital building to a new one; and conducting a major research effort. A model that is particularly well suited to the control of such major projects is the subject of this chapter.

While various diagrams, often informal, have long been used to represent sequences and interrelationships that characterize multiactivity projects, it was not until the late 1950s that formal network methods were proposed to plan, schedule, and control such projects. The two different network models that were developed concurrently and independently wound up being amazingly similar. Except for minor structural and notational differences, each model had one main ingredient that was absent in the other. The PERT model (performance evaluation review technique or program evaluation review technique) originally permitted three different time estimates for each individual task, while CPM (critical path method) permitted only a single time estimate. On the other hand, CPM identified time-cost trade-off points, whereas PERT did not. During the years since their origin the two methods have essentially been merged, with the current product incorporating the advantages of each model as well as many later developments. In our discussion of project management we will make no distinction between PERT and CPM.[1]

CONTENTS OF PERT/CPM

To plan and to control a project require two pieces of basic information about each task:

1. The length of time to complete each task
2. The tasks that must be completed before another task can begin

We will present these and the other fundamental ideas of PERT/CPM within the framework of a seminar development project, a commonly occurring one in any service agency.

A Seminar Development Project: An Illustration

Suppose the state council on mental health and mental retardation has developed an information system that it expects will provide the council with state-wide program information and the many county agencies with local program and client information. Realizing that such an information/evaluation system requires user understanding and cooperation, the council is planning to conduct a number of 3-day seminars at key locations throughout the state.

Ann Maxall is responsible for coordinating the seminars. She has identified the activities that must be completed prior to the seminars themselves. She has also identified which activities must be completed prior to any one activity and has estimated the number of weeks needed to perform each activity. With these

Table 12-1 Activities, predecessors, and time estimates in the seminar planning project

Activity	Description	Immediate predecessors	Estimated time (weeks)
A	Plan seminar content	—	2
B	Obtain speakers	*A*	1
C	Select seminar sites	—	2
D	Prepare and mail flyer/invitations	*B*, *C*	3
E	Accept reservations	*D*	3
F	Notify press	*D*	1

[1] Actually we will be using the terminology of PERT and the network analysis of CPM.

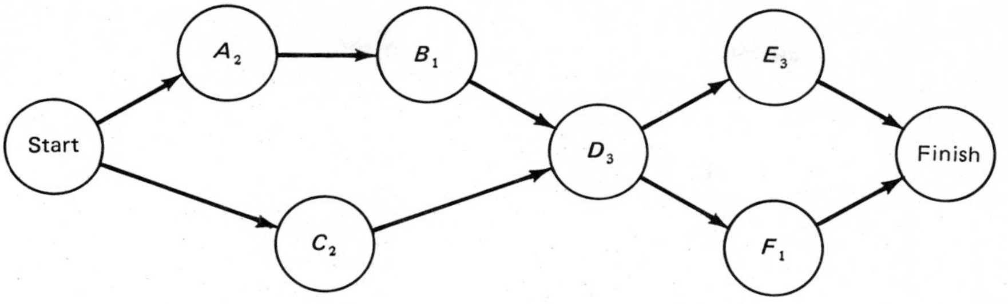

Figure 12-1 PERT diagram of the seminar planning project with activity completion times.

two pieces of basic information, the list of immediate predecessors and the estimated time for each activity, the planning project for the seminars is described as in Table 12-1.

Project Network

The immediate predecessor of activity *B* is activity *A*; this means that activity *A*, "plan seminar content," must be completed before activity *B*, "obtain speakers," can be started. In using the network diagram to illustrate the project, activities are represented by circles and sequencing is represented by arrows. For example, the arrow from activity *A* to activity *B* shows that activity *A* is the immediate predecessor of activity *B*. Once the network is complete, the estimated time of each activity can be inserted in the circle representing that activity. Figure 12-1 is the network diagram of the seminar planning project.

Note in Table 12-1 that activities *B* and *C* are both predecessors of activity *D*; in the diagram this is represented by arrows drawn from both *B* and *C* to *D*. Similarly, since activity *D* is the immediate predecessor of both *E* and *F*, arrows are drawn from *D* to both *E* and *F*. The activities represented by the "start" circle and "finish" circle are not real activities but merely signify the beginning and end of the project. The estimated time for each activity can be used to estimate the time for the whole project; in particular the time estimates will lead us to the *critical path* for the project.

THE CRITICAL PATH

A series of connected activities is called a *path*. In the seminar planning project, one path consists of activities *A*, *B*, *D*, *E*; another path consists of *C*, *D*, *F*. There are two other paths through the entire project from start to finish (can you find them?). The length of time associated with the path is the sum of the time estimates associated with each of the activities on the path. For instance, *ABDF* has a time estimate of 7 weeks, and *CDE* has a time estimate of 8 weeks. The path with the greatest time estimate is called the *critical path.* The critical path in our illustration is *ABDE,* which requires 9 weeks. The time required to complete the critical path is the shortest amount of time in which the entire project can be completed. Delays along the critical path result in a delay of the project; if the project is to be completed in less than the time estimate of the critical path, then one or more activities on the critical path must be hurried or *crashed* so that their combined completion time becomes less than the original estimate. On the other hand, crashing an activity not on the critical path will provide no benefits; for example, if activity *C* could be hurried to require 1 week instead of 2, activity *D* still could not start until after the completion of sequence *A* and *B*, which together require 3 weeks. Thus, there would be no benefit to crashing activity *C*. Furthermore, a delay in a noncritical activity will have no effect on the project finish time; for example, activity *F* could be delayed up to 2 weeks with no consequent delay in the completion of the project.

For a network as simple as Figure 12-1 the critical path can be determined by sight. In a more complex project, however, a more formal method of determining the critical path is needed. Such a systematic method is now considered.

Early Time, Late Time, and Slack

In order to find the critical path of a network, we first determine the *early start time* (ES) and *late start time* (LS) for each activity. ES is the earliest that an activity can start after all preceding tasks are completed. LS is the latest that an activity can start without delaying the entire project.

The difference LS − ES is called *slack;* it represents the amount by which an activity can be delayed without delaying the project. An activity *that has no slack is called a critical activity; the path of critical activities is the critical path.*

Find ES and EF by passing through the network from start to finish as follows:

1. The early start time of an activity with no predecessors is zero.
2. The early finish time (EF) of each activity is the sum of its early start time plus the time required to complete it.
3. The early start time of any other activity is the latest of its immediate predecessors' early finish times.

The early start time (ES) and the early finish time (EF) for each activity of Figure 12-1 are determined in the following way.

The ES for activity *A* (ES_A) is 0 since nothing has to happen before activity

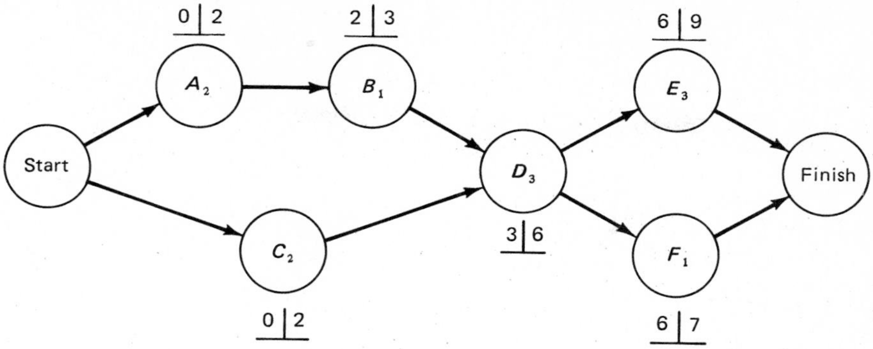

Figure 12-2 PERT diagram of the seminar planning project with early start (ES) and early finish (EF) times written as ES|EF.

A starts. The early finish time for activity A (EF_A) is:

$$ES_A = 0 \qquad EF_A = ES_A + t_A$$
$$= 0 + 2$$
$$= 2$$

Similarly,

$$ES_C = 0 \qquad EF_C = ES_C + t_C$$
$$= 0 + 2$$
$$= 2$$

The early start time of any other activity is equal to the largest of the early finish times of all of its immediate predecessors. ES_B equals EF_A since B's only predecessor is A; that is,

$$ES_B = EF_A$$

D has two immediate predecessors, B and C:

$$EF_B = 3 \qquad \text{and} \qquad EF_C = 2$$

and so

$$ES_D = 3$$

Figure 12-2 contains ES and EF of all activities in the network. Note there that since activity D requires both B and C to be completed before it can begin, ES_D equals the larger of EF_B and EF_C.

The next step in finding the critical path is to determine the late start (LS) and late finish (LF) for each activity. The *late start time* for any activity is the latest that that activity can commence without delaying the whole project. The *late finish time* of any activity is the latest that that activity can finish without delaying the whole project. In order to determine LS and LF of each activity, pass through the network backwards, from finish to start as follows:

1. The late finish time of an activity with no successors equals the project's finish time.
2. The late start time of any activity is its late finish time minus the time to complete it.
3. The late finish time of any other activity is the smallest of its successor's late start times.

The last activities in our network are E and F. The early finish times for those activities are 9 and 7; thus the earliest that the entire project can finish is 9, which becomes the finish time for the project. The LF of the last activity on any path is equal to the finish time of the project. Thus

$$\mathrm{LF}_E = 9 \qquad \text{and} \qquad \mathrm{LF}_F = 9$$

The LS for any activity is its LF minus its completion time.

$$\mathrm{LF}_E = 9 \qquad \mathrm{LS}_E = \mathrm{LF}_E - t_E = 9 - 3 = 6$$

Similarly,

$$\mathrm{LF}_F = 9 \qquad \mathrm{LS}_F = \mathrm{LF}_F - t_F = 9 - 1 = 8$$

Activity D is the predecessor of more than one activity. The LF of such an activity is the smallest of the LS values of its successors.

$$\mathrm{LS}_E = 6 \qquad \text{and} \qquad \mathrm{LS}_F = 8$$

and so

$$\mathrm{LF}_D = 6$$

Figure 12-3 gives LS and LF as well as ES and EF of all the activities in the network.

Slack is the amount of time an activity can be delayed without delaying the entire project. For example, activity C can begin as early as week 0; it can also begin as late as week 1 without delaying the project. Hence, activity C can be delayed 1 week without delaying the project; that is, it has 1 week of slack. In general, the slack for an activity is found by getting the difference between its LS and its ES. (Equivalently, this is also the difference between its LF and EF.) In our illustration F has two weeks of slack and C has one week of slack.

Shared slack is shared with the other activities in sequence with it. In Figure 12-5, activity B and activity D each have 3 days slack; however, a delay in activity B reduces D's slack time. *Free slack* is the amount of time an activity can be delayed without delaying or reducing the slack of any other activity. Exercise 12-5 focuses on the distinction between the two kinds of slack.

Activities with 0 slack are termed *critical activities*. A, B, D, and E all have 0 slack, and are thus critical activities of Figure 12-3. A delay in any critical

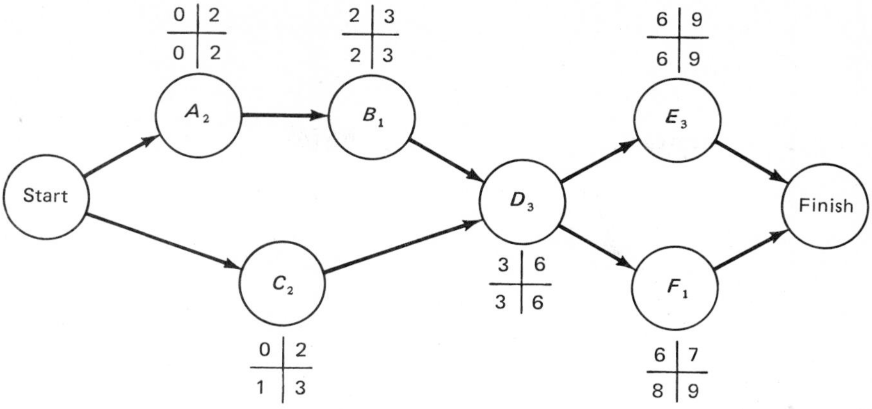

Figure 12-3 PERT diagram with $\frac{ES|EF}{LS|LF}$

activity will delay the entire project. *A sequence of critical activities forms a critical path.*

The above method generates ES and LS for each activity, and so will always find the critical path. It may happen that there is more than one critical path. In Figure 12-3, if the estimated time of *F* were 3 weeks rather than 1 week, then *ABDF* as well as *ABDE* would be a critical path, and a delay in either *E* or *F* would delay the complete project. As one can imagine, complex projects generate rather complex networks. There are many computer programs available for computing the slack and finding the critical path, provided one knows the sequence and estimated times of activities.

Having found the project completion time, one can then determine when the project must start in order for it to be completed on time. Suppose in our illustration the seminars are to be started on Monday, May 12; then the planning, which requires 9 weeks, must start on Monday, March 10. If it is already March 17, then it is quite reasonable to ask which activity times can be shortened or crashed, in order to speed up the project. We now consider this aspect of project management.

CRASHING ACTIVITY TIMES

The costs of a project are of three basic kinds:

1. Direct costs of activities
2. Indirect costs of supervision, administration, and so forth
3. Opportunity costs including late penalties and forfeited early bonuses

Generally, as the overall length of a project increases, the direct costs decrease

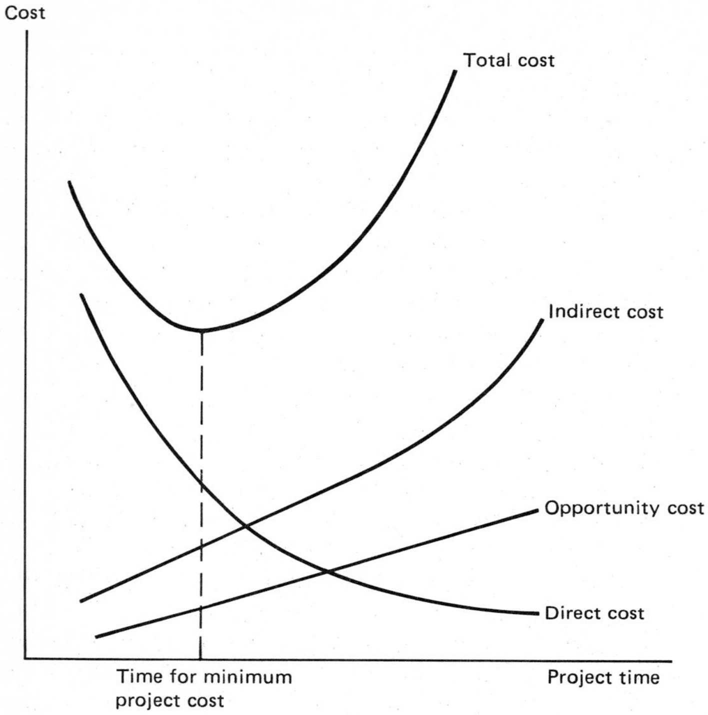

Figure 12-4 Cost-time relationship for a typical project.

but the indirect and opportunity costs increase, as depicted in Figure 12-4. Consequently, crashing activities may decrease *total* project costs while increasing *direct* costs. Costs here include monetary outlays and nonmonetary effects.

Estimated activity times are ordinarily based on normal working conditions. The length of time required to complete an activity can sometimes be shortened, at a price. In some instances that price may be a dollar cost; for instance, additional personnel may have to be hired temporarily or regular personnel may be asked to work overtime. In other instances, crashing the activity may lessen the quality of the activities; for instance, the surface of a highway

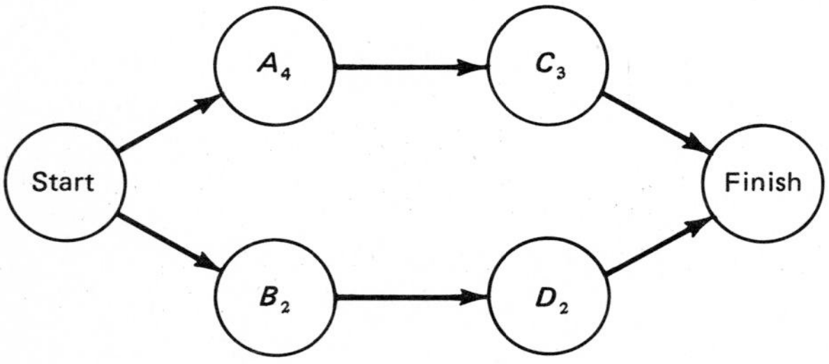

Figure 12-5 PERT network with critical path *AC*.

Table 12-2 A simple network with crash times

	Time (days)		Cost (dollars)	
Activity	Regular	Crash	Regular	Crash
A	4	2	$ 400	$ 800
B	2	1	300	450
C	3	2	500	600
D	2	$1\frac{1}{2}$	300	350
			$1500	$2200

may not be quite smooth if the smoothing operation has been rushed, or an agency report may be less informative if charts have to be omitted in the rush, or, in our illustration, the proper equipment may not be available if the sites have to be hurriedly selected. If it is necessary to speed up the project, then it is worthwhile determining (1) which activities are worth crashing and (2) which of those activities can be crashed at least cost, either monetary or otherwise.

We will first illustrate the time-cost trade-offs with a simple dollar example. Then we will return to the seminar planning illustration in which the costs may be nonmonetary.

Consider the simple PERT network of Figure 12-5. The regular time and cost, and the crash time and cost, are as in Table 12-2.

Consider critical activities *A* and *C*; we determine the marginal cost per day crashed so that crashing can be done as cheaply as possible. Here we assume that the cost of crashing *A* from 4 to 3 days is the same as the cost of crashing it from 3 to 2 days; that is, we assume the time-cost trade-off to be linear. If this were not the case, the logic would be the same but the computation would be a bit more involved. Table 12-3 focuses on the incremental cost per day for crashing critical activities.

If it is necessary to crash the project by 1 day, then *C* should be crashed. Its crash time is only $100 for the day, whereas crashing *A* one day would cost $200. If the project has to be crashed 2 days, then *C* should be crashed 1 day, and *A* should be crashed 1 day, resulting in a crash cost of $300. Finally if the project has to be crashed 3 days, then both *A* and *C* would be crashed completely. The crash cost would be $500 above the regular project cost.

If the critical path were crashed as much as possible, its completion time would be 4 days. Since the regular completion time of path *BD* is 4 days, it

Table 12-3 Crashing critical activities

Activity	Days shortened	Additional cost	Marginal cost per day
A	2	$400	$200
C	1	100	100

Table 12-4 The simple network revised

	Time (days)		Cost (dollars)	
Activity	Regular	Crash	Regular	Crash
A	4	2	$ 400	$ 800
B	2	1	300	450
C	3	2	500	600
D	3	2	300	400
			$1500	$2200

makes no sense to crash *B* and *D*. Ordinarily only the activities on the critical path are likely candidates for crashing. An exception occurs when the critical path crash time is less than the noncritical path regular time; then we consider crashing noncritical activities. Suppose activity *D* had a regular time of 3 days and a crash time of 2 days; the revised network is as in Table 12-4. The regular completion time of path *BD* would then be 5 days, whereas its crash time would be 3 days. If it is necessary to crash the project completion time from the regular time of 7 days to the crash time of 4 days, then path *BD* must also be crashed by 1 day. Since it is cheaper to crash *D* than *B*, *D* would be crashed by a day. When the crash time of the critical path is less than the regular time of a noncritical path, then noncritical activities may also have to be crashed.

Crashing with Nonmonetary Costs

We return now to the problem facing Ann Maxall, who is responsible for coordinating the forthcoming seminars for the state mental health and mental retardation (MH-MR) council. The seminars are to begin May 12, just 8 weeks from today, March 17. After developing the project network, she realizes that the regular completion time of the planning project is 9 weeks. Hence, she has to try to save a week somewhere. Her reasoning is as follows.

Ann estimates that if she reduces the time spent on planning the content of the seminar, it is quite likely that some important aspects of the information/evaluation system will be left out. She may think of it later, but then it may be too late to get the right speaker for that topic. She does not believe she can reduce the time to obtain speakers below the regular time of 1 week.

Preparing and mailing the flyer/invitations is an important step because the flyer will hopefully attract the county MH-MR personnel to the seminar. The state council is trying to avoid the "big stick" approach, by encouraging agency personnel to participate. Having it poorly prepared or short-cutting the mailing phase would run the risk of not getting "the word" to all the appropriate agency people. The consequence would be to have fewer participants at the seminar and subsequently have MH-MR personnel improperly using the information system.

Finally, the period for accepting reservations could be reduced from 3 to 2 weeks at the risk of not giving people sufficient advance notice, and hence getting the system off on the wrong foot by creating a "rush job" image. Alternatively, Ann could accept reservations for 2 weeks and then permit desk registration at the seminar. This would mean she would not have a good estimate of the number of participants, which she needs to be able to choose rooms of the right size, to have sufficient supplies, and to notify the seminar sites of the numbers for lunch and dinner.

Ann realizes that it is not impossible to crash most of the activities, but there is a price for any hurrying. Time saved in crashing *C* or *F* will have no effect on the project completion time, and so she has not even considered crashing them. To aid her own choice and to get counsel from her colleagues, she has summarized the crashing possibilities and their consequences. The summary is presented in Table 12-5.

After some thought and discussion, Ann finally arrives at a priority order for crashing the critical activities. Activity *D* is given top priority (it should be the last one to be crashed), since the seminar cannot possibly be successful if the county agency personnel do not attend. The second priority is given to activity *A*; if the personnel are not sold on using the system and do not learn how to use it properly, then the system has little chance of ultimate success. The last priority is given to activity *E*; the poor image can be avoided by encouraging but not demanding agency personnel to respond. Not knowing exactly how many will participate does pose some problem, but Ann feels she can easily have more supplies on hand than might be needed. Not knowing how many meals to serve will be a nuisance to the food service, will probably generate criticism of those running the seminar, but—this is important to Ann and the state council—will not involve the participants.

Accordingly, activity *E* is the one chosen to be crashed. Planning for the seminars now goes forward as originally outlined except for the shortened participants' response period. The seminars should be ready to start May 12.

Table 12-5 Crashing critical activities

	Time (weeks)		
Activity	Regular	Crash	Consequence of crashing
A	2	1	Important topics omitted; improper selection of speakers.
B	1	1	Crashing is infeasible.
D	3	2	Flyer not well prepared; some county agency personnel not on mailing list.
E	3	2	Rush-job image or unknown number of participants.

Determining time-cost trade-offs in PERT/CPM is analogous to sensitivity analysis in linear programming and, more accurately, to postoptimality analysis in goal programming. The time-cost trade-off of network management is a contribution specifically made by CPM. The contribution made particularly by PERT relaxes the requirement that there be a single time estimate to be treated as a constant and allows the network to be based on variable activity times. We will consider this aspect of project management in our next section.

VARIABLE ACTIVITY TIMES

The time required by most activities, especially those depending on human performances, is rarely a constant. Rather than make a single estimate of the activity time, three estimates are made. The three different estimates and their symbols are:

- a *The optimistic time*. This is the shortest amount of time the activity would need under the most favorable circumstances short of a miracle. The probability is very small that the activity could actually be completed in this amount of time.
- m *The most likely time*. This is the amount of time that the activity is most likely to require.
- b *The pessimistic time*. This is the amount of time the activity needs under the most unfavorable circumstances short of an act of God or some man-made catastrophe. The probability is small that this amount of time would actually be needed by the activity.

From these three estimates of activity time the mean, or *expected activity time*, is found by getting a weighted average of the three estimates. Intuitively it seems reasonable that the most likely time m should be given a greater weight than either the optimistic time a or the pessimistic time b. The equation for the expected activity time supports this notion; it is[2]:

$$t = \frac{a + 4m + b}{6}$$

[2] The equations for the expected activity time and standard deviation of activity time actually come from a *beta* probability distribution. The beta distribution is continuous over a finite range of values from a to b with mode m. We simply point out that the equations used have not been pulled from a hat; they come from the theoretical beta distribution, which repeated applications have shown to be an appropriate description of the activity time. It is beyond the scope of this book to examine the details of the beta distribution, how well it describes actual activity times, or the derivation of the equations for expected activity time t and standard deviation of activity time σ.

Example If

$$a = 2$$

$$m = 2\tfrac{1}{2}$$

$$b = 6$$

then

$$t = \frac{2 + 4(2\tfrac{1}{2}) + 6}{6} = 3$$

With a and b defined as they were, we can estimate the standard deviation of activity time. Assuming that the range $b - a$ covers six standard deviations,[3] the equation for the standard deviation is:

$$\sigma = \frac{b - a}{6}$$

Example Suppose that the simple network of Figure 12-5 has multiple time estimates as given in Table 12-6, columns headed "a," "m," and "b."

The mean or expected completion time of activity C is found by

$$t_c = \frac{a + 4m + b}{6}$$

$$= \frac{1 + (4)2\tfrac{1}{2} + 7}{6}$$

$$= \frac{18}{6}$$

$$= 3$$

The standard deviation of the completion time of activity C is given by

$$\sigma = \frac{b - a}{6}$$

$$= \frac{7 - 1}{6}$$

$$= 1$$

The mean and standard deviations are found in like manner for the other activities.

[3] In the normal distribution 99.73 percent of the distribution falls within the six-standard-deviation range; regardless of its form, at least 89 percent of any distribution falls within this range.

Table 12-6 Multiple time estimates

Activity	a	m	b	$t = \frac{a + 4m + b}{6}$	$\sigma = \frac{b - a}{6}$	σ^2
A	2	4	6	4	.67	.45
B	1	2	3	2	.33	.11
C	1	$2\frac{1}{2}$	7	3	1.0	1.0
D	1	$1\frac{1}{2}$	5	2	.67	.45

Expected Time and Standard Deviation of a Path

A path is a sequence of separate tasks or activities. The time to complete a path is the sum of the completion times of the activities on the path. To find the expected completion time and the standard deviation of the completion time for a path, we use two results from probability theory:

1. The expected value of a sum of variables is the sum of the expected values.
2. The variance of a sum of variables is the sum of the variances, provided the variables are statistically independent.

Example The expected completion time of path AC is

$$t_{AC} = t_A + t_C$$
$$= 4 + 3 = 7$$

To find the standard deviation of the completion time of AC, we first find its variance. The variance of AC, assuming its activity times are independent, is given by:

$$\sigma^2_{AC} = \sigma^2_A + \sigma^2_C$$
$$= .45 + 1.0 = 1.45$$

The standard deviation of the path completion time is

$$\sigma_{AC} = \sqrt{1.45} = 1.20$$

One finds expected completion time and standard deviation of completion time of any path in the same way. With these two pieces of information probability statements become meaningful. Of particular interest are probability statements about the critical path and about the whole project.

Completion Time and Probabilities

To be able to make a probability statement about a path's completion time (for example, the probability of completing the path in 4 weeks is .90), its probability distribution must be known. Since most projects have a large number of

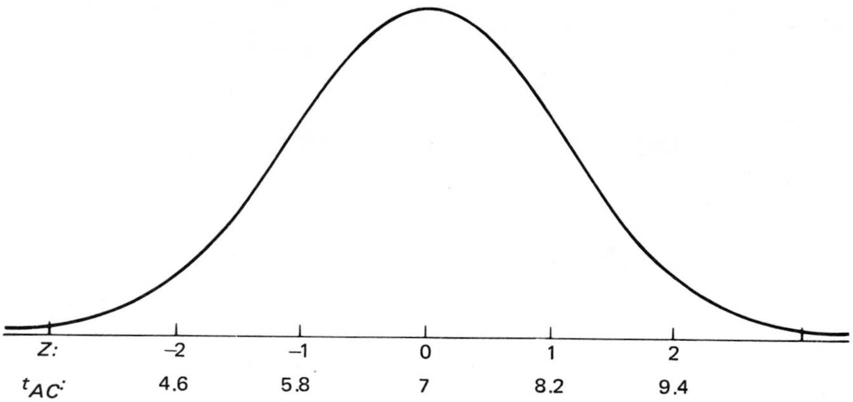

Figure 12-6 Normal probability of path completion time, with $t_{AC} = 7$ and $\sigma_{AC} = 1.2$.

activities, we can focus on those without much loss. If a path has many activities, then its completion time will be approximately normally distributed.[4]

Example With only two activities on the critical path the assumption of normality is a rather coarse approximation. Assuming for the moment, however, that the critical path completion time is approximately normally distributed with a mean of 7 days and a standard deviation of 1.2 days, the critical path completion time follows the probability distribution illustrated in Figure 12-6. Assuming a normal distribution, we can find the probability that the project will be completed within any given number of days.[5] The probability that path AC will be completed within 8.2 days is given by

$$P(t_{AC} \leq 8.2) = P(Z \leq 1) = .8413$$

The probability that the project will be completed within 9 days is found as follows:

$$P(t_{AC} \leq 9) = P\left(Z \leq \frac{9-7}{1.2}\right) = P(Z \leq 1.67) = .952$$

Finding these probabilities assumes that the critical path completion time is normally distributed, which is more closely adhered to when the path has many activities. Determining the mean and the standard deviation from the three estimates assumes that the activity time is approximately beta-distributed. If either of these assumptions is not satisfied, then the network may best be analyzed by simulation rather than by a direct analysis.

[4] According to the *central limit theorem* of probability theory, the sum of n independent variables tends to be normally distributed as n tends toward infinity.

[5] Finding normal probabilities is described in Chapter 3. The standard normal table is Table 2 of the Appendix to this text.

Finding probabilities of the critical path completion time, to the exclusion of the completion times of other paths, is deficient because a noncritical path may take longer than the critical path because of the variability of the activity times. Hence, especially if noncritical paths have completion times close to the critical path completion time, their expected completion times should be included in the analysis.

Example Suppose the network of Figure 12-7 has the estimated completion times as given in Table 12-7.

Path *ABD* is critical with $t_{ABD} = 9$ days, and path *CE* is almost critical with $t_{CE} = 8$. Here it is important to find the probability of both paths being completed in the specified number of days. Means and standard deviations of path completion times for the two paths are:

Path	t	σ
ABD	9	1.53
CE	8	1.20

To determine the probability that the project will be completed within 10 days, first determine the probability that each path will be completed within 10 days. These probabilities are found by

$$P(t_{ABD} \leq 10) = P\left(Z \leq \frac{10 - 9}{1.53}\right) = P(Z \leq .65) = .743$$

Similarly, $$P(t_{CE} \leq 10) = P\left(Z \leq \frac{10 - 8}{1.20}\right) = P(Z \leq 1.67) = .953$$

The project is complete only when *both ABD and CE* are complete.

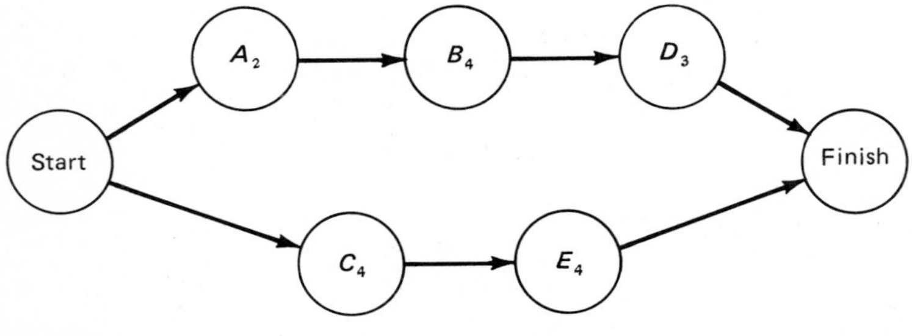

Figure 12-7 A critical path and an almost critical path.

Table 12-7 A critical path and an almost critical path

Activity	a	m	b	$t = \frac{a + 4m + b}{6}$	$\sigma = \frac{b - a}{6}$	σ^2
A	1	2	3	2	.33	.11
B	2	3	10	4	1.33	1.77
C	2	$3\frac{1}{2}$	8	4	1.00	1.00
D	2	$2\frac{1}{2}$	6	3	.67	.45
E	2	4	6	4	.67	.45

Assuming that the paths are independent, the probability multiplication rule (Chapter 2) applies.

$$\begin{aligned} P(t_{\text{project}} \leq 10) &= P(t_{ABD} \leq 10) \cdot P(t_{CE} \leq 10) \\ &= (.743) \cdot (.953) \\ &= .71 \end{aligned}$$

The closer the expected times of a noncritical and a critical path, the more likely it is that the noncritical path will actually wind up taking longer than the critical path. If the paths share resources (personnel or machinery or vehicles, for instance) or if the paths have a common activity (in the seminar planning project, activity *D* was common to paths *ABDE* and *CDF*), then the paths are not independent. In such a case the simple multiplication rule would not apply. If the project is complex with many conditional probabilities, simulating the network would be the wisest approach.

PERT/CPM AND PROJECT DECISION MAKING

Development of an initial project network is time consuming, but it greatly enhances understanding the project. As the project unfolds, and actual times and costs are used to update the network, reassessment of critical activities and paths provides ongoing planning and control. It helps to identify alternative ways of achieving the project management objectives related to time, cost, and quality. A large-scale project may have hundreds or thousands of activities. The corresponding network would most assuredly be computerized, but even so, the voluminous printout requires time, patience, and commitment if the technique is to contribute to project management and control. As with all management aids, the decision of whether to employ it depends on whether the improvement it provides outweighs the resources it consumes. While there are a few extensions of PERT/CPM, one in particular focuses on the cost aspects of project management.

PERT/Cost

PERT/Cost is a cost accounting extension to project management; it groups costs by activities rather than by organizational lines, fitting quite well with project management. PERT/Cost provides information on activity cost-to-date, which can be compared to activity completion-to-date. The mechanism allows for better control of each activity and the project as a whole.

Like any model or mechanism, PERT in any form or extension has its shortcomings.

Limitations

Project management is not without its problems, which include difficulties in estimating completion times, estimating regular and crash costs, the validity of statistical independence of activities, the validity of applying the beta distribution to activity times and the normal distribution to project times. There are also less technical difficulties. The effort required both to develop and to update the network is sometimes seen as extraneous both to the project and to its operational control.

Our discussion of project management will conclude with an application of a project network to a local referendum.

APPROVING A BOND ISSUE: AN APPLICATION[6]

Ordinary revenue is the usual source for expenses associated with day-to-day and year-to-year operations of a municipality or school district. Extraordinary expenses, arising from the construction of a new sanitary system, water purification plant, or a new school building, are often satisfied by grants from a higher authority (federal or state) or from funds invested by the public to be returned with interest at a later date. The latter source, through a bond issue, often requires voter approval. The process of gaining voter approval through a referendum must convince the voters of the real need for the bond issue, identify the time and places of polling, and record and publicize the results of the referendum. Such a project, then, is composed of many activities. Coordinating and planning such a project may benefit from a network representation. Here we present a simplified version of the activities that would comprise gaining voter approval for a school district's bond issue. The activities listed below are identified by number in the project network in Figure 12-8.

1. Establish need within long-range plans.
2. List resources and timed needs.

[6] This application is an adaptation of H. W. Handy and K. M. Hussain, *Network Analysis for Educational Management,* Prentice-Hall, Inc., Englewood Cliffs, N.J., 1969, pp. 79–83.

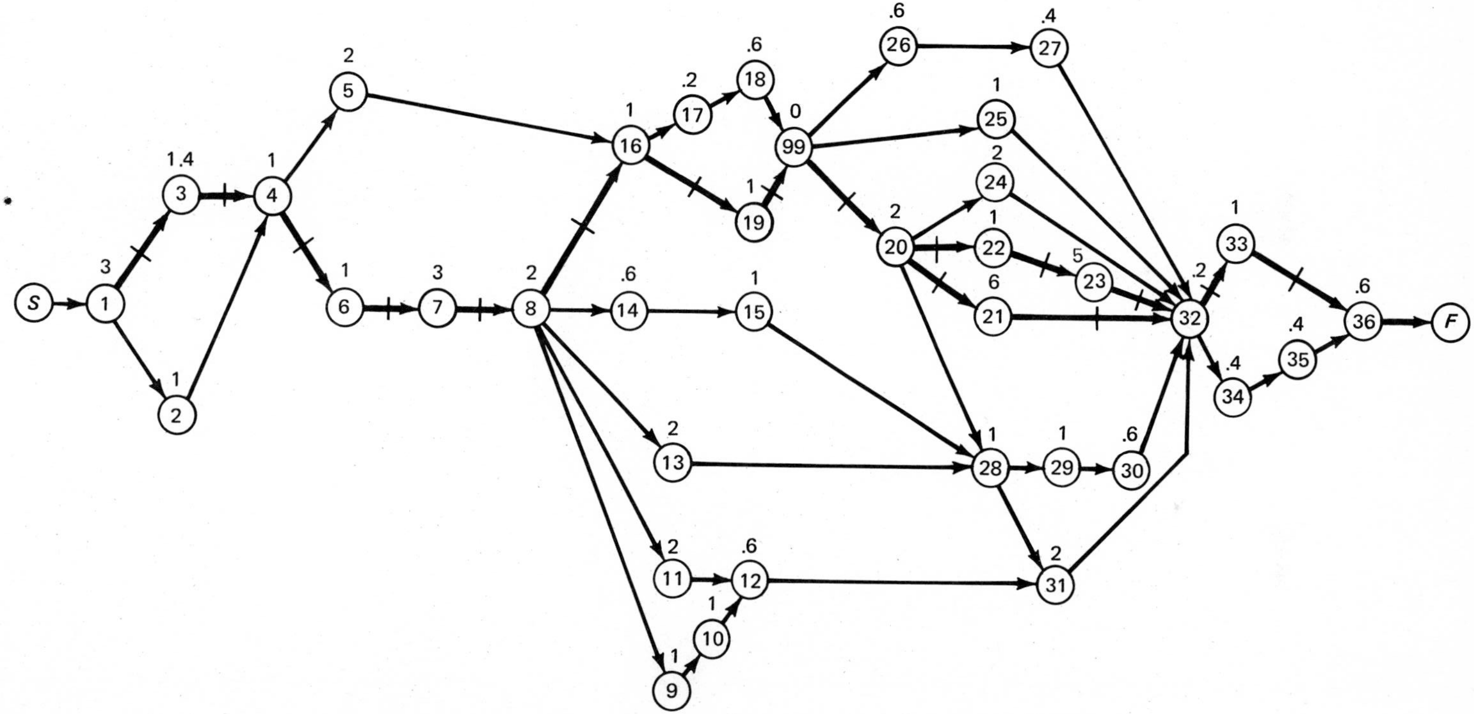

Figure 12-8 School bond issue PERT network (critical path: 23.2 weeks).

3. Form citizens' planning committee.
4. Identify campaign objectives and amount of bond issue.
5. Seek support of board members.
6. Organize information committees.
7. Plan promotion strategy and costs.
8. Develop master chart of dates and events.
9. Activate a speakers bureau.
10. Arrange for speakers and audiences.
11. Prepare campaign literature.
12. Distribute materials.
13. Solicit volunteer workers.
14. Solicit aid of a volunteer worker leader.
15. Organize materials to be given to volunteers.
16. Petition school board for elections.
17. Set election date.
18. Check for conflict with other elections.
19. Verify sufficiency of petition.
20. Determine polling places and district boundaries.
21. Declare election (with 6-week waiting period).
22. Obtain group endorsements of bond issue.
23. Run advertising campaign in media.
24. Conduct PTA voter registration drive.
25. Select election personnel.
26. Print election materials.
27. Deliver election materials.
28. Assign districts to volunteers.
29. Hold house-to-house campaign.
30. Arrange for baby-sitting and transportation.
31. Have speakers make presentation to their groups.
32. Hold election.
33. Apply for no litigation certificate (1-week delay required).
34. Canvas election results.
35. Publicize results.
36. Make official record of proceedings.
99. Dummy activity.

The network requires a minimum of 23.2 weeks for completion.

The estimated time for each activity, in weeks, appears above the activity circle in the diagram. The critical path, indicated by a heavy line, requires 23.2 weeks for completion. Note the parallel critical paths from activity 20 to activity 32, the election itself. A *dummy activity,* 99, has been inserted after activities 18 and 19 to simplify the network. Three activities, 20, 25, and 26, depend on the completion of activities 18 and 19. In such a case, the use of a dummy activity avoids the jumble of many intersecting sequence arrows.

One of the advantages of developing such a project network is that it provides greater opportunity for identifying all the activities, and indicates when each one should start. This helps to avoid omitting a necessary or at least helpful activity, or starting it so late that the result is less than desirable. This is particularly the case in a "soft" project such as the bond issue, where the election will take place even if some of the prerequisite activities have not been completed. For example, the election will be held on the declared day even if sufficient time has not been given to the voter registration drive, and even if the advertising campaign never got into full swing, and even if house-to-house campaigning reached only a few voters. In a "hard" project, such as the construction of a building, prerequisite activities are less easily omitted but may be started late with the ultimate effect of delaying the project.

SUMMARY

Management of projects which are rather unique combinations of activities is appropriately in the realm of a network model. A hybrid of PERT and CPM requires identifying the project activities, the activity times, and the sequencing information. From that, the earliest possible time an activity can start (ES) and the latest it can start without delaying the project (LS) are calculated. The difference LS − ES yields the slack time for each activity. Activities with zero slack are critical activities. A sequence of critical activities forms a critical path; the completion time of the critical path is the project's completion time. Critical activities may be able to be crashed at a price. PERT/CPM helps one find the right activities to crash to keep the cost of crashing to a minimum. Especially when those costs are nonmonetary, network analysis helps to assess the time-cost trade-offs in much the same way that goal programming helps to assess goal priorities.

Where activity times are random variables, one makes three different time estimates:

The optimistic, a
The most likely, m
The pessimistic, b

From these, the expected completion time

$$t = \frac{a + 4m + b}{6}$$

and the standard deviation of completion time

$$\sigma = \frac{b - a}{6}$$

can be estimated.

Assuming that the activity times are independent and the path completion time is normally distributed provides the basis for probability statements about the project completion time. Where any of these assumptions are severely lacking, simulation of the project network may be necessary.

Various extensions of this network technique have been developed which provide ways of building resource constraints into the network and which keep track of costs as well as time. A PERT-type network is not only useful in the planning stage but also helpful in monitoring the project once it is underway.

BIBLIOGRAPHY

Archibald, Russell Daw, and R. L. Zilloria: *Network-Based Management System (PERT/CPM)*, John Wiley & Sons, Inc., New York, 1967.

Calvin, George M., Jr., and Anthony F. Fielding: "A PERT Application to Curriculum Planning," *Educational Technology,* vol. 15, October 1975, pp. 9–21.

Handy, H. W., and K. M. Hussain: *Network Analysis for Educational Management,* Prentice-Hall, Inc., Englewood Cliffs, N.J., 1969.

——— and R. P. Lutz: "PERT: The Critical Path to Curriculum Development," *School Board,* vol. 10, September 1967, pp. 8–10.

Hanson, R. S.: "Moving the Hospital to a New Location," *Industrial Engineering,* vol. 4, no. 11, November 1972.

Kittleson, Howard, and Michael McCarthy: "PERT and Plays: Project Management in the Theatre Arts," *Educational Theatre Journal,* vol. 25, March 1973, pp. 95–101.

Levin, Richard I., and Charles A. Kirkpatrick: *Planning and Control with PERT/CPM,* McGraw-Hill Book Company, New York, 1966.

Moder, J. J., and C. R. Phillips: *Project management with CPM and PERT,* Van Nostrand Reinhold Company, New York, 1970.

Vazsonyi, Andrew: "l'Historie de Grandeur et de la Decadence de la Methode PERT," *Management Science,* vol. 16, April 1970, pp. B449–B455.

Whitehouse, Gary E.: *Systems Analysis and Designs Using Network Techniques,* Prentice-Hall, Inc., Englewood Cliffs, N.J., 1970.

Weist, J. D., and F. K. Levy: *A Management Guide to PERT/CPM,* Prentice-Hall, Inc., Englewood Cliffs, N.J., 1969.

EXERCISES

Extensions of chapter examples

12-1 Refer to the seminar planning project. (See p. 247.) How is the network affected in sequence and time if the seminar selection site C is dependent on the seminar content A?

12-2 Refer again to the seminar planning project. Ann Maxall realizes, as an afterthought, that the single time estimates that she originally made were really the most likely times to complete the activities. Upon further reflection she identifies an *optimistic* and a *pessimistic* time for each activity; they are as follows:

For A: 1 and 4
For B: $\frac{1}{2}$ and 2
For C: 1 and 3
For D: 2 and 4
For E: 2 and 6
For F: $\frac{1}{2}$ and 2

(*a*) What is now the expected project completion time?

(*b*) What is the probability that the project will be completed within the 9 weeks originally planned for?

12-3 Refer to problems 12-1 and 12-2. Suppose the time estimates of problem 12-2 apply to the network in which activity *C* depends on the completion of activity *A*.

(*a*) What is the expected completion time?

(*b*) What is the probability that the project will be completed within 9 weeks?

(*c*) What does this suggest about developing the proper sequence of activities?

12-4 Refer to the referendum application of Figure 12-8. Consider the portion of the network from activity 8 to activity 32, including only the critical paths and activities 13, 14, 15, 28, 29, and 30.

(*a*) Draw the network diagram.

(*b*) Calculate ES, EF, LS, and LF for all activities.

(*c*) Find the slack time of all activities.

(*d*) Find the critical path of the diminished network.

12-5 Refer to exercise 12-4.

(*a*) What is the slack time of activity 13?

(*b*) If activity 13 is 5 days late in getting started, how much slack will activity 28 still have?

(*c*) How much can activity 13 be delayed without delaying activity 28? This portion of the slack time is referred to as *free slack,* the difference between the ES of a successor activity and EF of the activity itself. The remainder of activity 13's slack is shared with activities 28, 29, and 30, those activities in series with it.

Other Applications

12-6 A project consists of the following activities:

Activity	Immediate predecessors	Estimated time (days)
A	—	2
B	—	3
C	*A*	3
D	*B*, *C*	1
E	*D*	4
F	*D*	2
G	*E*, *F*	1

(*a*) Draw a project diagram.

(*b*) Compute the ES, EF, LS, and LF for each activity.

(*c*) What is the project completion time?

12-7 Refer to problem 12-6. If activity *D* is not an immediate predecessor of activity *E*, but *B* and *C* are predecessors of *E*, what change should be made in the network diagram? Revise the project completion time.

12-8 In case it should be necessary to hurry the project of problem 12-6, the crash times of the activities have been identified. At the same time, estimates of costs under regular and crash conditions have also been identified. The time estimates and cost estimates for both regular and crash conditions are shown in the table on page 296.

(*a*) Find the regular project cost.

(*b*) Identify the time-cost trade-offs in the order in which they should be made, depending on the extent of crashing necessary.

(*c*) Find the cost of crashing 2 days.

12-9 Refer to problem 12-8. Suppose activity *D* is no longer a predecessor of activity *E*. Revise the order in which time-cost trade-offs should be taken.

	Time (days)		Cost	
Activity	Regular	Crash	Regular	Crash
A	2	1	$200	$ 300
B	3	2	300	400
C	3	$1\frac{1}{2}$	400	700
D	1	—	200	—
E	4	2	700	1000
F	2	1	300	500
G	1	$\frac{1}{2}$	200	300

12-10 The State Department of Public Welfare has had separate contracts with data processing firms to service its needs. It has just been decided that the payroll, client status/eligibility, and cash assistance/medical assistance functions will henceforth be handled internally on the department's own new computer system. Besides the authorization to enter into a leasing agreement for the equipment, the department has also been given hiring authority to secure programmers who will develop and maintain the system. Programmers who are hired will be responsible for developing the payroll program (P) and the client status/eligibility (CS/E) program, and for testing and maintaining the cash assistance/medical assistance (CA/MA) program, that will actually be written by the management services division of the Bureau of the Budget (BOB). Certain aspects of the cash assistance/medical assistance program depend on the client status/eligibility program. The director of systems support has attempted to identify the various activities that must be executed to get the complete set of programs running on the system that will be shortly installed. The activities and their expected completion times are described in the following table.

Symbol	Activity	Time (weeks)	Predecessors
A	Compare computer systems; notify manufacturer of choices.	8	
B	Await delivery of computer.	16	*A*
C	Hire programmers.	4	*A*
D	Flow chart P program.	6	*C*
E	Flow chart CS/E program.	10	*C*
F	Code P program.	3	*D*
G	Code CS/E.	5	*E*
H	Consult with BOB staff on CA/MA program.	4	*A*
I	Flow chart CA/MA program.	8	*E*, *H*
J	Code CA/MA program.	8	*G*, *I*
K	Test P and CS/E programs.	2	*F*, *G*
L	Debug P and CS/E programs.	2	*K*
M	Install and test new computer system.	2	*B*

N	Test P and CS/E programs on new computer.	2	*L, M*
O	Prepare P and CS/E program manuals.	4	*K*
P	Test CA/MA program on new computer.	2	*J, M*
Q	Prepare CA/MA program manual.	3	*P*
R	Implement P and CS/E programs.	2	*N*
S	Implement CA/MA program.	2	*P*
T	Thoroughly acquaint hired programmers with CA/MA program.	3	*N, P*

(*a*) How long will it take for the three programs to be up and running and under the control of department programmers?

(*b*) Which activities are critical in meeting the schedule of part *a*?

(*c*) How long will it be before the department can do an internal audit on client eligibility on the new computer?

12-11 This problem, though greatly simplified, is based on the Kittleson and McCarthy (1973) article, which concludes with, "It is clear that producing a play is a complex systems management problem. What was surprising to the director was the sheer usefulness of PERT in perceiving the interrelationships of the large number of activities".

The Community Theatre starts its Shakespearian Festival on Monday, June 30. It has identified the following tasks necessary for the production.

Activity	Description	Predecessors	Time (weeks)
A	Selection of plays		5
B	Casting	*A*	6
C	Set design	*A*	4
D	Costume design	*A*	5
E	Set construction	*C*	6
F	Rehearsals	*B*	5
G	Dress rehearsals	*D, E, F*	4
H	Printing tickets and programs	*B*	8
I	Festival presentations	*G, H*	2

(*a*) On what date must the selection of plays begin?

(*b*) It is now 2 weeks after that date. Propose alternatives for crashing, presenting the cost of crashing each activity.

Project problems

12-12 Pick some project you are or will be involved in, such as a recruiting effort to fill some position(s), the implementation of a new system, the development of some legislation, a research paper, or other undertaking. List its components, or activities, and their predecessors, and estimate times. Construct a project network. Identify the critical path and any almost critical paths.

12-13 The Calvin and Fielding (1975) article presents an application of a modification of PERT in an area that is not always considered the domain of management techniques.

(*a*) In what way is PERT modified in this application?

(*b*) What contributions did PERT make?

(*c*) Can you think of another potential application from an unlikely area?

CHAPTER

THIRTEEN

QUEUING

Waiting in line, or in a queue, is part of everyday life. Waiting "too long" at the Bureau of Motor Vehicles might be inconvenient. Waiting "too long" for an ambulance might prove fatal. The cost of improving service and decreasing waiting time might mean that the library must purchase an additional copy of a popular book, but that the airport must construct another runway and supporting facilities. Since the consequences of waiting and improving service vary greatly, those responsible for providing the service will make varying degrees of effort to understand the nature of waiting and providing a service. The decision maker or manager of the system that provides the service is concerned both with whether adequate service is being rendered (or the clients have to wait too long) and with whether the service facility is being used efficiently (or the facility is idle too much). In some situations deciding on the number of service providers is made easy by having available a supply of servers who can be otherwise employed; for example, librarians generally have worthwhile tasks when there are no borrowers claiming their attention. In other situations, a decision to maintain a particular number of servers must not be taken lightly; for example, enlarging the clinic or increasing the number of toll booths and approach lanes represents a commitment in a facility that cannot be alternately employed.

Waiting lines and service processes generally have three common elements: arrivals, servers, and the provision of service. Some typical examples of such situations from the public domain are presented in Table 13-1.

Table 13-1 Some common queues

Situation	Arrivals	Servers	Service
Post office	Patrons	Clerks	Stamps, letter registration, etc.
Clinic	Patients	Doctors, nurses	Medical treatment
School registration	Students	Clerks	Course cards, etc.
Airport	Airplanes	Runways	Landing and taking off
Telephone switchboard	Calls	Operator and switching equipment	Connection
Computer maintenance	"Down" computer	System engineer	Repair
Intersection	Automobiles	Policeman and/or traffic lights	Passage
Library I	Borrowers	Librarian	Return or check out
Library II	Requester	A particular book	Borrowed
Bureau of Motor Vehicles	Drivers	Clerks, records, computers, etc.	Registration, renewal, etc.

Generally, the faster arrivals come for service, the longer the line tends to be; the slower the server provides the service, the longer the line tends to be. Hence the arrival rate and service rate are the critical elements for determining the length of the line, the amount of time an arrival must wait for service, and the proportion of time that the server is idle. We shall also see that the variability in service time, as well as the average service time, greatly affects the length and the other characteristics of the queue.

Our intention here is not to provide a thorough and detailed discourse on all the possibilities in queuing, but rather to present some basic notions of queuing and to emphasize how the results of a waiting-line situation are related to decisions.

DECISION MAKING AND QUEUING

As the decision problem is defined, the salient features are abstracted. If the decision situation can be depicted as the arrival of units into a system where they will be serviced, and then leave the system (or perhaps continue on for further servicing, as in a multiphase model), then it is worthwhile to determine whether the relationships among the components satisfy certain assumptions that permit the use of an analytical queuing model.

If the assumptions are not satisfied, an analytical queuing model would not be appropriate, but simulation may be useful.

A queuing model is essentially a descriptive one that is used to predict the consequences (for example, the time an airplane waits for a runway or the idle time of physicians in a clinic) of various controllable decision alternatives (for example, the number of operating runways or the use of physician assistants alongside physicians). It is the decision situation itself rather than the model that generates the various alternatives. The model determines the consequences of each alternative so the decision maker can better evaluate it. This scheme is presented in Figure 13-1 within the context of our original decision-making paradigm.

As one abstracts the problem essentials and formulates the model, certain properties identify the appropriate model.

Queue Characteristics

In many cases service is provided in a sequence of steps. Our discussion of queuing will focus only on the simpler situation of service in a single step, or a single-phase facility.

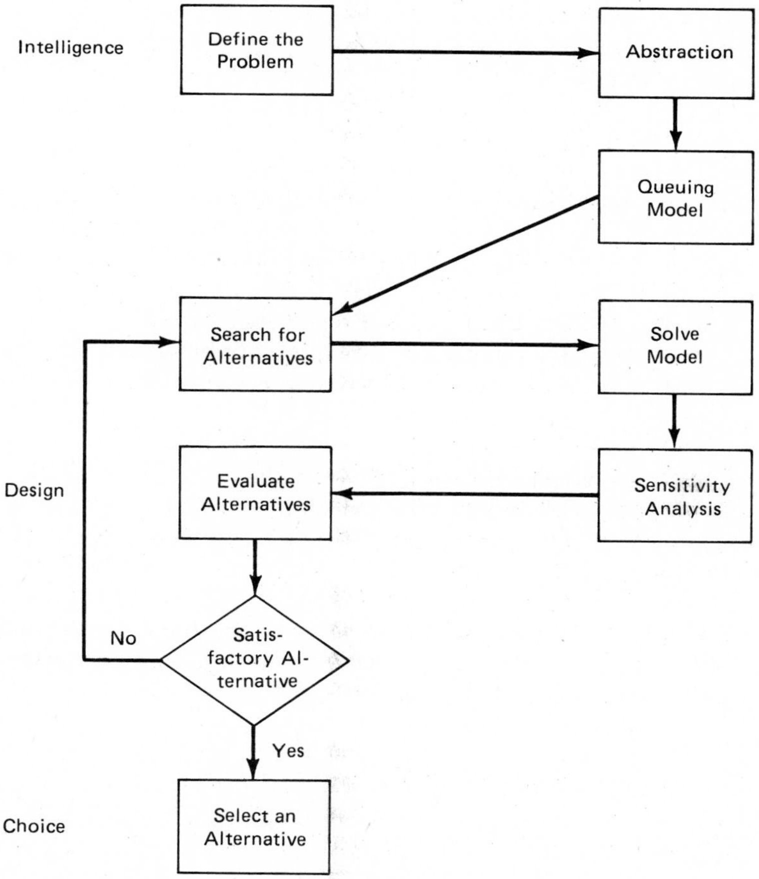

Figure 13-1 The use of queuing in the decision process.

Example Service at a medical clinic often involves registration at the clinic, measurement and recording of vital statistics, examination by a physician, laboratory tests, x-rays, and payment for services. As most of us have all too frequently experienced, each stage may have its own waiting line. Such a situation is referred to as a multiple-phase facility.

Queuing situations may be described according to the following characteristics:

1. Number of service facilities
2. Number of waiting lines
3. Queue discipline—whether arrivals are served on a first-come, first-served basis, or according to a priority classification, or in some other fashion
4. Arrival behavior—whether arrivals will refuse to join or be prohibited from joining a queue if it is too long, leave it if service is too slow, or pick one server over another because of the kind of service provided
5. Queue capacity
6. Size of population of arrivals
7. Arrival rate into the queue
8. Service rate

Queuing situations can be characterized according to the number of service facilities and whether a waiting line forms for each facility or a single waiting line leads to all facilities. Some of the examples from Table 13-1 fit into each of these categories.

Example Airplanes waiting to land at a single runway or borrowers waiting to be checked out by a single librarian are examples of a single-service facility, represented in Figure 13-2.

Example Patrons in line at the various windows in the post office and automobiles lined up at the toll booths on a bridge or highway exemplify multiple-service facilities with each facility having its own waiting line, as represented in Figure 13-3.

Example Patients arriving at the emergency room of the hospital and employees arriving at the interagency motor pool form a single queue for multiple facilities, as depicted in Figure 13-4.

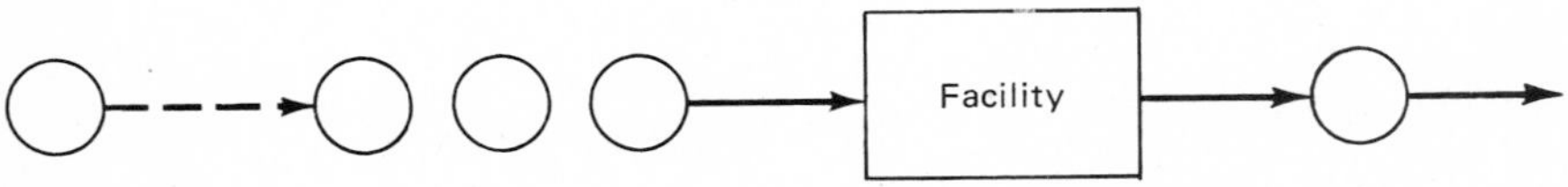

Figure 13-2 Arrivals form a single queue for a single facility.

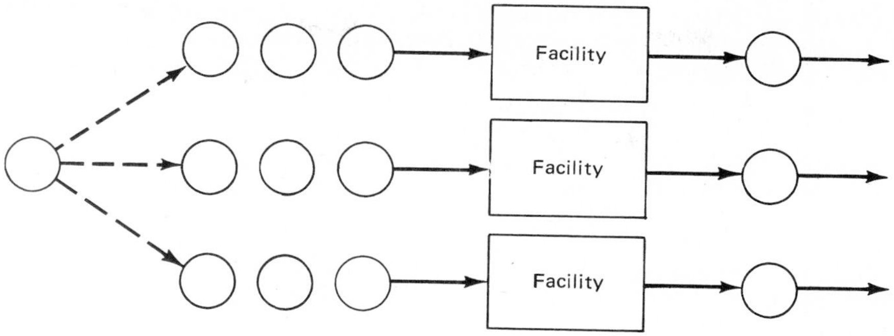

Figure 13-3 Arrivals form multiple queues for multiple facilities.

Each of these three queuing situations is analyzed differently. It is sometimes the objective of the analysis to determine the appropriate number of facilities to have, and so we will consider each of them.

In accordance with our intention of presenting the basic ideas of queuing, we will consider only those with the following characteristics:

1. Arrivals are served on a first-come, first-served basis; that is, there is no priority classification for any arrivals.
2. Arrivals do not "balk" or refuse to get into the queue because it may be too long.
3. Once in the queue an arrival will not "renege" or leave the line because he is not progressing fast enough.
4. Where there are many service facilities, we assume all servers provide the same service; arrivals do not go to a particular server for a particular service.
5. The capacity of a queue is infinite.
6. Service rate is independent of line length; servers do not go faster because the line is longer.

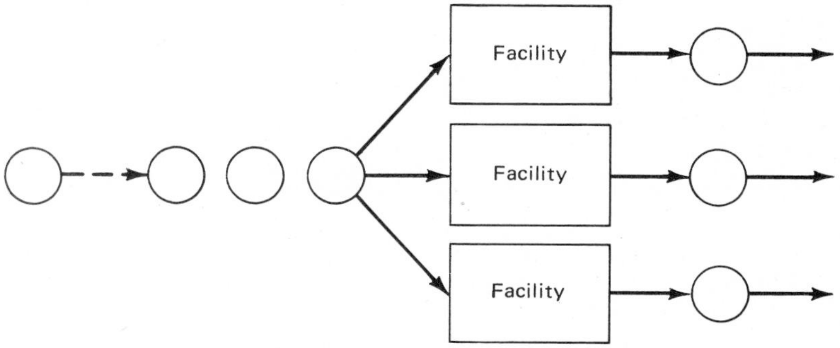

Figure 13-4 Arrivals form a single queue for multiple facilities.

Aside from the extremely simple case of constant arrival rate and constant service rate, we will consider four different types of queues summarized as follows:

Arrival rate	Service time	Population	Servers
1. Constant	Constant	Infinite	1
2. Poisson	Arbitrary	Infinite	1
3. Poisson	Exponential	Infinite	1
4. Poisson	Exponential	Infinite	Many
5. Poisson	Exponential	Finite	1

Throughout the discussion we assume that the situation has been operating long enough to permit formulas for average characteristics to be valid. This is referred to as the *steady state*.

CONSTANT ARRIVAL RATE, CONSTANT SERVICE TIME

The first very simple queuing case is helpful in setting the stage for other cases. A couple of examples and a statement of the main results will suffice.

Example If patrons arrive at the post office window exactly 3 minutes apart, or at the rate of 20 per hour, and the postal clerk requires exactly 3 minutes to perform the service, or can serve patrons at the rate of 20 per hour, then there will never be a line and the clerk will always be busy. If the clerk can serve patrons faster than 20 per hour, say 30 per hour, then there will never be a line, and the clerk will be busy two-thirds of the time. The clerk will take 2 minutes delivering the service and then wait 1 minute for the next arrival.

If the clerk can service only 15 patrons per hour, then he or she will always be busy and the length of the line will continue to increase. Thus if the service rate is less than the arrival rate, the facility cannot keep up with the arrivals.

Generally, when the arrival rate λ (Greek letter *lambda*) and the service rate μ (*mu*) are constant, then:

If $\lambda \leq \mu$, there is no waiting, and the proportion of server idle time is equal to $1 - \lambda/\mu$.

If $\lambda > \mu$, waiting time increases indefinitely, the server is always busy, and the service system fails.

The ratio $\rho = \lambda/\mu$ is referred to as the *traffic intensity,* or *average utilization.* (ρ is *rho*.) For this model,

If $\rho > 1$, the system fails. and
If $\rho \leq 1$, ρ is the proportion of time the system is busy.

Example There is one exact-change lane on the Parkway Bridge. Suppose drivers take exactly 15 seconds to drive into place, deposit the toll, and get a green-light response. That is, suppose service rate is a constant 4 per minute ($\mu = 4$).

(*a*) During a certain time of day, autos arrive at that toll booth lane at the constant rate of 4 per minute ($\lambda = 4$). Since $\lambda = \mu$, there is no waiting. Idle time of the toll booth $= 1 - \lambda/\mu = 0$; that is, the booth is never idle.

(*b*) During the early morning hours, cars arrive at that lane every minute ($\lambda = 1$).

Since $\lambda < \mu$, there is no waiting; and since $1 - \lambda/\mu = \frac{3}{4}$, the booth is idle 75 percent of the time.

(*c*) As rush hour approaches, cars arrive at that lane 6 per minute.

Since $\lambda > \mu$, the booth is never idle and the line increases indefinitely. The situation is resolved by opening another exact-change lane.

SOME GENERAL RELATIONSHIPS

The condition of constant arrival and constant service rate applies, however, only to highly mechanized and routinized situations, such as an assembly line where parts arrive at a completely automated station for further processing. Where human beings are involved in both arriving and servicing, the assumption of constant rates is highly inappropriate. Moreover, the services required by human arrivals are usually not exactly the same and therefore may require different amounts of time. In other words, a variable arrival rate and a variable service rate are more applicable and more likely to occur.

For the remainder of this chapter we focus on situations with variable arrival rate and service rate. First we consider the situation with the arrivals following a Poisson process, and the service rate varying but following no particular probability distribution. Then we consider the situation with both the arrivals and services Poisson-distributed. We next consider that situation extended to multiple-service facilities; last we consider situations in which the population of potential arrivals is so small that the probability of an arrival during any time period depends on the number already in the queue.

The relationship between service rate and service time is basic to understanding the service portion of a queuing situation. The speed with which service is provided can be expressed in either of two ways. The *service rate* describes the number of services provided during a particular time period. The *service time* describes the amount of time needed to perform a service. Service rates and service times are reciprocals of each other, and either is sufficient to describe the capacity of the service facility. A facility with an average service rate of μ has an average service time of $1/\mu$.

Example A runway is able to service 30 planes per hour, a doctor is able to service 4 patients per hour, and the postal clerk is able to service 60 patrons per hour. Equivalently, the runway has an average service time of 2 minutes, the doctor has an average service time of 15 minutes, and the postal clerk has an average service time of 1 minute.

The commonly used steady-state characteristics and their symbols are:

L_s = expected number of units in the system

L_q = expected number of units in the queue

W_s = expected time a unit spends in the system

W_q = expected time a unit spends in the queue

The relationships among these characteristics for a single-server facility are here presented only with some intuitive justification. If λ is the average arrival rate, then $1/\lambda$ is the average time between arrivals. Thus, the mean waiting time W_q (or mean time in the system W_s) is the product of the average time between arrivals $1/\lambda$ and the average line length L_q (or the average number in the system L_s). Symbolically,

$$W_q = \frac{1}{\lambda} L_q = \frac{L_q}{\lambda}$$

and

$$W_s = \frac{1}{\lambda} L_s = \frac{L_s}{\lambda}$$

Since the difference between average time in the system W_s and average time in the queue W_q is the average time being served,

$$W_s = W_q + \frac{1}{\mu}$$

Putting the three equations together yields

$$\frac{L_s}{\lambda} = W_s = W_q + \frac{1}{\mu} = \frac{L_q}{\lambda} + \frac{1}{\mu}$$

$$\frac{L_s}{\lambda} = \frac{L_q}{\lambda} + \frac{1}{\mu}$$

and

$$L_s = L_q + \frac{\lambda}{\mu}$$

Another view of the last result follows this line of reasoning. The difference between the expected number in the system L_s and the expected number in the queue L_q is the expected number being served. Since the server is busy, or is serving 1 unit, λ/μ of the time, and is idle or is serving 0 units, $1 - \lambda/\mu$ of the time,

$$\text{Expected number being served} = 1\left(\frac{\lambda}{\mu}\right) + 0\left(1 - \frac{\lambda}{\mu}\right) = \frac{\lambda}{\mu}$$

Consequently

$$L_s = L_q + \frac{\lambda}{\mu}$$

Example Suppose in the post office, $\lambda = 30$, $\mu = 40$, and $L_q = 3$; then

$$W_q = \frac{L_q}{\lambda} = \frac{3}{30} = .1$$

$$W_s = W_q + \frac{1}{\mu} = .1 + \frac{1}{40} = .125$$

Since $W_s = L_s/\lambda$,

$$L_s = \lambda W_s = 30(.125) = 3.75$$

One can verify

$$L_s = L_q + \frac{\lambda}{\mu}$$

easily enough with the given specifics.

Unlike the preceding example, L_q must usually be found. L_q depends on λ, μ, and the probability distributions of arrival and service rates. Because the arrival rate often follows a Poisson distribution, it is worthwhile examining the Poisson process before considering the other queuing models.

A POISSON PROCESS

Consider the telephone in an administrator's office. The probability of having a call arrive between 4:25 a.m. and 4:26 a.m. is certainly much smaller than the probability of having a call arrive between 9:30 a.m. and 9:31 a.m. However, if we restrict ourselves to a particular time, 9:00 a.m. to 10:00 a.m. for instance, it may very well be that the probability that a call will arrive during any minute is the same as for any other minute. Furthermore, it may be that whether a call has arrived during the preceding minute has no effect on whether a call will arrive during the present minute. If these conditions apply, the arrival process is called a *Poisson process*.

Summarily, in a Poisson process:

1. The probability that one event will occur during a particular unit of time is constant. (Two occurrences cannot occur in a single time unit.)
2. The occurrence of the event in any minute is independent of what has come before or will come after.

From the probability that a call will arrive during any minute, we can determine the *arrival rate,* which is the average number of arrivals in a particular period of time.

Example If

$$P(\text{a call will arrive in any minute}) = .20$$

then the average arrival rate of calls per hour (60 minutes) is:

$$\lambda = .20 \times 60 = 12 \text{ calls per hour}$$

Furthermore, if the arrivals follow a Poisson process, then the actual number of arrivals in an hour (or any extended period of time) is said to follow a Poisson probability distribution. Specifically, if λ is the average number of calls per hour, then

$$p = \frac{e^{-\lambda T}(\lambda T)^r}{r!}$$

is the probability of having exactly r calls in T hours. Equations for queue characteristics, where arrivals follow a Poisson process, have already taken the above probability expression into account. Thus it is unnecessary for us to make any calculations using it.

For the remainder of this chapter we make the assumption that arrivals to the service facility follow a Poisson process. Where necessary we focus attention on particular segments of time so that the assumption is reasonably well approximated.

POISSON ARRIVALS, ARBITRARY SERVICE TIME

In this section we assume that arrivals follow a Poisson process with an average arrival rate of λ. We make no similar assumption about service; we require only that we know the average service rate μ, or equivalently the average service time $1/\mu$, and the standard deviation of service time σ.

Since the general results relating W_s, W_q, L_s, and L_q apply to the single-server case, all that is needed is a way of finding any one of them. Although the proof is beyond the scope of this book, we accept the relationship

$$L_q = \frac{(\lambda\sigma)^2 + (\lambda/\mu)^2}{2(1 - \lambda/\mu)}$$

The steady-state averages can now be found.

A Referral Center Example

In an effort to improve the performance of a referral service center (for example, Drug and Alcohol, Family Planning, Rehabilitation), certain management efforts are appropriate. Such steps do not mean that greater efficiency will lead to decreased effectiveness. In fact, while maintaining the same quality level of care, it may be possible to improve the efficiency of the center and to reduce the client's total cost of obtaining assistance. Especially in the case of publicly funded centers, clients are frequently hourly employees who are not paid for time absent from the job. As a result, time spent waiting for assistance is a direct cost to the client. If this cost becomes overly burdensome, either because the wait is too long or the wages lost are too high, the low-income person may be inclined to forgo or delay noncompulsory services.

Such a center usually operates on a walk-in basis; some appointments are made, usually for follow-up visits. It is fairly common that such arrivals follow a Poisson distribution.[1]

We assume that most clients' needs are quickly satisfied since this center's main task is to refer clients to other centers that provide service.

Suppose for the center

	$\lambda = 4$	Expected number of clients arriving per hour
	$\mu = 5$	Expected number of clients being serviced per hour
or	$\frac{1}{\mu} = \frac{1}{5}$ hour	Expected service time per client
and	$\sigma = \frac{2}{5}$ hour	Standard deviation of service time per client

The utilization factor is

$$\rho = \frac{\lambda}{\mu} = \frac{4}{5}$$

which means the counselor is busy 80 percent of the time and is idle 20 percent of the time.

We want to describe the situation in terms of how long clients wait and how many clients are waiting at any one moment. We first use:

[1] In actual practice, the arrival rates are noted and compared to a Poisson probability distribution by a *goodness-of-fit* test. If the empirical rates "fit" the theoretical distribution, then the process is accepted as being Poisson. A description of the goodness-of-fit procedure can be found in many basic statistical texts.

$$L_q = \frac{(\lambda\sigma)^2 + (\lambda/\mu)^2}{2(1 - \lambda/\mu)}$$

$$= \frac{(4 \cdot \frac{2}{5})^2 + (\frac{4}{5})^2}{2(1 - \frac{4}{5})}$$

$$= \frac{64/25 + 16/25}{2(1/5)}$$

$$= 8$$

Then

$$W_q = \frac{1}{\lambda} L_q$$

$$= \frac{1}{4} \cdot 8$$

$$= 2$$

$$W_s = W_q + \frac{1}{\mu}$$

$$= 2.2$$

$$L_s = L_q + \frac{\lambda}{\mu}$$

$$= 8.8$$

Clients have an average wait of 2 hours for the average 12-minute service. One alternative is to hire a second counselor; another is to try to reduce the variability in service time. To see how the four mean queue characteristics depend on the standard deviation, we compare the results for $\sigma = \frac{1}{5}$ and $\sigma = \frac{2}{5}$, keeping $\lambda = 4$ and $\mu = 5$ for both. Although it is not particularly realistic to consider that service times at such a center would be constant, and hence $\sigma = 0$, we include that case for the sake of comparison. Results are presented in Table 13-2.

A comparison of the expected number of units in the system and the expected waiting time for the various values of standard deviation clearly shows that the variation in service time is extremely important in determining the

Table 13-2 Queue length and waiting time for fixed λ and μ and variable σ

	For $\lambda = 4$, $\mu = 5$;			
σ	L_q	L_s	W_q	W_s
$\frac{2}{5}$	8.0	8.8	2.0	2.2
$\frac{1}{5}$	3.2	4.0	.8	1.0
0	1.6	2.4	.4	.6

queue characteristics. This means that in analyzing a queue, care must be taken to estimate properly that variation.

Of particular importance in queuing analysis is the situation in which the service time follows an exponential distribution; that is, the services, as well as the arrivals, constitute a Poisson process.

POISSON ARRIVALS, EXPONENTIAL SERVICE TIME

Just as the rate of arrivals may be a Poisson process, so too the rate of service completions may be a Poisson process. One reasonable condition on the service provision is that the service rate can be Poisson only while there are individuals being serviced.

If the Poisson probability distribution gives the probability that a specific number of events will occur during a given segment of time, then the *exponential distribution* gives the probability of waiting a specific amount of time between successive occurrences. Applying this to the service rate and service time, if the service rate is described by a Poisson distribution, then the service time is described by an exponential distribution. For this reason this kind of queue is referred to either as Poisson-Poisson or Poisson-exponential.[2]

The relationships in a Poisson-exponential queue provide more information than those in a Poisson-arbitrary queue. We present them without proof. As before, the probability, or the proportion of time, that the server is idle is

$$P_0 = 1 - \frac{\lambda}{\mu}$$

A result not applicable to arbitrary service times gives the probability, or the proportion of time, that a specific number of units n are in the system (the service facility *and* the waiting line)

$$P_n = \left(\frac{\lambda}{\mu}\right)^n P_0$$

It is sometimes of particular interest to know the probability, or proportion of time, that the number of units equals or exceeds a particular value k. This is given by

$$P_{n \geq k} = \left(\frac{\lambda}{\mu}\right)^k$$

The average length of a Poisson-exponential queue is given by

$$L_q = \frac{\lambda}{\mu} \frac{\lambda}{(\mu - \lambda)}$$

[2] For a brief discussion of the Poisson and exponential distributions and how they are related, see the Appendix to this chapter.

Table 13-3 Relations in the Poisson-exponential queue

Characteristics	Symbol	Expression
Mean arrival rate	λ	
Mean service rate	μ	
Mean service time	$\frac{1}{\mu}$	
Average utilization	ρ	$\frac{\lambda}{\mu}$
Proportion of time:		
System is busy		$\frac{\lambda}{\mu}$
System is idle	P_0	$1 - \frac{\lambda}{\mu}$
System has n units	P_n	$\left(\frac{\lambda}{\mu}\right)^n P_0$
System has k units or more	$P_{n \geq k}$	$\left(\frac{\lambda}{\mu}\right)^k$
Expected:		
Number in queue	L_q	$\frac{\lambda^2}{\mu(\mu - \lambda)}$
Number in system	L_s	$\frac{\lambda}{\mu - \lambda}$
Time in queue	W_q	$\frac{\lambda}{\mu(\mu - \lambda)}$
Time in system	W_s	$\frac{1}{\mu - \lambda}$

The earlier general relationships provide the remaining average characteristics. The Poisson-exponential queue relationships are summarized in Table 13-3.

The Referral Center Revisited

If the service rate in our referral center illustration is a Poisson-service rate, then the queue characteristics are[3]:

$$\lambda = 4, \ \mu = 5$$

$$L_q = \frac{4^2}{5(5 - 4)} = \frac{16}{5} = 3.2$$

$$L_s = \frac{4}{5 - 4} = 4$$

[3] These agree with the results found previously for $\sigma = \frac{1}{5}$. This is because, for the exponential distribution, the standard deviation of service time equals the average service time, $\sigma = 1/\mu$. Thus, the results here coincide with those for $\lambda = 4$, $\mu = 5$, and $\sigma = \frac{1}{5}$.

$$W_q = \frac{4}{5(5-4)} = .8$$

$$W_s = \frac{1}{5-4} = 1$$

The values given by the formulas are the *averages* over a suitably long period of time. It should not be interpreted, for example, that the length of the line is usually 3.2 or close to it. In fact, since

$$P_0 = 1 - \tfrac{4}{5} = .20$$

we know that the counselor is idle about 20 percent of the time. We know too that since

$$P_1 = \tfrac{4}{5} \cdot \tfrac{1}{5} = .16$$

the counselor is with a client but there is no one in the waiting room about 16 percent of the time. Thus, more than one-third of the time there is either no one in the system or no one waiting. Going toward the other extreme, since

$$P_5 = (\tfrac{4}{5})^5 \tfrac{1}{5} = .0655$$

we know there are five people in the clinic (one being seen and four waiting) more than 6 percent of the time. The relationship that identifies the relative frequencies of extremes is useful in describing queue characteristics.

Here the probability that there are 10 or more clients in the system is given by

$$P_{n \geq 10} = (\tfrac{4}{5})^{10} = .107$$

and hence almost 11 percent of the time the system is extremely crowded, with one person being served and nine or more waiting for service. As with any other situation being described by statistics, the mean tells only part of the

Table 13-4 Queue characteristics depending on λ, with μ = 10

Arrival rate λ	Utilization, $\frac{\lambda}{\mu}$	Mean number in system, $L_S = \frac{\lambda}{\mu - \lambda}$	Mean time in system, $W_S = \frac{1}{\mu - \lambda}$	Probability ($n \geq 5$), $P_{n\geq 5} = \left(\frac{\lambda}{\mu}\right)^5$
1	.1	.111	.111	.00001
2	.2	.250	.125	.0003
3	.3	.429	.143	.002
4	.4	.667	.167	.010
5	.5	1.000	.200	.031
6	.6	1.500	.250	.078
7	.7	2.333	.333	.168
8	.8	4.000	.500	.328
9	.9	9.000	1.000	.590
9.9	.99	99.000	10.000	.951

story. Some knowledge of the relative frequency of extremes in either direction is necessary for making reasonable decisions.

For the special case in which the service time is exponentially distributed, or equivalently when the service rate is Poisson-distributed, the mean arrival rate and mean service rate are the important parameters. In fact, the ratio of arrival rate to service rate is critical to describing the system. For relatively small values of expected utilization λ/μ, the line length and the waiting times will be relatively small; for λ/μ closer to 1, the line length and the waiting time will tend to be large. As the arrival rate gets closer to the service rate, the expected line length and waiting time increase without bound. Table 13-4 compares a few queue characteristics for different arrival rates with service rate $\mu = 10$. The effect of the arrival rate getting close to the service rate is presented graphically in Figure 13-5. The arrival rate must be less than the service rate, for otherwise the queuing system fails. When the arrival rate approaches the service rate in an actual application, two alternatives are possible: (1) In-

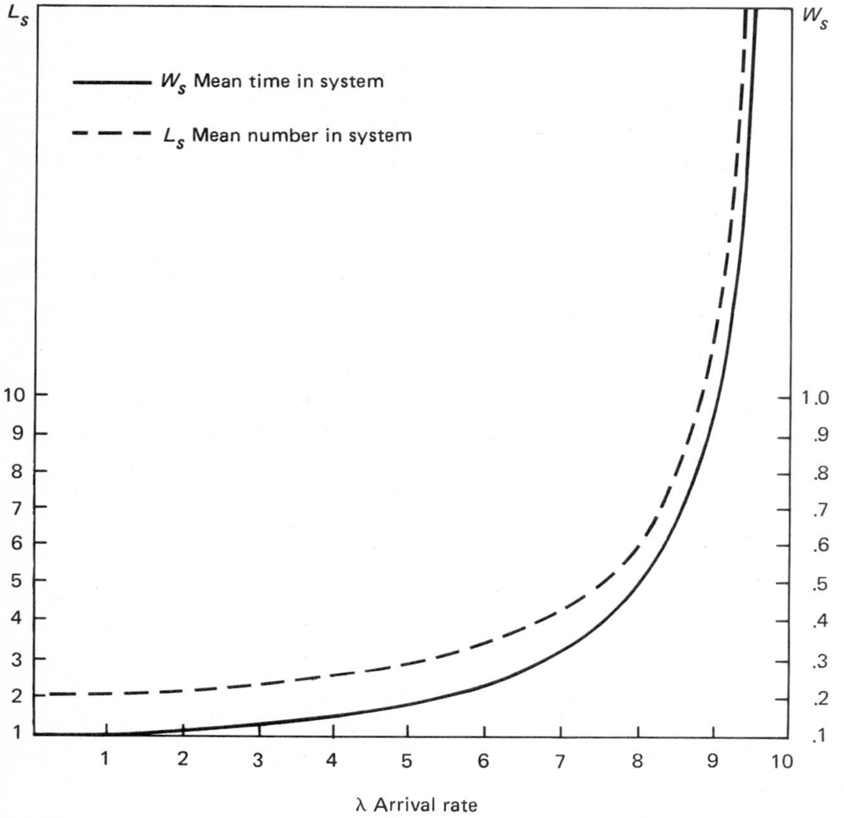

Figure 13-5 L_s and W_s increase indefinitely as arrival rate λ approaches service rate $\mu = 10$.

crease the service rate by developing better methods or using different equipment; or (2) increase the number of servers or service facilities in the system. We now consider this situation.

MULTIPLE-SERVICE CHANNELS

Many waiting-line situations actually have more than a single server to provide the service. Some examples include a clinic with more than one doctor, an airport with more than one runway, a post office with more than a single clerk, and a highway with more than one toll booth. Before proceeding further to analyze a queue with multiple-service channels, we first examine the ways in which arrivals form a queue.

Arrivals may form a separate waiting line for each service facility; in this case the analysis considers each server as a single server, with the arrival rate for that server equal to a portion of the total arrival rate.

Example Suppose a toll bridge has four toll booths; cars form lines at each toll booth. Then, if cars are arriving at the rate of 100 per hour, we consider an effective arrival rate for each toll booth as 25 per hour. The system can then be analyzed by considering the four lines and servers independently.

In some cases where arrivals tend to go toward the shorter line rather than the longer line, and once in line may do some line-switching, the foregoing method of analysis may have to be abandoned in favor of a simulation approach.

A second way in which the arrivals may wait for service is to form a single line, from which the next individual to be served will move to the next available server. Some banks have experimented with a single line leading to a number of different tellers. This approach is certainly as applicable to a post office or motor vehicle registration office as it is to a bank. As we shall see, such a waiting line is generally more efficient from the arrivals' point of view. Since it is not always perceived that way by those waiting in line, some offices have resorted to multiple lines even though their own objective analysis indicates a single line is better for their customers.

Here we consider a number of service channels with Poisson arrivals forming a single queue. We assume that all servers have the same mean service time and that the service time for each is exponentially distributed. That is, the service rate for each is Poisson. The equations that describe the queue characteristics are noticeably more complicated for multiple channels than for a single channel.

For a Poisson-Poisson multiple-channel-service facility with mean arrival rate λ, mean service rate μ, and the number of service channels C, the queue characteristics are given by the following equations.

The probability that the system is completely idle is given by[4]:

$$P_0 = \left[\frac{(\lambda/\mu)^C}{C!(1 - \lambda/C\mu)} + 1 + \frac{(\lambda/\mu)}{1!} + \frac{(\lambda/\mu)^2}{2!} + \cdots + \frac{(\lambda/\mu)^{C-1}}{(C-1)!}\right]^{-1}$$

The probability that there is any particular number of units in the system is given by one of two equations, depending on whether that number n is less than or equal to, or greater than, the number of channels C. Hence

$$\text{If } n \leq C: \qquad P_n = P_0 \frac{(\lambda/\mu)^n}{n!}$$

$$\text{If } n > C: \qquad P_n = P_0 \frac{(\lambda/\mu)^n}{C!C^{n-c}}$$

With a service rate of μ for each of the C service channels, the system is actually capable of a combined average service rate of μC. With an arrival rate of λ, the *utilization* of the system is given by $\lambda/\mu C$.

The other queue characteristics are as follows.

The mean number in the queue, or the mean queue length, is given by

$$L_q = \frac{(\lambda/\mu)^{C+1}}{C \cdot C!(1 - \lambda/C\mu)^2} P_0$$

Once the mean line length has been found, the other queue characteristics follow more readily from the earlier general relationships. They are given by:

$$L_s = L_q + \frac{\lambda}{\mu}$$

$$W_q = \frac{L_q}{\lambda}$$

$$W_s = W_q + \frac{1}{\mu}$$

To simplify the calculations, Table 5 of the Appendix contains the idle probability, P_0, and the mean number in the queue, L_q, for given values of λ/μ and for $C = 1$ to 10.

[4] The idle probability can also be represented by a more compact notation as

$$P_0 = \left[\frac{(\lambda/\mu)^C}{C!(1 - \lambda/C\mu)} + \sum_{i=0}^{C-1} \frac{(\lambda/\mu)^i}{i!}\right]^{-1}$$

The exponent -1 means "multiplicative inverse of" or "reciprocal of." For example,

$$3^{-1} = \frac{1}{3} \qquad \text{and} \qquad \left(\frac{\mu}{\mu - \lambda}\right)^{-1} = \frac{\mu - \lambda}{\mu}$$

The Service Center with More than One Server

Previously, we considered that the *referral* center had an arrival rate of 4 per hour and a service rate of 5 per hour, with a single counselor providing services. In determining whether a second counselor should be hired to serve at the center, it is worthwhile to know the consequences of having a second counselor and then to compare the queue characteristics for the two alternatives. So we have

for $\lambda = 4,\ \mu = 5,\ C = 2$:
$$P_0 = \left[\frac{(\frac{4}{5})^2}{2![1 - 4/2(5)]} + 1 + \frac{\frac{4}{5}}{1!}\right]^{-1}$$
$$= [2.33]^{-1}$$
$$= .43$$

Thus about 43 percent of the time both counselors will be idle. If we further determine the probability that there is only one patient in the system, we find that

$$P_1 = .43(\tfrac{4}{5}) = .34$$

Combining these two results, we note that about 77 percent of the time either one or both counselors will be idle; that is, only about 23 percent of the time will both counselors be busy.

Continuing, we find the other queue characteristics.

$$L_q = \frac{(\frac{4}{5})^3}{2(2)[1 - 4/2(5)]^2}(.43) = .153 \text{ persons}$$

$$L_s = .153 + \frac{4}{5} = .953 \text{ persons}$$

$$W_q = \frac{.153}{4} = .038 \text{ hours}$$

$$W_s = .038 + .2 = .238 \text{ hours}$$

Since the service time does not change when additional counselors are added, the queue characteristics that should be compared are the average line length L_q and the average waiting time W_q. We note that with the second counselor there is a sizable decrease from the previous values, $L_q = 3.2$ and $W_q = .8$.

Alternatively, each arrival may be met by a receptionist or an aid, who registers the arrival and assigns him to one of the counselors, effectively creating a separate queue for each server. Provided the assignments are made in some equalizing pattern (for example, with few exceptions, an arrival is to be assigned to the counselor with the shortest waiting line), the arrival rate to each counselor is half the arrival rate for the center. In this situation with average arrival rate equal to 2 and average service rate equal to 5, the waiting line for each counselor is characterized by:

For $\lambda = 2,\ \mu = 5,\ C = 1{:}\ L_q = \dfrac{4}{5(3)} = .267$ persons

$$W_q = \frac{.267}{2} = .134 \text{ hours}$$

The average number of people waiting in the clinic is $2\lambda = .534$.

For ease in comparing, the mean line length and waiting time for the three alternatives are here summarized:

	C	L_q	Average number waiting	W_q
	1	3.2	3.2	.8
Single queue	2	.153	.103	.038
Multiple queues	2	.267	.534	.134

Whether the center would decide to obtain the services of a second counselor would depend upon how the clients' waiting time is evaluated relative to the cost. The concepts of cost-benefit analysis as well as basic queuing theory provide the basis for the approach used in an actual application to be described in the next section.

QUEUING IN A MEDICAL CLINIC: AN APPLICATION[5]

A particular outpatient clinic is operated by a university medical center in order to deliver high-quality health care to the medically indigent in the area, and to serve as an educational clinic for interns and residents. A staff of doctors is assigned to the clinic for a month at a time, after which each doctor returns to the clinic 1 day per week to see patients whose treatment he or she initiated.

Patients given appointments are asked to report to either the morning or the afternoon clinic, without any particular time being designated. Patients without a scheduled appointment are also seen by the clinic; all patients are seen on a first-come, first-served basis. As patients arrive at the clinic, they are assigned to the doctor who has been treating them or to whom they have been referred; if their appointment is with no specific doctor or if their doctor is not in the clinic, patients are assigned to the doctor whose scheduled patient load is the

[5] This illustration is based on T. F. Keller and D. J. Laughhunn, "An Application of Queuing Theory to a Congestion Problem in an Outpatient Clinic," *Decision Science*, vol. 4, no. 3, July 1973, pp. 379–393.

lightest that day. Doctors are assigned to the clinic to see either new patients or returning patients, but not both types on a given day.

Patients arrive at the registration desk and are then directed to a particular doctor, which means that individual waiting lines form for each doctor, with the arrival rate being approximately the same for each doctor. Observing periodic congestion in the clinic as well as periodic idleness prompted the medical center to try to determine the "best" number of doctors C to serve the clinic. The meaning of "best" usually generates the actual criterion. In this particular application, the total cost of staff's working time and patients' lost working time was decided on as the criterion; the number of doctors that keeps the total cost to a minimum was then taken to be the best number.

Observing the clinic in operation led to the following analysis of actual arrival and service rates. Statistical analysis of the data revealed that the arrival rate followed a Poisson distribution, but the service rate did not. Furthermore, new patients required much more time than returning patients. Table 13-5 presents the observed values for the clinic, with $C\lambda$ representing the overall arrival rate. The arrival rate λ for each of the physician waiting lines is the overall arrival rate divided by the number of physicians available.

Determining the costs involved in staffing the clinic and in the patients' waiting is not without difficulty. The clinic was interested in controlling actual costs incurred by the clinic itself and by the patients. The cost incurred by the patients was assumed to be lost wages at the rate of \$3.20 per hour. Since this cost is one that is incurred as long as the patient is at the clinic, either waiting or being treated, the total time in clinic is the relevant value. Rather than try to assess the physicians' time by a value based on the national income of doctors, or the social benefits of physicians being available, the clinic directly calculated the cost of an intern's services on the basis of the salary paid to the intern or resident (\$10,000 per year) and the approximate number of hours worked (2000); thus, the physician cost of \$5.00 per hour was used. The cost for a 4-hour clinic session is the sum of the physicians' cost and patients' waiting-time costs. From the time spent in the clinic by each patient, the total time spent in clinic by all patients can be determined; from that, the total lost wages can be found.

Table 13-5 Clinic arrival and service values

Clinic	Actual average number of physicians	Clinic arrival rate $C\lambda$	Physician service rate μ	Service time	
				Mean $\frac{1}{\mu}$	Standard deviation σ
Morning, return	10.36	11.44	1.52	.658	.12
Afternoon, return	9.90	6.78	1.52	.658	.12
Morning, new	4.10	3.20	.72	1.39	.14
Afternoon, new	4.32	1.48	.72	1.39	.14

Recall that

$$L_q = \frac{\lambda^2\sigma^2 + (\lambda/\mu)^2}{2(1 - \lambda/\mu)} = \frac{\lambda^2(\sigma^2 + 1/\mu^2)}{2(1 - \lambda/\mu)}$$

$$W_q = \frac{L_q}{\lambda} \quad \text{and} \quad W_s = W_q + \frac{1}{\mu}$$

The last value is the appropriate one to use since we are concerned with the average time spent by a patient in the clinic.

For purposes of illustration we present the analysis for just the fourth clinic. Having more physicians available decreases the effective arrival rate at each physician's office. In the afternoon new-patient clinic, $C\lambda = 1.48$ and $\mu = .72$; therefore, there must be more than two physicians available or otherwise the arrival rate for each physician would be greater than the service rate, and the service facility would not be able to keep pace with the demand for service.

Regardless of the number of physicians, the service time and standard deviation of service time remain unchanged. The overall arrival rate at the clinic is 1.48 for the afternoon new-patient clinic; the arrival rate at the office of a physician varies with the number of physicians. Since the number of physicians available must be greater than 2, we find the average waiting time and total cost for three and four physicians, and then indicate why it is unnecessary to determine waiting time and cost for more than 4 physicians.

For three physicians, $\lambda = 1.48/3 = .493$, $\mu = .72$, $1/\mu = 1.39$, $\sigma = .14$.

$$W_q = \frac{.493(.0196 + 1.932)}{2(1 - .685)} = 1.53 \text{ hours}$$

$$W_s = 1.53 + 1.39 = 2.92 \text{ hours}$$

For four physicians, $\lambda = 1.48/4 = .37$, $\mu = .72$, $1/\mu = 1.39$, $\sigma = .14$.

$$W_q = \frac{.37(.0196 + 1.932)}{2(1 - .514)} = .74 \text{ hours}$$

$$W_s = .74 + 1.39 = 2.13 \text{ hours}$$

Based on the average patient time in clinic W_s, the patients' hourly wage H_p, the doctors' hourly wage H_D, and the number of doctors C, the total cost for a 4-hour session can be determined as follows:

$$\text{Total cost} = 4CH_D + 4C\lambda W_s H_p$$

$$\begin{aligned}\text{Total cost (with } C = 3) &= 4(3)(\$5.00) + 4(1.48)(2.92)(\$3.20) \\ &= \$60.00 + \$55.32 \\ &= \$115.32\end{aligned}$$

$$\begin{aligned}\text{Total cost (with } C = 4) &= 4(4)(\$5.00) + 4(1.48)(2.13)(\$3.20)\\ &= \$80.00 + \$40.35\\ &= \$120.35\end{aligned}$$

Three physicians is better than four, but should there be a fifth? The cost of each additional physician for the 4-hour session is \$20. With four physicians, the average waiting time is only .74 hour. The cost of the patients' waiting time is

$$\begin{aligned}\text{Waiting time cost} &= 4(1.48)(.74)(\$3.20)\\ &= \$14.02\end{aligned}$$

No matter how many physicians are added, the service time will not change; so the patients' cost cannot be reduced by more than the \$14.02. It is not economically worthwhile to assign a fifth physician to the afternoon new-patient clinic. Hence, the best number of physicians for that clinic is three.

In a similar way the best number of physicians for each of the other clinics was determined. By checking clinic records, it was possible to determine the actual number of physicians assigned to each clinic. The best and the actual number of physicians for each clinic are presented in Table 13-6. Although it is impossible to eliminate congestion or idleness entirely whenever arrivals and services are random, a comparison of the actual with the best staff sizes shows that reassigning the current staff rather than increasing the staff size is the first step toward efficiency.

Decision makers will note that the best staff size should not be determined solely on the basis of the actual costs of assigned doctors to the clinic and the cost of wages lost to patients while in clinic. Other considerations must be taken into account when actually assigning physicians to specific clinics; for example, other hospital assignments may preclude a physician's being available in a specific morning session rather than an afternoon session, in spite of the optimum assignment. Since the clinic serves educational purposes for the interns and residents, it may be advisable to assign a physician to a particular clinic in contradiction to the "best" assignment pattern. If physicians can be on duty in the clinic only at specific times because of their other hospital obliga-

Table 13-6 Number of physicians in clinic

Clinic	Actual average	Best
Morning, return	10.36	12
Afternoon, return	9.90	7
Morning, new	4.10	7
Afternoon, new	4.32	3
	28.68	29

tions, it may be possible to alter the arrival rates for the various clinics. One way is to schedule more patients in the afternoon, since the morning clinics were understaffed and the afternoon clinics were overstaffed.

A common way of resolving problems, especially in the public domain, relies on additional personnel or equipment. As this illustration clearly shows one can provide improvement not only by more but also by a different use of present resources. Occasionally improvement may be served in a rather unexpected manner. In the current application management hoped to eliminate unnecessary congestion by finding more appropriate staff sizes and then by assigning physicians differently. During the data-collection stage it was observed that the clinic started seeing patients on the average 1 hour after the registration desk opened, even though patients were always present at the official clinic opening time. The queue that developed during this first hour caused congestion during the entire clinic session, occasionally requiring doctors to remain after the official closing time. It is fairly common practice to have patients arrive before doctors are ready to see them in order to avoid expensive physician idle time. The results of a delay in starting must be examined relative to the overall objective of the clinic.

Thus far our discussion of characteristics has assumed that the Poisson arrivals come from an infinite population. Here the population is so large that having some of its members already in the queue has no effect on the arrival rate. We now turn our attention to a finite population, in which having some members in the queue does affect the arrival rate.

FINITE POPULATION, EXPONENTIAL SERVICE TIME

If arrivals come from a relatively small population, then having some members of the population being serviced or in the queue waiting for service affects the arrival rate of subsequent arrivals. For example, if an agency has one computer terminal and four computer analysts, then the probability of an arrival when no one is using the terminal is greater than when one analyst is using it and one is waiting for it. Thus the probability of an arrival is not independent of what has previously occurred. It may be, however, that the service time and the time between an individual's services are exponentially distributed. Then we can express the queue characteristics using the following symbols:

$\frac{1}{\lambda}$ = mean time between services

$\frac{1}{\mu}$ = mean service time

m = size of population

n = number in the queue or being serviced

$k = m - n$ = number not in the queuing system

The probability that the entire population m is being serviced or is waiting for service is

$$P_m = \left[1 + \frac{1}{1!}\frac{\mu}{\lambda} + \frac{1}{2!}\left(\frac{\mu}{\lambda}\right)^2 + \cdots + \frac{1}{m!}\left(\frac{\mu}{\lambda}\right)^m\right]^{-1}$$

This probability can be used to determine the probability of any number n being in the system.

$$P_n = \frac{1}{(m-n)!}\left(\frac{\mu}{\lambda}\right)^{m-n} P_m$$

In particular the probability that the system is idle, or that the entire population is outside the queuing system, is given by:

$$P_0 = \frac{1}{m!}\left(\frac{\mu}{\lambda}\right)^m P_m$$

The idle probability is then used to determine the basic queue characteristics:

$$L_q = m - \frac{\lambda + \mu}{\lambda}(1 - P_0)$$

$$L_s = L_q + (1 - P_0)$$

$$W_q = \frac{L_q}{(m - L_s)\lambda}$$

$$W_s = W_q + \frac{1}{\mu}$$

Example Suppose each of 4 analysts spends an average of 2 days doing desk work and then goes to a computer terminal for an average of a half day; that is,

$$\frac{1}{\lambda} = 2, \frac{1}{\mu} = \frac{1}{2}, \frac{\mu}{\lambda} = 4, \text{ and } m = 4$$

Then

$$P_m = \left[1 + 4 + \frac{1}{2!}(4)^2 + \frac{1}{3!}(4)^3 + \frac{1}{4!}(4)^4\right]^{-1}$$

$$= [1 + 4 + 8 + 10.67 + 10.67]^{-1}$$

$$= [34.33]^{-1}$$

$$= .029$$

$$P_0 = \frac{1}{4!}(4)^4(.029)$$

$$= .309$$

$$L_q = 4 - \frac{2 + \frac{1}{2}}{\frac{1}{2}}(1 - .309)$$
$$= .545$$
$$L_s = .545 + (1 - .309)$$
$$= 1.236$$

Noting the time between services and the average service time, it might appear to the unsophisticated that the computer terminal is well able to keep up with the needs of the analysts. However, because both arrivals and services are random, this is not the case. From the queue characteristics we note that all four computer analysts will be at their desks only 31 percent of the time. This could very well give rise to the perception that "those jokers wait more than they work." The effect of being able to reduce the average service time or of being able to increase the average time between services is left to be determined in Exercise 13-3.

It is sometimes suggested that the finite-population situation can be approximated by using the ordinary infinite-population formulas. This is quite inappropriate however. It should be noted that the mean time between services is 2 days per analyst. With 4 analysts, the average arrival rate is 2 per day. Since the service rate is also 2 per day, the equations for a Poisson-exponential queuing system would not apply, and the length of the queue and the waiting time would both increase without bound.

The computations needed to analyze the finite-population queuing situation are rather unwieldy; for multiple-service channels the complexity is even greater. Fortunately, extensive tables have been developed to assist in analysis of finite populations.[6]

SUMMARY

Waiting in line is a common experience; the consequences vary from inconvenience to extreme costs and even fatalities. The essential components of a queuing system are arrivals from some population, servers, and the provision of service.

We have considered only a select few simple queuing models. Where the arrivals are independent, it is not uncommon that they form a Poisson process which greatly facilitates the analysis. A similar assumption is less frequently satisfied by the service times. Accordingly we have considered general as well as exponential service times for a single-service queue. Two extensions of a simple queue have been considered, namely the multiple-server Poisson-exponential queue, and the finite-population exponential service time queue.

[6] See A. Desclous, *Delay Tables,* McGraw-Hill Book Company, New York, 1962; and L. G. Peck and R. N. Hazlewood, *Finite Queuing Tables,* John Wiley & Sons, Inc., New York, 1958.

There are many other queuing situations, some of which can be analyzed directly, not too unlike the approach used here.

A simulation approach may be needed where queue discipline is complicated; for example, where service is provided on a priority basis, arrivals switch from one line to another, service is faster with longer lines, customers refuse to join the queue or leave it if the line or the waiting time is too long, and where arrival and service distributions are not so neatly described. Chapter 14 will present a simulation of a complex queue.

BIBLIOGRAPHY

Brill, Edward A.: "A Model of a Traffic Jam behind a Bottleneck," *Operations Research,* vol. 20, July–August 1972, pp. 791–799.

Dei Rossi, J. A., G. F. Mills, and C. C. Summer: "A Telephone-Access Biomedical Information Center," *Operations Research,* vol. 20, May–June 1972, pp. 643–667.

Erikson, W. J.: "Management Science and the Gas Shortage," *Interfaces,* August 1974, pp. 47–51.

Harris, Carl M., and T. R. Thiagarajan: "Queuing Models of Community Correctional Centers in the District of Columbia," *Management Science,* vol. 22, October 1975, pp. 167–171.

Keller, P. F., and D. J. Laughhunn: "An Application of Queuing Theory to a Congestion Problem in an Outpatient Clinic", *Decision Science,* vol. 4, no. 3, July 1973, pp. 379–393.

Kolesar, Peter, Kenneth L. Rider, Thomas B. Crabill, and Warren E. Walker: "A Queuing-Linear Programming Approach to Scheduling Police Patrol Cars," *Operations Research,* vol. 23, November–December 1975, pp. 1045–1062.

Koopman, Bernard O.: "Air-Terminal Queues under Time-Dependent Conditions," *Operations Research,* vol. 20, November–December 1972, pp. 1089–1114.

Lee, A. M.: *Applied Queuing Theory,* McMillan and Co., Ltd., London 1966.

Little, John D. C.: "Proof for the Queuing Formula: $L = W$," *Operations Research,* vol. 9, May–June 1961, pp. 383–387.

Reid, Richard A., Betty J. Ebersole, Lois Gonzales, Naomi L. Quenk, Robert Oseasohn: "Rural Medical Care: An Experimental Delivery System," *American Journal of Public Health,* vol. 65, no. 3, March 1975, pp. 266–271.

Whitehouse, Gary E., and Ben L. Wechsler: *Applied Operations Research,* John Wiley & Sons, Inc., New York, 1976.

APPENDIX: THE POISSON AND EXPONENTIAL DISTRIBUTIONS

Assume interest is focused on whether an event will occur during a unit of time, for example, whether a telephone will ring in the next minute. If the probability that the event will occur during any minute is constant throughout the period 9:00 a.m. to 5:00 p.m., and is independent of whether calls have arrived during preceding minutes, then the process is called a Poisson process. As interest focuses on how many calls arrive over a continuous period of time, the probability distribution that is generated is called the Poisson distribution.

The Poisson Distribution

Suppose for example, telephone calls come, on the average, 5 per hour. The probability distribution for the number of calls n during the morning work period of 4 hours is given by the Poisson distribution formula:

$$P(n \text{ calls}) = \frac{e^{-5(4)}(5 \cdot 4)^n}{n!}$$

For example, the probability of getting exactly 10 calls is

$$P(10 \text{ calls}) = \frac{e^{-5(4)}(5 \cdot 4)^{10}}{10!}$$

which requires a good deal of computation. Fortunately there are tables available for the Poisson probability distribution in most basic statistics and probability texts.

In general

$$P(n \text{ events in } T \text{ hours}) = \frac{e^{-\lambda T}(\lambda T)^n}{n!}$$

is the probability of having n events occur during T hours when the average number of events per hour is λ. The mean number of calls during T hours is λT. The Poisson distribution has the special property that its variance is equal to its mean; thus the standard deviation of the number of events to occur during time T is $\sqrt{\lambda T}$.

A special case of the Poisson distribution is the probability that no events will occur during time T; that is,

$$P(0 \text{ events in } T \text{ hours}) = \frac{e^{-\lambda T}(\lambda T)^0}{0!} = e^{-\lambda T}$$

Another way of saying the same thing is that this is the probability that T hours will lapse without an event occurring. Focusing on this form gives rise to a related probability distribution, considered next.

The Exponential Distribution

Instead of focusing on the number of events to occur during a given time period, we can consider the probability of having to wait a certain amount of time before an event occurs. This yields the probability distribution for the waiting time t between successive events, or the service time or interarrival time in the queuing context. The probability function is called the exponential probability density function and appears as

$$f(t) = \lambda e^{-\lambda t} \qquad \text{with } 0 \leq t \leq \infty$$

The probability of having to wait T hours or more for the next event is[7]

$$P(t \geq T) = e^{-\lambda T}$$

which is identical to the Poisson probability that no events occur in time T. The mean of the exponential distribution is $1/\lambda$, and the variance is $1/\lambda^2$. That is, the standard deviation and the mean of the exponential distribution are both $1/\lambda$.

The Poisson distribution and exponential distribution provide two ways of saying the same thing. For example, if patients can be served at a clinic at an average rate of 5 per hour following a Poisson probability distribution, then the service time averages one-fifth of an hour following the exponential probability distribution. When the rate is Poisson-distributed, the time is exponentially distributed.

EXERCISES

Extensions of chapter examples

13-1 In the afternoon new-patient clinic described in the application in this chapter, the average arrival rate is 1.48 patients per hour. Assume doctors' service time is exponentially distributed with a mean rate of .72 per hour. Using the clinic's cost estimates and criterion, determine whether the best number of doctors is 3 or 4 or 5. (See p. 319.)

13-2 Refer to problem 13-1. Assume the clinic's operation is changed so that patients form a single queue and are seen by the first available physician.

(*a*) What is the best number of physicians?

(*b*) Compare the queue characteristics L_S, L_q, W_S, and W_q for 4 physicians in the original problem, in problem 13-1, and in this problem.

13-3 The analyst problem (see p. 323) assumed that each analyst would use the computer on the average every 2 days, with the between-service time exponentially distributed and with the service time also exponentially distributed with a mean of $\frac{1}{2}$ day. If new diagnostic material were made available, the service time would be reduced to $\frac{1}{3}$ of a day, still exponentially distributed. How does the decrease affect the queue characteristics:

(*a*) The probability that all analysts are working at their desks

(*b*) The probability that no analysts are working at their desks

(*c*) The average number of analysts waiting

(*d*) The average amount of time between arrival and completion of service

13-4 If problem 13-3 were analyzed as if there were a large number of analysts (treating the population as if it were infinite), then the effective arrival rate would be 2 per day, with the service time exponentially distributed with a mean of $\frac{1}{3}$ of a day.

(*a*) Contrast the probability that all analysts are working and the average number of analysts waiting with the results of the previous problem.

(*b*) What accounts for the discrepancy in answers? Comment on the appropriateness of using the regular queuing equations to analyze a finite-population queuing situation.

[7] With the probability density function $f(t) = \lambda e^{-\lambda t}$, the probability of having to wait T or more hours is given by the cumulative probability function $P(t \geq T) = \int_T^\infty \lambda e^{-\lambda t}\,dt = -e^{-\lambda t}\Big|_T^\infty = 0 + e^{-\lambda T}$.

Other applications

13-5 A department chief is feeling the effect of a budget crunch and is anxious to find ways of cutting costs while retaining a quality level of service. Currently there are five typists, each of whom types the letters from a single staff member. One of the typists will retire next January 1. It has been suggested to the department chief that the position could go unfilled and the remaining four typists could serve as a typing pool for the five staff members with little change in service level. Currently the time to complete a typing task is exponentially distributed with a mean of about 20 minutes. Each staff member requests about 15 typing jobs in the course of the $7\frac{1}{2}$-hour day. Assume that typing requests arrive at the typists' desks according to a Poisson distribution. Using an analysis of the queuing situation as the basis, make a recommendation concerning filling or not filling the position to be vacated next January.

13-6 DuVent City Airport has two runways. The north runway serves only jet aircraft; the west runway serves only propeller craft. The arrival of jets into the area follows a Poisson distribution with a mean arrival rate of 10 per hour; the arrival of props into the area follows a Poisson distribution with a mean of 6 per hour. Either runway can serve 15 aircraft per hour, with the service time being exponentially distributed. The FAA has estimated a cost of $1500 per jet and $600 per prop for each hour that an aircraft spends circling.

(*a*) If the two runways act independently, what is the average daily cost of unproductive flying?

(*b*) If the two runways act as two service facilities serving a single queue, what is the average daily cost of unproductive flying? (Assume that both runways have the facilities to service either kind of craft and that the combined arrival rate of jets and props is Poisson-distributed.)

13-7 It has been estimated that the court time of a particular type of criminal case averages $\frac{1}{2}$ day and is exponentially distributed. Cases arrive at the court for trial at the rate of eight per week with the arrival rate being Poisson-distributed. (Assume an 8-hour day and a 5-day week; a case arriving at the opening of court on Friday and heard at the opening of court on Monday would be said to have waited 1 day.) Analyze the backlog of court cases.

13-8 Refer to problem 13-7.

(*a*) If a judge assigned to court regularly takes an unscheduled absence of $\frac{1}{2}$ day per week from court, what is the effect on the backlog of cases?

(*b*) Similarly, what is the effect of an unscheduled full day off the bench?

(*c*) In either case what recommendations would you make to eliminate such a backlog? What other information would you want prior to making an actual recommendation?

13-9 Metropolitan Hospital receives ambulance calls that are Poisson-distributed with a mean of 3 per hour. The length of the ambulance round trip is exponentially distributed and averages 30 minutes. Ten percent of the ambulance patients are in critical condition, meaning that a delay in hospital treatment could seriously affect the patient's chances of survival; about 30 percent of the cases are serious, meaning that a delay in hospital service will aggravate the situation and require a longer recovery time; about 60 percent of the cases are simply classified as general, meaning that a delay in hospital service will not seriously affect the patient's condition. It costs $2000 a month to maintain an ambulance in service, $1500 for personnel, and $500 for amortization, insurance, maintenance, and supplies.

(*a*) Recommend to the hospital the number of ambulances it should have on call.

(*b*) Identify any assumptions made and values imputed in the analysis.

13-10 Metropolitan Hospital has a quick-service maintenance contract with a nearby fleet-maintenance corporation. Ambulances suffer a breakdown about once a month, requiring an average of 2 days to be serviced. Both working time (time between breakdowns) and repair time are exponentially distributed.

(*a*) If the hospital maintains a fleet of four ambulances, what is the probability that all four will be available at any given time?

(*b*) What is the probability that none of them will be available at a given time?

(*c*) On the average, how many ambulances are available for call?

13-11 Metropolitan Hospital has decided that it wishes to have four ambulances on call as a general policy.

(*a*) If the breakdown and service rates are as in problem 13-10, then how many ambulances must the hospital have in order to be 95 percent sure of having four ambulances on call?

(*b*) Reflecting on the costs of having an ambulance on call (see problem 13-9), how would the cost of a fifth substitute ambulance compare with the cost of one of the four original ambulances?

13-12 Assume the arrival rate of ships at a canal is Poisson-distributed with a mean of 4 per day, and the service time of a canal pilot has an unknown probability distribution with a mean of $\frac{1}{5}$ of a day and standard deviation of $\frac{2}{5}$ of a day. The Canal Authority has two options: (1) install equipment that would reduce the standard deviation to $\frac{1}{5}$ of a day but would maintain the average passage time of $\frac{1}{5}$ of a day; (2) install equipment that would reduce the passage time on the average to $\frac{1}{8}$ of a day, keeping the standard deviation at $\frac{2}{5}$ of a day. Compare the two alternatives in terms of the queue characteristics: queue length, time in the queue, and time in the system. Which option would you recommend?

Project problems

13-13 Describe a queuing situation with which you are familiar.

(*a*) Refer to the list on page 304 and hypothesize concerning its characteristics, including arrival rate and distribution and service rate and distribution.

(*b*) Do any of the models described in this chapter represent the situation? If so, which one? If not, which requirements do not hold?

13-14 Read Harris and Thiagarajan's 1975 article, "Queuing Models of Community Correctional Centers in the District of Columbia." Even though the model used is not one we have considered, certain main ideas are readily discernible.

(*a*) What are the objectives of the analysis?

(*b*) What are the main constraints?

(*c*) Compare the two solutions presented on the last page. Which would you recommend in light of parts *a* and *b*?

13-15 Read Erikson's article "Management Science and the Gas Shortage" (1974).

(*a*) What role does queuing play?

(*b*) What are some decisions or recommendations that might result from such an analysis?

CHAPTER

FOURTEEN

SIMULATION

At one time or another each of us has been involved in a simulation through playing "cops and robbers" or *Monopoly* or through taking part in a school play. Each of these instances satisfies the broad meaning of simulation insofar as each assumes the appearance or characteristics of reality. In this sense any model is a simulation. As it is used in management science, simulation not only *represents* reality but also *imitates* it in some fashion.

Simulation is one of the most flexible and consequently most used techniques in management science. Simulation can represent many decision situations which cannot be handled by an analytic model either because the assumptions of an analytic model are not met in the real situation or because the method of solving the model is highly impractical in the particular setting. This chapter will present the meaning and types of simulation, some in brief and some in detail; its relation to the decision-making process; the advantages and disadvantages of simulation; some applications; and heuristic methods, which are closely associated with simulation.

SIMULATION DEFINED

A simulation model represents some real system or situation and imitates it in some fashion. Accordingly, it provides a way of experimenting that would be impossible in the real system itself.

A simulation model is either physical, analog, or digital. A wind tunnel is a physical model used to imitate the atmosphere. An electrical network representing a waterway is an analog model, one physical system representing another. A digital simulation involves numerical manipulation of mathematical relationships. Our interest is in digital simulation models.

Simulation models based on mathematical relationships are either deterministic or stochastic and either static or dynamic. *Deterministic* simulations include only variables that are fixed for each application, whereas *stochastic* simulations include random variables. Some analysts include only the latter in defining simulations. In a *static* simulation the variables and parameters are independent of time, whereas in a *dynamic* simulation properties change with time. Most simulations of administrative and economic interest are dynamic.

Four types of simulation are included here in successively greater detail: artificial intelligence, merely indicating its meaning, objectives, and limitations; heuristic programming, showing its approach to problem solving and describing an application; deterministic system simulation, giving an overview and a conceptual application in urban dynamics; and finally stochastic simulation, giving the fundamental ideas and procedures of the Monte Carlo method through simple examples and real applications.

ARTIFICIAL INTELLIGENCE

Our brief reference to the general field of artificial intelligence is motivated not by a history of success but by the attention given to it from philosophical, psychological, and technological perspectives. Much of the early work, called *cognitive simulation,* attempted to get machines to match human problem-solving behavior. The technique involved getting human subjects to report their thoughts in problem solving and analyzing the reports to discover the rules that the subjects used. There has been some success with simulating human thought processes on certain simple problems, but we are still in the primitive stages of real machine simulation of human thought.

Another approach, referred to more specifically as "artificial intelligence," attempted to build machines capable of intelligent behavior, without necessarily simulating human behavior. Advancement on this frontier resembles the previously mentioned attempt.

Factors limiting advancement include finding practical methods of storage and retrieval of all the facts potentially relevant to a problem. These and other problems come back to two underlying difficulties: "1, how to restrict the class of possibly relevant facts while preserving generality, and 2, how to choose among possibly relevant facts those which are actually relevant."[1]

[1] Hubert L. Dreyfus, *What Computers Can't Do,* Harper & Row, Publishers, New York, 1972, p. 171.

HEURISTIC METHODS

A heuristic is sometimes described as a rule of thumb for solving some particular problem or some aspect of a problem. A collection of such rules of thumb for solving a whole complex problem is called a *heuristic program*.

A heuristic approach is relied on when there is no analytical procedure for solving the problem or when the theory-based procedure for finding the optimum solution is prohibitively impractical. Such would be the case where a more advanced analytical technique like integer programming or dynamic programming would require months of computer time to achieve the optimal solution to a complex problem. The cost of finding a solution, as well as the value of the solution, must be considered. A heuristic approach may settle for something less than optimum in exchange for a much cheaper method of solution.

A heuristic method can also be used when the objective(s) is (are) not sufficiently well defined to make optimizing even meaningful. The Stimson method of relative utilities (Chapter 6) is a type of heuristic that aims at finding an acceptable solution to a multiple-objective problem in a group decision-making setting.

A heuristic method generally aims at finding a satisfactory solution rather than an optimal one. The specific heuristic is justified on the basis of experimentation, either real or simulated, rather than on deductive reasoning.

The use of heuristics in everyday decision making is readily accepted.

Example The economy-minded supermarket shopper follows the rule of buying the store brand, even though he knows that making a comparison for each selected item will uncover some instances in which the national brand is less expensive. Exceptions will be explicitly made for specific items when the difference in quality more than offsets the difference in price.

Example The driving commuter may follow the rule of taking Main Street when the ramp to the freeway is congested, even though she knows that sometimes the ramp is crowded when the freeway itself is quite clear.

Example The beginning bridge player may always follow the rule of leading fourth from the top in the longest and strongest against a no-trump bid, although a more detailed decision rule might identify better alternatives in some instances.

Heuristic programs are not ordinarily as general as algorithms, and consequently they are used only for the specific situation for which they were designed, or one very similar. Heuristic programs for all but the simplest of cases are actually executed on a computer. For these reasons a detailed description of any one heuristic is beyond the intent of this text; it also would reap little benefit because of the limited generality. Rather we will describe a heuristic application.

Location of Health Care Facilities

Originally developed for warehouses,[2] the heuristic program for locating facilities has been successfully applied to locating prepaid ambulatory care centers.[3] The method does not result in a guaranteed optimum solution, but the original developers report obtaining near optimal ones.

While there are hundreds of potential center locations and more clusters of potential patients, the heuristic program requires that not very many have to be considered. The essential steps of the program are:

1. Get the expected enrollment from each population cluster for each center.
2. Eliminate locations with a maximum expected enrollment below a specified minimum.
3. Select two centers with the highest maximum expected enrollment.
4. Check each of the remaining centers:
   a. Include it if the maximum number of centers has not been reached and it satisfies cost restrictions.
   b. Substitute it for a previously included center if the maximum number has been reached and the new combination of centers has a better enrollment/cost ratio than the previous one.
   c. Remove a center if its enrollment drops below the specified minimum as a result of including some other center.
5. If either of the first two centers of step 3 has been replaced by another center in step 4*b*, check it (as in step 4*a*) to see if it should be included in the final list of centers.

The most difficult part is in step 1, estimating the proportion of any population cluster that will enroll in each potential medical care center. The key factor is the distance from the home to the center. Different relationships between distance and the enrolling proportion, as well as different values for minimum enrollment of a center and maximum number of centers, can be used to arrive at alternative solutions. The choice of a solution is made on the basis of estimated total enrollment, which depends on number and location of centers; total cost, which depends on number of centers and number enrolled in each center; and resources available, which determines the maximum number of centers.

Heuristic methods are often evaluated by simulating the decision situation. Simulation models sometimes include specific heuristics as the alternatives of the decision. Hence while heuristics are not, strictly speaking, simulation methods, they are closely related to simulation.

[2] Alfred A. Kuehn and Michael J. Hamburger, "A Heuristic Program for Locating Warehouses," *Management Science,* vol. 9, July 1963, pp. 643–666.

[3] Larry J. Shuman, C. Patrick Hardwick, and George A. Huber, "Location of Ambulatory Care Centers in a Metropolitan Area," *Health Services Research,* vol. 8, Summer 1973, pp. 121–138.

DETERMINISTIC SYSTEM SIMULATION

Simulation is often described in the context of systems analysis. A system is a purposeful set of interacting entities (people, buildings, vehicles) having attributes (skills and needs, location and capacity, cost and speed). Figure 14-1 represents a greatly simplified version of what a simulation model does for the decision maker in understanding a real system. One way of understanding the behavior of a real system is to observe it directly. Another way is to develop a model that imitates the system in whatever ways are deemed relevant and can practically be included in the model. Based on what is known about the real system, a model is developed. The behavior of the model is then observed, and from that behavior, inference is drawn about the behavior of the real system. A coarse simulation model will provide only gross information about reality, and a more detailed and complex simulation model will provide more refined information about reality.

Systems Dynamics

A methodology for simulating complex dynamic systems, called "systems dynamics," was first developed by Jay W. Forrester and his colleagues for the industrial environment.[4] The method has four levels of organization:

1. *Closed boundary,* which includes the entities necessary to represent the behavior of interest. Forces outside the boundary affect conditions in the system but not the way in which the system responds.
2. *Feedback loops,* through which the dynamic response of the system is initiated.

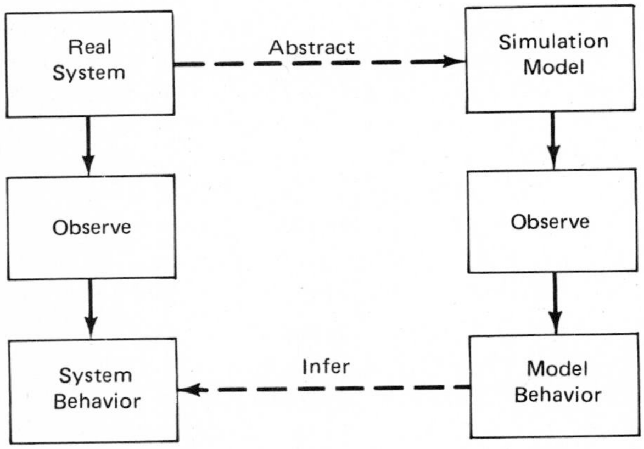

Figure 14-1 Understanding a system's behavior through simulation.

[4] J. W. Forrester, *Industrial Dynamics,* Cambridge, Mass., The M.I.T. Press, 1961. For other applications of the concepts, see the same author's *Urban Dynamics,* 1969, and *World Dynamics,* 1971, from the same publisher.

3. *Levels* or accumulations of objects and *rates* or flows of objects within feedback loops. Rates change levels and depend on information feedback.
4. *Components of a rate variable,* which consist of desired levels and observed levels. Discrepancies here trigger adjustments in the rate variables.

Originally the approach developed for industrial and economic systems was called *industrial dynamics*. Later the same methodology was applied to urban systems and global systems; the labels used then were "urban dynamics" and "world dynamics," respectively. Here we will consider briefly urban dynamics.[5]

Urban Dynamics

The goal of urban dynamics is the construction of a simulation model that would embody the essential characteristics of an urban area, assumed to be within the closed boundary. The levels of population, housing, industry, and taxation are the level variables of the model. The relationships among the variables are expressed in time-dependent equations that describe the construction, decline, and demolition of industry and housing, and changes in the population levels for management and professional workers, skilled workers, and unskilled workers. Some of the most important equations in the model describe the rate of arrival into and departure from the city for each of the three population groups. The rates are dependent on the size of that segment of the population and the attractiveness of the city to that segment. The model provides for estimating how various programs, such as the job training and slum clearance programs, affect the attractiveness of the city and ultimately the city itself. In response to criticism that the model is a conceptual one only and that its parameters are uncalibrated and untested, Forrester suggests that the aim of the model is not to predict the condition of the city at any point in time but rather to estimate the directions of changes that result from specific public policies.

Before proceeding with the more detailed discussion of stochastic simulation, the most frequently used type, we will present some of its benefits and limitations and relate its use to the decision process.

BENEFITS AND LIMITATIONS OF SIMULATION

The increased use of simulation is due to a number of factors, including the following:

1. The manager can experiment with different variables in order to answer "what if . . . ?" questions in a way that would be impossible with the

[5] Although technically well advanced, systems dynamics is too young for sufficient comparisons of models with reality.

system itself. Using simulation in this experimental mode is widely considered to be its greatest benefit.
2. Complex systems often must be greatly simplified to be expressed in an analytical form; simulation can provide a solution when analytical models fail to do so.
3. Simulation models are often more realistic than other models since they require fewer restrictive assumptions.
4. Simulation, though expensive, is not as expensive as altering the system itself in order to understand its behavior.
5. Simulation provides *time compression,* which provides in minutes what would require years of observing the system itself.
6. The mathematics of simulation is often not complex. If the system is complex, the model will be complex, but perhaps only because there are many elementary relationships and interdependencies.

With all its advantages, simulation experienced a great rise in use and popularity in the 1960s, sometimes being used in decision situations for which a direct analytical solution should have been preferred. Through experience certain disadvantages of simulation have been recognized, which serve not to preclude its use but rather to include it as only one of many quantitative methods to support decision making. Some limitations are:

1. Simulation is descriptive, and therefore an optimal solution is not identified. Since simulation is descriptive rather than normative, decision alternatives are evaluated by trial and error; that is, the simulation is run for each of the identified alternatives and the one yielding the best system consequences is accepted as the best of the available alternatives.
2. The data collection, design, and validation necessary for a simulation model are frequently slow and costly processes. If there are many feasible alternatives, simulating them all is costly for even moderately large-scale applications.
3. Inferences from a simulation are usually not applicable to other problems because the model incorporates the characteristics unique to the situation at hand. The methodology, however, is more likely to be transferable.

On balance simulation is an effective, highly applicable quantitative technique used in support of decision making. We now present two examples of simulation so that we will be better able to relate its use to the decision process.

Emergency Room Arrival

The arrival of patients at the emergency room of a hospital is often of such a nature that analysis based on "first-come, first-served" and "any patient to any service room" assumptions will not be satisfied, so that an analytical model such as queuing will not be appropriate. A simulation model of the emergency room uses such entities as the frequency of arrivals; the special services required by some arrivals, such as immediate transfusions or immediate transfer to an operating room; the priority status given to special categories of patients, so that they will be served by the next available attendant; the preemptive status given some categories of patients, so that an attendant will interrupt servicing another patient in order to care for the preempting patient; and the relative frequency of multiple arrivals, as from an industrial explosion or multiple-vehicle accident.

Various configurations of medical personnel on duty in the emergency room, or on duty in the hospital and just on call to the emergency room, different kinds of equipment available in the emergency room, and alternatives for the physical layout of the emergency room itself can be included in different versions of the simulation model. Seeing how each version of the model behaves under different simulated conditions of patient arrival rates and needs, one infers how the actual emergency room will operate under the corresponding real conditions. It is much easier to rearrange the components of the simulated system than of the real system in order to understand its behavior. While the simulation model does not find an optimum solution, it does provide information about the behavior of the system, and through that understanding it can lead to at least a good design of the real system.

The New York City Fire Project[6]

A major issue in the 1969 contract negotiations between New York City and fire-fighting units was work load. The union demanded that the city create one new fire unit for each "overworked" unit to share the work load. Depending on the definition of "overworked," the proposal would have required adding between 40 and 75 new units at a cost of up to $45 million a year. Investigations focused on the location of the overworked units, the time of day during which units were overworked, and the operational consequences of units being overworked. The investigation revealed that the very high frequency of calls occurred between 3:00 p.m. and 1:00 a.m. in specific areas of the city, and resulted in a response less than the standard "3 and 2." (Standard practice at the time was to assign three pumpers and two hook and ladders to respond to each fire call.) When units near the fire call were already busy at another call, neighboring units would be assigned to respond. The result, of course, was that during peak times in particular areas, calls were responded to by units some distance away, often greatly increasing the response time.

A simulation model was developed, making use of years of data giving the relative frequency of calls by location, time of day, state of the fire when the call was made, type of fire, and equipment actually needed. Using the model, different fire deployment policies were evaluated. For one thing, it was learned that adding new units would not reduce the work load of the overworked units,

[6] For a fuller account see Edward H. Blum, "The New York City Fire Project," in Alvin W. Drake, Ralph L. Keeney, and Philip M. Morse (eds.), *Analysis of Public Systems,* The M.I.T. Press, Cambridge, Mass., 1972, pp. 94–132.

but would relieve the lighter working units who otherwise would have assisted. Furthermore, it was found that much of the new units' capability would simply permit the standard response of "3 and 2" when, without the unit, the response would have been smaller. Both sides in the negotiations used the results of the simulation model, which showed rather effectively that there would be no appreciable lightening of the work load of the hardest working units. Other deployment policies were tried, including using an adaptive response rather than the standard "3 and 2" response. Eventually an adaptive response policy was implemented, wherein vehicles were assigned to a fire depending on the time of day, the location of the call, and the likelihood of different types of alarms. As the model had predicted, the policy resulted in quicker average response to a call, quicker arrival of "3 and 2" when needed than under the standard response policy, and the saving of between \$5 and \$20 million per year. It would have been unthinkable to consider experimenting in reality with the many different policies that could be examined in the simulation.

The application of simulation is limited only by man's imagination and the breadth of the problems that face him. Other areas in which simulation has provided an improved understanding include other urban systems, ambulance response and location; police patrol patterns; the flight to the moon; national economies; traffic flow; airport and runway operation; pollution dynamics, including sources and concentrations; reservoirs and waterways to determine the effect of various operating policies and weather on freshwater supplies, irrigation, and hydroelectric output; blood banking; university operations; movement of the criminal population through the criminal justice system; and allocation of resources. While this list is not meant to be complete, it does give some indication of the diversity of simulation applications.

DECISION MAKING AND SIMULATION

Simulation is a descriptive technique rather than a normative one, insofar as it attempts to describe the system's behavior under certain conditions rather than seek an optimum solution under those conditions. Whatever assumptions, conditions, and relationships are deemed relevant are included in the simulation model that is constructed. The model itself does not identify alternatives although it helps to suggest them. Identifying the alternatives is essentially a task for humans rather than for a model. As one identifies alternatives, one modifies the model; running the modified model aims at predicting the behavior of the system under that modification so the decision maker can view the consequences of the alternative. Figure 14-2 depicts the role of simulation in the decision-making process. The alternatives are identified on the decision-making side of the diagram rather than on the model side of the diagram. In contrast to this, in linear programming alternatives are identified in the execution of the model itself, insofar as the constraints of the problem dictate the feasible region, which consists of all allowable alternatives.

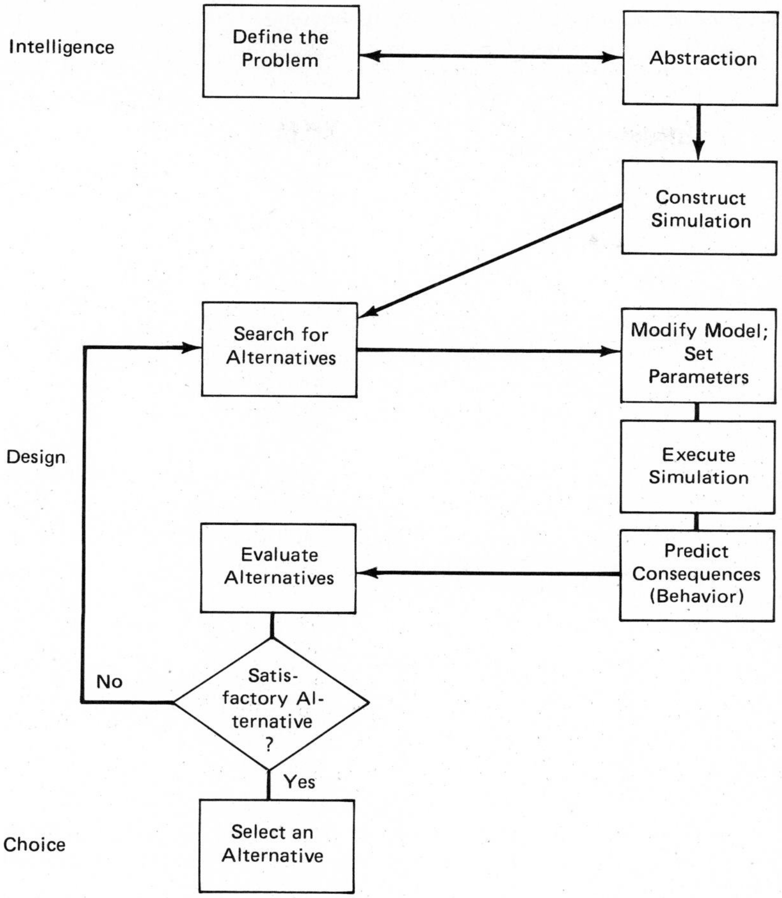

Figure 14-2 Simulation and the decision process.

Proper use of a simulation model requires close interaction between the decision maker (or advisor or staff assistant) and the model maker (who may be a staff assistant to the decision maker). It may be this great involvement of the decision maker in the development and running of the model that makes simulation more acceptable to management than some of the analytical techniques, which they perceive as more mysterious and removed from them.

STOCHASTIC SIMULATION

In the 1940s John von Neumann and Stanislaus Ulam used a simulation to solve a problem at the Los Alamos Science Laboratory. The essence of their approach involved the generation of an approximate solution by a roulette wheel;

Table 14-1 Distribution of emergency room arrivals by patient category*

Category of patient	Frequency	Relative frequency or probability
Regular	450	.90
Priority	35	.07
Preemptive:		
Extensive care	5	.01
Transient care	10	.02
	500	1.00

* Hospital records would reveal the frequency column; the probability or relative frequency column is computed from the frequency column.

the code name "Monte Carlo" was used. Aside from being the name of the famous gambling principality, Monte Carlo has become the name for generating simulated events according to the laws of chance. The essence of Monte Carlo simulation will be presented in a brief illustration.

Emergency Room Arrivals: An Illustration

Suppose patients arriving at a hospital emergency room (ER) are generally taken care of on a first-come, first-served basis. There are two exceptions to this service rule: Patients with a "priority" classification (based on reported symptoms) are attended to by the next available physician without having to wait in the line; patients with a "preemptive" classification are seen immediately by the ER on-duty physician, even if that physician is currently attending to another patient. In some instances the preempting patient is attended to extensively by the ER physician and in other cases is attended to only briefly by him while en route to some special-purpose hospital facility (for example, an operating room or sterile burn unit). The hospital would like to know the effects on the operation of the emergency room of various staffing policies; for example, whether to have physicians assigned only to the ER or assigned to the hospital and on call to the ER when the waiting line reaches a certain length.

Hospital records indicate the frequency of each category of patients. Based on the frequency of occurrence a relative frequency distribution or probability distribution can be developed. Table 14-1 presents an illustrative distribution of emergency room arrivals by patient category.

In initiating the ER activity, simulated arrivals are randomly assigned to one of the four patient categories in a way that will reflect the relative frequencies of the categories. One easy way to do this is to write the numbers 1 to 100 on a hundred pieces of paper and drop them into a hat. Arbitrarily assign numbers to each category to reflect the relative frequencies. One such arbitrary assignment follows.

Category	Numbers 1–100
Priority	3, 18, 26, 41, 58, 77, 92
Preemptive:	
Extensive care	14
Transient care	46, 83
Regular	All the others

It is easier to assign the numbers in order; that is, to assign 1–90 to regular, 91–97 to priority, 98 to preemptive extensive care, and 99–100 to preemptive transient care. This method of assignment corresponds exactly to the cumulative relative frequency and is the method usually used. The last column of Table 14-2 shows the random numbers assigned to each category, based on cumulative relative frequencies.

Rather than pick numbers out of a hat, either a random-number table or a special computer program, called a *random-number generator,* is used. Whether a number with one, two, three, or more digits is used depends solely on what is needed to reflect the relative frequencies. The cumulative probability column of Table 14-2, shows that two-digit numbers are appropriate for the ER simulation.

By picking numbers from a hat, or by reading numbers from a random-number table, or by having the computer program generate them, arrivals can be simulated. For example, suppose the first 10 two-digit random numbers picked are 07, 30, 50, 96, 46, 12, 25, 99, 50, and 12. The simulated sequence of arrivals would be: Arrival 4 is a priority patient, arrival 8 is a preemptive transient-care patient, and all others are regular patients. The arrivals would be treated in the simulation as the ER policy provides.

Needless to say, the operation of an emergency room depends on many

Table 14-2 Distribution of emergency room arrivals by patient category*

Category of patient	Frequency	Relative frequency or probability	Cumulative probability	Random numbers
Regular	450	.90	.90	01–90
Priority	35	.07	.97	91–97
Preemptive:				
Extensive care	5	.01	.98	98
Transient care	10	.02	1.00	99–00
	500	1.00		

* Hospital records would reveal the frequency column; the probability or relative frequency column is computed from the frequency column. Subtotals in the probability column are accumulated to get the cumulative probability column. Random numbers are assigned to each category according to the cumulative probabilities.

characteristics other than simply the category of the patient. Accordingly, the simulation of an emergency room would contain many components other than the choice of a random number to represent the simulated patient arrival. The more closely the model represents the real situation, the more components must be included in the simulation. We will return to this illustration shortly in order to see a fuller model.

In the Monte Carlo method, events are simulated by associating random numbers with random occurrences by means of the cumulative probability distribution. The process is formalized in the next section.

The Monte Carlo Process

A decision situation can be simulated by the Monte Carlo method using the following basic steps:

1. Identify the relevant features of the decision situation. Identify the probabilistic elements, and find the probability distribution of each.
2. Construct the cumulative probability distribution for each probabilistic element.
3. Assign random numbers to each event corresponding to its cumulative probability distribution.
4. Use random numbers to represent the occurrence of the random events, describing the simulated system as each occurs.
5. Continue step 4 for the desired amount of time, or until the desired number of events have occurred, or until some system performance indicator stabilizes. This step will receive further attention later.
6. Repeat steps 1 to 5 for the various systems alternatives or decision alternatives.

We now apply these steps to the simulation of a hospital emergency room. Since our main purpose is illustrative, we will not consider the emergency room in its grand complexity but will expand somewhat on the version presented in the last section.

1. *Identify relevant features, specifying the probabilistic elements.* For the sake of this illustration, we assume the emergency room has three service rooms and a waiting room. Each service room can handle the same kinds of cases, but none can handle major operations or extreme burn treatments. The hospital is trying to decide whether to staff the emergency room with two on-duty physicians or one on-duty physician with a second physician on duty elsewhere in the hospital and on call for service in the emergency room.

The operation of the emergency room is essentially like this: Patients arrive and are formally registered with means of payment recorded. If one of the service rooms is available, the patient is brought there; otherwise the patient waits in a common waiting room. Patients are brought from the waiting room to the service room on a first-come, first-served basis. Exceptions to this rule

Table 14-3 Distribution of time between patients' arrivals

Interarrival time (minutes)	Frequency	Probability	Cumulative probability	Random numbers
10	44	.11	.11	01–11
20	108	.27	.38	12–38
30	120	.30	.68	39–68
40	80	.20	.88	69–88
50	28	.07	.95	89–95
60	20	.05	1.00	96–00
	400	1.00		

apply to priority patients, who are assigned to the next available service room and are seen by the next available physician, and preemptive patients, who are seen immediately by a physician on duty who will even interrupt caring for another patient. This is done by having the preemptive patient brought immediately to a service room; if none is vacant, a screen is drawn, effectively creating two small service rooms. In most cases preemptive care is transient while the patient is enroute to a specialized facility within the hospital. About one-third of the preempting patients require more extensive care in the emergency room.

The probabilistic elements of the situation are patient arrival rate, patient category, and physician's service rate. For the time between successive arrivals, based on a sample of 400 patients, Table 14-3 presents the frequency distribution, resulting probability and cumulative probability distributions, and the assigned random numbers. Since the cumulative probabilities have only two digits, two-digit random numbers are appropriate. For the same sample, the distribution of physician service time is presented in Table 14-4. Preemptive patients who arrived during the sampling time were not included in the sample; it was generally agreed, however, by the emergency room personnel that two-

Table 14-4 Physicians' service time for regular and priority patients*

Service time (minutes)	Frequency	Probability	Cumulative probability	Random numbers
20	100	.25	.25	01–25
30	140	.35	.60	26–60
40	100	.25	.85	61–85
50	32	.08	.93	86–93
60	16	.04	.97	94–97
90	12	.03	1.00	98–00
	400	1.00		

* Service time for preemptive extensive care is 60 minutes, and for preemptive transient care, 10 minutes.

thirds of such patients require about 10 minutes (transient care) and the remaining require about an hour (extensive care).

2. *Construct cumulative probability distributions.* By taking subtotals of the probability values, the cumulative probability distributions are developed. These are presented in Tables 14-2 to 14-4.

3. *Assign random numbers.* Using the cumulative probability distribution as the basis, random numbers are assigned to each possible outcome of each probabilistic event. These numbers appear in the last column of each of the tables. For convenience, the random numbers assigned to patient categories are repeated in Table 14-5.

4. *Use random numbers to represent occurrences.* A table of random numbers is presented in Table 14-6. For best unbiased results in using a random-number table, some predetermined pattern of picking the numbers is recommended. In picking our random numbers, we will simply start with the last column and pick numbers from the top down; then we will go to the second-last column and continue in that way. One for the interarrival time, one for the patient category, and one for the physician service time lead to the arrival times, categories, and service start and completion times as in Table 14-7. For purposes of illustration, simulating 8 hours is sufficient.

5. *Continue simulation of the desired number of events.* Since our purposes are merely illustrative, we simulate one 8-hour shift. Ordinarily, the simulation would continue until a full day (or week or other period) has been simulated, or until some indicator stabilizes; for example, it becomes clear that the number of people in the waiting room never exceeds four, is always zero or one, or the queue continually increases in size.

6. *Repeat the process for various decision alternatives.* The simulation would then be repeated for the emergency room in which there is one on-duty physician with a second physician on call if needed. The meaning of "is needed" would have to be specified; for example, when the queue exceeds two patients, the second physician will be called. Such a modification and reexecution of the simulation is left for exercise 14-2.

In summarizing the results of the simulation, we first note that the only patients who arrived while another patient was being served are patients 3, 8, 11,

Table 14-5 Random numbers for patient categories

Category	Random numbers
Regular	01–90
Priority	91–97
Preemptive:	
Extensive	98
Transient	99–00

12, and 16. Since this simulation run assumed that two physicians were on duty, there was never any waiting time. A full summary of the simulation run follows:

Number of physicians	2 on duty
Total simulated time[7]	510 min = 8 hr 30 min
Number of patients served	16
Total patients' waiting time	0
Average waiting time	0
Average line length	0
Percent of time:	
Both physicians busy	.216
One busy	.549
None busy	.235
Number of priority patients	3
Number of patients "bumped" by priority patients	0
Number of preemptive patients	2
Number of patients "bumped" by preemptive patients	0

In this simple illustration the summary statistics above can be easily found by a quick review of the simulation. In a longer simulation run or a more complicated situation, it is advisable to track important statistics throughout the simulation. For example, when a patient waits 10 minutes in the waiting room, the total waiting time would be increased by 10; if 3 patients were waiting for those 10 minutes, then the waiting time would be increased by 30. At the conclusion of the simulation run, the total patient waiting time would be divided by the number of patients served to determine the average waiting time. When the simulation is computerized, cumulative totals are maintained as the simulation is run, so that summary statistics can be easily calculated.

The behavior of the simulated system, and by inference the behavior of the real system, is described by the various summary statistics. The effects of various alternatives can be assessed by interpreting the appropriate statistics.

Validation and Estimation

Simulation provides the basis for drawing inferences about a system's actual behavior. Quality inferences require that we be attentive to two aspects of simulation, namely, validation and estimation. Our purpose here is simply to call attention to these rather than to provide detailed steps.

[7] We have chosen to simulate 8 hours = 480 minutes; we include services started before 480 and finishing after, but do not include arrivals at or after 480. The effect in a longer run of such arbitrary choice is minimal.

Table 14-6 Random numbers

11 29 01 95 80	49 34 35 86 47	87 02 22 57 51	68 69 80 95 44
89 74 39 82 15	08 58 94 34 74	39 77 32 77 09	79 57 92 36 59
87 80 61 65 31	09 71 91 74 25	28 06 24 25 93	22 45 44 84 11
59 73 19 85 23	53 33 65 97 21	97 67 63 99 61	80 45 67 93 82
66 56 45 65 79	45 56 20 19 47	69 30 16 09 05	53 58 47 70 93
53 77 57 68 93	60 61 97 22 61	33 73 99 19 87	26 72 39 27 67
45 60 33 01 07	98 99 46 50 47	87 14 77 43 96	43 00 65 98 50
56 65 05 61 86	90 92 10 70 80	99 53 93 61 28	52 70 05 48 34
22 87 26 07 47	86 96 98 29 06	93 86 52 77 65	15 33 59 05 28
49 18 09 79 49	74 16 32 23 02	18 46 23 34 27	85 13 99 24 44
08 13 13 85 51	55 34 57 72 69	07 10 63 76 35	87 03 04 79 88
82 63 18 27 44	69 66 92 19 09	92 38 70 96 92	52 06 79 79 45
55 66 12 62 11	08 99 55 64 57	00 57 25 60 59	46 72 60 18 77
27 80 30 21 60	10 92 35 36 12	24 98 65 63 21	47 21 61 88 32
49 99 57 94 82	96 88 57 17 91	28 10 99 00 27	12 73 73 99 12
77 45 85 50 51	79 88 01 97 30	87 63 93 95 17	81 83 83 04 49
29 18 94 51 23	14 85 11 47 23	08 61 74 51 69	92 79 43 89 79
72 65 71 08 86	50 03 42 99 36	08 52 85 08 40	48 40 35 94 22
89 37 20 70 01	61 65 70 22 12	89 85 84 46 06	64 71 06 21 66
81 30 15 39 14	81 83 17 16 33	42 29 72 23 19	06 94 76 10 08
20 21 14 68 86	84 95 48 46 45	79 53 36 02 95	94 61 09 43 62
85 43 01 72 73	14 93 87 81 40	79 93 96 38 63	34 85 52 05 09
59 97 50 99 52	24 62 20 42 31	97 48 72 66 48	53 16 71 13 81
72 68 49 29 31	75 70 16 08 24	26 97 05 73 51	88 46 38 03 58
88 02 84 27 83	85 81 56 39 38	06 87 37 78 48	65 88 69 58 39

Validation attempts to determine whether the model accurately represents the problem situation. There are two components of this process: *Internal validation* determines whether the model does what was intended, or is free from logical and programming errors; *external validation* determines how well the model imitates real behavior. Internal validation is conducted through comparing simulation results to analytic results that may be available from a similar problem. Pencil and paper checking of a computer program simulation can be used to validate segments of the program. External validation requires a comparison of the model results with results of the real system, gathered in the past

Table 14-7 Representation of random occurrences (with two physicians)

Patient	RN for	Inter-arrival time	Time patient arrives	RN for	Category*	RN for	Service time	Time to start service	Time to complete service	No. of minutes two physicians busy
1	44	30	30	59	R	11	20	30	50	0
2	82	40	70	93	P	67	40	70	110	0
3	50	30	100	34	R	28	30	100	130	10
4	44	30	130	88	R	45	30	130	160	0
5	77	40	170	32	R	12	20	170	190	0
6	49	30	200	79	R	22	20	200	220	0
7	66	30	230	08	R	62	40	230	270	0
8	09	10	240	81	R	58	30	240	270	30
9	39	30	270	95	P	36	30	270	300	0
10	84	40	310	93	P	70	40	310	350	0
11	27	20	330	98	$P:e$		60	330	390	20
12	48	30	360	05	R	24	20	360	380	20
13	79	40	400	79	R	18	20	400	420	0
14	88	40	440	99	$P:t$		10	440	450	0
15	04	10	450	89	R	94	60	450	510	0
16	21	20	470	10	R	43	30	470	500	30

* R = regular patient; P = priority; $P:e$ = preemptive: extended care; $P:t$ = preemptive: transient care.

or after the simulation experiment. In testing its validity one must avoid using the same data that was used in constructing the model.

When simulation is used for estimating system characteristics such as the mean waiting time, the mean cost per day, and so forth, we must keep in mind that each simulation is similar to a single sample. As such the results provide a *point estimate* of the mean and standard deviation, and any other desired parameter. Just as we interpret sample results in terms of levels of confidence and plus or minus an error term, so too we should not expect a single simulation to be a perfect reflection of the real situation. As the sample size or simulation run size increases, the estimate is more likely to be close to the real parameter. This settling down to the *steady-state value* is known as *stochastic convergence*. To know how close a simulation statistic is to the real parameter, the usual methods of statistical inference should be employed. Such methods are standard topics in any basic statistics book.

Inasmuch as simulations are generally computerized, we make a brief mention of special simulation computer languages before our concluding applications.

Simulation Computer Languages

Without the use of a computer, simulations of complex systems or long-run simulations of even simple systems would be impossible in the practical sense. Programming a simulation model on a computer has been greatly facilitated by the development of specially designed simulation languages. Two such languages are DYNAMO and GPSS. The language DYNAMO has been developed to simplify a systems dynamic simulation. The equations relating levels and rates are easily programmed, and the output of the program is in a readily interpreted form.

General Purpose System Simulation (GPSS) was originally developed for complex queuing simulations. Entries (patients, emergency calls, vehicles, and so forth) are tracked as they progress through the system of waiting lines and service facilities. The output presents summary statistics on each waiting line and each service facility. Any system that can be described in terms of lines, service facilities, and movement from one system entity to another can be rather readily simulated in GPSS.

POLICE PATROL ANALYSIS: AN APPLICATION[8]

This section focuses on simulating different strategies for assigning police patrol cars to calls. Police cars patrolling their area of responsibility are either on preventive patrol or are responding to a call. A central dispatcher assigns a car to answer a call as he receives it.

[8] This application is based on Richard C. Larson, *Urban Police Patrol Analysis,* The M.I.T. Press, Cambridge, Mass., 1972, chap. 6.

Here we assume that assignments are made on a precinct-wide basis; that is, a patrol car can be assigned to cover any incident or respond to any call anywhere in the precinct.[9] Suppose further that the precinct is composed of nine sectors as represented in Figure 14-3. Each sector has associated with it one car; that car performs preventive patrol within that sector but will respond to any call to which it is assigned. When an incident occurs within any sector, the car assigned to that sector is dispatched to it. If that sector's car is busy with a previous incident, then another car is assigned to cover the current call. There are various methods for making nonsector assignments; the dispatcher may assign a car from any adjacent sector, or may assign the car from the sector that is closest to the location of the current incident. As an illustration, suppose an incident occurs at point A in sector 2. If any adjacent sector car is to be assigned, then the dispatcher would be indifferent to choosing cars 1, 3, or 5. If the car in the sector closest to the incident is to be dispatched, then the dispatcher would choose car 3. These methods of assigning nonsector cars to incidents are referred to as *strict center-of-mass dispatching* and *modified center-of-mass dispatching,* respectively.

If there are no cars available to respond to the call, the call is placed in a

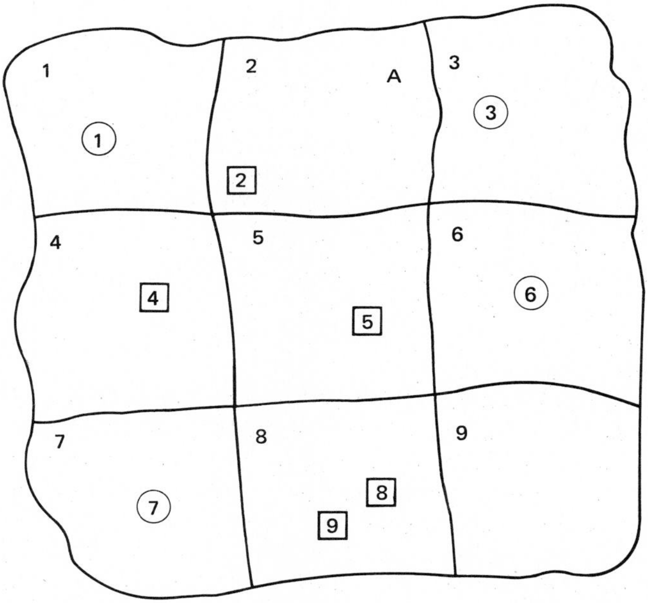

Figure 14-3 A precinct with nine patrol sectors. (1), car 1 is on preventive patrol; [2], car 2 is responding to a call. Note that car 9 is responding in sector 8.

[9] The same model could be used if assignments were made on a different basis; for example, a group of precincts, an entire municipality, or any other appropriate region could serve as the total area of response.

waiting line or queue. There are various ways of reassigning a car that becomes available to answer a call in a queue. The term ''reassignment'' is used when a car is dispatched to a call immediately upon completion of a previous call, without having resumed preventive patrol. A car may be reassigned to the call that is waiting the longest, or to the call that represents the closest incident, or to the call that is considered most important.

Incidents can be either prioritized or considered to be of equal importance. The purpose for the current simulation is to determine the effects of prioritizing calls on the operation of the patrol. We now describe the simulation.

The decision situation involves a precinct as previously described and as depicted in Figure 14-3. The precinct is divided into nine sectors, each of which is patroled by a car. There are three probabilistic elements in the decision situation: (1) Once a car arrives at the scene of the incident, the service time required is exponentially distributed with a mean of 40 minutes; (2) the arrival of calls is Poisson-distributed with a mean of 11.4 per hour; (3) the location of incidents is uniformly distributed over the entire precinct, that is, an incident is as likely to occur at one point in the precinct as it is at any other point in the precinct. Aside from these three probabilistic elements, if calls are to be prioritized, then the priority of the incoming call is also a probabilistic element. The associated probability distribution will be described in presenting the two decision alternatives.

There are two decision alternatives:

1. Calls are not prioritized; a modified center-of-mass dispatching strategy is used; cars are reassigned to the call waiting the longest.
2. Calls are prioritized without any preemption; a modified center-of-mass dispatching strategy is used; cars are reassigned to waiting calls in their order of priority and to the closest incident within a priority class; a maximum travel distance for each priority class is prescribed.

Example In alternative 2, when a car becomes available, it is reassigned to a priority 1 waiting call. If there are two calls of priority 1, the car is reassigned to the closest one. If there are no calls of priority 1, the car is reassigned to the closest priority 2 call provided it is within the prescribed maximum travel distance. If there is no nearby priority 2 call, the car returns to its sector, if it is not already there, for preventive patrol. If while tentatively resuming preventive patrol, the car passes within the prescribed maximum distance of the waiting incident, it is dispatched to that incident.

When prioritized, the priority classes of incidents are:

Priority 1 includes reported crimes in progress, officers in trouble, serious automobile accidents, and so forth; response time is critical for this class of call, which represents 5 percent of all calls.

Priority 2 calls include reported crimes which occurred in the past, family disputes, miscellaneous disturbances, etc. About 45 percent of all calls are in this class.

Priority 3 calls include open fire hydrants, parking violations, etc. Response time is least important for this class, which represents about 50 percent of all calls.

The prescribed response speeds for the three classes are: 15 miles per hour for class 1, 12 miles per hour for class 2, and 10 miles per hour for class 3. Under the nonprioritized alternative, the response speed averages 15 miles per hour. Certain maximum allowable response distances are prescribed for each priority class; these distances depend on the status of the responding car as well as the priority of the incident. The status of a car being considered for assignment is one of the following: (1) on preventive patrol; (2) at the point of completing a previous assignment; (3) in the process of resuming preventive patrol. The maximum allowable distances are summarized in Table 14-8. There is no limit on the distance for priority 1 calls; for Priority 2 calls, a car will be dispatched any distance from preventive patrol, but it will be reassigned to that incident only if it is within 1 mile. A car returning to preventive patrol will be assigned to a priority 2 incident if it is within 2 miles.

Random numbers are used for each of the probabilistic elements; interarrival time, incident location, service time, and for the second decision alternative, priority level. Table 14-9 presents the summary characteristics of a 2-hour simulation, executed for both the nonprioritized and the prioritized alternatives.

The actual arrival rate of calls varies with the time of day; when the arrival rate is less than nine calls per hour, the benefit of prioritizing calls is not very apparent. With a service time of 40 minutes and an average travel time of 5 minutes, the average total time per call is about 45 minutes. This means that with nine cars, the system capacity is 12 calls per hour. With an arrival rate of 11.4 calls per hour, the utilization factor is about .95. At this level the effect of prioritizing calls is readily apparent, as Table 14-9 indicates.

Priority 1 calls are responded to from any distance, and priority 2 and 3

Table 14-8 Maximum allowable travel distance (miles)*

	Status of car		
Priority of call	Preventive patrol	Completing previous assignment	Resuming patrol
1	None	None	None
2	None	1	2
3	2	0	2

* Each sector is about 1 mile by 1 mile.

Table 14-9 Police patrol system characteristics
Average arrival rate = 11.4 calls per hour
Average service time = 45 minutes; 9 cars

	Calls not prioritized	Calls prioritized		
		Priority 1	Priority 2	Priority 3
Average travel time	5	7.5	4.8	6
Average wait (before dispatch)	20	3.6	20	42
Average total response time	25	11.1	24.8	48
Percent of intersector assignments	.83	.85	.66	.52

calls have prescribed maximum travel distances. Hence, it is more likely that priority 1 calls will be served by cars at a greater distance. This explains why there is an increase in the average travel time for priority 1 calls over the nonprioritized alternative. However, the considerable decrease in waiting time for such calls more then compensates for the increased travel time. The critical factor is the total response time which at 11.1 minutes for priority 1 calls is considerably lower than 25 for nonprioritized calls. The total response time for priority 2 is about the same as for nonprioritized calls even though the response speed is 3 miles per hour slower for priority 2 calls than under the nonprioritized alternative.

The simulation can be repeated for any other patrol and dispatch alternatives. In a third alternative, the effect of permitting priority 1 calls to preempt priority 2 or priority 3 calls can be determined by including that factor in the simulation. Determining the effect of this modification or any other alternative without the aid of simulation would require experimental periods of actual implementation, during which time the human dispatcher would have to change his dispatching strategy rather frequently. The increased understanding of the real situation without tampering with it is one of the advantages of simulation as a decision aid.

Regardless of whether or not calls are prioritized, system characteristics may be improved by taking the cars' exact locations into account when dispatching a car to a call. Such a car-locator system provides constantly updated information which the dispatcher can use in making dispatch decisions. Such a system, an example of a decision information system, will be included in our discussion of management information systems in the next chapter.

NATIONAL PARK MANAGEMENT: AN APPLICATION[10]

The National Park Service (NPS) is charged with the responsibility of providing recreational activities throughout the vast system of the nation's national parks. Accordingly, the Department of the Interior employs a sizable contingent of personnel for administration of the system and to provide direct services such as information, instruction in a variety of outdoor activities, and tour guidance. Driven by a commitment to improve and expand upon opportunities available to the public, NPS is about to introduce a new section of scenic wilderness in an area where the demand for such a recreational outlet has been notably high.

The new scenic wilderness area is designed to provide naturalists with a series of trails, each characterized by a particular theme of flora and fauna. The trails have also been tailored in length to offer recreation to the rugged, as well as to the less vigorous, outdoorsperson. The series of trails is depicted in Figure 14-4.

NPS is trying to determine the number of trail guides that it should hire to adequately staff the new operation. Some disagreement exists in the Division of Planning as to the exact number of trail guides which will be necessary. While NPS does not have a comparable arrangement elsewhere, enough information exists throughout the system of national parks to be able to estimate the approximate use rate of the trails. This information appears in Tables 14-10 and 14-11.

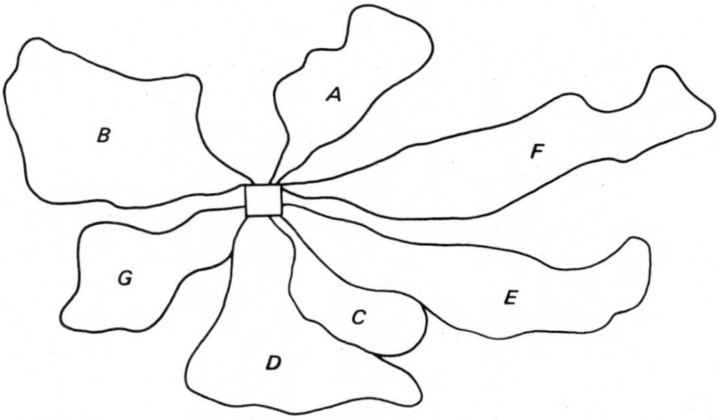

Figure 14-4 Nature trails for scenic wilderness project.

[10] This application is based on Kerry V. Smith, David B. Webster, and Norman A. Heck, "The Management of Wilderness Areas: A Simulation Model," *Decision Sciences,* vol. 7, July 1976, pp. 524–537.

Table 14-10 Distribution of time between naturalist group arrivals

Interarrival time (minutes)	Frequency	Probability	Random numbers
10	7	.11	01–11
20	10	.15	12–26
30	35	.54	27–80
40	5	.08	81–88
50	6	.09	89–97
60	2	.03	98–00
	65	1.00	

Additionally, by actually walking each trail, the service can predict the approximate round-trip time required to guide a naturalist group over a particular trail. This information is provided in Table 14-12.

The Division of Planning decided to conduct an experiment using the available information to simulate the operation's three busiest days to determine the maximum staff necessary to provide trail guidance.

The results of the simulation are provided in Table 14-13.

Using a 7:30 a.m. to 5:00 p.m. work schedule with $\frac{1}{2}$ hour for lunch, it is evident that at least two trail guides will be necessary. Table 14-13 indicates that guide 1 and guide 2 are busy approximately the same amount of time. The decision to hire a third guide hinges on the amount of time that a group must wait with two guides. Table 14-13 shows that for the 3-day period, only 10 of the 53 groups, 19 percent, were required to wait for a guide. Of these groups, none was required to wait more than 20 minutes. Based upon these observations, the Planning Division concludes that there is ample justification for employing two full-time guides, but a third guide is not warranted at this time.

Table 14-11 Distribution for naturalist group trail selection

a.m.			p.m.		
Trail	Probability	Random numbers	Trail	Probability	Random numbers
A	.11	01–11	*A*	—	—
B	.29	12–40	*B*	.50	01–50
C	.11	41–51	*C*	.16	51–66
D	.11	52–62	*D*	.16	67–82
E	.28	63–90	*E*	—	—
F	.05	91–95	*F*	—	—
G	.05	96–00	*G*	.18	83–00

Table 14-12 Mean guide round-trip travel time by trail

Trail	*A*	*B*	*C*	*D*	*E*	*F*	*G*
Mean travel time (minutes)	25	60	20	50	55	65	20

UNIVERSITY FACULTY POLICY PLANNING: AN APPLICATION[11]

In universities and colleges, next year's faculty will differ only slightly from this year's faculty. It is these slight year-to-year differences, however, that provide the opportunity for

Maintaining faculty vitality
Developing new academic initiatives
Maintaining economic viability

in the face of

Inflation and recession
Declining birthrates
Possible changing attitudes toward higher education

The policy-oriented planning model allows the various constituencies in an academic institution (including administrators, planners, and faculty groups) to evaluate the effects of present and proposed policies on their institution's long-term future and to select those policies that will result in shaping the composition of faculty to meet the institution's objectives.

In brief, six interrelated policy variables can be controlled directly:

Hiring, in terms of the rank, age, sex, race, and salary levels of new hires
Tenure, particularly the fraction of those eligible who are granted tenure
Promotion from one grade to the next
Retirement, including the option of early retirement and mandatory retirement ages
Salary
Substitution of part-time faculty for full-time faculty

As shown in Figure 14-5, next year's faculty is the same as this year's faculty except for the addition of new hires and the losses through attrition.

[11] This simulation model, presented in part here, was developed by Paul Gray and described more fully in "A Faculty Model for Policy Planning," Rep. M23, Center for Futures Research, Graduate School of Business Administration, University of Southern California, 1976.

Table 14-13 Simulation results

	Naturalist group	Random numbers for arrival time	Time of next arrival	Random numbers for trail	Trail selected	Service time	Time to start	Time to return	Trail guide
Day 1: Area opens 7:30 a.m.	1	97	8:10	65	*E*	55	8:10	9:05	1
	2	42	8:40	95	*F*	65	8:40	9:45	2
	3	75	9:10	01	*A*	25	9:10	9:35	1
	4	30	9:40	51	*C*	20	9:40	10:00	1
	5	94	10:30	05	*A*	25	10:30	10:55	1
	6	11	10:40	02	*A*	25	10:40	11:05	2
	7	77	11:10	70	*E*	55	11:10	12:05	1
	8	52	11:40	05	*A*	25	11:40	12:05	2
Half-hour lunch period	9	29	12:40	36	*B*	60	12:40	1:40	1
	10	13	1:00	63	*C*	20	1:00	1:20	2
	11	03	1:10	83	*G*	20	* 1:20	1:40	2 Wait 10 min for guide 2
	12	36	1:40	41	*B*	60	1:40	2:40	1
	13	00	2:40	07	*B*	60	2:40	3:40	1
	14	81	3:20	88	*G*	20	3:20	3:40	2
	15	77	3:50	86	*G*	20	3:50	4:10	1
	16	46	4:20	82	*D*	50	4:20	5:10	1
Area closes 5:00 p.m.	17	43	4:50	70	*D*	50	4:50	5:40	2
Day 2: Area opens 7:30 a.m.	18	88	8:00	18	*B*	60	8:00	9:00	1
	19	02	8:10	23	*B*	60	8:10	9:10	2
	20	83	8:50	42	*C*	20	* 9:00	9:20	1 Wait 10 min for guide 1
	21	90	9:40	62	*D*	50	9:40	10:30	1
	22	11	9:50	54	*D*	50	9:50	10:40	2
	23	98	10:50	94	*F*	65	10:50	11:55	1

	24	24	11:10	14	*B*	60	11:10	12:10	2
	25	96	12:00	67	*E*	55	12:00	12:55	1
Half-hour lunch period	26	83	1:10	18	*B*	60	1:10	2:10	2 (Due to lunch for guide 1)
	27	49	1:40	54	*C*	20	1:40	2:00	1
	28	24	2:00	35	*B*	60	2:00	3:00	1
	29	94	2:50	40	*B*	60	2:50	3:50	2
	30	75	3:20	65	*C*	20	3:20	3:40	1
	31	94	4:10	51	*C*	20	4:10	4:30	1
	32	65	4:40	37	*B*	60	4:40	5:40	1
Area closes 5:00 p.m.	33	05	4:50	69	*D*	50	4:50	5:40	2
Day 3: Area opens 7:30 a.m.	34	64	7:50	83	*E*	55	7:50	8:45	1
	35	34	8:20	71	*E*	55	8:20	9:15	2
	36	76	8:50	68	*E*	55	8:50	9:45	1
	37	55	9:20	38	*B*	60	9:20	10:20	2
	38	25	9:40	64	*E*	55	* 9:45	10:40	1 Wait 5 min for guide 1
	39	97	10:30	56	*D*	50	10:30	11:20	2
	40	41	11:00	05	*A*	25	11:00	11:25	1
	41	13	11:20	50	*C*	20	11:20	11:40	2 Lunch to 12:30
	42	34	11:50	71	*E*	55	11:50	12:45	1 Lunch to 1:15
Half-hour lunch period	43	74	12:50	36	*B*	60	12:50	1:50	2
	44	73	1:20	31	*B*	60	1:20	2:20	1
	45	66	1:50	19	*B*	60	1:50	2:50	2
	46	23	2:10	04	*B*	60	* 2:20	3:20	1 Wait 10 min for guide 1
	47	16	2:30	69	*D*	50	* 2:50	3:40	2 Wait 20 min for guide 2
	48	36	3:00	03	*B*	60	* 3:20	4:20	1 Wait 20 min for guide 1
	49	57	3:30	26	*B*	60	* 3:40	4:40	2 Wait 10 min for guide 2
	50	42	4:00	87	*G*	20	* 4:20	4:40	1 Wait 20 min for guide 1
	51	24	4:20	81	*D*	50	* 4:40	5:30	1 Wait 20 min for guide 1
	52	60	4:50	95	*G*	20	4:50	5:10	2
Area closes 5:00 p.m.	53	02	5:00	84	*G*	20	* 5:00	5:20	2 Wait 10 min for guide 2

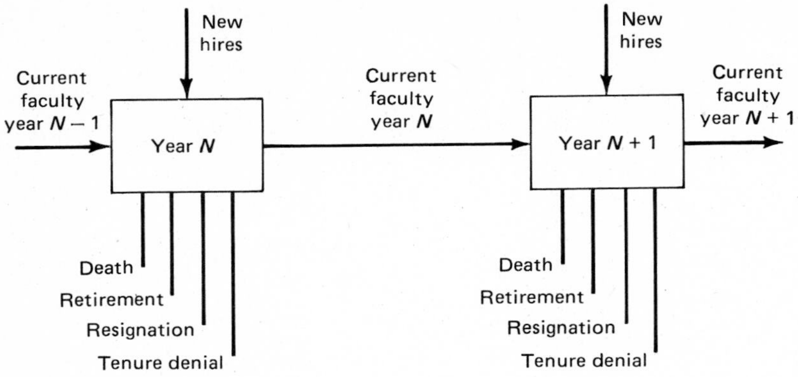

Figure 14-5 Faculty flow.

Losses result from death and resignation (uncontrollable) and retirement and tenure denial (controllable). In general:

Next year's faculty = continuing faculty + hires − terminations

As shown in Figure 14-6, the model requires two sets of inputs, one set representing the present and anticipated environment and the other the policies to be followed. The model traces the faculty through the environment according to the policies specified and produces statistics on the implications of these policies over the time horizon.

Policy Decisions

The policy variables are directly related to policy decisions. In executing the simulation, these are changed to represent different sets of planning policies.

Retirement policy is represented by the probability that an individual, who has not yet retired, will retire in any given year. Mandatory retirement at age 65 with no early retirement is represented by:

Age	60	61	62	63	64	65
Probability	0	0	0	0	0	1

One representation of early retirement is:

Age	60	61	62	63	64	65
Probability	.05	.05	.30	.10	.10	1

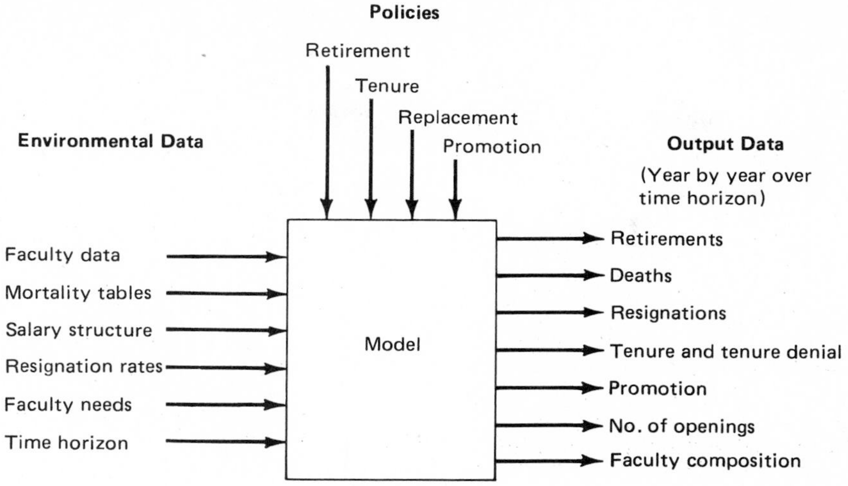

Figure 14-6 Basic structure of the model.

Tenure policy by rank is represented by the proportion of those eligible who are granted tenure. Hiring policy is represented by the probability distribution for the rank of the newly hired. Promotion policy is represented by the probability of an individual being promoted in any given year. Limits can be imposed including minimum and maximum number of years since tenure.

Environmental Factors

Some inputs to the model are not affected by policy decisions. The current faculty is described by age, rank, salary, sex, year of tenure or tenure decision, and department. Mortality tables provide the probability of death by age and sex. The time horizon is simply the long-range planning period; various values can be specified. Faculty size can be held constant or altered for expected growth or decline. Salary structure shows the annual increments and rank changes. It can be modified to reflect anticipated changes. Resignation rate represents the average percentage of faculty in each rank who leave for reasons other than tenure denial, death, or retirement. Salary structure and resignation are indirectly affected by policy decisions. Salary structure is controllable within limits, but it is considered a given rather than one of the policy variables. Resignation rate may be affected by significant changes in tenure policy; where this belief is held, the resignation rate may be adjusted.

A Comparison of Benign, Conservative, and Draconian Policies

To illustrate the uses of the model, consider the result of sample runs made under the assumption of constant faculty size over 10 years. Three policies, ar-

Table 14-14 Definition of benign, conservative, and draconian policies

Policy variable	Rank	Benign policy				Conservative policy				Draconian policy			
Probability of *tenure*	Professor	1				1				0.8			
	Associate Professor	1				1				0.8			
	Assistant Professor	0.75				0.25				0.10			
Probability of *quitting* in any year	Professor	0.025				0.025				0.04			
	Associate Professor	0.02				0.02				0.04			
	Assistant Professor	0.05				0.105				0.15			
		P	AP	aP	I	P	AP	aP	I	P	AP	aP	I
Replacement of vacancies	Professor	1	—	—	—	.25	.15	.60	—	.1	—	.9	—
	Associate Professor	.3	.7	—	—	.10	.25	.65	—	—	.1	.9	—
	Assistant Professor	—	.25	.75	—	.01	.05	.94	—	—	—	1.0	—
	Instructor	—	—	—	1	—	—	—	1	—	—	—	1
Retirement		Retire at 65				Retire at 65				Early retirement possible,* mandatory at 65			
Promotion from associate to full professor	Maximum number of Years in Rank	20				10				7			
	Maximum Age	65				45				45			
	Probability of promotion each year	.25				.08 year 1, 2 after tenure; .15 thereafter				.05			

* In technical terms, the probability of retiring at any age between 60 and 64 is .20, if not already retired.

bitrarily labeled "benign," "conservative," and "draconian" were assumed. These policies are defined in Table 14-14. The conservative policy is based roughly on historical experience. As indicated in Table 14-14, this school has tenured 25 percent of its assistant professors and has experienced an annual turnover of 10.5 percent in this rank. Associate professors have had an 8 percent chance of being promoted to full professor during each of the first 2 years after tenure and a 15 percent chance thereafter. No one has been promoted to full professor if more than 10 years in rank or over 45. Retirement takes place at 65. Replacements are principally at the assistant professor level, but a significant number of senior appointments are made.

In the benign policy, tenure becomes highly likely (75 percent). It is assumed that this policy reduces the assistant professor turnover due to resignation from 10.5 to 5 percent per year. Promotions to full professor are more rapid and have few restrictions. Replacements are typically made at the same level or at a higher level.

In the draconian policy, on the other hand, the situation is reversed. Tenure is awarded only 10 percent of the time. This policy is assumed to increase the annual resignation rate of assistant professors to 15 percent. Those appointed at associate or full rank are not assured tenure. Resignations at these ranks are assumed to increase slightly in response to the less pleasant environment. Early retirement is encouraged, and replacements are almost exclusively at the assistant professor level.

The purpose, then, was to compare the conservative policy's effects with the effects of "soft" or "hard" environments on the future of three different schools having between 110 and 140 faculty members. The results obtained from averaging five runs for school *B* are plotted in Figure 14-7. Four sets of data are shown in the figure:

Percent faculty tenured
Average faculty age
Average faculty salary (constant 1974–1975 dollars)
Total number of positions opened

In interpreting the plot of number of openings, we should recognize that the numbers are cumulative over the years and represent the number of people hired rather than the number of the initial faculty who leave. Thus some positions become open and are filled several times during a 10-year period.

Table 14-15 shows the potential spread of each of the four variables in 1984–1985 for the three schools. Data are presented for all three policies, and 1974–1975 values are recorded for comparison. The lowest and highest value observed in five runs are listed together with the average of these five runs to indicate the range of outcomes that can be anticipated.

Although Figure 14-7 refers specifically to school *B*, the trends are similar for the other two schools analyzed. First, the "conservative" policy does quite well in creating a sizable number of new positions, keeping the faculty

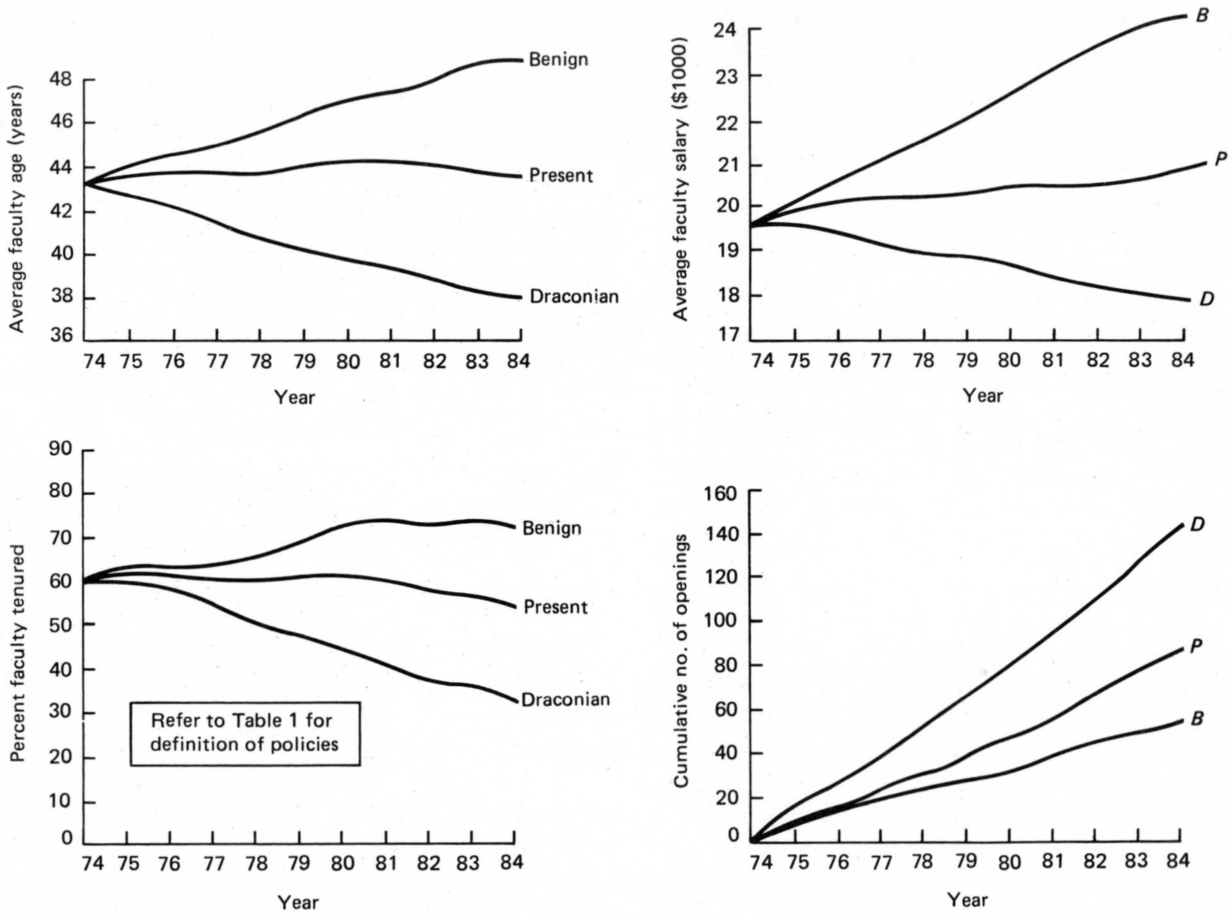

Figure 14-7 Anticipated faculty composition under three policies, school *B*.

Table 14-15 Range of variables in 1984–1985

School	Variable	1974–1975 actual	Benign Low	Benign Avg	Benign High	Conservative Low	Conservative Avg	Conservative High	Draconian Low	Draconian Avg	Draconian High
A	Total number of openings		40	44.6	48	67	82	91	122	128	133
	Total faculty cost	1872	2298	2310	2349	1904	1956	2021	1728	1766	1801
	Avg faculty age	43.3	48.7	49.1	49.5	47.4	43.3	44.4	37.5	38.6	39.4
	% tenured	55.0	71.0	75.2	79.0	51.0	56.2	63.0	29.0	34.2	37.0
B	Total number of openings		51	54	62	81	86	91	132	144	152
	Total faculty cost	2220	2740	2751	2774	2301	2348	2374	1936	2017	2090
	Avg faculty age	43.1	48.2	48.4	48.6	42.6	43.2	43.9	36.9	37.7	30.1
	% tenured	61.2	68.1	72.0	76.1	50.4	53.6	56.6	25.7	31.7	39.8
C	Total number of openings		52	61	70	112	116	119	165	179	181
	Total faculty cost	2416	2912	2951	2976	2414	2446	2494	2082	2132	2207
	Avg faculty age	40.9	45.9	46.4	47.0	40.6	40.9	41.7	36.2	37.1	38.1
	% tenured	53.0	68.6	73.3	75.7	46.4	49.9	52.9	30.0	32.1	34.3

Notes: Total number of openings are cumulative between 1975–1976 and 1984–1985. Faculty cost in thousands of dollars. Based on data from five replications. Faculty sizes are: school *A*, 110; school *B*, 113; school *C*, 140.

from aging, and keeping costs relatively level in constant dollar terms. The policy actually reduces the fraction tenured by 8 percent, mostly because 13 retirements are anticipated. A draconian policy would reduce faculty age and salary costs and would create an average of six more openings per year. As is to be expected, a benign policy has the opposite effect since more of the present faculty stay. Therefore, there are fewer hiring opportunities, and the average age, percent tenured, and cost/faculty all increase. Almost the entire faculty become full professors. The cost increases are quite significant for a 10-year horizon. For example, the total cost for faculty salaries in school *B* would increase by $530,000 in constant dollar terms.

Early retirement, which is introduced in the draconian policy, generates few additional openings. The principal effect of instituting early retirement appears to be that a few additional positions become vacant in the immediate future, but thereafter the system is in equilibrium and no additional gain in additional positions is obtained.

Perhaps the most intriguing result is that, under steady-state conditions, the conservative policy was able to generate an 8 percent annual turnover. This means that over a 5-year period there is a 40 percent turnover, certainly enough for a school to undertake major initiatives over a relatively short period of time.

The model was further employed in a sensitivity analysis to determine the relative importance of the individual policy variables. Further model modifications considered the effects of hiring females in and above the proportion in the availability pool and the effects of changing faculty size. None of these extensions is within our intent of merely introducing the model.

SUMMARY

Simulation is a process whereby relevant features of a system are included in a model which imitates the real system in some way.

Cognitive simulation is an attempt to get machines to match human problem-solving behavior. Artificial intelligence attempts to build machines capable of intelligent behavior without necessarily simulating human behavior. Both are still in the formative stage.

Heuristic programming is a collection of workable successful heuristics, or rules of thumb. Such methods are used when analytic methods are either inapplicable or impractical; they aim at finding a satisfactory but not necessarily optimal solution. Since heuristic programs are usually developed for a particular type of problem, they are not as broadly applicable as analytic methods.

System simulation refers to large-scale complex simulation models. Urban dynamics is a conceptual application of systems dynamics which models a system by describing the relationships among the systems boundary, feedback loops, levels and rates, and rate components.

A stochastic model identifies probabilistic components of a system, determines the probability distributions for such components, and then simulates events by using random numbers that reflect the probabilities. This is referred to as the Monte Carlo method.

In this chapter we have suggested a few different application areas for which simulation may be appropriate. Taking into account the advantages and disadvantages of simulation, we have placed simulation in the context of the decision process. The Monte Carlo method was described in some detail using a hospital emergency room as a simple example. Applications exist in many fields; the chapter concludes with models of police patrol, forest management, and university planning.

BIBLIOGRAPHY

Angel, R. D., R. N. Caudle, and A. Whinston: "Computer-Assisted School Bus Scheduling," *Management Science,* vol. 18, no. 6, 1972, pp. B279–288.

Blewett, F., D. M. Grove, A. Massinas, J. M. Norman, and K. M. Southern: "Computer Simulation Models for a Multi-Specialty Ward," *Operational Research Quarterly,* vol. 23, June 1972, pp. 139–149.

Bodin, Lawrence D., T. Owen Carroll, Allen Lee, and Sally Stout: "Financing Mental Health Services in the State of New York," *Operations Research,* vol. 20, September–October 1972, pp. 942–954.

Choralas, Dimitris M.: *System and Simulation,* Academic Press, New York, 1965.

Davis, Otto A., and Frederick H. Rueter: "A Simulation of Municipal Zoning Decisions," *Management Decisions,* vol. 19, December 1972, pp. 39–77.

Drake, Alvin W., Ralph L. Keeney, and Philip M. Morse (eds.): *Analysis of Public Systems,* The M.I.T. Press, Cambridge, Mass., 1972.

Dreyfus, Hubert L.: *What Computers Can't Do,* Harper & Row, Publishers, New York, 1972.

Emshoff, James R., and Roger L. Sisson: *Design and Use of Computer Simulation Models,* McMillan Co., Ltd., London, 1970.

Forrester, Jay W.: *Industrial Dynamics,* The M.I.T. Press, Cambridge, Mass., 1961.

———: *Urban Dynamics,* The M.I.T. Press, Cambridge, Mass., 1969.

———: *World Dynamics,* The M.I.T. Press, Cambridge, Mass., 1971.

Frerichs, Ralph R., and Joan Prawon: "A Computer Simulation Model for the Control of Rabies in an Urban Area of Colombia," *Management Science,* vol. 22, December 1975, pp. 411–421.

Geoffrion, A. M., J. S. Dyer, and A. Feinberg: "An Interactive Approach for Multi-Criterion Optimization, with an Application to the Operation of an Academic Department," *Management Science,* vol. 19, December 1972, pp. 357–368.

Goldberg, Michael A.: "Simulation, Synthesis and Urban Public Decision-Making," *Management Science,* vol. 20, December 1973, pp. 629–643.

Gordon, Geoffrey: *System Simulation,* Prentice-Hall, Inc., Englewood Cliffs, N. J., 1969.

———: *The Application of GPSSV to Discrete System Simulation,* Prentice-Hall, Inc., Englewood Cliffs, N.J., 1975.

Gray, Paul: "A Faculty Model for Policy Planning," Rep. M23, Center for Futures Research, Graduate School of Business Administration, University of Southern California, 1976.

Guthrie, Harold W.: 'Microanalytic Simulation Modeling for Evaluation of Public Policy," *Urban Affairs Quarterly,* vol. 7, June 1972, pp. 403–418.

Hamilton, H. R., et al.: *Systems Simulation for Regional Analysis,* The M.I.T. Press, Cambridge, Mass., 1969.

Harnden, Boyd M., P. Michael Maher, and Gregory A. Martin: "Forest Fire Detection Systems Design," *Management Science,* vol. 20, December 1973, pp. 617–628.

Hershey, John C., William J. Abernathy, and Nicholas Baloff: "Comparison of Nurse Allocation Policies: A Monte Carlo Model," *Decision Sciences,* vol. 5, January 1974, pp. 58–72.

Kate, A. Ten: "A Comparison between Two Kinds of Decentralized Optimality Conditions in Nonconvex Programming," *Management Science,* vol. 18, August 1972, pp. 734–743.

Kilpatrick, Kerry E., Richard S. Mackenzie, and Allen G. Delaney: "Expanded-function Auxiliaries in General Dentistry: A Computer Simulation," *Health Services Research,* vol. 7, Winter 1972, pp. 288–300.

Kolesar, Peter, and W. E. Walker: "An Algorithm for the Dynamic Relocation of Fire Companies," *Operations Research,* vol. 22, March–April 1974, pp. 249–274.

Kuzdroll, Paul J., N. K. Kwak, and Homer H. Schmitz: "The Monte Carlo Simulation of Operating-Room and Recovery-Room Usage," *Operations Research,* vol. 22, March–April 1974, pp. 434–440.

Kwak, N. K., P. J. Kuzdrall, and Homer H. Schmitz: "The GPSS Simulation of Scheduling Policies for Surgical Patients," *Management Science,* vol. 22, no. 9, 1976, pp. 982–989.

Larson, Richard C.: *Urban Police Patrol Analysis,* The M.I.T. Press, Cambridge, Mass., 1972.

Lutz, R. R., M. D. Devine, H. J. Kumin, and W. C. Smith: "An Application of Operations Research to School Desegregation," *Management Science,* vol. 19, December 1972, pp. 17–26.

Mass, Nathaniel J. (ed.): *Readings in Urban Dynamics,* The M.I.T. Press, Cambridge, Mass., 1974.

Meadows, B. H., et al.: *The Limits to Growth,* Universe Books, New York, 1972.

Mesarovic, M., and E. Pestel: *Mankind at the Turning Point,* E. P. Dutton/Reader's Digest Press, New York, 1974.

Nolan, Richard L., and Michael G. Sovereign: "A Recurursive Optimization and Simulation Approach to Analysis with an Application to Transportation Systems," *Management Science,* vol. 18, August 1972, pp. 676–690.

Perkins, William C., and Paul E. Paschke: "A Simulation Model of the Higher Education System of a State," *Decision Sciences,* vol. 4, April 1973, pp. 194–215.

Rabinowitz, Manus: "Blood Bank Inventory Policies: A Computer Simulation," *Health Services Research,* vol. 8, Winter 1973, pp. 271–282.

Raser, John R.: *Simulation and Society: An Exploration of Scientific Gaming,* Allyn & Bacon, Inc., Boston, 1969.

Sackman, Morris: "Make Your Own Simulations to Train Public Managers in Collective Bargaining," *Public Personnel Management,* vol. 4, July–August 1975, pp. 231–237.

Sass, Margo A., and William D. Wilkinson, eds.: *Computer Augmentation of Human Reasoning,* Spartan Books, Inc., Washington, D.C., 1965.

Schmitz, Homer H., and N. K. Kwak: "Monte Carlo Simulation of Operating-Room and Recovery-Room Usage," *Operations Research,* vol. 20, November–December 1972, pp. 1171–1180.

Shuman, Larry J., C. Patrick Hardwick, and Geoge A. Huber: "Location of Ambulatory Care Centers in a Metropolitan Area," *Health Services Research,* vol. 8, Summer 1973, pp. 121–138.

Smith, V. Kerry, David B. Webster, and Norman A. Heck: "A Prototype Simulation Model of a Wilderness Area," *Operational Research Quarterly,* vol. 25, December 1974, pp. 529–539.

Thoreson, I., and J. Littschwager: "Legislative Districting by Computer Simulation," *Behavioral Science,* vol. 12, 1967, pp. 237–247.

Uyeno, Dean H.: "Health Manpower Systems: An Application of Simulation to the Design of Primary Health Care Teams," *Management Science,* vol. 20, February 1974, pp. 981–989.

Vora, Jay A.: "Heuristics and Optimizing Techniques Applied to Long Range Facility Planning for Hospital Ancillary Departments," *Management Science,* vol. 21, December 1974, pp. 409–417.

EXERCISES

Extension of chapter examples

14-1 The hospital emergency room example (see p. 340) simulated only 8 hours. Assume the arrival rate is appropriate around the clock. Continue the simulation for the remainder of a 24-hour day.

(*a*) What pattern did you choose for selecting random numbers?

(*b*) What are the summary system characteristics? (Use the same ones used in summarizing the system on p. 345.)

(*c*) Compare the system characteristics with those of the 8-hour simulation.

(*d*) Compare your results with the results of others who may have used different random number selection strategies. What does this suggest about the use of simulation?

14-2 In the hospital emergency room simulation in the chapter, two physicians were on duty in the emergency room. Repeat the simulation using the same set of random numbers, for the emergency room in which there is one on-duty physician and a second physician who will be called when there are three patients in the waiting room.

(*a*) Execute the simulation for 8 hours, and for 24 hours.

(*b*), (*c*) Answer questions *b* and *c* of problem 14-1.

(*d*) Compare the two sets of results in the simulation experiment; recommend one of the alternatives. Using the same set of random numbers for the two alternatives is similar to a controlled experiment in which "other factors" are held constant.

14-3 Refer to Table 14-7. The next patient would arrive at time = 480. If we arbitrarily choose to include that patient in the analysis, what is the effect on the summary statistics? (From Table 14-6, the three random numbers for that patient are 05, 13, 03.)

14-4 Refer to the National Park management application on p. 353.

(*a*) Based on Table 14-10, what is the average arrival rate?

(*b*) Based on Tables 14-11 and 14-12, what is the mean service rate?

(*c*) Assuming there are two guides, and based on parts *a* and *b*, what is the average utilization?

(*d*) Based on the simulation in Table 14-13, what is the average utilization?

(*e*) Comment on the relationship between part *c* and part *d*.

(*f*) Can this kind of comparison be used in establishing internal validity? External validity?

Other applications

14-5 It frequently happens that after a problem has been formulated as an analytic model, a short-cut or heuristic is identified. Refer to the linear program formulation of exercise 8-10.

A heuristic for allocating the accident prevention budget might simply apply the maximum allowable amount to the most cost-effective alternative, then to the second most cost-effective, and so forth. Determine the specific allocations of the $220,000 budget on the basis of the heuristic.

14-6 A project consists of seven tasks. The activity time for each task is a random variable, with the probability distribution as given in the table on p. 368.

(*a*) Draw the network diagram.

(*b*) Identify the critical path and expected project time on the basis of expected times. (Compare these with exercise 12-6.)

(*c*) Simulate the project, using random numbers to determine the task times. Find the critical path and project time. Compare with part *b*.

(*d*) Repeat the simulation four more times. Is the same path critical in all simulations? Compare the project times with the expected project time.

(*e*) Compare your results with those of others, and make a combined frequency distribution on project times. Discuss the frequency distribution with particular reference to the expected project time, and to the distribution based on the central limit theorem (Chapter 12).

Activity	Immediate predecessors	Activity time (days) Probability
A	—	1 2 3 .3 .4 .3
B	—	1 3 5 .2 .6 .2
C	*A*	2 3 4 5 .3 .5 .1 .1
D	*B, C*	1
E	*D*	2 3 4 5 .1 .1 .5 .3
F	*D*	1 2 3 .3 .4 .3
G	*E, F*	1

Project problems

14-7 Find a simulation model in your field of interest, from either a journal article or a report.

(*a*) Describe the situation, listing the main areas of uncertainty and the decision alternatives.

(*b*) Describe the model, listing the main entities of the simulation and indicating which are probabilistic.

(*d*) Do heuristics play a role in the simulation model?

(*e*) How long was the model run in simulated time or number of events? How was execution length decided upon?

(*f*) How was the model validated? How would you proceed in evaluating it?

(*g*) Present the major conclusions and recommendations resulting from the model.

CHAPTER
FIFTEEN
MANAGEMENT INFORMATION SYSTEMS

Decisions are made to leave things as they are or to alter them according to whether our view of "things as they are" agrees or disagrees with our view of "things as they should be." Our view of "things as they are" is derived from gathering information past and present, qualitative and quantitative, objective, subjective and impressionistic, that helps to describe it. For example, in driving a car, certain bits of data about the speed and direction of our own car, the speed, direction, and proximity of other cars, road conditions and prevailing speed limits are all used in our vehicle operating decisions. Other bits of data are received by us and discarded as being irrelevant; for example, the color of a nearby car is usually not used in making a decision. (There are exceptions, as when a large *red* truck is behind us.) Information is distinguished from data in that the former serves to influence decisions, often by reducing the uncertainty in a decision situation. The set of procedures that provides information in support of decision making is referred to as an *information system.* Decision makers have always had sources of information; an information system uses the sources and makes the information available to decision makers in an orderly and timely manner.

In driving an automobile there is no need for a complex system to provide the decision maker with needed and timely information. The automobile itself has an information system that provides the driver with the not immediately obvious but necessary information, such as fuel level, battery-charging status, oil pressure, speed, and engine temperature. It is usually up to the driver to seek information on the driving environment. Sources include radio traffic reports and citizen band radios monitoring travel and road conditions. In operating an airplane, however, more detailed and greater amounts of information about the vehicle and its environment are necessary if the decision maker, the pilot, is to make reasonable decisions. Accordingly, there is a more sophisticated information system that involves the airplane's own control system, the pilot, control towers at airports, and intermediate contact points. There are many decisions to be made in piloting the airplane; some are rather unstructured, including choosing the destination. Others are quite structured, including aeronautical corrections to maintain balance and proper direction. The information system is such that the pilot is provided with the information necessary to make the unstructured decisions, and the control system is provided with and uses information necessary for structured decisions without pilot intervention. For example, the balance control mechanism makes automatic adjustments to the bearing of the craft on the basis of current and desired craft posture, without requiring the pilot's attention.

Generally speaking, information systems can be simple or complex depending on the decision situation; they may provide information to the decision maker, make a decision, or generate a response on the basis of the information that is generated. (Have you ever received a computer-written letter concerning a charge account? That is an example of a response based on certain information.) In situations in which the information is derived in a complex way from raw data, or where the decision requires large amounts of information, or where time is a critical factor in providing information, a formal information system, often involving a computer, may be appropriate.

In this chapter we will consider what a management information system (MIS) is and present a few typical settings. After seeing an MIS in the context of the decision-making process, we will consider some of the benefits and some of the cautions in developing and using an MIS. Noting that both MIS and quantitative models relate to the decision system, we will consider how they relate to each other. We will conclude the chapter with an historical summary of the issue of privacy.

DEFINITION OF A MANAGEMENT INFORMATION SYSTEM

To speak of *a*, or worse, *the*, definition of "management information system" is sheer folly. A few definitions are presented here to provide a basis for the rest of our discussion, and to suggest a kind of consensus as to what really constitutes a management information system. Lucas (1978) suggests that

> An information system is an organized procedure which provides information to support decision making.

Schwartz (1970) defines it as a

> System of people, equipment, procedures, documents, and communication that collects, validates, operates on, transforms, stores, retrieves, and presents data for use in planning, budgeting, accounting, controlling, and other management processes.

Cougar (1968) says that the purpose of an information system is to

> Capture or generate all data pertinent to [an organization's] operation . . . process that data in the most efficient and economical manner utilizing management sciences to the fullest extent possible . . . produce precise and timely information as required by each level of management, for optimum execution of its functional objective.

The definition given by Dickey and Arya (1970) is

> An approach to information system design that conceives the . . . enterprise as an entity composed of interdependent systems and subsystems which, with the use of automated data processing systems, attempts to provide timely and accurate management information which will permit optimum management decision making.

The concept presented by Duersch (1968) is particularly appealing to the public decision maker:

> An information system provides management with the information it requires to monitor progress, measure performance, detect trends, evaluate alternatives, make decisions, and take corrective action.

Without suggesting that any one definition is inherently superior to all others, or that the various definitions differ in more than perspective and/or emphasis, we will take as our working definition the following: *A management information system (MIS) consists of the persons, equipment, and processes that provide for the flow of timely and relevant information in support of identifying and making decisions.* Some would suggest that "process" rather than "system" is the appropriate term for whatever is done to transform data into information, and to provide that information to the right people at the right time. Since the term system generally connotes a broader perspective than process, and since system is the term more commonly used in this context, we will follow convention. The purpose of an MIS suggests discussing the relationship of the information system to the decision-making process.

MIS AND THE DECISION PROCESS

In placing the various management science tools and processes in the context of decision making, we have generally associated the use of the model with one or two phases of the decision-making process. However, since we realize that the stages of the decision process are part of a continuum rather than a sequence of discrete steps, we realize that the use of a model has some impact on each of the phases. So much more is this the case concerning the role of an MIS in the decision-making process. Figure 15-1 depicts the relationship between a management information system and the decision process. In the intelligence phase, the decision maker becomes aware of a problem and gathers data about it. The data is processed, which may mean summarized, tabulated, compared,

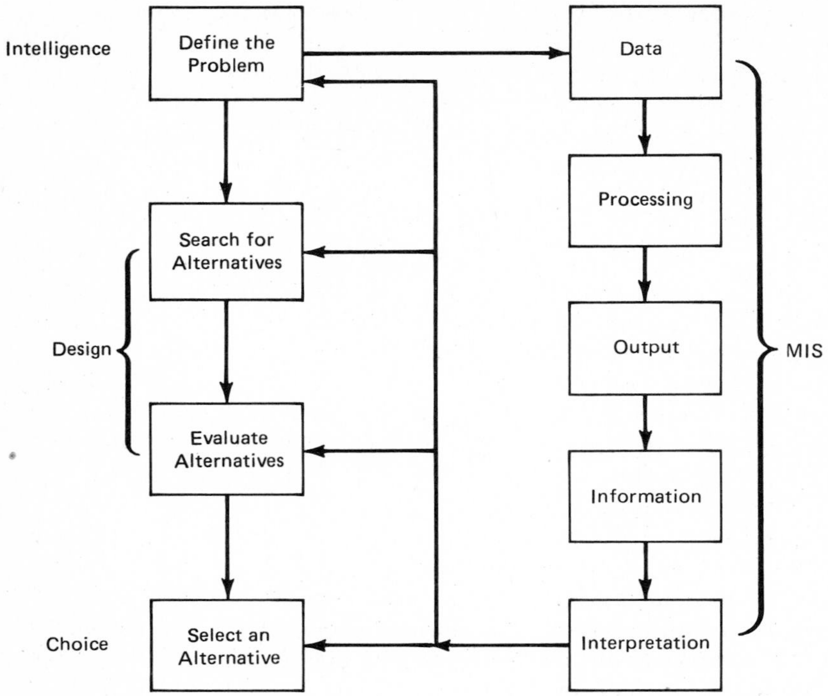

Figure 15-1 The relationship of an MIS to the decision process.

or projected—in brief, analyzed—and the processing yields results or output. When put in the proper context, the output is considered to be information. The information is interpreted by decision makers, advisors, and antagonists. Information and the ensuing interpretation have an impact on the problem definition itself by causing it to be revised or confirmed. Alternatives are found by considering the information about the decision situation and its environment, often accompanied by a good dose of imagination and intuition. Alternatives are evaluated by considering the projected impact of each alternative. If alternatives have been unequivocally evaluated, the selection phase is a simple one. However, information and the different interpretations that are made by interested parties do not always provide an indisuputable selection of an alternative.

Example Consider a claim made in the governor's office that the rising level of state welfare payments is a problem greatly in need of "solution." An analysis of the present welfare roles suggests that payment in the current fiscal year will far exceed budgeted amounts. Comparisons with last year suggest that next year's payments will be much greater than this year's. There are three different interpretations made of this information: (1) State unemployment problems have increased the number of people on welfare; (2) welfare fraud has become so prevalent that much of the increase is attributable to duplicate payment and illegal recipients; (3) the legislature passed the budget prior to and without taking into account new, higher legislated payment amounts. In order to take any meaningful action, the true problem must be identified. Moreover, it is possible that the correct interpretation is a combination of two or all three of the above interpretations. Other data and resulting information can help to shed light on the real welfare problem.

Most existing information systems relate to structured, or repetitive, operational decisions. This is not surprising since structured decisions are more easily understood and therefore more easily automated; furthermore, the day-to-day operation of an agency or department depends on many operational systems of one type or another. As more information systems are developed and implemented, more semistructured and unstructured decisions are addressed, and the application moves from operational decisions toward management decisions and strategic planning.

Many processes aimed at improving planning and management in government (for example, planning-programming-budgeting system, management by objectives, and program evaluation) depend on a good management information system for their own success. The relationship of the MIS to the decision process, and the impact of interpretation on problem definition, emphasize the need for the user of the information to be involved in developing the information system. Much has been written suggesting that user participation is essential if an information system is to be successful; Lucas sees the role of the user as so important that he argues that *the user should design the system* with technical assistance and guidance from the systems designer.[1] Our attention here is not to examine all the details of designing and implementing a management information system. Rather we will briefly describe the stages in the development and use of an information system.

MIS LIFE CYCLE

A management information system should facilitate the flow of information in support of decision making. There is no inherent need that computers be part of an MIS, but since many decision situations depend on a complex information flow, it is frequently taken for granted that computers will be part of the MIS. The computer system that supports the information system is comprised of various kinds of machines, *hardware,* and various sets of instructions, *software* or *programs,* that essentially tell the machines what to do. There are many

[1] See Henry C. Lucas, Jr., *The Analysis, Design, and Implementation of Information Systems,* McGraw-Hill Book Company, 1976, pp. 59ff; and Lucas, *Toward Creative System Design,* Columbia University Press, New York, 1974.

Table 15-1 Summary of the MIS life cycle

Considerations	Phases	Results
Definition of project Alternate approaches Scope and value of project	Analysis	Preliminary user specifications Development plan Management approval
Methods Mathematical models Equipment configuration Data requirements	Conceptual design	Assurance of feasibility Methods and techniques System specifications Management approval
Programs and documentation Manuals and procedures Equipment specifications Training methods	Detailed design	Operating procedures Computer programs Documentation Training program Management approval
Coordination of conversions System testing Correction of test problems Training schedules	Implementation	Tested system Trained personnel Conversion to new system Termination of old system
Equipment failures Personnel errors System logic problems New needs	Maintenance	Correction of problems Monitoring of compliance System improvements

books that describe information systems, some concentrating on particular aspects. The Bibliography for this chapter presents some fine examples. A thorough understanding of an MIS from either the designer's or the manager's perspective would require becoming familiar with a few such works.

From the identification of a need to the ultimate operating use, an MIS is developed in stages. It is not being suggested that these steps are discrete, and that one is completely finished when the next begins. Rather, the passage from one to the next is gradual, and the steps themselves may considerably overlap. Nevertheless, in one way or another these steps must be completed in the development of an information system. The five steps, summarized in Table 15-1, are as follows.[2]

1. *System analysis*. The rather general need which originated the project is investigated. The first step is to develop a concept with specific objectives and general boundaries; then users' needs are better defined and become requirements on the system's end product.

[2] The life-cycle view of system development is a frequently used one; see, for example, Don Q. Matthews, *The Design of the Management Information System,* Petrocelli/Charter, New York, 1976.

As the needs are better understood and various approaches are examined, the time constraints, the resources required, and the responsibilities will start to become clear. Here the value of the project and its likelihood of success are examined. ("Success" means the eventual use of the system to support management.)

2. *Conceptual design.* The system concept is subjected to detailed evaluation to determine the best methods to achieve the objective.

The goals were identified in the analysis phase; the methods to achieve these goals are developed in the conceptual-design phase. Each alternative method must be evaluated for its feasibility, precision, and economy. A main component of this phase is the logical flow; exposing errors and identifying missing links is an essential part. It is at this stage that the use of any models is considered, both for the development of the information system itself, for example, PERT or simulation, and for eventual use in the final MIS, for example, decision theory, linear programming, PERT, simulation, or other.

3. *Detailed design.* The results of analysis are expanded into a detailed design, and these design details are recorded.

This phase includes identifying hardware and needed facilities and developing computer programs with a description of exactly what the program does (called *documentation*); manuals and procedures which describe how the system is to be used and what it does; computer operating procedures, including special data handling techniques, emergency directions, and equipment failure procedures; and training materials to enable the system operators to understand the system's characteristics.

4. *Implementation.* The individual elements of the detailed design are produced, integrated, and collectively tested; then the system is placed into operation.

Probably the most difficult phase of the system life cycle, implementation, requires great coordination to recognize and correct the unpredictable problems that invariably occur. During the design phase, the various components of the system were tested individually; here they are tested as a single system. This testing should be done in as real an environment as possible. Correcting the system now is far easier than correcting it while the system is in operation and supporting day-to-day activities and decisions. The extent of testing can vary from running in a simulated environment, to actual use for an extended period (perhaps 6 months) while the original information system is still in place. The final stage of implementation, called *cutover,* is the start of actual operation of the information system in its real environment.

5. *Maintenance*. The useful operating life of the system covers several years and requires maintenance, evaluation, modification, and improvement.

No matter how much testing is done during the implementation stage, unexpected problems are bound to occur after the system is running. Each problem must be identified and corrected to prevent a decline of system performance. The first element in the system is data, which usually involves human handling. Therefore there is the possibility of introducing data not in compliance with system requirements. In such a case, either procedures have to be established to assure compliance or the system must be adjusted to accept the data in various forms. In the course of time, management will identify new needs to support new decisions; to support these decisions and needs, the information system will be improved. This *evaluation* of the system—determining whether the system is doing what is currently required of it—is an ongoing process that is sometimes identified as a separate stage in the development and use of an MIS.

Information systems have been around since man made his first decision. Purposefully developing such a system rather than permitting it to happen is the thrust of "information systems." Having an MIS should not be regarded as a cure-all for management's ills; nevertheless, a well-thought-out information system provides support for the operation of a program or organization. A few practical instances are presented in the next section.

MIS IN PRACTICE

With a new process or technique—or even an old process or technique with a new name—come two premature and false conclusions. The first is that the innovation will eventually prove to be absolutely useless and extremely expensive; the second is that the innovation will ultimately provide solutions for so many problems that it is cheap at any price. After some time, and often not too long a time, the newcomer follows its predecessors into disuse, amidst expressions of disappointment and "I told you so." The frustration generally is derived from two sources: the black box has been either oversold or underunderstood. As with other attempts to assist in the decision-making process, MIS has met with success and failure. One can reasonably expect a well-designed MIS to help alleviate a problem related to information flow. A situation described by social conditions and/or lack of resources is not likely to be improved by an MIS no matter how well designed, although it may help to understand the situation and thus indirectly contribute to improvement. For instance, an information system that is designed to reduce fraud in welfare payments has a reasonable chance at success. One that is set up to alleviate the causes of welfare is doomed to failure; and since any large-scale information system is expensive, it will be an expensive failure. As with any other undertaking, care must be taken to assure that the process at hand is appropriate for the objective in mind.

An information system can support various levels of decision making. Starting with the lowest level, and presenting some examples, they are:

1. Transaction processing, basically a clerical activity, which may be automated, for which little, if any, decision making is necessary; for example, posting tax receipts, and imposing a fine for late payment of taxes
2. Operational control, seeing that tasks are performed efficiently and effectively; for example, ensuring that arrests are made in accordance with policy and legal requirements, and short-term investing of idle municipal funds
3. Managerial control, often requiring the subjective judgment, using resources efficiently and effectively to achieve the organization's objectives; for example, assignment of staff in accordance with their capabilities and organization's needs, and decisions based on cost-benefit analysis
4. Strategic planning, choosing objectives and means to them, noting the relationship between an organization and its environment; for example, a land-use plan, and selection of sites in a new program.

We now present five MIS applications to show the varied areas of applications and the different levels of decision making that information systems can support.

A Fire Command System[3]

In 1971, the San Francisco voters approved an $8 million bond issue, $1.8 million of which was for a computerized fire command system. Prior to the installation of such a system, whenever an alarm was received, a coded bell sequence was sounded in every fire station. The location and the extent of the emergency, and the availability of the units, dictated which unit would actually respond. The actual response was determined at each fire house. Therefore, each watch officer had to monitor the status of all units and keep assignment rules for the entire city. This resulted in considerable delay and error, especially during busy periods.

The core of the new system is a dispatch center equipped with a radio console (for widespread communication), a microfiche unit (for storing very much displayable information), a video display computer terminal (like a television screen), and a specially designed keyboard (for entering requests and special instructions). The heart of the system is two medium-sized computers. The

[3] A fuller description of the San Francisco Fire Department's SAFER system (System for Assignment of Fire Equipment and Resources) can be found in Robert E. Rose, "A Computerized Command and Control System," *Fire Command!*, March 1975, and reproduced in Richard A. Bassler and Norman L. Enger (eds.), *Computer Systems and Public Administrators*, College Reading, Inc., Alexandria, Va., 1976, pp. 50–52.

computers' data files contain a geographic description of the entire city and routing information to every alarm box from the nearest fire station; it can be updated to reflect temporary street closures and hazard information.

A call can be received from an alarm box or a telephone. Telephoned alarms are handled as though they have come from the nearest fire alarm box, except that the address is forwarded to the responding commander enroute to the fire. The system controller enters the call into the electronic system, which then determines and displays the proper assignment. A dispatcher can either accept the computer assignment or modify it at his operating keyboard. When the dispatcher activates the assignment, an alarm is sounded in the assigned fire houses, while the station's teletype machines print emergency location, routing, and hazard information. The computer updates its own list of available apparatus, which is represented on a lighted board display in the central dispatch office. As units arrive on the scene the site commander reports to the dispatcher who feeds the information into the system. If warranted, the system will initiate the next higher level of response. It will also update a running incident status report that is visually displayed in the dispatch center. By constantly maintaining the level of need of each emergency and the status of each piece of apparatus, the system is able to generate accurate tailored responses more quickly. This problem, with its delayed and/or erroneous assignments, was one which could reasonably be addressed by improving information flow. By doing so, the new system enables the fire department to provide more effective fire protection.

A Criminal Case Management System[4]

The Massachusetts superior court consists of the Chief Justice and 45 associate justices, who are assigned on a modified circuit basis to sit in the state's 14 counties, holding criminal sessions in 19 different locations. With approximately 90 percent of the criminal cases being heard in the 8 most populous county courts, those courts are constantly active while the other courts have only two or three intensely active periods while criminal sessions are being heard.

Some undesirable symptoms became evident to the Chief Justice in 1969. Among them were: "a seven month delay in reaching trial, a growing case load, an exploding backlog, generally low productivity of court personnel, an apparent general lack of control, direction, or management of the court's operation, and an increasingly poor public image of the court and its role in the administration of justice."

[4] A more complete description of the information system can be found in Burton Kreindel and John P. Moreschi, "A Statewide Superior Court Criminal Case Management System for Massachusetts," *The Advocate,* Spring 1975, which was reprinted in Richard A. Bassler and Norman L. Enger (eds.), *Computer Systems and Public Administrators,* College Reading, Inc., Alexandria, Va., 1976, pp. 239–245.

The court-initiated study was determined to avoid two common pitfalls. One assumes that "automating" is needed primarily to do an existing job more efficiently, without taking the time to develop a basic understanding of the court's overall information needs. The result is often the "automation" of an ineffective system. The other approach is to bring in an outside expert to convert the court to automated data processing. With restricted funds, little understanding of the court problems, and little interaction with the court's managers, the results are either hazy concepts for information system improvement or rigid procedures for the court to follow. Either approach often leads to the generation of thick reports that go unused; the resulting system has little chance for implementation. The criminal case management system (CCMS) is the result of an orderly assessment of the court organization, functions, and responsibilities.

The new system concept was a computerized "information and communication system that would provide the court's operating personnel with the records, calendars, notices, dockets, and other data required for daily operation, using remote computer display terminals connected to a central statewide data base and computer. The system concept included many features that were simply impossible to accomplish under the overburdened manual system. Such features included time-of-day case scheduling; telephone reschedule capability; automatic production of jail lists; participant notification for every court appearance; conflict-free schedule dates; case information for assignment judges, including the number of previous continuances; preprinted data collection forms; and many other operational features." Utilizing the same data base, management received "listings of potential participant conflicts, reports of cases which exceed a predetermined case movement schedule, reports of excessive case loads for private or public defenders, prosecutors or courts, and many others."

Each participant in the criminal case process and each charge are tracked as the case moves from indictment to final disposition, with different necessary reports being provided to judges, probation and certain prosecution offices, and clerks of the courts. Thus, the system is designed to provide information while tracking a case through the court and to issue summary reports and management information while maintaining the selective use of the information by authorized personnel.

Automatic Car Locator System

In the preceding chapter we considered simulating dispatch strategies for assigning patrol cars to calls for police assistance. In that illustration we assumed only that a police car was in a given sector of a precinct; knowing the exact location of each car at each instant would not necessarily alter the dispatching strategy but rather would provide more information for the dispatcher to use in making an assignment.[5]

[5] A fuller description of automatic car locator systems can be found in Richard C. Larsen, *Urban Police Patrol Analysis,* The M.I.T. Press, Cambridge, Mass., 1972, chap. 7.

By means of a radar-type system or the use of signal transmitters and receivers, the location of each car is monitored. The amount of error in the location identification depends on the type of system used. The evaluation of such an information system can be assessed prior to its installation by simulating the control situation. While it might appear that having such detailed information should greatly improve the system's response to calls, simulation analysis concludes otherwise. For example, in a nine-sector precinct (similar to the one analyzed in the illustration in Chapter 13) the reduction in mean travel time generated by including the car locator system is generally not more than 20 percent, and considerably less than that when the arrival rate of calls is close to system capacity. The reduction in average travel time is accompanied by an increased number of intersector assignments. For the modest benefits, there are great system disadvantages.

Before embarking on such a technologically advanced decision information system, decision makers would very likely want to consider in greater detail its costs and benefits. A simulation model can sometimes help to predict the benefits. The system—as with any process aimed at supporting decision making—should be implemented or not according to its projected impact on decision making. An MIS is designed not for what it is in itself, but for what it can contribute to the decision process.

A Cooperative Urban Information System

Local and county government often believe they are too small to afford computer equipment for a modern information system. Decreasing equipment costs offer some relief, although it is only partial relief because personnel and other system costs are not decreasing.

Sharing the system and therefore the costs is another approach to the problem. Since local units' jurisdictions overlap, sharing a system helps to avoid much of the duplication in identifying data needs, collecting and analyzing data, interpreting information, and publishing evaluative information. Recognizing that such cooperation among governmental units has its own political and behavioral difficulties, we present a brief description of a cooperative venture.

Spurred on by two basic common needs, integration of research efforts and generation of local data necessary for policy decisions, the city of Wichita, Kansas, Sedgewick County, Unified School District 259, Wichita State University, and about 60 other public, quasipublic, and individual members supported an Interagency Research Committee.[6] The committee provided a framework for the coordinated activities.

[6] Richard E. Zody and Ronald E. Enlow, *An Operational Urban Information System,* Urban Affairs Paper 1, National Association of Schools of Public Affairs and Administration, Washington, D.C., December 1976.

The system was designed to address decisions at all levels:

1. *Transaction processing.* The annual county enumeration of residents by name, address, and age as required by Kansas state law; the mandated Sedgewick County annual dog census; legally required socioeconomic data
2. *Operational control.* Monitoring refuse collection; determining manpower needs; determining eligibility for rehabilitation loans and grants
3. *Managerial control.* Land-use plan and forecast; program evaluation; environmental impact studies
4. *Strategic planning.* Problem identification and need determination; goal setting and affirmative action programs; selection of sites and services for senior citizens

Without the cooperative venture, not only would there have been significant duplication of effort but much of the evaluative information would simply have been unavailable.

An Evaluation Information System: Mental Health Centers

As with most social service agencies, community mental health centers routinely gather demographic, clinical, and other patient data. The National Institute of Mental Health has specified objectives for federally funded community mental health centers. A study group precisely formulated some of those objectives[7] that relate to admission, service delivery, and termination. Without requiring additional data collection, the group specified evaluative procedures for those objectives. Without discussing the details of the rationale or methodology, we present the objectives and evaluative procedures for two reasons: (1) to underscore the evaluative purpose of the system and (2) to show that the same data ordinarily used for summary and descriptive purposes can contribute to the management and planning functions.

The objectives and evaluative procedures are:

1. *Objective:* The center shall admit residents according to the needs of the population in the service area, without regard to ethnicity or socioeconomic level.
   Procedure: Determine the variations between the percentages of various ethnic and socioeconomic groups in the general population and the percentages of these groups in the center's population.
2. *Objective:* The various socioeconomic and ethnic groups should receive treatment according to their needs.

[7] For a fuller description, see Carole Siegel and Ann B. Goodman, "An Evaluative Paradigm for Community Mental Health Centers Using an Automated Data System," *Community Mental Health Journal,* vol 12, no. 2, 1976, pp. 215–227.

Procedure: Determine the variations among groups of patients in type and quantity of treatment received.

3. *Objective:* The client should receive continuous, nondisruptive care as long as it is therapeutically necessary.
Procedure: (*a*) Determine the proportion of clients who are no-shows and the variation of this proportion among groups of patients; (*b*) among terminated patients, determine the proportions of those who withdrew without notification and those who were unresponsive or for whom further care was indicated but unavailable.

Although most current information systems support transactions processing and operational decisions rather than managerial or strategic decisions, there is movement toward developing them for the higher-level decisions. Regardless of the level of the decisions, there are a few characteristics that every MIS should have.

CHARACTERISTICS OF AN MIS

If an MIS is to be effective in support of planning, evaluation, and management, it must possess certain characteristics:

1. It should be *selective* in providing relevant information to a decision maker. The image of a bureau chief receiving a 6-inch stack of computer printout as a monthly activity report underscores the need to provide the manager only with the information needed. If the needed information is buried in a stack of the irrelevant, it may just as well not be provided at all. This further suggests that *who* needs *what* information should be considered in the design of the information system.

   Example The chief administrator of a medical center should not be deluged with the occupancy pattern of each department within the hospital. His or her needs would be better served by exception reports, such as a summary of the departments consistently underutilized.

2. The MIS should be *integrated* so that various interacting departments, and levels within departments, are considered in relation to each other.

   Example The decision of the Department of Transportation to repave certain streets leaves something to be desired when the Sewer Authority is planning to install new pipes under those same streets in 3 months.

3. The MIS is *organization oriented,* matching information provided to a manager with the manager's responsibility and authority within the organi-

zation. This focus on organization needs can sometimes uncover elements of performance that have become no one's responsibility.

Example A professional degree program at a university may remain current by adding to its curriculum courses on new and relevant developments; there is usually a specific mechanism for tracking the faculty and administration approval of a new course. There may be a parallel requirement that courses not taught for a certain number of years should be deleted from the list of available courses. Designing an academic information system may identify the fact that no one has been charged with actually removing the course from the official curriculum or from the school catalog.

4. Ths MIS should *distinguish between planning and control requirements* within the organization. The two main features of this distinction involve time and organization. The control function of management may be served by reports covering relatively short periods and including such features as day-to-day use of facilities, number of program participants, and indicators of compliance with regulation. Such reports generally follow lines of organizational responsibility and authority. The planning and policy-making responsibilities, however, involve longer periods of time and involve expected changes in population characteristics, outside influences, and economic and social trends. Planning does not follow the organizational lines of responsibility and authority; rather it should cut across such lines.

Whether these properties characterize a particular MIS is not a yes-no question. These qualities are generally present, but it is the degree to which they are present that strengthens the support that the MIS provides the decision-making functions. Since quantitative models also support decision making, management information systems and models will meet in their supportive roles. How they might meet is discussed next.

MIS AND QUANTITATIVE MODELS

The transformation from data to information includes analysis of the data. The analysis can include developing models that represent particular decision situations. Here we will describe in brief how an information system might develop appropriate numerical quantities for use in some of the quantitative models that have been described earlier in this text.

MIS and Basic Probability

In most decision situations that use probability, and therefore in decision models that include probability values, past experience is relied on to provide relative frequencies, from which probability distributions are developed.

Example A personnel management information system provides hiring characteristics for each agency. Included in the information system could be a summary of employees hired according to sex, race, and age. Not only could each agency be compared to the state overall, but the system could include a statistical indicator to indicate whether such a history would be likely to occur by random chance rather than by bias or design. The indicator in turn could be used to develop management by exception reports that would identify those agencies whose staffs differ greatly from what might be expected. The interpretation of this information should be that the exceptions are worth a closer look, rather than that there is something wrong.

MIS and Decision Theory

The probability of each of various states of nature is usually estimated on the basis of considerable information. The estimation of consequences of various alternatives also depends on considerable information. The information system that generates these estimates might very well include a way of combining and presenting them in summary form to the relevant decision maker.

Example In the gas drilling venture of Chapter 4, the likelihood of the presence of gas and the various economic consequences depend on extensive information from various sources. Some formal system is necessary to pull these together. A useful by-product of the system would summarize the estimates in tabular form and even apply various decision criteria. The information system and the associated decision model do not make the decision. Decisions are linked to the interpretation of information; the information system and the model provide part of the basis for various interpretations.

MIS and Linear Programming

Some decision problems lend themselves to formulation as a linear program. In that event, there are numerous constants that must be inserted as the program is being formulated. Some are inserted on the basis of some a priori consideration; for example, the objective function in the personnel assignment problem in the power inspection illustration of Chapter 8 has an objective function that is simply the number of inspections completed. Other constants in the linear program depend on data; the amount of time required to complete any kind of inspection may be arrived at by checking past records, and the amount of time available may come from personnel assignment records. In solving the ensuing program, the information system identifies feasible solutions and chooses the one that is optimal according to the specific objective function.

MIS and PERT

There are two distinct ways in which MIS and PERT can be mutually supportive. The first involves using PERT in managing the design and implementation of an MIS. Although the phases described earlier apply to establishing any MIS, each MIS is in some ways unique since the organization and its information needs are somewhat unique. Thus, each MIS development is a one-time-only project, the components of which are frequently encountered. Although the number and complexity of programs that will be needed in the design stage are not usually completely known in the analysis stage, using a project management tool even with coarse time estimates provides some basis for management and control. As the project progresses from the analysis to the design stage, more uncertainties will be resolved, better time estimates can be made, and a more refined PERT representation will be developed. This enables the MIS developers to shift resources, where possible, to those activities most likely to be critical.

The second way in which MIS and PERT are related is in the management of any project, whether it be building a roadway, floating a bond issue, or moving facilities. The management of the project requires that certain information concerning progress, difficulties, and constraints be accessible to management. The project management information system that facilitates the flow of information can at the same time compare the progress with preset mileposts. PERT, or an extension of it, can be built into the MIS and used to control the project.

MIS and Simulation

Simulations rely extensively on historical data to characterize the relationships among the elements of the system and to develop frequency distributions for probabilistic events. This set of historical data can be produced by an MIS. The MIS and the simulation can be tied together, so that the simulation uses the historical information generated by the information system.

The simulation is then executed for whatever controllable characteristics management predetermines. The results of the simulation are transmitted to management as part of the output of the information system. In effect this produces projected results which are then used by management in choosing an alternative.

The criteria by which simulation results are to be judged suggest—and may form—the bases for evaluating the real situation itself. The MIS must monitor those real criteria and report appropriately to the decision makers.

Quantitative methods and information systems together provide neither a style of managing nor a solution manual for decision making. When applied properly to appropriate situations, they assist in identifying problems, finding alternatives, and choosing solutions to be implemented.

Our concluding section will present an historical overview of privacy issues in information systems.

ISSUES OF PRIVACY[8]

To address the privacy issue in information systems, we will survey particularly relevant documents: The Freedom of Information Act of 1966, Fair Credit Reporting Act of 1971, The Federal Privacy Act of 1974, the proposed Comprehensive Right to Privacy Act, and the reports of H.E.W. Advisory Committee on Automated Personal Data Systems, The Domestic Council Committee on the Right of Privacy, and The Privacy Protection Study Commission.

Freedom of Information Act of 1966

The Freedom of Information Act of 1966, amended in 1974, requires each agency to make available to citizens its documents, manuals, staff reports, and indexes to data, on a quarterly basis. Defense secrets, trade secrets, and law enforcement records are among those exempt from this act, which was the first step in granting public access to government data.

Fair Credit Reporting Act of 1971

This act is the most significant piece of privacy legislation to affect the private sector. It was created to protect consumers from inaccurate or obsolete credit reports and to ensure that agencies conform to the requirements of the act. Under this act, consumers may review their credit file, correct or delete data, and make brief statements concerning their files.

This law applies to any person or organization that (1) provides written or oral information on consumers to third parties for fees or on a cooperative basis and/or (2) assembles or evaluates information on a consumer's credit worth, general character, or personal character.

H.E.W. Advisory Committee on Automated Personal Data Systems

This committee was formed in 1972 to "analyze harmful consequences that might result from automated personal data systems, and . . . make recommendations about safeguards that might protect individuals against potentially harmful consequences and afford them redress for any harm."[9]

The development of computer files on personal information and the ability to access them by remote terminals had caused concern with the record-keeping practices of the government and private agencies. It was this issue that the committee investigated. They were trying to determine the best way to balance the power between citizens' rights and the organization's record system. This balancing of interests led to a concept known as "mutuality," in which the

[8] The assistance of Greg Shawley in developing this section is gratefully acknowledged.

[9] This and the two subsequent quotations are from W. H. Ware, "Records, Computers and the Rights of Citizens," *Datamation,* September 1973, pp. 112–114.

committee defined privacy as ". . . procedures that afford the individual a right to participate in deciding what the content of the record will be and what disclosure and use will be made of the identifiable information in it. . . ."

The committee proposed five principles which define fair information practice as they relate to mutuality in record keeping. They are as follows:

1. No personal data record-keeping system is secret.
2. Means should be provided for an individual to find out what information is collected on him or her and its use.
3. This information is to be prevented from being collected for one purpose and used or disseminated for another.
4. There must be a way to correct or amend a record.
5. An organization must assure the reliability of the data.

The Domestic Council Committee on the Right to Privacy[10]

This committee was established in February 1974 to study individual privacy and the collection of personal data. It endorsed the recommendations of the H.E.W. Advisory Committee and suggested that no one bill should be enacted to enforce all the provisions suggested since balancing the privacy rights of the individual and the organization is quite complex.

They recommended legislation that would include confidentiality and security for:

1. Federal data banks
2. Criminal justice information systems
3. Tax information
4. Preemployment personal background investigations

The recommendations were for federal government agencies, but it was hoped they might be used for other levels of government and the private sector.

The council more recently suggested the creation of the Information Protection Agency.[11] This agency would be responsible for:

1. Developing a national information systems policy
2. Developing relevant legislation for both the public and private sectors
3. Monitoring enforcement of such legislation
4. Monitoring the proposed development of future systems to ensure they have appropriate information protection procedures.

[10] See D. W. Metz and G. B. Trubow, "The Complexity of Privacy," in Richard A. Bassler and Norman L. Enger (eds.), *Computer Systems and Public Administrators,* College Reading, Inc., Alexandria, Va., 1976, p. 65–66.

[11] B. J. Cohen, "Rights to Privacy: Can We Cope with the Issues?" *Financial Executive,* August 1977, pp. 26–29.

The agency would be assisted by an advisory committee with members from academic, local government, and private sectors.

The Federal Privacy Act of 1974

The purpose of this act is to provide safeguards for personal privacy for individuals against the federal government. The act provides the following:

1. It permits an individual access to information held about him by federal agencies.
2. It provides the chance to correct inaccurate material and supplement the data.
3. It places controls on agency dissemination of individual information.
4. It requires federal agencies to publish annually in the Federal Register a description of each system of records about citizens, uses of the records, storage, access, and disposal.[12]

The act also applies to recipients of federal contracts and establishes a Privacy Protection Study Commission to make a study of data banks, automated data processing programs, and information systems of governmental and private organizations.

William E. Porter identified technical ambiguities in the act, which may create litigation problems resulting from noncompliance with the act. The areas he identified as possibly being ambiguous were inconsistent and interchangeable usage of terms and omissions in making the agency liable for negligence.[13]

Some of the potential impacts of the act were fewer records kept, conflict with other laws, and increased cost. Officials said fewer records would be kept in the future and millions of existing records would be destroyed in order to assure agency compliance with the act. The law may also conflict with other acts or agency functions. The Privacy Act does not change the Freedom of Information Act, but it may require a court interpretation for disclosure of some information. The act may also conflict with the Federal Reports Act of 1942, which allows agencies to transfer among themselves information that was collected for one purpose and is to be used for another. It may also restrict use of personal data collected for program evaluations.[14]

[12] P. B. Demitriades, "Administrative Secrecy and Data Privacy Legislation," *Journal of Systems Management,* October 1976, pp. 24–29.

[13] W. E. Porter, "The Privacy Act of 1974: A Look at It from a Combined Technical and Legal Perspective," *Computers and People,* December 1976, pp. 10–13.

[14] R. E. Cohen, "New Privacy Law To Have Major Impact on Government Data," *National Journal Reports,* January 4, 1975, pp. 20–22.

Privacy Protection Study Commission[15]

The Privacy Protection Study Commission was an outgrowth of the Privacy Act of 1974. The mandate of the commission was broad, but its dominant task was to determine the extent to which the provisions of the Privacy Act should be extended to the private sector. It also examined confidentiality of federal tax records, mailing lists, the role of social security numbers, and federal agencies' compliance with the provisions of the Privacy Act.

In its final report, the commission's general overall recommendation was to maintain openness and fairness in record keeping. The commission concluded that (1) record keeping in government was very different from that in the private sector, and (2) the behavior of institutions and managers is very different from that in government agencies; consequently, a blanket omnibus law covering the private sector would be inappropriate. The detailed recommendations are a blend of fair information practices, limits on collection and disclosure, propagation of corrections, a restriction on the use of some items for decision making, a separation between certain types of records on the same individual, an emphasis on accuracy of record keeping, control of access on a strict need-to-know basis, disclosure of only the pertinent portion of the record for a stated purpose, and a number of behavioral constraints levied on the institution per se rather than on its record-keeping system.

Comprehensive Right to Privacy Act

This bill, purposely numbered HR1984, was introduced in 1975, and would apply the provisions of the Privacy Act to the private sector. Its positive aspect is that it would establish consistency in applying privacy legislation among the states in both the public and private sectors and on manual and computerized systems. Opponents of the bill say it would be extremely difficult and expensive to implement and would severely impede the operations of government and industry.

As of this writing, there is no comprehensive privacy legislation. The issues have not been resolved. By examining the legislation and reports of the various study commissions, we have merely identified some of the privacy issues closely related to information systems.

SUMMARY

A management information system is seen as the persons, things, and procedures that facilitate the flow of information in support of decision making. The system that processes data resulting in interpretable information relates to all stages of the decision-making process. The development of an MIS involves

[15] See W. H. Ware, "Handling Personal Data," *Datamation*, October 1977, pp. 83–87.

analysis, design, implementation and operation, and maintenance and evaluation. An MIS is appropriate in any decision-making environment; we have considered a few. A useful MIS is selective, integrated, and organization- and planning-oriented. An MIS is seen as mutually supportive of quantitative models—both are decision aids rather than styles of management or solutions to problems. A survey of legislation and study group reports provides an overview of the significant privacy issues in information systems.

BIBLIOGRAPHY

Ackoff, Russel L.: "Management Misinformation System," *Management Science,* December 1967, pp. 147–56. Reprinted in Efraim Turban and N. Paul Loomba: *Readings in Management Science,* Business Publications, Inc., Dallas, Texas, 1976.

Bassler, Richard A., and Norman L. Enger (eds.): *Computer Systems and Public Administrators,* College Reading, Inc., Alexandria, Va., 1976.

Bostwick, Gary L.: "Privacy of Personal Information: California Faces the Issues," *Public Affairs Report,* vol. 18, Feb. 1, 1977, pp. 1–6.

Brounstein, Sidney H., and Murray Kamrass (eds.): *Operations Research in Law Enforcement, Justice and Societal Security,* Lexington Books, Lexington, Mass., 1976.

Couger, J. Daniel: "Seven Inhibitors to a Successful Management Information System," *Systems and Procedures Journal,* January–February 1968.

Davis, Gordon V.: *Management Information Systems: Conceptual Foundations, Structure, and Developments,* McGraw-Hill Book Company, New York, 1974.

Dickey, P. M., and N. S. Arya: "MIS and International Business," *Journal of Systems Management,* vol. 21, no. 6, June 1970, pp. 8–12.

Duersch, R. R.: "Business Information System Design," Rep. 68-C-281, General Electric Company, Schenectady, N.Y., August 1968.

Eldin, Hamed K., and F. Max Croft: *Information Systems: Management Science Approach,* Petrocelli/Charter, New York, 1974.

Hoos, Ida R.: "Information Systems and Public Planning," *Management Science,* vol. 17, no. 10, June 1971, pp. B-658–B-671.

Kreindel, Burton, and John P. Moreschi: "A Statewide Superior Court Criminal Case Management System for Massachusetts," *The Advocate,* Spring 1975. Reprinted in Bassler and Enger: *Computer Systems and Public Administrators.*

Larson, Richard C.: *Urban Police Patrol Analysis,* The M.I.T. Press, Cambridge, Mass., 1972.

Lucas, Henry C., Jr.: *Toward Creative Systems Design,* Columbia University Press, New York, 1974.

———: *The Analysis, Design, and Implementation of Information Systems,* McGraw-Hill Book Company, New York, 1976.

———: *Information Systems Concepts for Management,* McGraw-Hill Book Company, New York, 1978.

Maier, J. E. et al.: "Drug Information Processing Concepts," in Sidney H. Brounstein and Murray Kamrass (eds.), *Operations Research in Law Enforcement, Justice and Societal Security,* pp. 89–98.

Maltz, Michael D.: "Privacy, Criminal Records, and Information Systems," in Sidney H. Brounstein and Murray Kamrass (eds.), *Operations Research in Law Enforcement, Justice and Societal Security,* pp. 247–262.

Matthews, Don Q.: *The Design of the Management Information System,* Petrocelli/Charter, New York, 1976.

Murdick, Robert G., and Joel E. Ross: *Information Systems for Modern Management,* 2d ed., Prentice Hall, Inc., Englewood Cliffs, N.J., 1975.

Rose, Robert E.: "A Computerized Command and Control System," *Fire Command!* March 1975. Reprinted in Bassler and Enger (eds.), *Computer Systems and Public Administrators.*

Schuyler, Howard: "Using a Social Service MIS in a Court Environment," in Sidney H. Brounstein and Murrary Kamrass (eds.), *Operations Research in Law Enforcement, Justice and Societal Security.*

Schwartz, M. H.: "MIS Planning," *Datamation,* vol. 16, no. 10, September 1970, pp. 28–31.

Siegel, Carole, and Ann B. Goodman: "An Evaluative Paradigm for Community Mental Health Centers Using an Automated Data System," *Community Mental Health Journal,* vol. 12, no. 2, 1976, pp. 215–227.

Ware, W. H.: "Records, Computers and the Rights of Citizens," *Datamation,* September 1973, pp. 112–114.

Welf, Ronald T.: "Designing and Implementing a Prosecutor's Management Information System," in Sidney H. Brounstein and Murray Kamrass (eds.), *Operations Research in Law Enforcement, Justice and Societal Security.*

Wendler, Clifford C.: "Where Are the Earmarks of Effective Total Systems?", *Systems and Procedures Journal,* vol 17, no. 4, July–August 1966, pp. 29–31.

Williams, Kristen M.: "The Use of Criminal Justice Information Systems," in Sidney H. Brounstein and Murray Kamrass (eds.), *Operations Research in Law Enforcement, Justice and Societal Security.*

Zody, Richard E., and Ronald E. Enlow: "An Operational Urban Information System," Urban Affairs Paper 1, National Association of Schools of Public Affairs and Administration, Washington, D.C., December 1976.

EXERCISES

Extension of chapter examples

15-1 Brief descriptions of five information systems were presented in the section "MIS in Practice." (See pp. 376–382.) For each system, identify:

(*a*) Some data that enter the system
(*b*) Some information that the system produces
(*c*) A decision supported by the system
(*d*) The level of the decision
(*e*) Is a different level decision also being supported?

Other applications

15-2 Assume you are taking a course at a college or university. At registration time you have to complete a number of forms. Some of the data that you record on the forms are necessary for the record-keeping operations of the college.

(*a*) What are some of these record-keeping operations of the college?

(*b*) The same or other data that you have entered on the forms may ultimately be used for the college's decision making. What are some such decisions?

(*c*) Who might be making those decisions?

(*d*) How might the data that you record ultimately be transformed into information for those decision makers?

15-3 Refer to exercise 12-10. Assume the ideal situation wherein the department implements a program only after it has prepared the program manuals and trained program maintenance personnel.

(*a*) Make the necessary changes in the list of predecessors.
(*b*) Make the corresponding adjustments in the project network.
(*c*) What is the new project time?

Project problem

15-4 Read an article or an agency report on MIS within your field of interest. Describe it, identifying the source of data, information needed, decisions supported, and whether any mathematical model is part of the system.

POSTSCRIPT

THE FUTURE OF ANALYSIS

The sophistication and acceptance of decision aids may change in the course of time. The presence of contradictory goals and conflicting demands will persist in a pluralistic and relatively free society. Public decision makers choose to consider or disregard information and models while applying complex value systems in a political environment. Long-range goals and objectives, although indeed appropriate, are not soon rewarded. The recommendations of analysis are tempered by the claims of the vocal public—minority and majority—and the omnipresence of the next election. This is the nature of public decision making. The future role of analysis has been well expressed by James Schlesinger:

> What then can systems analysis accomplish? The question is perhaps most relevant for the long run, since we must recognize the problem of transition. The qualities that make for a good analysis—detachment, breadth, interdisciplinary sympathies—do not appear like manna from heaven. It will take time to train an adequate supply of personnel and to produce good analysis. One cannot put new wine into old bottles. Even though the language of cost-effectiveness analysis is adopted by the agencies, one cannot expect a miraculous change of attitudes. At best, it will be years before analysis begins to have a significant influence in many agencies.
>
> Nonetheless, even in the shorter run analysis will serve an educative function. In ways that may go unrecognized, analysis will begin to reshape the way that agencies view their own problems. While the desire to preserve empires will not disappear, the concept of the agency's functions will undergo change. Perhaps this is the major accomplishment of analysis: it sharpens and educates the judgments and intuitions of those making decisions. Even when analytical drapings are employed consciously or unconsciously as a camouflage for prejudged issues, the intuitions will have become sharper.[1]

[1] James R. Schlesinger, "Systems Analysis and the Political Process," in Frederick S. Lane (ed.), *Current Issues in Public Administration,* St. Martin's Press, New York, 1978, pp. 364–365.

APPENDIX

Table 1 The cumulative binomial probability distribution $P(r \geq R$, for $n, p)$ for selected values of n

n = 4

r \ p	.01	.02	.03	.04	.05	.06	.07	.08	.09	.10
1	.0394	.0776	.1147	.1507	.1855	.2193	.2519	.2836	.3143	.3439
2	.0006	.0023	.0052	.0091	.0140	.0199	.0267	.0344	.0430	.0523
3	.0000	.0000	.0001	.0002	.0005	.0008	.0013	.0019	.0027	.0037
4	.0000	.0000	.0000	.0000	.0000	.0000	.0000	.0000	.0001	.0001

	.11	.12	.13	.14	.15	.16	.17	.18	.19	.20
1	.3726	.4003	.4271	.4530	.4780	.5021	.5254	.5479	.5695	.5904
2	.0624	.0732	.0847	.0968	.1095	.1228	.1366	.1509	.1656	.1808
3	.0049	.0063	.0079	.0098	.0120	.0144	.0171	.0202	.0235	.0272
4	.0001	.0002	.0003	.0004	.0005	.0007	.0008	.0010	.0013	.0016

	.21	.22	.23	.24	.25	.26	.27	.28	.29	.30
1	.6105	.6298	.6485	.6664	.6836	.7001	.7160	.7313	.7459	.7599
2	.1963	.2122	.2285	.2450	.2617	.2787	.2959	.3132	.3307	.3483
3	.0312	.0356	.0403	.0453	.0508	.0566	.0628	.0694	.0763	.0837
4	.0019	.0023	.0028	.0033	.0039	.0046	.0053	.0061	.0071	.0081

	.31	.32	.33	.34	.35	.36	.37	.38	.39	.40
1	.7733	.7862	.7985	.8103	.8215	.8322	.8425	.8522	.8615	.8704
2	.3660	.3837	.4015	.4193	.4370	.4547	.4724	.4900	.5075	.5248
3	.0915	.0996	.1082	.1171	.1265	.1362	.1464	.1569	.1679	.1792
4	.0092	.0105	.0119	.0134	.0150	.0168	.0187	.0209	.0231	.0256

	.41	.42	.43	.44	.45	.46	.47	.48	.49	.50
1	.8788	.8868	.8944	.9017	.9085	.9150	.9211	.9269	.9323	.9375
2	.5420	.5590	.5759	.5926	.6090	.6252	.6412	.6569	.6724	.6875
3	.1909	.2030q	.2155	.2283	.2415	.2550	.2689	.2831	.2977	.3125
4	.0283	.0311	.0342	.0375	.0410	.0448	.0488	.0531	.0576	.0625

n = 5

r \ p	.01	.02	.03	.04	.05	.06	.07	.08	.09	.10
1	.0490	.0961	.1413	.1846	.2262	.2661	.3043	.3409	.3760	.4095
2	.0010	.0038	.0085	.0148	.0226	.0319	.0425	.0544	.0674	.0815
3	.0000	.0001	.0003	.0006	.0012	.0020	.0031	.0045	.0063	.0086
4	.0000	.0000	.0000	.0000	.0000	.0001	.0001	.0002	.0003	.0005

	.11	.12	.13	.14	.15	.16	.17	.18	.19	.20
1	.4416	.4723	.5016	.5296	.5563	.5818	.6061	.6293	.6513	.6723
2	.0965	.1125	.1292	.1467	.1648	.1835	.2027	.2224	.2424	.2627
3	.0112	.0143	.0179	.0220	.0266	.0318	.0375	.0437	.0505	.0579
4	.0007	.0009	.0013	.0017	.0022	.0029	.0036	.0045	.0055	.0067
5	.0000	.0000	.0000	.0001	.0001	.0001	.0001	.0002	.0002	.0003

Example: $P(r \geq 2$ for $n = 4$, $p = .35) = .4370$.

Source: Thanks to Charles Jackson, Penn State University—Capitol Campus Computing Center, for developing this table.

n = 5 (Continued)

r \ p	.21	.22	.23	.24	.25	.26	.27	.28	.29	.30
1	.6923	.7113	.7293	.7464	.7627	.7781	.7927	.8065	.8196	.8319
2	.2833	.3041	.3251	.3461	.3672	.3883	.4093	.4303	.4511	.4718
3	.0659	.0744	.0836	.0933	.1035	.1143	.1257	.1376	.1501	.1631
4	.0081	.0097	.0114	.0134	.0156	.0181	.0208	.0238	.0272	.0308
5	.0004	.0005	.0006	.0008	.0010	.0012	.0014	.0017	.0021	.0024
	.31	..32	.33	.34	.35	.36	.37	.38	.39	.40
1	.8436	.8546	.8650	.8748	.8840	.8926	.9008	.9084	.9155	.9222
2	.4923	.5125	.5325	.5522	.5716	.5906	.6093	.6276	.6455	.6630
3	.1766	.1905	.2050	.2199	.2352	.2509	.2670	.2835	.3003	.3174
4	.0347	.0390	.0436	.0486	.0540	.0598	.0660	.0726	.0796	.0870
5	.0029	.0034	.0039	.0045	.0053	.0060	.0069	.0079	.0090	.0102
	.41	.42	.43	.44	.45	.46	.47	.48	.49	.50
1	.9285	.9344	.9398	.9449	.9497	.9541	.9582	.9620	.9655	.9688
2	.6801	.6967	.7129	.7286	.7438	.7585	.7728	.7865	.7998	.8125
3	.3349	.3525	.3705	.3886	.4069	.4253	.4439	.4625	.4813	.5000
4	.0949	.1033	.1121	.1214	.1312	.1415	.1522	.1635	.1752	.1875
5	.0116	.0131	.0147	.0165	.0185	.0206	.0229	.0255	.0282	.0312

n = 6

r \ p	.01	.02	.03	.04	.05	.06	..07	.08	.09	.10
1	.0585	.1142	.1670	.2172	.2649	.3101	.3530	.3936	.4321	.4686
2	.0015	.0057	.0125	.0216	.0328	.0459	.0608	.0773	.0952	.1143
3	.0000	.0002	.0005	.0012	.0022	.0038	.0058	.0085	.0118	.0158
4	.0000	.0000	.0000	.0000	.0001	.0002	.0003	.0005	.0008	.0013
5	.0000	.0000	.0000	.0000	.0000	.0000	.0000	.0000	.0000	.0001
	.11	.12	.13	.14	.15	.16	.17	.18	.19	.20
1	.5030	.5356	.5664	.5954	.6229	.6487	.6731	.6960	.7176	.7379
2	.1345	.1556	.1776	.2003	.2235	.2472	.2713	.2956	.3201	.3446
3	.0206	.0261	.0324	.0395	.0476	.0560	.0655	.0759	.0870	.0989
4	.0018	.0025	.0034	.0045	.0059	.0075	.0094	.0116	.0141	.0170
5	.0001	.0001	.0002	.0003	.0004	.0005	.0007	.0010	.0013	.0016
6	.0000	.0000	.0000	.0000	.0000	.0000	.0000	.0000	.0000	.0001
	.21	.22	.23	.24	.25	.26	.27	.28	.29	.30
1	.7569	.7748	.7916	.8073	.8220	.8358	.8487	.8607	.8719	.8824
2	.3692	.3937	.4180	.4422	.4661	.4896	.5128	.5356	.5580	.5798
3	.1115	.1250	.1391	.1539	.1694	.1856	.2023	.2196	.2374	.2557
4	.0202	.0239	.0280	.0326	.0376	.0431	.0492	.0557	.0628	.0705
5	.0020	.0025	.0031	.0038	.0046	.0056	.0067	.0079	.0093	.0109
6	.0001	.0001	.0001	.0002	.0002	.0003	.0004	.0005	.0006	.0007
	.31	.32	.33	.34	.35	.36	.37	.38	.39	.40
1	.8921	.9011	.9095	.9173	.9246	.9313	.9375	.9432	.9485	.9533
2	.6012	.6220	.6422	.6619	.6809	.6994	.7172	.7343	.7508	.7667
3	.2744	.2936	.3130	.3328	.3529	.3732	.3937	.4143	.4350	.4557
4	.0787	.0875	.0969	.1069	.1174	.1286	.1404	.1527	.1657	.1792
5	.0127	.0148	.0170	.0195	.0223	.0254	.0288	.0325	.0365	.0410
6	.0009	.0011	.0013	.0015	.0018	.0022	.0026	.0030	.0035	.0041
	.41	.42	.43	.44	.45	.46	.47	.48	.49	.50
1	.9578	.9619	.9657	.9692	.9723	.9752	.9778	.9802	.9824	.9844
2	.7819	.7965	.8105	.8238	.8364	.8485	.8599	.8707	.8810	.8906
3	.4764	.4971	.5177	.5382	.5585	.5786	.5985	.6180	.6373	.6562
4	.1933	.2080	.2232	.2390	.2553	.2721	.2893	.3070	.3252	.3438
5	.0458	.0510	.0566	.0627	.0692	.0762	.0837	.0917	.1003	.1094
6	.0048	.0055	.0063	.0073	.0083	.0095	.0108	.0122	.0138	.0156

n = 7

r \ p	.01	.02	.03	.04	.05	.06	.07	.08	.09	.10
1	.0679	.1319	.1920	.2486	.3017	.3515	.3983	.4422	.4832	.5217
2	.0020	.0079	.0171	.0294	.0444	.0618	.0813	.1026	.1255	.1497
3	.0000	.0003	.0009	.0020	.0038	.0063	.0097	.0140	.0193	.0257
4	.0000	.0000	.0000	.0001	.0002	.0004	.0007	.0012	.0018	.0027
5	.0000	.0000	.0000	.0000	.0000	.0000	.0000	.0001	.0001	.0002

n = 7 (Continued)

r \ p	.11	.12	.13	.14	.15	.16	.17	.18	.29	.20
1	.5577	.5913	.6227	.6521	.6794	.7049	.7286	.7507	.7712	.7903
2	.1750	.2012	.2281	.2556	.2834	.3115	.3396	.3677	.3956	.4233
3	.0331	.0416	.0513	.0620	.0738	.0866	.1005	.1154	.1313	.1480
4	.0039	.0054	.0072	.0094	.0121	.0153	.0189	.0231	.0279	.0333
5	.0003	.0004	.0006	.0009	.0012	.0017	.0022	.0029	.0037	.0047
6	.0000	.0000	.0000	.0000	.0001	.0001	.0001	.0002	.0003	.0004

	.21	.22	.23	.24	.25	.26	.27	.28	.29	.30
1	.8080	.8243	.8395	.8535	.8665	.8785	.8895	.8997	.9090	.9176
2	.4506	.4775	.5040	.5298	.5551	.5796	.6035	.6266	.6490	.6706
3	.1657	.1841	.2033	.2231	.2436	.2646	.2861	.3081	.3304	.3529
4	.0394	.0461	.0536	.0617	.0706	.0802	.0905	.1016	.1134	.1260
5	.0058	.0072	.0088	.0107	.0129	.0153	.0181	.0213	.0248	.0288
6	.0005	.0006	.0008	.0011	.0013	.0017	.0021	.0026	.0031	.0038
7	.0000	.0000	.0000	.0000	.0001	.0001	.0001	.0001	.0002	.0002

	.31	.32	.33	.34	.35	.36	.37	.38	.39	.40
1	.9255	.9328	.9394	.9454	.9510	.9560	.9606	.9648	.9686	.9720
2	.6914	.7113	.7304	.7487	.7662	.7828	.7987	.8137	.8279	.8414
3	.3757	.3987	.4217	.4447	.4677	.4906	.5134	.5359	.5581	.5801
4	.1394	.1534	.1682	.1837	.1998	.2167	.2341	.2521	.2707	.2898
5	.0332	.0380	.0434	.0492	.0556	.0625	.0701	.0782	.0869	.0963
6	.0046	.0055	.0065	.0077	.0090	.0105	.0123	.0142	.0164	.0188
7	.0003	.0003	.0004	.0005	.0006	.0008	.0009	.0011	.0014	.0016

	.41	.42	.43	.44	.45	.46	.47	.48	.49	.50
1	.9751	.9779	.9805	.9827	.9848	.9866	.9883	.9897	.9910	.9922
2	.8541	.8660	.8772	.8877	.8976	.9068	.9153	.9233	.9307	.9375
3	.6017	.6229	.6436	.6638	.6836	.7027	.7213	.7393	.7567	.7734
4	.3094	.3294	.3498	.3706	.3917	.4131	.4346	.4563	.4781	.5000
5	.1063	.1169	.1282	.1402	.1529	.1663	.1803	.1951	.2105	.2266
6	.0216	.0246	.0279	.0316	.0357	.0402	.0451	.0504	.0562	.0625
7	.0019	.0023	.0027	.0032	.0037	.0044	.0051	.0059	.0068	.0078

n = 8

r \ p	.01	.02	.03	.04	.05	.06	.07	.08	.09	.10
1	.0773	.1492	.2163	.2786	.3366	.3904	.4404	.4868	.5297	.5695
2	.0027	.0103	.0223	.0381	.0572	.0792	.1035	.1298	.1577	.1869
3	.0001	.0004	.0013	.0031	.0058	.0096	.0147	.0211	.0289	.0381
4	.0000	.0000	.0001	.0002	.0004	.0007	.0013	.0022	.0034	.0050
5	.0000	.0000	.0000	.0000	.0000	.0000	.0001	.0001	.0003	.0004

	.11	.12	.13	.14	.15	.16	.17	.18	.19	.20
1	.6063	.6404	.6718	.7008	.7275	.7521	.7748	.7956	.8147	.8322
2	.2171	.2480	.2794	.3111	.3428	.3744	.4057	.4366	.4670	.4967
3	.0487	.0608	.0743	.0891	.1052	.1226	.1412	.1608	.1815	.2031
4	.0071	.0097	.0129	.0168	.0214	.0267	.0328	.0397	.0476	.0563
5	.0007	.0010	.0015	.0021	.0029	.0038	.0050	.0065	.0083	.0104
6	.0000	.0001	.0001	.0002	.0002	.0004	.0005	.0007	.0009	.0012
7	.0000	.0000	.0000	.0000	.0000	.0000	.0000	.0000	.0001	.0001

	.21	.22	.23	.24	.25	.26	.27	.28	.29	.30
1	.8483	.8630	.8764	.8887	.8999	.9101	.9194	.9278	.9354	.9424
2	.5257	.5538	.5811	.6075	.6329	.6573	.6807	.7031	.7244	.7447
3	.2255	.2486	.2724	.2967	.3215	.3465	.3718	.3973	.4228	.4482
4	.0659	.0765	.0880	.1004	.1138	.1281	.1433	.1594	.1763	.1941
5	.0129	.0158	.0191	.0230	.0273	.0322	.0377	.0438	.0505	.0580
6	.0016	.0021	.0027	.0034	.0042	.0052	.0064	.0078	.0094	.0113
7	.0001	.0002	.0002	.0003	.0004	.0005	.0006	.0008	.0010	.0013
8	.0000	.0000	.0000	.0000	.0000	.0000	.0000	.0000	.0001	.0001

	.31	.32	.33	.34	.35	.36	.37	.38	.39	.40
1	.9486	.9543	.9594	.9640	.9681	.9719	.9752	.9782	.9808	.9832
2	.7640	.7822	.7994	.8156	.8309	.8452	.8586	.8711	.8828	.8936
3	.4736	.4987	.5236	.5481	.5722	.5958	.6189	.6415	.6634	.6846
4	.2126	.2319	.2519	.2724	.2936	.3153	.3374	.3599	.3828	.4059
5	.0661	.0750	.0846	.0949	.1061	.1180	.1307	.1443	.1586	.1737
6	.0134	.0159	.0187	.9218	.0253	.0293	.0336	.0385	.0439	.0498
7	.0016	.0020	.0024	.0030	.0036	.0043	.0051	.0061	.0072	.0085
8	.0001	.0001	.0001	.0002	.0002	.0003	.0004	.0004	.0005	.0007

n = 8 (Continued)

r \ p	.41	.42	.43	.44	.45	.46	.47	.48	.49	.50
1	.9853	.9872	.9889	.9903	.9916	.9928	.9938	.9947	.9954	.9961
2	.9037	.9130	.9216	.9295	.9368	.9435	.9496	.9552	.9602	.9648
3	.7052	.7250	.7440	.7624	.7799	.7966	.8125	.8276	.8419	.8555
4	.4292	.4527	.4762	.4996	.5230	.5463	.5694	.5922	.6146	.6367
5	.1895	.2062	.2235	.2416	.2604	.2798	.2999	.3205	.3416	.3633
6	.0563	.0634	.0711	.0794	.0885	.0982	.1086	.1198	.1318	.1445
7	.0100	.0117	.0136	.0157	.0181	.0208	.0239	.0272	.0310	.0352
8	.0008	.0010	.0012	.0014	.0017	.0020	.0024	.0028	.0033	.0039

n = 9

r \ p	.01	.02	.03	.04	.05	.06	.07	.08	.09	.10
1	.0865	.1663	.2398	.3075	.3698	.4270	.4796	.5278	.5721	.6126
2	.0034	.0131	.0282	.0478	.0712	.0978	.1271	.1583	.1912	.2252
3	.0001	.0006	.0020	.0045	.0084	.0138	.0209	.0298	.0405	.0530
4	.0000	.0000	.0001	.0003	.0006	.0013	.0023	.0037	.0057	.0083
5	.0000	.0000	.0000	.0000	.0000	.0001	.0002	.0003	.0005	.0009
6	.0000	.0000	.0000	.0000	.0000	.0000	.0000	.0000	.0000	.0001
	.11	.12	.13	.14	.15	.16	.17	.18	.19	.20
1	.6496	.6835	.7145	.7427	.7684	.7918	.8131	.8324	.8499	.8658
2	.2599	.2951	.3304	.3657	.4005	.4348	.4685	.5012	.5330	.5638
3	.0672	.0833	.1009	.1202	.1409	.1629	.1861	.2105	.2357	.2618
4	.0117	.0158	.0209	.0269	.0339	.0420	.0512	.0615	.0730	.0856
5	.0014	.0021	.0030	.0041	.0056	.0075	.0098	.0125	.0158	.0196
6	.0001	.0002	.0003	.0004	.0006	.0009	.0013	.0017	.0023	.0031
7	.0000	.0000	.0000	.0000	.0000	.0001	.0001	.0002	.0002	.0003
	.21	.22	.23	.24	.25	.26	.27	.28	.29	.30
1	.8801	.8931	.9048	.9154	.9249	.9335	.9411	.9480	.9542	.9596
2	.5934	.6218	.6491	.6750	.6997	.7230	.7452	.7660	.7856	.8040
3	.2885	.3158	.3434	.3713	.3993	.4273	.4552	.4829	.5102	.5372
4	.0994	.0114	.1304	.1475	.1657	.1849	.2050	.2260	.2478	.2703
5	.0240	.0291	.0350	.0416	.0489	.0571	.0662	.0762	.0870	.0988
6	.0040	.0051	.0065	.0081	.0100	.0122	.0149	.0179	.0213	.0253
7	.0004	.0006	.0008	.0010	.0013	.0017	.0022	.0028	.0035	.0043
8	.0000	.0000	.0001	.0001	.0001	.0001	.0002	.0003	.0003	.0004
	.31	.32	.33	.34	.35	.36	.37	.38	.39	.40
1	.9645	.9689	.9728	.9762	.9793	.9820	.9844	.9865	.9883	.9899
2	.8212	.8372	.8522	.8661	.8789	.8908	.9017	.9118	.9210	.9295
3	.5636	.5894	.6146	.6390	.6627	.6856	.7076	.7287	.7489	.7682
4	.2935	.3173	.3415	.3662	.3911	.4163	.4416	.4669	.4922	.5174
5	.1115	.1252	.1398	.1553	.1717	.1890	.2072	.2262	.2460	.2666
6	.0298	.0348	.0404	.0467	.0536	.0612	.0696	.0787	.0886	.0994
7	.0053	.0064	.0078	.0094	.0112	.0133	.0157	.0184	.0215	.0250
8	.0006	.0007	.0009	.0011	.0014	.0017	.0021	.0026	.0031	.0038
9	.0000	.0000	.0000	.0001	.0001	.0001	.0001	.0002	.0002	.0003
	.41	.42	.43	.44	.45	.46	.47	.48	.49	.50
1	.9913	.9926	.9936	.9946	.9954	.9961	.9967	.9972	.9977	.9980
2	.9372	.9442	.9505	.0563	.9615	.9662	.9704	.9741	.9775	.9805
3	.7866	.8039	.8204	.8359	.8505	.8642	.8769	.8889	.8999	.9102
4	.5424	.5670	.5913	.6152	.6386	.6614	.6836	.7052	.7260	.7461
5	.2878	.3097	.3322	.3551	.3786	.4024	.4265	.4509	.4754	.5000
6	.1109	.1233	.1366	.1508	.1658	.1817	.1985	.2161	.2346	.2539
7	.0290	.0334	.0383	.0437	.0498	.0564	.0637	.0717	.0804	.0898
8	.0046	.0055	.0065	.0077	.0091	.0107	.0125	.0145	.0169	.0195
9	.0003	.0004	.0005	.0006	.0008	.0009	.0011	.0014	.0016	.0020

n = 10

r \ p	.01	.02	.03	.04	.05	.06	.07	.08	.09	.10
1	.0956	.1829	.2626	.3352	.4013	.4614	.5160	.5656	.6106	.6513
2	.0043	.0162	.0345	.0582	.0861	.1176	.1517	.1879	.2254	.2639
3	.0001	.0009	.0028	.0062	.0115	.0188	.0283	.0401	.0540	.0702
4	.0000	.0000	.0001	.0004	.0010	.0020	.0036	.0058	.0088	.0128
5	.0000	.0000	.0000	.0000	.0001	.0002	.0003	.0006	.0010	.0016
6	.0000	.0000	.0000	.0000	.0000	.0000	.0000	.0000	.0001	.0001
	.11	.12	.13	.14	.15	.16	.17	.18	.19	.20
1	.6882	.7215	.7516	.7787	.8031	.8251	.8448	.8626	.8784	.8926
2	.3028	.3417	.3804	.4184	.4557	.4920	.5270	.5608	.5932	.6242
3	.0884	.1087	.1308	.1545	.1798	.2064	.2341	.2628	.2922	.3222
4	.0178	.0239	.0313	.0400	.0500	.0614	.0741	.0883	.1039	.1209
5	.0025	.0037	.0053	.0073	.0099	.0130	.0168	.0213	.0266	.0328
6	.0003	.0004	.0006	.0010	.0014	.0020	.0027	.0037	.0049	.0064
7	.0000	.0000	.0001	.0001	.0001	.0002	.0003	.0004	.0006	.0009
8	.0000	.0000	.0000	.0000	.0000	.0000	.0000	.0000	.0001	.0001
	.21	.22	.23	.24	.25	.26	.27	.28	.29	.30
1	.9053	.9166	.9267	.9357	.9437	.9508	.9570	.9626	.9674	.9718
2	.6536	.6815	.7079	.7327	.7560	.7778	.7981	.8170	.8345	.8507
3	.3526	.3831	.4137	.4442	.4744	.5042	.5335	.5622	.5901	.6172
4	.1391	.1587	.1794	.2012	.2241	.2479	.2726	.2979	.3239	.3504
5	.0399	.0479	.0569	.0670	.0781	.0904	.1037	.1181	.1337	.1503
6	.0082	.0104	.0130	.0161	.0197	.0239	.0287	.0342	.0404	.0473
7	.0012	.0016	.0021	.0027	.0035	.0045	.0056	.0070	.0087	.0106
8	.0001	.0002	.0002	.0003	.0004	.0006	.0007	.0010	.0012	.0016
9	.0000	.0000	.0000	.0000	.0000	.0000	0001	.0001	.0001	.0001
	.31	.32	.33	.34	.35	.36	.37	.38	.39	.40
1	.9755	.9789	.9818	.9843	.9865	.9885	.9902	.9916	.9929	.9940
2	.8656	.8794	.8920	.9035	.9140	.9236	.9323	.9402	.9473	.9536
3	.6434	.6687	.6930	.7162	.7384	.7595	.7794	.7983	.8160	.8327
4	.3772	.4044	.4316	.4589	.4862	.5132	.5400	.5664	.5923	.6177
5	.1679	.1867	.2064	.2270	.2485	.2708	.2939	.3177	.3420	.3669
6	.0551	.0637	.0732	.0836	.0949	.1072	.1205	.1348	.1500	.1662
7	.0129	.0155	.0185	.0220	.0260	.0305	.0356	.0413	.0477	.0548
8	.0020	.0025	.0032	.0039	.0048	.0059	.0071	.0086	.0103	.0123
9	.0002	.0003	.0003	.0004	.0005	.0007	.0009	.0011	.0014	.0017
10	.0000	.0000	.0000	.0000	.0000	.0000	.0000	.0001	.0001	.0001
	.41	.42	.43	.44	.45	.46	.47	.48	.49	.50
1	.9949	.9957	.9964	.9970	.9975	.9979	.9983	.9986	.9988	.9990
2	.9594	.9645	.9691	.9731	.9767	.9799	.9827	.9852	.9874	.9892
3	.8483	.8628	.8764	.8889	.9004	.9111	.9209	.9298	.9379	.9453
4	.6425	.6665	.6898	.7123	.7340	.7547	.7745	.7933	.8112	.8281
5	.3922	.4178	.4436	.4696	.4956	.5216	.5474	.5730	.5982	.6230
6	.1834	.2016	.2207	.2407	.2616	.2832	.3057	.3288	.3526	.3770
7	.0626	.0712	.0806	.0908	.1020	.1141	.1271	.1410	.1560	.1719
8	.0146	.0172	.0202	.0236	.0274	.0317	.0366	.0420	.0480	.0547
9	.0021	.0025	.0031	.0037	.0045	.0054	.0065	.0077	.0091	.0107
10	.0001	.0002	.0002	.0003	.0003	.0004	.0005	.0006	.0008	.0010

n = 15

r \ p	.01	.02	.03	.04	.05	.06	.07	.08	.09	.10
1	.1399	.2614	.3667	.4579	.5367	.6047	.6633	.7137	.7570	.7941
2	.0096	.0353	.0730	.1191	.1710	.2262	.2832	.3403	.3965	.4510
3	.0004	.0030	.0094	.0203	.0362	.0571	.0829	.1130	.1469	.1841
4	.0000	.0002	.0008	.0024	.0055	.0104	.0175	.0273	.0399	.0556
5	.0000	.0000	.0001	.0002	.0006	.0014	.0028	.0050	.0082	.0127
6	.0000	.0000	.0000	.0000	.0001	.0001	.0003	.0007	.0013	.0022
7	.0000	.0000	.0000	.0000	.0000	.0000	.0000	.0001	.0002	.0003

r \ p	.11	.12	.13	.14	.15	.16	.17	.18	.19	.20
1	.8259	.8530	.8762	.8959	.9126	.9269	.9389	.9490	.9576	.9648
2	.5031	.5524	.5987	.6417	.6814	.7179	.7511	.7813	.8085	.8329
3	.2238	.2654	.3084	.3520	.3958	.4392	.4819	.5234	.5635	.6020
4	.0742	.0959	.1204	.1476	.1773	.2092	.2429	.2782	.3146	.3518
5	.0187	.0265	.0361	.0478	.0617	.0778	.0961	.1167	.1394	.1642
6	.0037	.0057	.0084	.0121	.0168	.0227	.0300	.0387	.0490	.0611
7	.0006	.0010	.0015	.0024	.0036	.0052	.0074	.0102	.0137	.0181
8	.0001	.0001	.0002	.0004	.0006	.0010	.0014	.0021	.0030	.0042
9	.0000	.0000	.0000	.0000	.0001	.0001	.0002	.0003	.0005	.0008
10	.0000	.0000	.0000	.0000	.0000	.0000	.0000	.0000	.0001	.0001

r \ p	.21	.22	.23	.24	.25	.26	.27	.28	.29	.30
1	.9709	.9759	.9802	.9837	.9866	.9891	.9911	.9928	.9941	.9953
2	.8547	.8741	.8913	.9065	.9198	.9315	.9417	.9505	.9581	.9647
3	.6385	.6731	.7055	.7358	.7639	.7899	.8137	.8355	.8553	.8732
4	.3895	.4274	.4650	.5022	.5387	.5742	.6086	.6416	.6732	.7031
5	.1910	.2195	.2495	.2810	.3135	.3469	.3810	.4154	.4500	.4845
6	.0748	.0905	.1079	.1272	.1484	.1713	.1958	.2220	.2495	.2784
7	.0234	.0298	.0374	.0463	.0566	.0684	.0817	.0965	.1130	.1311
8	.0058	.0078	.0104	.0135	.0173	.0219	.0274	.0338	.0413	.0500
9	.0011	.0016	.0023	.0031	.0042	.0056	.0073	.0094	.0121	.0152
10	.0002	.0003	.0004	.0006	.0008	.0011	.0015	.0021	.0028	.0037
11	.0000	.0000	.0001	.0001	.0001	.0002	.0002	.0003	.0005	.0007
12	.0000	.0000	.0000	.0000	.0000	.0000	.0000	.0000	.0001	.0001

r \ p	.31	.32	.33	.34	.35	.36	.37	.38	.39	.40
1	.9962	.9969	.9975	.9980	.9984	.9988	.9990	.9992	.9994	.9995
2	.9704	.9752	.9794	.9829	.9858	.9883	.9904	.9922	.9936	.9948
3	.8893	.9038	.9167	.9281	.9383	.9472	.9550	.9618	.9678	.9729
4	.7314	.7580	.7829	.8060	.8273	.8469	.8649	.8813	.8961	.9095
5	.5187	.5523	.5852	.6171	.6481	.6778	.7062	.7332	.7587	.7827
6	.3084	.3393	.3709	.4032	.4357	.4684	.5011	.5335	.5654	.5968
7	.1509	.1722	.1951	.2194	.2452	.2722	.3003	.3295	.3595	.3902
8	.0599	.0711	.0837	.0977	.1132	.1302	.1487	.1687	.1902	.2131
9	.0190	.0236	.0289	.0351	.0422	.0504	.0597	.0702	.0820	.0950
10	.0048	.0062	.0079	.0099	.0124	.0154	.0190	.0232	.0281	.0338
11	.0009	.0012	.0016	.0022	.0028	.0037	.0047	.0059	.0075	.0093
12	.0001	.0002	.0003	.0004	.0005	.0006	.0009	.0011	.0015	.0019
13	.0000	.0000	.0000	.0000	.0001	.0001	.0001	.0002	.0002	.0003

r \ p	.41	.42	.43	.44	.45	.46	.47	.48	.49	.50
1	.9996	.9997	.9998	.9998	.9999	.9999	.9999	.9999	1.0000	1.0000
2	.9958	.9966	.9973	.9979	.9983	.9987	.9990	.9992	.9994	.9995
3	.9773	.9811	.9843	.9870	.9893	.9913	.9929	.9943	.9954	.9963
4	.9215	.9322	.9417	.9502	.9576	.9641	.9697	.9746	.9788	.9824
5	.8052	.8261	.8454	.8633	.8796	.8945	.9080	.9201	.9310	.9408
6	.6274	.6570	.6856	.7131	.7392	.7641	.7875	.8095	.8301	.8491
7	.4214	.4530	.4847	.5164	.5478	.5789	.6095	.6394	.6684	.6964
8	.2374	.2630	.2898	.3176	.3465	.3762	.4065	.4374	.4686	.5000
9	.1095	.1254	.1427	.1615	.1818	.2034	.2265	.2510	.2767	.3036
10	.0404	.0479	.0565	.0661	.0769	.0890	.1024	.1171	.1333	.1509
11	.0116	.0143	.0174	.0211	.0255	.0305	.0363	.0430	.0506	.0592
12	.0025	.0032	.0040	.0051	.0063	.0079	.0097	.0119	.0145	.0176
13	.0004	.0005	.0007	.0009	.0011	.0004	.0018	.0023	.0029	.0037
14	.0000	.0000	.0001	.0001	.0001	.0002	.0002	.0003	.0004	.0005

n = 20

r \ p	.01	.02	.03	.04	.05	.06	.07	.08	.09	.10
1	.1821	.3324	.4562	.5580	.6415	.7099	.7658	.8113	.8484	.8784
2	.0169	.0599	.1198	.1897	.2642	.3395	.4131	.4831	.5484	.6083
3	.0010	.0071	.0210	.0439	.0755	.1150	.1610	.2121	.2666	.3231
4	.0000	.0006	.0027	.0074	.0159	.0290	.0471	.0706	.0993	.1330
5	.0000	.0000	.0003	.0010	.0026	.0056	.0107	.0183	.0290	.0432
6	.0000	.0000	.0000	.0001	.0003	.0009	.0019	.0038	.0068	.0113
7	.0000	.0000	.0000	.0000	.0000	.0001	.0003	.0006	.0013	.0024
8	.0000	.0000	.0000	.0000	.0000	.0000	.0000	.0001	.0002	.0004
9	.0000	.0000	.0000	.0000	.0000	.0000	.0000	.0000	.0000	.0001

r \ p	.11	.12	.13	.14	.15	.16	.17	.18	.19	.20
1	.9028	.9224	.9383	.9510	.9612	.9694	.9759	.9811	.9852	.9885
2	.6624	.7109	.7539	.7916	.8244	.8529	.8773	.8982	.9159	.9308
3	.3802	.4369	.4920	.5450	.5951	.6420	.6854	.7252	.7614	.7939
4	.1710	.2127	.2573	.3041	.3523	.4010	.4496	.4974	.5439	.5886
5	.0610	.0827	.1083	.1375	.1702	.2059	.2443	.2849	.3271	.3704
6	.0175	.0260	.0370	.0507	.0673	.0870	.1098	.1356	.1643	.1958
7	.0041	.0067	.0103	.0153	.0219	.0304	.0409	.0537	.0689	.0867
8	.0008	.0014	.0024	.0038	.0059	.0088	.0127	.0177	.0241	.0321
9	.0001	.0002	.0005	.0008	.0013	.0021	.0033	.0049	.0071	.0100
10	.0000	.0000	.0001	.0001	.0002	.0004	.0007	.0011	.0017	.0026
11	.0000	.0000	.0000	.0000	.0000	.0001	.0001	.0002	.0004	.0006
12	.0000	.0000	.0000	.0000	.0000	.0000	.0000	.0000	.0001	.0001

r \ p	.21	.22	.23	.24	.25	.26	.27	.28	.29	.30
1	.9910	.9931	.9946	.9959	.9968	.9976	.9982	.9986	.9989	.9992
2	.9434	.9539	.9626	.9698	.9757	.9805	.9845	.9877	.9903	.9924
3	.8230	.8488	.8716	.8915	.9087	.9237	.9365	.9474	.9567	.9645
4	.6310	.6711	.7085	.7431	.7748	.8038	.8300	.8534	.8744	.8929
5	.4142	.4580	.5014	.5439	.5852	.6248	.6625	.6981	.7315	.7625
6	.2297	.2657	.3035	.3427	.3828	.4235	.4643	.5048	.5447	.5836
7	.1071	.1301	.1558	.1838	.2142	.2467	.2810	.3169	.3540	.3920
8	.0419	.0536	.0675	.0835	.1018	.1225	.1455	.1707	.1982	.2277
9	.0138	.0186	.0246	.0320	.0409	.0515	.0640	.0784	.0948	.1133
10	.0038	.0054	.0075	.0103	.0139	.0183	.0238	.0305	.0385	.0480
11	.0009	.0013	.0019	.0028	.0039	.0055	.0074	.0100	.0132	.0171
12	.0002	.0003	.0004	.0006	.0009	.0014	.0019	.0027	.0038	.0051
13	.0000	.0000	.0001	.0001	.0002	.0003	.0004	.0006	.0009	.0013
14	.0000	.0000	.0000	.0000	.0000	.0000	.0001	.0001	.0002	.0003

r \ p	.31	.32	.33	.34	.35	.36	.37	.38	.39	.40
1	.9994	.9996	.9997	.9998	.9998	.9999	.9999	.9999	.9999	1.0000
2	.9940	.9953	.9964	.9972	.9979	.9984	.9988	.9991	.9993	.9995
3	.9711	.9765	.9811	.9848	.9879	.9904	.9924	.9940	.9953	.9964
4	.9092	.9235	.9358	.9465	.9556	.9634	.9700	.9755	.9802	.9840
5	.7911	.8173	.8411	.8626	.8818	.8989	.9141	.9274	.9390	.9490
6	.6213	.6574	.6918	.7242	.7546	.7829	.8090	.8329	.8547	.8744
7	.4305	.4693	.5079	.5460	.5834	.6197	.6547	.6882	.7200	.7500
8	.2591	.2922	.3268	.3624	.3990	.4361	.4735	.5108	.5478	.5841
9	.1340	.1568	.1818	.2087	.2376	.2683	.3005	.3341	.3688	.4044
10	.0591	.0719	.0866	.1032	.1218	.1424	.1650	.1897	.2163	.2447
11	.0220	.0279	.0350	.0434	.0532	.0645	.0775	.0923	.1090	.1275
12	.0069	.0091	.0119	.0154	.0196	.0247	.0308	.0381	.0466	.0565
13	.0018	.0025	.0034	.0045	.0060	.0079	.0102	.0132	.0167	.0210
14	.0004	.0006	.0008	.0011	.0015	.0021	.0028	.0037	.0049	.0065
15	.0001	.0001	.0001	.0002	.0003	.0004	.0006	.0009	.0012	.0016
16	.0000	.0000	.0000	.0000	.0001	.0001	.0001	.0002	.0002.	.0003

r \ p	.41	.42	.43	.44	.45	.46	.47	.48	.49	.50
1	1.0000	1.0000	1.0000	1.0000	1.0000	1.0000	1.0000	1.0000	1.0000	1.0000
2	.9996	.9997	.9998	.9998	.9999	.9999	.9999	1.0000	1.0000	1.0000
3	.9972	.9979	.9984	.9988	.9991	.9993	.9995	.9996	.9997	.9998
4	.9872	.9898	.9920	.9937	.9951	.9962	.9971	.9977	.9983	.9987
5	.9577	.9651	.9714	.9767	.9811	.9848	.9879	.9904	.9924	.9941
6	.8921	.9078	.9217	.9340	.9447	.9539	.9619	.9687	.9745	.9793
7	.7780	.8041	.8281	.8501	.8701	.8881	.9042	.9186	.9312	.9423
8	.6196	.6539	.6868	.7183	.7480	.7759	.8020	.8261	.8482	.8684
9	.4406	.4771	.5136	.5499	.5847	.6207	.6546	.6873	.7186	.7483
10	.2748	.3064	.3394	.3736	.4086	.4443	.4804	.5166	.5525	.5881
11	.1480	.1705	.1949	.2212	.2493	.2791	.3104	.3432	.3771	.4119
12	.0679	.0810	.0958	.1123	.1308	.1511	.1734	.1977	.2238	.2517
13	.0262	.0324	.0397	.0482	.0580	.0694	.0823	.0969	.1133	.1316
14	.0084	.0107	.0136	.0172	.0214	.0265	.0326	.0397	.0480	.0577
15	.0022	.0029	.0038	.0050	.0064	.0083	.0105	.0133	.0166	.0207
16	.0004	.0006	.0008	.0011	.0015	.0020	.0027	.0035	.0046	.0059
17	.0001	.0001	.0001	.0002	.0003	.0004	.0005	.0007	.0010	.0013
18	.0000	.0000	.0000	.0000	.0000	.0001	.0001	.0001	.0001	.0002

n = 25

r \ p	.01	.02	.03	.04	.05	.06	.07	.08	.09	.10
1	.2222	.3965	.5330	.6396	.7226	.7871	.8370	.8756	.9054	.9282
2	.0258	.0886	.1720	.2642	.3576	.4473	.5304	.6053	.6714	.7288
3	.0020	.0132	.0380	.0765	.1271	.1871	.2534	.3232	.3937	.4629
4	.0001	.0014	.0062	.0165	.0341	.0598	.0936	.1351	.1831	.2364
5	.0000	.0001	.0008	.0028	.0072	.0150	.0274	.0451	.0686	.0980
6	.0000	.0000	.0001	.0004	.0012	.0031	.0065	.0123	.0210	.0334
7	.0000	.0000	.0000	.0000	.0002	.0005	.0013	.0028	.0054	.0095
8	.0000	.0000	.0000	.0000	.0000	.0001	.0002	.0005	.0011	.0023
9	.0000	.0000	.0000	.0000	.0000	.0000	.0000	.0001	.0002	.0005
10	.0000	.0000	.0000	.0000	.0000	.0000	.0000	.0000	.0000	.0001
r \ p	.11	..12	.13	.14	.15	.16	.17	.18	.19	.20
1	.9457	.9591	.9692	.9770	.9828	.9872	.9905	.9930	.9948	.9962
2	.7779	.8195	.8543	.8832	.9069	.9263	.9420	.9546	.9646	.9726
3	.5291	.5912	.6483	.7000	.7463	.7870	.8226	.8533	.8796	.9018
4	.2934	.3525	.4123	.4714	.5289	.5837	.6352	.6829	.7266	.7660
5	.1331	.1734	.1283	.2668	.3179	.3707	.4241	.4772	.5292	.5793
6	.0499	.0709	.0965	.1268	.1615	.2002	.2425	.2875	.3347	.3833
7	.0156	.0243	.0359	.0509	.0695	.0920	.1185	.1488	.1827	.2200
8	.0041	.0070	.0113	.0173	.0255	.0361	.0495	.0661	.0859	.1091
9	.0009	.0017	.0030	.0050	.0080	.0121	.0178	.0252	.0348	.0468
10	.0002	.0004	.0007	.0013	.0021	.0035	.0055	.0083	.0122	.0173
11	.0000	.0001	.0001	.0003	.0005	.0009	.0015	.0024	.0037	.0056
12	.0000	.0000	.0000	.0000	.0001	.0002	.0003	.0006	.0010	.0015
13	.0000	.0000	.0000	.0000	.0000	.0000	.0001	.0001	.0002	.0004
14	.0000	.0000	.0000	.0000	.0000	.0000	.0000	.0000	.0000	.0001
	.21	.22	.23	.24	.25	.26	.27	.28	.29	.30
1	.9972	.9980	.9985	.9990	.9992	.9995	.9996	.9997	.9998	.9999
2	.9789	.9838	.9877	.9907	.9930	.9947	.9961	.9971	.9979	.9984
3	.9204	.9360	.9488	.9593	.9679	.9748	.9804	.9848	.9883	.9910
4	.8013	.8324	.8597	.8834	.9038	.9211	.9358	.9481	.9583	.9668
5	.6270	.6718	.7134	.7516	.7863	.8174	.8452	.8696	.8910	.9095
6	.4325	.4816	.5299	.5767	.6217	.6644	.7044	.7415	.7755	.8065
7	.2601	.3027	.3471	.3927	.4389	.4851	.5308	.5753	.6183	.6593
8	.1358	.1658	.1989	.2349	.2735	.3142	.3565	.3999	.4440	.4882
9	.0614	.0788	.0993	.1228	.1494	.1790	.2115	.2465	.2838	.3231
10	.0240	.0325	.0431	.0560	.0713	.0893	.1101	.1338	.1602	.1894
11	.0082	.0117	.0163	.0222	.0297	.0389	.0502	.0636	.0795	.0978
12	.0024	.0036	.0053	.0076	.0107	.0148	.0199	.0264	.0345	.0442
13	.0006	.0010	.0015	.0023	.0034	.0049	.0069	.0096	.0130	.0175
14	.0001	.0002	.0004	.0006	.0009	.0014	.0021	.0030	.0043	.0060
15	.0000	.0000	.0001	.0001	.0002	.0003	.0005	.0008	.0012	.0018
16	.0000	.0000	.0000	.0000	.0000	.0001	.0001	.0002	.0003	.0005
17	.0000	.0000	.0000	.0000	.0000	.0000	.0000	.0000	.0001	.0001
	.31	.32	.33	.34	.35	.36	.37	.38	.39	.40
1	.9999	.9999	1.0000	1.0000	1.0000	1.0000	1.0000	1.0000	1.0000	1.0000
2	.9989	.9992	.9994	.9996	.9997	.9998	.9998	.9999	.9999	.9999
3	.9932	.9949	.9961	.9971	.9979	.9984	.9989	.9992	.9994	.9996
4	.9737	.9793	.9838	.9874	.9903	.9926	.9944	.9958	.9968	.9976
5	.9254	.9390	.9504	.9600	.9680	.9745	.9799	.9842	.9877	.9905
6	.8344	.8593	.8813	.9006	.9174	.9318	.9441	.9546	.9633	.9706
7	.6981	.7343	.7679	.7987	.8266	.8517	.8742	.8940	.9114	.9264
8	.5319	.5747	.6163	.6561	.6939	.7295	.7626	.7932	.8211	.8464
9	.3639	.4057	.4482	.4908	.5332	.5748	.6152	.6542	.6914	.7265
10	.2213	.2555	.2919	.3300	.3697	.4104	.4517	.4933	.5347	.5754
11	.1188	.1424	.1686	.1975	.2288	.2624	.2981	.3355	.3743	.4142
12	.0560	.0698	.0859	.1044	.1254	.1490	.1751	.2036	.2346	.2677
13	.0230	.0299	.0383	.0485	.0604	.0745	.0907	.1093	.1303	.1538
14	.0083	.0112	.0149	.0196	.0255	.0326	.0412	.0515	.0637	.0778
15	.0026	.0036	.0050	.0069	.0093	.0124	.0163	.0212	.0271	.0344
16	.0007	.0010	.0015	.0021	.0029	.0041	.0056	.0075	.0100	.0132
17	.0002	.0002	.0004	.0005	.0008	.0011	.0016	.0023	.0032	.0043
18	.0000	.0000	.0001	.0001	.0002	.0003	.0004	.0006	.0008	.0012
19	.0000	.0000	.0000	.0000	.0000	.0001	.0001	.0001	.0002	.0003
20	.0000	.0000	.0000	.0000	.0000	.0000	.0000	.0000	.0000	.0001
	.41	.42	.43	.44	.45	.46	.47	.48	.49	.50
1	1.0000	1.0000	1.0000	1.0000	1.0000	1.0000	1.0000	1.0000	1.0000	1.0000
2	1.0000	1.0000	1.0000	1.0000	1.0000	1.0000	1.0000	1.0000	1.0000	1.0000
3	.9997	.9998	.9998	.9999	.9999	1.0000	1.0000	1.0000	1.0000	1.0000
4	.9983	.9987	.9991	.9993	.9995	.9997	.9998	.9998	.9999	.9999
5	.9927	.9945	.9958	.9969	.9977	.9983	.9988	.9991	.9994	.9995
6	.9767	.9816	.9856	.9888	.9914	.9934	.9950	.9963	.9972	.9980
7	.9394	.9505	.9599	.9677	.9742	.9796	.9840	.9876	.9904	.9927
8	.8692	.8894	.9071	.9227	.9361	.9477	.9575	.9658	.9727	.9784
9	.7593	.7897	.8177	.8431	.9660	.8865	.9046	.9205	.9343	.9461
10	.6151	.6535	.6902	.7250	.7576	.7880	.8160	.8415	.8646	.8852

n = 25 (Continued)

r \ p	.41	.42	.43	.44	.45	.46	.47	.48	.49	.50
11	.4548	.4956	.5363	.5765	.6157	.6538	.6902	.7249	.7574	.7878
12	.3029	.3397	.3780	.4174	.4574	.4978	.5382	.5780	.6171	.6550
13	.1797	.2080	.2387	.2715	.3063	.3429	.3808	.4199	.4598	.5000
14	.0941	.1127	.1336	.1569	.1827	.2109	.2413	.2740	.3086	.3450
15	.0431	.0535	.0656	.0797	.0960	.1145	.1353	.1585	.1841	.2122
16	.0171	.0220	.0280	.0353	.0440	.0543	.0663	.0803	.0964	.1148
17	.0058	.0078	.0103	.0134	.0174	.0222	.0281	.0352	.0438	.0539
18	.0017	.0023	.0032	.0044	.0058	.0077	.0102	.0132	.0170	.0216
19	.0004	.0006	.0008	.0012	.0016	.0023	.0031	.0041	.0055	.0073
20	.0001	.0001	.0002	.0003	.0004	.0005	.0008	.0011	.0015	.0020
21	.0000	.0000	.0000	.0000	.0001	.0001	.0002	.0002	.0003	.0005
22	.0000	.0000	.0000	.0000	.0000	.0000	.0000	.0000	.0001	.0001

n = 30

r \ p	.01	.02	.03	.04	.05	.06	.07	.08	.09	.10
1	.2603	.4545	.4990	.7061	.7854	.8437	.8866	.9180	.9409	.9576
2	.0361	.1205	.2269	.3388	.4465	.5445	.6306	.7042	.7657	.8163
3	.0033	.0217	.0601	.1169	.1878	.2676	.3513	.4346	.5145	.5886
4	.0002	.0029	.0119	.0306	.0608	.1026	.1550	.2158	.2825	.3526
5	.0000	.0003	.0019	.0063	.0156	.0315	.0553	.0874	.1277	.1755
6	.0000	.0000	.0002	.0011	.0033	.0079	.0162	.0293	.0481	.0732
7	.0000	.0000	.0000	.0001	.0006	.0017	.0040	.0082	.0152	.0258
8	.0000	.0000	.0000	.0000	.0001	.0003	.0008	.0020	.0041	.0078
9	.0000	.0000	.0000	.0000	.0000	.0000	.0001	.0004	.0010	.0020
10	.0000	.0000	.0000	.0000	.0000	.0000	.0000	.0001	.0002	.0005
11	.0000	.0000	.0000	.0000	.0000	.0000	.0000	.0000	.0000	.0001

r \ p	.11	.12	.13	.14	.15	.16	.17	.18	.19	.20
1	.9697	.9784	.9847	.9892	.9924	.9946	.9963	.9974	.9982	.9988
2	.8573	.8900	.9159	.9362	.9520	.9641	.9733	.9803	.9856	.9895
3	.6558	.7153	.7670	.8113	.8486	.8796	.9051	.9259	.9425	.9558
4	.4234	.4929	.5594	.6215	.6783	.7295	.7748	.8144	.8484	.8773
5	.2295	.2882	.3499	.4129	.4755	.5365	.5947	.6491	.6993	.7448
6	.1049	.1431	.1871	.2363	.2894	.3453	.4028	.4605	.5174	.5725
7	.0407	.0606	.0858	.1165	.1526	.1936	.2390	.2880	.3397	.3930
8	.0136	.0221	.0339	.0497	.0698	.0945	.1240	.1582	.1968	.2392
9	.0039	.0069	.0116	.0184	.0278	.0403	.0563	.0763	.1004	.1287
10	.0010	.0019	.0035	.0059	.0097	.0150	.0224	.0323	.0451	.0611
11	.0002	.0005	.0009	.0017	.0029	.0049	.0078	.0120	.0179	.0256
12	.0000	.0001	.0002	.0004	.0008	.0014	.0024	.0040	.0062	.0095
13	.0000	.0000	.0000	.0001	.0002	.0004	.0007	.0011	.0019	.0031
14	.0000	.0000	.0000	.0000	.0000	.0001	.0002	.0003	.0005	.0009
15	.0000	.0000	.0000	.0000	.0000	.0000	.0000	.0001	.0001	.0002
16	.0000	.0000	.0000	.0000	.0000	.0000	.0000	.0000	.0000	.0001

r \ p	.21	.22	.23	.24	.25	.26	.27	.28	.29	.30
1	.9992	.9994	.9996	.9997	.9998	.9999	.9999	.9999	1.0000	1.0000
2	.9924	.9945	.9961	.9972	.9980	.9986	.9990	.9993	.9995	.9997
3	.9663	.9745	.9808	.9857	.9894	.9922	.9943	.9959	.9970	.9979
4	.9016	.9217	.9383	.9517	.9626	.9712	.9780	.9834	.9875	.9907
5	.7854	.8213	.8525	.8793	.9021	.9213	.9373	.9505	.9612	.9698
6	.6249	.6739	.7192	.7604	.7974	.8302	.8590	.8839	.9053	.9234
7	.4470	.5008	.5533	.6039	.6519	.6969	.7384	.7762	.8102	.8405
8	.2850	.3333	.3834	.4345	.4857	.5362	.5853	.6324	.6770	.7186
9	.1611	.1975	.2376	.2807	.3264	.3739	.4226	.4718	.5206	.5685
10	.0806	.1039	.1311	.1620	.1966	.2346	.2756	.3190	.3645	.4112
11	.0357	.0485	.0642	.0833	.1057	.1317	.1613	.1943	.2305	.2696
12	.0140	.0200	.0280	.0381	.0507	.0660	.0845	.1061	.1310	.1593
13	.0049	.0073	.0108	.0155	.0216	.0295	.0395	.0518	.1667	.0845
14	.0015	.0024	.0037	.0056	.0082	.0117	.0164	.0225	.0303	.0401
15	.0004	.0007	.0011	.0018	.0028	.0041	.0061	.0087	.0123	.0169
16	.0001	.0002	.0003	.0005	.0008	.0013	.0020	.0030	.0044	.0064
17	.0000	.0000	.0001	.0001	.0002	.0004	.0006	.0009	.0014	.0021
18	.0000	.0000	.0000	.0000	.0001	.0001	.0001	.0002	.0004	.0006
19	.0000	.0000	.0000	.0000	.0000	.0000	.0000	.0001	.0001	.0002

n = 30 (Continued)

r \ p	.31	.32	.33	.34	.35	.36	.37	.38	.39	.40
1	1.0000	1.0000	1.0000	1.0000	1.0000	1.0000	1.0000	1.0000	1.0000	1.0000
2	.9998	.9999	.9999	.9999	1.0000	1.0000	1.0000	1.0000	1.0000	1.0000
3	.9985	.9989	.9993	.9995	.9997	.9998	.9998	.9999	.9999	1.0000
4	.9931	.9950	.9963	.9974	.9981	.9987	.9991	.9993	.9995	.9997
5	.9768	.9823	.9866	.9899	.9925	.9944	.9959	.9971	.9979	.9985
6	.9386	.9512	.9615	.9700	.9767	.9822	.9864	.9898	.9924	.9943
7	.8671	.8903	.9102	.9271	.9414	.9533	.9631	.9712	.9776	.9828
8	.7570	.7920	.8235	.8515	.8762	.8977	.9163	.9321	.9454	.9565
9	.6148	.6590	.7007	.7395	.7753	.8078	.8371	.8631	.8861	.9060
10	.4586	.5060	.5529	.5985	.6425	.6842	.7235	.7599	.7934	.8237
11	.3112	.3549	.4000	.4460	.4922	.5382	.5833	.6270	.6689	.7085
12	.1909	.2255	.2631	.3031	.3452	.3889	.4337	.4790	.5242	.5689
13	.1053	.1292	.1563	.1865	.2198	.2559	.2945	.3353	.3778	.4215
14	.0520	.0664	.0835	.1034	.1263	.1523	.1813	.2133	.2481	.2855
15	.0229	.0305	.0399	.0514	.0652	.0815	.1006	.1226	.1475	.1754
16	.0090	.0125	.0170	.0228	.0301	.0391	.0501	.0632	.0788	.0971
17	.0031	.0045	.0065	.0090	.0124	.0167	.0222	.0291	.0377	.0481
18	.0010	.0015	.0022	.0032	.0045	.0063	.0088	.0119	.0160	.0212
19	.0003	.0004	.0006	.0010	.0014	.0021	.0031	.0043	.0060	.0083
20	.0001	.0001	.0002	.0003	.0004	.0006	.0009	.0014	.0020	.0029
21	.0000	.0000	.0000	.0001	.0001	.0002	.0002	.0004	.0006	.0009
22	.0000	.0000	.0000	.0000	.0000	.0000	.0001	.0001	.0001	.0002

r \ p	.41	.42	.43	.44	.45	.46	.47	.48	.49	.50
1	1.0000	1.0000	1.0000	1.0000	1.0000	1.0000	1.0000	1.0000	1.0000	1.0000
2	1.0000	1.0000	1.0000	1.0000	1.0000	1.0000	1.0000	1.0000	1.0000	1.0000
3	1.0000	1.0000	1.0000	1.0000	1.0000	1.0000	1.0000	1.0000	1.0000	1.0000
4	.9998	.9999	.9999	.9999	1.0000	1.0000	1.0000	1.0000	1.0000	1.0000
5	.9989	.9993	.9995	.9996	.9998	.9998	.9999	.9999	1.0000	1.0000
6	.9959	.9970	.9978	.9985	.9989	.9992	.9995	.9996	.9998	.9998
7	.9869	.9901	.9926	.9946	.9960	.9971	.9979	.9985	.9990	.9993
8	.9656	.9731	.9792	.9841	.9879	.9909	.9932	.9950	.9964	.9974
9	.9231	.9378	.9501	.9603	.9688	.9757	.9813	.9857	.9892	.9919
10	.8510	.8751	.8964	.9148	.9306	.9440	.9553	.9647	.9724	.9786
11	.7456	.7799	.8112	.8396	.8650	.8874	.9070	.9239	.9384	.9506
12	.6125	.6545	.6945	.7322	.7673	.7996	.8290	.8555	.8790	.8998
13	.4660	.5107	.5551	.5986	.6408	.6813	.7196	.7555	.7888	.8192
14	.3251	.3666	.4095	.4533	.4975	.5417	.5852	.6277	.6687	.7077
15	.2062	.2398	.2760	.3146	.3552	.3973	.4406	.4845	.5285	.5722
16	.1180	.1419	.1687	.1984	.2309	.2661	.3037	.3434	.3849	.4278
17	.0606	.0754	.0928	.1128	.1356	.1613	.1899	.2214	.2556	.2923
18	.0278	.0358	.0456	.0574	.0714	.0878	.1068	.1286	.1533	.1808
19	.0113	.0151	.0199	.0260	.0334	.0426	.0536	.0668	.0822	.1002
20	.0040	.0056	.0077	.0104	.0138	.0183	.0238	.0307	.0391	.0494
21	.0013	.0018	.0026	.0036	.0050	.0069	.0093	.0124	.0164	.0214
22	.0003	.0005	.0008	.0011	.0016	.0022	.0031	.0043	.0060	.0081
23	.0001	.0001	.0002	.0003	.0004	.0006	.0009	.0013	.0019	.0026
24	.0000	.0000	.0000	.0001	.0001	.0001	.0002	.0003	.0005	.0007
25	.0000	.0000	.0000	.0000	.0000	.0000	.0000	.0001	.0001	.0002

n = 40

r \ p	.01	.02	.03	.04	.05	.06	.07	.08	.09	.10
1	.3310	.5543	.7043	.8046	.8715	.9158	.9451	.9644	.9770	.9852
2	.0607	.1905	.3385	.4790	.6009	.7010	.7799	.8406	.8860	.9195
3	.0075	.0457	.1178	.2145	.3233	.4335	.5375	.6306	.7106	.7772
4	.0007	.0082	.0314	.0748	.1382	.2173	.3063	.3993	.4908	.5769
5	.0000	.0012	.0067	.0210	.0480	.0896	.1454	.2132	.2897	.3710
6	.0000	.0001	.0012	.0049	.0139	.0309	.0581	.0967	.1465	.2063
7	.0000	.0000	.0002	.0010	.0034	.0091	.0199	.0376	.0639	.0995
8	.0000	.0000	.0000	.0002	.0007	.0023	.0059	.0127	.0242	.0419
9	.0000	.0000	.0000	.0000	.0001	.0005	.0015	.0037	.0081	.0155
10	.0000	.0000	.0000	.0000	.0000	.0001	.0003	.0010	.0024	.0051
11	.0000	.0000	.0000	.0000	.0000	.0000	.0001	.0002	.0006	.0015
12	.0000	.0000	.0000	.0000	.0000	.0000	.0000	.0000	.0001	.0004
13	.0000	.0000	.0000	.0000	.0000	.0000	.0000	.0000	.0000	.0001

n = 40 (Continued)

r \ p	.11	.12	.13	.14	.15	.16	.17	.18	.19	.20
1	.9905	.9940	.9962	.9976	.9985	.9991	.9994	.9996	.9998	.9999
2	.9438	.9612	.9734	.9820	.9879	.9919	.9947	.9965	.9977	.9985
3	.8312	.8739	.9071	.9324	.9514	.9655	.9757	.9831	.9884	.9921
4	.6548	.7232	.7816	.8302	.8698	.9016	.9265	.9458	.9605	.9715
5	.4532	.5331	.6080	.6762	.7367	.7890	.8533	.8701	.9000	.9241
6	.2738	.3464	.4213	.4958	.5675	.6346	.6958	.7504	.7980	.8387
7	.1445	.1980	.2586	.3245	.3933	.4631	.5316	.5971	.6583	.7141
8	.0668	.0996	.1405	.1890	.2441	.3044	.3682	.4337	.4991	.5629
9	.0272	.0443	.0677	.0980	.1354	.1797	.2301	.2857	.3451	.4069
10	.0098	.0175	.0290	.0453	.0672	.0952	.1296	.1702	.2167	.2682
11	.0032	.0062	.0111	.0188	.0299	.0454	.0657	.0916	.1233	.1608
12	.0009	.0019	.0038	.0070	.0120	.0194	.0301	.0446	.0636	.0875
13	.0002	.0005	.0012	.0023	.0043	.0075	.0124	.0196	.0297	.0432
14	.0001	.0001	.0003	.0007	.0014	.0026	.0047	.0078	.0126	.0194
15	.0000	.0000	.0001	.0002	.0004	.0008	.0016	.0028	.0048	.0079
16	.0000	.0000	.0000	.0000	.0001	.0002	.0005	.0009	.0017	.0029
17	.0000	.0000	.0000	.0000	.0000	.0001	.0001	.0003	.0005	.0010
18	.0000	.0000	.0000	.0000	.0000	.0000	.0000	.0001	.0002	.0003
19	.0000	.0000	.0000	.0000	.0000	.0000	.0000	.0000	.0000	.0001

r \ p	.21	.22	.23	.24	.25	.26	.27	.28	.29	.30
1	.9999	1.0000	1.0000	1.0000	1.0000	1.0000	1.0000	1.0000	1.0000	1.0000
2	.9991	.9994	.9996	.9998	.9999	.9999	.9999	1.0000	1.0000	1.0000
3	.9946	.9964	.9976	.9984	.9990	.9993	.9996	.9997	.9998	.9999
4	.9797	.9857	.9900	.9931	.9953	.9968	.9979	.9986	.9991	.9994
5	.9430	.9578	.9691	.9776	.9840	.9886	.9920	.9945	.9962	.9974
6	.8729	.9011	.9240	.9423	.9567	.9679	.9765	.9830	.9878	.9914
7	.7640	.8078	.8454	.8773	.9038	.9255	.9430	.9569	.9678	.9762
8	.6235	.6799	.7314	.7775	.8180	.8530	.8828	.9076	.9281	.9447
9	.4694	.5312	.5910	.6476	.7002	.7480	.7909	.8286	.8612	.8890
10	.3238	.3821	.4419	.5017	.5605	.6169	.6701	.7193	.7641	.8041
11	.2038	.2517	.3038	.3589	.4161	.4740	.5315	.5875	.6410	.6913
12	.1167	.1514	.1912	.2359	.2849	.3371	.3918	.4478	.5040	.5594
13	.0609	.0830	.1100	.1421	.1791	.2209	.2669	.3165	.3687	.4228
14	.0289	.0415	.0578	.0782	.1032	.1329	.1674	.2065	.2498	.2968
15	.0124	.0189	.0277	.0394	.0544	.0733	.0964	.1240	.1560	.1926
16	.0049	.0078	.0121	.0181	.0262	.0370	.0509	.0683	.0897	.1151
17	.0017	.0030	.0048	.0076	.0116	.0171	.0246	.0345	.0473	.0633
18	.0006	.0010	.0018	.0029	.0047	.0072	.0109	.0160	.0229	.0320
19	.0002	.0003	.0006	.0010	.0017	.0028	.0044	.0068	.0101	.0148
20	.0000	.0001	.0002	.0003	.0006	.0010	.0016	.0026	.0041	.0063
21	.0000	.0000	.0000	.0001	.0002	.0003	.0005	.0009	.0015	.0024
22	.0000	.0000	.0000	.0000	.0000	.0001	.0002	.0003	.0005	.0009
23	.0000	.0000	.0000	.0000	.0000	.0000	.0000	.0001	.0002	.0003
24	.0000	.0000	.0000	.0000	.0000	.0000	.0000	.0000	.0000	.0001

r \ p	.31	.32	.33	.34	.35	.36	.37	.38	.39	.40
1	1.0000	1.0000	1.0000	1.0000	1.0000	1.0000	1.0000	1.0000	1.0000	1.0000
2	1.0000	1.0000	1.0000	1.0000	1.0000	1.0000	1.0000	1.0000	1.0000	1.0000
3	.9999	1.0000	1.0000	1.0000	1.0000	1.0000	1.0000	1.0000	1.0000	1.0000
4	.9996	.9998	.9998	.9999	.9999	1.0000	1.0000	1.0000	1.0000	1.0000
5	.9983	.9989	.9993	.9995	.9997	.9998	.9999	.9999	1.0000	1.0000
6	.9940	.9958	.9971	.9981	.9987	.9991	.9994	.9996	.9998	.9999
7	.9827	.9875	.9911	.9937	.9956	.9970	.9980	.9986	.9991	.9994
8	.9580	.9685	.9766	.9829	.9876	.9911	.9937	.9956	.9970	.9979
9	.9123	.9315	.9472	.9598	.9697	.9775	.9835	.9880	.9914	.9939
10	.8393	.8697	.8957	.9175	.9356	.9503	.9621	.9715	.9788	.9844
11	.7376	.7796	.8171	.8500	.8785	.9028	.9232	.9400	.9537	.9648
12	.6130	.6639	.7115	.7552	.7947	.8299	.8608	.8874	.9101	.9291
13	.4777	.5323	.5857	.6371	.6857	.7309	.7722	.8095	.8426	.8715
14	.3467	.3989	.4524	.5061	.5592	.6109	.6602	.7067	.7497	.7888
15	.2333	.2779	.3257	.3759	.4279	.4807	.5334	.5851	.6351	.6826
16	.1450	.1791	.2175	.2597	.3054	.3538	.4043	.4560	.5081	.5598
17	.0830	.1065	.1343	.1662	.2022	.2422	.2858	.3323	.3813	.4319
18	.0436	.0583	.0764	.0981	.1239	.1536	.1875	.2253	.2668	.3115
19	.0210	.0293	.0399	.0534	.0699	.0900	.1138	.1415	.1732	.2089
20	.0093	.0135	.0192	.0266	.0363	.0485	.0636	.0820	.1040	.1298

r \ p	.31	.32	.33	.34	.35	.36	.37	.38	.39	.40
					n 40 (Continued)					
21	.0038	.0057	.0084	.0122	.0173	.0240	.0327	.0438	.0575	.0744
22	.0014	.0022	.0034	.0051	.0075	.0109	.0154	.0214	.0292	.0392
23	.0005	.0008	.0012	.0020	.0030	.0045	.0066	.0096	.0136	.0189
24	.0001	.0002	.0004	.0007	.0011	.0017	.0026	.0039	.0058	.0083
25	.0000	.0001	.0001	.0002	.0004	.0006	.0009	.0015	.0022	.0034
26	.0000	.0000	.0000	.0001	.0001	.0002	.0003	.0005	.0008	.0012
27	.0000	.0000	.0000	.0000	.0000	.0001	.0001	.0002	.0002	.0004
28	.0000	.0000	.0000	.0000	.0000	.0000	.0000	.0000	.0001	.0001

r \ p	.41	.42	.43	.44	.45	.46	.47	.48	.49	.50
1	1.0000	1.0000	1.0000	1.0000	1.0000	1.0000	1.0000	1.0000	1.0000	1.0000
2	1.0000	1.0000	1.0000	1.0000	1.0000	1.0000	1.0000	1.0000	1.0000	1.0000
3	1.0000	1.0000	1.0000	1.0000	1.0000	1.0000	1.0000	1.0000	1.0000	1.0000
4	1.0000	1.0000	1.0000	1.0000	1.0000	1.0000	1.0000	1.0000	1.0000	1.0000
5	1.0000	1.0000	1.0000	1.0000	1.0000	1.0000	1.0000	1.0000	1.0000	1.0000
6	.9999	.9999	1.0000	1.0000	1.0000	1.0000	1.0000	1.0000	1.0000	1.0000
7	.9996	.9998	.9998	.9999	.9999	1.0000	1.0000	1.0000	1.0000	1.0000
8	.9986	.9991	.9994	.9996	.9998	.9998	.9999	.9999	1.0000	1.0000
9	.9958	.9971	.9980	.9987	.9991	.9994	.9996	.9998	.9999	.9999
10	.9887	.9919	.9943	.9960	.9973	.9981	.9988	.9992	.9995	.9997
11	.9735	.9803	.9856	.9896	.9926	.9948	.9964	.9975	.9983	.9989
12	.9447	.9575	.9677	.9758	.9821	.9869	.9906	.9933	.9953	.9968
13	.8964	.9175	.9351	.9496	.9614	.9708	.9782	.9840	.9884	.9917
14	.8240	.8551	.8821	.9053	.9249	.9413	.9546	.9654	.9740	.9808
15	.7270	.7679	.8051	.8382	.8674	.8927	.9143	.9324	.9474	.9597
16	.6102	.6586	.7043	.7468	.7858	.8209	.8522	.8795	.9031	.9231
17	.4833	.5348	.5855	.6346	.6815	.7255	.7662	.8033	.8365	.8659
18	.3589	.4083	.4590	.5101	.5609	.6107	.6585	.7039	.7463	.7852
19	.2484	.2912	.3370	.3851	.4349	.4857	.5365	.5867	.6354	.6821
20	.1594	.1930	.2305	.2714	.3156	.3624	.4112	.4614	.5122	.5627
21	.0946	.1184	.1461	.1776	.2130	.2521	.2946	.3400	.3878	.4373
22	.0516	.0669	.0855	.1074	.1331	.1627	.1961	.2333	.2740	.3179
23	.0259	.0348	.0460	.0598	.0767	.0969	.1206	.1482	.1796	.2148
24	.0118	.0165	.0226	.0305	.0405	.0530	.0683	.0867	.1086	.1341
25	.0049	.0072	.0102	.0142	.0196	.0265	.0354	.0465	.0602	.0769
26	.0019	.0028	.0042	.0060	.0086	.0121	.0167	.0228	.0305	.0403
27	.0006	.0010	.0015	.0023	.0034	.0050	.0072	.0101	.0140	.0192
28	.0002	.0003	.0005	.0008	.0012	.0019	.0028	.0041	.0058	.0083
29	.0001	.0001	.0002	.0002	.0004	.0006	.0010	.0015	.0022	.0032
30	.0000	.0000	.0000	.0001	.0001	.0002	.0003	.0005	.0007	.0011
31	.0000	.0000	.0000	.0000	.0000	.0000	.0001	.0001	.0002	.0003
32	.0000	.0000	.0000	.0000	.0000	.0000	.0000	.0000	.0001	.0001

n = 50

r \ p	.01	.02	.03	.04	.05	.06	.07	.08	.09	.10
1	.3950	.6358	.7819	.8701	.9231	.9547	.9734	.9845	.9910	.9948
2	.0894	.2642	.4447	.5995	.7206	.8100	.8735	.9173	.9468	.9662
3	.0138	.0784	.1892	.3233	.4595	.5838	.6892	.7740	.8395	.8883
4	.0016	.0178	.0628	.1391	.2396	.3527	.4673	.5747	.6697	.7497
5	.0001	.0032	.0168	.0490	.1036	.1794	.2710	.3711	.4723	.5688
6	.0000	.0005	.0037	.0144	.0378	.0776	.1350	.2081	.2928	.3839
7	.0000	.0001	.0007	.0036	.0118	.0289	.0583	.1019	.1596	.2298
8	.0000	.0000	.0001	.0008	.0032	.0094	.0220	.0438	.0768	.1221
9	.0000	.0000	.0000	.0001	.0008	.0027	.0073	.0167	.0328	.0579
10	.0000	.0000	.0000	.0000	.0002	.0007	.0022	.0056	.0125	.0245
11	.0000	.0000	.0000	.0000	.0000	.0002	.0006	.0017	.0043	.0094
12	.0000	.0000	.0000	.0000	.0000	.0000	.0001	.0005	.0013	.0032
13	.0000	.0000	.0000	.0000	.0000	.0000	.0000	.0001	.0004	.0010
14	.0000	.0000	.0000	.0000	.0000	.0000	.0000	.0000	.0001	.0003
15	.0000	.0000	.0000	.0000	.0000	.0000	.0000	.0000	.0000	.0001

r \ p	.11	.12	.13	.14	.15	.16	.17	.18	.19	.20
1	.9971	.9983	.9991	.9995	.9997	.9998	.9999	1.0000	1.0000	1.0000
2	.9788	.9869	.9920	.9951	.9971	.9983	.9990	.9994	.9997	.9998
3	.9237	.9487	.9661	.9779	.9858	.9910	.9944	.9965	.9979	.9987
4	.8146	.8655	.9042	.9330	.9540	.9688	.9792	.9863	.9912	.9943
5	.6562	.7320	.7956	.8472	.8879	.9192	.9428	.9601	.9726	.9815

n = 50 (Continued)

r \ p	.11	.12	.13	.14	.15	.16	.17	.18	.19	.20
6	.4760	.5647	.6463	.7186	.7806	.8323	.8741	.9071	.9327	.9520
7	.3091	.3935	.4789	.5616	.6387	.7081	.7686	.8199	.8624	.8966
8	.1793	.2467	.3217	.4010	.4812	.5594	.6328	.6996	.7587	.8096
9	.0932	.1392	.1955	.2605	.3319	.4071	.4832	.5576	.6280	.6927
10	.0435	.0708	.1074	.1537	.2089	.2718	.3403	.4122	.4849	.5563
11	.0183	.0325	.0535	.0824	.1199	.1661	.2203	.2813	.3473	.4164
12	.0069	.0135	.0242	.0402	.0628	.0929	.1309	.1768	.2300	.2893
13	.0024	.0051	.0100	.0179	.0301	.0475	.0714	.1022	.1405	.1861
14	.0008	.0018	.0037	.0073	.0132	.0223	.0357	.0544	.0791	.1106
15	.0002	.0006	.0013	.0027	.0053	.0096	.0164	.0266	.0411	.0607
16	.0001	.0002	.0004	.0009	.0020	.0038	.0070	.0120	.0197	.0308
17	.0000	.0000	.0001	.0003	.0007	.0014	.0027	.0050	.0087	.0144
18	.0000	.0000	.0000	.0001	.0002	.0005	.0010	.0019	.0036	.0063
19	.0000	.0000	.0000	.0000	.0001	.0001	.0003	.0007	.0013	.0025
20	.0000	.0000	.0000	.0000	.0000	.0000	.0001	.0002	.0005	.0009
21	.0000	.0000	.0000	.0000	.0000	.0000	.0000	.0001	.0002	.0003
22	.0000	.0000	.0000	.0000	.0000	.0000	.0000	.0000	.0000	.0001
	.21	.22	.23	.24	.25	.26	.27	.28	.29	.30
1	1.0000	1.0000	1.0000	1.0000	1.0000	1.0000	1.0000	1.0000	1.0000	1.0000
2	.9999	.9999	1.0000	1.0000	1.0000	1.0000	1.0000	1.0000	1.0000	1.0000
3	.9992	.9995	.9997	.9998	.9999	1.0000	1.0000	1.0000	1.0000	1.0000
4	.9964	.9978	.9986	.9992	.9995	.9997	.9998	.9999	.9999	1.0000
5	.9877	.9919	.9948	.9967	.9979	.9987	.9992	.9995	.9997	.9998
6	.9963	.9767	.9841	.9893	.9930	.9954	.9970	.9981	.9988	.9993
7	.9236	.9445	.9603	.9720	.9806	.9868	.9911	.9941	.9961	.9975
8	.8523	.8874	.9156	.9377	.9547	.9676	.9772	.9842	.9892	.9927
9	.7505	.8009	.8437	.8794	.9084	.9316	.9497	.9635	.9740	.9817
10	.6241	.6870	.7436	.7934	.8363	.8724	.9021	.9260	.9450	.9598
11	.4864	.5552	.6210	.6822	.7378	.7871	.8299	.8663	.8965	.9211
12	.3533	.4201	.4878	.5544	.6184	.6782	.7329	.7817	.8244	.8610
13	.2383	.2963	.3585	.4233	.4890	.5539	.6163	.6749	.7287	.7771
14	.1490	.1942	.2456	.3023	.3630	.4261	.4901	.5534	.6145	.6721
15	.0862	.1181	.1565	.2013	.2519	.3075	.3669	.4286	.4912	.5532
16	.0462	.0665	.0926	.1247	.1631	.2075	.2575	.3121	.3703	.4308
17	.0229	.0347	.0508	.0718	.0983	.1306	.1689	.2130	.2623	.3161
18	.0105	.0168	.0259	.0384	.0551	.0766	.1034	.1359	.1741	.2178
19	.0045	.0075	.0122	.0191	.0287	.0418	.0590	.0809	.1080	.1406
20	.0018	.0031	.0054	.0088	.0139	.0212	.0314	.0449	.0626	.0848
21	.0006	.0012	.0022	.0038	.0063	.0100	.0155	.0232	.0338	.0478
22	.0002	.0004	.0008	.0015	.0026	.0044	.0071	.0112	.0170	.0251
23	.0001	.0001	.0003	.0006	.0010	.0018	.0031	.0050	.0080	.0123
24	.0000	.0000	.0001	.0002	.0004	.0007	.0012	.0021	.0035	.0056
25	.0000	.0000	.0000	.0001	.0001	.0002	.0004	.0008	.0014	.0024
26	.0000	.0000	.0000	.0000	.0000	.0001	.0002	.0003	.0005	.0009
27	.0000	.0000	.0000	.0000	.0000	.0000	.0001	.0001	.0002	.0003
28	.0000	.0000	.0000	.0000	.0000	.0000	.0000	.0000	.0001	.0001
	.31	.32	.33	.34	.35	.36	.37	.38	.39	.40
1	1.0000	1.0000	1.0000	1.0000	1.0000	1.0000	1.0000	1.0000	1.0000	1.0000
2	1.0000	1.0000	1.0000	1.0000	1.0000	1.0000	1.0000	1.0000	1.0000	1.0000
3	1.0000	1.0000	1.0000	1.0000	1.0000	1.0000	1.0000	1.0000	1.0000	1.0000
4	1.0000	1.0000	1.0000	1.0000	1.0000	1.0000	1.0000	1.0000	1.0000	1.0000
5	.9999	.9999	1.0000	1.0000	1.0000	1.0000	1.0000	1.0000	1.0000	1.0000
6	.9996	.9997	.9998	.9999	.9999	1.0000	1.0000	1.0000	1.0000	1.0000
7	.9984	.9990	.9994	.9996	.9998	.9999	.9999	1.0000	1.0000	1.0000
8	.9952	.9969	.9980	.9987	.9992	.9995	.9997	.9998	.9999	.9999
9	.9874	.9914	.9942	.9962	.9975	.9984	.9990	.9994	.9996	.9998
10	.9710	.9794	.9856	.9901	.9933	.9955	.9971	.9981	.9988	.9992
11	.9409	.9563	.9683	.9773	.9840	.9889	.9924	.9949	.9966	.9978
12	.8916	.9168	.9371	.9533	.9658	.9753	.9825	.9878	.9916	.9943
13	.8197	.8564	.8874	.9130	.9339	.9505	.9635	.9736	.9811	.9867
14	.7253	.7732	.8157	.8524	.8837	.9097	.9310	.9481	.9616	.9720
15	.6131	.6698	.7223	.7699	.8122	.8491	.8805	.9069	.9286	.9460
16	.4922	.5530	.6120	.6679	.7199	.7672	.8094	.8462	.8770	.9045
17	.3734	.4328	.4931	.5530	.6111	.6664	.7179	.7649	.8070	.8439
18	.2666	.3197	.3760	.4346	.4940	.5531	.6105	.6653	.7164	.7631
19	.1786	.2220	.2703	.3227	.3784	.4362	.4949	.5533	.6101	.6644
20	.1121	.1447	.1826	.2257	.2736	.3255	.3805	.4376	.4957	.5535

n = 50 (Continued)

r \ p	.31	.32	.33	.34	.35	.36	.37	.38	.39	.40
21	.0657	.0882	.1156	.1482	.1861	.2289	.2764	.3278	.3824	.4390
22	.0360	.0503	.0685	.0912	.1187	.1513	.1890	.2317	.2788	.3299
23	.0184	.0267	.0379	.0525	.0710	.0938	.1214	.1540	.1916	.2340
24	.0087	.0133	.0196	.0282	.0396	.0544	.0730	.0960	.1236	.1562
25	.0039	.0061	.0094	.0141	.0207	.0295	.0411	.0560	.0748	.0978
26	.0016	.0026	.0042	.0066	.0100	.0149	.0216	.0306	.0423	.0573
27	.0006	.0011	.0018	.0029	.0045	.0070	.0106	.0155	.0223	.0314
28	.0002	.0004	.0007	.0012	.0019	.0031	.0048	.0074	.0110	.0160
29	.0001	.0001	.0002	.0004	.0007	.0012	.0020	.0032	.0050	.0076
30	.0000	.0000	.0001	.0002	.0003	.0005	.0008	.0013	.0021	.0034
31	.0000	.0000	.0000	.0000	.0001	.0002	.0003	.0005	.0008	.0014
32	.0000	.0000	.0000	.0000	.0000	.0001	.0001	.0002	.0003	.0005
33	.0000	.0000	.0000	.0000	.0000	.0000	.0000	.0001	.0001	.0002
34	.0000	.0000	.0000	.0000	.0000	.0000	.0000	.0000	.0000	.0001
	.41	.42	.43	.44	.45	.46	.47	.48	.49	.50
1	1.0000	1.0000	1.0000	1.0000	1.0000	1.0000	1.0000	1.0000	1.0000	1.0000
2	1.0000	1.0000	1.0000	1.0000	1.0000	1.0000	1.0000	1.0000	1.0000	1.0000
3	1.0000	1.0000	1.0000	1.0000	1.0000	1.0000	1.0000	1.0000	1.0000	1.0000
4	1.0000	1.0000	1.0000	1.0000	1.0000	1.0000	1.0000	1.0000	1.0000	1.0000
5	1.0000	1.0000	1.0000	1.0000	1.0000	1.0000	1.0000	1.0000	1.0000	1.0000
6	1.0000	1.0000	1.0000	1.0000	1.0000	1.0000	1.0000	1.0000	1.0000	1.0000
7	1.0000	1.0000	1.0000	1.0000	1.0000	1.0000	1.0000	1.0000	1.0000	1.0000
8	1.0000	1.0000	1.0000	1.0000	1.0000	1.0000	1.0000	1.0000	1.0000	1.0000
9	.9999	.9999	1.0000	1.0000	1.0000	1.0000	1.0000	1.0000	1.0000	1.0000
10	.9995	.9997	.9998	.9999	.9999	1.0000	1.0000	1.0000	1.0000	1.0000
11	.9986	.9991	.9994	.9997	.9998	.9999	.9999	1.0000	1.0000	1.0000
12	.9962	.9975	.9984	.9990	.9994	.9996	.9998	.9999	.9999	1.0000
13	.9908	.9938	.9958	.9973	.9982	.9989	.9993	.9996	.9997	.9998
14	.9799	.9858	.9902	.9933	.9955	.9970	.9981	.9988	.9992	.9995
15	.9599	.9707	.9789	.9851	.9896	.9929	.9952	.9968	.9980	.9987
16	.9265	.9443	.9585	.9696	.9780	.9844	.9892	.9926	.9950	.9967
17	.8757	.9025	.9248	.9429	.9573	.9687	.9774	.9839	.9888	.9923
18	.8051	.8421	.8740	.9010	.9235	.9418	.9565	.9680	.9769	.9836
19	.7151	.7617	.8037	.8406	.8727	.8998	.9225	.9410	.9559	.9675
20	.6099	.6638	.7143	.7608	.8026	.8396	.8718	.8991	.9219	.9405
21	.4965	.5539	.6099	.6635	.7138	.7602	.8020	.8391	.8713	.8987
22	.3840	.4402	.4973	.5543	.6100	.6634	.7137	.7599	.8018	.8389
23	.2807	.3316	.3854	.4412	.4981	.5548	.6104	.6636	.7138	.7601
24	.1936	.2359	.2826	.3331	.3866	.4422	.4989	.5554	.6109	.6641
25	.1255	.1580	.1953	.2375	.2840	.3343	.3876	.4431	.4996	.5561
26	.0762	.0992	.1269	.1593	.1966	.2386	.2850	.3352	.3885	.4439
27	.0432	.0584	.0772	.1003	.1279	.1603	.1975	.2395	.2858	.3359
28	.0229	.0321	.0439	.0591	.0780	.1010	.1286	.1609	.1981	.2399
29	.0113	.0164	.0233	.0325	.0444	.0595	.0784	.1013	.1289	.1611
30	.0052	.0078	.0115	.0166	.0235	.0327	.0446	.0596	.0784	.1013
31	.0022	.0034	.0053	.0079	.0116	.0167	.0236	.0327	.0445	.0595
32	.0009	.0014	.0022	.0035	.0053	.0079	.0116	.0166	.0234	.0325
33	.0003	.0005	.0009	.0014	.0022	.0035	.0053	.0078	.0114	.0164
34	.0001	.0002	.0003	.0005	.0009	.0014	.0022	.0034	.0052	.0077
35	.0000	.0001	.0001	.0002	.0003	.0005	.0009	.0014	.0021	.0033
36	.0000	.0000	.0000	.0001	.0001	.0002	.0003	.0005	.0008	.0013
37	.0000	.0000	.0000	.0000	.0000	.0001	.0001	.0002	.0003	.0005
38	.0000	.0000	.0000	.0000	.0000	.0000	.0000	.0001	.0001	.0002

Table 2 The standard normal probability distribution

Area under the standard normal curve from 0 to z, shown shaded, is $A(z)$.

Example: If Z is the standard normal random variable and $z = 1.54$, then

$$A(z) = P(0 < Z < z) = .4382$$
$$P(Z > z) = .0618$$
$$P(Z < z) = .9382$$
$$P(|Z| < z) = .8764$$

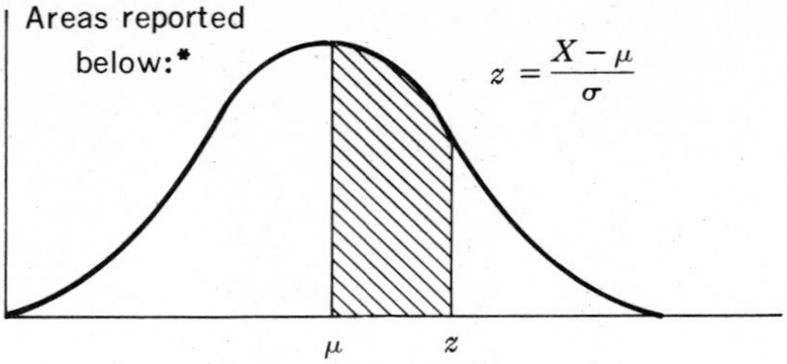

z	.00	.01	.02	.03	.04	.05	.06	.07	.08	.09
0.0	.0000	.0040	.0080	.0120	.0160	.0199	.0239	.0279	.0319	.0359
0.1	.0398	.0438	.0478	.0517	.0557	.0596	.0636	.0675	.0714	.0753
0.2	.0793	.0832	.0871	.0910	.0948	.0987	.1026	.1064	.1103	.1141
0.3	.1179	.1217	.1255	.1293	.1331	.1368	.1406	.1443	.1480	.1517
0.4	.1554	.1591	.1628	.1664	.1700	.1736	.1772	.1808	.1844	.1879
0.5	.1915	.1950	.1985	.2019	.2054	.2088	.2123	.2157	.2190	.2224
0.6	.2257	.2291	.2324	.2357	.2389	.2422	.2454	.2486	.2518	.2549
0.7	.2580	2.612	.2642	.2673	.2704	.2734	.2764	.2794	.2823	.2852
0.8	.2881	.2910	.2939	.2967	.2995	.3023	.3051	.3078	.3106	.3133
0.9	.3159	.3186	.3212	.3238	.3264	.3289	.3315	.3340	.3365	.3389
1.0	.3413	.3438	.3461	.3485	.3508	.3531	.3554	.3577	.3599	.3621
1.1	.3643	.3665	.3686	.3708	.3729	.3749	.3770	.3790	.3810	.3830
1.2	.3849	.3869	.3888	.3907	.3925	.3944	.3962	.3980	.3997	.4014
1.3	.4032	.4049	.4066	.4082	.4099	.4115	.4131	.4147	.4162	.4177
1.4	.4192	.4207	.4222	.4236	.4251	.4265	.4279	.4292	.4306	.4319
1.5	.4332	.4345	.4357	.4370	.4382	.4394	.4406	.4418	.4429	.4441
1.6	.4452	.4463	.4474	.4484	.4495	.4505	.4515	.4525	.4535	.4545
1.7	.4554	.4564	.4573	.4582	.4591	.4599	.4608	.4616	.4625	.4633
1.8	.4641	.4649	.4656	.4664	.4671	.4678	.4686	.4693	.4699	.4706
1.9	.4713	.4719	.4726	.4732	.4738	.4744	.4750	.4756	.4761	.4767
2.0	.4772	.4778	.4783	.4788	.4793	.4798	.4803	.4808	.4812	.4817
2.1	.4821	.4826	.4830	.4834	.4838	.4842	.4846	.4850	.4854	.4857
2.2	.4861	.4864	.4868	.4871	.4875	.4878	.4881	.4884	.4887	.4890
2.3	.4893	.4896	.4898	.4901	.4904	.4906	.4909	.4911	.4913	.4916
2.4	.4918	.4920	.4922	.4925	.4927	.4929	.4931	.4932	.4934	.4936
2.5	.4938	.4940	.4941	.4943	.4945	.4946	.4948	.4949	.4951	.4952
2.6	.4953	.4955	.4956	.4957	.4959	.4960	.4961	.4962	.4963	.4964
2.7	.4965	.4966	.4967	.4968	.4969	.4970	.4971	.4972	.4973	.4974
2.8	.4974	.4975	.4976	.4977	.4977	.4978	.4979	.4979	.4980	.4981
2.9	.4981	.4982	.4983	.4983	.4984	.4984	.4985	.4985	.4986	.4986
3.0	.4987	.4987	.4987	.4988	.4989	.4989	.4989	.4989	.4990	.4990
3.5	.4997									
4.0	.4999683									

Source: Donald H. Sanders, A. Franklin Murph, and Robert J. Eng, *Statistics—A Fresh Approach,* McGraw-Hill Book Company, New York, 1976.

Table 3 Single-payment present worth factors

	Interest or discount rates							
n	.04	.05	.06	.08	.10	.15	.20	*n*
1	0.9615	0.9524	0.9434	0.9259	0.9091	0.8696	0.8333	1
2	0.9246	0.9070	0.8900	0.8573	0.8264	0.7561	0.6944	2
3	0.8890	0.8638	0.8396	0.7938	0.7513	0.6575	0.5787	3
4	0.8548	0.8227	0.7921	0.7350	0.6830	0.5718	0.4823	4
5	0.8219	0.7835	0.7473	0.6806	0.6209	0.4972	0.4019	5
6	0.7903	0.7462	0.7050	0.6302	0.5645	0.4323	0.3349	6
7	0.7599	0.7107	0.6651	0.5835	0.5132	0.3759	0.2791	7
8	0.7307	0.6768	0.6274	0.5403	0.4665	0.3269	0.2326	8
9	0.7026	0.6446	0.5919	0.5002	0.4241	0.2843	0.1938	9
10	0.6756	0.6139	0.5584	0.4632	0.3855	0.2472	0.1615	10
11	0.6496	0.5847	0.5268	0.4289	0.3505	0.2149	0.1346	11
12	0.6246	0.5568	0.4970	0.3971	0.3186	0.1869	0.1122	12
13	0.6006	0.5303	0.4688	0.3677	0.2897	0.1625	0.0935	13
14	0.5775	0.5051	0.4423	0.3405	0.2633	0.1413	0.0779	14
15	0.5553	0.4810	0.4173	0.3152	0.2394	0.1229	0.0649	15
16	0.5339	0.4581	0.3936	0.2919	0.2176	0.1069	0.0541	16
17	0.5134	0.4363	0.3714	0.2703	0.1978	0.0929	0.0451	17
18	0.4936	0.4155	0.3503	0.2502	0.1799	0.0808	0.0376	18
19	0.4746	0.3957	0.3305	0.2317	0.1635	0.0703	0.0313	19
20	0.4564	0.3769	0.3118	0.2145	0.1486	0.0611	0.0261	20
21	0.4388	0.3589	0.2942	0.1987	0.1351	0.0531	0.0217	21
22	0.4220	0.3418	0.2775	0.1839	0.1228	0.0462	0.0181	22
23	0.4057	0.3256	0.2618	0.1703	0.1117	0.0402	0.0151	23
24	0.3901	0.3101	0.2470	0.1577	0.1015	0.0349	0.0126	24
25	0.3751	0.2953	0.2330	0.1460	0.0923	0.0304	0.0105	25
26	0.3607	0.2812	0.2198	0.1352	0.0839	0.0264	0.0087	26
27	0.3468	0.2678	0.2074	0.1252	0.0763	0.0230	0.0073	27
28	0.3335	0.2551	0.1956	0.1159	0.0693	0.0200	0.0061	28
29	0.3207	0.2429	0.1846	0.1073	0.0630	0.0174	0.0051	29
30	0.3083	0.2314	0.1741	0.0994	0.0573	0.0151	0.0042	30
31	0.2965	0.2204	0.1643	0.0920	0.0521	0.0131	0.0035	31
32	0.2851	0.2099	0.1550	0.0852	0.0474	0.0114	0.0029	32
33	0.2741	0.1999	0.1462	0.0789	0.0431	0.0099	0.0024	33
34	0.2636	0.1904	0.1379	0.0730	0.0391	0.0086	0.0020	34
35	0.2534	0.1813	0.1301	0.0676	0.0356	0.0075	0.0017	35
40	0.2083	0.1420	0.0972	0.0460	0.0221	0.0037	0.0007	40
45	0.1712	0.1113	0.0727	0.0313	0.0137	0.0019	0.0003	45
50	0.1407	0.0872	0.0543	0.0213	0.0085	0.0009	0.0001	50

Source: Thanks to Robert J. Brown, Associate Professor of Finance, Penn State University—Capitol Campus, for the development of this table.

Table 4 Uniform-series present worth factors

	Interest or discount rates							
n	.04	.05	.06	.08	.10	.15	.20	*n*
1	0.962	0.952	0.943	0.926	0.909	0.870	0.833	1
2	1.886	1.859	1.833	1.783	1.736	1.626	1.528	2
3	2.775	2.723	2.673	2.577	2.487	2.283	2.106	3
4	3.630	3.546	3.465	3.312	3.170	2.855	2.589	4
5	4.452	4.329	4.212	3.993	3.791	3.352	2.991	5
6	5.242	5.076	4.917	4.623	4.355	3.784	3.326	6
7	6.002	5.786	5.582	5.206	4.868	4.160	3.605	7
8	6.733	6.463	6.210	5.747	5.335	4.487	3.837	8
9	7.435	7.108	6.802	6.247	5.759	4.772	4.031	9
10	8.111	7.722	7.360	6.710	6.144	5.019	4.192	10
11	8.760	8.306	7.887	7.139	6.495	5.234	4.327	11
12	9.385	8.863	8.384	7.536	6.814	5.421	4.439	12
13	9.986	9.394	8.853	7.904	7.103	5.583	4.533	13
14	10.563	9.899	9.295	8.244	7.367	5.724	4.611	14
15	11.118	10.380	9.712	8.559	7.606	5.847	4.675	15
16	11.652	10.838	10.106	8.851	7.824	5.954	4.730	16
17	12.166	11.274	10.477	9.122	8.022	6.047	4.775	17
18	12.659	11.690	10.828	9.372	8.201	6.128	4.812	18
19	13.134	12.085	11.158	9.604	8.363	6.198	4.843	19
20	13.590	12.462	11.470	9.818	8.514	6.259	4.870	20
21	14.029	12.821	11.764	10.017	8.649	6.312	4.891	21
22	14.451	13.163	12.042	10.201	8.772	6.359	4.909	22
23	14.857	13.489	12.303	10.371	8.883	6.399	4.925	23
24	15.247	13.799	12.550	10.529	8.985	6.434	4.937	24
25	15.622	14.094	12.783	10.675	9.077	6.464	4.948	25
26	15.983	14.375	13.003	10.810	9.161	6.491	4.956	26
27	16.330	14.643	13.211	10.935	9.237	6.514	4.964	27
28	16.663	14.898	13.406	11.051	9.307	6.534	4.970	28
29	16.984	15.141	13.591	11.158	9.370	6.551	4.975	29
30	17.292	15.372	13.765	11.258	9.427	6.566	4.979	30
31	17.588	15.593	13.929	11.350	9.479	6.579	4.982	31
32	17.874	15.803	14.084	11.435	9.526	6.591	4.985	32
33	18.148	16.003	14.230	11.514	9.569	6.600	4.988	33
34	18.411	16.193	14.368	11.587	9.609	6.609	4.990	34
35	18.665	16.374	14.498	11.655	9.644	6.617	4.992	35
40	19.793	17.159	15.046	11.925	9.779	6.642	4.997	40
45	20.720	17.774	15.456	12.108	9.863	6.654	4.999	45
50	21.482	18.256	15.762	12.233	9.915	6.661	4.999	50

Source: Thanks to Robert J. Brown, Associate Professor of Finance, Penn State University—Capitol Campus, for the development of this table.

Table 5 Idle probability and average queue length for multiple channel queues (Poisson arrivals and exponential service times)

	NUMBER OF CHANNELS									
λ/μ	1	2	3	4	5	6	7	8	9	10
0.1	0.9000	0.9048	0.9048	0.9048	0.9048	0.9048	0.9048	0.9048	0.9048	0.9048
	0.0111	0.0003	0.0000	0.0000	0.0000	0.0000	0.0000	0.0000	0.0000	0.0000
0.2	0.8000	0.8182	0.8187	0.8187	0.8187	0.8187	0.8187	0.8187	0.8187	0.8187
	0.0500	0.0020	0.0001	0.0000	0.0000	0.0000	0.0000	0.0000	0.0000	0.0000
0.3	0.7000	0.7391	0.7407	0.7408	0.7408	0.7408	0.7408	0.7408	0.7408	0.7408
	0.1286	0.0069	0.0004	0.0000	0.0000	0.0000	0.0000	0.0000	0.0000	0.0000
0.4	0.6000	0.6667	0.6701	0.6703	0.6703	0.6703	0.6703	0.6703	0.6703	0.6703
	0.2667	0.0167	0.0013	0.0001	0.0000	0.0000	0.0000	0.0000	0.0000	0.0000
0.5	0.5000	0.6000	0.6061	0.6065	0.6065	0.6065	0.6065	0.6065	0.6065	0.6065
	0.5000	0.0333	0.0030	0.0003	0.0000	0.0000	0.0000	0.0000	0.0000	0.0000
0.6	0.4000	0.5385	0.5479	0.5487	0.5488	0.5488	0.5488	0.5488	0.5488	0.5488
	0.9000	0.0593	0.0062	0.0006	0.0001	0.0000	0.0000	0.0000	0.0000	0.0000
0.7	0.3000	0.4815	0.4952	0.4965	0.4966	0.4966	0.4966	0.4966	0.4966	0.4966
	1.6333	0.0977	0.0112	0.0013	0.0001	0.0000	0.0000	0.0000	0.0000	0.0000
0.8	0.2000	0.4286	0.4472	0.4491	0.4493	0.4493	0.4493	0.4493	0.4493	0.4493
	3.2000	0.1524	0.0189	0.0024	0.0003	0.0000	0.0000	0.0000	0.0000	0.0000
0.9	0.1000	0.3793	0.4035	0.4062	0.4065	0.4066	0.4066	0.4066	0.4066	0.4066
	8.1000	0.2285	0.0300	0.0042	0.0005	0.0001	0.0000	0.0000	0.0000	0.0000
1.0	*******	0.3333	0.3636	0.3673	0.3678	0.3679	0.3679	0.3679	0.3679	0.3679
	*******	0.3333	0.0455	0.0068	0.0010	0.0001	0.0000	0.0000	0.0000	0.0000
	NUMBER OF CHANNELS									
λ/μ	1	2	3	4	5	6	7	8	9	10
1.1	*******	0.2903	0.3273	0.3321	0.3328	0.3329	0.3329	0.3329	0.3329	0.3329
	*******	0.4771	0.0664	0.0106	0.0016	0.0002	0.0000	0.0000	0.0000	0.0000
1.2	*******	0.2500	0.2941	0.3002	0.3011	0.3012	0.3012	0.3012	0.3012	0.3012
	*******	0.6750	0.0941	0.0159	0.0026	0.0004	0.0001	0.0000	0.0000	0.0000
1.3	*******	0.2121	0.2638	0.2712	0.2723	0.2725	0.2725	0.2725	0.2725	0.2725
	*******	0.9511	0.1303	0.0230	0.0040	0.0006	0.0001	0.0000	0.0000	0.0000
1.4	*******	0.1765	0.2360	0.2449	0.2463	0.2466	0.2466	0.2466	0.2466	0.2466
	*******	1.3451	0.1771	0.0325	0.0060	0.0010	0.0002	0.0000	0.0000	0.0000
1.5	*******	0.1429	0.2105	0.2210	0.2228	0.2231	0.2231	0.2231	0.2231	0.2231
	*******	1.9286	0.2368	0.0448	0.0086	0.0016	0.0003	0.0000	0.0000	0.0000
1.6	*******	0.1111	0.1872	0.1993	0.2014	0.2018	0.2019	0.2019	0.2019	0.2019
	*******	2.8444	0.3129	0.0605	0.0122	0.0023	0.0004	0.0001	0.0000	0.0000
1.7	*******	0.0811	0.1657	0.1796	0.1821	0.1826	0.1827	0.1827	0.1827	0.1827
	*******	4.4261	0.4095	0.0803	0.0168	0.0034	0.0006	0.0001	0.0000	0.0000
1.8	*******	0.0526	0.1460	0.1616	0.1646	0.1652	0.1653	0.1653	0.1653	0.1653
	*******	7.6737	0.5321	0.1052	0.0228	0.0048	0.0009	0.0002	0.0000	0.0000
1.9	*******	0.0256	0.1278	0.1453	0.1487	0.1494	0.1495	0.1496	0.1496	0.1496
	*******	17.5872	0.6884	0.1360	0.0303	0.0066	0.0014	0.0003	0.0000	0.0000
2.0	*******	*******	0.1111	0.1304	0.1343	0.1351	0.1353	0.1353	0.1353	0.1353
	*******	*******	0.8889	0.1739	0.0398	0.0090	0.0019	0.0004	0.0001	0.0000

Example: If $C = 2$, $\lambda/\mu = 1.7$, then $P_0 = .0811$ and $L_q = 4.4261$.

Source: Thanks to Charles Jackson, Penn State University—Capitol Campus, for developing this table.

NUMBER OF CHANNELS

λ/μ	1	2	3	4	5	6	7	8	9	10
2.1	*******	*******	0.0957	0.1169	0.1213	0.1222	0.1224	0.1224	0.1225	0.1225
	*******	*******	1.1488	0.2204	0.0515	0.0121	0.0027	0.0006	0.0001	0.0000
2.2	*******	*******	0.0815	0.1046	0.1094	0.1105	0.1107	0.1108	0.1108	0.1108
	*******	*******	1.4909	0.2772	0.0659	0.0159	0.0037	0.0008	0.0002	0.0000
2.3	*******	*******	0.0683	0.0933	0.0987	0.0999	0.1002	0.1002	0.1003	0.1003
	*******	*******	1.9511	0.3464	0.0835	0.0207	0.0049	0.0011	0.0002	0.0000
2.4	*******	*******	0.0562	0.0831	0.0889	0.0903	0.0906	0.0907	0.0907	0.0907
	*******	*******	2.5888	0.4306	0.1048	0.0266	0.0065	0.0015	0.0003	0.0001
2.5	*******	*******	0.0449	0.0737	0.0801	0.0816	0.0820	0.0821	0.0821	0.0821
	*******	*******	3.5112	0.5331	0.1304	0.0339	0.0086	0.0021	0.0005	0.0001
2.6	*******	*******	0.0345	0.0651	0.0721	0.0737	0.0742	0.0742	0.0743	0.0743
	*******	*******	4.9328	0.6582	0.1610	0.0427	0.0111	0.0027	0.0006	0.0001
2.7	*******	*******	0.0249	0.0573	0.0648	0.0666	0.0671	0.0672	0.0672	0.0672
	*******	*******	7.3535	0.8115	0.1976	0.0533	0.0142	0.0036	0.0009	0.0002
2.8	*******	*******	0.0160	0.0502	0.0581	0.0601	0.0606	0.0608	0.0608	0.0608
	*******	*******	12.2735	1.0002	0.2412	0.0660	0.0180	0.0047	0.0012	0.0003
2.9	*******	*******	0.0077	0.0437	0.0521	0.0543	0.0548	0.0550	0.0550	0.0550
	*******	*******	27.1927	1.2345	0.2929	0.0812	0.0227	0.0061	0.0015	0.0004
3.0	*******	*******	*******	0.0377	0.0466	0.0490	0.0496	0.0497	0.0498	0.0498
	*******	*******	*******	1.5283	0.3542	0.0991	0.0282	0.0078	0.0020	0.0005

NUMBER OF CHANNELS

λ/μ	1	2	3	4	5	6	7	8	9	10
3.1	*******	*******	*******	0.0323	0.0417	0.0441	0.0448	0.0450	0.0450	0.0450
	*******	*******	*******	1.9019	0.4269	0.1203	0.0349	0.0098	0.0026	0.0007
3.2	*******	*******	*******	0.0273	0.0372	0.0398	0.0405	0.0407	0.0407	0.0408
	*******	*******	*******	2.3857	0.5130	0.1453	0.0428	0.0123	0.0034	0.0009
3.3	*******	*******	*******	0.0227	0.0330	0.0358	0.0366	0.0368	0.0369	0.0369
	*******	*******	*******	3.0273	0.6152	0.1745	0.0522	0.0153	0.0043	0.0011
3.4	*******	*******	*******	0.0186	0.0293	0.0322	0.0331	0.0333	0.0334	0.0334
	*******	*******	*******	3.9061	0.7367	0.2086	0.0633	0.0190	0.0054	0.0015
3.5	*******	*******	*******	0.0148	0.0259	0.0290	0.0298	0.0301	0.0302	0.0302
	*******	*******	*******	5.1650	0.8816	0.2485	0.0762	0.0232	0.0068	0.0019
3.6	*******	*******	*******	0.0113	0.0228	0.0260	0.0269	0.0272	0.0273	0.0273
	*******	*******	*******	7.0898	1.0553	0.2948	0.0913	0.0283	0.0085	0.0024
3.7	*******	*******	*******	0.0081	0.0200	0.0233	0.0243	0.0246	0.0247	0.0247
	*******	*******	*******	10.3471	1.2646	0.3488	0.1089	0.0343	0.0105	0.0031
3.8	*******	*******	*******	0.0051	0.0174	0.0209	0.0219	0.0222	0.0223	0.0224
	*******	*******	*******	16.9370	1.5187	0.4116	0.1293	0.0413	0.0129	0.0038
3.9	*******	*******	*******	0.0025	0.0151	0.0187	0.0198	0.0201	0.0202	0.0202
	*******	*******	*******	36.8595	1.8302	0.4846	0.1529	0.0495	0.0157	0.0048
4.0	*******	*******	*******	*******	0.0130	0.0167	0.0178	0.0182	0.0183	0.0183
	*******	*******	*******	*******	2.2165	0.5695	0.1801	0.0590	0.0190	0.0059

NUMBER OF CHANNELS

λ/μ	1	2	3	4	5	6	7	8	9	10
4.1	*******	*******	*******	*******	0.0111	0.0149	0.0160	0.0164	0.0165	0.0166
	*******	*******	*******	*******	2.7029	0.6685	0.2115	0.0701	0.0229	0.0072
4.2	*******	*******	*******	*******	0.0093	0.0132	0.0144	0.0148	0.0149	0.0150
	*******	*******	*******	*******	3.3273	0.7839	0.2476	0.0828	0.0275	0.0088
4.3	*******	*******	*******	*******	0.0077	0.0117	0.0130	0.0134	0.0135	0.0136
	*******	*******	*******	*******	4.1493	0.9191	0.2890	0.0975	0.0328	0.0107
4.4	*******	*******	*******	*******	0.0063	0.0104	0.0117	0.0121	0.0122	0.0123
	*******	*******	*******	*******	5.2682	1.0778	0.3365	0.1143	0.0389	0.0129
4.5	*******	*******	*******	*******	0.0050	0.0091	0.0105	0.0109	0.0110	0.0111
	*******	*******	*******	*******	6.8624	1.2650	0.3910	0.1336	0.0460	0.0155
4.6	*******	*******	*******	*******	0.0038	0.0080	0.0094	0.0098	0.0100	0.0100
	*******	*******	*******	*******	9.2893	1.4869	0.4535	0.1556	0.0542	0.0185
4.7	*******	*******	*******	*******	0.0027	0.0070	0.0084	0.0089	0.0090	0.0091
	*******	*******	*******	*******	13.3821	1.7520	0.5251	0.1807	0.0636	0.0220
4.8	*******	*******	*******	*******	0.0017	0.0061	0.0075	0.0080	0.0081	0.0082
	*******	*******	*******	*******	21.6408	2.0711	0.6073	0.2093	0.0744	0.0261
4.9	*******	*******	*******	*******	0.0008	0.0053	0.0067	0.0072	0.0074	0.0074
	*******	*******	*******	*******	46.5655	2.4593	0.7017	0.2418	0.0867	0.0307
5.0	*******	*******	*******	*******	*******	0.0045	0.0060	0.0065	0.0066	0.0067
	*******	*******	*******	*******	*******	2.9376	0.8104	0.2788	0.1006	0.0361

NUMBER OF CHANNELS

λ/μ	1	2	3	4	5	6	7	8	9	10
5.1	*******	*******	*******	*******	*******	0.0038	0.0053	0.0058	0.0060	0.0061
	*******	*******	*******	*******	*******	3.5363	0.9357	0.3207	0.1165	0.0423
5.2	*******	*******	*******	*******	*******	0.0032	0.0047	0.0052	0.0054	0.0055
	*******	*******	*******	*******	*******	4.3009	1.0805	0.3683	0.1345	0.0493
5.3	*******	*******	*******	*******	*******	0.0027	0.0042	0.0047	0.0049	0.0050
	*******	*******	*******	*******	*******	5.3028	1.2486	0.4222	0.1549	0.0573
5.4	*******	*******	*******	*******	*******	0.0021	0.0037	0.0042	0.0044	0.0045
	*******	*******	*******	*******	*******	6.6611	1.4444	0.4833	0.1779	0.0664
5.5	*******	*******	*******	*******	*******	0.0017	0.0032	0.0038	0.0040	0.0040
	*******	*******	*******	*******	*******	8.5902	1.6736	0.5527	0.2039	0.0767
5.6	*******	*******	*******	*******	*******	0.0013	0.0028	0.0034	0.0036	0.0037
	*******	*******	*******	*******	*******	11.5185	1.9438	0.6314	0.2332	0.0884
5.7	*******	*******	*******	*******	*******	0.0009	0.0025	0.0030	0.0032	0.0033
	*******	*******	*******	*******	*******	16.4462	2.2643	0.7208	0.2662	0.1016
5.8	*******	*******	*******	*******	*******	0.0006	0.0021	0.0027	0.0029	0.0030
	*******	*******	*******	*******	*******	26.3732	2.6482	0.8226	0.3033	0.1165
5.9	*******	*******	*******	*******	*******	0.0003	0.0018	0.0024	0.0026	0.0027
	*******	*******	*******	*******	*******	56.2996	3.1130	0.9385	0.3451	0.1332
6.0	*******	*******	*******	*******	*******	*******	0.0016	0.0021	0.0024	0.0024
	*******	*******	*******	*******	*******	*******	3.6830	1.0709	0.3920	0.1519

NUMBER OF CHANNELS

λ/μ	1	2	3	4	5	6	7	8	9	10
6.1	*******	*******	*******	*******	*******	*******	0.0013	0.0019	0.0021	0.0022
	*******	*******	*******	*******	*******	*******	4.3937	1.2226	0.4447	0.1730
6.2	*******	*******	*******	*******	*******	*******	0.0011	0.0017	0.0019	0.0020
	*******	*******	*******	*******	*******	*******	5.2981	1.3968	0.5039	0.1966
6.3	*******	*******	*******	*******	*******	*******	0.0009	0.0015	0.0017	0.0018
	*******	*******	*******	*******	*******	*******	6.4796	1.5977	0.5705	0.2230
6.4	*******	*******	*******	*******	*******	*******	0.0007	0.0013	0.0015	0.0016
	*******	*******	*******	*******	*******	*******	8.0771	1.8306	0.6455	0.2525
6.5	*******	*******	*******	*******	*******	*******	0.0006	0.0012	0.0014	0.0015
	*******	*******	*******	*******	*******	*******	10.3406	2.1019	0.7298	0.2855
6.6	*******	*******	*******	*******	*******	*******	0.0004	0.0010	0.0012	0.0013
	*******	*******	*******	*******	*******	*******	13.7701	2.4200	0.8249	0.3223
6.7	*******	*******	*******	*******	*******	*******	0.0003	0.0009	0.0011	0.0012
	*******	*******	*******	*******	*******	*******	19.5323	2.7960	0.9323	0.3634
6.8	*******	*******	*******	*******	*******	*******	0.0002	0.0008	0.0010	0.0011
	*******	*******	*******	*******	*******	*******	31.1272	3.2446	1.0536	0.4092
6.9	*******	*******	*******	*******	*******	*******	0.0001	0.0007	0.0009	0.0010
	*******	*******	*******	*******	*******	*******	66.0548	3.7856	1.1911	0.4603
7.0	*******	*******	*******	*******	*******	*******	*******	0.0006	0.0008	0.0009
	*******	*******	*******	*******	*******	*******	*******	4.4472	1.3473	0.5174

NUMBER OF CHANNELS

λ/μ	1	2	3	4	5	6	7	8	9	10
7.1	*******	*******	*******	*******	*******	*******	*******	0.0005	0.0007	0.0008
	*******	*******	*******	*******	*******	*******	*******	5.2697	1.5253	0.5810
7.2	*******	*******	*******	*******	*******	*******	*******	0.0004	0.0006	0.0007
	*******	*******	*******	*******	*******	*******	*******	6.3138	1.7289	0.6521
7.3	*******	*******	*******	*******	*******	*******	*******	0.0003	0.0005	0.0006
	*******	*******	*******	*******	*******	*******	*******	7.6747	1.9627	0.7315
7.4	*******	*******	*******	*******	*******	*******	*******	0.0003	0.0005	0.0006
	*******	*******	*******	*******	*******	*******	*******	9.5111	2.2325	0.8204
7.5	*******	*******	*******	*******	*******	*******	*******	0.0002	0.0004	0.0005
	*******	*******	*******	*******	*******	*******	*******	12.1088	2.5457	0.9198
7.6	*******	*******	*******	*******	*******	*******	*******	0.0002	0.0004	0.0004
	*******	*******	*******	*******	*******	*******	*******	16.0392	2.9118	1.0314
7.7	*******	*******	*******	*******	*******	*******	*******	0.0001	0.0003	0.0004
	*******	*******	*******	*******	*******	*******	*******	22.6357	3.3432	1.1566
7.8	*******	*******	*******	*******	*******	*******	*******	0.0001	0.0003	0.0004
	*******	*******	*******	*******	*******	*******	*******	35.8982	3.8563	1.2976
7.9	*******	*******	*******	*******	*******	*******	*******	0.0000	0.0002	0.0003
	*******	*******	*******	*******	*******	*******	*******	75.8269	4.4736	1.4567
8.0	*******	*******	*******	*******	*******	*******	*******	*******	0.0002	0.0003
	*******	*******	*******	*******	*******	*******	*******	*******	5.2266	1.6367

NUMBER OF CHANNELS

λ/μ	1	2	3	4	5	6	7	8	9	10
8.1	*******	*******	*******	*******	*******	*******	*******	*******	0.0002	0.0002
	*******	*******	*******	*******	*******	*******	*******	*******	6.1608	1.8411
8.2	*******	*******	*******	*******	*******	*******	*******	*******	0.0001	0.0002
	*******	*******	*******	*******	*******	*******	*******	*******	7.3444	2.0740
8.3	*******	*******	*******	*******	*******	*******	*******	*******	0.0001	0.0002
	*******	*******	*******	*******	*******	*******	*******	*******	8.8845	2.3406
8.4	*******	*******	*******	*******	*******	*******	*******	*******	0.0001	0.0002
	*******	*******	*******	*******	*******	*******	*******	*******	10.9597	2.6474
8.5	*******	*******	*******	*******	*******	*******	*******	*******	0.0001	0.0001
	*******	*******	*******	*******	*******	*******	*******	*******	13.8914	3.0025
8.6	*******	*******	*******	*******	*******	*******	*******	*******	0.0001	0.0001
	*******	*******	*******	*******	*******	*******	*******	*******	18.3226	3.4166
8.7	*******	*******	*******	*******	*******	*******	*******	*******	0.0000	0.0001
	*******	*******	*******	*******	*******	*******	*******	*******	25.7532	3.9032
8.8	*******	*******	*******	*******	*******	*******	*******	*******	0.0000	0.0001
	*******	*******	*******	*******	*******	*******	*******	*******	40.6832	4.4807
8.9	*******	*******	*******	*******	*******	*******	*******	*******	0.0000	0.0001
	*******	*******	*******	*******	*******	*******	*******	*******	85.6127	5.1742
9.0	*******	*******	*******	*******	*******	*******	*******	*******	*******	0.0001
	*******	*******	*******	*******	*******	*******	*******	*******	*******	6.0186

NUMBER OF CHANNELS

λ/μ	1	2	3	4	5	6	7	8	9	10
9.1	*******	*******	*******	*******	*******	*******	*******	*******	*******	0.0001
	*******	*******	*******	*******	*******	*******	*******	*******	*******	7.0644
9.2	*******	*******	*******	*******	*******	*******	*******	*******	*******	0.0000
	*******	*******	*******	*******	*******	*******	*******	*******	*******	8.3873
9.3	*******	*******	*******	*******	*******	*******	*******	*******	*******	0.0000
	*******	*******	*******	*******	*******	*******	*******	*******	*******	10.1066
9.4	*******	*******	*******	*******	*******	*******	*******	*******	*******	0.0000
	*******	*******	*******	*******	*******	*******	*******	*******	*******	12.4204
9.5	*******	*******	*******	*******	*******	*******	*******	*******	*******	0.0000
	*******	*******	*******	*******	*******	*******	*******	*******	*******	15.6861
9.6	*******	*******	*******	*******	*******	*******	*******	*******	*******	0.0000
	*******	*******	*******	*******	*******	*******	*******	*******	*******	20.6179
9.7	*******	*******	*******	*******	*******	*******	*******	*******	*******	0.0000
	*******	*******	*******	*******	*******	*******	*******	*******	*******	28.8825
9.8	*******	*******	*******	*******	*******	*******	*******	*******	*******	0.0000
	*******	*******	*******	*******	*******	*******	*******	*******	*******	45.4799
9.9	*******	*******	*******	*******	*******	*******	*******	*******	*******	0.0000
	*******	*******	*******	*******	*******	*******	*******	*******	*******	95.4101

INDEX

INDEX